T3-BUM-694

# OLD GOVERNMENT / NEW PEOPLE

## Readings for the New Politics

Alfred deGrazia
University of the New World, Valais, Switzerland
R. Eric Weise
University of Cincinnati
John Appel
University of Michigan

# OLD GOVERNMENT NEW PEOPLE

## Readings for the New Politics

Scott, Foresman and Company
Glenview, Illinois London

Library of Congress Catalog Card Number: 70-167646


Regional offices of Scott, Foresman and Company
are located in Dallas, Oakland, N.J., Palo Alto, and Tucker, Ga.

**Acknowledgements**

"Are We in the Middle of a Second American Revolution?" by David McReynolds, *et al.*, from *The New York Times Magazine*, May 17, 1970. © 1970 by The New York Times Company.

"Explosive Changes," reprinted by permission of the publishers from *The Strength of Government* by McGeorge Bundy. Cambridge, Mass.: Harvard University Press, Copyright, 1968, by the President and Fellows of Harvard College.

"How to Compete with Government," condensed from *Reclaiming the American Dream*, by Richard C. Cornuelle. Copyright © 1965 by Richard C. Cornuelle. Reprinted by permission of Brandt & Brandt, Random House, Inc., and the author.

"Methods of Survey Research," original title, "Survey Research Methods," reprinted from *Political Behavior of the American Electorate* by William H. Flanigan (Boston: Allyn & Bacon, 1968), pp. 117-121, by permission of the publisher.

"A Misperception of Public Opinion," original title "Electoral Myth and Reality: The 1964 Election" by Philip E. Converse, Aage R. Clausen and Warren E. Miller, reprinted from *American Political Science Review*, LIX, No. 2, June 1965, pp. 332-335, by permission of the publisher and the authors.

"Personal Feelings upon the Death of a President," reprinted from *Children and the Death of a President* by Martha Wolfenstein and Gilbert Kliman. Copyright © 1965 by Martha Wolfenstein and Gilbert Kliman. Reprinted by permission of Doubleday & Company, Inc.

"Letter from Birmingham Jail," by Martin Luther King, Jr., reprinted from *Nonviolence in America: A Documentary History*, ed., Staughton Lynd (Indianapolis, Ind.: The Bobbs-Merrill Company, Inc., 1966), pp. 461-481, by permission of the American Friends Service Committee.

"Social Control of Escalated Riots," reprinted from *Social Control of Escalated Riots* by Morris Janowitz, The University of Chicago Center for Policy Study, © The University of Chicago 1968, by permission of the author.

"The Cost of Threats in World Affairs," by James L. Payne, reprinted from *The American Threat: The Fear of War as an Instrument of Foreign Policy*, by James L. Payne, editor, 1970 Markham Publishing Company. Copyright 1970 by James L. Payne.

"Report from Iron Mountain" reprinted from *Report from Iron Mountain on the Possibility and Desirability of Peace* with Introductory Material by Leonard C. Lewin. Copyright © 1967 by The Dial Press, Inc. and used by permission of the publisher and William Morris Agency, Inc.

"The Times They Are A-Changin': The Music of Protest," by Robert A. Rosenstone, reprinted from *The Annals of the American Academy of Political and Social Science*, Vol. 82, March 1969, pp. 131-144, by permission of the publisher and the author.

"Mothers Versus Fathers as 'Mind-Invaders'" by M. Kent Jennings and Kenneth P. Langton, reprinted from *The Journal of Politics*, May 1969, pp. 329-357, by permission of the publisher.

"American History Through Communist Eyes," reprinted from O. Lawrence Burnette, Jr. and William C. Haygood (eds.) *A Soviet View of the American Past* (Chicago: Scott, Foresman and Company, 1960), pp. 40-50.

"The Effects of Political Broadcasts," reprinted from "Political Broadcasting: What's Its Impact on Elections?" by Herbert E. Alexander, The Center for Information on America, 1964, pp. 3-15, by permission of the publisher.

"The Press Versus Government," reprinted from *Friendly Adversaries: The Press and Government* by George Berdes, pp. 88-94. Milwaukee, Wisconsin: The Center for the Study of the American Press of the College of Journalism, Marquette University, 1969.

"Political Activities of Unions and Company Managers" by the Staff, *Issues in Industrial Society,* Vol. 1, No. 2 (1969), New York State School of Industrial and Labor Relations, © Cornell University, pp. 10-13.

"A Do-It-Yourself Presidential Election Forecasting Kit," reprinted with permission of the author and the Macmillan Company from *The Democratic Party in American Politics* by Ralph M. Goldman. Copyright © 1966 by Ralph M. Goldman.

"Secrets of Advancemanship" by Robert C. Terry, reprinted from *Guide for Political Advancemen,* 1968, reprinted by permission of the author.

"The Day of Senator Monroney," reprinted from Chapter 3 of *On Capitol Hill: Studies in the Legislative Process,* by John Bibby and Roger Davidson. Copyright © 1967 by Holt, Rinehart and Winston, Inc. Reprinted by permission of Holt, Rinehart and Winston, Inc.

"Three Cases of Command," reprinted from *Presidential Power* by Richard E. Neustadt (New York: John Wiley & Sons, Inc., 1960), pp. 9-32, by permission of the publisher.

"Romney Decides To Withdraw," original title, "Romney Decision Urged by His Aides" by Robert B. Semple, Jr., from *The New York Times*, March 1, 1968. © 1968 by The New York Times Company. Reprinted by permission.

"An Inside View of LBJ's Decision Not To Run" by Jean Heller is from the *New York Post,* April 8, 1968, p. 8. Reprinted by permission of the Associated Press.

"The Police and the Supreme Court," reprinted from *Behind the Shield* by Arthur Niederhoffer. Copyright © 1967 by Arthur Niederhoffer. Reprinted by permission of Doubleday & Company, Inc. and the author.

"Due Process of Law in Military and Industrial Organizations," by William M. Evan, reprinted from *Administrative Science Quarterly,* August 1967, pp. 189-207, by permission of the publisher and the author.

"The Commerce Power Without Bounds," reprinted from *The Commerce Clause: Its Inception and Its Significance* by Newton Morton (Kent, Ohio: Bureau of Economic and Business Research, Kent State University, 1966), pp. 29-34. Reprinted by permission of Mrs. Newton Morton.

"Congressional Predictions of Judicial Behavior" by S. Sidney Ulmer, reprinted from *PROD* (now the American Behavioral Scientist), Vol. III, No. 7 (March 1960), pp. 15-17, by permission of the author and the Publisher, Sage Publications, Inc.

"Bureaucratic Barriers and the Exhaustion of Reform," original title, "City's Efforts To Speed Planning Stalled in Interagency Red Tape" by Richard Reeves from *The New York Times,* March 25, 1966. © 1966 by The New York Times Company. Reprinted by permission.

"New Moves in Federal-Local Relations," original title, "The Relationship of Federal to Local Authorities" by Daniel P. Moynihan, reprinted by permission of the author and *Daedalus,* Journal of the American Academy of Arts and Sciences, Boston, Massachusetts, Vol. 96, No. 3 (Summer 1967).

"Trial by Battle: History of a Smear," reprinted from *History of a Smear* by Edward Lamb, by permission of the Center for the Study of Democratic Institutions and the author.

"The Burden of Mr. Strobel," reprinted from *All Honorable Men* by Walter Goodman, by permission of the author and Atlantic-Little, Brown and Co. Copyright © 1963, by Walter Goodman.

"The Life and Death of Project Camelot" by Irving Louis Horowitz, reprinted from *Trans-Action,* III, No. 1, November-December 1965, pp. 3-7, 44-47, by permission of the publisher and the author. Copyright © 1965 by Washington University, St. Louis, Mo.

"The Rise of the National Institutes of Health Empire," reprinted from "The Rise of a Research Empire: NIH, 1930 to 1950" by Donald C. Swain, *Science,* Vol. 138, No. 3546, December 14, 1962, pp. 1233-1237, by permission of the publisher and the author.

"Government by Commissions" by Amitai Etzioni, reprinted from *The Record,* Vol. 69, No. 6, March 1968, pp. 563-565, by permission of the publisher and the author.

"The Politically Impossible," original title, "What is Meant by 'Politically Impossible'?" by Carl J. Friedrich is reprinted from *PROD* (predecessor to the *American Behavioral Scientist*), Vol. I, No. 5 (May, 1958), pp. 3-6, by permission of the Publisher, Sage Publications, Inc.

"The Rudiments of Apportionment," reprinted from *Essay on Apportionment and Representative Government* by Alfred de Grazia (Washington, D.C.: American Enterprise Institute, 1963), pp. 1-15, by permission of the publisher and the author.

"Statistics: Achilles' Heel of Government" by Murray N. Rothbard, reprinted from *The Freeman*, June 1961, pp. 40-44, by permission of the publisher and the author.

"The Need for More Behavioral Science in Government," original title, "A Magna Carta for the Social and Behavioral Sciences," by Hubert H. Humphrey, reprinted from the *American Behavioral Scientist*, Vol. V. No. 6, (February, 1962), pp. 11-15, by permission of the Publisher, Sage Publications, Inc.

"Using Computers in Foreign Affairs," reprinted from *The Computer and Foreign Affairs, Some First Thoughts* by Fisher Howe, Department of State, publication 8156, U. S. Government Printing Office, by permission of the author.

"Expert Predictions of Foreign Threats and Remedies," original title, "Predictions of Threats and Beliefs About How to Meet Them," by T. W. Milburn and J. F. Milburn, reprinted from the *American Behavioral Scientist*, Vol. IX, No. 7 (March 1966), pp. 3-7, by permission of the authors and the Publisher, Sage Publications, Inc.

"Slums: Now and Hereafter," original title, "The Current Scene and Future Prospects," reprinted from Lawrence M. Friedman, *Government and Slum Housing,* © 1968 by Rand McNally & Company, Chicago, pp. 173-183. Reprinted by permission of Rand McNally & Company.

"Drugs: The Addiction to Controls," original title, "Practical Aspects of Drug Legislation," by Lloyd N. Cutler, reprinted from *Drugs in Our Society* edited by Paul Talalay (Baltimore: The Johns Hopkins Press, 1964), pp. 149-159, by permission of the publisher.

"The Atomic Energy Commission Breeds Its Power," original title, "Nuclear Energy by Contract: The AEC Experience" adapted from *Contracting for Atoms* by Harold Orlans, Brookings Research Report 63 (Washington, D.C.: The Brookings Institution, 1967), pp. 1-9, by permission of the publisher.

"Environmental Degradation by Government," original title, "The Federal Government as an Inadvertent Advocate of Environmental Degradation" by Charles R. Ross, reprinted from *The Environmental Crisis*, edited by Harold W. Helfrich, Jr. Copyright © 1970 by Yale University. Reprinted by permission of Yale University Press.

"The Impact of Public Spending upon Freedoms," reprinted from *Public Spending* by R. N. McKean. Copyright © 1968 by McGraw-Hill, Inc. Used by permission of McGraw-Hill Book Company.

"The Future Planners" by Andrew Kopkind, reprinted by permission of the author and *The New Republic,* © 1967, Harrison-Blaine of New Jersey, Inc.

# Preface

The student confronts two contradictory facts in American government—stable legal framework and explosive environment. Critics of change demand loyalty to the framework hoping that the explosion will subside. They exalt constitutional principles as truths which, if relied upon, would resolve the conflicts that tear at the social and political fabric of the United States. But Oliver Wendell Holmes, in his oft-quoted opinion, suggested that in a true democracy "truth is that which can be sold in the market place." And bombs are today being exploded in the market places of ideas. Herein is the dilemma for the American Republic in the latter decades of the twentieth century. Which methods and procedures can indeed be sold to the public in the market place? Will these be *adequate* "truths"? Will they develop a better consensus in the future than in the past?

This volume of selected readings is not supposed to solve problems but to introduce them to argument. It lets the reader understand the scope of conflict and change present in the American system. But, more than that, the book samples the various methods by which political scientists and politicians try to know what they are talking about. The book also samples the kinds of documents—speeches, orders, and so on—that are the stock in trade of political communication.

We are in an America that is in mid-revolution in the twentieth century. Old issues remain, but new issues of great urgency have arisen. If the men who still run the country choose to belittle this fact, they do so at their own peril. There is nothing new about the fact that half the American people are women, a third are young, and a tenth or more are black. But the new fact is that in all three of these groups, which together make up three quarters of the population, profound changes are stirring. Once our leaders understand what some of the new issues in American government are going to be, they will be ready for the next step—finding solutions to these issues.

We do not hold much hope for the present generation of American leaders. They are glued to the fabric of the establishment: feckless political parties, sluggish courts, impersonal corporate and governmental bureaucracies, and stagnant backwaters of popular opinion—sometimes called the "silent majority." By the time the present leaders take the two steps just described, they will be hurled from power by a new leadership and choked in the dust of history. In ordinary times, leaders average twenty-five or more years older than the upcoming leaders-to-be; in unsettled times, the gap can drop almost to parity. If those young leaders who are intent upon change wish to control the power they are seizing, they will have to learn to bypass useless, irrelevant, and misleading knowledge—which lies mountain high before all institutional careers—and head directly for knowledge that counts in making political and social decisions. This book is intended to contribute to that goal. Its materials can be used in introductory American government courses; they would also be congenial to the study of sociology and psychology in social science survey courses.

We are indebted to the authors, publishers, and editors who granted permission to use their work in this volume. We are also grateful to Miss Susan Peters and Miss Roberta Lewis, whose constant secretarial assistance was invaluable.

# Contents

PHOTO CREDITS

| | |
|---|---|
| **Revolution: Fact or Fancy?** | *Fred W. McDarrah* |
| **"Let's Do Something"** | *Gerald L. Sloan* |
| **The Public Pulse** | *Françoise Nicolas* |
| **Double Trouble** | *Burt Glinn—Magnum* |
| | *U. S. Army Photograph* |
| **Manipulating Political Behavior** | *J. Asquith and Joe Meinike (Photo)* |
| **Top Leadership** | *Bureau of Engraving and Printing* |
| **The Long Arm of the Law** | *U.P.I.* |
| **The City** | *Françoise Nicolas* |
| **"Happenings" in Government** | *Françoise Nicolas* |
| **The Knowable and Possible** | *Harvey Shaman* |
| **How To Torture a Public Policy** | *Michael Alexander* |
| **Budgets and the Good Life** | *J. Asquith and John Moore (Photo)* |

# OLD GOVERNMENT / NEW PEOPLE

## Readings for the New Politics

# Revolution:

1

# Fact or Fancy?

Two points are clear to a great many observers of the United States today: the country is speeding along through a technological and social revolution that is uncontrolled, and it needs a reconstituted leadership and program—the sooner the better. A revolution consists simply of deep changes achieved rapidly in many areas of life. A great many Americans feel that such a revolution is necessary. Now what stops the majority of the people and prevents the show from getting on the road is an uneasy satisfaction with their material lives and the distrust and fear of the unknown—the post-revolutionary social system. This resistance to change has led inevitably to conflict and violence.

Generally speaking, the people who feel most acutely the need for revolution and who suffer most now are the people who dislike violence and coercion most. The extremist, however, whether leftist revolutionary or vigilante upholder of "law and order," is most prone to violence, adept at it, and possessed of the means of violence. Notice how the opinions in the following article are saturated with feelings about violence, even though, in principle, revolutions need not be violent and need not coerce any more people than are continually being coerced by society.

The article is the result of a *New York Times Magazine* symposium in which six commentators were asked to answer the following questions:

> The United States is at the beginning of its "Second Revolution," spokesmen for the New Left have taken to saying. Is it true? Is America today in such a state that a revolution—i.e., the overthrow of the present system, by force if necessary—is justified? With what would the revolutionaries replace the present system? What chance of success do they have?

The six commentators are David McReynolds, the field secretary of the War Resisters League; Richard H. Rovere, author of the "Letter from Washington" column in the *New Yorker;* David Gelber, writer for *Liberation Magazine* and contributor to *The Village Voice;* Arthur Schlesinger, Jr., former White House aide; Ayn Rand, author of *The Fountainhead, Atlas Shrugged,* and other books; and Paul Cowan, author of *The Making of an Un-American.*

# 1

## David McReynolds
## *Are We in the Middle of the "Second American Revolution"?*

Are we in the beginning of a Second American Revolution? Yes and no. Paradox: revolutions can occur only after they have occurred. Marx's call for revolution in 1848 was based on the revolutionary changes that had already occurred—the emergence of the proletariat. Revolution as we usually use the word means the violent effort to create new institutions to help share power among new social forces. In England and in the Scandinavian countries, the creation of democratic political parties (a debt we owe the Marxists), trade unions and cooperatives all served to distribute political power to the proletariat without a violent convulsion. In Russia, the revolution occurred less because of the proletariat—a small group in 1917—than because of the inflexibility of Russian institutions combined with the disaster of the war. When the Czar stumbled from power in April, 1917, it was a surprise to everyone, including Lenin. (Which suggests that while we may talk about revolutions, we cannot predict them.)

Revolutions do not occur because of revolutionaries but because of massive social tensions that demand change, combined with a political establishment unwilling or unable to make those changes..That situation exists today in America. Nixon has made the fatal mistake of declaring war on our youth (through his noisome little mouthpiece, Spiro Agnew) and of seeking the allegiance of Southern whites rather than the confidence of American blacks and American youth. In the short run, it is a successful strategy. In the long run, it will prove a disaster.

Blacks, Chicanos, Puerto Ricans, and youth do not constitute a majority, but they are a massive force of social energy and they are unable to feel respect for—or any sense of shared power in—the present white Establishment, made up of the military, the corporations, the conservative A.F.L.-C.I.O. The Chicago trial, the search and destroy missions the police carry out against the Black Panthers, the nomination of Carswell, the absolutely unconstitutional expansion of the war into Cambodia, the failure of the Government to check inflation or to wage a meaningful war on poverty—all of these provoke a loss of confidence in the legitimacy of the Establishment. (The hypocrisy of the "respectable Establishment" is demonstrated by New York Times editorials demanding immediate criminal prosecution of the handful of terror bombers in our nation while failing to demand similar criminal prosecution of Nixon and all officers of the Government who have conspired in the massive bombing of Vietnam and the waging of a war in which more than a million have died and an entire nation has been ravaged.)

The Pentagon is a greater threat to American institutions than the Weathermen. Spiro Agnew is the real organizer for the violent fringe—every speech he makes drives a few more deeply concerned youths into the tragic tactic of armed resistance. The most "revolutionary agent" of the moment is simply the war itself, which daily persuades more Americans of the criminal nature of the central Government.

When is a revolution justified? Is America in such a bad state that a revolution is justified now? Revolutions are like earthquakes. They are tragic, they cannot be predicted, they do not require justification, they cannot really be organized. Revolutions occur when they occur. They are not caused by conspiracies but, as the Russian theologian Nicholas Berdyaev pointed out, by the indifference and inhumanity and inflexibility of existing institutions. America is in a bad state now and it would be in a bad state after a violent revolution.

What is the aim, beyond destroying the system, of present-day revolutionaries? Revolutions, from our own of 1776 through the Russian, Chinese and Cuban, share a common set of values: freedom, justice, wider distribution of power to previously powerless and oppressed elements of the society. Few revolutions have a blueprint of what they will actually do, and those blueprints are usually scrapped as unusable once the revolution has occurred. For myself, I favor wider distribution of power away from the central Government directly to communities. And I favor the unilateral dismantling of our military machine, so that it cannot oppress us or anyone else. (I would fear a revolutionary military machine as much as I fear the present one.) Such an act would more likely revolutionize the world as a whole, including the Soviet Union, than lead to our facing an invasion. The large corporations need to be broken into smaller units with ownership and control vested in communities and regions. Centralization of economic or political power is dangerous to a free society.

What chances of success do the revolutionaries have? On our own, very little. The central Government still commands the support of the vast majority of citizens, though discussion of revolution helps to remind people that revolution is a very American process. Terror bombings do more to build support for a police state than for revolution, and I suspect that Government agents are involved in some of the bombings. It is possible there will be no revolution but that America, the most advanced power in the world, will prove unable to govern itself in any way and sink into chaos. Youths need to read less Lenin and Mao and more about America. Chants of "Ho, Ho, Ho Chi Minh" are not revolutionary. Ho didn't win power in Vietnam by chanting about Russia or China, but by dealing with Vietnamese problems. The breakfast program of the Panthers is far shrewder than their earlier display of guns. The nonviolence of César Chavez and the nonviolence of the draft-resistance movement suggest that the compassionate tradition of American radicalism, the tradition of Eugene Debs and Martin Luther King, is not yet played out.

Is the revolution here? Something is happening, Mr. Jones, but I'm not sure what it is. The bombings. The campus unrest. Hundreds jailed for resisting the draft, thousands jailed on drug charges, tens of thousands fleeing into Canada, black leaders shot to death in their beds by Chicago cops. Listen to rock music. Observe the culture heroes of the youth.

Popular as Nixon and Agnew may be with a frightened middle America, they lack the charisma needed to sustain the kind of police state the Attorney General is trying so hard to fashion. I won't try to predict the future—just urge those of us who believe in democracy and nonviolence to keep struggling. The editor of Crawdaddy, a leading "rock culture" paper, put the thing perfectly when he said: "Agnew, Nixon and Mitchell have set to sea in a sieve." Sink they will—nothing in today's politics is more certain. The question is whether America will sink with them.

P.S. Just as I prepared to turn this in, I learned troops opened fire on students at Kent State in Ohio, killing four and wounding others. The military junta that rules us is in the open. The chances for a nonviolent and democratic solution—such as Congressional impeachment of Nixon and Agnew—fade hour by hour.

## Richard H. Rovere

So many things are out of joint in this country that if they were all, or nearly all, set right, or nearly right, the changes, by whatever means accomplished, would constitute a revolution of great magnitude.

None of us can know, at this point in our history, how much in the way of change is within the realm of the possible—a realm in which time is now a crucial dimension. If we go by the form sheets—election returns, opinion polls—we have to see ourselves as a conservative people, and getting more so from month to month. Yet the conservative powers-that-be are capable of at least some innovation—e.g., family-assistance programs. And some kinds of change seem to commend themselves on an almost wholly non-ideological basis—e.g., protection of the environment, abortion reform. But this seems to me about to exhaust the categories. Most of the rest involve struggle. Power has to change hands. Wealth has to be redistributed. Institutions have to be junked or reshaped. Most social and political change is brought about through social and political conflict.

Conflict can and usually does take many forms, one of which is violence. For my own part, I see little point in discussing violence as a means toward revolutionary ends in this country in this part of this century. I think I would oppose it under almost any circumstances because I find it abhorrent and corrupting. But even if I felt otherwise and felt also that conditions in this country were so intolerable as to justify an attempt at revolution by violence, I would still oppose it on the ground that the likeliest—indeed, the certain—outcome would be to make conditions even more intolerable. There have been exceptions (fewer than are claimed, though), but this has been the general history of violence, and I should suppose that anyone in possession of his wits and able to give the matter a few moments of thought would find this conclusion inescapable. This country might benefit from revolutionary change, but the overwhelming majority of its people think otherwise. Our society may be deteriorating, but the news hasn't reached deeply into the masses. Of those it has reached, probably a majority blame the deterioration on those who would make the revolution.

In other words a revolution would be quite promptly crushed. Before that happened, a few, perhaps many, edifices would topple, and guerrillas might make life hazardous for a time. But the more bombings there were and the more guerrillas in the streets, the bloodier the retribution and the more repressive the repression. This is not Vietnam. The masses may be deceived and exploited, but political education has not brought them to the point of much awareness on this score. Nor are they apathetic. They are overwhelmingly on the side of authority, legitimate or otherwise, and wish it were used less sparingly than it is. And although certain outbreaks of violence—particularly in the ghettoes—may have had some value as "demonstration effect," the kind of concerted violence that is revolution would bring into the streets not only the police and the military but millions of self-appointed and well-armed vigilantes and counter-revolutionaries.

I said—or tried to say—some of this to some young revolutionaries on a television show recently and was quickly put down as a "cynic" and a "defeatist." My analogies were all from the past–where else can one find any?–and one of them enjoined me to forget history and "study the future." I plead not guilty to cynicism, but guilty of first-degree defeatism when it comes to the proposition of turning this country leftward with guns and bombs. That, at least, is what my study of "the future" leads me to conclude.

Beyond this, I conclude very little. I have my visions of what I would like this country to be and do in the world, and I think they accord with at least some of those who are in the process of persuading themselves that violence is the only answer. I am not sure they are wrong in believing there is no hope in any of the other approaches. In other words, it could be that our American situation is hopeless. But I see no choice but to proceed on the assumption that there is hope. The argument, in any case, is not closed as of now. The record of democracy, where it has been practiced in some limited fashion, is often far from exhilarating, particularly when it comes to wars and other instruments of foreign policy. It has produced injustices as gross as those produced in many totalitarian societies. But it has had its triumphs, and it is the only system that I know of to be worth trying to bring to something approaching perfection. It cannot be improved or perfected by revolutionary violence. But it can surely be wrecked by counterrevolutionary violence.

## David Gelber

In the first place, this symposium is a hustle. We've been asked to respond to four cosmic questions (which insinuate that the principle threat of violent revolution comes from the left) in 1,000 words. Leaving no space for a coherent, substantiated case for views which rarely make their way into the mass media, this format effectively reinforces the smug clichés about "simple-minded leftist fanatics" while giving the reader the illusion that he has "heard both sides."

Schlesinger, Rovere, Rand et al may not be very convincing either, but they are very much at home in a business-dominated system which subordinates human development to the production of anesthetizing (and murderous) objects. We're not. They accept the capitalist/warfare state (and the distorted human relationships which inevitably follow) as the loftiest attainable by man. We don't. But if neither side is convincing the status quo wins another round.

The Times, meanwhile, does its bit by focusing on the relatively insignificant violence of the left instead of the massive, legalized violence of Agnew, Mitchell, Nixon and Laird, who are busily hacking away at the Constitution. If The Times called a symposium on the right-wing counter-revolution now under way, it might, God forbid, anger Spiro Agnew. In the hoary tradition of liberal spinelessness, The Times would rather fight the left while caving in to the right.

It is, of course, revolutionary these days to talk about people controlling their own government. Just that. Black and poor white communities have no say as to how or by whom they are policed. Polluting the air is a sacred prerogative of private industry and will remain so as long as profit is the sanctum sanctorum of American values. Voters don't even know what wars their Government is fighting, and, as many Americans have just discovered, it wouldn't make a hell of a lot of difference if they did. So, in the context of violent counterrevolutionaries running things in Washington, you can be a revolutionary if you just take the Constitution seriously.

At the same time, the U.S., which controls 60 per cent of the earth's natural resources for 6 per cent of the world's population, is the chief target of a world revolution. Washington's attempt in Vietnam, and now Laos and Cambodia, to suppress that global revolution has accelerated natural divisions in American society and gives some hope that forces will emerge and unite to make a second American Revolution. In heavy industry, where real wages are declining because of war-induced inflation, young workers are rejecting sweetheart contracts at an unprecedented rate. Blacks, forced to fight a white man's war, have never been so disposed to use militant tactics to achieve dignity in a white-supremacist society. Students are refusing to live out the acquisitive roles slated for them by elders whose enthusiasm for the domination of nonwhites by whites spurred on the U.S. rape of Southeast Asia. In the past decade, millions of blacks, women, soldiers, students, prisoners, homosexuals, young workers and professionals have been sensitized to the intricate patterns of domination and privilege on which the American system rests. Deference to our rulers (or "patriotism," if you will) is a vanishing phenomenon, even among sectors of the population too dulled to put up a fight. All this is enough to justify the assertion that a second American Revolution (inseparable from a world revolution) has at least begun.

In case you haven't noticed, we're not living in a nice, relatively humdrum country like Denmark where the Social Democrats tinker around enough to make life in a class-ridden society tolerable. Those who tenaciously rely on liberalism for gradual solutions to social crises need a strong dose of history.

Liberals have been knocking around for 70 years now without giving us a positive solution to even one major social problem of modern American society. Poverty and unemployment were "solved" not by the New Deal but rather by war and, since World War II, by the production of ecocidal trash. The trusts which engaged the bully-boy progressives in 1900 are more powerful than ever. Eighty per cent of Americans cannot afford the cost of a major illness. The system's answer to the race problem–integration–has integrated 1 per cent of black school children in the South since Brown *v.* Board of Education. Reform-administered cities are unlivable and will get worse as long as private profit determines how money is spent in America. And two of our last three Presidents, self-avowed messengers of the liberal, humanist tradition, were mass murderers.

Irving Howe intoned in these pages recently that he is "sick and tired" of those who would forsake moderate reformers like Ralph Nader and Sam Brown. In fact, we've had Naderesque muckrakers around since the beginning of time begging Congress to regulate big business, yet consumer products are gaudier and less reliable than ever. As for Sam Brown, less than a month after Howe's article appeared, Brown tucked in his tail and closed down the Moratorium business, having already prevented it from possibly developing into a general-strike movement he and Gene McCarthy could not control. Enough of such timidity. It is a delusion to think that we can create a decent society without first taking power away from the private industrialists, generals and politicians who set the course of this indecent society.

With what would the left replace the present system? The question is misleading. What is positive in the American tradition is not threatened by the left; it is daily being destroyed by the right. Or what do *you* make of midnight raids on Black Panthers by uniformed murderers? Of laws which make a state of mind illegal? Another misleading implication here is the supposed dividing line between revolution (which The Times reduces to simply a destructive event) and the postrevolutionary system of government. In a revolution worthy of the name (such as the Vietnamese), radically advanced social institutions and human relationships develop in the course of the revolutionary struggle itself.

An example close to home: Last year, the radical community in Berkeley converted a useless piece of land into a people's park. [Governor] Reagan and the university's Board of Regents correctly saw the park struggle as a threat to the principle of private ownership of land. As a result, the Berkeley radicals are up against a coordinated attack spearheaded by Reagan, who declared himself in favor of a juvenicidal bloodbath, the Berkeley City Council, which is about to purchase two surveillance helicopters, and the more liberal University of California, which prefers to destroy the radical community with a housing policy that would convert Berkeley into a well-heeled suburb for professors, obedient scholars and San Francisco executives.

In self-defense, the Berkeley people increasingly are forming supportive community structures: free schools, food cooperatives, democratic living arrangements, rent-strike units and free professional services. This is *not* the latest utopian flight from the real world. It is a self-conscious effort to strengthen the community for a fight for survival which lies in the imminent future. It is also a partial embodiment of the vision of the revolutionary society which inspires the young left.

The prospects for revolutionary change in America will not be enhanced if the Government is able to murder, exile and jail revolutionary leaders while scaring millions of others into depressive passivity. We may have to face an indefinite period during which the only permissible dissidence will be insipid happenings like Earth Day or privatistic acts such as smoking dope or growing sideburns.

Ten years ago, however, no symposiast in his right mind would have anticipated the emergence of a left potent enough to send one President into retirement and to discredit (in the academic world, at least) liberal imperialists like Arthur Schlesinger, who approve of global interventionism as long as the U.S. can get away with it.

Recent disturbances at state universities and working-class community colleges suggest that the spirit of radical resistance is seeping down the social class ladder. It is not surprising. Lower-middle-class kids who attend college to learn how to feed computers also share in a culture which exalts peace, good sex, generational solidarity and, in general, better aspirations than flooring a Mustang. The anti-authoritarianism inherent in the young left is politicized by a growing resentment against the socially destructive aims and alienating work of modern industry. This may mean that, within five to ten years, the new generation of workers will be taking over plants and offices insisting (as some French workers did in 1968) on the establishment of work-place democracy and popular control of investment and production decisions. That would not be compatible with the continued hegemony of wealthy shareholders and a managerial élite. For that to happen, the left (the student left, the antiwar left, the women's liberation left, the antipollution left, etc.) will have to come together far more than it has. If these forces manage to join together against a natural target, like polluter-warmaker General Motors (which the U.A.W. will probably strike against next fall), the revolution will seem a lot nearer—and The Times will have to call another symposium.

## Arthur Schlesinger, Jr.

The notion of a New Left revolution in the United States—in the sense of a forceful overthrow of the present system—remains a fantasy in spite of the revolutionary stimulus recently provided by President Nixon with his invasion of Cambodia and his encouragement of action against the "bums" on campus. The New Left has revolutionary dreams, not revolutionary plans. It has no program for overthrowing the system and no program for imposing or constructing a new system. For the New Left, revolution is what they term in their patois a "life style"; it is not an overarching conspiracy.

New Leftists, in short, are fantasts of revolution. They see politics as theater and seek to make cautionary and symbolic points against the rigidities and hypocrisies of contemporary life. By being systematically outrageous, they aim to expose and explode the cant that envelops them. When their fantasy maintains touch with reality—as was once the case with Tom Hayden as a reformer and may still be the case with Abbie Hoffman as a satirist—they can be effective. Many criticisms launched by the New Left are uncomfortably close to the mark. By forcing the rest of us to take a fresh look at injustices too complacently accepted or too benignly neglected, the New Leftists have played an undoubted role in stimulating the national conscience.

But saying something like this drives many New Leftists into a fury. Their obsessive anxiety is that society may absorb them as licensed rebels and professional entertainers. Some New Leftists invite such roles, of course, and display obvious relish when offered the chance to bring their act into college lecture halls or television studios. But the more angry among them are propelled by the fear of "cooptation" into drastic attitudes and actions. When this happens, their fantasy loses touch with reality. It has carried some of them into realms of hysteria where their gospel of love becomes an injunction to hate and they seek to verify fantasy by violence.

The more literally they take their revolutionary dreams, the more they jeopardize the revolution of which they dream. If, through their cult of disruption and destruction, the New Leftists should ever succeed in turning American society into a competition of unreason, hysteria and guerrilla warfare, do these play-boys of insurrection really believe that Jerry Rubin, Eldridge Cleaver and Herbert Marcuse will bring more armed men into the streets than George Wallace, Ronald Reagan and John Mitchell? Should the New Left bring down the fabric of civility in our society and make force the final court of appeal, they seal their own fate and hand the future to the right. The New Leftists can't make a revolution, but they might conceivably make a counter-revolution.

Obviously there are times and places when revolution is justified. The Declaration of Independence offers a lucid explanation of the conditions that make revolution legitimate and necessary. But, however deplorable the present situation of the United States, it can hardly be said that we have exhausted nonrevolutionary remedies. Still the fashion of revolutionary talk—the fact that The Times should stage this symposium—ought to convey a warning to our leaders.

For, though our internal divisions are not revolutionary, they are acute and ominous. President Nixon announced after the election that his purpose was to "bring us together," but his policies have only driven us further apart. Instead of trying to bring the estranged and excluded Americans into the national community, he has evidently decided to accept and exploit the division and side with those he considers the majority. Instead of a politics of reconciliation, he has chosen the politics of polarization and has unleashed the Vice President for this purpose.

One of the few remaining institutions of reconciliation, for example, has been the Supreme Court; to this, almost alone in the panoply of Washington, the alienated groups felt they could look for justice. President Nixon's determination to convert the Supreme Court into one more arm of the established order can only deprive rebels against the system of a last reason to retain faith in the constitutional process. His determination to intensify and widen the Vietnam war in spite of Congressional and popular opposition can only increase disenchantment with the democratic process.

Should the Administration thus continue to make our institutions more rigid and regressive, our internal divisions will certainly deepen. As John F. Kennedy once said, "Those who make peaceful revolution impossible will make violent revolution inevitable." But also, in the words of Adam Smith, there is a lot of ruin in a country. The further hardening of the Nixon policies will, I trust, lead to an overthrow of the Government, but through elections, not explosions.

## Ayn Rand

The New Left does not portend a revolution, as its press agents claim, but a *Putsch*. A revolution is the climax of a long philosophical development and expresses a nation's profound discontent; a *Putsch* is a minority's seizure of power. The goal of a revolution is to overthrow tyranny; the goal of a *Putsch* is to establish it.

Tyranny is any political system (whether absolute monarchy or fascism or communism) that does not recognize individual rights (which necessarily include property rights). The overthrow of a political system by force is justified only when it is directed against tyranny: it is an act of self-defense against those who rule by force. For example, the American Revolution. The resort to force, not in defense, but in violation, of individual rights, can have no moral justification; it is not a revolution, but gang warfare.

No revolution was ever spearheaded by wriggling, chanting drug addicts who are boastfully antirational, who have no program to offer, yet propose to take over a nation of 200 million, and who spend their time manufacturing grievances, since they cannot tap any authentic source of popular discontent.

Physically, America is not in a desperate state, but intellectually and culturally she is. The New Left is the product of cultural disintegration; it is bred not in the slums, but in the universities; it is not the vanguard of the future, but the terminal stage of the past.

Intellectually, the activists of the New Left are the most docile conformists. They have accepted as dogma all the philosophical beliefs of their elders for generations: the notions that faith and feeling are superior to reason, that material concerns are evil, that love is the solution to all problems, that the merging of one's self with a tribe or a community is the noblest way to live. There is not a single basic principle of today's Establishment which they do not share. Far from being rebels, they embody the philosophic trend of the past 200 years (or longer): the mysticism-altruism-collectivism axis, which has dominated Western philosophy from Kant to Hegel to James and on down.

But this philosophic tradition is bankrupt. It crumbled in the aftermath of World War II. Disillusioned in their collectivist ideals, America's intellectuals gave up the intellect. Their legacy is our present political system, which is not capitalism, but a mixed economy, a precarious mixture of freedom and controls. Injustice, insecurity, confusion, the pressure-group warfare of all against all, the amorality and futility of random, pragmatist, range-of-the-moment policies are the joint products of a mixed economy and of a philosophical vacuum.

There *is* a profound discontent, but the New Left is not its voice; there is a sense of bitterness, bewilderment and frustrated indignation, a profound anxiety about the intellectual-moral state of this country, a desperate need of philosophical guidance, which the church-and-tradition-bound conservatives were never able to provide and the liberals have given up.

Without opposition, the hoodlums of the New Left are crawling from under the intellectual wreckage. Theirs is the Anti-Industrial Revolution, the revolt of the primordial brute—no, not against capitalism, but against capitalism's roots—against reason, progress, technology, achievement, reality.

What are the activists after? Nothing. They are not pulled by a goal, but pushed by the panic of mindless terror. Hostility, hatred, destruction for the sake of destruction are their momentary forms of escape. They are a desperate herd looking for a Führer.

They are not seeking any specific political system, since they cannot look beyond the "now." But the sundry little Führers who manipulate them as cannonfodder do have a mongrel system in mind: a statist dictatorship with communist slogans and fascist policies. It is their last, frantic attempt to cash in on the intellectual vacuum.

Do they have a chance to succeed? No. But they might plunge the country into a blind, hopeless civil war, with nothing but some other product of antirationality, such as George C. Wallace, to oppose them.

Can this be averted? Yes. The most destructive influence on the nation's morale is not the young thugs, but the cynicism of respectable publications that hail them as "idealists." Irrationality is not idealistic; drug addiction is not idealistic; the bombing of public places is not idealistic.

What this country needs is a *philosophical* revolution—a rebellion against the Kantian tradition—in the name of the first of our Founding Fathers: Aristotle. This means a reassertion of the supremacy of reason, with its consequences: individualism, freedom, progress, civilization. What political system would it lead to? An untried one: full, laissez-faire capitalism. But this will take more than a beard and a guitar.

## Paul Cowan

I'm writing this a few hours after the Ohio National Guard murdered four students at Kent State; a few days after President Nixon incited such violence by calling students "bums," announced the invasion of Cambodia, resumed the bombings of North Vietnam. New declarations of war on two fronts, a redeclaration of war on one. Who knows what will have happened by the time this is printed?

We got rich too quickly in this country, defined our freedom as the right to exploit others, replaced our cultural and moral roots with a crazed desire to chase the big buck. We prided ourselves on an undefeated, untied, unscoredupon war record, lost all personal feeling for what it's like to be devastated. We decided that our affluence was willed by God and immunized ourselves to the complexity and tragedy of life, the suffering of others.

I have serious doubts about presenting a fuller, reasoned argument here. Are there words that will persuade you that The New York Times, Time and Newsweek should print articles exploring the psyches of the clean-cut generals who order the wanton destruction of thousands of Asians, not of radicals who respond to such provocations by fighting? That the white-collar fascists in power now hope to gain total control of this country by insulting, imprisoning and even murdering young people, black people and poor people? Can you be convinced that Richard Nixon and his advisers are war criminals who should be tried accordingly? That there are no conventional means at all by which the problems of this country can be solved?

Here are seven proposals. Some readers may have mind sets that make it hard for them to take such suggestions seriously. To me, and many people I've talked to, such ideas—not necessarily these specific ones—represent the minimum necessary for survival.

(1) Force the United States to admit and accept defeat in Southeast Asia.

(2) That means that the end of the war in Indochina—and of the war against dissenters at home—must become the absolute first priority of every American institution.

Strikes can be organized like those on the campuses. Social workers can force their agencies to join clients in combating the war and its disastrous effect on poor people. Teachers and students; poverty lawyers and their clients; doctors, nurses and their patients can enter into similar sorts of alliances. People in agencies like the Peace Corps and AID can organize to shut down those operations. Liberal Justice Department lawyers, if there still are any, can disrupt the functioning of that thoroughly corrupt agency. Federal employes in agencies like Health, Education and Welfare and the O.E.O. can stage massive demonstrations at the Pentagon for a reversal of national priorities. Workers throughout the country can organize antiwar strikes in their unions. Such actions could inspire a nationwide general strike.

(3) Also, petition the United Nations General Assembly (where the U.S. has no veto) to brand this country the aggressor in Southeast Asia and recruit an international army to fight it in a sort of reverse Korea.

(4) Impeach Nixon—then the rest of the ghostly parade of successors who have complied with the United States' criminal policies: Agnew, John McCormack, Richard Russell, etc.

(5) Force the Government, private institutions and large corporations to recognize that America's affluence is largely based on the exploitation of domestic colonies. Negotiate reparations treaties with blacks, Indians, Puerto Ricans, Mexican-Americans. Free political prisoners like Huey Newton, Bobby Seale and Martin Sostre, some of the bravest, most far-sighted members of their communities.

(6) Establish new communities, "liberated zones," in cities or sections of states.

There we can build the kind of humane institutions we believe in—schools, hospitals, child-care centers, old peoples' homes, mental institutions that are dedicated to serving people. Our loyalties will not be to the piggish United States, but to people throughout the world. In such communities, we will have to learn to transcend the racism, egotism and product addition that we have developed during our lives in this culture of greed—to undergo personal revolutions that parallel the political revolution we are trying to bring about.

If we can create such communities and defend them, people throughout the country will relate to them enthusiastically, see them and the politics and life style they represent as vibrant alternatives to the horrors of Nixonia.

(7) Work toward the eventual dissolution of the United States into a number of smaller autonomous regions. Only indispensible technological systems like communications and transportation should be continental—and those should include Canada and Mexico as equal partners with the rest of the separate North American states.

In some regions, of course, people will form alliances with Europeans, Asians, Africans or Latins that are closer than their alliances with other parts of the present United States.

This nation is too big for any group to govern it humanely. Few people really identify with it except in a commercial sense: they get tears in their eyes when they go overseas and hear some patriotic or popular song that reminds them of the hamburgers or huge hunks of steak they miss. Living in smaller, self-governing regions, Americans might recover some of the roots they lost when they came to this country, recover some of the modesty. We might become decent citizens of the world.

But maybe that is impossible. Maybe our history has injected a poison into our blood stream that forces us to be violent. Then, I would rather see Kansans fight Oklahomans than be part of a country where Kansans and Oklahomans are drafted into an army which forces them to drop bombs on Cambodians, Laotians, Vietnamese, their houses, schools and hospitals.

My slogan is: Dissolution before decay!

Of course, much of America's ruling class will suffer if any such ideas are adopted. The Nixon Administration knows that. It is terrified by all threats to its greedy plans to turn the United States into a giant factory town and use its mechanized people to control this planet and space.

It will try to stifle even small threats with repression at first, as it is doing now. Perhaps, when that doesn't work, there will be a military dictatorship. If that happens, the bloodshed will be ghastly. Could anything humane survive the wreckage that would be in store for this country?

I often think that the name of the thing we are headed for is not fascism, not revolution, but national suicide.

“Let’s Do

# 2

LAWS
THE GHETTO
GYPPED
of black
are greatful to
HERBERT Colbert, J. REYNOLDS, FRANK SHEPPARD, Johnnie
BOB LUCAS, JIM TILMAN, BUZZ PALMER, SOIDINE, Miss S. CARTER, CHRIS
FOR SAVING THE WALLS
following COMMUNITY SERVICES.. DAY CHILD CARE
SERVICES, LEGAL SERVICES,
HOUSING.
Black Power!
All Together
Join NOW!

# Something"

The Americans, for as long as they have had a separate identity as a people, have been known to be pragmatic and reformist. They want to do something about their problems and generally are not resigned to fate. They are initiators, activists. At least this is the prevailing mood in the country, although the United States, like every other country, has a large group of citizens who are passive or apathetic.

A goodly number of Americans, especially today, share the view of the Christian ex-soldier and bishop, Tertullian, who lived in the Roman Empire during its apogee and who could still say:

> I owe no obligation to forum, campus, or senate. I stay awake for no public function, I make no effort to monopolize the platform, I pay no heed to any administrative duty, I shun the voters' booth, the juryman's bench . . . I serve neither as magistrate nor soldier, I have withdrawn from the life of secular society. . . . My only concern is for myself, careful of nothing except that I should have no care. . . . . Man who is destined to die for himself is not born for another . . . .
>
> For us nothing is more foreign than the commonwealth. We recognize but one universal commonwealth, that is the world.

Still other Americans are cynical about the effectiveness of political action. If those above are Tertullians, these are Gorgians, for it was the ancient Greek Sophist, Gorgias, who once declared:

> Nothing exists.
> If it did exist, we couldn't know it.
> If we did know it, we couldn't communicate it to anyone.

However, the prevailing tendency of American political activists is toward reform, but this does not mean that there is agreement about the means or even the objectives. The following selections present two divergent views as to where our energies should be directed.

McGeorge Bundy was a Harvard dean and a special assistant to the president for national security affairs between 1961 and 1966. Thereafter he became head of the Ford Foundation, which subsidizes a fair proportion of all nongovernmentally supported studies and research in the United States. He believes we need not fear central government but should realize that it is the only realistic means of solving our vast, far-reaching problems. He feels that only a strong central executive can set a national policy and give it intelligent direction.

Richard Cornuelle also was active in foundations (the Volker Fund) prior to becoming vice-president of the National Association of Manufacturers. He was later chairman of President-elect Nixon's Task Force on Voluntary Action and is a consultant to government agencies and private associations. He believes that voluntary creative effort is the mainspring of American society and government. His message, as opposed to McGeorge Bundy's, is that the willing action of an individual or group is worth much more than the action coerced or ordered by the state. He discusses how the independent sector—nongovernmental, private institutions—can help to solve our national problems.

# 2

## McGeorge Bundy
## *Explosive Changes*

The more we learn about problems of race and poverty, the more we feel the force of two great contrasting propositions: The first is that these problems are enormously complex and deep-rooted, and the second is that they can be solved. It is this double awareness, on which the Negro himself has learned to insist, that makes these problems explosive, and there will be only explosions, not solutions, if there is not action by the government.

The components of the problem are now usually seen in four parts: jobs, housing, welfare, and education—and in all four fields the role of government has clear public recognition. . . .

No one really knows what it will cost to end poverty and racial unfairness in America. . . . My own estimate is that the kind of new money we need . . . is of the order of 20 or 30 billions a year. . . . This kind of continuing cost inevitably means federal action. . . .

When we consider what the government has done to affect men's thinking in the last 25 years, it becomes absurd to disconnect it from this problem. . . .

And very often . . . it will be only from Washington that the necessary action can come. The example of the schools is familiar, but I myself think the matter of equal access to real estate may be still more fundamental: This country cannot have real decency in its race relations until it turns clear away from the belief that the ownership of a piece of property carries with it the right to decide that no black man shall own it next. . . .

The average real-estate man must change his position, and there is no reason to suppose that he will do so until that position becomes a federal offense. . . .

We are rich enough, and we can be decent enough, to end poverty and racism. . . . We shall need federal law and federal money—in short, federal government for freedom.

### *'Powerful Arguments'*

When we look at the means of communication, we encounter all the . . . powerful arguments against excessive governmental activity . . . suggested by the magical words "free enterprise" . . . and "free speech." [These] are among the freedoms . . . government must serve. . . .

We are at the early stages of an explosion in this field, whose depth and variety create needs which only government can meet. . . .

The simplest and most powerful element in this explosion is technological.

Within this generation . . . we shall be able to put all sorts of information in all sorts of places in ways . . . not dreamed of till now. . . . The living room can readily become a place with the combined advantages of Widener Library [Harvard's nearly 2½ million-volume collection] and the total information net of the press, business, and government combined.

It may be that we shall "borrow books" by tuning in on the public-library channel, or that we shall do our shopping by two-way TV, and pay our bills the same way. On other channels we may conduct . . . meetings without ever leaving our rooms. . . .

A host of unanswered questions will have to be resolved as these extraordinary instruments become possible:

Are we talking about a new kind of common carrier, or . . . an information service as a form of free press? What is the place . . . for competition . . . ? . . . Should such a system . . . be directly assimilated to the processes of public education. . . ? What about governments as consumers of this information as well as regulators?

The first role of the government here will be legislative and regulatory . . . and the legislative and regulatory role itself requires kinds of strength and skill the government does not now have. . . .

A more subtle task for the government is to find the right way of supporting public-service research in this field. . . .

Let me suggest that if we consider first the attitudes of preschool children toward TV; second, the critical social value of a real head start in reading; third, the amount of money that commercial television spends to hold the children's interest; and fourth, the amount of money our educational system now spends to teach reading, there is suggested the possibility that a few . . . hundreds of millions of dollars for research and development in preschool teaching might give a lot of our children a built-in head start that would repay the investment in every possible way. . . . In a field which does not offer profits, [such as investment] can only mean government. . . .

*Decisions Demanded*

By its very nature the explosive force of the [atomic] nucleus has forced upon this country a series of decisions . . . which can only be made by government. . . .

The systems of safeguards which are designed to give us both alertness against attack and protection against accident are not inhuman—they require men. Those men are a part of government. Without some confidence in them, not one of us could responsibly turn to any other problem at all. . . .

There will be need for . . . unremitting excellence in their performance. . . . There will also be continuing need for a process of government in which they and we can continue to believe. No weak government can control the bombs indefinitely. . . .

### A 'DANGEROUSLY WEAK' BRANCH

The American System of Government is today far too weak to do the job now assigned to it, let alone the job that it ought to be given. . . . The simplest demonstration of the weakness of the executive branch is its subordination to the Congress in matters of appropriation and taxation. . . .

There is a classic instance of this perennial difficulty before us now: The executive branch has believed for six months that the country needs increased taxes, and for six months the central business of the executive branch has been to try to persuade the Congress to act on this need.

It is a pardonable exaggeration to say that during that period, the convictions of Wilbur Mills [chairman of the House Ways and Means Committee, which has bottled up the President's tax bill] have had more influence on the programs of the executive branch than [have] the convictions of President Johnson. . . .

In using his power to the limit to serve the purpose he thinks right, Mr. Mills is simply doing what we must expect any determined politician to do–indeed what we must want him to do. It is not the strength of Mr. Mills but the relative weakness of the whole executive branch that I am complaining of. . . .

### *Flexible Rates Urged*

Flexible tax rates are now quite simply indispensable to the effective management of economic policy–and so to strong and stable economic growth. . . .

The government . . . can [not] meet its present responsibilities effectively if it cannot change basic tax rates–perhaps up to 20 percent in either direction–with much greater speed than our system now permits. . . .

The executive branch is also dangerously weak in its own internal capacity for sustained, coordinated, and energetic action. . . .

The contest between the President and the bureaucracy is as real today as ever, and there has been no significant weakening in the network of triangular alliances which unite all sorts of interest groups with their agents in the Congress and their agents in the bureaucracy. . . .

The executive branch remains woefully short of first-class executive agents of the President. . . . The trouble is at the Cabinet level of the government, certainly, but it derives overwhelmingly from the nature of the office and not from the nature of the men who have occupied it. . . . Even very good Cabinet officers tend to become special pleaders at the White House for at least some of the interest groups that are strong in their departments. . . . They should run their part of government for the administration–not run to the administration for the interests of their part of the government. . . . At a test–unless he means to resign–the secretary should always be the president's agent, not the other way round. . . .

### *President's Problem*

The most compelling present example of this need for stronger Cabinet-level government is in the struggle against racism and poverty. . . . What is wrong . . . is the absence of the clearly concentrated authority and responsibility which have become characteristic of the Defense Department in recent years. . . . It is a safe prediction that the war against poverty will not be won until its high command in Washington is properly organized. . . .

[Two other weaknesses of the executive branch] are the underrepresentation of the public interest and the inadequacy of the interconnection of parties with legitimate concerns. The first weakness can be seen clearly in the area of communications policy and the second in the field of nuclear weapons.

The federal body which is supposed to set communications policy for the nation is the Federal Communications Commission. Its weakness is a national scandal. . . . The staff of the commission has a traditionally high level of ability, but it is absurdly small because the Congress keeps it that way. . . .

I do not mean to imply that the Congress has been suborned by the communications industry. . . . I do mean to suggest . . . that when there is a clash between public and private interests in the field of communications, there is bound to be caution in the Congress. . . .

I think the building blocks of a solution lie somewhere in a combination of judicious amendment of the Federal Communications Act, substantial reinforcement of the FCC, and a quite explicit strengthening of the machinery of the executive branch. It may also prove wise . . . to strengthen the president's own ability to influence both the membership and the agenda of the FCC. . . .

The nuclear problem illustrates many terrible and hopeful facts about our modern life. . . . The age of explosions . . . requires both special knowledge and understanding across the boundaries of . . . special knowledge. . . . The most critical of all the lines of connection here is from the scientist to the politician. . . .

My real point about the military in nuclear matters is not that they have contests with one another, but that they have found it so hard to communicate back and forth with others in the government about the real and hard questions of weapons choice, strategic doctrine, and arms control. . . .

This difficulty of understanding from one specialist to another is not unique to the nuclear field. . . . It is part of the nature of our age; there are parallel difficulties in the field of communications and in the war against racism and poverty. Specialists are indispensable, but specialists who do not know how to talk to others outside their field are dangerous. . . .

## AUTHORITY—AND PARTICIPATION

First . . . the need for effective government can often be demonstrated case by case. Social security, medical care, and now education are notable cases where visible need has gradually overcome shibboleths. . . .

A second familiar element in these arguments is a demonstration that even at its largest and most demanding, the government in fact remains quite small. . . .

The third necessity for a new concept of effective government is that we should reverse the whole pattern of our thinking about public officials. We should make it the explicit rule, and not the undiscussed exception, that they should have ample executive authority. To me the simplest and most straightforward demonstration of such confidence would be to establish pay scales and rules of appointment which will allow a senior governmental executive to get the men he wants. . . .

One enormous advantage . . . of . . . the White House is that if you can't get the best men in the country to help you, it's really your own fault. . . .

But there is only one White House, and truly effective government in the executive branch requires quality and energy and staff work out in the departments. For that kind of leadership we need salaries roughly twice the size of those which are now permitted. . .

But . . . executives need release also from other normal constraints: from laws so loaded with detail that discretionary responsibility is crushed; from patterns of power in which their nominal subordinates are in fact almost wholly autonomous; from legislative oversight which mistakes the trees for the woods, and even from trivial presidential intrusion which in the past has often been a necessary antidote to inertia or impotence.

And behind these . . . needs . . . is: a new level of public support for strong government. The American people, in their own true interest, need to learn to give their government more credit for action than for avoiding error, more honor for initiative than for standing pat, and more credit for what it does in the common interest of all than for what it does in the special interest of each. . . .

I remind you that I am claiming to talk not merely about strong government, but about strong government for freedom. In that concept I emphatically include . . . the general idea that one great part of freedom is to have a part in your own government, especially when it affects you directly. . . .

I will not back off one inch from what I have said about the need for energetic and effective public authority. Yet I also insist on the rightness of maximum practicable participation. Do I assert a contradiction?

I say that I do not. . . . I assert that if you want maximum practicable participation, you must first have something to participate in—and that the way to give a share of power to the people in these cases is first to give real power to an agency of government. . . . I think the accountable executive is much more likely to give real participation to the poor—and to other constituencies—if he has some power to share than if he does not. . . .

There is a need for authority; there is a need for participation. The challenge to the philosopher of freedom in our age is not to reject either necessity, but to point the way to their creative reconnection.

### *Need Pinpointed*

The president necessarily knows much that the people do not know about . . . nuclear matters. But if the president and the people do not have a good mutual understanding on the basic elements of the problem, then the president is flying blind. It follows that there must be good communication from the government to the public and back again on this issue. . . .

The task of interconnection between the people and their government grows harder. . . . It will be assisted, certainly, by progress in the interconnection of experts and specialists in and out of government. . . . But in the end . . . [it] is a problem for the president himself, in direct touch with the nation. . . .

In arguing for extending the reach of the presidency . . . I am [not] talking about extending the naked power of the president as an individual. The president who indulges his personal whims . . . is taking political risks which presidents simply do not like to take. . . . Limited discretionary power over tax rates seems to me likely to decrease and not increase the risk of capricious . . . action at moments of change in economic climate. . . .

The Constitution, our tradition, the private and the public interests unite to make [the president's] office the right source of new executive strength—which he must share beyond his own staff.

# 3

## Richard C. Cornuelle
## *How to Compete with Government*

Competition with government is really a competition for the confidence of the American people. As we saw in Chapter 10, we send representatives to Congress to decide for us what the public business is and who shall do it. Government's recent growth means simply that it has been able to convince Congress that it can perform better than independent or commercial institutions. The independent sector is clearly failing in this competition. It fails for two reasons. Either:

(1) it has left some important piece of public business undone or poorly done

or

(2) it has done a good job but has failed to get its story across to the public and its representatives in Congress.

Thus, the independent sector's competitive problem is very much like the competitive problem businesses face every morning. And businesses, to compete effectively, have to do four things:

(1) Find out what people want.
(2) Develop a product to meet that demand.
(3) Produce it economically.
(4) Sell it vigorously.

The independent sector needs to do the same things:

(1) *Research:* to find real human needs, their extent, their cause.
(2) *Development*: to find the best ways the independent sector can meet these needs.
(3) *Mobilization:* to get the independent sector to adopt these new methods.
(4) *Information:* to sell what it accomplished to the public.

In a simpler America, this wasn't necessary. We could see needs and remedies more easily. But today we can't see the public business so clearly. We have to take problems apart and look hard to find their cures. We have to plan carefully. We have to use up-to-date production methods, and often must create new organizational machinery. We have to report the results systematically to the public.

## RESEARCH

The government is quick to perceive emerging human needs. It is never stuck for a solution. This is as it should be. In a complex society, we would overlook many public problems if someone weren't looking for them. But, predictably, people who push federal programs often present biased evidence. They tend to exaggerate our problems. They say these problems are caused by factors only the government can fix. They understate what anybody else is doing and can do.

Author John Steinbeck, a man with a practiced eye for human misery, drove across America lately to see how we were doing. In a splendid book, *Travels With Charley* (Viking, 1963), he gave a generally favorable report. He found a friendly, if restless, nation of good people. Aside from heart-sickening racial turmoil, we seemed to be doing all right.

But officially, we are on the brink of moral, economic, and cultural collapse. We are in deep statistical distress.

Our unemployment rate is dangerously high.
Our growth rate has been dangerously low.
We need thousands more public school classrooms, and the situation is getting worse.
One fourth of us live in abject poverty.
Most older people can't get decent medical care.
By 2000, we will need three times as many places to play as we have now.
We need thousands more engineers, teachers, physicists, social workers, and recreationists right now.

Such "official" figures, fortunately, tell us only where the hard sell is on. Federal statistics often depend less on human need than on what is needed to make a political sale. President Roosevelt pioneered the system: he saw "one-third of the nation ill-housed, ill-clad, ill-nourished." Donald Richberg, who worked with Roosevelt on the speech, tells us where the figure came from. Richberg, reporting on their work together over the text in his autobiography *My Hero* (G. P. Putnam's Sons, 1954), said, "I protested that there were no statistics which could possibly be marshalled to support such a statement. . . . I ventured to suggest that if one were going to pull a figure out of the sky, it would at least be safer to say one-fourth. . . . But F.D.R. had a certain feeling for numbers. . . . He liked the one-third and he wasn't particularly bothered by using a fraction which, even if it could not be supported, could not be disproved."

These days, political statistics are worked up much more carefully. For example:

> Congress recently passed a program to help colleges. They had been told: Between 1960 and 1970, college enrollment will double. We face a national emergency. "There are simply not enough classrooms, laboratories, or libraries for the rising flood of applicants. Nothing less is at stake than our national strength, progress and survival."
>
> Only the federal government can do the job.

If these things are really true, could Congress fail to assign responsibility to government?

But many experts doubt these facts. Researcher Roger Freeman of Stanford's Hoover Institution points out that college enrollment will not grow as fast in the eight years beginning 1962 as it did in the eight years before 1962. A researcher for the Fund for the Advancement of Education says, "If classrooms were used to the greatest extent possible . . . present classrooms could handle four times the number of students." Journalists Benjamin Fine and Sidney Eisenberg polled 3,000 schools; 795 reported vacancies.

We are told one in twenty workers can't find a job. So we need a bigger federal job program. But the figures include:

> people who have quit their jobs to look for better ones,
> people who can't work for a while because other workers are on strike,
> people looking for part-time jobs,
> seasonal workers,
> handicapped people who can't work.

Many economists think that fewer than a million people are having real trouble finding a suitable job.

Government figures now tell us a fourth of our people still live in poverty. No doubt many do. But according to *Fortune's* Edmund V. Faltermayer, if we applied the same yardstick to Britain, we would find that three fourths of the British are poor. Opinion analyst Samuel Lubell writes: "The statistics being used of the people who are supposed to be living in poverty are not good figures at all." An honest concern for the poor does not justify imaginary statistics to scare off non-government competitors in the public business of helping the poor. . . .

The government sector's boosters overstate public problems. They also say problems have causes only the government can remedy. And government often reasons backward—from remedy to cause. Government can move resources around. It can tax and spend. It can restrict and punish. But our most urgent new public problems can't be solved with such crude instruments. . . .

Most experts agree that if you have to pick one cause, bad family life is the prime contributor to juvenile crime. But federal programs are entirely "based on the belief that obstacles to economic and social betterment among low income groups are the main cause of delinquency." Why does the government sector focus a one-track mind on this diagnosis when the evidence points another way? You can "better" people economically by spending money. You can't improve family life or the community that fosters better family life that way. . . .

The problems of education? The government says the schools need money. But many education experts disagree. "Education is weak, but it is not undernourished," writes Ernest van den Haag. "It is weak partly from obesity, partly from faulty diet, and above all, from lack of exercise." And the late Beardsley Ruml, liberal inventor of pay-as-you-go income taxes, wrote, "New money is not needed in anything like the amounts presently estimated. Many of the necessary funds are already at the disposal of the colleges, but are being dissipated through wastes in the curriculum and in methods of instruction."

Nor do the government sector's advocates waste much time boosting their competition. They often look briefly at the commercial and independent sectors. These are, they almost always find, "inadequate."

Early in his administration, President Eisenhower told his Secretary of Health, Education and Welfare to find out what non-governmental agencies could do to give older people the medical care they needed. The Department got to work. Several months later they reported. Their search for voluntary solutions was "futile." You can imagine how hard federal employees looked for a program that wouldn't require any federal employees. . . .

The commercial sector spends millions looking for new markets, getting ready for new demands. The government sector spends millions looking for new items of public business. The independent sector spends next to nothing. Yet of the three, it knows least about its own strength and how and where and when to put it to work.

## DEVELOPMENT

As the independent sector develops its own sense of what needs to be done in modern America, it must then work out specific ways to act. The basic know-how is at hand. In response to the increasingly technical requirements of business and government, a whole new industry, the research and development industry, has sprung up. These organizations, some commercial but many independent, will, it seems, tackle anything—from the economic planning of Disneyland to the launching of Telstar. They know how to find answers. We are beginning to discover how to ask the questions.

New ways to use physical materials could revolutionize independent action, just as they have revolutionized commercial production and distribution. We can see some results already.

One researcher designed a round hospital. He claims it can cut costs in half. Others have developed hospital beds which work electrically. They pay for themselves in two years in saved nurses' time. Intercoms save 15 per cent of the nurses' trips to patients. A $5,000 analyzer frees two $4,000 employees for other duties. Ultrasonic devices to clean equipment would save $19.5 million each year, if all hospitals used them. Throw-away syringes for injections save 25 per cent of the cost, add to safety.

A builder in Detroit designed apartments for poor older people and rented them for $22 a month. In the cultural field, new know-how in electronics, plastics, and optics can sharply cut down the cost of staging an opera.

These achievements promise even larger ones, as R&D technology is systematically focused on the problems of independent institutions, but there is a much larger challenge. For the independent sector's great crime is not that it wastes things, but that it wastes people. . . .

The commercial sector's energy exploded because it released the energy of people, discovered their most valuable specialty, and put them to work at it. In Detroit, a man takes his place on the line, does a job he can understand and handle, and contributes in combination with thousands of other specialists to the production of a car he couldn't build by himself in a thousand years. His work has been organized for him, and his productivity multiplies.

The independent sector has not learned how to use people. There are millions of people longing to be called to service. But there is no longer much they can do. We have professionalized the independent sector's work force. All the citizen can do is pay or persuade others to pay. Experts, we are told, must find the jobs for the hard-core unemployed. Only trained people can deal with juvenile crime. Only social workers can help troubled families. . . .

Thus, the great potential of the independent sector is bottled up. Its energy is reduced to a trickle that is forced through the narrow professional funnel. . . .

Many unusually enterprising individuals, moved by deep concern and guided by common sense, find satisfying roles for themselves. New York publisher Lyle Stuart was disturbed one night in a Brooklyn library by a noisy street gang. When he complained, he found out they had nowhere else to go, had no adult leadership. He won their confidence, learned they wanted jobs, helped them in their search.

As a result, Harrison Salisbury reported in the *New York Times:*

> The roughhouse gang that used to disrupt the library has vanished. The youngsters are working afternoons and Saturdays. There is still plenty of delinquency at Fort Greene, and gang problems as well. Not all of Mr. Stuart's boys will be straight. But a warm heart, common sense and civic responsibility have done much.

Elmer L. Winter, president of Milwaukee-based Manpower, Inc., heard that many young people in the Milwaukee area would probably be out of work in the summer months. He set up Youthpower, Inc., donated an office, typewriters, and office supplies, and helped it decide what to do. In a few weeks Youthpower found summer jobs for over a thousand boys and girls. Mr. Winter probably knows more about part-time employment than anybody in America. Probably no one else could have put Youthpower together. . . .

In Hazleton, Pennsylvania, Dr. Ed Dessen saw his town on the skids as its mines shut down. He set up CANDO to attract new industry. In five years, CANDO had created eleven thousand new jobs.

None of these men are professional social workers. They are laymen, exercising their independent responsibility with unusual conscientiousness. They invest their time in public service carefully and imaginatively, matching their particular skills to problems at hand.

But such enterprisers are, in the nature of things, rare. Most of us have the same impulse which moves them, but need guidance in how our particular skills can best be applied to the problems we see about us. "What can I do?" people ask. I can imagine no more urgent research task than to find answers

Bold innovation in methods of organizing the service impulse has become as important to the independent sector as assembly-line production and the corporate form of organization were to the commercial sector. I can only guess what forms these innovations will take. They will not be developed abstractly, but, I expect, will develop as effective competition with government makes them increasingly necessary.

Some general prospects are clear. For example, the franchising principle, so widely used in commerce, seems uniquely adaptable to some of the independent sector's unfinished business. Franchising blends central expertise with local initiative and responsibility. The Sears Foundation, in a project mentioned earlier, has pioneered this principle. Any determined rural community that needs and wants a team of doctors and a clinic can get expert guidance from the Foundation at every step of the way. But initiative and responsibility rest wholly with the community itself.

DATA International in Palo Alto, California, is pioneering in another promising technique. This organization keeps a careful skill bank, with which technicians of all types all over the country register. Simultaneously, DATA encourages people working abroad to ask for help with their problems. As these are reported, DATA assigns them to technicians who know how to help. Assignments have ranged from construction of chicken houses in Indonesia to ridding tomatoes of fungus to the development of a telephone exchange in Turkey. But DATA's principle—that specialized skills should be systematically linked up to specific problems—doubtless has a much wider application.

The independent sector obviously has a staggering development job to do. But the skills needed to get it done are there, waiting to be put to work.

## MOBILIZATION

As the independent sector develops new and better ways of applying its energy to the public business, it will find, as we did in student loans, that these plans will have to be promoted skillfully and persistently. . . .

But independent groups don't copy new methods. The know-how often stays at its point of origin. Look at Saul Alinsky's conquest of America's worst slum, at Henry Viscardi's success in putting the handicapped to work, at Cleo Blackburn's work in rebuilding slums, at the Menningers' work in mental health, at Millard Roberts' work in education. These operations rarely reach far beyond what these gifted and strong-willed men can do themselves.

In commerce it's different. Edison lighted not only Menlo Park but the whole world. Ford put a whole nation behind the wheel of the Model T. But the independent sector doesn't copy sound practices automatically. . . .

There are some striking isolated illustrations of effective mobilization of the independent sector. I was deeply impressed by the polio immunization program as it was handled in our county. The coverage was nearly total. The program was beautifully planned. The press, radio, and television played their part. The medical society pitched in to man the immunization stations. Hundreds of volunteers handled the crowds, and were so skillfully briefed that there were few hitches, even though several hundred thousand people were involved. We were asked as we left to put a quarter in a can if we wanted to, more if we chose, or nothing. When the books were closed, there was a surplus of nearly $100,000. I served on a committee that distributed the surplus among local charities.

But examples like this are rare. The independent sector has not, on the whole, learned to mobilize its resources promptly and sensibly. This lethargy will be cured to some extent when the independent sector's competitive spirit is restored. But in the modern world, salesmanship is a permanent imperative. Those who think the independent sector will be restored if we simply collect "good ideas" and print bulletins about them are in for heartbreak. We can no longer vaguely admonish independent institutions to "do better." Nor can we expect national action from magazine articles titled "What Cucamonga Can Do Your Town Too Can Do."

Government uses tax money to buy talent. And this method requires much less promotional and organizational skill than does persuading independent individuals and institutions to work more effectively. However, competitive pressure has developed in the commercial sector a breed of gifted promoters and organizers of commercial action. We need to create such a breed in the independent sector. They are our scarcest resource.

## INFORMATION

To compete with government and win, you have to perform. But that's not enough; you also have to let the public know you're performing. Government is the master huckster of its plans and programs. The independent sector–humble and reticent, mute and invisible–has been no good at all. The public forgets it exists.

This is, in part, natural. The groups which are good at getting things done are often no good at politics. The groups best at getting results–Alcoholics Anonymous, for example–shun publicity, spurn outside money, and go quietly about helping such people as alcoholics. Our best writers avoid the spotlight. Our poor ones hire people to keep them in it.

The people who do the country's work keep busy at it. Others talk to Congress about what they could do with more money and more power. Some people like to work; other people like to talk. Neither group is good at what the other does well. So it isn't natural for the independent sector to crow about what it does, to sell itself. Its institutions are scattered. They speak with no single voice. But they must find ways to overcome reticence, to find a single voice and to amplify it in public debate.

The press has become passive. The initiative has largely been reversed. You don't find the press looking for news as much as you find news looking for the press. Those who go after attention get it; those who don't, don't. Thus, while the press reports what goes on in commerce and government, it neglects what the independent sector does. For example, at the time the press hailed the Peace Corps as a bold innovation, 33,000 Americans, sponsored mainly by religious groups, were working quietly on a voluntary basis in 146 countries, doing the same things in the same places we were planning to send the Peace Corpsmen. These groups had been at it since 1809.

The sector of American society Tocqueville thought most important has become largely invisible and inaudible. The press covers golf more fully than independent action—partly because the independent sector doesn't do much new work, but partly because it doesn't make noise.

Again, a competitive posture will force a new realism about the independent sector's public and political relations. For years, Ford proudly refused to advertise. He thought the merit of his product was manifest and advertising superfluous, if not degrading. But as you may have noticed, competition in time forced him to advertise.

In political relations, the independent sector has some special problems. Clearly, the federal bureaucracy's convenient monopoly on the ear of Congress will be hard to break. There is virtually no limit on the bureaucracy's access to Congress. But independent institutions, if tax-exempt, cannot legally appear before Congress in pursuit of new responsibility or to beg that responsibility not be wrested from them. It is imperative that the right of the independent sector to defend itself and to seek new responsibility be clearly affirmed.

I would go further. I've proposed elsewhere that Congress establish an office, similar to the General Accounting Office, charged to inform Congress systematically of the achievements and potential of non-governmental institutions. Like the GAO, this agency would be responsible only to Congress, thus independent of the executive. It could help Congress perform its natural function by performing the role of the public defender and advocate of the independent sector, making certain it was fairly and vigorously defended. Such an agency would best be financed by private funds.

Here, then, are the elements of a strategy for independent action. It must find out for itself what needs to be done in America, develop modern answers to modern problems, mobilize, and tell the public what it's doing. The next chapters speculate on how a few of our principal independent institutions might put this strategy to work in specific ways.

3

# The Public Pulse

The United States publics are many, but its political activists are few. Perhaps only three persons out of a hundred in the general public are politically active. Many more, of course, are active in special associations (unions, churches, etc.) that ultimately contribute to the political energies of the nation. How do you find out what the people think about issues? One method is survey research, about which every student of American government, no matter how elementary his interest, should be informed.

Professor William H. Flanigan of the University of Minnesota, where numerous studies pioneering in the field of political behavior began, describes the essentials of survey research. Much of the information contained in modern American textbooks on government is gathered by the survey method. This method can produce a great variety of information about the views that people hold from a sample of a thousand or more persons. Indeed, almost everything can be studied in some form by the survey method, and almost any student can perform his own sample survey on any question of public opinion or behavior that concerns him. It will be a rare one who does not eventually in some way take part in a sample survey.

Sampling as described here is only about fifty years old. The Bureau of the Census uses it increasingly to obtain information about both individuals and groups, such as business and voluntary organizations. The results of a properly conducted survey can be as accurate and in some respects more accurate than an election. Many people, perhaps 50 per cent or more, do not participate in elections, but their opinions are represented in a properly selected sample of people. But if these people do not vote, why are public opinion polls politically important? Do polls reflect public opinion, or do they influence it?

The measurement of public opinion is discussed in the article by Philip Converse, Aage R. Clausen, and Warren Miller, who pioneered in this field at the University of Michigan and who founded the Survey Research Center, a major source of innovation and development of sample survey research. In this article they used the survey method to determine how Barry Goldwater and his advisers misunderstood the state of opinion in the country, at least as it related to the possible Goldwater vote in November 1964. The survey was conducted by the University of Michigan Survey Research Center. We note from the findings that the active public is quite small. Only 15 per cent of the American public has ever sent a letter to a public official. In running a campaign, the politician and his staff have to make many decisions in a fog over public reactions. In addition to polls and other factual evidence, they use a kind of inner steering to assess the state of the public mind. In Goldwater's case the outburst of letterwriting in his favor and the intense conviction of the pro-Goldwater people created a delusion. Since a vote is only a slight measure of intensity of feeling, intense feelings on the part of a few people do not indicate that the vote will be in favor of their candidate. This article suggests that the small number of politically active voters do not have much influence on the opinions of others. What do you think influences the voting behavior of most people?

One influence on voting behavior is discussed in the last article in this chapter, by Martha Wolfenstein and Gilbert Kliman. It focuses on the belief systems of the American people and the ways in which they react to shock. Such beliefs are the facts of political life as much as civil service examinations or the opinions of the Supreme Court. The survey method is less prominent in this study, which is a summary of a number of studies, some conducted by the survey method, some by prolonged psychoanalytic interviews.

As foreseen by a number of early American leaders, the presidency has become a veritable "cult of personality," whereby the President is believed to have qualities beyond those of an ordinary person. When a leader dies or especially when he is assassinated, as Sebastian de Grazia has shown in his early book *The Political Community* (1948), a society falls into a state, hopefully temporary, of acute anomie (a feeling of anxiety and isolation). This was the experience of the American people following President John F. Kennedy's death.

Many people in all age groups experienced psychological disturbances after the assassination. Protest took the form of disbelief and primitive rage reactions. Personality disorganization occurred as well as turmoil, distress, anxiety, regression to infantile behavior, sickness (especially of the digestive tract), and feelings of helplessness (acute anomie). The reorganization of personality was notable because many people were more willing to accept the former President's ideas and programs, which received much more support after his death than they had received before. How important do you think personality is, as compared to issues, in influencing political behavior?

# 4

## William H. Flanigan
## *Methods of Survey Research*

So many data have come from survey research and so much analysis has been based on findings from survey research that some description of these methods may be necessary to establish their appropriateness. During the last thirty years social scientists have developed an impressive array of techniques for discovering and measuring individual attitudes and behavior. Basically survey research relies on giving a standard questionnaire to the individuals to be studied, and in most major studies of the national electorate trained interviewers ask the questions and record the responses in a face-to-face interview with each respondent. A few studies depend on the respondents to fill out the questionnaires themselves without using interviewers.

There are four data collection phases of survey research: 1) sampling, 2) interviewing, 3) questions, and 4) coding. At most points the methods of the Survey Research Center at the University of Michigan will be described.

### SAMPLING

It may seem inappropriate to analyze the entire American electorate with studies composed of fewer than two thousand individuals, . . . [but it] would be prohibitively expensive to interview the entire electorate, and the only way to study public opinion nationally is by interviewing relatively few individuals who accurately represent the entire electorate. *Probability sampling is the method used to assure that the individuals selected for interviewing will be representative of the total population.*

Probability sampling attempts to select respondents in such a way that every individual in the population has an equal chance of being selected for interviewing. If the respondents are selected in this way, the analyst can be confident that the characteristics of the sample are approximately the same as those of the whole population. It would be impossibly difficult to make a list of every adult in the United States and then draw names from the list randomly so the Survey Research Center departs from such strict random procedures in three basic ways: the sample is *stratified, clustered,* and *of households.*

Stratification means that random selection occurs within subpopulations and in the United States customarily the sample is selected within regions to guarantee that all sections are represented and within communities of different sizes as well. Clustering means that within the geographical areas selected for sampling the interviews are to be made may be picked by stratified sampling procedures but at interviewers. Finally, the Survey Research Center samples households rather than individuals (although within households individuals are sampled and interviewed) and this means that within sampling areas households are enumerated and selected at random. (This sampling procedure means that there are no interviews on military bases, in hospitals and prisons, or in other places where people do not live in households.)

An alternative procedure for selecting respondents is quota sampling and is employed commonly by commercial polling organizations. The areas where interviews are to be made may be picked by stratified sampling procedures but at the last stage of selection the interviewer is given discretion to choose respondents according to quotas. Quotas usually cover several social characteristics but the intention is to create a collection of respondents with proportions of quota-controlled characteristics identical to those in the population. For example, the quota might call for half the respondents to be men, half to be women; for one-third to be grade school educated, one-third high school educated and one-third college educated; and so forth. The advantage of this procedure is that it is much faster and less expensive than probability sampling, but the disadvantages are severe. With quota sampling the analyst cannot have confidence that respondents are representative of the total population because the interviewers introduce conscious or unconscious biases when selecting respondents. Both methods of sampling depend heavily on the ability and integrity of the interviewers, but probability sampling does not permit interviewers to introduce biases. Most statistical manipulations depend on using probability sampling.

## INTERVIEWING

The selection of the sample depends on the interviewer but even more important is the role of the interviewer in asking questions of the respondent and recording the answers. Motivated, well-trained interviewers are crucial to the success of survey research. The interviewer has several major responsibilities: first, he selects the respondent according to sampling instructions; second, the interviewer must develop rapport with the respondent so he will be willing to go through with the interview which may last an hour or more; third, the interviewer must ask the questions in a friendly way and encourage the respondent to answer fully without distorting the answers; finally, the interviewer must record the answers of the respondent fully and accurately. In order to accomplish these tasks with a high level of proficiency the survey organizations train and retrain a permanent staff of interviewers.

## QUESTIONS

Ordinarily in survey questionnaires several types of questions will be used. Public opinion surveys began years ago with forced choice questions to which a respondent was asked to give a simple answer. For example, forced choice questions frequently take the form of stating a position on public policy and asking the respondent to "agree" or "disagree" with the statement. . . . [A richer supply of answers] is produced on forced choice questions in which respondents . . . [are] asked to "agree strongly," "agree," "disagree," or "disagree strongly." Some respondents give qualified answers that do not fit into these prearranged categories, or have no opinions.

The major innovation associated with the Survey Research Center is an alternative form of questioning called "open-ended." Open-ended questions give the respondent the opportunity to express his opinion in his own way without being forced to select among categories provided by the questionnaire. Questions like "Is there anything in particular you like about the Democratic Party?" or "What are the most important problems facing the country today?" permit the respondent to answer in his own terms. Survey Research Center interviewers encourage respondents to answer such questions as fully as they can with "probes" like "Could you tell me more about that," "anything else," and similar remarks that draw forth more discussion. There is no doubt that open-ended questions are a superior method of eliciting accurate expressions of opinion.

There are two major disadvantages in open-ended questioning: one is that it places much more of a burden on interviewers to record the responses, and the other is that the burden of reducing the many responses to a dimension that can be analyzed is left for the coders. For example, in the United States if people are asked, "Do you think of yourself as a Democrat, a Republican or an independent?" almost all of the responses will fit usefully into the designated categories:

1. Democrat
2. Independent
3. Republican
4. Other party
5. I'm nothing, apolitical

6. Don't know
7. Refused to say
8. Not ascertained

On the other hand, if a relatively unstructured, open-ended question is used like "How do you think of yourself politically?" some people would answer with "Democrat," "Republican," etc. but many others would give answers that were quite different and not easily compared with the partisan categories. Often analysts intend to force responses into a single dimension like partisanship whether the respondents would have volunteered an answer along that dimension or not. This is essential if they are to develop single dimensions for analytic purposes. Modern survey research includes questions and techniques considerably more complex than these examples for establishing dimensions, but for the most part these methods have not been applied in political studies.

## CODING

Once the interviewers administer the questionnaires to respondents, the coders take over and reduce the verbal information to a numerical form according to a "code." The numeric information unlike verbal information can be processed and manipulated by high speed data processing equipment. The coders' task may be simple or complex. For example, to code the respondent's sex requires a simple code:

1. Male
2. Female

This means that on an IBM card which contains information on the respondent a column will be designated for indicating the respondent's sex. A "I" punch in the column will indicate men and a "2" punch will indicate women. The code shown above for partisan categories gives the numbers that would stand for various responses.

Some coding is very complicated in that it requires elaborate arrays of categories and many columns on an IBM card. For example, coding of the responses to a question like "Is there anything in particular you don't like about the Democratic Party?" might include fifty or a hundred categories and these categories would cover such details as: "I like the party's farm policies," "I like the party's tax program," "I've just always been a Democrat." Some codes require the coders to make judgments about the respondents' answers and in political surveys these codes have covered judgments on the level of sophistication of the respondents' answers and judgments as to the main reason for respondents' vote choices. After the coders have converted the verbal information into numbers according to the coding instructions, the numbers are punched into IBM cards and readied for analysis. At this point the survey research process ends and the political analyst takes over to make what use of the data he can.

There are a number of good texts on survey research methods. The Survey

Research Center has a *Manual For Interviewers* and a *Manual For Coders;* these provide simple, thorough introductions to two phases of the data collection process. Leslie Kish's *Survey Sampling* is by far the most authoritative and difficult work on sampling. Kahn and Cannel have provided a description and defense of the Survey Research Center interviewing in *The Dynamics of Interviewing.* The best discussion of the use of survey research from the perspective of the social analyst is Herbert Hyman's *Survey Design and Analysis.* . . .

# 5

## Philip Converse, Aage R. Clausen and Warren Miller
## *A Misperception of Public Opinion*

Goldwater lost the 1964 election . . . [but many in his camp] thought he had a chance to win. What most of our descriptions of the election year have had in common is a sort of chronic miscalculation of electoral reality: miscalculations of standing strength, of new strength that might be won, and of what appeals were necessary to win that new strength. Since "electoral reality" is at many points a nest of uncertainties, and since we are told that in the face of uncertainty personal needs are likely to color perceptions the more strongly, there is little surprising in the fact that Goldwater overestimated his strength and drawing power. But as these misperceptions of Goldwater and his aides went grossly beyond what many observers felt were the margins of uncertainty, they deserve closer comment.

Rather than write off these perceptions as figments of imagination, let us suppose that to persist in the way many electoral misperceptions of the right wing have persisted, there must be some sustaining reality bases; and let us ask instead what such bases might be. For "public opinion" is a protean thing, and we shall discover that there are perfectly sound ways of measuring public opinion during the 1964 campaign which, instead of illustrating Johnson's towering lead in the opinion polls, would actually have shown Goldwater enjoying a slight margin.

As is well known, public opinion was spoken of and roughly gauged long before the operations of public opinion polling were developed. What was gauged was opinion from a variety of kinds of sources: informal reactions to events among ancillary elites around the centers of government; the writings of intellectuals and newspaper editors; representations from leaders of interest groups, and the like.

While it was apparent that this conglomerate of opinion came disproportionately from relatively elite and informed sources and hence need not have coincided with what the "real public" thought, beyond mass elections themselves there were (and *are*, for those who totally distrust the polls) few further ways of understanding what the public below an elite level was thinking. One of those few ways of "digging down" into the real population was letters of opinion: letters sent from unassuming constituents to public officals, "letters to the editor" composed by non-professional writers reacting to daily events and even, in no few cases, to the opinions of the editor himself. This was one level of public opinion that seemed to be generated below the elite level and that, for the observer interested in opinion beyond the localisms of municipal government, could be monitored regularly on a wide geographic base.

In our 1964 interview schedule we spent some time investigating the behavior of our respondents with respect to the writing of politically relevant letters. We ascertained first whether or not they had ever written such a letter either to any kind of public official, or to the editor of a newspaper or magazine. Then, among the minority who could recall ever writing such a letter, we went on to ask about the frequency of such activity—whether any of the letters had been written in the past four years, and if so, roughly how many such letters the respondent would estimate he had written to each of the two types of targets over the recent period.

Many aspects of these data remain intriguing despite their general predictability. Thus, for example, the materials demonstrate handsomely that the large bulk of letters to public officials or the printed media come from a tiny fraction of the population, which tends to write very repetitively. Thus, . . . [from our sample survey of Americans] we find that only about 15 percent of the adult population reports ever having written a letter to a public official, and of the total stream of such letters from the grass-roots, two-thirds are composed by about 3 percent of the population. Where letters to newspapers or magazines are concerned, the constituency is even more restrictive still: only about 3 percent of the population recalls ever having written such a letter, and two-thirds of such letters are turned out by not more than half of one percent of the population. Needless to say, there is fair overlap between those who write to the printed media and those writing to public officials, so that the observer monitoring both lines of communication would tend to count the same people twice.

Furthermore, as these few people write more and more letters over time, they are counted again and again, and this of course is the phenomenon that interests us. What we have done is to reconstruct our data on various preferences relevant to the 1964 election *not* by a raw head-count, which is what a mass election measures, but rather with each individual's preference on an item weighted by the number of letters that he has reported writing to either target in the four preceding years. This provides a basis, within reasonable limits, for a fair replication of the different kind of "public opinion" as it might be assessed by a hypothetical observer.

Figure 1 contrasts "public opinion" in the head-count sense, with that form of public opinion as measured by letter-writing. We suggest that this figure may usher us into the reality world on which many of Goldwater's assessments and stratagems were based. This is not to say that Goldwater had no other bases from which to calculate public opinion. He had, among other things, public opinion as measured by the polls, and he did not entirely discredit this information. Yet as we have noted there was evidence that poll data perplexed him, not simply because they customarily brought bad news, but also because they failed to square with all of his other intuitive impressions as to what the public was thinking. In the measure that these impressions came from a variety of sources not very different from the letter-writers among the public (*i.e.*, from party activists, from campaign personnel and from informal associations), it is not hard to believe that they may have been displaced from the head-count of public opinion in much the same ways.

If we accept letter-writing for the moment then as a relevant indicator of public opinion, we see a rather marvelous change in the state of political affairs. In Figure 1(a), instead of trailing Johnson sadly in the anonymous crowd in mid-campaign, Goldwater holds a visible lead. Moving back to the time of the San Francisco convention (b), Goldwater is no longer the candidate of a small minority among Republicans and Independents, but rather is the toast of an absolute majority, even counting "no preferences" against him. In (c), we discover that not only is a vast majority of the public interested in the problem of the growing strength of the federal government,[1] but those upset by this growing strength outnumber their opponents by a ratio approaching 3 to 1! In Figure 1(d), the displacement of "letter opinion" from public opinion is much less, in part because the item wording brought a relatively consensual response. However, it is clear that Goldwater's "hard" inclinations in foreign policy are somewhat overrepresented as well in the letter-writing public.

In some ways, Figure 1(e) contains more grist than any of the others, however. First, the very form of the distributions of ideological preference differs rather dramatically. Where "public opinion" is concerned, nearly half the population falls in the "zero" category, making no affective distinction whatever between conservatives and liberals.[2] In addition, the clustering around this zero-point is very tight: over three-quarters of the population is located within one category of the zero-point. The distribution of "letter opinion," however, is quite different. The central mode of indifference or ignorance shrinks dramatically, and voices from more extreme positions on the continuum gain in strength. Other analyses show

[1] The wordings of the issue items involved in Figure 1 (c) and (d) were as follows:

> *(For 1c) Some people are afraid the government in Washington is getting too powerful for the good of the country and the individual person. Others feel that the government in Washington has not gotten too strong for the good of the country. . . . What is your feeling?*
>
> *(For 1d) Some people think our government should sit down and talk to the leaders of the Communist countries and try to settle our differences, while others think we should refuse to have anything to do with them. . . . What do you think?*

[2] It is likely that this contingent is roughly coterminous with that 40-50 percent of the American electorate which we have described elsewhere as having no impression as to what such terms as "conservative" and "liberal" mean. See Philip E. Converse, "The Nature of Belief Systems in Mass Publics," in David E. Apter, ed., *Ideology and Discontent* (New York, 1964), pp, pp. 206-61. The data presented there were gathered in 1960. In the 1964 study we collected the same data on recognition of ideological terms, thinking that perhaps the nature of the Goldwater campaign might render these terms and meanings more salient to a wider public. The data show that it did not.

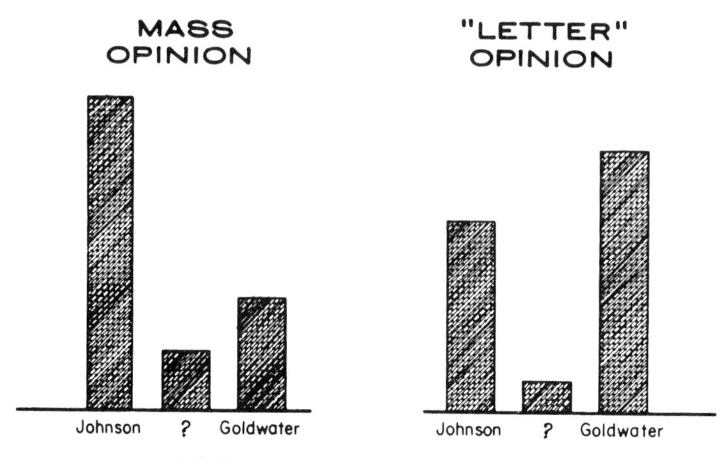


(a.) EARLY VOTE INTENTION

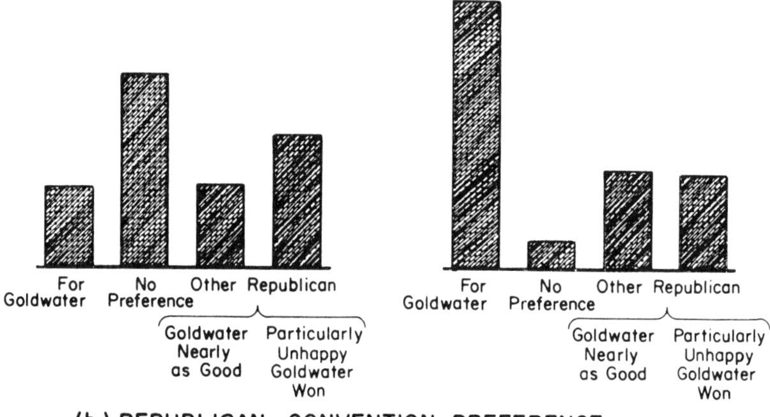


(b.) REPUBLICAN CONVENTION PREFERENCE
(Among Independents and Republicans Only)

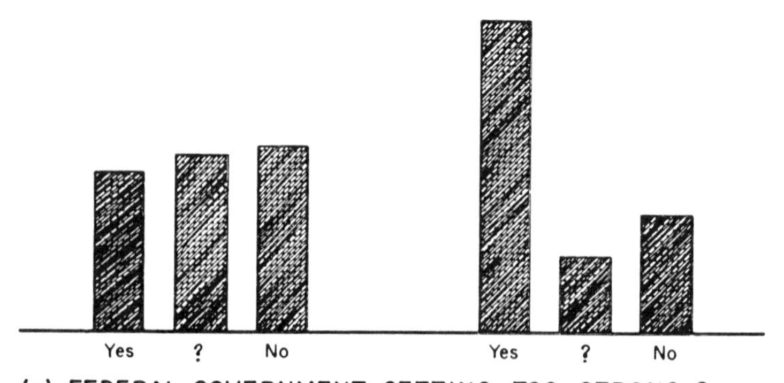


(c.) FEDERAL GOVERNMENT GETTING TOO STRONG ?

Figure 1(e) is based on a set of questions that asked people to indicate their affective reactions toward a variety of groups, including "conservatives" and "liberals." The scores for the figure are based on the difference in reaction to the two stimuli.

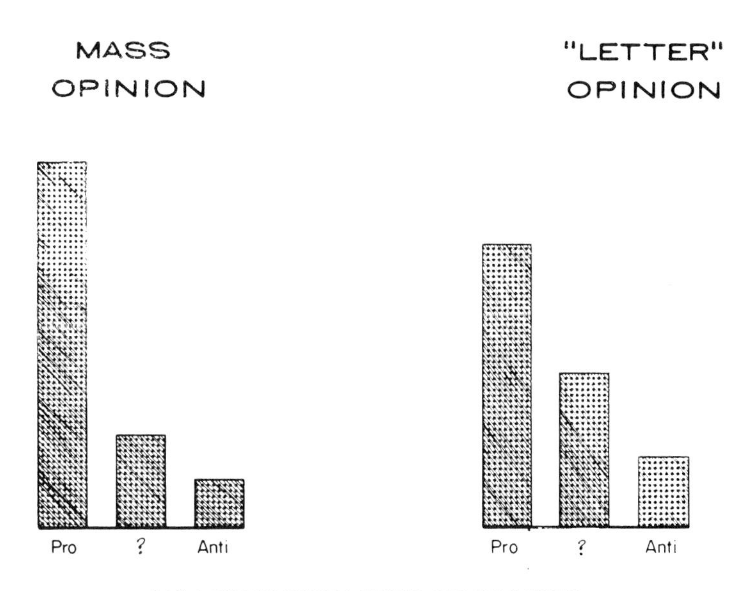


(d.) NEGOTIATION WITH COMMUNISTS

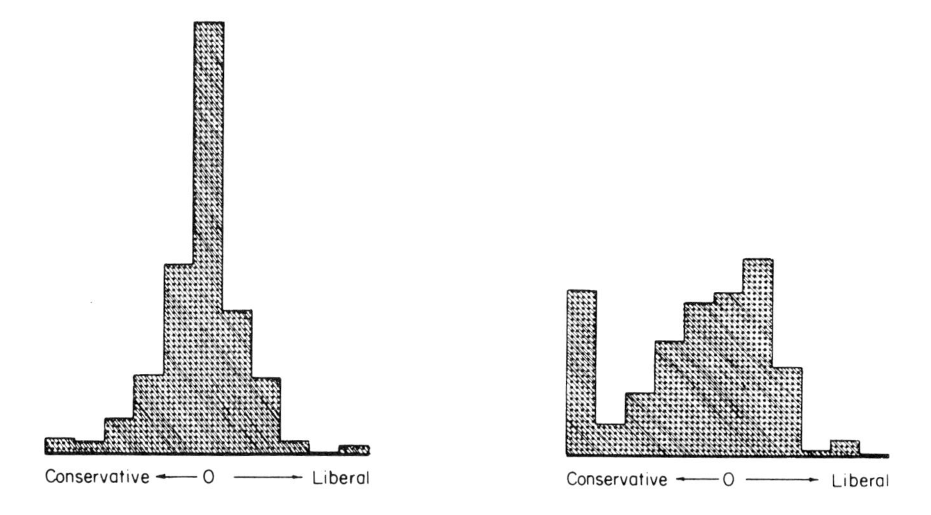


(e.) IDEOLOGY

that virtually all letter-writers rank very high on measures we have used of ideological sensitivity. Hence those who remain toward the middle of the continuum in the right half of Figure 1(e) are not there through indifference or ignorance: they understand the ideological alternatives and place themselves toward the middle of the road with forethought. And, as the bimodal shape of the distribution suggests, political discourse becomes most notably a dialogue between very mild liberals and ultra-conservatives.

It is to the world of letter opinion or one like it that the Goldwater campaign, in its original design, was addressed. At least until its late stages, it assumed an electorate with near-total ideological comprehension and sensitivity. The appeal to the Southern conservative tradition in any abstract vein was indeed joyfully received in the South, and created great ferment among a part of the Southern population. Except as this theme became concretized in day-to-day problems with Negroes, however, the part of the population affected was tiny, even though in the letter-writing and related senses it was so visible as to appear to be "most of the South," politically speaking.

Similarly, the distribution of the population in this world of letter opinion helped maintain persistent overestimations of strength. Empirically speaking, the center of Goldwater support lay roughly in the third bar of the figure on the conservative side. It weakened rapidly with any further steps toward the center, and was relatively solid in the outer two bars of the graph. If one looks at "letter opinion" with this zone in mind, it would appear that the base of standing Goldwater support was very substantial. Goldwater hoped to firm up the support on his side of the center sufficiently to create a majority, and in this figure it would have taken only a modest extension of influence to achieve this. In the world of public opinion relevant for mass elections, however, the distribution of actual and potential support was radically different. Rather than starting from a solid base of support on the conservative wing, the initial springboard was scarcely populated at all. To win a majority, a much deeper penetration into the center would have been required.

# 6

## Martha Wolfenstein and Gilbert Kliman

## *Personal Feelings Upon the Death of a President*

In the days immediately following the death of President Kennedy, a major feeling we had was one of unanimity. There was the sense of a great and terrible event, which had affected us all, and of grief shared throughout the nation and the world. This feeling of all being joined in a common emotion has been voiced recurrently when a nation suffers the loss of a great man. In his "Ode on the Death of the Duke of Wellington," Tennyson wrote:

> *Bury the Great Duke*
> *With an empire's lamentation;*
> *Let us bury the Great Duke*
> *To the noise of the mourning of a mighty nation.*

The sense of all joining in a common response has much emotional value for the mourner. He is not alone in his suffering. There is general acknowledgment of great cause for distress. Feelings flow more freely from the awareness of re-enforcement from others. The mourner experiences a sense of increased poignancy and at the same time assuagement from this sharing of emotion. Also in a culture like ours, where mourning for private losses tends to be curtailed, the national mourning for the President probably released many feelings for past griefs incompletely expressed before. "Then can I drown an eye, unus'd to flow."

It is undoubtedly true that in such a circumstance the individual finds some of his feelings echoed to an exceptional degree by a great number of other people. However, the assassination and its sequels constituted a series of complex events, from which different individuals could select and on which they could elaborate according to their varying susceptibilities. The most comprehensive generalization we can make about the studies in this volume is that they all deal with differences in reactions: differences between children and adults, between younger and older children, boys and girls, normal and disturbed, upper and lower class, science students and liberal arts students, as well as a great variety of individual differences. In this concluding chapter we shall attempt to sum up the major differences that were observed. We will also try to show basic themes running through our material, common motives, which manifested themselves in a variety of ways.

Let us start with differences between adults and children. Adults acknowledged more outspoken grief than children did: more adults said that they had wept. There is also the impression that adults underestimated children's reactions. We have to do here with differences related to age, and also with the complicated interchange between children and their elders. In situations of emotional stress generally, communication between children and parents is often disrupted. Or perhaps we should say that at such times their usual difficulties in understanding each other become more noticeable. Adults tend to find distress in children hard to bear. Parents often try to protect their children from the impact of grievous events by suppressing information. Children, on their side, are subject to certain inhibitions in expression of emotion, and also tend to mask their feelings in the presence of adults. Thus distress in children may be both muted and disguised, while adults more readily overlook it because of their need to see their children as untouched by suffering.

The general questions may be raised: when is emotion infectious, so that one is drawn into feeling what another feels, and when does the expression of emotion in another stimulate a different reaction? We know that anxiety is readily communicated from mothers to their young children. How is it with grief? On the weekend of the assassination children saw their parents in an unaccustomed state of distress, sometimes weeping, generally depressed, and less able to respond to the children's demands than usual. We would suppose that, rather than stimulating grief in the children, these manifestations in their parents would have provoked anxiety and some resentment. This would vary with the age of the children and the degree of their dependence on the parents. Our findings show much greater anxiety in younger than in older children, which we would ascribe in part to the effect of seeing their parents in such an unusual emotional state.

Differences in tempo of emotional response also set parents and children at odds. Children cannot tolerate distress for long, while adults can sustain more protracted grief. We have reported on children who cried briefly over the President's death but were then anxious to pursue their usual amusements during that weekend. This precipitated conflicts with their parents. Parents' impressions that children were unfeeling may be related to the short sadness span in children.

The fact that adults more frequently acknowledged weeping than children raises interesting questions. We touch here on the little understood psychology of crying in relation to phases of the life cycle. Infants and small children cry readily at any physical or psychic distress. Later an inhibition against crying sets in. This inhibition extends through the latency period well into adolescence. There is also a strong conscious feeling of shame associated with crying. In our studies, young adolescents repeatedly mentioned that when other children cried over the President's death, when they themselves finally broke down and cried, they were not ashamed. It was as if feelings of shame had to be overcome before they could permit themselves to cry. College boys who admitted that they and their friends were moved to tears had to qualify this by saying "not weeping so much as tears coming out of eyes." The marked sex typing that prevails in our culture in regard to weeping is evident here. It is more permissible for girls and women to weep than it is for boys and men. Thus among our subjects boys denied crying (sometimes contrary to what their parents reported) more than girls did. For either sex it is considered brave not to weep over personal misfortune. We may recall how often people praised Mrs. Kennedy for being brave in not weeping openly at the funeral ceremonies. The strong sentiment in our culture that it is brave not to weep and shameful to give way to tears interferes with the free expression of sad feelings.

How do we account for the fact that adults acknowledged weeping more than children did? Our studies of reactions to a death in the family have shown that while adults manifest outspoken grief, children and adolescents tend to suffer from an affective inhibition. It is our impression that the capacity for a protracted mourning reaction develops only after adolescence. In response to the death of a beloved leader we would expect this capacity for mourning to be more manifest in adults. Also the struggle for control over emotions and impulses is less severe in adults than in children. The long childhood restraint of sexual impulses has subsided; there is greater freedom for emotional release generally. While children contend against their impulses and feelings, adults have gained the sense that they may under appropriate circumstances give free expression to their emotions. When it comes to sad feelings, it is particularly permissible to express them when the occasion is one that involves sympathy for others rather than personal misfortune. We did not find adults speaking of feelings of shame when they acknowledged weeping for the President. The less frequent acknowledgment of weeping on the part of children may have been due in some instances to their being ashamed to admit it. We would suppose, however, that there was a greater affective inhibition than in adults. Also for both adults and children who did not acknowledge outspoken grief there may well have been lesser emotional involvement with the President.

In the introduction we spoke of the phases of reaction to loss: protest, disorganization, and reorganization. We would like to see now from our various findings how these appeared in reaction to the President's death. Protest appeared in the feeling of disbelief, which was the most common initial reaction in all age groups. There was a strong unwillingness to accept the reality of what had happened. Related to this were frequent thoughts and fantasies of how the fatality could have been prevented, undoing it in imagination. Feelings of anger also characterize this phase. Lindemann has pointed out the component of rage in grief. This rage is initially inchoate and objectless. It is a primitive reaction to being frustrated and cruelly deprived. Subsequently it seeks an object on which to vent itself. Following the President's death it took the form of vengeful feelings against the assassin, of directing blame against various groups and agencies, of disputes between people who had different interpretations of the events.

The phase of protest was variably prolonged in different age groups. It was most protracted in adolescents. Younger children achieved a quicker acceptance of what had happened because they had not as yet become so emotionally involved with the President. Adults underwent a process of mourning, which, however, was accomplished in a much more condensed time span than mourning for a personal loss. Distress of an acute nature tended to subside relatively quickly. However grievous the loss was, it required less massive reorganization of emotions, habits, and expectations than does the loss of a person with whom one is intimately involved in one's daily life. Feelings of affection, admiration, and regret no doubt remained attached to the dead President. But the initial sense of protest, of inability to believe it, gave way to an acceptance of what had happened.

It was in adolescents that the sense of disbelief persisted longest. We can relate this to their unreadiness, in their phase of development, to carry through the work of mourning. They felt a continuing sense of not being able to accept the loss of someone to whom they had become so attached. But also we would suppose that our youngest President had a particularly strong appeal for this age group. He seemed close to them, someone who could understand them; for the younger adolescents, an ideal parent figure, for the older ones, the model of what they should strive to become. This applies particularly to young men. For young girls we may suppose that the President figured more as a love object than as an ego ideal. Among older adolescents, the girls found it even more difficult than the young men to reconcile themselves to his loss.

The phase of disorganization is difficult to observe. It consists of inner turmoil, inchoate distress, anxiety, restlessness, thoughts in disarray. The process of putting feelings into words is a step toward reorganization. Our subjects, in talking with us, in writing about what they had experienced, in responding to structured forms of inquiry such as questionnaires, were by these very activities getting reorganized. Probably we ourselves in pursuing research in a time of crisis were partly motivated by a need to bring order out of chaos.

We may observe nevertheless many indications of emotional disorganization. Anxiety and apprehension of other bad things happening were widespread. Generally those who have experienced a sudden disaster become fearful that it will be repeated. This apprehension has no realistic relation to the future. It is rather a continuing reverberation of the disaster already undergone, which has not yet been assimilated. Also deep-seated, often unconscious beliefs in benevolent, protective powers keeping us safe from harm are seriously shaken. The apprehensiveness occasioned by a disaster, like the rage in grief of which we spoke, may at first be without definite object. Then it attaches itself to more specific dangers. Following the assassination young children frequently expressed the fear that the assassin might be lurking in their neighborhood. This sinister figure became condensed with the attacker in the night who already had haunted their fantasies. Other young children, most impressed with the fact that the father of children like themselves had died, became anxious about separation from their parents, or fearful that something might happen to them. Many adults, as we know, expressed apprehensions about bad things happening to our country, or the outbreak of another war. We might say that the President, as a good father figure, was trusted to keep aggression under control. The fact that he himself was killed showed that he was unable to do this; hence the fear of the outbreak of aggressive acts, whether the child's fear of the lurking assassin, or the adult's apprehension of a nuclear war. Younger children more than adolescents or adults were subject to anxiety following the assassination. We would relate this to their greater susceptibility to separation anxiety and their greater fear of aggression (their own and that which they project onto others) getting out of control. These vulnerabilities, combined with the unsettling effect of seeing their parents weeping and distraught, occasioned much anxiety.

Among the defenses noted against the anxiety thus provoked were regression and a massive blanking out of the events. Young disturbed children were observed to revert temporarily from games of fighting and killing to more infantile behavior: sucking their thumbs, clinging to a favorite toy which had previously been given up, wanting to sit on the therapist's lap. Other disturbed children showed a tendency to ward off the alarming stimuli, not to react, to take in the facts in a detached rote manner, later to forget everything connected with these events. It was observed conversely that the children who could tolerate an emotional response were better able to retain knowledge and understanding of what had happened.

Feelings of malaise also characterized the phase of disorganization. Children and adults alike spoke of feeling sick. This referred both to diffuse feelings of psychic distress and somatic reactions. On the large-scale questionnaire study, younger children acknowledged more somatic disturbances—difficulty in sleeping, loss of appetite, headaches—than adolescents. This may be related to the higher anxiety level in the younger children. But it may be also that the alternatives offered in the questionnaire did not cover the range of somaticized reactions. Thus in more spontaneous reporting, adolescents spoke, for instance, of an empty feeling in the stomach, feeling as if the breath was knocked out of them when they heard the news.

Feelings of helplessness were expressed, sometimes of wishing to do something, but there being nothing one could do. There was a sense of inability to carry on usual occupations or complete loss of interest in them. This again varied with age, younger children pursuing more readily than adolescents or adults their usual activities. It is characteristic of a true mourning reaction that the disturbing sense of loss permeates the mourner's mind and makes everything else unimportant. In younger children, their lesser involvement or their intolerance for protracted distress facilitated a greater isolation of the event; its effect was not all-absorbing. There is also evidence that among adolescents it was the more disturbed ones who tended quickly to push the event aside. Even if they had been very upset immediately following, they were anxious to have fun that weekend. In their inability to sustain painful feelings they resembled younger children.

Some college students spoke of not knowing how to react, of watching those around them to get cues. We may suppose that they were in conflict about expressing or restraining unusual emotions. Also there may have been some persisting sense of unreality, entailing a postponement of reaction. Confused thoughts and conflicting feelings were probably frequent, but difficult to observe. We see this kind of inner turmoil in the young adolescent girl who wanted to kill the assassin and also felt like killing herself. She seems to have suffered a diffuse rage reaction, without knowing how to direct it. We could also infer that feelings of guilt were stirred up, which may have motivated the suicidal thoughts. An older adolescent girl, when she heard that the President had been shot, found herself praying that he should not die. She had for some time before this ceased to believe in God. Under the stress of a great threat, older feelings, which she thought she had given up, came to the surface.

Adolescents and adults both reported that they felt compelled to think intensively about what had happened. This thinking often took the form of propounding a question to which there appeared to be no answer: how could such a thing happen? It seemed that the murder of the President had shattered basic assumptions about how the world is arranged. It constituted an appalling discrepancy. We suppose that on a deeper level there was horror at the violation of an awesome taboo, a sense that perhaps the laws of conscience are not laws of nature. Feelings and fantasies from deeply repressed levels were stirred. The intensive effort to think represented a struggle to reorganize the moral and rational surface structure of the mind, shaken by confused and alien feelings from the depths. In the phase of disorganization angry feelings also persisted. These now found many different objects of attack. We shall consider particularly vengeful feelings against the assassin.

We have spoken of the complexity of the assassination and its sequels, and how different individuals could select as the focus of their response the aspect most related to their emotional preoccupations. Two major aspects of the sequence of events were: loss of a loved and admired leader and a series of crimes of violence. For some people, grief for loss appeared to be the predominant reaction; others seemed preoccupied with murder and retribution. Our studies suggest that these two kinds of reaction tended to be mutually exclusive. For those who mourned, punishment of the assassin seemed relatively unimportant. Those who were filled with vengeful feelings seemed less susceptible to grief. Perhaps, however, these contrasting emotions occurred in the same subjects over time. The impression of their mutual exclusiveness may derive from our having tapped subjects at moments when one or the other emotion was temporarily in the ascendant.

Absorption in the crime and its punishment was expressed in the wish that the police would have shot Oswald down immediately, in many fantasies of cruel tortures that should have been inflicted on him, and in approbation of his being murdered by Ruby. We have found a number of variables related to these vengeful feelings. Younger more than older children expressed the wish for immediate and often cruel vengeance. Talion punishment dominates their moral outlook. The severity with which they condemn the aggressive impulses in themselves, with which they are still waging dubious battle, is readily turned against others. An external conflict is substituted for an internal one; the force of their primitive and cruel conscience can be directed against another, who has carried into action the bad wishes they themselves are holding in check.

Within a given age group (young adolescents) disturbed children were found to be more vengeful than normal children. In their lesser capacity to solve problems of aggression, they resemble younger children. With increasing age (on the level of high school seniors) lower-class children showed greater persistence of vengeful feelings than upper-class children. We would suppose that they, like the younger and the more disturbed children, have achieved less sublimation and moderation of aggression.

Among college students, a striking difference appeared between athletes and those more intellectually oriented. In the latter group there was weeping. As one of these young men put it, "My sense of loss overwhelms my feelings for revenge." The athletes were dry-eyed, and rather scornful of other students who were not. They were occupied with thinking up and discussing gruesome tortures that they would have liked to inflict on Oswald. From this predominance of vengeful feelings in the athletes, we would infer that they also are far from having solved the problems of aggression.

Children's understanding and acceptance of legal procedures are related to the exigencies of their emotional development. Intelligent, normal children in latency and prepuberty told us that Oswald should not have been given a trial, he should have got immediate death because he killed a very important man. They seem to see a trial as a postponement of punishment in cases where the crime is not too grave. We may find a counterpart to this in what they have probably experienced as reactions to their own misdeeds. If they commit a minor misdemeanor, their parents may palaver about what is to be done. This corresponds to a trial. If they do something really bad, their parents are provoked to immediate chastisement. A trial would thus mean a delay of retribution, which is allowed only for minor crimes. We may also discern deeper motives behind the demand for immediate punishment of the murderer. Theodor Reik has pointed out that when a murder has been committed, members of the community tend to feel an urgent anxiety to identify the criminal. While he remains unknown, suspicion may attach to all. In the case of a particularly horrible crime a similar urgency may be felt to confirm the guilt of the culprit by his prompt punishment. Then doubts as to the innocence of others may be set at rest. The tendency of younger children to say that Oswald should have been shot down immediately may derive in part from uneasy feelings of vicarious guilt. With increasing age, as we move into adolescence, there is a progressive acceptance of the necessity for fair trial. This greater tolerance for the law's delays would seem to be related to reduced intensity of inner conflicts about aggressive impulses.

Speculations about a possible conspiracy represent another aspect of response to the crime and feelings about justice. Children were much less inclined than adults to consider that there might have been a conspiracy. For them it seemed clear that the assassin did it. We would suppose that this is partly due to children's having fewer concepts of intricate and indirect social connections, and less concern with the sifting of details of evidence. Also their fantasies of aggression tend to focus on direct interpersonal action. For the considerable number of adults who believed in a conspiracy, we would think that an underlying motive was a sense of disproportion between cause and effect, between the mad impulse of an insignificant man and the fall of the leader of a great nation. Children, whose fantasies and stories are full of small protagonists overcoming big giants, would be less likely to feel this discrepancy. While children had little doubt that the assassin did it, they were less ready than adults to commit themselves as to possible reasons for his act. In this know-nothing attitude we see their need to dissociate themselves from the crime.

That oedipal impulses and related guilt were activated by the assassination is evidenced, or may be inferred from clinical and other findings. In one group of adolescent patients, the boys in contrast to the girls avoided mention of the assassination in the first therapeutic session following it. This avoidance was ascribed to the arousal of vicarious guilt for a crime that bore the latent significance of parricide. Other clinical reports, of later responses, showed that manifest parricidal fantasies emerged. Some boy patients also produced fantasies in which they assumed an assassin's role.

With the President's death, many thoughts and feelings were turned toward his young widow. College boys who were interviewed were scrupulous about denying that she could be thought of as a possible love object. In praising her they acknowledged, "This is what the college guy would like to marry." But they went on to say that she could never marry again; it would just not be possible. They were concerned about whether her emotional restraint might have meant less than total devotion to her husband. It seemed as though they wanted her to assure them that she was forever taboo, dedicated to perpetual mourning.

While the parricidal significance of the assassination was the most disturbing on deeper emotional levels, incestuous impulses were also stimulated. These appeared both in provocative behavior of child patients toward their parents and in fantasies about the President and his wife. Some boy patients reported amorous fantasies about Mrs. Kennedy. It was striking that some girl patients acknowledged similar daydreams about Mr. Kennedy. An event corresponding to the male oedipal crime had been translated by them into feminine oedipal terms. We would speculate that if a couple, emotionally equated to the parental couple, is separated by death, either partner may seem available as a love object. Daydreams, as we know, override barriers of both convention and reality. It should be added that where such amorous fantasies were admitted it was likely to be with compunction and shame.

Negative feelings toward the dead are generally repressed or suppressed. *De mortuis nihil nisi bonum.* When Lois Murphy proposed to include in her questionnaire on the assassination a question about criticisms of the late President, her colleagues were censorious. There is no doubt that following the death of President Kennedy a strongly intensified idealization of him was widespread. We shall have more to say about this presently. However, there were minor indications of negative feelings. In reports of reactions in schools to the announcement of the assassination, there were recurrent references to some child who laughed. This was generally viewed with reprobation. A child patient who had laughed reported how he had suffered from the vindictive behavior of his schoolmates, and that he really felt terrible. This momentary laughter may be related to the frequent thought at first hearing the news that it was a joke. It may also be taken as a reaction to extreme tension. But we are struck by the fact that this incidental laughter was so repeatedly recalled. The sick jokes about the Kennedy family that appeared later re-enforce the impression that there is a theme here of some significance.

Fenichel has said that persons who feel like laughing at a funeral are expressing mastery over anxiety and triumph over the dead. Strong scruples militate against such feelings of triumph. Nevertheless a covert sense of how the mighty have fallen may make itself felt. In a democracy there are many defenses against envy of those who attain high position. Since the race is officially open to all, citizens cannot feel if they are low and others high that this is divinely ordered as it is in a hereditary monarchy or aristocracy. The ancient Greeks believed in *hubris,* an inevitable retribution against the great who vaunted themselves too highly. This may be interpreted as a projection of the envy of their fellow citizens. In our democracy we have many defenses against envy of the great. Among these are vicarious pleasure in their success, diversion of antagonism against their opponents, an emphasis on the sufferings of the great, a leveling view according to which a man in high office is just doing another job. The Kennedy family, with their many extraordinary advantages and successes, strained the usual defenses against envy. This was why there was so much joking about them. We suggest that this was also why the minor note of someone laughing at the news of the assassination remained memorable and Kennedy jokes began to reappear in the guise of sick jokes.

The phase of reorganization includes reduction of distress, perpetuation of the lost person in memory and in other internal and external ways, transfer of some feelings to substitute figures, and assimilation of what has happened into a coherent view of the world. Since our data were gathered shortly after the President's death the signs of reorganization that we can indicate are necessarily incomplete. Following disasters generally there is a recurrent wish that out of evil good will come. The thought is expressed that grievous things happen for a purpose. The survivors resolve that they will hereafter strive to do better. Both adults and children expressed some positive expectations that we would become better, that our country would become better, as a consequence of the President's death. These ideas tended to be vague, without concrete content. We might see in them the positive counterpart to the conspiracy theories, which generally lacked any specification of what the plot was. In both these views, of plot and positive purpose, we see a striving to find a meaning, to integrate a disturbing event into an organized view of the world. That these efforts to find a larger meaning, for good or ill, remained incomplete suggests the obsolescence of teleological thinking in our time.

On a deeper emotional level, there is the tendency to idealize a lost object and to identify with it in various ways. It is evident that affection and admiration for President Kennedy were intensified by his death. Our studies show that children and adolescents felt more positively toward him than they had before. Those who had had some negative feelings tended to change over. Those who were already attached to him experienced a strengthening of this attachment. This is similar to what we have observed in children who have lost a parent, but we would expect it to have different consequences in relation to a national leader. When a parent dies, children tend to idealize him and intensify their attachment to him. In their own secret thoughts and feelings, they refuse to give him up and reject possible substitutes. No one else can compare with the idealized lost parent to whom they cling. Idealization and strengthened feeling for a national leader who has died would seem to have more positive effects. He has not occupied such a unique personal position in the emotional life of his followers. There is less resistance to his being replaced. Feelings of resentment toward Johnson for replacing Kennedy were expressed by some children and adolescents. However, this was a minor theme, whether because it was little felt or because it was considered inappropriate to express it. The opposite sentiment was also voiced, of gratification that our country was so arranged that we had a new President ready to take charge and with whom we could face the world. Also estimates of Mr. Johnson rose almost immediately on his assuming the Presidency. This has been regularly observed in response to any new incumbent.

A major way in which someone who has died is perpetuated is through those who live on identifying with his traits and aims. The superego and ego ideal of children are initially modeled on their parents as they perceive them. As they develop they turn increasingly to other models, from life or fiction, who seem to them to embody ideal qualities. These admired figures enter into the further formation of the ideal image that the young person strives to realize. A President, in life, appears generally in an idealized light. He is one of many from among whom the young may choose models. With his death, and particularly a death that resembles martyrdom, he not only becomes still more idealized, but there is a strong tendency to want to perpetuate him. There is considerable evidence that children and adolescents have become much occupied with the life of John F. Kennedy. This is partly an effort to recapture a valued person whose sudden loss has evoked strong regret. We would suppose also that his idealized image may enter into the formation of the ego ideal in those in whom it is still developing. It is difficult at this point to know what the image is or how lasting its effect will be. We would suppose that for young boys it is a hero image, of the sort they so prize; for adolescents, perhaps one of dedication to a career that is not merely self-seeking.

The murder of a leader, according to Freud, evokes strong posthumous obedience in his followers. They feel that they must take it upon themselves to carry out his behests. We would speculate that following the murder of the President a sense of this imperative was widely felt in the adult population. In the time between the assassination and the election of the next year, President Johnson became established in people's minds as dedicated to helping us carry out what President Kennedy had wanted done. The fact that he received an unprecedented popular majority in the election may be ascribed in part to posthumous obedience to the murdered leader.

How the death of President Kennedy will be remembered later is again a matter for speculation. Personal memories of such an event are difficult to preserve since they become overlaid with many publicly repeated versions of what happened. However, we would predict that for young children, to the extent that their personal experience survives, it will be remembered as an isolated event of an uncanny nature. The world around them, at school, at home, was in an upset state such as they had not known. Even their familiar television programs were suspended. What they watched was disturbing and bewildering. Their incomprehension of the grown-up world was intensified, with a sense of things being radically out of control. They were distressed, but they fell back on the resources of their age for escaping distress. They went out and played. Of course much was explained to them. They got some organized idea of the sequence of events, varying with their age and health of mind. But if some twinges of their own feelings from that time are revived later they will evoke something strange, something that intruded into the usual round of life and could not be quite assimilated.

For young adolescents we would predict that it will be remembered by many as their first experience of grief. It was for them an initiation into the experience of painful loss which none escapes in life. Perhaps this experience of grief, which they were helped to bear by sharing it with so many others, will have prepared them to some extent to tolerate later losses.

For older adolescents it meant the sudden tragic end of a career with which they were much identified. There was a young President to whom they felt unusually close. They wanted him to succeed; they felt empathic hurt in his fall. He would never achieve all that he had set out to do. Perhaps in later years, when they think back on the high hopes of their youth, which for them, as for other generations, will be incompletely fulfilled, their nostalgic regrets for lost youth will be mingled with their feelings for their young President cut off in mid-career.

We should like to add a few methodological reflections. A wide range of methods was used in the different studies in this volume. It does not seem necessary to recapitulate here the advantages and limitations of each of them. Comparisons, for instance, between what can be obtained from questionnaire studies of a large population and more intensive studies of a limited number of subjects, based on interviewing or clinical material, are familiar to students of the social sciences. Nor shall we repeat well known arguments pro and con as to how much can be extrapolated from clinical findings that is applicable to normal subjects. We shall confine ourselves to a few methodological points raised by our studies, which may be of use to other researchers.

A problem was posed for all our investigations by a character trait that generally prevails in our culture, namely, inarticulateness, especially in spoken words, about strong feelings. Our tendency is toward understatement rather than verbal exuberance. We have delegated to public speakers, such as television commentators and political orators, the role of expressor of what the majority cannot themselves articulate. We also often rely on music to evoke what we are unable to say. This is typically exemplified in the use of the musical sound track in films. For instance, in *High Noon,* Gary Cooper carried out his fated and lonely role with a look of tragic determination on his face, while on the sound track one heard the moving song, "Do not forsake me, oh my darling," which expressed what he felt and could not say.

Articulateness about feelings varies with the medium of expression. We would compare particularly what our subjects were able to express in spoken and in written words. It is our impression that on all age levels spoken words were inadequate to express much of what was felt. A young boy voiced what were probably massive feelings of distress on hearing the news of the assassination by saying, "I didn't like it a bit." His elders were not much more articulate, frequently experiencing a painful sense of the inadequacy of words. Often more could be expressed in writing than orally. A ten-year-old boy wrote, "*Please* Lord, *please.* Tell me this was a publicity stunt. *Please.*" It seems unlikely that he could have spoken such words either to age-mates or to his elders. Among adolescents particularly, at an age when considerable mastery of written expression has been achieved, we found a strong striving to evoke and record in writing what they had experienced, and they produced moving documents. This finding suggests the importance of the written medium for obtaining expression of strong feelings.

In evoking the experiences of our subjects another alternative was whether we were asking for recall or recognition: that is, whether we asked for a spontaneous recapitulation of events, as in an essay, or whether we tried to elicit various details by a series of questions, on a questionnaire or in an interview. The relative effectiveness of these methods varies with the age of the subject. The less directive method has the greater possibility for eliciting unanticipated responses. However, it presupposes a considerable capacity to organize and formulate one's experiences. Younger children as compared with adolescents were less able to do this. The stimulus of specific questions, in questionnaires or interviews, facilitated their expression of the range of their reactions.

We have had to do throughout with the problems of young people communicating with their elders. Such communication varies with the age of the child, the person with whom he is communicating, and the medium of communication. Particularly relevant here are children's changing images of adults, and their preferences at different ages as to whom they most want to communicate with. A case in point is the group interviewing of college students, which proved highly evocative. It seems possible that these adolescents could not have talked as freely in individual interviews as they did when interviewed in groups of familiar age-mates. They were at an age when they were most anxious to talk with each other about their thoughts and feelings. They felt the need to check their responses against those of their peers, and having done so could move from more tentative to more outspoken statements. Confronted with a highly structured questionnaire, adolescents seemed to play down their feelings. They may have felt that the preconceptions of the adult questioner hampered their freedom of expression. With their demand for autonomy and their powers of introspection and organization they were able to report more intense emotional reactions in more open-ended communication. Young adolescents were able to confide anonymously in writing to unknown adults whom they could imagine to be sympathetic and understanding. We do not know whether this mode of communication would have appealed equally to older adolescents, who feel less longing to confide in an ideal parent figure.

The way in which the adult shared or failed to share the child's experience was of particular importance in therapeutic situations. Therapists found themselves in a relatively unprecedented situation in which they were agitated by an event that affected them as much as, or more than, their patients. Since they had little or no preparation for confronting such a crisis with their patients, procedure varied widely. We can readily suppose that whether the therapist dismissed his patients on the afternoon of the assassination, or listened to the news reports with them, had significant effects for subsequent communication. In the reports from the children's home, we saw how the staff lived through the crisis and its aftermath with the children. Over a period of time the children moved from idiosyncratic, mutually unrelated reactions to some assimilation of what had happened into a unifying group experience. Initial tendencies toward avoidance and withdrawal were counteracted. The children gained some sense of an event that had become history, and were then moved to ask about the past and future of the institution of which they formed a part, to add an historic dimension to their own lives and those of the adults who cared for them. In this instance, as in therapy generally, the responses observed were in the process of being modified by the observers.

It has been brought out in connection with clinical studies how important it is in assessing the impact of an event to know what was going on in the subject beforehand. For instance, fantasies about killing and rescue operations, which followed the assassination, might have been ascribed to its impact if there had not been observations of the child's previous preoccupation with such themes. At times it seemed as though the assassination only provided children with a new cast of characters for their habitual fantasies. However, comparisons of the functioning of child patients before and after the event showed some shifts in the breakthrough of impulses and in the marshaling of defenses against what were felt to be threats from without and within. These observations suggest the importance of antecedent knowledge of our subjects in assessing the effect a major event has on them.

We have had to do with an event that produced much emotional disorganization. A major problem for our studies was to get an adequate picture of this state of mind, in which the individual is assailed by confusing and opposite feelings. Probably we were not very clearly aware of this problem at the time of starting our researches. As we have said, the very fact of responding to a formal inquiry may make the subject present a coherent account that is at variance with his inner turmoil. We would say that the less structured the method of investigation, and the more it enabled one to obtain expressions of the subject over time, the more disorganization could be observed. In interviews, conflicting emotions, contradictory attitudes, and feelings of bewilderment and confusion were manifest. Essays revealed similar material. Clinical observation showed many shifts of reactions over time, initial avoidance yielding to intense preoccupation, or a nonchalant attitude giving way to painful guilt-ridden feelings. As to more structured methods, we would suggest that, when applied to subjects who may be expected to be in a state of disorganization, they should include questions that make possible the expression of a number of opposite feelings and opinions.

Those studies in which the subjects could be observed for some time after the event had the advantage of following them into the beginnings of reorganization, showing in some instances positive acquisitions from the mastery of what they had experienced. We would suggest that wherever reactions to an event may be expected to manifest a series of phases, as here, it would be desirable to provide for observations over time, or follow-up studies.

We are aware of the limitations of our investigation. As far as regional distribution is concerned, our researches were carried out only in the East and Middle West. It would have been interesting to have had observations of southern children, about whose negative feelings toward President Kennedy there were many rumors. Another limitation is that we have relatively little observation of parent-child interactions. All our studies had to be improvised in haste in the effort to observe the impact of an unexpected event closely following its occurrence. These investigations had few precedents, and there was little time for the preparatory reflection and planning usual in research undertakings. We have tried, however, to understand something of what the death of a national leader means to his people, and, for the first time, how such an event affects children.

# 4

# Double Trouble

American society today appears to many observers to be profoundly different from its earlier stages. America has always been a country of restless people. Today the restlessness seems to be more accentuated and political in character. The usual trouble is compounded because it seems to be centered in newly agitated groups in the population—young people, women, blacks, and dissidents within the intelligentsia and the business world. Our selections in this chapter deal with three of the areas of dissention—passive resistance and the right to demonstrate, the control of mass disorder, and that bogeyman, the military-industrial complex.

The current era of political activism and dissent in America began with the demands for black equality in the 1950's. Dr. Martin Luther King, Jr., became the principal leader of this movement. Controversial, prudent, calm, intelligent, courageous, and persistent, Dr. King possessed a rare combination of powers at a critical moment in the social crisis of the black people. In the first selection, from a twenty-page letter to some churchmen who had warned against the acceptance of his methods of mass demonstration and passive resistance, he tells why he went to Birmingham and why he went to jail.

A number of great men have expressed themselves and their ideas in letters, among them St. Paul; the Roman, Pliny the Younger; and Thomas Jefferson. Even in this day of oral and visual communication, there is something powerful and unique about a letter. This one was written in a jail. Jail is the place for the agitator: saint or sinner, he usually spends some time there.

The movement Dr. King led resulted in new laws for equality in voting, the use of public accommodations, and open housing. But it did not bring economic opportunity rapidly enough to the thousands of impoverished black people living in major cities. Rioting occurred in the black ghettos in many cities in the 1960's. The problem of social disorder in the United States is not new, and the recent race riots, which were not so much racial as just riots, have caused some loss of life and a considerable loss of property. Proportionately, the loss has been perhaps less now than in past periods of social unrest if one measures the destruction against the enormous gain in property values in America. Some call it instant slum clearance, implying that what has been destroyed was well worth destroying. There has been a remarkably small loss of life.

Morris Janowitz, Professor of Political Science at the University of Chicago, is concerned in the second selection not so much with arguing the issues of the poor and who has the right, if any, to riot as with the varieties of rioting and the many means of handling riots. His work should dispel any notion of the simplicity of the problem and bring out a point that many have made and more will make: rioting and crowds have been frequent actors on the stage of history and are in fact an illegal form of casting a vote against the system. We say that millions of refugees in Europe and Asia have voted against communism and for America with their feet. One could say that thousands of Americans have burned and looted in a vote against the American system.

Another area of dissent concerns the military and foreign policy. The war in Vietnam has provoked not only demonstrations and dissent but also a reappraisal by many people of American foreign policy and the role of the military in both foreign and domestic policy. The discussion by James L. Payne, Professor of Government at Wesleyan University in Connecticut, presents, first of all, a common contradiction between informed professional views on world events and less informed people's views. More than that, it says that you cannot participate in world affairs unless you do unpleasant and costly things, like order soldiers to their deaths on a cold calculation to make your threats credible, to show that you mean what you say. Might it be that the only way out of this perpetual, mutually degrading game between nations is an overwhelming drive for a world order in which conflict among nations would be as limited as it is among individuals within nations? Then the nations might concentrate upon greatly reducing the violence of such internal conflicts as well.

The last selection in this chapter, "The Report from Iron Mountain," discusses the advantages of war. War is a costly tutor, but teach it does. This selection tells not only what it teaches but what its positive advantages are especially if it is carefully managed. There are many theoretically superior avenues to economic progress, but they are not so easy to follow as the road to war. This report is partly a hoax; it was presented as a true account of a meeting in which matters were resolved so dangerously and unpopularly that the report was suppressed. Actually, the beginnings of the book probably occurred in a sponsored meeting, but the rest was a serious joke with a false ending.

Nevertheless, it reflects a certain class of arguments that need to be considered and which people generally refuse to consider. No one has argued, for example, in any public place that a solid reason for taking the casualties and the cost of the war in Vietnam is future savings. Yet, if the two million American troops that were trained in Vietnam had to be committed in a large-scale war with a much larger enemy, the losses in a few months of warfare would be measurably reduced because of the experience of the American forces in Vietnam, and the total cost of the Vietnam war would be wiped out several times over. Are the points discussed in this article valid reasons for waging war? In what other ways could these advantages be obtained?

# 7

## Martin Luther King, Jr.
## *Letter from Birmingham Jail*

*My dear Fellow Clergymen,*

While confined here in the Birmingham City Jail, I came across your recent statement calling our present activities "unwise and untimely." Seldom, if ever, do I pause to answer criticism of my work and ideas. If I sought to answer all of the criticisms that cross my desk, my secretaries would be engaged in little ,else in the course of the day and I would have no time for constructive work. But since I feel that you are men of genuine goodwill and your criticisms are sincerely set forth, I would like to answer your statement in what I hope will be patient and reasonable terms.

I think I should give the reason for my being in Birmingham. . . .

. . . I am in Birmingham because injustice is here. . . .

Moreover, I am cognizant of the interrelatedness of all communities and states. I cannot sit idly by in Atlanta and not be concerned about what happens in Birmingham. Injustice anywhere is a threat to justice everywhere. We are caught in an inescapable network of mutuality tied in a single garment of destiny. Whatever affects one directly affects all indirectly. Never again can we afford to live with the narrow, provincial "outside agitator" idea. Anyone who lives inside the United States can never be considered an outsider anywhere in this country.

You deplore the demonstrations that are presently taking place in Birmingham. But I am sorry that your statement did not express a similar concern for the conditions that brought the demonstrations into being. . . .

In any nonviolent campaign there are four basic steps: (1) collection of the facts to determine whether injustices are alive; (2) negotiation; (3) self-purification; and (4) direct action. We have gone through all of these steps in Birmingham. There can be no gainsaying of the fact that racial injustice engulfs this community. Birmingham is probably the most thoroughly segregated city in the United States. Its ugly record of police brutality is known in every section of this country. . . .

. . . My friends, I must say to you that we have not made a single gain in civil rights without determined legal and nonviolent pressure. History is the long and tragic story of the fact that privileged groups seldom give up their privileges voluntarily. Individuals may see the moral light and voluntarily give up their unjust posture; but as Reinhold Niebuhr has reminded us, groups are more immoral than individuals.

We know through painful experience that freedom is never voluntarily given by the oppressor; it must be demanded by the oppressed. Frankly I have never yet engaged in a direct action movement that was "well timed," according to the timetable of those who have not suffered unduly from the disease of segregation. For years now I have heard the word "Wait!" It rings in the ear of every Negro with a piercing familiarity. This "wait" has almost always meant "never." . . .

I guess it is easy for those who have never felt the stinging darts of segregation to say wait. But when you have seen vicious mobs lynch your mothers and fathers at will and drown your sisters and brothers at whim; when you have seen hate filled policemen curse, kick, brutalize, and even kill your black brothers and sisters with impunity; when you see the vast majority of your twenty million Negro brothers smothering in an air-tight cage of poverty in the midst of an affluent society; when you suddenly find your tongue twisted and your speech stammering as you seek to explain to your six-year-old daughter why she can't go to the public amusement park that has just been advertised on television, and see tears welling up in her little eyes when she is told that Funtown is closed to colored children, and see the depressing clouds of inferiority begin to form in her little mental sky, and see her begin to distort her little personality by unconsciously developing a bitterness toward white people; when you have to concoct an answer for a five-year-old son asking in agonizing pathos: "Daddy, why do white people treat colored people so mean?" . . . then you will understand why we find it difficult to wait. There comes a time when the cup of endurance runs over, and men are no longer willing to be plunged into an abyss of injustice where they experience the bleakness of corroding despair. I hope, sirs, you can understand our legitimate and unavoidable impatience.

You express a great deal of anxiety over our willingness to break laws. This is certainly a legitimate concern. Since we so diligently urge people to obey the Supreme Court's decision of 1954 outlawing segregation in the public schools, it is rather strange and paradoxical to find us consciously breaking laws. One may well ask, "How can you advocate breaking some laws and obeying others?" The answer is found in the fact that there are two types of laws; There are *just* laws and there are *unjust* laws. I would be the first to advocate obeying just laws. One has not only a legal but moral responsibility to obey just laws. Conversely, one has a moral responsibility to disobey unjust laws. I would agree with Saint Augustine that "An unjust law is no law at all."

Now what is the difference between the two? How does one determine when a law is just or unjust? A just law is a man-made code that squares with the moral law or the law of God. An unjust law is a code that is out of harmony with the moral law. To put it in the terms of Saint Thomas Aquinas, an unjust law is a human law that is not rooted in eternal and natural law. Any law that uplifts human personality is just. Any law that degrades human personality is unjust. All segregation statutes are unjust because segregation distorts the soul and damages the personality. It gives the segregator a false sense of superiority and the segregated a false sense of inferiority. To use the words of Martin Buber, the great Jewish philosopher, segregation substitutes an "I-it" relationship for the "I-thou" relationship, and ends up relegating persons to the status of things. So segregation is not only politically, economically, and sociologically unsound, but it is morally wrong and sinful. . . .

. . . I was arrested Friday on a charge of parading without a permit. Now there is nothing wrong with an ordinance which requires a permit for a parade, but when the ordinance is used to preserve segregation and to deny citizens the First Amendment privilege of peaceful assembly and peaceful protest, then it becomes unjust.

I hope you can see the distinction I am trying to point out. In no sense do I advocate evading or defying the law as the rabid segregationist would do. This would lead to anarchy. . . .

I had hoped that the white moderate would understand that law and order exist for the purpose of establishing justice, and that when they fail to do this they become the dangerously structured dams that block the flow of social progress. . . .

. . . I am further convinced that if our white brothers dismiss us as "rabble rousers" and "outside agitators"—those of us who are working through the channels of nonviolent direct action—and refuse to support our nonviolent efforts, millions of Negroes, out of frustration and despair, will seek solace and security in black nationalist ideologies, a development that will lead inevitably to a frightening racial nightmare.

Oppressed people cannot remain oppressed forever. The urge for freedom will eventually come. . . .

I hope the Church as a whole will meet the challenge of this decisive hour. But even if the Church does not come to the aid of justice, I have no despair about the future. I have no fear about the outcome of our struggle in Birmingham, even if our motives are presently misunderstood. We will reach the goal of freedom in Birmingham and all over the nation, because the goal of America is freedom. Abused and scorned though we may be, our destiny is tied up with the destiny of America. Before the pilgrims landed at Plymouth, we were here. Before the pen of Jefferson etched across the pages of history the majestic words of the Declaration of Independence, we were here. For more than two centuries our foreparents labored in this country without wages; they made cotton "king"; and they built the homes of their masters in the midst of brutal injustice and shameful humiliation—and yet out of a bottomless vitality they continued to thrive and develop. If the inexpressible cruelties of slavery could not stop us, the opposition we now face will surely fail. We will win our freedom because the sacred heritage of our nation and the eternal will of God are embodied in our echoing demands. . . .

. . . If I have said anything in this letter that is an understatement of the truth and is indicative of my having a patience that makes me patient with anything less than brotherhood, I beg God to forgive me.

. . . Let us all hope that the dark clouds of racial prejudice will soon pass away and the deep fog of misunderstanding will be lifted from our fear-drenched communities and in some not too distant tomorrow the radiant stars of love and brotherhood will shine over our great nation with all of their scintillating beauty.

*Yours for the cause of*
*Peace and Brotherhood*
MARTIN LUTHER KING, JR.

# 8

## Morris Janowitz
## *Social Control of Escalated Riots*

In the building of institutions to reduce and eliminate race rioting in urban centers of the United States, two "sociological" assumptions supply a point of departure. There is a considerable body of evidence to support these assumptions, but it is best to consider them as assumptions.

1. Social tensions generated by discrimination, prejudice and poverty offer essential but only partial explanations of Negro mass rioting in the urban centers of the United States. Allen Grimshaw, one of the most careful students of race riots, concluded in 1962 that "there is no direct relation between the level of social tension and the eruption of social violence."

Because of the complex meaning of the term "no direct relation" it is not necessary to accept all that this proposition implies. It is enough to reemphasize the obvious fact that in the United States, social tension exists where riots break out, and to accept his alternative formulation that "in every case where major rioting has occurred, the social structure of the community has been characterized by weak patterns of external control."

2. Among elements that account for the outbreak of mass rioting are both (*a*) the organizational weaknesses and professional limitations of law enforcement agencies and (*b*) a moral and social climate that encourages violence. Of particular importance is the widespread availability of weapons and the impact of the mass media, both in its imagery of violence and in its specific treatment of riots and law enforcement agencies. In the language of the sociologist, a key element in the outbreak of riots is a weakness in the system of social control.

Race riots are an expression of the position of the Negro in American society, for the history of the Negro has been markedly different from that of the other immigrant and minority groups. Institution-building aimed at political, social and economic reform is at the heart of short and long range programs designed to alter the status of the Negro. One cannot overlook the fact that militant action by Negro groups, and even the occurrence of riots have dramatized the plight of Negroes and have focused public attention on the necessity for reform. Arbitrary and mechanical demands for law and order have been voiced by particular leadership groups as a device for inhibiting social change and political reform. If public policy is concerned merely with police action, both the short term and long term consequences are certain to be self-defeating. Yet there is a core problem in the handling of urban violence, for continued massive violence would hardly serve the objectives of the Negro community and would disrupt the growth of programs required for social change.

Therefore, my basic point of view is that in addition to institution-building aimed at social and economic reform, social control of rioting requires independent efforts in the deescalation of violence; domestic disarmament, if you will. In strengthening social control, a fusion of two elements is involved. First, the law enforcement agencies and the mass media need to develop policies which articulate with the realities of new forms of urban violence that have emerged in recent years. Second, this is not merely a technical problem in the management of violence. It is essential to recognize that political and moral considerations are overriding. Thus, for example, the concept of the constabulary is an effort to base the practices of law enforcement agencies on fundamental political and moral commitments. The constabulary function as applied to urban violence emphasizes a fully alert force committed to a minimum resort to force and concerned with the development and maintenance of conditions for viable democratic political institutions. The constabulary approach implies a continuing review of the division of responsibility between local and federal authorities, as well as of the social prestige and professional self-concept of the police. While the elimination of race riots is at the center of the constabulary concept, we are dealing with a wide range of issues of social control, especially, the legitimacy of law enforcement agencies in the United States. . . .

The stark reality of the new type commodity riot is in the use of weaponry. It is truly an escalated riot. In the old fashioned communal riot, the police were armed with pistols and an occasional rifle. The national guard or federal units carried rifles tipped with bayonets, plus limited amounts of heavy infantry weapons. . . . The central fact about the commodity riots is the wide dispersal of small arms and rifles among the rioters. These firearms are partially the result of individual stockpiling. . . .

The new type of rioting [as contrasted with the U.S. history of riots] is likely to be set off by an incident involving the police in the ghetto, which is defined as police brutality, where some actual violation of accepted police practice has taken place. The very first phase is generally nasty and brutish, while the police are being stoned, crowds collect and tension mounts. The second stage is reached with the breaking of glass windows. Local social control breaks down and the population recognizes that a temporary opportunity for looting is available. The atmosphere changes quickly, and this is when positive enthusiasm is released. But all too briefy. If the crowds are not dispersed and order restored, the third stage of the riot is the transformation wrought by sniper fire, widespread destruction and the countermeasures created by police and uniformed soldiers.

There can be no doubt that the countermeasures employed deeply influence the course of rioting—even in prolonging the period of reestablishing law and order. One is, of course, struck by the great variation in local response to escalated rioting and in the skill and professionalism of the forces in their counter efforts. . . .

. . . The objective is to seek to prevent the spread of contagion. No special steps are taken to prevent routine police performance from developing into incidents which might provoke tension. But if an incident becomes the focal point for tension and the collection of a crowd, the police respond early and in depth in order to prevent the second stage from actually expanding. Numerous police are sent to the scene or kept in reserve nearby. The police seek to operate by their sheer presence, not to provoke further counteraction. They seek to prevent the breaking of windows and the starting of looting which would set the stage for an escalated riot. If actual rioting is threatening, one element is the early mobilization of local national guard units and their ready reserve deployment in inner city garrisons. In part, this is designed to reduce the time required for their deployment on city streets and in part as a containment policy which enables the local police to commit their reserves and feel that they have a supporting force available.

Once a commodity riot enters the second phase of widespread looting and especially during the third phase of extensive scattered sniper fire, effective countermeasures are difficult and require highly trained and specialized units. It is, in some respects, a type of military situation, but the notion of an insurrection has little meaning, for snipers have no intention or capability for holding territory, nor are they part of a scheme to do so even temporarily. The sniper fire exposes police officers and national guard units without battle experience (or without simulated battlefield training experience) to fire fight with which they are not accustomed. The amount of firepower is not very high, although personal risk is clearly present. The basic problem is the scattered source of fire which envelops the law enforcement units. It is this envelopment fire, especially from behind, which has led to the use of the term guerilla tactics, but the guerilla concept is also not relevant since guerillas are part of an organization, proceed with a plan, prepare paths of withdrawal and develop sanctuaries.

The police feel surrounded and, in the absence of effective command and control, they often respond with indiscriminate and uncontrolled fire. The immediate result is that they expose numerous civilians to danger. Such fire does not eliminate snipers, which can only be eliminated by carefully directed fire and counter-sniper procedures. In fact, the initial counterfire can actually mobilize new rioters into the fire fight.

In a major riot, law enforcement officers are exposed to an environment which most have not previously experienced. Their behavior is conditioned by the sheer feeling of the unreality of the rioting situation and the physical disruption which takes place. One response, elimination of street lights by rifle fire, turns an advantage to the snipers and contributes to the sense of unreality. In effect, for prompt control of snipers, special teams of police and national guardsmen are required, using highly exact fire or semi-automatic weapons and trained to respond directly to the source of sniper fire and avoid general displays of fire power. At night, they require support by massed beacon-lights to illuminate the area rather than to plunge it into darkness.

Some police forces had organized, by the summer of 1967, special anti-sniper teams, but such police resources are limited and there is considerable variation in planning and training from one police department to another.

Likewise, the recent summers of 1964 through 1967 demonstrate wide variations in the capacity of national guard units to respond to and assist local police. On the whole, national guard units have received little specific training in riot control and the contents of such training would not appear particularly germane to contemporary problems. The level of effectiveness derives from their military preparedness in general. The performance of national guard units in Newark and in Detroit has been judged by expert observers as deficient. By contrast, the behavior of the national guard units in Maryland and in Wisconsin (Milwaukee) has been reported as much more in accordance with the requirements of the constabulary function. The basic question is fire control and an effective communications network. By contrast, federal troops used in Detroit were highly professional units with extensive training who clearly displayed a higher degree of unit control and were less prone to employ unnecessary fire. The superiority of the federal troops reflects past experience and indicates that more effective military training per se (even without additional civil disorder training), and more effective officers, produces more appropriate responses.

A central index to national guard effectiveness is the failure to integrate units. Because of its fraternal spirit, the national guard has been able to resist federal directives and Negroes account for less than two percent of its personnel. Units in Detroit and Newark were not integrated, while Chicago based units that were employed during the summer disturbances of 1965 were integrated and had Negro officers. Charles Moskos, Northwestern University sociologist who witnessed these events, has reported that integration clearly contributed to the local populations' acceptance of these units and their legitimacy.

## NEXT STAGE: POLITICAL VIOLENCE

There is reason to believe that the mechanisms for preventing and controlling escalated rioting can be improved in the United States. A number of concrete proposals for strengthening social control by police and military units are described below, some of which were partially being implemented by local authorities after the Newark and Detroit experiences. Many measures will require federal intervention and federal assistance.

There is also reason to believe that the socio-economic position of the Negro in American society will continue to improve, especially as federal programs of assistance become more effective. Much social learning has taken place since the initial phase of the "war against poverty." The main lines of effective innovation are beginning to emerge; federal assistance in family planning, radical modification of the present welfare system including a negative income tax, and special youth work training enterprises. Of special importance are the efforts to locate employment opportunities in depressed areas. Experience to date indicates that such industrial establishments become training stations which serve to incorporate youngsters into the labor market for the first time and that, after a short period of work experience, give them incentives to seek additional training or better employment in the wider labor market. No doubt, regardless of their limited immediate impact, some of the community organizations being developed in Negro areas with foundation, trade union and federal funds serve as a learning experience for training new leadership. It also appears that there is a social learning process for both the Negro community and for the larger society when a mass riot takes place, which inhibits the repetition of another similar outburst.

However, expected changes in the socio-economic position of the Negro during the period from 1967 to 1968 or from 1967 to 1970, and even from 1967 to 1972, do not lead to an estimate that social tensions will decline so drastically that problems of social control will become minor. In fact, in our open society, it is necessary to realize that the present commodity riots bear a parallel to the outbursts of militancy in the trade union movement in the 1930's which displayed their vigor not during the depth of the depression, but during 1936 and 1937, a period of halting but increasing prosperity. In the present period, trade union organizations do not supply an effective or adequate channeling of the Negro protests, demands, and aspirations; community and political organizations must serve the equivalent function. . . .

Escalated rioting and the rioting of commodity looting appears to be giving way to more specific, more premeditated and more regularized uses of force. It is as if the rioters learned the lesson emphasized in the mass media, that mass destruction achieves no tangible benefits. New outbursts appear to have more of a goal; a diffuse goal at times, at other times a very specific one. It is almost appropriate to describe these outbursts as political violence or political terror. It is not inaccurate to describe this shift as one from expressive outburst to a more instrumental use of violence. . . .

It is almost as if one were dealing with a form of defiance politics. As these activities increase and become institutionalized, they supply a new power base in the Negro community. In the past, the rackets and the periphery of the political party organizations made use of violence to extract a financial toll from slum communities. These groups confined violent outbursts to the maintenance of the flow of economic privilege. Practitioners of political violence and political terror are now more open in advocating violence and opposition to the larger society. It represents an effort to achieve goals much broader and vaguer than those of the racketeer. There are crude ideological overtones and especially a desire to carry violence into the white community. . . .

. . . Emerging Negro groups seem to reflect various elements of organization such as aspects of the Mafia, as well as paramilitary groups with overtones of a "liberation" outlook. Their style is most outspoken and they seem prone to personal factionalism. But since they are based on racial identification, are difficult to penetrate because of their narrow local recruitment, and have easy access to weapons, their potential for disruption should not be underemphasized.

## TOWARD THE CONSTABULARY FUNCTION

. . . In the management of violence, there is a wide gulf between official doctrine and actual practice. The revolution in police and military training of the last twenty years has been based on the notion that classroom instruction and exposure to training manuals are incomplete and at times somewhat self-deceptive approaches. Training requires simulation of real situations. It was therefore inevitable that, after the escalated riots of the summer of 1967, the United States Army would stage full scale exercises of riot control. In October, 1967, 3,000 law enforcement officials observed army troops break up a simulated riot by 200 "hippies," who were given the opportunity to set fire to a number of buildings, overturn autos and loot stores. It is noteworthy that the object of control was hippies rather than Negroes, indicating that there are political limitations in organizing simulated training operations. In the Chicago area, a similar training exercise was held at the Great Lakes Training Base, where abandoned buildings were destroyed in order to give national guard units realistic experience. While these exercises have a public relations overtone, they do reflect increased consciousness of the real problems involved in the control of escalated riots.

Under the constabulary concept, the bayonet would be eliminated. The bayonet in the American military is a strange example of the power of tradition. The United States armed forces have placed greater emphasis on the bayonet than have most major powers. If it had real relevance at some point in the development of military operations, the advent of the machine gun and the tank eliminated its effectiveness. It remains an instrument of training with the implied justification that it contributes to battle effectiveness by developing the "fighter spirit." The most powerful counterargument is that particular modern armies, from the Wehrmacht to the Israeli, have trained men to perform effectively without such devices. In fact, the bayonet is a symbolic effort to maintain the distinctiveness of the military from civilian occupations and professions.

In any case, the bayonet is completely useless as an instrument of riot control and the management of civil disorder. As a device for separating hostile groups or controlling mobs, it has some of the impact of a police dog, in that it produces countereffects that are not desired. It is not a weapon which reassures soldiers, especially national guardsmen; federal troops tend to avoid its use. Even in the most difficult riot control situations which faced British forces, as for example in Hong Kong, the bayonet was absent.

Instead, riot control forces require helmets, water hose equipment, batons, wicker shields, and the like. They must opt for a minimum use of force if they are to achieve their goals effectively and quickly. If the riot involves gunfire, trained counter-sniper tactics are required, as described above, not display of the ceremonial bayonet. In each case the emphasis is on a selective response and a concern with the minimum application of force. The response of some police departments to engage in widespread arming of their personnel with rifles or to plan to procure armored personnel vehicles does not appear to be appropriate.

The constabulary approach of riot control also requires extensive and ever widening gun control and widespread disarmament programs. Local city ordinances can immediately eliminate the dangers of the acquisition of guns by looting; this can be accomplished by the requirement that all types of guns be rendered inoperative while being stored for sale. Local and state ordinances are required to develop effective gun control but, fundamentally, comprehensive federal legislation is needed. Four years after the assassination of President John F. Kennedy, no such legislation has been passed, and prospects for this action appear to be increasing only gradually. The symbolic and moral significance of any type of gun control legislation should not be overlooked. It might well be possible to take the first steps by concentrating on heavy automatic weapons and making their possession illegal.

The likelihood of effective gun control legislation would probably increase if clearer recognition were given to the need to develop alternative institutions for dealing with the desires of the public to engage in hunting and various types of target practice. Public shooting galleries for target shooters could be established in urban areas, where owners could store their rifles and pistols. The old fashioned Western tradition of checking your gun when in town requires a modern equivalent. Any gun control legislation should include positive incentives for voluntary "turning in of weapons." Prestige incentives could be used, such as badges and other types of material rewards. A bounty system properly controlled would serve to stimulate disarmament in the civilian population. For many persons, especially for youngsters, a gun represents an investment for which a payment is required if he is to give it up. . . .

Effective riot control requires better coordination between municipal and county police, and between local police and national guard units. As riots develop in suburban enclaves, county police will have to be supported by central city forces. There are technical questions of special communication circuits which are easily solved. More difficult is the establishment of unified field command procedures when different units are employed. In the absence of a metropolitan police force, national guard units must maintain, at least during summer months, some small fully alerted units which are resident in local garrisons. These units need to be available for use in the early stages of unrest. They would be under the field command of police officers. While such national guard units would include specialists to handle sniper fire, in effect they would serve as police reenforcements and would have appropriate equipment and directives to that end. In the event of a deeper emergency where it was deemed necessary to mobilize significant numbers of national guard units, the command hierarchy would come under their own direction.

## THE IMPACT OF THE MASS MEDIA

Another important institution of social control which has special relevance for racial violence is the mass media. A complex debate has raged among social scientists since the early 1930's when the Payne Foundation underwrote a group of University of Chicago social scientists in the first large scale study of the impact of the mass media; in this case, the consequences of movies for young people.

The mass media both reflect the values of the larger society and at the same time are agents of change and devices for molding tastes and values. It is a complex task to discern their impact since they are at the same time both cause and effect. Controversies about the mass media focus particularly on the issue of their contribution to crime and delinquency and to an atmosphere of lawlessness. Among social scientists, it is generally agreed that consequences of the mass media are secondary as compared with the influence of family, technology, and the organizational structures of modern society. But differences in the meaning and importance attributed to this "secondary factor" among social scientists is great. "Secondary" can mean still important enough to require constructive social policy; or "secondary" can mean that a factor is trivial and unimportant.

Two separate but closely linked issues require attention. First, what are the consequences of the mass media with its high component of violence on popular attitudes toward authority and on conditioning and acceptance of violence in social relations? Second, what have been the specific consequences of the manner in which the mass media have handled escalated rioting since the period of Watts? Civil liberties groups have supported the managers of the mass media who run their enterprises on a profit basis so that the content of channels of communication, especially television, in the United States, have a distinct "violence flavor" as contrasted with other nations. Thus, for example, the British Broadcasting Corporation operates under strict limitations as to the amounts and times when American television shows can be disseminated. In the United States, it should be noted that the comic book industry, under its own self-regulation, has greatly reduced the amount of horror and sadism in its content; sales to be obtained as an educational medium were found to be more profitable than serving the popular demand for criminal content.

Scholarly debate about the impact of the mass media is not limited to social scientists. Humanists have rejected the whole argument among social scientists and the type of evidence that social scientists utilize as being rather unimportant. For them it is apparent that fundamental principles of morality and aesthetics lead to a rejection of current American practices. Mortimer Adler has been one of the earliest critics of the mass media, holding that it was self-evident that popular emphasis of violence was socially and morally undesirable. In their view, the resources of mass media are limited and should therefore be used for beneficial and useful ends. But the pragmatic bent of American public opinion has not been deeply impressed by the first principles argument, and has been more concerned with empirically demonstrating the impact of the same media.

In my judgment, the cumulative evidence collected by social scientists over the last thirty years has pointed to a discernible, but limited, negative impact of the media on social values and on personal controls required to inhibit individual disposition into aggressive actions. Other students of the same data have concluded that their impact is so small as to not warrant intervention. In part, the research methodology limited more definitive results.

Many studies on media impact are based on limited amounts of exposure, as contrasted to the continuous exposure of real life. Other studies make use of *ex post facto* sample surveys which are too superficial to probe the psychological depths of these issues. More recent research employing rigorous experimental methods has strengthened the conclusion that high exposure to violence content in the mass media weakens personal and social controls. These new findings are based on probing fantasy and psychological responses of young people after exposure to violence content.

They have special importance for lower class groups because of the high exposure of these groups to television. These lower class groups have less involvement in printed media which has less violence material; in addition the symbolic impact of this medium appears to be much less dramatic.

In a democratic society, the content of mass media must be determined by self regulation. But there is reason to believe that the United States could be a more effectively integrated society if popular features on violence and crime were drastically reduced. In achieving such an objective, government agencies, especially those charged with regulating radio and television, have a positive and facilitating role to play. They need to stimulate the television managers to rethink their programing and to review their procedures of self regulation. The mass media have become sensitive to these issues and have attempted to respond by presenting police and law enforcing agencies in a favorable light. But the issue goes much deeper; to end a half hour program of violence with a closing flash favorable to the police is not to alter the fundamental psychological message and its effect on the fantasy life of the next generation. The issue runs deeper in that a long range objective is to make effective and positive use of the mass media to strengthen democratic values.

This means improving mass media coverage of the achievements and aspirations of youth groups. It means broadening the access of youth groups to the mass media to supply an outlet for their creative talents. There can be no doubt that the increased production of alternative suitable materials by foundations and public educational groups if supplied free to the networks would be of important assistance.

It is also necessary to assess the coverage of the riots themselves by television and the impact of this coverage on social control. While there are no adequate statistical studies, it appears that the contemporary coverage of racial violence conforms to the crime wave pattern. The national crisis produced by escalated riots warranted massive coverage according to existing standards of mass media performance. However, the result had a secondary effect of bringing into the scope of coverage violent events which would not have been reported under "normal circumstances." Likewise, the media have been criticized for imbalance in coverage and for not adequately reporting successful accomplishments in police and law enforcement agencies. During the summer of 1967, congressmen called for a review of press and television practices.

Television has served as the main instrument for impressing the grim realities of the riots onto the mass consciousness of the nation. On the spot reportage of the details of the minor riots and their aftermath was extensive and was buttressed by elaborate commentaries. If the fullest coverage of these events is deemed to be necessary as a basis for developing constructive social policy, costs of such media coverage should not be overlooked. It is impossible to rule out the contention that detailed coverage of riots has had an effect on potential rioters and on the public at large.

Such a contention does not rest on the occasional instance where the television camera focused on the riot scene and led either rioters or police to play to the television audience. The television camera thus served to exacerbate tensions and aggressive behavior. Some observers feel that the mere presence of a television crew on the street serves to stimulate excitement and unrest.

Of greater importance is the impact of pictures of the rioting on a wider audience. Again we are dealing with a process of social learning, especially for potential participants. Rioting is based on contagion, the process by which the mood and attitudes of those who are actually caught up in the riot are disseminated to a larger audience on the basis of direct contact. Television images serve to spread the contagion pattern throughout urban areas and the nation. Large audiences see the details of riots, the manner in which people participate in them, and especially the ferment associated with looting and obtaining commodities which was so much at the heart of riot behavior. Television presents detailed information about the tactics of participation and the gratifications that were derived. The media disseminates symbols of identification used by the rioters and their rationalizations. One is struck by the fact that many snipers are portrayed by magazines and television wearing elements of costumes, especially headdress which the snipers believe to have national African elements. The mass media serve to reenforce and spread a feeling of consciousness among those who participate or sympathize with extremist actions regardless of the origins. In particular, television, seeking to expand and hold its audiences, gives great attention to minor extremist leaders far beyond their actual newsworthiness.

Knowledge of the riot would spread in any case, but immediate extensive and detailed coverage both speeds up the process and gives it a special reality. On balance, I would argue that these images serve to reenforce predispositions to participate and even legitimate participation. To generate mass media coverage, especially television coverage, becomes an element in the motivation of the rioters. The sheer ability of the rioters to command mass media attention is an ingredient in developing legitimacy. In highbrow intellectual circles in the United States, a language of rationalization of violence has developed. The mass media serve to disseminate a popular version of such justification. The commentaries on television were filled with pseudo-sociological interpretations and the rioters themselves given ample opportunity to offer a set of suitable rationalizations.

In past periods when rioting was of the contested area variety, the newspapers were the major mass media. In many areas they developed an operational code, informally and formally, to deal with news about rioting. The practice was to apply an embargo on news about a riot during the actual period of the riot. After the event, it would be covered. The goal was to prevent the newspapers from serving as a means for mobilizing rioters, as was the case in the riots of Chicago in 1919. With the growth of television and the intensification of competition between the press and television, this practice broke down. . . .

Since the end of World War II, the mass media have been helping to modify the imagery of the Negro and thereby weaken the prejudiced symbolism. The advances of the Negro in economic, social and political life have supplied a basis by which the mass media could project a more realistic and more favorable picture of the Negro. The reasoned and moral arguments in defense of racial equality by Negro and white leaders supply the basis for extensive editorial commentary in the mass media. Mass media images of the Negro were enhanced by the role of Negro troops in the Korean conflict and by the increasing presentation of the Negro as policemen. Regardless of Negro leadership opinion on the war in South Vietnam, the Negro soldier's role has served to modify in a positive direction the image of the Negro in both white and Negro communities. The early phase of the civil rights movement with its emphasis on orderly and controlled demonstrations served also to alter the symbolism of the Negro from that of a weak powerless figure. The climax of this phase of change, as presented by the mass media, was the dramatic events of the march on Washington led by Martin Luther King. As an event in the mass media, it was unique. The national media were focused on a predominantly Negro assemblage moving in an orderly and powerful fashion. In a real sense, it was a symbolic incorporation of the Negro into American society because of the heavy emphasis on religion and the setting in the nation's Capital. By contrast to the case of the Jew, these events were internal rather than external. The development of black nationalism in tropical Africa, while contributing strongly to Negro self-consciousness, has not produced a clear cut image in American public opinion. The disorders in the Congo and the general instability of these regimes have not produced a favorable response in popular attitudes.

In the elimination of prejudiced imagery, the Negro in the United States obviously has had to face much greater psychological barriers than those of the Jew or any other minority group. Hostility and prejudice formed on the axis of color runs deep. Nevertheless, the secular trend in negative stereotypes toward the Negro from 1945 to 1965 has shown a dramatic decline.

The impact of the riots, as noted above, has not brought about a reversal of commitment to social equality for the Negro although it has temporarily modified attitudes about the pace of change. If the riots served as a basis of group cohesion among the minority of Negroes who are prepared to accept the slogans and tactics of extremist black power, and revolted the bulk of the Negro population, it also introduced, or strengthened, if only temporarily, a strong element of irrationality into the response of white persons to Negroes. The trend toward a transformation in the underlying psychological imagery of the Negro has been interrupted. The view of personal competence and responsible group strength of the Negro was for the moment shattered. Instead, the image of the explosive irrationality of the Negro has been dramatized. The use of sheer strength for destructive purposes, rather than to achieve a goal that the white population could define as reasonable and worthwhile, has served only to mobilize counterhostility and counteraggression.

Most persons live in a limited social space. Their personal contacts are with a limited number of relatives and friends, plus their work associates. The mass media serve as links to the larger society, and these linkages have special relevance for the imagery of race relations. Most white people have few direct contacts with Negroes, although the range of these contacts is gradually broadening. We face the hopeful situation that more often than not these contacts are satisfactory or at least neutral. They are at variance with the imagery of the violent explosiveness of riots and race tensions as projected in the mass media. This is not to underestimate the actual unsatisfactory contacts between whites and Negroes. But let it not be forgotten that the victims of Negro criminal behavior are mainly Negroes and not whites. Most unsatisfactory contacts across race lines take place at the boundaries of residential ghettos, particularly lower class residential areas.

Generally speaking, the most stable interracial contacts take place in occupational settings and the bulk of them are satisfactory. Moreover, the broadening range of interracial contact is between middle class groups, in educational and voluntary associations, especially church settings, among groups best prepared for such contact. In short, for many persons, interpersonal contacts with Negroes, when they have them, are more satisfactory than the recent imagery presented in the mass media. Only when the mass media operate with standards of performance which reflect the satisfactory content of interracial contacts, can they be said to be filling their social responsibility. At the moment, in the guise of reporting the news, they present a most distorted image of social reality. In particular they are searching for evidence of conspiratorial action, rather than explaining the dynamics of rioting. Moreover, the mass media need to develop techniques of reporting which disseminate the essential news, but yet do not serve to weaken patterns of social control or to legitimate resort to violence.

Effective social control involves a delicate balance of a wide range of institutions; the family, the school, religious organizations, and voluntary associations. The goal of social control in a political democracy is to enhance the personal competence and personal control of the individual. Racial equality, if it is to be more than mechanical compliance, must make use of personal controls and individual decisions. This analysis has focused on the police and the mass media. It is in error to think of them as institutions whose inherent operations weaken personal controls. Their effective management can directly contribute to strengthening such controls or to easing the conditions for effective contributions by other institutions.

# 9

## James L. Payne
## *The Cost of Threats in World Affairs*

### WHY THE STATESMAN VALUES A CREDIBLE THREAT MORE THAN THE CITIZEN DOES

Americans generally place a lower value on having a credible threat than do their statesmen. When Americans have supported military action abroad it has rarely been because they thought maintaining a threat was worth these sacrifices. Motives of patriotism, anticommunism or humanitarianism account for most of the popular support of, or acquiescence to, foreign involvement. When presented with the theory of deterrence most citizens would find, it seems, "a credible threat" a flimsy reason for sacrificing American boys or risking American society. When, for example, opponents of the war in Vietnam argued within the deterrence framework, they regularly concluded that the reputation we would have lost by withdrawing from Vietnam would not have been worth the sacrifices we were making. In this judgment these citizens disagree with four Presidents, their Secretaries of State, and virtually all their diplomatic advisors who approved the policy of involvement in Vietnam. Apparently the statesmen have felt the sacrifices are worth it.

The statesman seems to feel that having a coercive threat is a desperately important matter; the citizen finds that, while probably necessary, it is secondary or peripheral to the issues of the day. Which view is more likely to be correct? An answer may be approached by examining how this difference in perspectives arises.

The citizen can believe in a basically benign world; the statesman cannot. The citizen can believe that aggression and war are highly unusual phenomena; he can believe that most international disputes "take care of themselves," that "negotiations" and "diplomacy" are substitutes for war and the threat of war. The citizen can believe that "negotiations," not bullets and a threat of atomic war, brought the Korean conflict to an end, that "diplomacy" settled the situation in Laos in 1961-62. He can believe that aggression does not take place in Burma, Berlin, Venezuela, Nigeria, Pakistan, Quemoy or Turkey simply because aggression is a foolish, uncivilized enterprise which no one would attempt anyway.

The statesman's full-time job is grappling with aggression and war. He cannot consider aggression an unusual phenomenon. He remembers, in his own lifetime, dozens of cases. His list includes not only the crises which citizens have forgotten or overlooked, but confrontations which were resolved before they became public. Crossing his desk are daily intelligence reports on enemy troop movements, political plots, conspiracies, infiltration, and clandestine diplomatic maneuvers. His files are full of plans and counterplans for military contingencies. For the statesman, violence, war, and the threat of war are not far-off improbabilities; they surround his daily life. The statesman knows that international conflicts do not settle themselves; the statesman must take grave risks or make great sacrifices to manage a solution. Negotiation and diplomacy are not substitutes for violence but are often the manipulation of violence, actual or potential.

The citizen can believe in a simple world containing only a few danger points. He imagines only three or four contingencies in which threats might be useful. When, for example, one defends our Vietnam involvement as necessary to maintain our threat and thus discourage aggression elsewhere, one is likely to hear the incredulous response: "Do you mean to say that if we had withdrawn from Vietnam the Russians would invade Europe on the following day?" What the citizen has not assimilated is that there are hundreds of dangerous contingencies around the world; the few illustrations he has in mind are among the least likely to occur. Naturally, then, he attaches little importance to keeping our threat credible.

The statesman is watching all these danger points. He keeps this long list in the forefront of his mind. The Chinese could begin a war of liberation against Burma; the North Vietnamese could push for the communist conquest of Laos; the Chinese could bomb Quemoy; the Russians could send "military advisors" to a procommunist African nation attacking its neighbor; the Chinese could give atomic weapons to Egypt; Cuba could land a battalion of guerrillas in Haiti. A few contingencies are probable; most, at the moment, improbable. But together they form an imposing case for maintaining a secure deterrent threat.

Furthermore, the statesman realizes that the failure to deal successfully with certain challenges to the status quo opens up sequences of new problems. Avoidance of one challenge does not cause the other dangers and possibilities to disappear; it is likely to aggravate them. An American withdrawal from Vietnam would not have ended our problems in Southeast Asia. There still would be dangers in Laos, Thailand, Cambodia, Burma, and Malaysia. And these difficulties, which a Vietnam withdrawal would likely exacerbate, would raise grave and agonizing dilemmas similar to the ones we might hope to escape by withdrawing from Vietnam.

The answer to the incredulous citizen who asked above, "Do you mean to say?" is "No, not exactly. Our failure to confront this problem will result in a *worsening situation.* If we continue to face challenges with the lack of determination implied in your demand for withdrawal in this case, we are likely to get into more serious trouble where dreadful events, perhaps even the one you mention, become possible."

In the words of a practitioner, Dean Rusk (referring to American concern about Laos in 1961): "If you don't pay attention to the periphery, the periphery changes. And the first thing you know the periphery is the center." Because he is not aware of the numerous types of actual and potential challenges and the continuous gradations between them, the citizen conceives of the "center" as a distinct entity which will somehow take care of itself. In this view, action at the "periphery" is, necessarily, peripheral.

The citizen in his ignorance is overconfident; the statesman is not. The citizen believes that events which look improbable, are improbable. The statesman knows that the improbable sometimes happens and, therefore, no possibilities can be dismissed. Would China use nuclear weapons against Japan? The citizen feels that that is improbable and the possibility should be dismissed. The statesman knows that it *seems* improbable, but it could still happen and he must act accordingly. It seemed improbable that the Russians would place missiles in Cuba. But they did. One could imagine this dialogue in January 1962:

> Statesman: We must maintain a highly credible threat.
> Citizen: What for?
> Statesman: Well, to give one of a score of possibilities, if the Russians come to doubt our firmness they might, for example, put missiles in Cuba.
> Citizen: Now, really, aren't you being fanciful? They'll never do that.

Finally, the citizen disregards the unforeseen; the statesman constantly prepares for it. The citizen is content to imagine that the future will resemble the past—or be an improvement over the past. Therefore one need not make special preparations. But history is full of unexpected events. And, sometimes, these events produce confrontations in which one desperately needs a credible threat. One would not have supposed, early in 1967, that the American threat would come in handy in the Mid-East later that year. Unexpected developments made it so. Egypt violated the status quo by blockading the Gulf of Aqaba; Israel reacted with a stunning re-violation. And the Russians stood timidly by while Israel gobbled up tons of Russian arms and miles of Arab territory. Why did they remain aloof? And why, following the victory, was Israel able to ignore the Russian demands for a withdrawal? Surely in the face of a Russian threat to intervene, during the war or after, Israel would have immediately retreated. But there was a countervailing American threat. The Russians assumed that if they went in, we might go in. The Israelis understood this. And why did the Russians seem to believe that if they went in, we would? Because the President of the United States was the kind of person who will take risks and make sacrifices to counter the advances of his opponents. What gave them that impression? Did the Russians believe the same thing about Harold Wilson or Indira Ghandi?

The statesman wants to maintain a highly credible threat not only to guard against all the existing dangers, but to have a margin of safety for the unexpected. China may now be relatively prudent in her foreign affairs. But an adventurous leadership could suddenly come to power. These leaders might, for example, be tempted to invade India before India could acquire nuclear weapons. The justification for a preemptive or preventive war might appear quite compelling to them. Whether or not they do invade would depend heavily upon what they believe the American response will be.

Or, suppose the Chinese do invade India and we wish to stop them. The President of the United States may tell the Chinese that we shall come in with everything we have, including nuclear weapons, unless they withdraw. If the Chinese believe him a great disaster will be averted. If, however, they believe that the United States is timid, not willing to make sacrifices to protect faraway lands, overwhelmed by a fear of using nuclear weapons . . . When the President has to voice that ultimatum it will be too late to do anything about the Chinese belief in our determination. The job of teaching them that we mean what we say had to be done, if at all, in earlier Koreas and Vietnams.

For these reasons, then, the statesman values a coercive threat more highly than the citizen. He is willing to pay more to keep that threat credible.

There is one other point which should be noted concerning the differing attitudes of the statesman and the citizen. The statesman, in his thinking about threats, is consistent and disciplined; the citizen's thinking on the same subject is inconsistent and superficial.

Few people reject the basic logic of deterrence. One has to search long to find someone who does not believe that the threat of war is ultimately the only effective instrument to counter an opponent willing to use force to further his international goals. But although citizens easily make "Then we'll threaten them with. . . ." statements, they are not at all consistent when it comes to the implications of such positions. They do not consider the grave and complicated issues involved in making any threat credible, but simply assume that to "say" is to threaten. And they do not consider the consequences of actually carrying out the threat that they voice—consequences so awesome that, in practice, they would probably be unwilling to carry out their own threat.

Some time ago, I witnessed a conversation which took place between a colleague of mine and a campus visitor. The visitor, it quickly turned out, was strongly opposed to the American involvement in Vietnam. My colleague questioned him about his proposal for dealing with the problem and the following dialogue ensued:

> Q. What would you do?
>
> A. All right. Here's my solution. We tell Ho that he can have South Vietnam, only he's got to give us two years to get out, before we turn it over to him. In this time, we relocate all the South Vietnamese who want to leave before the communists take over—in other Asian nations or even the United States. If we accept Hungarian or Cuban refugees, why not from South Vietnam?
>
> Q. And what do we get in return?
>
> A. I'm getting to that. In return, Ho agrees to get his troops out of Laos and Thailand and to stay out.
>
> Q. But what if he doesn't agree? Or what if, after we get out of South Vietnam, he starts attacking Laos and Thailand again?
>
> A. Then we'll tell the North Vietnamese we will bomb them.
>
> Q. What ?! We're already bombing and it isn't changing their minds! It's already being tried. Or do you mean—?
>
> A. No, not nuclear. Conventional.
>
> Q. Then you mean more . . . ?
>
> A. Yes, more.
>
> Q. Like what?
>
> A. The cities.
>
> Q. You mean bomb the cities, the civilian population?
>
> A. (He nodded).

Q. But that's "genocide"! That's something that even the administration hawks don't want to do!

A. (Somewhat flustered).

Here we have a threat theorist, certainly. But not a thoughtful one. He has, as my colleague pointed out, voiced a threat which U.S. policymakers—and probably he himself if it came to that—would be unwilling to carry out. But even more importantly, he has not considered how he is going to make this threat credible. Indeed, his plan contains a step which practically ensures that his threat will not be believed: the withdrawal from South Vietnam. Such a step demonstrates, in fact, that he is not willing to make sacrifices to defend Southeast Asian countries from North Vietnamese conquest. If he really were willing to make such sacrifices, then why should he want to give up South Vietnam in the first place?

Furthermore, he assumed that all Americans—senators, students, college professors—would join together to carry out *his* threat. Surely this was an unreasonable expectation—particularly in light of the fact that he himself was working to undermine someone else's threat (to defend South Vietnam).

This illustration points up one of the general shortcomings of the many arguments for "redrawing our defense perimeters:" how can we make these new lines *real?* A child with a crayon and a map can draw lines of containment, but what will they mean? What will they mean to us and to our opponents? If these new lines are—as has been the case in recent proposals—merely a device to avoid the difficult defense of old lines, then line-drawing is a sophistic technique for appeasement. Our opponents can trust us—or our sons—to draw more new lines every time they challenge old ones.

Moreover, the lines as they have come to exist are real. They reflect the axis of great power conflict; they represent the interface of the value conflicts between the hostile camps. While we may not be united and enthusiastic about making a particular defense of the existing status quo, we are definitely disunited when it comes to selecting alternatives. The line-drawers are unable to agree upon a new line. Some want us to defend Thailand, others do not. Some say to include Malaysia, others say to leave it out. Some are for Taiwan, others against defending it. Such confusion arises because people are attempting to draw lines without regard to the underlying national values, traditions, and world expectations which would make such lines meaningful. They believe in deterrence. They agree that lines must be drawn and war threatened if they are crossed or undermined. But they have paid insufficient attention to the problems of making their threats real.

The citizen, then, seldom rejects deterrence theory outright. What brings him into conflict with the statesman is his superficial application of the theory. The citizen picks and chooses, almost absent-mindedly, the elements of threat policy which seem obvious, emotionally satisfying, or reasonable on an abstract level. The statesman cannot be inconsistent; he has to seek out and accept the practical, the difficult and the subtle implications of deterrence.

Ultimately, as I said, deciding how credible our threat ought to be is a matter of judgment. But the citizen should understand this threat, its vast application, and its many implications before he decides.

## SACRIFICES OR RISKS?

Sacrifices are men killed, cities destroyed, and moralities trampled. Risks are probabilities of sacrifices, probabilities of losing men, having cities demolished, and acting counter to moral principles. For the statesman, risks and sacrifices are roughly commensurable. To sacrifice 10,000 men is about as bad as taking a moderate risk of sacrificing 100,000 and clearly preferable to accepting a high risk of losing 500,000.

The American public does not treat sacrifices and risks as commensurable. When a President takes a grave risk and things come out well, the only major consequence is a jump in his Gallup rating. Perhaps academics will, for a few months, quietly reflect on past dangers. When the President makes sacrifices, even modest ones, a steady and corrosive wave of opposition builds. Public criticism is vigorous, persistent, and widespread. Let the President risk war in Iran, in a Berlin airlift, or in a Cuban missile crisis, and his action is unnoticed or, if noticed, "heroic." Let him make sacrifices in a Korea or a Vietnam and he is scorned, battered, and driven from office.

Did it not proceed from ignorance, the illogical public attitude toward risks and sacrifices would be seriously hypocritical. Sacrifices are, after all, the result of taking risks which turn out badly. If one is to oppose the sacrifices, then he should oppose taking the risk which may lead to those sacrifices. It makes no sense to remain silent while the gambler places his bets, cheer when he wins but release a storm of abuse when he loses.

In March-April of 1961, the United States moved to the brink of war in Laos to induce the communists to halt their conquest of that country. Had they not halted, Kennedy was apparently prepared to commit American Marines to the defense of Laos. There is no reason to suppose that one Marine regiment would have been enough. Probably the Pathet Lao would intensify recruitment; probably North Vietnam would increase infiltration of troops and supplies; probably more American troops would have to be committed. It might have become necessary to bomb North Vietnam to hold down infiltration. Thus, a war in Laos could have resulted which would have resembled the Vietnam war in almost every particular: a far-off country, "on the Asian mainland," "of no strategic value," undergoing civil war, with incompetent local troops, its "undemocratic local regime," and "civilian casualties."

Surely, anyone who opposed the war in Vietnam should have implored Kennedy not to take the risk. Yet, where were the publicists, the demonstrators, the draft-card burners, the Mothers, Psychiatrists, and Salesmen for Peace? Where was the National Council of Churches, the British Labor Party and the Center for the Study of Democratic Institutions? Most people never knew what was happening—let alone why it was happening. Of the few that realized war was being risked, many could not realistically grasp the blood and destruction of war and therefore did not really fear it.

The willingness of the American public to accept risks while at the same time rejecting any policy of sustained sacrifice may have profound and potentially disastrous consequences. To a certain extent, it is possible for the statesman to substitute risks for sacrifices. Eisenhower chose to risk a serious escalation of the Korean war by threatening to use atomic weapons against China. The risk paid off and the sacrifices of a protracted ground struggle were avoided. Had the threat of escalation failed, a larger war would probably have resulted.

But a deterrence policy based entirely on risks would be neither viable nor safe. A risk is accepting the probability of a sacrifice. If one has a standing policy of making no sacrifices, then one cannot take any risks. In effect, then, one cannot project a threat. If it is well-known that the United States will not accept the sacrifices of fighting a war, then we simply shall be unable to threaten war. Ultimately, the only way we can prove that we will make sacrifices is to make some.

In practice, a serious attempt to substitute risks for sacrifices would deprive us of the option of limited war, which involves sustained sacrifice, and place full reliance on a nuclear threat. When violations of the status quo occurred, we would either have to accept them or threaten to use nuclear weapons. Although this nuclear threat might work sometimes, it is unlikely to work in every case. In many cases the threat of a nuclear response will be incredible because such a response would dramatically violate the rule of proportionality. If two hundred guerrillas infiltrate Thailand from North Vietnam, would we use atomic bombs on Hanoi and Haiphong? Moreover, if we did carry out such a disproportional response, our opponents would rightly treat our action as aggression and feel compelled to take equivalent counteraction. If Red China dropped atomic bombs on Formosa in reaction to a Nationalist commando raid on the mainland, could we idly stand by?

The option of limited war provides us with a proportional and, therefore, credible and coercive response to marginal violations of the status quo. Eliminating this option will not prevent aggression and it will not end the bargaining or threatening process between hostile states. If all we have to threaten is a general conflagration, then that is the threat we will use. In this imperfect world full of miscalculations and accidents, such a threat will, on occasion, fail. And then we shall have the conflagration.

The genesis of World War I illustrates the great dangers of an all-or-nothing deterrence system. In those days (indeed, until the 1950's), limited war was often technologically impossible. Aggression in one theater could not be successfully resisted in the specific locality alone because the defender could not get enough forces and supplies to the area. Nations bargained with the threat of general war—avoiding war for many years. But one miscalculation was enough. Austria sought to invade Serbia. Russia was determined to prevent this aggression. But she could not successfully resist Austria in Serbia. Russia could not get troops and supplies there. If she was not to retreat again, Russia had to mobilize to attack Austria directly. Had the C-47 transport existed in those days, a limited war in Serbia might have been substituted for a World War.

We would be ill-advised, then, to substitute a purely atomic deterrence system for the option of limited war. Limited war gives us a margin of safety. It enables us to say to a reckless actor—such as the North Koreans or North Vietnamese—"See, you have miscalculated," and still live through it.

The American public must learn to accept the sacrifices of limited war. If the war-protesters ever succeed in depriving our statesmen of the option of limited war—and that is, in effect, what they are attempting to do—they shall have placed us still closer to the cataclysm we all dread.

It would not be the first time in history that an honest but naive search for peace has led further down the road toward war.

## THE PAST AND THE FUTURE

A complete inventory of all the resources which the United States has to work its will abroad would fill an entire volume. This brief study has explored only one: the American threat of war. This resource has been a central instrument of American foreign policy since the Second World War. All our Presidents have used it, knowingly and perhaps unknowingly too. The threat of American military action, that is, war, lurks behind the frowns of our Ambassadors, hides between the lines of our diplomatic messages, and darts in and about Presidential press conferences.

What have we accomplished with American power in the world over the past 25 years? What beneficial effects does our threat have today?

First, we have not had total war, or even a major war. That is something no other 20th century generation can say for itself. To point out that total war would be a miscalculation does not diminish the magnitude of the achievement. Both the First and Second World Wars were also miscalculations, as winners and losers would readily admit. They happened nevertheless. The opportunity for miscalculation still exists today. We have had many miscalculations: the Berlin blockade was one; there were two in Korea, one theirs, one ours; the Cuban missile crisis. The war in Vietnam is probably another; one doubts that Hanoi and its supporters would have acted as they did had they foreseen the consequences.

These and other postwar miscalculations have not led to major war because they took place in marginal confrontations and to marginal degrees. The United States, by exerting pressure at the margins of the struggle against the aggression of its opponents, by correcting the miscalculations that take place there, has made it difficult for its enemies to make major miscalculations. Because they *see* us fighting at the periphery they *know* we will fight elsewhere. A Russian invasion of West Germany or a Chinese invasion of India—events which would lead to major war—are today most improbable. And so not only have we not had major war, but such war seems less likely today than before.

To withdraw from marginal areas under communist guns would seem to be the road to a major miscalculation. Our opponents would learn that we definitely will not fight at the margins and come to guess that we might not fight at more "central" areas. Or, to put it another way, they would be unable to recognize what was marginal and what was not. It has been suggested that Kennedy's policy of "non-provocation" during 1961-62 led to the serious Russian miscalculation in the Cuban missile crisis. And, after all, Kennedy retreated very little. But the Russians came to believe we would tolerate something we, in fact, considered intolerable. This same pattern would be repeated on a grander, more dangerous scale by larger, more dramatic American retreats.

American power has also made at least two major tactics of aggression impractical. The first is nuclear blackmail. It would be possible for either Russia or China to dangle nuclear weapons over the heads of neighboring countries and thereby terrify them into submission. But because everyone believes that the United States might respond in kind, aggressive nuclear threats have little coercive value. The way to bring nuclear blackmail on the world stage is to convince everyone that we are panicked at the thought of nuclear war, and are unwilling to risk war or make sacrifices to protect the free world.

The massive land invasion has gone out of style. Since 1950 the communists have attempted no major land invasion. Korea was, clearly, some sort of turning point—but it remains a turning point only because everyone continues to suppose that the United States, with or without the United Nations, is unlikely to tolerate the open communist invasion of a free-world country. It is not unreasonably optimistic to hope that American success in Vietnam would bring us a similar lull in the use of the so-called "peoples' war" strategy of aggression.

Back in the 1950's, there was much talk about the spread of nuclear weapons, and dire predictions were voiced about the "nth" nation possibility. At the time the letter "n" stood for a large and indeterminate number of nations with nuclear arsenals. Today, a decade later, "n" is not large nor highly indeterminate. It seems to equal five. What has happened?

Although many do not realize it, we live in an unusually peaceful world. Nations do not live in mortal fear of annihilation by their neighbors. Aggression does not flourish. Few small nations tremble in the shadow of larger ones. This stabilized world scene contrasts markedly with the ominous, menacing atmosphere that prevailed in periods such as 1933-1939. The peaceful world situation is, in large measure, the result of the American deterrent threat. Russia, East Germany, China, North Korea, North Vietnam, and Cuba: American power has blocked these aggressive states and caused them to moderate their expansionist orientations.

The only thing about the future we can say with certainty is that the threat of war will continue to play a central role in international affairs. Even in our own country, after almost two centuries of nationhood, the threat of force is necessary to discipline political sub-units. When, in 1957, the governor of Arkansas defied the federal court order to integrate Central High School of Little Rock, the President of the United States sent federal troops to ensure compliance. And the basic problem of threatening to use force—that of credibility—also remains. If President Eisenhower had shown himself unwilling to use force to have a federal court order obeyed in Little Rock, then other state governments would have doubted his determination to use force against them in similar circumstances.

If we cannot eliminate the threat of force from our own intergovernmental relations, how could it be eliminated between nations divided by more profound conflicts and where no unit has a monopoly of force? Even should we succeed in eliminating war in the distant future, it will be eliminated only because, and as long as, the threat of war compels nations to accept non-violent processes for the resolution of conflict.

The United States will be in the business of deterrence when our grandchildren grow old. The job may become easier—as we hope—or more difficult. The Cold War axis may disappear only to be replaced by another alliance and perception system.

We may find ourselves attempting to deter a reckless and aggressive Brazil or Japan or France. But we will still be manipulating our threat of war.

Unfortunately, the American tradition of debate on foreign policy practically ignores the role of threats and their beneficial consequences. About the evil effects of power, we are well-informed. The tragedy of war is repeatedly emphasized. We question and criticize our motives with energy. Our moralistic, critical tradition of free debate on foreign policy focuses upon the dangers of using force for evil purposes.

We do not have, however, a tradition of debate which protects us against the evil consequences of a failure to use force. If a war appears moral or necessary in an immediate, compelling way, we support it. But we have not grasped the inextricable link between war and the threat of war. And we have not understood that our threat of war, properly managed, reduces the occurrence of war. As a consequence, the public debate on foreign policy is unbalanced, taking place over the immediate pros and cons of a particular American involvement with little attention given to the indirect and future effects.

This situation is in no way surprising or unusual. It is, unfortunately, characteristic of public opinion that it fixes upon the direct and immediate perception of issues and ignores the indirect and future aspects. Machiavelli pointed this out some time ago:

> If we consider now what is easy and what difficult to persuade a people to, we may make this distinction: either what you wish to persuade them to represents at first sight gain or loss, or it seems brave or cowardly. And if you propose to them anything that upon its face seems profitable and courageous, though there be really a loss concealed under it which may involve the ruin of the republic, the multitude will ever be most easily persuaded to it. But if the measure proposed seems doubtful and likely to cause loss, then it will be difficult to persuade the people to it, even though the benefit and welfare of the republic were concealed under it.

In the management of foreign policy, the inability of the public to weigh concealed gains and losses is profoundly dangerous. Being unable to grasp the connection between a present war which involves obvious loss and future wars which cannot be seen, the desire is to avoid the present loss. Distracted by the circumstantial issues it happens to perceive in a particular conflict, the public fails to apprehend the connection between that particular challenge and the enduring national values. These values will not be dead; they would merely be dormant. We would eventually return to defending them—and probably with a vengeance. Then military action will seem courageous. And our enemies, misled by our failure to defend our values consistently, will have miscalculated.

The public, with its gaze fixed upon the immediate and obvious, wants, in effect, to fight only those wars which are morally compelling or necessary for national survival. But wars which are morally compelling or necessary for survival are the ones which should never have to be fought. They are the catastrophes.

If we are to avoid such tragedy, we must grasp the relationships between

American action–or inaction–in the present and the indirect and future consequences of that action. The focus for understanding these relationships is our nation's most powerful foreign policy instrument: the American threat of war.

# 10

# *The Functions of War: Report from Iron Mountain*

As we have indicated, the preeminence of the concept of war as the principal organizing force in most societies has been insufficiently appreciated. This is also true of its extensive effects throughout the many nonmilitary activities of society. These effects are less apparent in complex industrial societies like our own than in primitive cultures, the activities of which can be more easily and fully comprehended.

We propose in this section to examine these nonmilitary, implied, and usually invisible functions of war, to the extent that they bear on the problems of transition to peace for our society. The military, or ostensible, function of the war system requires no elaboration; it serves simply to defend or advance the "national interest" by means of organized violence. It is often necessary for a national military establishment to create a need for its unique powers–to maintain the franchise, so to speak. And a healthy military apparatus requires regular "exercise," by whatever rationale seems expedient, to prevent its atrophy.

The nonmilitary functions of the war system are more basic. They exist not merely to justify themselves but to serve broader social purposes. If and when war is eliminated, the military functions it has served will end with it. But its nonmilitary functions will not. It is essential, therefore, that we understand their significance before we can reasonably expect to evaluate whatever institutions may be proposed to replace them.

## ECONOMIC

The production of weapons of mass destruction has always been associated with economic "waste." The term is pejorative, since it implies a failure of function. But no human activity can properly be considered wasteful if it achieves its contextual objective. The phrase "wasteful but necessary," applied not only to war expenditures but to most of the "unproductive" commercial activities of our society, is a contradiction in terms.

> . . . The attacks that have since the time of Samuel's criticism of King Saul been leveled against military expenditures as waste may well have concealed or misunderstood the point that some kinds of waste may have a larger social utility.

In the case of military "waste," there is indeed a larger social utility. It derives from the fact that the "wastefulness" of war production is exercised entirely outside the framework of the economy of supply and demand. As such, it provides the only critically large segment of the total economy that is subject to complete and arbitrary central control. If modern industrial societies can be defined as those which have developed the capacity to produce more than is required for their economic survival (regardless of the equities of distribution of goods within them), military spending can be said to furnish the only balance wheel with sufficient inertia to stabilize the advance of their economies. The fact that war is "wasteful" is what enables it to serve this function. And the faster the economy advances, the heavier this balance wheel must be.

This function is often viewed, oversimply, as a device for the control of surpluses. One writer on the subject puts it this way:

> Why is war so wonderful? Because it creates artificial demand . . . the only kind of artificial demand, moreover, that does not raise any political issues: *war, and only war, solves the problem of inventory. . . .*

The *principal* economic function of war, in our view, is that it provides just such a flywheel. It is not to be confused in function with the various forms of fiscal control, none of which directly engages vast numbers of men and units of production. It is not to be confused with massive government expenditures in social welfare programs; once initiated, such programs normally become integral parts of the general economy and are no longer subject to arbitrary control.

But even in the context of the general civilian economy war cannot be considered wholly "wasteful." Without a long-established war economy, and without its frequent eruption into large-scale shooting war, most of the major industrial advances known to history, beginning with the development of iron, could never have taken place. Weapons technology structures the economy. According to the writer cited above,

> Nothing is more ironic or revealing about our society than the fact that hugely destructive war is a very progressive force in it. . . . War production is progressive because it is production that would not otherwise have taken place. (It is not so widely appreciated, for example, that the civilian standard of living *rose* during World War II.)

This is not "ironic or revealing," but essentially a simple statement of fact.

It should also be noted that war production has a dependably stimulating effect outside itself. Far from constituting a "wasteful" drain on the economy, war spending, considered pragmatically, has been a consistently positive factor in the rise of gross national product and of individual productivity. A former Secretary of the Army has carefully phrased it for public consumption thus:

> If there is, as I suspect there is, a direct relation between the stimulus of large defense spending and a substantially increased rate of growth of gross national product, it quite simply follows that defense spending *per se* might be countenanced *on economic grounds alone* [emphasis added] as a stimulator of the national metabolism.

Actually, the fundamental nonmilitary utility of war in the economy is far more widely acknowledged than the scarcity of such affirmations as that quoted above would suggest. . . .

Although we do not imply that a substitute for war in the economy cannot be devised, no combination of techniques for controlling employment, production, and consumption has yet been tested that can remotely compare to it in effectiveness. It is, and has been, the essential economic stabilizer of modern societies.

## POLITICAL

The political functions of war have been up to now even more critical to social stability. It is not surprising, nevertheless, that discussions of economic conversion for peace tend to fall silent on the matter of political implementation, and that disarmament scenarios, often sophisticated in their weighing of international political factors, tend to disregard the political functions of the war system within individual societies.

These functions are essentially organizational. First of all, the existence of a society as a political "nation" requires as part of its definition an attitude of relationship toward other "nations." This is what we usually call a foreign policy. But a nation's foreign policy can have no substance if it lacks the means of enforcing its attitude toward other nations. It can do this in a credible manner only if it implies the threat of maximum political organization for this purpose—which is to say that it is organized to some degree for war. War, then, as we have defined it to include all national activities that recognize the possibility of armed conflict, is itself the defining element of any nation's existence vis-à-vis any other nation. Since it is historically axiomatic that the existence of any form of weaponry insures its use, we have used the word "peace" as virtually synonymous with disarmament. By the same token, "war" is virtually synonymous with nationhood. The elimination of war implies the inevitable elimination of national sovereignty and the traditional nation-state.

The war system not only has been essential to the existence of nations as independent political entities, but has been equally indispensable to their stable internal political structure. Without it, no government has ever been able to obtain acquiescence in its "legitimacy," or right to rule its society. The possibility of war provides the sense of external necessity without which no government can long remain in power. The historical record reveals one instance after another where the failure of a regime to maintain the credibility of a war threat led to its dissolution, by the forces of private interest, of reactions to social injustice, or of other disintegrative elements. The organization of a society for the possibility of war is its principal political stabilizer. It is ironic that this primary function of war has been generally recognized by historians only where it has been expressly acknowledged—in the pirate societies of the great conquerors.

The basic authority of a modern state over its people resides in its war powers. (There is, in fact, good reason to believe that codified law had its origins in the rules of conduct established by military victors for dealing with the defeated enemy, which were later adapted to apply to all subject populations.) On a day-to-day basis, it is represented by the institution of police, armed organizations charged expressly with dealing with "internal enemies" in a military manner. Like the conventional "external" military, the police are also substantially exempt from many civilian legal restraints on their social behavior. In some countries, the artificial distinction between police and other military forces does not exist. On the long-term basis, a government's emergency war powers—inherent in the structure of even the most libertarian of nations—define the most significant aspect of the relation between state and citizen.

In advanced modern democratic societies, the war system has provided political leaders with another political-economic function of increasing importance: it has served as the last great safeguard against the elimination of necessary social classes. As economic productivity increases to a level further and further above that of minimum subsistence, it becomes more and more difficult for a society to maintain distribution patterns insuring the existence of "hewers of wood and drawers of water." The further progress of automation can be expected to differentiate still more sharply between "superior" workers and what Ricardo called "menials," while simultaneously aggravating the problem of maintaining an unskilled labor supply.

The arbitrary nature of war expenditures and of other military activities make them ideally suited to control these essential class relationships. Obviously, if the war system were to be discarded, new political machinery would be needed at once to serve this vital subfunction. Until it is developed, the continuance of the war system must be assured, if for no other reason, among others, than to preserve whatever quality and degree of poverty a society requires as an incentive, as well as to maintain the stability of its internal organization of power.

### SOCIOLOGICAL

Under this heading, we will examine a nexus of functions served by the war system that affect human behavior in society. . . .

In general, the war system provides the basic motivation for primary social organization. In so doing, it reflects on the societal level the incentives of individual human behavior. The most important of these, for social purposes, is the individual psychological rationale for allegiance to a society and its values. Allegiance requires a cause; a cause requires an enemy. This much is obvious; the critical point is that the enemy that defines the cause must seem genuinely formidable. Roughly speaking, the presumed power of the "enemy" sufficient to warrant an individual sense of allegiance to a society must be proportionate to the size and complexity of the society. Today, of course, that power must be one of unprecedented magnitude and frightfulness.

It follows, from the patterns of human behavior, that the credibility of a social "enemy" demands similarly a readiness of response in proportion to its menace. In a broad social context, "an eye for an eye" still characterizes the only acceptable attitude toward a presumed threat of aggression, despite contrary religious and moral precepts governing personal conduct. The remoteness of personal decision from social consequence in a modern society makes it easy for its members to maintain this attitude without being aware of it. A recent example is the war in Vietnam; a less recent one was the bombing of Hiroshima and Nagasaki. In each case, the extent and gratuitousness of the slaughter were abstracted into political formulae by most Americans, once the proposition that the victims were "enemies" was established. The war system makes such an abstracted response possible in nonmilitary contexts as well. A conventional example of this mechanism is the inability of most people to connect, let us say, the starvation of millions in India with their own past conscious political decision-making. Yet the sequential logic linking a decision to restrict grain production in America with an eventual famine in Asia is obvious, unambiguous, and unconcealed.

What gives the war system its preeminent role in social organization, as elsewhere, is its unmatched authority over life and death. It must be emphasized again that the war system is not mere social extension of the presumed need for individual human violence, but itself in turn serves to rationalize most nonmilitary killing. It also provides the precedent for the collective willingness of members of a society to pay a blood price for institutions far less central to social organization than war. To take a handy example, ". . . rather than accept speed limits of twenty miles an hour we prefer to let automobiles kill forty thousand people a year." A Rand analyst puts it in more general terms and less rhetorically:

> I am sure that there is, in effect, a desirable level of automobile accidents—desirable, that is, from a broad point of view; in the sense that it is a necessary concomitant of things of greater value to society.

The point may seem too obvious for iteration, but it is essential to an understanding of the important motivational function of war as a model for collective sacrifice.

5

# Manipulating Political Behavior

The child is father of man and mother of woman. A few years ago millions of young Americans and Europeans were listening intently to Bob Dylan singing "All I Really Want To Do." This song expresses a hatred of manipulation, whether in family or intimate relations or in society. Here, in brief, is an attitude that cannot help but collide strongly against established social institutions, against authority in all its forms.

Where do we go from here? There is enough heat generated to crack many a social iceberg. What new institutions would arise if the old were to melt? Or is it possible to have a society where no one is manipulated, an anarchy of mutually respectful and affectionate humankind? While the reader is kindly answering these questions, we move on hastily to several studies of the influences on political behavior.

Five types of studies are presented which describe different sources of belief and influences on political opinion. The study by two associate professors at the University of Michigan, M. Kent Jennings and Kenneth P. Langton, is a fairly tight, systematic exploration of the beginnings of political attitudes in the family setting, which influence not only political behavior but every other aspect of adult life. It is not as easy as children believe to think independently of their parents. Nor can one prove very readily in what ways parents influence their children's thoughts. Here a national sample survey is used skillfully to marshal data on behalf of the thesis that parents do influence the political views of their children and that it is usually the mother's views that triumph in cases where the parents do not agree.

The selection from the *Great Soviet Encyclopedia* is intended to stimulate discussion of how history is written and rewritten, both consciously and unconsciously, as part of the great waves of influence that affect whole generations and their cultural outlook, including their political behavior. History is rewritten continuously as men change their minds about events, discover new information, and acquire new ways of looking at the past. Contemporary totalitarian governments have made this principle of the "sociology of history" a public policy. Soviet historians have the same faults as most American historians: they "buy" the prevailing vocabulary, and they are ruled by the prevailing fads. But they are also controlled, and there are no exceptions for the "bad boys" of the historical profession. A Soviet historian thus rewrites history more consciously, more often, and to a greater degree. This document is a verbatim translation of what the *Great Soviet Encyclopedia,* the official work for all Soviet citizens, has to say about contemporary American history. The footnotes are by an American historian and correct some of the factual errors.

This article illustrates how history can be manipulated to give students certain desired attitudes. Do you think American students are also taught a version of history that emphasizes America's good points and minimizes its bad ones? If so, what attitudes do you think are derived from our history courses?

Another source of political opinion is the press, by which we mean newspapers, magazines, movies, radio, and television. Because television appears to be having a considerable impact upon campaign habits, upon the character of candidates, upon the casting of ballots, and upon the cost of politics, a study is included by Herbert Alexander, who directs continuous studies of political campaign processes in America with special attention to the costs of campaigning. This selection is a general survey of the field and is not intended to be a tight cause-and-effect study.

The influence of television can rarely be proved except by the most careful and systematic, not to mention costly, research projects. However, its impact seems undeniable, perhaps because there is always an immediate response to shocking news. People will change their habits upon learning about a traffic jam, shipwreck, tornado, or political murder. So it is obvious that people are affected in the immediate sense, but over the longer haul, such as a political campaign, it is not so easy to establish cause and effect. Simply asking people whether they prefer the way Richard Nixon debated to the way John Kennedy debated would not necessarily give valid and reliable responses. One would have to know a great deal about the people themselves—whether they were already committed, how typical they were of the electorate, whether the effect of the debate was long lasting, and so on. The same might be said of the debate in California not quite eight years later between the younger brother of John Kennedy, the late Senator Robert Kennedy, and Senator Eugene McCarthy. In any event, the effects of television are of great concern to those who wish to improve the political process.

The press has traditionally functioned to keep the people informed about what the government is doing. It has also acted as a watchdog to expose dishonesty or ineptness in government. Does the government lie to the people? Does it distort news? Does it conceal bad news? Does it make some information difficult to get? At times, yes, indeed, it does all of these things and does so as a matter of course. After all, who doesn't? Officials are only human, and the problems of public life make them sometimes less than human.

The answer with government officials, as with ordinary people, is virtue, to be sure, plenty of moral education, and freedom from fear of honest revelation. Then one could trust well-designed and operated institutions, like the press or the press as it might be. The fourth document in this chapter, an interview of James Reston, a well-known and influential Washington correspondent, discusses the relationship between the press and the government. To what extent does the press cooperate with or fight the government in obtaining and presenting news about the government?

The first four articles in this section deal with influences that help shape the individual's political attitudes—his parents, his culture, and the press. The final article gives an example of how organizations seek to influence both public opinion and legislative decisions. Such activities are less important in shaping the individuals' attitudes, but they can be influential in determining government policy. This article compares the current activities of labor unions and companies in the electoral process and public opinion management. A thick volume of laws, both federal and state, limits and regulates the appetites of labor unions and business organizations for political power. Power is important; it means a more or less profitable stream of laws, rules, and orders coming from the halls of power. Modern government takes over $200 billion a year in taxes and charges, controls a quarter of the nation's jobs, owns a quarter of the nation's assets, regulates practically every industry to some degree, and defines the right to exist and work. All these aspects of modern government breed both a hostility toward the government, as we have seen, and widespread activity to influence the laws in one's favor. Here, as with Herbert Alexander's and many another study, it is well to realize that the study itself is likely to affect political attitudes and behavior. It is like cleaning a window: the purpose is to let everyone see through the glass, but the bustle of the work and its success in clearing the grime have something to do with what is going to be seen.

# 11

## Robert A. Rosenstone
## *"The Times They Are A-Changin'": The Music of Protest*

At the beginning of the 1960's, nobody took popular music very seriously. Adults only knew that rock n' roll, which had flooded the airwaves in the 1950's, had a strong beat and was terribly loud; it was generally believed that teen-agers alone had thick enough eardrums, or insensitive enough souls, to enjoy it. Certainly, no critics thought of a popular star like the writhing Elvis Presley as being in any way a serious artist. Such a teen-age idol was simply considered a manifestation of a subculture that the young happily and inevitably outgrew—and, any parent would have added, the sooner the better.

Today, the view of popular music has drastically changed. Some parents may still wonder about the "noise" that their children listen to, but important segments of American society have come to recognize popular musicians as real artists saying serious things.[1] An indication of this change can be seen in magazine attitudes. In 1964, the *Saturday Evening Post* derided the Beatles—recognized giants of modern popular music—as "corny," and *Reporter* claimed: "They have debased Rock 'n Roll to its ultimate absurdity." Three years later the *Saturday Review* solemnly discussed a new Beatles record as a "highly ironic declaration of disaffection" with modern society, while in 1968 *Life* devoted a whole, laudatory section to "The New Rock," calling it music "that challenges the joys and ills of the . . . world."[2] Even in the intellectual community, popular music has found warm friends. Such

[1] The definition of "popular music" being used in this article is a broad one. It encompasses a multitude of styles, including folk, folk-rock, acid-rock, hard-rock, and blues, to give just a few names being used in the musical world today. It does so because the old musical classifications have been totally smashed and the forms now overlap in a way that makes meaningful distinction between them impossible. Though not every group or song referred to will have been popular in the sense of selling a million records, all of them are part of a broad, variegated scene termed "pop." Some of the groups, like Buffalo Springfield, Strawberry Alarm Clock, or the Byrds, have sold millions of records. Others, like the Fugs or Mothers of Invention, have never had a real hit, though they are played on radio stations allied to the "underground." Still, such groups do sell respectable numbers of records and do perform regularly at teen-age concerts, and thus must be considered part of the "pop" scene.

[2] *Saturday Evening Post,* Vol. 237, March 21, 1964, p. 30; *Reporter,* Vol. 30, Feb. 27, 1964, p. 18; *Saturday Review,* Vol. 50, August 19, 1967, p. 18; *Life,* Vol. 64, June 28, 1968, p. 51.

sober journals as *The Listener, Columbia University Forum, New American Review,* and *Commentary* have sympathetically surveyed aspects of the "pop" scene, while in *The New York Review of Books*—a kind of house organ for American academia—composer Ned Rorem has declared that, at their best, the Beatles "compare with those composers from great eras of song: Monteverdi, Schumann, Poulenc."[3]

The reasons for such changes in attitude are not difficult to find: there is no doubt that popular music has become more complex, and at the same time more serious, than it ever was before. Musically, it has broken down some of the old forms in which it was for a long time straight-jacketed. With a wide-ranging eclecticism, popular music has adapted to itself a bewildering variety of musical traditions and instruments, from the classic Indian sitar to the most recent electronic synthesizers favored by composers of "serious" concert music.

As the music has been revolutionized, so has the subject matter of the songs. In preceding decades, popular music was almost exclusively about love, and, in the words of poet Thomas Gunn, "a very limited kind [of love], constituting a sort of fag-end of the Petrarchan tradition."[4] The stories told in song were largely about lovers yearning for one another in some vaguely unreal world where nobody ever seemed to work or get married. All this changed in the 1960's. Suddenly, popular music began to deal with civil rights demonstrations and drug experiences, with interracial dating and war and explicit sexual encounters, with, in short, the real world in which people live. For perhaps the first time, popular songs became relevant to the lives of the teen-age audience that largely constitutes the record-buying public. The success of some of these works prompted others to be written, and the second half of the decade saw a full efflorescence of such topical songs, written by young people for their peers. It is these works which should be grouped under the label of "protest" songs of the 1960's, for, taken together, they provide a wide-ranging critique of American life. Listening to them, one can get a full-blown picture of the antipathy that the young song writers have toward many American institutions.

Serious concerns entered popular music early in the 1960's, when a great revival of folk singing spread out from college campuses, engulfed the mass media, and created a wave of new "pop" stars, the best known of whom was Joan Baez. Yet, though the concerns of these folk songs were often serious, they were hardly contemporary. Popular were numbers about organizing unions, which might date from the 1930's or the late nineteenth century, or about the trials of escaping Negro slaves, or celebrating the cause of the defeated Republicans in the Spanish

[3] "The Music of the Beatles," *New York Review of Books,* Jan. 15, 1968, pp. 23–27. See also "The New Music," *The Listener*, Vol. 78, August 3, 1967, pp. 129–130; *Columbia University Forum* (Fall 1967), pp. 16–22; *New American Review,* Vol. 1 (April 1968), pp. 118–139; Ellen Willis, "The Sound of Bob Dylan," *Commentary,* Vol. 44 (November 1967), pp. 71–80. Many of these articles deal with English as well as American popular groups, and, in fact, the music of the two countries cannot, in any meaningful sense, be separated. This article will only survey American musical groups, though a look at English music would reveal the prevalence of most of the themes explored here.

[4] "The New Music," *loc. cit.,* p. 129.

Civil War. Occasionally, there was something like "Talking A-Bomb Blues," but this was the rare exception rather than the rule.[5]

A change of focus came when performers began to write their own songs, rather than relying on the traditional folk repertoire. Chief among them, and destined to become the best known, was Bob Dylan. Consciously modeling himself on that wandering minstrel of the 1930's, Woody Guthrie, Dylan began by writing songs that often had little to do with the contemporary environment. Rather, his early ballads like "Masters of War" echoed the leftist concerns and rhetoric of an earlier era. Yet, simultaneously, Dylan was beginning to write songs like "Blowin' In the Wind," "A Hard Rain's A-Gonna Fall," and "The Times They Are A-Changin'," which dealt with civil rights, nuclear war, and the changing world of youth that parents and educators were not prepared to understand. Acclaimed as the best of protest-song-writers, Dylan in mid-decade shifted gears, and in the song "My Back Pages," he denounced his former moral fervor. In an ironic chorus claiming that he was much younger than he had been, Dylan specifically made social problems the worry of sober, serious, older men; presumably, youths had more important things than injustice to think about. After that, any social comment by Dylan came encapsulated in a series of surrealistic images; for the most part, he escaped into worlds of aestheticism, psychedelic drugs, and personal love relationships. Apparently attempting to come to grips in art with his own personality, Dylan was content to forget about the problems of other men.[6]

The development of Dylan is important not only because he is the leading song writer, but also because it parallels the concerns of popular music in the 1960's. Starting out with traditional liberal positions on war, discrimination, segregation, and exploitation, song writers of the decade turned increasingly to descriptions of the private worlds of drugs, sexual experience, and personal freedom. Though social concerns have never entirely faded, the private realm has been increasingly seen as the only one in which people can lead meaningful lives. Now, at the end of the decade, the realms of social protest and private indulgence exist side by side in the popular music, with the latter perceived as the only viable alternative to the world described in the former songs.[7]

## THE NEGRO IN SONG

In turning to the protest songs of the 1960's, one finds many of the traditional characters and concerns of such music missing. Gone are exploited, impoverished people, labor leaders, "finks," and company spies. This seems natural in the affluent 1960's, with youths from middle-class backgrounds writing songs. Of course, there has been one increasingly visible victim of exploitation in this decade, the Negro; and the songsters have not been blind to his plight. But, egalitarian as

[5] *Time,* Vol. 80 Nov. 23, 1962, pp. 54–60, gives a brief survey of the folk revival.

[6] Wills, *op cit.,* gives a good analysis of his work. Though he is very quotable, there will, unfortunately, be no quotations from Dylan in this article because the author cannot afford the enormous fees required by Dylan's publisher for even the briefest of quotations.

[7] It must be pointed out that, in spite of the large amount of social criticism, most songs today are still about love, even those by groups such as Country Joe and the Fish, best known for their social satire.

they are, the white musicians have not been able to describe the reality of the black man's situation.[8] Rather, they have chronicled Northern liberal attitudes towards the problem. Thus, composer-performer Phil Ochs penned works criticizing Southern attitudes towards Negroes, and containing stock portraits of corrupt politicians, law officials, and churchmen trembling before the Ku Klux Klan, while Paul Simon wrote a lament for a freedom rider killed by an angry Southern mob.[9] Similarly white-oriented was Janis Ian's very popular "Society's Child," concerned with the problem of interracial dating. Here a white girl capitulates to society's bigotry and breaks off a relationship with a Negro boy with the vague hope, "When we're older things may change/But for now this is the way they must remain."[10]

Increasingly central to white-Negro relationships have been the ghetto and urban riots, and a taste of this entered the popular music. Phil Ochs, always on top of current events, produced "In the Heat of the Summer" shortly after the first major riot in Harlem in 1964. Partially sympathetic to the ghetto-dwellers' actions, he still misjudged their attitudes by ascribing to them feelings of shame–rather than satisfaction–in the aftermath of the destruction.[11] A later attempt, by Country Joe and the Fish, to describe Harlem ironically as a colorful vacation spot, verged on patronizing blacks, even while it poked fun at white stereotypes. Only the closing lines, "But if you can't go to Harlem . . ./Maybe you'll be lucky and Harlem will come to you," followed by sounds of explosion, thrust home what indifference to the ghetto is doing to America.[12] The most successful song depicting the situation of the Negro was "Trouble Coming Everyday," written by Frank Zappa during the Watts uprising in 1965. Though the song does not go so far as to approve of rioting, it paints a brutal picture of exploitation by merchants, bad schooling, miserable housing, and police brutality–all of which affect ghetto-dwellers. Its most significant lines are Zappa's cry, "You know something people, I ain't black, but there's a whole lots of times I wish I could say I'm not white." No song writer showed more empathy with the black struggle for liberation than that.[13]

## POLITICIANS

While the downtrodden are heroes of many traditional protest songs, the villains are often politicians. Yet, politics rarely enters the songs of the 1960's. Ochs, an

[8] This article is concerned almost exclusively with music written and performed by white musicians. While popular music by Negroes does contain social criticism, the current forms–loosely termed "soul music"–make comments about oppression similar to those which Negroes have always made. The real change in content has come largely in white music in the 1960's.

[9] Phil Ochs, "Talking Birmingham Jam" and "Here's to the State of Mississippi," *I Ain't Marching Any More* (Elektra, 7237); Simon and Garfunkel, "He Was My Brother," *Wednesday Morning 3 A.M.* (Columbia, CS 9049). (Songs from records will be noted by performer, song title in quotation marks, and album title in italics, followed by record company and number in parentheses.)

[10] Copyright 1966 by Dialogue Music, Inc. Used by permission.

[11] Ochs, *I Ain't Marching Any More.*

[12] "The Harlem Song," *Together* (Vanguard, VSD 79277). Copyright by Joyful Wisdom Music, Inc.

[13] Mothers of Invention, *Freak Out* (Verve, 65005). Copyright 1968 by Frank Zappa Music, Inc. All rights reserved.

unreconstructed voice from the 1930's, depicts vacillating politicians in some works, and Dylan mentions corrupt ones early in the decade. But the typical attitude is to ignore politics, or, perhaps, to describe it in passing as "A yardstick for lunatics, one point of view."[14] It is true that the death of President Kennedy inspired more than one song, but these were tributes to a martyr, not a politician.[15] If Kennedy in death could inspire music, Lyndon Johnson in life has seemed incapable of inspiring anything, except perhaps contempt. In a portrait of him, Country Joe and the Fish pictured the, then, President as flying through the sky like Superman ("It's a bird, it's a plane, it's a man insane/It's my President L. B. J."). Then they fantasized a Western setting:

> Come out Lyndon with your hands held high
> Drop your guns, baby, and reach for the sky
> I've got you surrounded and you ain't got a chance
> Send you back to Texas, make you work on your ranch.[16]

One traditional area, antiwar protest, does figure significantly in the music of the 1960's. With America's involvement in Vietnam and mounting draft-calls, this seems natural enough. Unlike many songs of this genre, however, the current ones rarely assess the causes of war, but dwell almost exclusively with the effect which war has on the individual. Thus, both Love and the Byrds sing about what nuclear war does to children, while the Peanut Butter Conspiracy pictures the effect of nuclear testing on everyone: "Firecracker sky filled with roots of fusion . . . /We're so far ahead we're losing."[17] Most popular of the antiwar songs was P. F. Sloan's "Eve of Destruction," which, for a time in 1965, was the best-selling record in the country (and which was banned by some patriotic radio-station directors). The title obviously gives the author's view of the world situation; the content deals mostly with its relationship to young men like himself: "You don't believe in war, but what's that gun you're totin'?"[18] There are alternatives to carrying a gun, and defiance of the draft enters some songs, subtly in Buffy St. Marie's "Universal Soldier" and stridently in Ochs' "I Ain't Marching Any More."[19] Perhaps more realistic in its reflection of youthful moods is the Byrds' "Draft Morning," a haunting portrait of a young man reluctantly leaving a warm bed to take up arms and kill "unknown faces." It ends with the poignant and unanswerable question, "Why should it happen?"[20]

[14] Strawberry Alarm Clock, "Incense and Peppermints," written by John Carter and Tim Gilbert, *Strawberry Alarm Clock* (Uni., 73014). Copyright by Claridge Music, Inc.

[15] Phil Ochs, "That Was the President," *"I Ain't Marching Any More*; the Byrds, "He Was A Friend of Mine," *Turn! Turn!* (Columbia, CS 9254).

[16] "Superbird," *Electric Music for the Mind and Body* (Vanguard, 79244). Copyright by Tradition Music Company.

[17] Love, "Mushroom Clouds," *Love* (Elektra, EKL 4001); the Byrds, "I Come and Stand at Every Door," *Fifth Dimension* (Columbia, CS 9349); Peanut Butter Conspiracy, "Wonderment," written by John Merrill, *Great Conspiracy* (Columbia, CS 9590). Copyright by 4-Star Music Company, Inc.

[18] Copyright 1965 by Trousdale Music Publishers, Inc.

[19] Buffy St. Marie, "Universal Soldier," Southern Publishing, ASCAP; Ochs, *I Ain't Marching Any More.*

[20] *The Notorious Byrd Brothers* (Columbia, CS 9575).

If many songs criticize war in general, some have referred to Vietnam in particular. The Fugs give gory details of death and destruction being wreaked on the North by American bombers, which unleash napalm "rotisseries" upon the world.[21] In a similar song, Country Joe and the Fish describe children crying helplessly beneath the bombs, and then comment ironically, "Super heroes fill the skies, tally sheets in hand/Yes, keeping score in times of war takes a superman."[22] No doubt, it is difficult to make music out of the horrors of war, and a kind of black humor is a common response. In a rollicking number, the Fugs, with irony, worry that people may come to "love the Russians" and scream out a method often advocated for avoiding this: "Kill, kill, kill for peace."[23] And one of Country Joe's most popular numbers contains the following:

> Well come on generals let's move fast
> Your big chance has come at last
> We gotta go out and get those reds
> The only good Commie is one that's dead
> And you know that peace can only be won
> When we blow 'em all to kingdom come.[24]

The injustice and absurdity of America's Asian ventures, perceived by the song writers, does not surprise them, for they feel that life at home is much the same. The songs of the 1960's show the United States as a repressive society, where people who deviate from the norm are forced into conformity—sometimes at gunpoint; where those who do fit in lead empty, frustrated lives; and where meaningful human experience is ignored in a search for artificial pleasures. Such a picture is hardly attractive, and one might argue that it is not fair. But it is so pervasive in popular music that it must be examined at some length. Indeed, it is the most important part of the protest music of the decade. Here are criticisms, not of exploitation, but of the quality of life in an affluent society: not only of physical oppression, but also of the far more subtle mental oppression that a mass society can produce.

## YOUTH AS VICTIM

Throughout the decade, young people have often been at odds with established authority, and, repeatedly, songs picture youth in the role of victim. Sometimes the victimization is mental, as when the Mothers of Invention complain of outworn thought patterns and say "All your children are poor/Unfortunate victims of lies/You believe."[25] On a much simpler level, Sonny Bono voices his annoyance

[21] "War Song," *Tenderness Junction* (Reprise, S 6280).

[22] "An Untitled Protest," *Together*. Copyright by Joyful Wisdom Music.

[23] "Kill for Peace," *The Fugs* (Esp. 1028).

[24] "I Feel Like I'm Fixin' to Die," *I Feel Like I'm Fixin' to Die* (Vanguard, 9266). Copyright by Tradition Music Company.

[25] *We're Only in It for the Money* (Verve, 65045). Copyright by Frank Zappa Music, Inc. All rights reserved.

that older people laugh at the clothes he wears, and he wonders why they enjoy "makin' fun" of him.[26] Now, Bono could musically shrug off the laughs as the price of freedom, but other songs document occasions when Establishment disapproval turned into physical oppression. Thus, Canned Heat tells of being arrested in Denver because the police did not want any "long hairs around."[27] The Buffalo Springfield, in a hit record, describe gun-bearing police rounding up teen-agers on the Sunset Strip, and draw the moral, "Step out of line the men come and take you away."[28] On the same theme, Dylan ironically shows that adults arbitrarily oppose just about all activities of youths, saying that they should "look out" no matter what they are doing.[29] More bitter is the Mothers' description of police killing large numbers of hippies, which is then justified on the grounds "They looked too weird . . . it served them right."[30] Though the incident is fictional, the Mothers clearly believe Americans capable of shooting down those who engage in deviant behavior.

Though the songs echo the oppression that youngsters have felt, they do not ignore the problems that all humans face in a mass society. Writer Tom Paxton knows that it is not easy to keep one's life from being forced into a predetermined mold. In "Mr. Blue" he has a Big-Brother-like narrator telling the title character, a kind of Everyman, that he is always under surveillance, and that he will never be able to indulge himself in his precious dreams of freedom from society. This is because society needs him to fill a slot, no matter what his personal desires. Of that slot, the narrator says, "You'll learn to love it/Or we'll break you." And then comes the chilling chorus:

> What will it take to whip you into line
> A broken heart?
> A broken head?
> It can be arranged.[31]

Though no other writer made the message so explicit, a similar fear of being forced into an unwelcome slot underlies many songs of the period.

The society of slotted people is an empty one, partly described as "TV dinner by the pool, /I'm so glad I finished school."[32] It is one in which people have been robbed of their humanity, receiving in return the "transient treasures" of wealth and the useless gadgets of a technological age. One of these is television, referred to simply as "that rotten box," or, in a more sinister image, as an "electronic shrine." This image of men worshipping gadgets recurs. In the nightmare vision of a

[26] "Laugh at Me," *Five West Cotillion,* BMI.

[27] "My Crime," *Boogie* (Liberty, 7541).

[28] "For What It's Worth." Copyright 1966 by Cotillion Music, Inc.—Ten East Music—Springaloo Toones. Reprinted by permission.

[29] "Subterranean Homesick Blues," *Bob Dylan's Greatest Hits* (Columbia, KCS 9463).

[30] *We're Only in It for the Money.* Copyright 1968 by Frank Zappa Music, Inc. All rights reserved.

[31] "Mr. Blue," written by Tom Paxton, *Clear Light* (Elektra, 74011). Copyright 1966 by Deep Fork Music, Inc. All rights reserved. Used with permission.

[32] Mothers of Invention, "Brown Shoes Don't Make It," *Absolutely Free* (Verve, 65013). Copyright 1968 by Frank Zappa Music, Inc. All rights reserved.

McLuhanesque world—where the medium is the message—Simon and Garfunkle sing of men so busy bowing and praying to a "neon god" that they cannot understand or touch one another. Indeed, here electronics seem to hinder the process of communication rather than facilitate it. People talk and hear but never understand, as the "sounds of silence" fill the world.[33] Such lack of communication contributes to the indifference with which men can view the life and death of a neighbor, as in Simon's "A Most Peculiar Man."[34] It also creates the climate of fear which causes people to kill a stranger for no reason other than his unknown origins in Strawberry Alarm Clock's "They Saw the Fat One Coming."[35]

Alienated from his fellows, fearful and alone, modern man has also despoiled the natural world in which he lives. With anguish in his voice, Jim Morrison of the Doors asks:

> What have they done to the earth?
> What have they done to our fair sister?
> Ravished and plundered and ripped her and bit her
> Stuck her with knives in the side of the dawn
> And tied her with fences and dragged her down.[36]

In a lighter tone but with no less serious an intent, the Lewis and Clark Expedition describe the way man has cut himself off from nature.

> There's a chain around the flowers
> There's a fence around the trees
> This is freedom's country
> Do anything you please

With a final thrust they add, "You don't need to touch the flowers/They're plastic anyway."[37]

This brings up a fear that haunts a number of recent songs, the worry that the technological age has created so many artificial things that nothing natural remains. Concerned with authenticity, the songsters are afraid that man himself is becoming an artifact, or, in their favorite word, "plastic." Thus, the Jefferson Airplane sing about a "Plastic Fantastic Lover," while the Iron Butterfly warn a girl to stay away from people "made of plastic."[38] The image recurs most frequently in the works of the Mothers of Invention. In one song, they depict the country as being run by a plastic Congress and President.[39] Then, in "Plastic People," they start with complaints about a girlfriend who uses "plastic goo" on her face, go on to a picture of teen-agers on the Sunset Strip—who are probably their fans—as being "plastic,"

[33] "Sounds of Silence," *Sounds of Silence* (Columbia, CS 9269).

[34] *Sounds of Silence.*

[35] *Wake Up . . . It's Tomorrow* (Uni., 73025).

[36] "When the Music's Over," *Strange Days* (Elektra, 74014). Copyright 1967 by Nipper Music, Inc. All rights reserved.

[37] "Chain Around the Flowers," *The Lewis and Clark Expedition* (Colgems, COS 105). Words and music by John Vandiver. Copyright 1967 by Screen Gems—Columbia Music, Inc. Used by permission. Reproduction prohibited.

[38] *Surrealistic Pillow* (Victor, LSP 3766); "Stamped Ideas," *Heavy* (Atco, S 33-227).

[39] "Uncle Bernie's Farm," *Absolutely Free.*

too, and finally turn on their listeners and say "Go home and check yourself/You think we're talking about someone else."[40] Such a vision is frightening, for if the audience is plastic, perhaps the Mothers, themselves, are made of the same phony material. And if the whole world is plastic, who can be sure of his own authenticity?

## LOVE RELATIONSHIPS

Toward the end of "Plastic People," the Mothers say, "I know true love can never be/A product of plasticity."[41] This brings up the greatest horror, that in a "plastic" society like the United States, love relationships are impossible. For the young song writers, American love is viewed as warped and twisted. Nothing about Establishment society frightens them more than its attitudes towards sex. Tim Buckley is typical in singing that older Americans are "Afraid to trust in their bodies," and in describing them as "Faking love on a bed made of knives."[42] Others give graphic portraits of deviant behavior. The Fugs tell of a "Dirty Old Man" hanging around high school playgrounds; the Velvet Underground portray a masochist; and the Mothers depict a middle-aged man lusting after his own thirteen-year-old daughter.[43] The fullest indictment of modern love is made by the United States of America, who devote almost an entire album to the subject. Here, in a twisted portrait of "pleasure and pain," is a world of loveless marriages, homosexual relationships in men's rooms, venomous attractions, and overt sadism—all masked by a middle-class, suburban world in which people consider "morality" important. To show that natural relationships are possible elsewhere, the group sings one tender love lyric; interestingly, it is the lament of a Cuban girl for the dead Ché Guevara.[44]

The fact that bourgeois America has warped attitudes towards sex and love is bad enough; the songsters are more worried that such attitudes will infect their own generation. Thus, the Collectors decry the fact that man-woman relationships are too often seen as some kind of contest, with a victor and vanquished, and in which violence is more acceptable than tenderness.[45] Perhaps because most of the singers are men, criticisms of female sexual attitudes abound. The Mothers say disgustedly to the American woman, "You lie in bed and grit your teeth," while the Sopwith Camel object to the traditional kind of purity by singing, "I don't want no woman wrapped up in cellophane."[46] This is because such a woman "will do you

[40] "Plastic People," *Absolutely Free.* Copyright 1968 by Frank Zappa Music, Inc. All rights reserved.

[41] *Ibid.*

[42] "Goodbye and Hello," written by Tim Buckley, *Goodbye and Hello* (Elektra, 7318). Copyright 1968 by Third Story Music, Inc. All rights reserved.

[43] *The Fugs;* "Venus in Furs," *The Velvet Underground and Nico* (Verve, V6-5008); "Brown Shoes Don't Make It," *Absolutely Free.*

[44] *The United States of America* (Columbia, CS 9614).

[45] "What Love," *The Collectors* (Warner Bros.-Seven Arts, WS 1746).

[46] *We're Only in It for the Money;* "Cellophane Woman," *The Sopwith Camel* (Kama Sutra, KLPS 8060). Copyright by Great Honesty Music, Inc.

in/Bending your mind with her talking about sin."[47] All the musicians would prefer the girl about whom Moby Grape sings who is "super-powered, deflowered," and over eighteen.[48]

Living in a "plastic" world where honest human relationships are impossible, the song writers might be expected to wrap themselves in a mood of musical despair. But they are young–and often making plenty of money– and such an attitude is foreign to them. Musically, they are hopeful because, as the title of the Dylan song indicates, "The Times They Are A-Changin'." Without describing the changes, Dylan clearly threatens the older generation, as he tells critics, parents, and presumably anyone over thirty, to start swimming or they will drown in the rising flood-waters of social change.[49]

In another work, Dylan exploits the same theme. Here is a portrait of a presumably normal, educated man, faced with a series of bizarre situations, who is made to feel like a freak because he does not understand what is going on. The chorus is the young generation's comment to all adults, as it mocks "Mr. Jones" for not understanding what is happening all around him.[50]

The changes going on are, not surprisingly, associated with the carefree, joyful experiences of youth. As Jefferson Airplane sings, "It's a wild time/I see people all around me changing faces/It's a wild time/I'm doing things that haven't got a name yet."[51] The most full-blown description of the changing world is Tim Buckley's "Goodbye and Hello," a lengthy and explicit portrait of what the youth hope is happening. Throughout the song the author contrasts two kinds of people and their environments. On the one hand are the "antique people" –godless and sexless–of an industrial civilization, living in dark dungeons, working hard, worshipping technology and money, sacrificing their sons to placate "vaudeville" generals, and blinding themselves to the fact that their "masquerade towers" are "riddled by widening cracks." Opposed to them are the "new children," interested in flowers, streams, and the beauty of the sky, who wish to take off their clothes to dance and sing and love one another. What's more, the "antique people are fading away"; in fact, they are already wearing "death masks." As the song says, "The new children will live because their elders have died."[52]

Buckley's vision of the new world that is coming is obviously that of a kind of idyllic Eden before the fall, a world in which men will be free to romp and play and indulge their natural desires for love. It is a pagan world, the antithesis of the Christian ideal that would postpone fulfillment to some afterlife. Elsewhere, Buckley explicitly condemns Christianity, saying "I can't hesitate and I can't wait

[47] "Cellophane Woman." Copyright by Great Honesty Music, Inc.

[48] "Motorcycle Irene," *Wow* (Columbia, CS 9613).

[49] *Bob Dylan's Greatest Hits.*

[50] "Ballad of a Thin Man/Mr. Jones," *Highway 61 Revisited* (Columbia, CS 9189). Though this song has obvious homosexual overtones, it also stands as youth's criticism of the older generation.

[51] "Wild Tyme (H)," *After Bathing at Baxter's* (Victor, LSO-1511). Copyright by Ice Bag Corporation.

[52] "Goodbye and Hello," written by Tim Buckley, *Goodbye and Hello.* Copyright 1968 by Third Story Music, Inc. All rights reserved.

for pleasant street."[53] Similarly, the Doors' Jim Morrison states, "Cancel my subscription to the resurrection," and in the same song literally shrieks, "We want the world and want it now."[54] Here is the impatient demand of youth that all problems be swept aside and the world be made into paradise without delay.

## HOW TO LIVE

Though the times may be changing, the songsters are well aware that–despite their brave words and demands–there is plenty of strength left in the old social order. Obviously, they can see the war continuing, Negro demands not being met, and the continuing hostility of society toward their long hair, music, sexual behavior, and experimentation with drugs. Faced with these facts, the musicians must deal with the problem of how to live decently within the framework of the old society. Here they tend toward the world of private experience mentioned earlier in this article in connection with Dylan. Many of their songs are almost programs for youth's behavior in a world perceived as being unlivable.

The first element is to forget about the repressive society out there. As Sopwith Camel says, "Stamp out reality . . ./Before reality stamps out you."[55] Then it is imperative to forget about trying to understand the outside world rationally. In a typical anti-intellectual stance, the Byrds describe such attempts as "scientific delirium madness."[56] Others combine a similar attitude with a strong measure of *carpe diem*. Spirit deride people who are "always asking" for "the reason" when they should be enjoying life, while H. P. Lovecraft admits that the bird is on the wing and states, "You need not know why."[57] What is important is that the moment be seized and life lived to the fullest. As Simon and Garfunkel say, one has to make the "moment last," and this is done best by those who open themselves fully to the pleasures of the world.[58]

The most frequent theme of the song writers is the call to freedom, the total freedom of the individual to "do his own thing." Peanut Butter Conspiracy carry this so far as to hope for a life that can be lived "free of time."[59] Circus Maximus and the Byrds–despite the fact that they are young men–long to recapture some lost freedom that they knew as children.[60] Such freedom can be almost solipsistic; Jimi Hendrix claims that even if the sun did not rise and the mountains fell into the

[53] "Pleasant Street," written by Tim Buckley. Copyright 1968 by Third Story Music, Inc. All rights reserved.

[54] "When the Music's Over," *Strange Days.* Copyright 1967 by Nipper Music Company, Inc. All rights reserved.

[55] "Saga of the Low Down Let Down," *The Sopwith Camel.* Copyright by Great Honesty Music, Inc.

[56] "Fifth Dimension," *Fifth Dimension.*

[57] "Topanga Window," *Spirit* (Ode, 212 44004); "Let's Get Together," *H. P. Lovecraft* (Phillips, 600-252).

[58] "Feeling Groovy," *Sounds of Silence.*

[59] "Time is After You," *West Coast Love-In* (Vault, LP 113).

[60] "Lost Sea Shanty," *Circus Maximus* (Vanguard, 79260); "Going Back," *The Notorious Byrd Brothers.*

sea, he would not care because he has his "own world to live through."[61] But for others, it can lead to brotherhood. As H. P. Lovecraft says, "C'mon people now, let's get together/Smile on your brother,/Try and love one another right now."[62]

A desire for freedom is certainly nothing new. What is different in the songs of the 1960's is the conviction that this freedom should be used by the individual in an extensive exploration of his own internal world. Central to the vision of the song writers is the idea that the mind must be opened and expanded if the truths of life are to be perceived. Thus, the importance of external reality is subordinated to that of a psychological, even a metaphysical, realm. The most extensive treatment of this subject is by the Amboy Dukes, who devote half of a long-playing record to it. Their theme is stated quite simply: "How happy life would be/If all mankind/Would take the time to journey to the center of the mind."[63] Like any mystical trip, what happens when one reaches the center of the mind is not easy to describe. Perhaps the best attempt is by the Iron Butterfly, who claim that an unconscious power will be released, flooding the individual with sensations and fusing him with a freedom of thought that will allow him to "see everything." At this point, man will be blessed with the almost supernatural power of knowing "all."[64]

Such a journey is, of course, difficult to make. But youth has discovered a short cut to the mind's center, through the use of hallucinogenic drugs. Indeed, such journeys are almost inconceivable without hallucinogens, and the so-called "head songs" about drug experiences are the most prevalent of works that can be classified as "protest."[65] In this area, the songs carefully distinguish between "mind-expanding," nonaddictive marijuana and LSD, and hard, addictive drugs which destroy the body. Thus, the Velvet Underground and Love both tell of the dangers of heroin, while Canned Heat warn of methedrine use and the Fugs describe the problems of cocaine.[66] But none of the groups hesitate to recommend "grass" and "acid" trips as a prime way of opening oneself to the pleasures and beauties of the universe. As the Byrds claim in a typical "head song," drugs can free the individual from the narrow boundaries of the mundane world, allowing him to open his heart to the quiet joy and eternal love which pervade the whole universe.[67] Others find the reality of the drug experience more real than the day-to-day world, and some even hope for the possibility of staying "high" permanently. More frequent is the claim that "trips" are of lasting benefit because they improve the

[61] "If 6 Was 9," *Axis* (Reprise, S 6281).

[62] H. P. Lovecraft, *"Let's Get Together,"* written by Chester Powers, *H. P. Lovecraft.* Copyright by Irving Music, Inc.

[63] "Journey to the Center of the Mind," *Journey to the Center of the Mind* (Mainstream, S 6112). Copyright 1968 by Brent Music Corporation.

[64] "Unconscious Power," *Heavy.*

[65] There are so many "head songs" that listing them would be an impossibly long task Some of the most popular protest songs of the decade have been such works. They include Jefferson Airplane, "White Rabbit," *Surrealistic Pillow;* the Doors, "Light My Fire," *The Doors* (Elektra EKS 74007); Strawberry Alarm Clock, "Incense and Peppermints," *Incense and Peppermints;* and the Byrds, "Eight Miles High," *Fifth Dimension.*

[66] "Heroin," *Velvet Underground;* "Signed D. C.," *Love* (Elektra, 74001); "Amphetamine Annie," *Boogie;* "Coming Down," *The Fugs.*

[67] "Fifth Dimension," *Fifth Dimension.*

quality of life of an individual even after he "comes down."[68] The Peanut Butter Conspiracy, claiming that "everyone has a bomb" in his mind, even dream of some day turning the whole world on with drugs, thus solving mankind's plaguing problems by making the earth a loving place.[69] An extreme desire, perhaps, but one that would find much support among other musicians.

## A REPRESSIVE SOCIETY

This, then is the portrait of America that emerges in the popular songs of the 1960's which can be labelled as "protest." It is, in the eyes of the song writers, a society which makes war on peoples abroad and acts repressively toward helpless minorities like Negroes, youth, and hippies at home. It is a land of people whose lives are devoid of feeling, love, and sexual pleasure. It is a country whose institutions are crumbling away, one which can presumably only be saved by a sort of cultural and spiritual revolution which the young themselves will lead.

Whether one agrees wholly, partly, or not at all with such a picture of the United States, the major elements of such a critical portrait are familiar enough. It is only in realizing that all this is being said in popular music, on records that sometimes sell a million copies to teen-agers, in songs that youngsters often dance to, that one comes to feel that something strange is happening today. Indeed, if parents fully understand what the youth are saying musically to one another, they must long for the simpler days of Elvis Presley and his blue suede shoes.

If the lyrics of the songs would disturb older people, the musical sound would do so even more. In fact, a good case could be made that the music itself expresses as much protest against the status quo as do the words. Performed in concert with electronic amplification on all instruments—or listened to at home at top volume—the music drowns the individual in waves of sound; sometimes it seems to be pulsating inside the listener. When coupled with a typical light show, where colors flash and swirl on huge screens, the music helps to provide an assault on the senses, creating an overwhelming personal experience of the kind that the songs advise people to seek. This sort of total experience is certainly a protest against the tepid, partial pleasures which other songs describe as the lot of bourgeois America.

Another aspect of the music which might be considered a kind of protest is the attempt of many groups to capture in sound the quality of a drug "trip," to try through melody, rhythm, and volume to—in the vernacular—"blow the mind" of the audience. Of course, youngsters often listen to such music while under the influence of hallucinogens. In such a state, the perceptive experience supposedly can have the quality of putting one in touch with regions of the mind and manifestations of the universe that can be felt in no other way. Such mysticism, such transcendental attitudes, are certainly a protest against a society in which reality is always pragmatic and truth instrumental.

[68] See Country Joe and the Fish, "Bass Strings," *Electric Music for the Mind and Body;* or United States of America, "Coming Down," *United States of America.*

[69] "Living, Loving Life," *Great Conspiracy.*

To try to explain why the jingles and vapid love lyrics of popular music in the 1950's evolved into the social criticism and mystical vision of the 1960's is certainly not easy. Part of it is the fact that performers, who have always been young, started writing their own songs, out of their own life experiences, rather than accepting the commercial output of the older members of tin pan alley. But this does not explain the popularity of the new songs. Here one must look to the youthful audience, which decided it preferred buying works of the newer kind. For it was the commercial success of some of the new groups which opened the doors of the record companies to the many that flourish today.

## THE FUNCTION OF MUSIC

Though one cannot make definitive judgments about this record-buying audience, some things seem clear. Certainly, it is true that with increasingly rapid social change, parents–and adults in general–have less and less that they can tell their children about the ways of the world, for adult life experiences are not very relevant to current social conditions. Similarly, institutions like the school and the press suffer from a kind of cultural lag that makes their viewpoints valueless for youth. Into the place of these traditional sources of information have stepped the youth themselves, and through such things as the "underground" press and popular music they are telling each other exactly what is happening. In this way, the music has achieved popularity–at least in part–because it telegraphs important messages to young people and helps to define and codify the mores and standards of their own subculture. A youngster may personally feel that there is no difference between his parents' drinking and his use of marijuana. Certainly, it is comforting to him when his friends feel the same way, and when popular songs selling millions of copies deliver the same message, there are even stronger sanctions for his "turning on." Thus, the lyrics of the music serve a functional role in the world of youth.

It is interesting to note that the popular music also puts youth in touch with serious, intellectual critiques of American life. Perhaps it starts only as a gut reaction in the song writers, but they have put into music the ideas of many American social critics. Without reading Paul Goodman, David Riesman, C. Wright Mills, or Mary McCarthy, youngsters will know that life is a "rat race," that Americans are a "lonely crowd," that "white-collar" lives contain much frustration, and that the war in Vietnam is far from just. And they will have learned this from popular music, as well as from their own observation.

The other side of the coin from criticism of contemporary life is the search for personal experience, primarily of the "mind-expanding" sort. As is obvious by now, such expansion has nothing to do with the intellect, but is a spiritual phenomenon. Here a final critique is definitely implicit. Throughout the music–as in youth culture–there is the search for a kind of mystical unity, an ability to feel a oneness with the universe. This is what drugs are used for; this is what the total environment of the light and music shows is about; and this is what is sought in the sexual experience—often explicitly evident in the orgasmic grunts and moans of performers. Through the search for this unity, the music is implicitly condemning the fragmentation of the individual's life which is endemic in the modern world. The songsters are saying that it is wrong to compartmentalize work and play, wrong to cut men off from the natural rhythms of nature, wrong to stifle sex and love and play in favor of greater productivity, wrong to say man's spiritual needs can be filled by providing him with more material possessions.

This is obviously a criticism that can only be made by an affluent people, but these youth do represent the most affluent of all countries. And rather than wallow in their affluence, they have sensed and expressed much of the malaise that plagues our technological society. The charge may be made against them that they are really utopians, but the feeling increases today that we are in need of more utopian thinking and feeling. And while one might not wish to follow their prescriptions for the good life, they have caught something of the desire for freedom that all men feel. What could be more utopian and yet more inviting in its freedom than the hopeful picture which the Mothers of Invention paint of the future:

> There will come a time when everybody
> Who is lonely will be free . . .
> TO SING AND DANCE AND LOVE
> There will come a time when every evil
> That we know will be an evil
> WE CAN RISE ABOVE
> Who cares if hair is long or short
> Or sprayed or partly grayed . . .
> WE KNOW THAT HAIR
> AINT WHERE IT'S AT
> (There will come a time when you
> won't even be ashamed if you are fat!)
>
> Who cares if you're so poor
> You can't afford to buy a pair
> Of mod a-go go stretch elastic pants
> THERE WILL COME A TIME
> WHEN YOU CAN EVEN
> TAKE YOUR CLOTHES OFF WHEN
> YOU DANCE[70]

[70] "Take Your Clothes Off When You Dance," *We're Only in It for the Money.* Copyright 1968 by Frank Zappa Music, Inc. All rights reserved.

# 12

## M. Kent Jennings and Kenneth P. Langton

## *Mothers Versus Fathers as "Mind-Invaders"*

The family has long been assigned an important if not central role in the political socialization process. While recent research has forced a reevaluation of its direct influence, there is little doubt that parents have a profound impact on the formation of certain political orientations. In talking about the place of the family, parents are usually treated as a unit and not distinguished according to their individual roles in the political socialization of their children. Moreover, when "parental" characteristics are specified, father attributes are commonly taken as a satisfactory description of the unit. Such assumptions are valid enough for many purposes, but to understand more fully the socialization process within the family circle it is necessary to differentiate the contributions of mothers versus fathers.

One area in which the family is undoubtedly important is in the transmission of party identification. Studies of adults and children show that when the recalled party preference of both parents is the same, up to 80% of the respondents also report that preference. How much each parent contributes to this high congruence is not clear; nor is this question easily resolved, given mother-father concordance. When parental partisanship is mixed or inconsistent, the identification of the offspring is more evenly divided between the parties. Little is known about the relative influence of parents on the child's party identification in these families. . . .

The prevailing view on intra-familial interaction is that the husband-father plays the dominant political role. McClosky and Dahlgren found, for example, that when husbands' and wives' inherited political preferences differed, "there was a tendency for women to switch more often to their husbands' preferences than the reverse." Campbell, Gurin, and Miller observed that "political influence in the marriage relationship seems to go predominantly in one direction," from husbands to wives. . . .

. . . [T]hree studies of young people based on limited samples and recall data report findings on the inter-generational transfer of party identification. In one, a group of college students had somewhat greater agreement with their mothers than with their fathers; in another, young adults agreed more with their mother than father when parents diverged in their party preferences. . . .

## RESEARCH DESIGN AND A BASIC MEASURE

We shall utilize data from a study of political socialization among American high school seniors. At the core of the study stands a national probability sample of 1669 seniors, distributed among ninety-seven secondary schools. . . .

Initially we must divide the parental pairs into like-minded versus conflicting combinations. The determination of the homogeneity-heterogeneity of parents' party identification was conditioned by a number of factors. First, this analysis starts with a set of parental pairs, the great majority of which are homogenous in party identification given most reasonable means of determination. Because the primary target of this study is families involving heterogenous parental pairs, we did not want to restrict unnecessarily the number of such pairs by insisting that they be bi-polar, that is, a combination of Democrat and Republican. In the analysis both the bi-polar pairs and other less marked cases of heterogeneity will be examined, sometimes separately and at other times in collapsed form. . . .

Therefore, for most analytical purposes we treated the parents' seven point measure of party direction as a three point scale by ignoring the distinction between strong, weak, and independent partisans. In other words, a Republican or Democratic parent would be anyone originally identified as (1) strong, (2) weak, or (3) Independent leaning toward a party. Independents consist of only "pure" types. This means that any parental mix of strong, weak, or Independent-Democrats would make a homogenous Democratic pair. Likewise any similar mix on the part of both parents and their student offspring would make a homogenous Democratic triple. . . .

. . . First are those completely homogenous triples, wherein the student, mother, and father all share the same general party affiliation. Fifty-seven percent of the cases fit this description. This figure belies the popular notion that the family unit is predominately like-minded. A second type is one in which mother and father are homogenous but the student deviates. For example, the parents are Democrats while the offspring is either a Republican or a pure Independent. Seventeen percent of the triples are of this nature. When this group is divided further it turns out that 59% of the children go to the opposite party, while the remainder become pure Independents. A final triadic pattern is one in which the parents are heterogeneous and the offspring agrees with one or, possibly neither. Illustratively, father might be Republican, mother Democratic, and the child Republican, i.e., child agrees with father. If the child in this particular instance were an Independent, he would be classified as agreeing with neither. Out of all triples, 26% fall into this category. Of this sub-total, some 54% embrace partisan-Independent parental pairs and 46% involve Democratic-Republican bi-polar combinations.

To summarize: 57% of the triples are broadly homogeneous; 17% have homogeneous parents and a deviating child; and 26% include heterogeneous parents. One immediate conclusion, then, is that the family circle is by no means monolithic in its partisan attachments. . . .

## TRIPLES WITH HOMOGENEOUS PAIRS

Although the cases marked by parental heterogeneity are of central concern to us, the homogeneous parents, because of their ubiquity, also bear brief scrutiny. One of the recurrent findings in the electoral behavior literature is that those people who recall both their parents as preferring one of the two major parties generally prefer that party themselves. Our data clearly support these findings; where parents agree, 76% of the students agree with them. Inter-party differences are present, however. Among Republican parents 68% of their offspring also prefer that party (Appendix). By comparison, among Democratic parents 85% of their offspring identify with the Democratic party. The Democratic party obviously enjoys greater retaining power among the children of like-minded parents. Moreover, when students do disagree with their homogeneously partisan parents, those with Republican parents are more likely to defect all the way to the opposing party (60%) than are students with Democratic parents (46%). In short, whatever the non-familial influences acting on today's adolescents, such as Democratic majorities in the nation or the partisan climate of the school community, they are somewhat stronger in the direction of the Democratic party than the Republican.

Of more immediate interest are the two subsets of triples with homogeneous parents. In the first subset are the students (76%) who succumb to their parents' identification, while the other group (24%) consists of those who fail to follow their parents. Our first analytic effort is to see if there are any prominent familial attributes which help set off these defecting students. That is, given like-minded parents, it is conceivable that one parent may be relatively more influential than the other in preventing the party deviation of the student. What happens, for example, when the mother is high and the father is low in politicization, or conversely, when the father is high and the mother is low? In order to examine this and similar questions we devised indices depicting the relative politicization and education of mothers versus fathers.

Against the backdrop of the generally assumed political dominance of the father in the family it is surprising to see his marginal strength in helping preserve triadic homogeneity. If either parent plays a more impressive role in maintaining the family homogeneity of party preferences, it seems to be the mother and not the father. Evidence for this conclusion emerges upon examining the relative politicization of the parents as determined by campaign activities. As expected, there are more families where the father shows greater politicization. But when mother is the more highly politicized, she has relatively more "pulling power" than father in maintaining the child's loyalty to his parents (Table 1). . . .

Better tests of the parental influence question can be conducted with parents who are more truly heterogeneous in character. As a first step, let us set aside momentarily the bi-polar parents and consider the less extreme case of partisan-Independent families. The findings for students in these families add additional evidence that fathers are by no means the decisive positive force in the establishment of children's party identification. In the first place the overall results

**TABLE 1** The Relation between the Campaign Activity Level of Mother and Father and Student Agreement with Party Identification of Homogeneous Parents

| Triples Involving Homogeneous Parents | | | | |
|---|---|---|---|---|
| *Relative Activity Level of Mother vs Father* | *Parents and Student Agree* | *Parents Agree, Student Differs* | | *N* |
| Mother higher | 85% | 15% | 100% | ( 71) |
| Approximately equal | 75% | 25% | 100% | (171) |
| Father higher | 73% | 27% | 100% | (128) |

**TABLE 2** Relation between Party Identification of Parents and Offspring among Parents with a Partisan-Independent Party Identification Mix

| *Parental Party Identification Mix* | | *Student Party Identification* | | | | |
|---|---|---|---|---|---|---|
| Mother | Father | Democrat | Independent | Republican | | N |
| Democrat | Independent | 51%[a] | 37 | 12 | 100% | (20) |
| Independent | Democrat | 39% | 40 | 21 | 100% | (20) |
| Republican | Independent | 21% | 34 | 45 | 100% | (14) |
| Independent | Republican | 43% | 17 | 40 | 100% | (15) |

[a] Percentages here and in other tables may not appear to be correct given the N's upon which they are based. This is a consequence of rounding off the weighted N's to integers.

show 39% of the students agreeing with mother, 37% with father, and 24% with neither. Second, out of all the possibilities for agreeing with the *partisan* parent among these partisan-Independent parent pairs, the students agree with the mother 53% of the time, and with the father 47%. Perhaps more significant is the amount of defection to the opposite party. When fathers are partisan, 44% of the students identify with the opposite party, whereas this is true of 24% when mother has the partisan role. . . .

. . . In those families with a Democratic-Independent parental mix, a partisan mother has more Democratic pulling power than a partisan father (12% difference) and there are fewer Republican defections (9% difference). Similarly, when mother is a Republican and father an Independent, she has slightly more partisan pulling power than does a Republican father when mother is an Independent. She also "allows" fewer defections to the Democratic party (22% difference).

The most severe instance of heterogeneous parents is the bi-polar type, that is, where one parent is a Republican and the other a Democrat. For the students this is potentially the most cross-pressured situation possible. In response to this, 26% of them adopt a position of Independence. Inasmuch as only 10% of students with homogeneous parents are Independents, it must be concluded that cross-pressures increase the likelihood of an Independent preference. One of the classic solutions to cross-pressures is to adopt an intermediate or neutral position. Temporarily, at least, a sizable fraction of our cross-pressured young adults have elected this course.

**TABLE 3** Relation between Party Identification of Bi-Polar Parents and Their Offspring

| *Parental Partisan Identification Mix* | | *Student Party Identification* | | | | |
|---|---|---|---|---|---|---|
| Mother | Father | Democrat | Independent | Republican | | N |
| Democrat | Republican | 44% | 21 | 35 | 100% | (37) |
| Republican | Democrat | 29% | 38 | 33 | 100% | (23) |

Appealing as the classic resolution of cross-pressures may be, it obviously is not the modal pattern. To the one-fourth who are Independents must be added two-fifths who identify with the mother's party compared with one-third sharing the father's party. Again the mother, by inference, exerts the stronger pull on the party loyalties of offspring. That the net difference between the "pull" of mothers compared with fathers is only 8% is not so significant as the fact that there is *any* difference in this direction.

An important question to ask at this point is whether mothers hold an edge in each of the two subsets of the larger set of bi-polar parents. That is, does a Democratic mother with a Republican husband exert the same pull as a Republican mother with a Democratic husband? Table 3 presents the relation between the party preference of bi-polar parents and their offspring with partisan direction clearly shown. In those bi-polar pairs consisting of a Democratic mother and a Republican father the proportion of Democratic offspring is greater (15% difference) than where the father is Democratic and the mother Republican. This is accomplished primarily by the reduction in the number of student Independents in those bi-polar families with a Democratic mother. When mother is a Republican and father a Democrat, both the father's influence and that of the Democratic majority culture are partly counteracted, while the ranks of the Independents are swelled. The classic middle-ground solution to the cross-pressure dilemma occurs more frequently where the mother is running contrary to national trends. It is as though the student, unable to jump completely to the trend-consistent preference of his father, edges away only to the Independent status.

Our analysis demonstrates that students fail to gravitate in disproportionate numbers to the party of their fathers. Indeed, there is a modest counter-movement, a pattern which tends to hold irrespective of particular varieties in identification mixes. Regardless of the direction in which the child leans, however, the question remains as to what prompts him to align with one parent versus the other. Are these idiosyncratic patterns or are there underlying regularities at work?

## CONCOMMITANTS OF DIFFERENTIAL INFLUENCE

Although we cannot say precisely why students agree more with mothers or fathers, it is possible to detect some familial properties accompanying such differences. We noted previously that parent-student sex combinations had some bearing on intergenerational agreement when heterogeneity was broadly defined.

Mother-daughter symmetry was higher while son's agreement was generally distributed more evenly between parents. A similar pattern occurs for the more tightly defined heterogeneous families, that is, the combination of both bi-polar and partisan-Independent parents. Nevertheless there is some tendency for same-sex agreement among both boys and girls. . . .

Dividing these triples even more finely highlights the strength of the mother-daughter agreement. Among both partisan-Independent and bi-polar families daughters continue to agree more with mothers at virtually identical rates. For boys this same-sex pattern is not as persistent. While boys more often follow father than mother in partisan-Independent families–33% mother, 44% father, 23% neither–they go with one parent as readily as the other in bi-polar families. Each parent may receive some advantage from same-sex imitation, but mother is clearly the chief beneficiary of this process. Psychological theories about parent-child links along same-sex lines appear to fit mothers and daughters better than fathers and sons.

One possible explanation for the mother's surprisingly competitive position in drawing agreement may lie in a natural reservoir of affective ties between mother and child. Identification links are first formed between a child and its mother, and these early bonds lay the basis for a lasting, intimate relationship. On the average children of all ages feel closer to their mothers than to their fathers. Certainly this is true of the twelfth graders. Among all students with heterogeneous parents 56% felt equally close to each parent, 39% felt closer to their mothers, and only 5% felt closer to their fathers than their mothers. . . .

. . . The data suggest that mothers do, indeed, benefit from the greater emotional attachment. . . . When the student feels equally close to each parent, he is less compelled to make a choice or to be drawn toward the mother, and the traditional pattern of male superiority prevails. Even in this instance of equally close attachments the father's absolute pull is not as high as that for mother when she is perceived more warmly. *The central point is that the closer relationship with mother helps reduce the typical product of typing father as the appropriate model for political identification. . . .*

. . . After mothers and fathers are categorized according to their relative campaign activity, and this in turn is crossed against parent-student agreement, a clear tendency emerges for the student to follow the more politicized parent (Table 4, panel 4). This pattern is most striking, however, when mother is the more active inasmuch as there is more agreement with her than with father when he is most active (23% net). Significantly, the greatest incidence of student independence occurs in those families where father is most active. . . .

We noted previously that both relative closeness to mother and mother's relative level of partisanship were positively related to taking mother's party identification. If the variables are combined, as in the top half of Table 5, the effect is to produce a rather extraordinary range. Thus when the child feels closer to mother and mother is the more partisan parent (upper left cell), nearly two-thirds of the students agree with her. At the other extreme, when the child feels equally close to each parent and father is the more partisan (lower right cell), agreement with mother is reduced to about one-sixth.

**TABLE 4** Agreement between Party Identification of Mother and Offspring among Parents with Heterogeneous Identifications, under two Sets of Control Conditions

| Relative Closeness to Parent | Partisanship Level of Mother versus Father | | | | | |
|---|---|---|---|---|---|---|
| | Mother | Higher | Equal | Father | Higher |
| Closer to mother | 64%[1] | (17) | 50% (14) | 40% | (17) |
| | 34% | (23) | 31% (21) | 16% | (25) |
| **Student Sex** | **Campaign Activity Level of Mother versus Father** | | | | |
| | Mother | Higher | Equal | Father | Higher |
| Girls | 70% | (08) | 50% (14) | 38% | (24) |
| Boys | 53% | (15) | 33% (31) | 23% | (28) |

[1] Cell entries show the percentage agreeing with mother out of the total N for that cell that is the number within the parentheses. Clearly each of the two characteristics has some impact, but the additive effects are perhaps even more impressive. . . .

A basic finding for party identification was that students with heterogeneous parents do not more often agree with their fathers; in fact, there is a persistent tendency for higher congruity with their mothers and less defection to the opposite party. Similar tests can be made with issue-orientations. Five issue-questions, producing dichotomous answers, will be employed. To these will be added political cynicism scale scores, divided into low, medium, and high categories. The dichotomous issues produce combinations analogous to bi-polar pairs on party identification. Illustratively:

| | Mother pro<br>Father con | Mother con<br>Father pro |
|---|---|---|
| Student pro | | |
| Student con | | |

If the agreement patterns (excluding cynicism) are analyzed in terms of the four-fold table shown above the tau-b correlations run from .03 to .23, thereby indicating greater mother-student congruence in every instance. These correlations are obviously modest, but they are perfectly suitable for rejecting the father-dominant model of value transmission.

It is also instructive to present the results in terms of percentage distributions. Without exception there is higher agreement with mother than father (Table 5, total column). Two of these differences are so slight as to be virtual ties. Yet even they are significant for rejecting the hypothesis of greater cue-taking from fathers. It would appear that the greater incidence of student-mother alignment is not confined to the extremely salient domain of party preference.

Dividing the students according to sex preserves, with one exception for each sex, the direction of the findings for the total. Girls are a shade more likely to agree with their fathers over the federal government's role in integrating the schools, whereas boys more often side with their fathers on the question of allowing prayers in public schools. . . .

**TABLE 5** Agreement between Heterogeneous Parents and Students on Six Issues, by Sex of Parent and Student

| | Girls | | | Boys | | | Total | | |
|---|---|---|---|---|---|---|---|---|---|
| *Issue* | *Agree With Mother* | *Agree With Father* | N | *Agree With Mother* | *Agree With Father* | N | *Agree With Mother* | *Agree With Father* | N |
| U.S. participation in United Nations | 80% | 20[a] | (15) | 53 | 47 | (35) | 61 | 39 | (50) |
| Allowing Communist to take office | 61% | 39 | (78) | 53 | 47 | (90) | 57 | 43 | (168) |
| Political cynicism | 56% | 44 | (127) | 58 | 42 | (139) | 57 | 43 | (266) |
| Federal role in integrating the schools | 47% | 53 | (59) | 61 | 39 | (67) | 54 | 46 | (126) |
| Allowing prayers in public schools | 64% | 36 | (34) | 42 | 58 | (48) | 51 | 49 | (82) |
| Allowing public speeches against religion | 52% | 48 | (62) | 51 | 49 | (89) | 51 | 49 | (151) |

[a] Percentages add to 100 going across each subdivision.

Once the forces of female political participation and rising education were set in motion, they were abetted by the structural properties of the family in accelerating the relative importance of the mother. Early affective ties and emotional dependencies between child and mother could now be expected to have some carryover into political matters, especially for those children who happened to have parents with dissimilar preferences. When parental conflict is present—regardless of whether the offspring recognizes it—the resolution is likely to favor the parent for whom affect is highest and expressive ties closest. This choice making can occur during the preadult years or during early adulthood when there is greater opportunity to exercise political preferences. Historically, then, a multiple effect occurred as legal and sociological-educational changes began to interact with the psychological properties of the nuclear family. The traditional view of differential parental influence fails to take account of these dynamics.

# 13

# The Great Soviet Encyclopedia

## *American History Through Communist Eyes*

*annotated by Fred Harvey Harrington*

### THE USA DURING THE FIRST WORLD WAR, 1914–1918

After the outbreak of the First World War, 1914–1918, the USA declared on August 4, 1914, that it would preserve neutrality. American monopolies took to themselves the role of providing food-stuffs, ammunition, and loans to the belligerent states, mainly the countries of the Entente. An economic recession impending in 1913–1914 had already changed, by 1915 as a result of the war situation, into an upswing. American monopolists (especially the financial group of Morgan) made huge profits in deliveries to the European countries. The USA took advantage of its period of neutrality for military, economic, political, and ideological preparation for entry into the war. . . . The desire of the American monopolies to maintain maximum profits inevitably pushed the USA towards direct participation in the war for the redivision of the world.

Points of opposition existed between the USA and the countries of the Entente, especially England; however, in this period the conflict between the USA and Germany became particularly intense. At the end of 1915 Colonel E. House, Wilson's special confidential agent, announced: "The USA cannot allow the defeat of its allies, leaving Germany dominant over the world through a military factor."[1] Economic ties between the USA and the countries of the Entente strengthened substantially during the years of neutrality. American financial barons granted credit and loans worth millions to the countries of the Entente and feared to lose them in the event of a German victory. Tension grew still more in the relations between the USA and Germany in connection with the ruthless submarine war conducted by Germany.[2]

[1] The House quotation should read: "It will not do for the United States to let the Allies go down and leave Germany the dominant military factor in the world." House to Assistant Secretary of State Polk, October 11, 1915. Charles Seymour, ed., *The Intimate Papers of Colonel House* (Bosand, New York, 1926), II, 82.

[2] Economic forces had much to do with American entry into World War I. This account, however, overstates these factors (especially the financier influence) as compared with other forces. For a good treatment of the economic factors, see C. C. Tansill, *America Goes to War* (New York, 1938); for other interpretations, Charles Seymour, *American Diplomacy During the World War* (New York, 1934), Walter Millis, *The Road to War* (New York, 1935), and Ernest R. May, *The World War and American Isolation, 1914–1917* (Cambridge, 1959).

On April 6, 1917, the USA declared war on Germany. The period of USA participation in the war was characterized by the intensification in the country of political reaction, by the increase of militarists, by the transition to a military economy, and by a still more open submission of government authority to the monopolies. During the years of the war the living standard of workers declined.[3] Prices increased on foodstuffs and articles of broad consumption: in 1917 prices on foods increased on an average of 57 per cent, and in 1918 by 87 per cent in comparison with 1913; prices on clothes correspondingly rose 49 per cent in 1917 and 105 per cent in 1918. The increase of prices, the huge increase in taxes, the compulsory subscriptions to war loans, the growth of exploitation, the difficult wartime routine, and the presence—despite the economic boom—of a large army of unemployed led to a worsening of the condition of the working class. The workers responded to the increase of exploitation by numerous strikes. In 1917 over 4,400 strikes took place.

Wilson's administration dealt brutally with the worker movement. An espionage law (June, 1917) declared any anti-war rally of the workers to be treason against the government. Left-wing Socialists and members of the organization, "Industrial Workers of the World," courageously protesting against war, were subjected to repressions. Prominent figures of the American workers' movement, W. Haywood and E. Debs, were arrested. A split occurred in connection with the imperialist war in the Socialist Party of the USA, the internationalist wing of which, protesting against war, organized the League of Socialist Propaganda in 1915. The right wing leadership of the Socialist Party openly supported an imperialist policy. The AFL pursued a policy of "class co-operation" with monopolies. A conference of the AFL in March, 1917, offered its assistance to the government in the event of entry into the war. The leader of the AFL, Gompers, was a member of a committee of the National Defense Committee.

Taking advantage of the fact that the strength of the European states was diverted by the war, the USA in these years increased its expansion in Latin America. . . . In 1916 the USA forced Denmark to sell it the Danish West Indies.[4] During the time of the war the USA concluded an agreement with Japan at the expense of China (Lansing-Ishii Agreement, *q.v.*). However, this agreement was not able to check further intensification of American-Japanese differences. The war brought unprecedented profits to American monopolists. The average annual income of USA corporations in 1916–1918 was approximately $4,000,000,000 more than the average annual income in 1912–1914.

The February bourgeois-democratic revolution of 1917 in Russia made American ruling circles, fearful of the withdrawal of Russia from the war, extremely uneasy. The USA hastened to recognize the bourgeois Provisional Government and supported it with huge loans.[5]

[3] Although the cost-of-living index rose as a result of wartime conditions, so did the index of real wages. See Paul Douglas, *Real Wages in the United States, 1890–1926* (Boston, 1930).

[4] Denmark was not forced to sell the Virgin Islands. Her voters and their Parliament were glad to accept the $25,000,000 offered by the United States. See C. C. Tansill, *The Purchase of the Danish West Indies* (Baltimore, 1932).

[5] The Wilson administration was far from satisfied with the Provisional Government, and never gave it all-out support. Recognition, however, was extended promptly—less than a

As a result of the First World War the USA was transformed from a debtor to the largest creditor, to whom the countries of Europe found themselves indebted for over ten billion dollars. Almost all the countries of the Entente fell into the debt of the USA. V. I. Lenin pointed out that American multimillionaires, more than anyone, profited by the war. The foreign trade of the USA grew substantially. Thus, in the period from 1913 to 1920 the trade of the USA with the countries of Latin America increased almost four times. Over half of the world's gold reserves was concentrated in the USA. The war stimulated further development of a number of branches of heavy industry. Several new areas of industry were developed. The process of centralizing capital grew. By the end of the First World War 1 per cent of the people controlled more than 50 per cent of all the wealth in the USA.[6]

## THE USA IN THE PERIOD BETWEEN THE TWO WORLD WARS

A general crisis of capitalism began in the period of the First World War, and especially as a result of the defection of Soviet Russia from the capitalistic system. After the First World War the development of the revolutionary workers' and farmers' movement began in the USA. The impact of the Great October Socialist Revolution was of profound significance in strengthening the revolutionary movement in the USA.[7] In 1919 the number of strikes in the USA grew substantially. The most important were the strike of 365,000 steel workers (of which the organizer was W. Foster) and the strike of 435,000 miners. In this same year powerful strikes occurred in the ports of New York and Seattle. Along with England and France, the USA became an accomplice in the intervention against Soviet Russia. The USA implemented open military intervention in the Soviet North and in the Soviet Far East (1918–1920).[8]

fortnight after the overthrow of the Tsar. Further, the United States Government advanced nearly $200,000,000 in loans to the Russian Provisional Government between the spring and fall of 1917. In contrast, the United States extended no credits to the Bolshevik Government (which took over control in November, 1917) and postponed recognition for sixteen years. See William Appleman Williams, *American-Russian Relations, 1781–1947* (New York, 1952) and George F. Kennan, *Russia Leaves the War* (Princeton, 1956).

[6] Although World War I did increase the concentration of economic control, the figures here presented are open to question. They are presumably drawn from Anna Rochester's heavily slanted *Rulers of America: A Study of Finance Capital* (New York, 1936), 144.

[7] Was there a strong revolutionary movement in the United States in 1919–1920, as this account suggests? This was the period of the Big Red Scare, when antilabor leaders and others insisted that the postwar strikes and unrest reflected a dangerous revolutionary trend. Historians, however, have found little evidence to support the theory that there was much danger of revolution.

[8] Some 5,000 Americans took part in an Allied landing at Archangel in northern Russia in 1918. One purpose of this expedition was to prevent supplies from falling into German hands. Nearly twice as many Americans were sent into eastern Siberia, to support anti-Bolshevik groups, to check Japan, and for other reasons. See, *e.g.*, Betty M. Unterberger, *America's Siberian Expedition, 1918–1920* (Durham, North Carolina, 1956) and George F. Kennan, *The Decision to Intervene* (Princeton, 1958).

In January, 1918, Wilson came forward with an imperialist program of peace—the so-called "Fourteen-Point program."[9] . . .

In conditions favorable for the growth of the masses' revolutionary movement, the Communist Party of the United States of America was founded in September, 1919, which carried on a struggle against the oppression of the capitalists and for the bettering of the position of the working class and of all workers. With the active participation of the Communists, large-scale strikes of dockworkers, who refused to load materials for the use of USA interventionist troops in Russia and for the White Guards, took place.

A campaign of protest against USA participation in anti-Soviet intervention unfolded across the entire country. American workers formed the "League of the Friends of Soviet Russia," which organized the gathering of signatures on a petition to the government to cease the intervention and blockade of Russia. Almost 100 trade unions joined in the petition. "Hands Off Russia" committees were also formed. In 1920 the American government was forced to recall its troops from Russia.[10]

In 1920 an economic crisis began in the USA, reaching its highest peak in 1921. In a number of branches of industry the volume of output declined 40 per cent or more. The number of unemployed reached 5,500,000. Wages were reduced. The crisis also gripped agriculture. Ruined farmers went to the cities, enlarging the ranks of the unemployed. The bourgeoisie intensified the attack on the rights of workers. Employers refused to negotiate with trade unions and broke off collective agreements. This policy was rebuffed by the working class. In 1921–1922 more than 2,500,000 workers participated in strikes. Over 600,000 miners took part in a strike of coal workers occurring in 1922. Railroad workers (about 500,000 men) were on strike simultaneously with the coal workers. The administration of the Republican President W. Harding (1921–1923), with the actual help of the AFL leadership, suppressed a number of strikes. The leaders of the AFL preached "class co-operation" with the capitalists, and helped them carry out the capitalist streamlining of manufacture leading to an increase in the exploitation of the working class.[11] The leadership of the AFL prevented the admittance into the AFL of Negroes and unskilled workers.

[9] Some of the Fourteen Points were anti-imperialist, and this Wilson peace program—whatever its faults—stands in sharp contrast to the divide-the-spoils arrangements of the "secret treaties" of the Allies. For a general treatment, see Thomas A. Bailey, *Woodrow Wilson and The Lost Peace* (New York, 1944).

[10] Pressure from American Communists and from non-Communist labor groups had little to do with the decision to end American intervention in northern Russia and Siberia. The collapse of Germany, Bolshevik successes, and general American reaction against overseas ventures, all figured in the picture, as did a growing realization of government officials and private citizens that the intervention had been ill-advised from the start.

It is worth noting, however, that the Communist Party of the United States is first mentioned in this account in connection with efforts to assist Russian Communists. Theodore Draper's recent book, *The Roots of American Communism* (New York, 1957), argues convincingly that the American Communist Party was Russian-dominated from the start.

[11] This section shows Soviet attitudes toward American labor leadership, as other sections show Soviet attitudes toward American business. Much can be said against the AFL in the 1920's. The organization was ineffective in that decade, and declined in membership. It failed to make headway in the new mass-production, assembly-line industries. Many of its unions did

The struggle of the Negro people for democratic rights, and against the intensification of racial discrimination, was crushed by means of severe repressions. In 1917–1919 Negro massacres took place in a number of cities. In July, 1919, in Chicago, according to official figures, substantially underestimated, thirty-eight persons were killed and over 500 were injured, and hundreds of homes were demolished or burned.

After the war the economic and political role of the USA in the capitalist world grew considerably. The USA became the center of the financial exploitation of the world. . . . In the period of partial, temporary stabilization of capital, which had begun in 1924, the chronic lack of employment remained; there existed underproduction in a number of branches of industry; the number of investors grew; and the export of capital increased (the export of capital in 1929 exceeded the prewar level more than four times). Capitalistic standardization led to the reinforcement of the exploitation of the workers and to an increase of the unemployed. The process of the ruination of farmers grew in strength.[12] In 1928 over 300,000 workers struck in the USA. Communists played an active role in leading the strikers.[13]

The defenders of American imperialism created a myth of so-called prosperity and of the "uniqueness" of American capitalism. They declared that American capitalism supposedly had its own proper development, completely different from the course of development of European capitalism, and that it did not fear economic crises. These "theories" about the "prosperity" and "uniqueness" of USA capitalism were propagandized in every possible way by reactionary trade union leaders and other reformists trying to delude the broad masses of workers. In actuality the stabilization of capitalism which was characterized by the sharpening of conflict between the workers and capitalists, between the imperialists and the peoples of the colonial countries and among the imperialists of various countries, was as partial and temporary in the USA as in all the capitalist countries.

During the time of the presidential elections of 1924, a so-called Progressive bloc was formed representing the interests of the farmers and the petty urban bourgeoisie and supported by part of the trade unions. Its origin was provoked by the dissatisfaction of the workers with the policy both of the Republican and Democratic parties. The bloc advocated a program directed at the negligible democratization of government apparatus and toward the bettering of the situation of workers and farmers. Senator R. La Follette, who was advanced as the presidential candidate of this bloc, received a substantial number of votes in the elections (after the elections the bloc collapsed).

exclude or otherwise discriminate against women, Negroes, and the unskilled. But for all of that, the AFL was not the antilabor force here pictured. For the question of AFL "cooperation" with capitalism, see Selig Perlman, *History of Trade Unionism in the United States* (New York, 1922).

[12] Although there was suffering in some quarters, the 1920's were a decade of prosperity for most Americans. For a general treatment, see George Soule, *Prosperity Decade, From War to Depression, 1917–1929* (New York, 1947).

[13] The Communists were unsuccessful in their efforts to secure control of the American labor movement in the 1920's. For a discussion of their efforts, see Daniel Bell, "The Background and Development of Marxian Socialism in the United States," in Donald Drew Egbert and Stow Persons, eds., *Socialism and American Life* (Princeton, 1952).

The candidate of the Republican Party, C. Coolidge (*q.v.*), who was Vice-President during the administration of Harding and who had taken the presidential post in 1923 because of the sudden death of Harding, was elected President. . . .

. . . In the 1920's Anglo-American oppositions became the principal conflicts within the capitalist world. A struggle for markets and for sources of raw materials, especially for oil, with the USA pressing England more and more, developed between the USA and England. In the middle of the twenties the export of capital from the USA was twice as large as the export of capital from England.

In the elections of 1928 the monopolist bourgeoisie sent to the office of President the candidate of the Republican Party, H. Hoover (President, 1929–1933). Hoover came into authority under the slogan of "prosperity." However, the destructive economic crisis of 1929–1933 graphically proved the failure of the "theories" of "prosperity" and the "uniqueness" of the course of the development of American capitalism. The world crisis most forcefully struck the principal capitalistic country–the USA, which by that time had concentrated in its hands approximately half of the production and consumption of the capitalist world. The economic crisis gripped industry, agriculture, trade, and the credit system; it was extremely severe and protracted. The crisis fell as a terrible burden on the shoulders of the workers. During the years of the crisis, wages of workers fell 60 per cent, and the income of farmers 59 per cent. In 1932 in the USA, according to official figures, there were 13,200,000 totally unemployed, an overwhelming majority of whom did not receive any kind of assistance from the government.

The crisis led to the sharpening of the class struggle. The development of the workers' movement began in the country; the movement of the unemployed masses spread, being under the direct leadership of the Communist Party.[14] The Communist Party organized demonstrations of the unemployed on March 6, 1930, in many cities, in which 1,250,000 persons took part. A "hunger march" of the unemployed was carried out in Washington in 1931 with demands for the introduction of unemployment insurance and the distribution of benefits. In 1932 there was a march of unemployed war veterans in Washington. Troops under the command of General D. MacArthur dealt brutally with the participants of this march. During 1929–1934 more than 3,500,000 workers participated in strikes. In 1932 and 1933, with the assistance of the Communist Party, national conventions of farmers took place which decided on the necessity of a united struggle–with the workers–against the yoke of the monopolies. The protest of the farmers against low purchase prices expressed itself in a refusal to sell farm products to monopolistic companies.

Hoover's administration, helping large-scale capital, placed the whole burden of the crisis on the shoulders of the workers. It established a financial corporation with a capital of $3,500,000,000, which was used for the subsidizing of monopolies with the object of saving them from collapse during the period of the crisis. At the same time the administration reinforced repressions against strikers. . . . The

[14] Although the Communists tried to assume "direct leadership" in the United States during the depression, they were notably unsuccessful. This account greatly overstates their influence.

organization of the Negro peoples' masses grew. In 1936 in Chicago there was a convention of the progressive National Negro Congress, which delegates from 551 Negro organizations, uniting 3,300,000 persons, attended. . . .

In the presidential elections of 1932, F. Roosevelt (*q.v.*), the candidate of the Democratic Party, won. . . .

After coming into office Roosevelt proclaimed the "New Deal," representing an attempt to overcome the crisis on the basis of "regulation" of private-capital activity, to strengthen the capitalistic system by strengthening government capitalism, and with the help of several concessions to the masses to keep them from revolutionary actions. Two acts, passed in 1933, underlay the "New Deal": The "National Industrial Recovery Act" (NIRA) and the "Agricultural Adjustment Act" (AAA). The NIRA established government regulation of industry, for which in various branches "fair practices codes" were introduced, fixing prices on products, fixing the level of production, regulating markets, establishing maximum working hours and minimum wages. The basic object of the codes consisted in mitigating the crisis by reducing production. A government administration, into which representatives of the large monopolies entered, was formed for the implementation of the NIRA. Having taken into their own hands the working-out of the "codes," the monopolists put into practice a policy of compulsory cartelizing, and reduced wages for workers. The profits of the monopolies increased sharply during the time of Roosevelt's presidency.

In practice, the National Labor Board established by Roosevelt guarded the interests of employers. The "Federal Emergency Relief Administration" attempted to solve the problem of unemployment by sending part of the unemployed to work camps for public works and by paying unemployment benefits. However, only a negligible part of the unemployed were occupied in public works, and only 20 per cent of the unemployed were given the small benefits.[15] At the same time, the government gave three billion dollars in aid to the banks.[16] A law regulating agriculture was supposed to raise prices on agricultural products. With this object the government distributed subsidies to the farmers for reducing the area under grain crops and for reducing livestock. The AAA was used with profit by the largest agricultural monopolies and market corporations, but, naturally, it could not prevent the mass ruin of the farmers.

In 1933 in the USA a slow rise in industrial production began, which, however, turned into its own depression. The attempt of Roosevelt's administration to overcome the depression and to prevent the approach of a new crisis with the help of the "New Deal" ended in failure.

[15] The emergency relief projects of the New Deal reached a larger number and had a larger effect than is here indicated. Although business men did help shape some of the first Roosevelt statutes (*e.g.*, NIRA), the New Deal had less of a Big Business flavor, and helped the bulk of the farmers and workers more than this account implies. See Basil Rauch, *History of the New Deal* (New York, 1944).

[16] The reference is presumably to a provision inserted by inflationary Congressmen in the Farm Relief and Inflation Act of 1933, whereby the President was given discretionary authority to inflate the currency by issuing $3,000,000,000 in new treasury notes ("greenbacks") or by reducing the gold content of the dollar by 50 per cent. Roosevelt did not issue the greenbacks. See Broadus Mitchell, *Depression Decade, From New Era to New Deal, 1929–1941* (New York, 1947), 137–138.

In 1933–1935 the strike battle of the proletariat grew in strength. In 1933, 1,695 strikes took place; in 1934, 1,856 strikes; in 1935, 2,014 strikes. In the strikes about four million strikers in all participated. Strikes gripped the textile, steel, coal, automobile, and other branches of industry. In 1934 a strike of textile workers took place. The general strike in San Francisco in 1934 had an extraordinary range, enveloping all of the Western seaboard. The Communist Party, constantly fighting for the united action of the working class and the farmers, was the organizer of many militant rallies. The Communist Party promoted an active struggle against the threat of fascism and war. The Ninth Congress of the Party (1936) called for the organization of a united democratic front of workers, farmers, petty bourgeoisie, and Negroes.

The Communist Party had substantial influence in left-wing trade unions, advocating the reorganization of the AFL on an industrial basis. In 1935 the Congress of Industrial Organizations (*q.v.*) was formed (the CIO, existing until 1938 under the name of the Committee for Industrial Organization).[17] In 1936 the reactionary leadership of the AFL expelled from the federation, trade unions (with one million members) which had joined the Committee for Industrial Organization. However, left-wing elements did not succeed in heading the CIO, whose leadership was seized by right-wing trade union leaders—Lewis, Murray, Carey, and others.

Under pressure of the workers, Roosevelt's administration made several concessions to the working class. In June, 1935, Congress passed the so-called Wagner Act (*q.v.*), in which the right of workers to conclude collective agreements with employers was declared. At the same time this act stipulated compulsory arbitration, with the object of breaking strikes.[18]

Under the conditions of a profound and lingering economic depression, the monopolies considered the majority of legislative enactments of the "New Deal" to be for themselves. When a transition to an economic revival began to appear, the attitude of the monopolies toward "planned" experiments changed sharply and they demanded their cancellation. As a result, the Supreme Court in 1935 and 1936 held the NIRA and AAA to be unconstitutional, which meant their abolition.[19]

The foreign policy of the Roosevelt Administration in a number of questions was carried out by somewhat different methods from the policies of former administrations. On November 16, 1933, the USA established diplomatic relations with the USSR. By this the most far-seeing American statesmen recognized that the establishment of diplomatic relations with the USSR corresponded to the interests of the USA.

In connection with the growth of the resistance of the peoples of Latin America to the expansion of the USA, Roosevelt proclaimed in 1933 the so-called "Good

[17] The wording here suggests that the Communists had a great deal to do with the formation of the CIO. Such was not the case.

[18] The failure to mention such significant New Deal legislation as the establishment of Social Security, the Federal Deposit Insurance Corporation, the Securities and Exchange Commission, etc., should be noted.

[19] Most businessmen had ceased to support NIRA and were opposed to AAA in 1935 and 1936. There is no evidence, however, that the Supreme Court overthrew NIRA and AAA because of pressure from business. Rather, the decisions reflected the constitutional reasoning and social philosophies of the sitting judges.

Neighbor Policy," which in actuality, however, served as a disguise for the old policy of intervention in the domestic affairs of the Latin American countries. Reactionary circles in the USA promoted the organization in Mexico of the rebellion of General Cedillo against the lawful government of Cardenas (1938).[20]

In 1935 a neutrality act was passed in the USA giving the President the right to prohibit the export of arms to countries in a state of war. Declaring the lawful Republican government of Spain to be "belligerent," the government of the USA deprived it of the right to buy arms in the USA. At the same time, the USA increased the export of strategic materials and arms to Italy and Germany, who were carrying out armed intervention in Spain (1936–1939). The USA did not consider Italy and Germany as "belligerents." In this way the USA took advantage of the Neutrality Act for the actual support of Italian-German intervention in Spain.[21] In March, 1938, the government prohibited the departure of American volunteers to Republican Spain, and in April, 1939, the USA officially recognized the government of Franco. Progressive forces in the USA actively protested against the Neutrality Act, demanding that help be given to the Spanish Republican government and that sanctions be used against Germany and Italy. Many American anti-Fascists went to Spain, where they fought in the international brigades.

In 1937 a new, world economic crisis began which again struck the USA the most severely of all the capitalist countries. Sixty per cent of the workers' families earned wages equal to only 50 per cent of subsistence wages, total unemployment benefits were reduced from $278,000,000 in 1936 to $96,000,000 in 1937, and public works were curtailed. In 1937 the number of strikes doubled in comparison with 1936 (4,740 strikes took place, in which 1,860,000 persons participated). The Communist Party strove for the united action of the working masses of the USA, demanding that aid be rendered to the unemployed, and fighting against racial discrimination.[22]

In the 1930's the activities of a number of reactionary organizations in the USA became more energetic: the Ku Klux Klan, the American Legion (formed in 1919), and others.

In the prewar years the so-called isolationists played an important role in the conduct of the USA's foreign policy. Under the pretence of giving up intervention in the affairs of Europe, Asia, and Africa, the isolationists, representing in those

[20] Under The Good Neighbor Policy as developed by Presidents Hoover and Roosevelt, the United States abandoned its "old policy" of military intervention in Latin America. By using diplomatic and economic rather than military methods, the United States was able to increase its influence in the area during the 1930's. Despite friction over Cardenas' expropriation measures, the Roosevelt Administration remained on friendly terms with Mexico in these years; and the United States Government assisted Cardenas during the Cedillo revolt. While some United States businessmen favored Cedillo, they failed to provide that general with effective support.

[21] A Congressional resolution of January, 1937, barred exports to "either of the opposing forces in Spain." This helped Franco, although American policy makers did not intend that it should. See F. J. Taylor, *The United States and The Spanish Civil War* (New York, 1954).

[22] During this period Communist parties throughout the world tried to form "popular front" cooperation with non-Communist political groups. Such efforts were not successful in the United States. The Socialists, Democrats, and organized labor all rejected united-front overtures; and the American Communist Party remained isolated and weak.

years the most reactionary circles of the American bourgeoisie, in fact supported Fascist aggression.[23] The USA refused to support the proposals of the USSR directed toward the execution of a policy of collective security, toward a struggle for the preservation of peace, and against Fascist aggression. The USA facilitated the Munich Pact of England and France with Hitlerian Germany and Facist Italy. Thus, the diplomatic representatives of the USA shortly before the conclusion of the Munich Pact (*q.v.*) carried on talks with the representatives of the ruling circles of Hitler's Germany, England, and France, from which it was obvious that the USA was not opposed to Hitler's aggression in the East. The USA's ambassador to Germany, H. Wilson, went to Prague in August, 1938, with the object of inducing the Czechoslovakian government to compromise with Hitler's Germany. The USA approved the negotiations of N. Chamberlain with Hitler in Berchtesgaden and Bad Godesberg (September, 1938). The policy of the USA, like the policy of England and France, helped unleash the Second World War, 1939–1945.[24]

## THE USA DURING THE PERIOD OF THE SECOND WORLD WAR, 1939–1945

Remaining formally a non-belligerent, the USA had already, with the very beginning of the war, come forward on the side of England and France. In November, 1939, Congress revised the Neutrality Act, allowing the sale of arms to the belligerents, which in practice meant authorization to export arms to England and France.

In the period of the Russo-Finnish War, 1939–1940, the government of the USA placed a "moral embargo" in 1939 on the export of goods to the Soviet Union, and gave the Finnish government a loan of ten million dollars. At the same time in the USA itself, persecution of the Communists and of all progressives increased. In 1940 Congress passed the Smith Act (*q.v.*), which subsequently was, in fact, used against progressive forces.

After the crushing defeat of France (June, 1940), the USA, preparing to enter the war, began carrying out a vast program of armament. In September, 1940, a law was passed for universal military service. The USA gave help to England in the fight against Germany. During the summer of 1940 it sold 1,000,000 rifles, 84,000 machine guns, and 2,500 pieces of ordnance to England. In March, 1941, the

[23] Very few American isolationists "supported Fascist aggression." American opponents of the isolationists did maintain, however, that isolationist strength reduced President Roosevelt's ability to oppose Hitler and his allies. See William L. Langer and S. Everett Gleason, *The Challenge to Isolation, 1937–1940* (New York, 1952), an antiisolationist view; for a contrasting interpretation, favorable to the isolationists, Charles Callan Tansill, *Back Door to War: The Roosevelt Foreign Policy, 1933–1941* (Chicago, 1952). See also Wayne S. Cole, *America First: The Battle Against Intervention 1940–1941* (Madison, Wisconsin, 1953).

[24] The argument here is that World War II could have been avoided if Britain, France, and the United States had joined the Soviet Union in boldly resisting Hitler, instead of trying to appease the Nazi dictator. Views differ on this; but it does appear that the American public did not favor active involvement in Europe in 1938.

Lend-Lease Act was passed in the USA, allowing a substantial increase in the export of arms and war materials (mainly to England). But at the same time as it supported England against Germany, the USA tried to take advantage of England's difficulty to establish American control over several English possessions and spheres of influence. According to an agreement of 1940 (finally drawn up in the form of a contract, March 27, 1941) the USA received from England, in exchange for fifty old destroyers, ninety-nine-year leases on territory for the establishment of a system of American naval and air bases in a series of strategically important points on the Atlantic. Subsequently in the course of the war the USA concluded a number of other agreements with England, aimed at establishing her financial-economic dependence on the USA.[25]

In July, 1940, the USA achieved the recognition, at an inter-American conference, of the so-called Act of Havana, which permitted "any American country" to occupy any European possession in the Western Hemisphere, if it thought that this possession might be seized by one European power from another. In April, 1941, the USA established military control over Greenland, and in November, 1941, over Dutch Guiana.

On June 22, 1941, Hitler's Germany treacherously attacked the Soviet Union. Repelling the attack of the aggressor, the USSR entered the war. The Great Patriotic War of the Soviet Union, 1941–1945, began. The USSR took upon itself the main attack on Fascist Germany. The Soviet-German front became the decisive front of the Second World War. A powerful anti-Hitler coalition headed by the Soviet Union, the USA, and Great Britian was formed, which joined into a united camp, setting for itself the object of crushing Hitler's Germany. The formation of the anti-Hitler coalition answered to the interests of all freedom-loving peoples.

The conflicts between the USA and Germany by this time were extremely acute. The USA came into conflict with Germany in the fight for the division of spheres of influence, colonies, and sources of raw materials. American capitalists were especially worried by the strengthening of the economic and political positions of Germany in Latin America. Together with this, the ruling circles of the USA and England could not leave out of account the desire of broad masses of their countries for close co-operation with the Soviet Union for a successful fight against Hitler's Germany.[26] On June 24 Roosevelt's government announced the support of the Soviet Union by the United States of America. On July 30 the personal representative of the President of the USA, H. Hopkins, arrived in Moscow, and on August 2 there was an exchange of notes between the USSR and the USA extending a working trade agreement for one year. On August 14 the Atlantic Charter was signed–a declaration of the governments of the USA and England regarding the war. From September 29 to October 1, 1941, there was a meeting of the representatives of the USSR, the USA, and England in Moscow, at which a decision

[25] American aid to Great Britain prior to our entry into the war was partially to offset the unfavorable balance created by the Hitler-Stalin nonaggression pact of 1939–1941, the existence of which is nowhere mentioned in the text above.

[26] There was little popular pressure in the United States for close co-operation with the Soviet Union, 1941–1945. Some Americans opposed co-operation. The majority agreed with President Roosevelt, who chose co-operation as a means of defeating Hitler.

was made on expanding the delivery of arms, equipment, and food supplies to the Soviet Union, and on the delivery by the Soviet Union of materials for England and the USA.

The military co-operation of the USSR, the USA, and England, which was established despite the differences in the economic and political systems of the countries entering into the anti-Hitler coalition, was extremely important in winning the victory over the bloc of fascist aggressors in the Second World War. The anti-Hitler coalition was a mighty union of freedom-loving peoples. The sympathy of wide masses of the American people increased more and more toward the Soviet people, who themselves carried the burden of the war with Hitler's Germany.

Side by side with the sharpening of the relations of the USA with Germany, the relations between the USA and Japan continued to grow worse. On December 7, 1941, Japan attacked the Pacific possessions and bases of the USA and England. American bases in the Pacific (Pearl Harbor) and in the Philippine Islands, on Guam and Wake Island, were subjected to attack. The American Navy suffered losses even in the first hours of the war. On December 8, 1941, the USA declared war on Japan. On December 11, 1941, Germany and Italy declared war on the USA. In June, 1942, the USA declared war on Bulgaria, Hungary, and Rumania. Thus the USA found itself in a state of war with Japan, and Germany and her associates (except Finland).

On June 11, 1942, a Soviet-American agreement was signed in Washington on the principle of mutual aid in conducting the war against the aggressor. In an Anglo-Soviet communique on a visit by V. M. Molotov, and a Soviet-American communique on the visit by V. M. Molotov to Washington, published June 12, 1942, in Moscow, London, and Washington, it was pointed out that at the negotiations "a full understanding was reached in regard to the urgent problems of the formation of a Second Front in Europe in the year 1942." Already by the summer of 1942 in England and Canada more than four million persons were in the army and in the USA more than two million; however, the Second Front was not opened either in 1942 nor in 1943.

Reactionary circles in the USA and England were not interested in the rapid conclusion of the war.[27] They wanted the mutual weakening of the USSR and Germany.

[27] As this account suggests, Russian wartime relations with the United States and Britain were less cordial than were Anglo-American relations. The Western Allies wanted to win the war as quickly as possible; but, in order to hold their casualties to the minimum, they postponed invasion of France until their armed forces were fully equipped for the operation. The Russians, who were suffering heavy losses, became impatient at the delay, and refused to consider the Western Allies' invasion of North Africa and Italy as the establishment of a true Second Front. See Herbert Feis, *Churchill, Roosevelt, Stalin* (Princeton, 1957), and William Hardy McNeill, *America, Britain and Russia: Their Co-Operation and Conflict, 1941–1946* (London, 1953).

# 14

## Herbert E. Alexander

## *The Effects of Political Broadcasts*

Not so long ago the only way to see and hear a Presidential candidate was by going to some rally where he was slated to speak.

Today, through the push of a button or turn of a knob, you can invite him right into your home.

The emergence of television as a major means of mass communication has had a tremendous impact on the American political system.

It has brought about the altering of certain campaign techniques:

It has helped build up—or tear down—political careers.

It has also become a major expense, adding considerably to the burden of financing campaigns.

### A REVOLUTION IN POLITICS

This revolution in politics dates back several decades to the time that radio first came into use. The total effect of radio broadcasting on American politics is complicated to measure—but a couple of examples will help show its extent. President Franklin D. Roosevelt, possessing the voice and technique for it, used radio tellingly and dramatically for his "fireside chats," which brought him into an intimate, face-to-face relationship with the listening citizenry. Roosevelt's use of radio was partly to offset the influence of the press, which for the most part opposed him.

Wide employment of radio was greatly influential in turning Wendell Willkie, Republican candidate for the Presidency, into a national figure—all within the brief period of a Presidential campaign.

With the advent of television, the entire practice and timetable of campaigning underwent change. Campaign itineraries were worked out in such a way that major speeches were scheduled for prime viewing hours, thus assuring maximum audiences at the nation's TV sets. Before the official start of the Presidential campaign, today's Nominating Conventions are planned with the aim of providing for the American people a maximum exposure to the proceedings. Every effort is made to put the Party, its operations, and its candidates in the best possible light.

One result has been to de-emphasize the smoke-filled room. Presidential candidates now seem chosen in the open, in state primaries and at the conventions, right in front of the television camera lenses.

As for the Presidential campaign itself, John F. Kennedy and Richard M. Nixon were able to reach more voters through the Great Debates than candidates previous to 1960 could possibly hope to get to during the entire race for the Presidency.

That television can build—or wreck—a political career is easily illustrated.

The crime hearings conducted before television in 1951 by Estes Kefauver, Chairman of the Senate Committee to Investigate Organized Crime, catapulted the Senator into a prominence which made him a serious contender for the Democratic Presidential nomination.

In 1952, Richard Nixon's prompt use of nationwide television to answer charges about the "Nixon Fund" effectively reached large audiences and saved his political career.

In 1958, Nelson Rockefeller made wide use of television to gain the smashing election victory that swept him into the Governorship of the State of New York.

In the 1960 Presidential campaign, the Great Debates are regarded as having been of major importance in John F. Kennedy's victory over Richard M. Nixon. With the election so close (Kennedy's margin of victory was 112,000 votes), many factors may be said to have determined the result. Yet it seems clear that Kennedy's position was enhanced by the Great Debates, while Nixon's was impaired.

Elmo Roper, the pollster, has reported that 57 percent of the voters in the 1960 Presidential election said their decision was influenced by the debates. An additional 6 percent, or 4 million voters, declared that the debates actually caused them to decide how they would vote. Of this key group, Roper reports that 72 percent decided on Kennedy, while 26 percent decided that their votes would go to Nixon.

The 1960 Debates are often compared with the classic Lincoln-Douglas encounters of 1858. But these debates of one hundred years ago were for a senatorial seat and reached only a comparatively small audience, even with the aid of newspaper reporting. What the 1960 Debates enabled Presidential candidates to do for the first time was to enter the homes of 40 million American families and jointly discuss the issues before this huge audience.

Naturally the impact on the Democratic and Republican Party organizations was to make them seek earnestly and eagerly to gauge the actual importance of such debates with regard to vote-getting potentialities. The search for answers still goes on. It has resulted in the spending of considerable funds on public opinion polls just to audit voter reaction to such debates.

As for the Great Debates themselves, as conducted, they have been both praised and criticized. They were conceded to be impressive in that they served to convey the sense of excitement and drama inherent in politics in direct and meaningful ways to tremendous numbers of citizens. The debates tended to equalize the maximum exposure of either standard bearer to the public view, doing so in all likelihood in a more influential manner than money spent in other ways could have bought for either candidate.

The unusually large audiences for the Great Debates drove home one important fact concerning television itself. The debates showed that political broadcasting can compete successfully with other forms of TV programming, including entertainment. But, to retain a favorable place in the competition for audiences, political broadcasting (the term applies to both TV and radio) will need to show considerable skill and inventiveness. This is something all candidates henceforth will wish to bear in mind. Besides competing with rival candidates, they must remember that they are competing for the attention of the TV viewer, with the hope not only of winning his attention and approval but also his vote. And the political broadcaster will have to compete, for the most part, without help of the fanfare that accompanied the Great Debates.

## INFLUENCE OF BROADCASTING ON THE QUALITY AND STYLE OF AMERICAN POLITICS

Competition for attention in the mass media of broadcasting is bound to affect the quality and style of American politics. TV makes it possible for candidates to reach the farthest corners of a constituency. It also can perform an immense service to candidates by making them well known and familiar to the electorate. But these opportunities come at a high dollar cost and at the cost of accentuating certain qualities in a candidate while minimizing or de-valuing others. Thus the medium of television would seem to be producing a shift in the grounds on which candidates are picked. The criteria for selection tend to shift to whether or not the candidate has good television presence. Does he have an attractive video personality? Does his family show up well on the screen?

One result of such standards for selection is that sometimes issues remain undefined and positions are left unclarified while a candidate emphasizes his personal image and appearance to attract attention. This projects irrelevancies into a campaign. Parties are downgraded and tend to become less important if candidates are nominated because they come over well on the screen and have an engaging grin, good voice, and pleasant and convincing manner. Selection on such grounds makes them campaign as popular personalities rather than as Party personages.

There is some cause to believe that a leader with access to radio and television facilities and a forum like the White House or Governor's Mansion has little need of Party organization and machinery to achieve electorial success. With this situation in mind, there are those who fear that the growth of political broadcasting will downgrade the Party system as an instrument for winning elections and for shaping national policies.

On the positive side, TV undoubtedly provides the means to produce a feeling of direct contact between the candidate or public official and the viewer—though the citizen, at the time he is watching, cannot himself take part or express his own opinion. Nevertheless the general effect of political broadcasting is to turn the whole nation into a huge town meeting. And the individual viewer gets his turn and can talk back when he votes.

Political broadcasting seems also to include the ability to cement the links between the political leadership in Washington and the citizenry at large. It tends to act as a connecting force between political leaders anywhere and the great mass of the people.

It is clear that TV has the capacity to enable the electorate to become direct witnesses of political history. This it can do whenever it has the opportunity to make available to the citizenry such events as congressional hearings, political conventions, debates between candidates, inaugurations, and addresses to Congress. It can do so, too, through news events, interviews, and documentaries.

Studies have shown that television, in its first decade, has not significantly elevated the level of political interest, nor has it increased the rate of political participation or heightened the level of political information. Nevertheless, a recent study has also revealed that 60 percent of the voters in 1960 received most of their information on the national election from television. Furthermore, it has been shown that in 1963, TV became the nation's primary news medium, for the first time surpassing newspapers. However, it also came out that those citizens most likely to seek information on television about political matters, or liable to be affected by what they see, are already the best informed concerning the campaign. In other words, television broadcasts seem more likely to reinforce predispositions, prejudices, and beliefs than to change them. Consequently one significant result of political broadcasting is that it helps mobilize sympathizers into voters. . . .

### COSTS

Talk is not cheap when directed to large audiences over major broadcasting facilities.

In 1952, and again in 1956, over one-third of the total funds spent by national-level political committees for Presidential campaigning went for radio and television broadcasting. The costs for 1960 must be comparably great, though exact figures are not available.

During the 1950's, broadcast costs appeared to be most significant at the national and statewide levels. Because they were high, they tended to crowd out other forms of campaign spending when only limited funds were available.

There is evidence, according to Federal Communications Commission surveys in 1960 and 1962, that political broadcast costs have risen perhaps most dramatically at the state and local level. But it is nationwide Presidential campaigning that bites off the biggest mouthful.

The Great Debates were not the only important innovation in political campaigning in 1960. Another important first was the nationwide Nixon Telethon, which took place on the day before the election. Costs of the Telethon and other Republican broadcasts, on that day, according to report, came to half a million dollars. In the last ten days of the campaign, the Republicans spent in the neighborhood of two million dollars in broadcasts.

As to the Democrats, they spent $2.6 million, according to report, in the last eighteen days of the campaign, though this figure probably includes some state and local broadcast expenditures.

As for total expenditures for political broadcasting at all levels, combining TV, FM, and AM networks and stations, they were almost one and a half times as high in the 1960 election period as in that of 1956. A Federal Communications

Commission survey of political broadcasting for 1960, covering the period from September 1 to Election Day, put total charges for all levels at $14,195,000. Of this total sum, the adjusted components were as follows: $7.5 million spent by the Republicans, $6.2 million by the Democrats, and $431,000 for all others. This is 44 percent more than the $9,818,000 spent for political broadcasting during the same period in 1956.

Charges for combined radio and TV network time and facilities—primarily for broadcasts by Presidential and Vice Presidential candidates and their supporters—were actually 7.5 percent less for the two major parties in 1960 than in 1956, chiefly because, in 1960, news and interview programs were exempted from the provisions of Section 315 of the Federal Communications Act (the "equal-time" provision). The total paid time in 1960 for television and radio network programs for the Presidential tickets was $3,006,102—roughly $1.9 million for the Republican standard bearers and $1.1 million for the Democratic. In 1960, charges for television were practically identical with those for 1956, but radio costs declined. The explanation for this is that free exposure enabled the candidates to make do with less paid time in 1960. Nevertheless, the fewer paid programs in 1960 cost more for both production and circulation.

As for 1962 (a non-Presidential election year), a survey by the Federal Communications Commission shows that political parties and candidates spent $20.2 million for broadcasting during the primary and general election campaigns. One explanation of why the 1962 total for all political broadcasting was higher than in 1960 is because in 1962 the FCC surveyed costs in primaries as well as in the general elections, whereas in 1960 it surveyed only the costs for general elections. The 1962 total was made up of about $12 million spent in the general election campaigns and about $8 million in the primaries. Republicans and Democrats spent almost equal amounts in the general election campaigns—$6 million for the Republicans and $5.7 million for the Democrats. In the primaries, however, the Democrats outspent the Republicans $6.3 million to $1.5 million—the most likely reason being that the Democrats had more numerous intraparty contests, particularly in the South, with Democratic nominations more valuable there than Republican because of greater likelihood of election, hence more highly contested. . . .

## REGULATION

By law, the FCC, in granting broadcasting licenses, is required to do so with a regard for "the public interest, convenience, and necessity." But the meaning of this phrase has never been fully defined either by Congress or the Commission.

In accordance with this provision, stations are required to give some public service to the community in which they are located. But this does not specifically compel them to give or sell time for political broadcasts.

As for the regulation of political broadcasting, the Federal Communications Act deals with this in its Section 315—the so-called equal-time provision, which might more accurately be referred to as the "equal opportunity" provision. Section 315 prohibits station licensees from selling paid time, or granting free time, to one candidate unless offering an equal amount of time on the same terms to all candidates for the office. The purpose is to prevent broadcasters from giving unfair advantage to one candidate over another, even on a news broadcast. In 1959, permanent exemption from the provisions of Section 315 was given to certain kinds of newscasts, including interviews, documentaries, or on-the-spot coverage of legally qualified candidates.

The effects of the equal opportunity provision have sometimes been to prevent debates or other programs presenting the major party candidates because the costs of providing equal time for minor party candidates or independents would for many stations be prohibitive.

Section 315 has worked least well in Presidential elections, in which almost invariably there are a dozen or more different candidates nominated by various minor parties. With this situation in mind, Congress in 1960 passed a temporary suspension of the provision as far as it concerns the Presidential and Vice Presidential campaigns. For 1964, the President's Commission on Campaign Costs has recommended a similar suspension.

The suspension of the "equal-time" provision enables the networks to make available prime viewing time without charge to the Presidential and Vice Presidential candidates of the two major parties. It also enabled them to present the Great Debates. This will likewise be possible in 1964.

In 1960, the two major parties were provided virtually equal amounts of free sustaining time. Total free television time for appearances of all Presidential and Vice Presidential candidates averaged 6:30 hours compared with 9:55 hours of paid time per station. Hence, in 1960, candidates on the Presidential ticket got well over 50 percent as much free time as time they paid for. It is interesting that additional free time offered in 1960 on some programs was actually turned down. Free time given to the major party Presidential candidates increased dramatically in 1960 over 1956.

In 1960 the costs to the networks of the free time provided for the Presidential campaign was around $4-$5 million. The cost of the four Kennedy-Nixon debates alone was probably over $2 million.

As for the value of the debates to both Kennedy and Nixon, it was phenomenally great in terms of audience coverage. A total of 115 million persons saw or heard one or more of the four debates. In this respect the cost equivalents are unimportant, for paid broadcasts in prime time periods attracted, according to one network, less than a third of the audience of 71 million persons, on the average, who viewed a Great Debate.

In 1962, when there was no Presidential election, an FCC survey showed that most of the nation's 5,300 broadcasting stations carried paid political broadcasts. Only some 1,200 stations, however, gave free time to candidates and their supporters. Only 5 percent of stations did no political broadcasting at all. Many stations sell only spot announcements. With just a few seconds available, these are so short that they can hardly be of much help in educating the electorate.

## THE PROBLEMS OF POLITICAL BROADCASTING

The issues and problems of political broadcasting are considerable and complex.

The area we are dealing with is a limited part of the public domain known as the broadcast spectrum. Broadcasters are licensed by the FCC on behalf of the people to use an allocated radio wave or television channel within this spectrum.

In democratic theory, every candidate should have the right to put his views before the electorate. It is clear that broadcasting facilities should not be used to favor certain candidates over others. Money should not influence elections and the ability to buy time should not permit dominance of the airwaves.

In the past, the broadcasting industry has put the burden of proof on defenders of Section 315. The industry says that this provision impedes the networks and broadcasters from presenting more candidates with free time. By way of rejoinder to this, it is suggested that, instead, the burden of proof rests with the broadcasting industry to show that it is giving free time where there are only two candidates. Just two candidates, in American elections, are the usual and typical thing. For example, in only nine out of thirty-nine senatorial elections in 1962 were there three or more candidates. Only forty-one out of 435 congressional elections had three or more candidates. And in thirty-five gubernatorial contests, only thirteen had more than two candidates to be voted on at the final election.

Looked at from within each state, in twenty-eight states there were only two candidates in each of the senatorial contests, whereas in eight states there were more than two candidates. Proportionately as many television stations in the eight states provided sustaining time for the senatorial candidates as in the twenty-eight states. In states in which there are candidates of only two major parties competing, broadcasters have less excuse for not providing some free time.

On occasion, as we have seen, offers of sustaining time by stations are not accepted. There are various reasons for this. Sometimes there is no request for equal time by one or another opposing candidate. The tactical interests of a candidate may not square with the broader interests of the electorate. Thus an incumbent may not want to debate a relatively unknown opponent, thereby giving him prominence and a sizable audience. Nevertheless the broader interests of the public could suggest that debates are desirable as a means for information and education on the issues.

In this particular matter, two points should be borne in mind. The first is that candidates need more exposure to public view than is provided through debates and interviews, and such exposure may be very costly. The second point is that while broadcasters are naturally concerned about format, they should be flexible and their concern should not be pressed to the point where broadcasters in effect dictate the candidate's strategy by putting offers of free time on a "take-it-or-leave-it" basis. Broadcasters should not be in a position to substitute their judgment for that of the candidates.

The incidence of two-candidate contests varies from year to year and place to place, but where there are three or more candidates the economics of broadcasting may not readily permit broadcasters to provide free time.

One suggested answer to the problem of political broadcasts at all levels would be a policy of "differential equality of access," in which major candidates for certain offices would receive free equal time, whereas minor candidates would receive free equal time but less than that afforded to major candidates whom the public would be most interested in hearing. This doctrine would recognize our predominant two-party system while also giving a chance to independent and minor party candidates, regardless of their seriousness or their chance of success. . . .

## HOW CAN THE VOTER MAKE THE BEST USE OF TELEVISION AND RADIO?

Television has lifted the voter from his living room into the convention city, not just into the convention hall. It has made it possible for the viewer to actually see far more of what is happening than any individual delegate can possibly observe.

Sight alone, which is the primary appeal of television, is completely inadequate to understand a convention. The sense of hearing is, perhaps, more important for comprehension.

The picture that television provides can almost be described as the frosting on the cake. It gives the viewer the "color" that is unique to national nominating conventions.

When the TV camera is on the keynote speaker, and the sound records his voice, it is simple to understand. But when the TV camera zeros in on a huddle of men on the convention floor during the balloting, sight alone is inadequate. You must listen to the explanation offered by the commentator.

Both Democratic and Republican convention officials do everything they can to schedule proceedings so the most important events will occur during prime viewing time.

But no matter how perfect the scheduling, convention events will not follow the clock. Hours of apparent inactivity will pass on the convention floor. This seemingly idle time is absolutely necessary for the convention machinery to sort out the "facts" presented by the delegates. It is a time for compromise, caucuses, debates, and more compromises until the choice is made.

The vacuum is filled by speeches. Not only do they consume time on the convention floor, they also provide an opportunity for a governor, a senator or key political figure to gain the home-town prestige of making a national convention speech. Network radio and TV may virtually ignore these speeches, but they will be given prominent coverage in local newspapers and even on local radio and television stations. Such speeches are important to the welfare of the party on the local or state level by adding prestige to the party leaders.

During these periods of local-interest speech-making when television commentators appear on the screen, viewers may be inclined to turn the set off and take a breather.

However, this can be a most important time for the viewer. The commentator can sum up four hours of convention proceedings in a few minutes. He can analyze the meaning of a caucus by a key state. He can interpret the convention for the viewer.

Despite its increasing flexibility, television still cannot cover the entire convention with pictures. For that matter, the greatest handicap of television is the inability to give a detailed report of daily doings of each state delegation. Only the newspapers with reporters concentrating on a single state or region can provide that data.

Beware of one thing while watching the convention on television. It is easy to get the false impression that the convention is being "swept" by some Presidential candidate because of a frenzied demonstration being staged in his behalf. The demonstrations at national conventions have become almost professional operations with the delegates in many cases being merely spectators.

The pretty girls, the banners and signs, the bands, all are brought onto the floor for the demonstration. These participants can't vote. Also, politicians take special precautions to keep a convention from being so stampeded.

Radio's primary advantage is that it provides convention proceedings at times and in places where television viewing is impossible or inconvenient. It can be considered the voice without the picture.

## A GREAT AND GROWING IMPACT

In politics, power to communicate is of greatest importance. Political broadcasting is an increasingly potent means for creating a candidate's and a party's image for election purposes.

Does it also have the power to raise the levels of political education and participation? This still needs to be proved, though such capacity has been demonstrated, at least fleetingly, by such practices as the broadcasting of Presidential Nominating Conventions, and also through such events as the Kennedy-Nixon debates.

One thing is sure. In politics, TV's impact is great—and it is growing.

# 15

**James Reston**
**George R. Berdes**

## *The Press Versus Government*

BERDES / In 1937, Leo Rosten wrote in his book, Washington Correspondents, "In a democracy we depend on the press for a presentation of the facts on which our political opinions are based and the issues around which our political controversies revolve but we know nothing of the men and women and the problems and the devices behind the dispatches and columns which begin with the portentous dateline 'Washington, D.C.' " My purpose is to obtain as much current information as possible about the daily functioning of that American institution known as the newspress which is charged with the responsibility of keeping democracy functioning. I would like to begin by asking what you think are some of the greatest obstacles to reporting the vast and complex machine known as the federal government in Washington. In other words, what are some of the inherent difficulties which a reporter has to overcome here to report the news intelligently so that his readers truly understand the crucial issues and can thereby function intelligently as citizens of a democracy?

RESTON / The first thing we have to try to do is put the press in its historical context. That means going back to the first article of the Bill of Rights, which instructs the Congress to do nothing to interfere with, or to abridge the freedom of the press. It is the root of our psychology as reporters. The theory of the Founding Fathers was that the press should be the watchman on the walls, that power corrupts, and the more power there is, the more there should be an outside skeptical eye watching the operations of the men who exercise power. That is the legal and psychological basis. If we follow the history of the press in the United States we can see the expansion and elaboration of the idea. The press was always skeptical of power; the press always tended to follow Mencken's idea that there was only one way to look at a politician, and that's down. In the nineteenth century there was the era of the little editor on the frontier, sitting with a gun in his desk, criticizing what went on, watching for corruption of all kinds, often having to defend his life in the process. The critical function was expanded later in periodical journalism, of course, by the muckrakers (and all the others). They also looked skeptically at power and particularly at government, assuming anything the government was doing which was hidden from the people was necessarily wicked and should be exposed.

Such an attitude is all very understandable and in many ways it has been the glory of the press during the days of our isolation. However, once the U.S. became a part, and indeed a leader, of a whole coalition of nations in issues involving the possibility of peace and war, then there were all kinds of different complications. Now the government of the United States, engaged in a cold war against a very cunning enemy, has to do all kinds of things of a clandestine nature in its own defense. The situation raises some interesting modern questions for the press: what should the press do about the organization by the CIA of a military landing against the government of Cuba? Does the press print it? In the past, editors would hold these people to be engaged in something actually against the treaty obligations of the United States. And yet if the press printed everything known at the time, following the older custom to expose anything of a secret nature, the press could expose the country to great danger. So, the press is now, I think, in the position of almost all institutions—the Church, the university, many great businesses—which forces them to ask whether the traditions of the past are adequate to the present. Because old habits of operating are not in some ways fully applicable today, we end up with a great deal of ambiguity which the press did not face in the nineteenth century.

We in the press, since the United States became involved in the world, have transferred the habits of county courthouse reporting and police reporting to the capitals of the world. The habits of police court and county courthouse reporting are quite simple. They deal not with the usual life of the community, but with the unusual. We don't report that most people in the community of Washington lived faithfully within the family over the last weekend; we report the one or two cases where violence or some abnormal action took place. We have tended, more and more, to do the same thing in world reporting. Even in political reporting here in the capital we are still thinking primarily in terms of reporting violence, of reporting conflict. The conflict in Berlin today is just as great as it ever was, but because there is no actual slanging back and forth between the Russians and ourselves over Berlin at the present moment, Berlin has vanished from the papers as if it didn't exist. Berlin has vanished because we're still following the old habits.

There are many, many other illustrations of the same thing, so my first observation is that a rapid movement of history now requires the press to re-examine its habits of the past, and then its principles, to see whether its habits are viable in the present day.

BERDES / One of the habits is the set of news evaluation standards which we use?

RESTON / Well, that's what I said. The most important thing going on in the world today may be an almost unmanageable increase in population. And yet, it's a slow process. The press occasionally mentions the problem, but it doesn't really deal with it in its historical significance the way, perhaps, a historian at the end of the century may look back on our time and say the really important development in the world in the decades of the fifties and the sixties was the enormous increase of the human population of the world. In other words, at the end of the century human energy may prove to be more important than atomic energy; but, today, we pay a great deal of attention to atomic energy and we don't pay much attention to the human energy that has been loosed upon the world.

BERDES / What about obstacles inherent to the structure which exists here in the capital itself—the complexity of the government establishment, its vastness?

RESTON / Yes, I think it's a problem. However, the press has done a better job of dealing with complex government than with creeping social changes, through the development of specialists. For example, the *New York Times* has developed specialist-writers in the field of labor news. A special writer like Louie Stark probably knew more about the labor union movement in this country through the thirties and the forties than anybody else in the country. John Pomfret carries on the same tradition in the labor field. Developing specialists has been increasingly expanded to other fields. Anthony Lewis has studied the Supreme Court and the problems of the Department of Justice, applying a combination of scholarship and aggressive newspapering to his job. I would say he has elevated the quality of coverage in his field beyond anything we have ever seen in this country. Specialization has occurred also in science. Since the early thirties, we've sent a whole generation of young reporters into the world with a knowledge of the Soviet problem, and to a lesser extent, the Chinese problem, but more generally, the problems of all foreign countries. All this represents a chapter in the history of American journalism which is very admirable.

The complexity and the size of the government, of course, add to the burden of the work which, to be sure, makes it extremely difficult for the average newspaper to provide the money, the manpower, and the talent to cover so vast a story. Therefore, we had to devise ways of dealing with the volume of coverage. We on the *Times* have felt the needed volume and breadth of reporting was not only a commercial opportunity but a national responsibility to make the reports of the specialists available through the service of the *Times* to papers all over the country. But, in spite of the effort of the *Times* and others, there is still another problem. In the nineteenth century the editor of a small paper probably knew as much about the tariff, land development, education, and other great issues of the day as anybody here in Washington. Today, the editor of a small paper faces great difficulty in knowing how the scientific probes of the moon are going, or whether we're on the right track in Vietnam, or what to do about the outflow of gold, or the balance of payments problem in the world, or whether structural employment can be dealt with by fiscal and monetary devices. Obviously editors are not any less intelligent than those on small papers a century ago. Rather, the world has become much more complicated, and what happens in Vietnam now influences the kids in his home town. They're drafted into the Army, they're sent to Vietnam, so Vietnam becomes a local story. But how is the local editor going to find time and energy to educate himself about Vietnam to the degree he could have done in the nineteenth century on a problem which was much simpler and closer to home?

BERDES / What is the effect on the reader which results from the basic inadequacy of most American newspapers, as you point out, to provide specialized reporting, understanding, and interpretive development?

RESTON / Well, the citizen has his responsibilities as well as the newspaper. There is no excuse for any intelligent man in this country to remain uninformed if he wants to understand what is going on in his world, what is going to influence his business, or maybe even jeopardize the lives of his children. There's nothing in the Constitution which insists he must read only his weekly newspaper. He can subscribe very cheaply to a body of information today, the like of which has never been seen in any country in the history of the nation-state. So, I'm not very sympathetic with the argument that "the poor fella can't get it out of his local paper." It visibly is impossible for the average newspaper to get and spend the money to do what your question implies it should be doing. How can an editor in a town of fifty thousand possibly give to his readers all the information they would like to have about all these things and still stay solvent? It's almost impossible. But the small-town reader has all the new means of communication of radio and television, as well as a more lively periodical journalism than he ever before had in America. He has a few papers which are undoubtedly the best in the world, and they'll sell him their papers if he cares enough about informing himself to buy and read them.

BERDES / You spoke earlier about the growing tendency toward specialization in reporting and the presence of many specialists in Washington. From your own experience in Washington, what are the general qualifications of experience and background a reporter should have to perform his work here intelligently and effectively?

RESTON / We'll need to break the question down. If we're talking in general, that's one thing, but you began your question with the specialist. If you ask about the specialist doing his job and meeting his responsibility, obviously his qualifications will differ from specialty to specialty. But I don't think I have anything particularly novel to add to the qualifications needed by a journalist. Surely, he needs a good, general, liberal arts education with more emphasis on economics now than ever before, because increasingly in both domestic and foreign affairs a knowledge of economics is essential to understand even political questions. The budget and the economic report which were issued this week probably contain a thousand different political issues. Until a reporter masters those documents, until he knows what is in the budget and what is in the economic report it will be very difficult for him to understand the background of the political issues.

I do have one thought on the matter of qualifications and educational preparation for the journalist; we have rejected too quickly and casually the English concept that shorthand is important. I know all the arguments against it—the reporter is thinking in terms of the little scribbles he's putting on a piece of paper rather than the substance of what the person is saying. But as we get more and more deeply involved in the world, and as the statements made, even by Congressmen and Senators, become issues which might affect our foreign policy, or our security policy overseas, the requirement for accuracy in quotation is fundamental. The greater the power of the nation, the greater the need for accuracy in the nation. Therefore, in my view (and I say this with some feeling, because I, myself, have suffered over the years from a lack of shorthand), this is a tool the good reporter should have. In the past we have not only failed to regard it as essential, but in some cases have even thought it not really a very good idea at all. The same is true to a certain extent of foreign languages today. In a world that is more and more mixed up—as it is now and will be in the future—we can't expect a man to do top flight reporting on issues involving other countries unless he can use one or two languages, not only to give him an entree to these countries, but to enable him to work in these countries. I'm talking now, of course, about world journalism. In my own case, I started as a sports reporter and thought the last thing I would ever need would be a foreign language. Therefore, I did a very bad job on foreign languages in college, although, now they would be more valuable to me than anything else.

I also believe news reporting is an intuitive business and that people ought to start in it when they're young. I would like to see a kid go through a normal high school education, but start working on a paper during the summer. There's one wrong way to do it: The kids who have been academic bums around the world until their middle twenties, who are married with a couple of kids, come in looking for jobs and say, "I think I'm kind of interested in the newspaper 'game.' " This is not the way to prepare for journalism, in my view. The earlier they start, the better and the more they develop the techniques of journalism so that they come naturally, almost as if they're playing baseball, the better it will be for them. . . .

BERDES / Could we change directions to discuss news management? It's a vast, involved subject, but I think Walter Lippmann expressed the whole problem very succinctly. He said:

> Because the raw news facts are indigestible, news has to be and will be managed. It will be selected, played up or played down, clarified, sometimes obfuscated, emphasized—sometimes for good reasons, sometimes for no reasons at all. And this great democracy will depend for the truth on the unending pulling and hauling between the good reporters wanting a true story and the official who believes, as the saying goes, that they are protecting the national interest.

Turner Catledge of the *New York Times* complemented that by saying:

> I don't think there is anything evil in managing the news. Alert and active newsmen should not be whining and complaining about it all the time.

RESTON / I happen to be responsible for the phrase, "managing the news," at a time when there were many charges that government officials were censoring the news or suppressing the news. I said before a congressional committee I wasn't so worried about people suppressing the news as I was about their managing the news. First of all, let me say this about it—everybody manages the news. George Washington managed the news; Lyndon Johnson manages the news. I have no doubt that the president of Marquette University manages the news, to the extent that when he goes before the public, he naturally places before the public the best possible story he can, and in the process he very often manages the news by emphasizing the best from his own point of view and minimizing the worst. Now you know it's true. Everybody does it. Every politician, every preacher, every publisher of a newspaper naturally emphasizes, puts the best light on his own story, whatever it is, when he comes before the public. The main question about it all at the government level is often overlooked. The main question is: Will all the reporters have access to the sources of information on the topic being publicized at the moment so that they can perform their proper function of questioning and checking out what has been put out publicly? The real question is whether we have access to do our function of questioning in a skeptical but honest way. If we don't have such access, we're in trouble because there are many kinds of things a government can do to put out information which may be too optimistic and not quite accurate. If they also close the door to questioning, it's very difficult for us to perform our proper function. So I begin with the proposition that they will manage the news; and, yet, I'm not awfully worried about it, frankly, because during the last generation there's been a counter-movement to the natural desire of governments to withhold information, not to let it get out. That is, we have now become so deeply involved with so many other countries, and the Executive branch of the government is now so dependent on the Congress for consent to the appropriations involved in foreign policy, and even security policy, that it is extremely difficult for governments to keep us from finding out what is happening, through the embassies, through the Congress, through the opposition, through the experts who are outside the government but are regularly brought in for consultation. Information is more widely disseminated now than it was a generation ago. We have to tell our allies before we move in order to assure in advance that we have their consent, or their agreement, or that, at least, we understand their opposition. In passing the questions from one government to another, a great many people who formerly didn't have access to such information now do have access, which gives a good, aggressive reporter a better chance than he had twenty-five years ago to find out what is going on and keep governments from distorting the truth.

BERDES / One form of news management is what I would call the "personal approach." It involves high government officials, often the President himself, attempting to influence the reporter through subtle means. The President may invite the reporter to a private dinner, for example, or a casual evening chat. By being made to feel personally "in" with the President, do reporters lose proper perspective?

RESTON / Some do and some don't.

BERDES / In reference to Arthur Sylvester's "right to lie" speech, you said before the Moss Committee in 1963 that "the Kennedys may have conned a few reporters into being more sympathetic than good reporters should be, but that is mostly the reporters' fault."

RESTON / That's exactly the way I feel about it. It is a question of integrity, pure and simple, an understanding of what your job is. It's also a question of understanding from the beginning that personal relationships of an intimate nature between the reporter and his sources of information are rather bad per se, because newspaper people who like to pretend they're very tough are really very sentimental people who are subject to all the ills of body and mind. They are subject to flattery. They are subject, thank God, to sympathy. Spending a lot of time around the President, watching the agony of decision, seeing all the problems he has, a reporter may become deeply involved personally with him as he goes through the decisions. A reporter can very easily lose his critical faculty. But with reporters, as with women, the first step is usually the most dangerous step, and he must know when to say no. He must know if he starts down the road, he's liable to get in trouble, but I guess women have learned, perhaps not as well as they should. I think reporters may not have learned it well enough, either.

# 16

## The Staff of the New York State School of Industrial and Labor Relations, Cornell University

### *Political Activities of Unions and Company Managers*

Samuel Gompers' doctrine of "voluntarism" opposed labor's heavy involvement in partisan politics. He believed in collective bargaining for economic gains, in lobbying only for specific legislation and in minimal political activity as needed to sway a critical election's balance. By the beginning of this century, however, the AFL had begun a friendly relationship with the Democratic party.

Before their merger in 1955, the CIO relied much more heavily than did the AFL on political organization. In 1943 CIO's permanent Political Action Committee (PAC) was established, and, in accordance with federal law, depended solely on voluntary contributions. Money was collected at the state levels and half of all contributions stayed within the states. PAC supported candidates at all levels through contributions, manpower commitments, and "educational" campaigns.

The activities of PAC pushed the AFL into forming Labor's League for Political Education (LLPE) in 1947 to perform the same services. When the AFL and CIO merged, the Committee on Political Education (COPE) superseded PAC and LLPE.

Gompers also opposed the idea of a separate labor party, and most labor leaders today agree that a formal labor party would be self-defeating in this country, insuring the election of anti-labor "reactionaries" since labor is a minority in the country. Several other factors argue against any separate labor party: The cost, effort, and pressure needed to supervise both union and party affairs would be tremendous; the size of the country and diversity of the nation's interests make it virtually impossible for a single-interest party to capture power; the traditions of local autonomy in both unions and national parties in the United States would make control of a national labor party very difficult; state laws favor traditional parties and voting habits since a candidate must, in most instances, reside in the district from which he runs and few districts are completely labor-oriented; most of labor's strength is concentrated in 10 to 12 states, a fact which would make a national party practically impossible.

Organized labor has, therefore, concentrated on pressure politics directed at the existing two parties. Through money and manpower, not to mention the possibility of votes, labor attempts to "reward friends and punish enemies." Union leaders, however, do not control a block of votes which can be swung as the leaders wish. Some studies indicate that workers who identify with a pro-Democratic union are likely to vote for Democratic candidates; but if the identification is missing or if the union does not favor the Democratic candidate, the member is as likely to vote Republican. In a telephone sample of 409 selected union members run by Public Opinion Surveys, Inc. of Princeton, New Jersey for the *New York Times* (10/9/68) 20 percent of the respondents said they always supported the union-endorsed candidate, 54 percent said they sometimes supported the endorsed candidate, 22 percent said they never did, and 4 percent did not know. In the same survey 53 percent knew that former Vice President Hubert Humphrey was the endorsed candidate of the AFL-CIO, 39 percent did not know, and 8 percent gave various answers. Labor's endorsement, however, may spell the difference between election and defeat for certain Democratic candidates, especially in urban areas.

Whether or not there is a labor vote in America is a question interesting not only to union leaders but also to politicians, academics, and businessmen. The weight of academic opinion, at least as far back as post-World War II and the monumental *House of Labor* by Maurice Neufeld and J. B. S. Hardman, is that labor leaders cannot deliver the vote of their members to favored candidates, despite a long history of effort. Corporate managers have been heard to say that union leaders have lost influence with their members also in persuading them to accept contracts bargained with employers. Perhaps, they add, there is general loss of union leadership credibility stemming from too much communication in areas like politics in which members do not concede union officers to be more expert than themselves. Perhaps it is a matter also of communication exposure; and like U.S. presidents, union leaders may have only so much communication potential, and if they use too much of it on secondary issues they will have too little to use on primary issues. Another speculation is that America's base of democratic power in recent years has greatly widened for whites as well as blacks, and that institutional messages, including those of labor, no longer gain acceptance just because they come from a unit of the establishment.

But despite the agreement among a variety of observers that labor has little political whamo, the fact remains that labor consistently has supported social legislation even from the days of Samuel Gompers, and that much of this legislation has become the law of the land. And labor leadership usually supports Democratic candidates and platforms, and whether or not as a result, the majority of union votes are cast for Democrats. In fact, the 56 percent of union family votes going to Humphrey in 1968 is less than in any election since the early New Deal (a report of the Gallup Poll, *New York Times,* 11/31/68). From 1936 to 1942 the labor vote was consistently more than 72 percent Democrat, and since John L. Lewis gave $469,000 to FDR's campaign in 1936, labor's financial commitment has been largely to the Democratic party. In 1952 Eisenhower cut labor's Democrat vote to 61 percent, and in 1956 to 57 percent, a 20-year low. In 1960 union voters were 65 percent for Kennedy, and in 1964 were 73 percent for Johnson. And since union leadership actively supported Democrats in these elections (nine of ten of them did so in 1958) it seems incontrovertible that there *is* a labor vote. Because their self-interests are similar, would the members' vote be the same as the union leadership's? The question is practically unanswerable, and perhaps even unimportant. One school of persuasive communicators admits that communication effectiveness cannot be measured by any other standard than the behavior of their audiences in conformity with their messages.

So, whether or not because COPE told them to, 56 percent of union families rallied to Hubert Humphrey in the final days of the 1968 campaign. Twenty-nine percent voted for Richard Nixon and 15 percent for George Wallace (*New York Times,* 11/31/68). Labor union voters shifted 15 percentage points toward Humphrey between early October and the election—largely at the expense of Wallace. The Gallup Poll listed the belief that "A vote for Wallace is a wasted vote" as the union voters' first reason for shifting to Humphrey.

Conservatives are inclined to take heart from the other side of this union voting picture: The total union vote going to Nixon and Wallace together was 44 percent. Could it be, they ask, the beginning of a trend, paralleling workers' affluence, toward workers' conservatism? The 29 percent of union families with income above $10,000 is larger than the percent of nonunion families with such incomes (25 percent). At any rate, resolutions are being made by the Republican party strategists to speak more directly to union voters in the 1972 campaign.

Historically, COPE has served the Republican party in an opposite role: as an incentive to businessmen that they had better contribute generously to Republican candidates or "Labor's candidates" will get them. And for businessmen who were Democrats, the COPE lesson was that, "because businessmen have failed to support the Democratic party, labor threatens to take over—and we must work to prevent our party from becoming a labor party."

## LABOR'S ORGANIZED SUPPORT

Organized labor can be especially effective in its use of manpower to support its desired candidates. The hands for envelope stuffing and the feet for door-to-door canvassing supplied from labor's rolls can often make a difference for a candidate. COPE and similar organizations print and distribute educational materials, man voter registration drives (on the assumption that a large turnout will work in labor's behalf), and help to get the voters to the polls on election day.

Money can also be a significant contribution from organized labor to a candidate's race. Labor's political spending is limited by law, and members' dues money cannot be spent on campaign contributions to candidates seeking office. Instead, campaign funds must be received from individual voluntary contributions, "the COPE dollar" which every union member is urged to contribute. The law does permit union dues to be spent on educational and citizenship projects which often may have indirect political effects. COPE generally contributes up to $25,000 to individual senatorial races and up to $10,000 to campaigns for the House of Representatives. This ability of the national organization to contribute monies to candidates in areas where labor may not be particularly strong has enabled labor to extend its influence nationally.

By many estimates labor's campaign dollars just about equal those of the top officials of the nation's largest businesses. Charles M. Rehmus felt in the middle of this decade that the "total value of the labor contribution of dollars and services to politics constitutes less than 5 percent of the whole amount that is spent by all political parties in American election years."

### *Labor Lobbying*

Unions must have favorable legislative atmosphere to succeed in their economic aims. While the political departments of organized labor try to insure the election of sympathetic legislators, others attempt to influence Congress on specific bills. Labor lobbies in much the same way any other organization does: either by direct approach to congressmen or by attempts at whipping up grass roots fervor. Generally, organized labor attempts to influence legislation that has direct bearing on union organizing and collective bargaining, that has some broad social aim with which labor is in general accord, or that will benefit the industry with which a specific union is connected.

The AFL-CIO maintains a Department of Legislation with the primary aim of maintaining legislative contacts and seeing that the "labor side" is presented on important questions. In addition to this department, several others are involved in legislative activities: research, social security, education, civil rights, public relations, and publications. Within the legislative department five men make up a full-time lobbying staff headed by the director of the department. Other unions also maintain active lobbying groups in Washington, and it is estimated that there are about 100 full- or part-time labor lobbyists in the nation's capitol. The AFL-CIO and other union lobbyists make up the National Legislative Council, a part of the AFL-CIO which plans and coordinates congressional strategy.

## BUSINESS

The average business executive about to be visited by an election year fund-raiser for his political party may be scheming to minimize rather than maximize his gift.

The likelihood that his contribution might gain him political favor seems to him remote indeed. Nonetheless, for his boss or for his boss's boss a tangible or intangible return on a campaign contribution may seem possible. One company has devised a sliding scale which "suggests" an up-to-3-percent-of-salary gift for men in the highest brackets. An executive salary of $20,000 seems a popular minimum to be eligible for solicitation, but at that level the amount asked is not likely to exceed one percent. It is reported (but always about some other company) that padded expense accounts sometimes are permitted to reimburse contributors, or that compensation comes in the form of bonuses. The vice presidents delegated to attend $100-a-plate testimonial dinners for candidates may feel justified in considering this a company expense. In 1956, a series of "Salute to Eisenhower" dinners reportedly grossed about $4,500,000 for the party.

In recent campaigns some managements have established soliciting organizations, so that the touch will be made by a peer and not by one's boss, an approach felt to be less intrusive and more genteel. Another advantage of the especially formed soliciting organization is that it makes less conspicuous the corporate origin of the money—except to the political recipient, of course. The Merrill, Lynch, Pierce, Fenner and Smith management utilized such an organization in 1968, called The Effective Government Association, to contribute to the campaigns of Representative William B. Widnell, (Rep. N.J.), of the House Banking Committee, and Representative Hale Boggs, (Dem., La.,), of the House Ways and Means Committee, among others. The organization received publicity in the *Washington Post* (10/18/68) and the *New York Times* (11/31/68) to the effect that it had donated similar amounts to both Republican and Democratic national committees, and had contributed also to Representative W. S. Stuckey, (Dem., Ga.), of both the Stuckey roadside candy family and the House Finance Subcommittee, although Stuckey was unopposed for reelection in 1968. The *Times* reported that he said that he used the contribution to pay off the deficit of a previous campaign, a legal use of the money.

Giving to the campaigns of competing candidates is not uncommon. The explanation offered by one such dual contributor was that this was just his way of supporting the two-party system. Another question of delicacy concerns manager's contributions to candidates in states other than the company's headquarters state. Senator Albert Gore rhetorically asked: "Do you think the people of South Dakota should elect their own senator, or should a California or Pennsylvania corporation undertake this function? I think the interstate movement of campaign funds is a definite threat to representative government, an attempt to usurp and subvert the rights of the people in other states." (Quoted by Duncan Norton Taylor, "How to Give Money to Politicians," *Fortune,* May 1965, p. 241.) The answer of most multiplant corporate managements would be that the presence of their plant in the state gives them an obvious and legitimate interest in government there.

The very large personal contributions, of course, come from the wealthy heads of major corporations. Duncan Norton Taylor observed in *Fortune,* "A man has to be a very humble person indeed to fork over tens of thousands of dollars to a political group and not acquire at least a feeling of possessiveness."

6

# Top Leadership

The caliber of our leaders and the conditions under which they are elected and work help determine our ability to solve national problems. Leaders may be studied macroscopically as a group of people having certain social origins, educational backgrounds, and political ideology. They may also be studied microscopically through the intensive analysis of the personality and practices of one leader. Such case studies can then be used to generalize about the dynamics of leadership. The study by John Bibby and Roger Davidson is an example of a microscopic study.

Since most of the top public offices in the United States are elective, we begin with a discussion of the election process. Predicting elections is a great American pastime. Ralph Goldman, Dean at San Francisco State University, presents an entertaining way of illustrating some propositions about the voting behavior of the electorate while assisting contestants in the game of prediction. In a way, it may be shown how prediction as a tool assists a party to gain control.

Trying to forecast the results of presidential elections may satisfy some voters, but others want to influence the results by plunging into politics. Once in a campaign, they are likely to meet and work with their candidate's advanceman, or perhaps they may even serve as an advanceman.

Robert Terry first found himself in politics as an advanceman in Senator Hubert H. Humphrey's campaign for the vice-presidency. He later was Advance Staff Director for Senator Eugene J. McCarthy's presidential campaign. To help train student volunteers, he wrote a *Guide for Political Advancemen,* of which chapter one is included here.

The task of the advanceman may seem to be merely bringing together a crowd to cheer on signal before whirring TV cameras. But in truth, advancemen cannot create enthusiasm and crowds; they can only tap political energy existing but latent in voters' feelings and then direct it into activities useful to their candidate. At their best, advancemen energize or create organizations which link the candidate with the voters and work on after the candidate and the press depart, thus strengthening the body politic. Would-be workers often say, "I've never campaigned before. What can I do?" The job of the advanceman is to help workers to discover their own skills and to contribute to the political process.

Once elected, the new official is faced with an extremely busy life. It is a wonder how many tough characters turn up who can cope with American politics and remain not only sane but more sane than most people. This is, of course, just a speculation based upon some experience and wide reading; there is no good study that compares the incidence of alcoholism, deviant sex behavior, criminal tendencies, corruption, and other extremities of behavior among politicians, whether successful or unsuccessful, with the leaders of other professions or with the population as a whole.

The selection by John Bibby and Roger Davidson describes the activities that occupied former senator Mike Monroney and his staff during a typical day. Senator Monroney has been one of the more productive, confident, and powerful of the recent generation of American leaders. This selection shows something of what he has coped with year in and year out. The life described is a tough one for anyone who seeks to spend time in deliberative thought. The deliberative and thoughtful mind is often found among politicians whose seats are safe. The rest can rarely stop to think. They must be cunning while running.

The next three selections focus on one important aspect of the politician's work—the making of decisions. The first one, by Richard Neustadt, the director of the John F. Kennedy Institute at Harvard University, gives a simplified account of the making of three major presidential decisions. He does not try to describe the millions of thoughts and actions that contribute to these decisions or to delineate the role of the watching public. Instead, he focuses on the culminating act and describes the conditions under which a President can make a major decision and have it executed immediately. He concludes that, "drastic action rarely comes at bargain rates." Such action is costly both to the President and to the country. Do you think that the difficulty in executing such decisions is detrimental to the national interest?

The next two selections are newspaper accounts of political decisions. Accounts such as these are the raw material upon which studies such as Neustadt's are based. Here, more than in the Neustadt selection, the emphasis is on the thoughts and actions that contribute to the making of a major decision. Note how the leader operates in the context of his supporters and advisers. Leadership is a group phenomenon, not a matter of an isolated individual doing as he pleases. Robert B. Semple, Jr., of the *New York Times* tells how George Romney arrived at his decision to withdraw from the race for the Republican presidential nomination in 1968. Jean Heller of the *New York Post* reports Lyndon Johnson's decision not to run for reelection in the same year. Unfortunately, few of the thousands of important decisions in politics and government are reported so completely.

# 17

## Ralph M. Goldman

## *A Do-It-Yourself Presidential Election Forecasting Kit*

Americans are inveterate score-keepers. Baseball scores, football scores, stock market reports, and, of course, election returns. Underlying all this is a cultural heritage that esteems vigorous but peaceful competition, decisive but fair play, and a pragmatic recognition that performance records tell us much about the expectations we may have for probable outcomes in future contests.

Thus, politicians and pundits begin interpreting the last election returns even before the votes are completely counted. Contending factions and prospective candidates start from the last set of votes as they build up for the next nominating contests. Party leaders study returns and opinion polls as sources of information about how and where best to direct their efforts in upcoming nomination, platform, campaign, and other party activities.

The statistical exercise below is a consequence of the author's own interest in presidential election score-keeping. However, the exercise also involves some useful propositions about the voting behavior of the electorate generally, and the presidential electorate specifically. These propositions—some of which will seem quite obvious—are as follows:

1. In its voting patterns for *particular offices* most constituencies maintain a high degree of consistency. The point emphasized here is the significance to be attached to the office being voted for. In a particular state, for example, its presidential electorate needs to be studied apart from its gubernatorial, senatorial, and other kinds of electorates. In the analysis below, we have studied the presidential electorate in each of the states, that is, the Democratic, Republican, and "other party" votes for state electors in the Electoral College.[1]

2. Because of this consistency in voting patterns, the returns from the last election normally tell us a great deal about how the parties will divide in the next election. Study of the last election is, in fact, the basis for most analyses currently made by practicing politicians. However, this one-election kind of evidence *wastes* a great deal of useful data readily available in the returns of earlier elections. A two-, three-, or four-election analysis may tell us a great deal more about the constituency's average behavior, trends, and degrees of relative volatility. Time series and trend analyses are the kinds of tools that business firms, for example, have in recent decades come to find indispensable for their production and sales decisions. In the analysis below, we have adopted the four-election time series; the forecast for 1964 was based upon the state returns of 1948–1960.[2]

3. In voting for particular offices, sub-constituencies—like soldiers marching to war or football players lining up on the field—tend to maintain a high degree of rank-order consistency. In other words, when voting for President, most states, as Electoral College sub-constituencies within the nation as a whole, tend to have the same neighbors on the pro-Democratic or pro-Republican side of the line-up; e.g., Ohio and Pennsylvania usually land close to each other. If the rank-orders of the states in several successive elections are studied, long-run shifts in party alignment become readily observable; e.g., Mississippi's and South Carolina's long-run shift from the Democratic end of the roster to the Republican. In the analysis below, the 1964 and 1968 rank-orders are forecasted and placed side by side.

4. There is a systematic relationship between nationwide swings in presidential preference and the way a state will vote in the Electoral College. As the informed citizen knows, the real decision of the Presidency is made in the Electoral College, whereas the Gallup Poll and other polls endeavor to predict how the voters-in-the-mass will divide proportionately. However, there has been no procedure for economically forecasting how a 65-35, a 56-44, or some other voters-in-mass division may affect the outcome in the Electoral College. In the analysis below, the procedure for finding the "Electoral College cut-off point" attempts this kind of forecast with substantial success.

Let us now examine the 1964 Electoral College Forecast below. Analyzing the

[1] The District of Columbia, with its three Electoral College votes, participated for the first time in 1964 and is omitted from this analysis.

[2] The statistical technique employed is the parabolic regression, although experiments have also been conducted with (a) linear regressions and (b) weighted means.

*1964 Electoral College Forecast*

| Predicted Stalemate Indexes, Ranked | State | Electoral College Vote |
|---|---|---|
| 70.6 | Alabama | 10 |
| 75.9 | Mississippi | 7 |
| 82.6 | Tennessee | 11 |
| 83.6 | Alaska | 3 |
| 84.5 | Oklahoma | 8 |
| 85.8 | Hawaii | 4 |
| 86.7 | Kentucky | 9 |
| 87.6 | So. Carolina | 8 |
| | cut-off point | |
| 91.0 | Nebraska | 5 |
| 91.9 | Indiana | 13 |
| 92.9 | Georgia | 12 |
| 93.4 | Missouri | 12 |
| 93.4 | Delaware | 3 |
| 93.9 | Kansas | 7 |
| 94.5 | No. Carolina | 13 |
| 95.2 | Ohio | 26 |
| 95.4 | Pennsylvania | 29 |
| 95.6 | Arizona | 5 |
| 95.8 | So. Dakota | 4 |
| 95.9 | Washington | 9 |
| 96.0 | Oregon | 6 |
| 96.0 | Iowa | 9 |
| 96.6 | Virginia | 12 |
| 97.5 | Colorado | 6 |
| 97.9 | California | 40 |
| 98.1 | West Virginia | 7 |
| 98.8 | Michigan | 21 |
| 98.9 | Arkansas | 6 |
| 99.6 | Wyoming | 3 |
| 99.6 | Illinois | 26 |
| 99.7 | Florida | 14 |
| 99.9 | Utah | 4 |
| 100.2 | Maine | 4 |
| 100.6 | Vermont | 3 |
| 101.6 | New Hampshire | 4 |
| 103.6 | Minnesota | 10 |
| 104.0 | Montana | 4 |
| 104.5 | New Mexico | 4 |
| 105.6 | No. Dakota | 4 |
| 105.6 | New Jersey | 17 |
| 106.0 | Idaho | 4 |
| 106.0 | Wisconsin | 12 |

*1968 Electoral College Forecast*

| Predicted Stalemate Indexes, Ranked | State | Electoral College Vote |
|---|---|---|
| 71.8 | No. Dakota | 4 |
| 73.6 | Mississippi | 7 |
| 75.4 | So. Dakota | 4 |
| 76.9 | Idaho | 4 |
| 83.2 | Nevada | 3 |
| 83.3 | Kansas | 7 |
| 83.5 | Nebraska | 5 |
| 83.8 | So. Carolina | 8 |
| 87.9 | Wyoming | 3 |
| 89.0 | Vermont | 3 |
| 90.0 | Montana | 4 |
| 90.6 | Iowa | 9 |
| 91.0 | Louisiana | 10 |
| 91.3 | Oregon | 6 |
| 93.4 | Wisconsin | 12 |
| 94.0 | California | 40 |
| 94.2 | Arizona | 5 |
| 94.9 | Florida | 14 |
| 95.9 | Virginia | 12 |
| 96.2 | Colorado | 6 |
| 97.4 | Indiana | 13 |
| 97.7 | Maryland | 10 |
| 97.7 | Minnesota | 10 |
| 98.1 | New Mexico | 4 |
| 99.9 | New Hampshire | 4 |
| | illustrative cut-off point | |
| 100.7 | Michigan | 21 |
| 101.0 | Illinois | 26 |
| 101.0 | Washington | 9 |
| 102.1 | Massachusetts | 14 |
| 102.1 | Maine | 4 |
| 103.7 | New York | 43 |
| 103.7 | Connecticut | 8 |
| 103.8 | Texas | 25 |
| 104.1 | New Jersey | 17 |
| 104.6 | Alabama | 10 |
| 104.8 | Delaware | 3 |
| 104.9 | Ohio | 26 |
| 106.2 | Pennsylvania | 29 |
| 106.5 | Tennessee | 11 |
| 106.8 | Missouri | 12 |
| 107.1 | Oklahoma | 8 |
| 107.5 | Utah | 4 |

| *1964 Electoral College Forecast* | | | *1968 Electoral College Forecast* | | |
|---|---|---|---|---|---|
| Predicted Stalemate Indexes, Ranked[a] | State | Electoral College Vote[b] | Predicted Stalemate Indexes, Ranked[a] | State | Electoral College Vote[b] |
| 107.1 | New York | 43 | 108.2 | Rhode Island | 4 |
| 108.0 | Maryland | 10 | 108.2 | No. Carolina | 13 |
| 109.7 | Nevada | 3 | 109.4 | Arkansas | 6 |
| 110.8 | Texas | 25 | 111.0 | Georgia | 12 |
| 111.1 | Connecticut | 8 | 111.0 | Alaska | 3 |
| 117.5 | Louisiana | 10 | 115.4 | West Virginia | 7 |
| 125.8 | Massachusetts | 14 | 116.6 | Kentucky | 9 |
| 129.7 | Rhode Island | 4 | 119.5 | Hawaii | 4 |

[a] See text for derivation of Electoral College cut-off point.

[b] The illustrative cut-off point hypothesizes an exact 50-50 split in popular preference for only two party nominees in 1968. The 1968 trend projection is based upon a four-election analysis of the returns for 1952–1964.

1948–1960 presidential Stalemate Indexes for each state by parabolic regression formula, the Predicted Stalemate Indexes for 1964 were found and listed in the first column.[3]

The Predicted State Stalemate Indexes were listed in rank order from 70.6 for Alabama, the most Republican on the roster, to 129.7 for Rhode Island as the most Democratic. Indexes below 100 show Republican leanings; those above 100 Democratic leanings.

Various statistical experiments by the author have confirmed that a fairly consistent relationship exists between each of these State Stalemate Indexes and the National Stalemate Index. The National Stalemate Index is simply the index derived from the nationwide, voters-in-the-mass percentage division of the presidential vote. Thus, if the nationwide vote divides, as it actually did in 1964, 61.0 per cent for Johnson, 38.4 per cent for Goldwater, and 0.6 per cent for others, the National Stalemate Index is 11.3.[4]

The next step was to add the National Stalemate Index (in this case, 11.3) to the Predicted State Stalemate Index that most nearly produces a sum of 100.0 (in this case, South Carolina's 87.6 plus 11.3 add up to 98.9, whereas Nebraska's 91.0 plus 11.3 amount to 102.3). An "Electoral College cut-off line" is then drawn just *below* the state that produces these results. In 1964, this would have been South Carolina, as shown in the 1964 Forecast column.

Next, tally up the votes of the states *above* the cut-off line; the total represents a predicted Republican Electoral College vote. This predicted outcome, based upon a

[3] The Stalemate Index is defined in Footnote 1 on page 137. By adding the constant 100 to each Stalemate Index, it was possible to produce results so that numbers below 100 could be classified as pro-Republican and those above 100 pro-Democratic.

[4] From 61.0 subtract 38.4, leaving 22.6. One half of 22.6 is 11.3, the National Stalemate Index. In this election, Goldwater would have had to move his proportion of the vote by 11.3 per cent in order to tie Johnson in popular votes cast.

61.0-38.4 Democratic-Republican split in the popular vote, would have been 60 Electoral College votes in 1964. Goldwater actually received 52 Electoral College votes. The sum of the state votes *below* the cut-off line would have been 475 for Johnson. Johnson actually received 483 Electoral College votes (not including the District of Columbia's three).

Notice, however, that this illustrative 1964 Electoral College Forecast is based upon the actual 61.0-38.4 popular vote split in 1964. What information do we have *before* Election Day in order to predict the National Stalemate Index we need to fix our Electoral College cut-off point? The answer is the poll findings–Gallup, Roper, and others–as they are reported during the presidential campaign. However, be sure that the poll percentages account for "other candidates," "undecided," etc., in order to produce an over-all 100 per cent for the total electorate.

In 1964 the author used the Gallup Poll report of October 18, which showed the nationwide presidential electorate divided 64.0 per cent for Johnson, 29.0 per cent for Goldwater, and 7.0 per cent "undecided" or for "others." Had the poll been perfect, of course, it would have forecast the 61.0-38.4-0.6 division that actually occurred. Nonetheless, using the Gallup 64.0-29.0 finding to produce a Predicted National Stalemate Index of 17.5, the author located the "Electoral College cut-off point" just below Tennessee (82.6 plus 17.5 add up to 100.1). On this basis, he forecast that Goldwater would receive 28 Electoral College votes (Alabama, Mississippi, and Tennessee) and Johnson 507 (not including D.C.).[5] The actual outcome was, as indicated above, 483-52.

To forecast the 1968 Electoral College outcome, the reader need only add the latest Gallup Poll data to the information in the 1968 Electoral College Forecast column above. This now is an easy do-it-yourself forecast kit.

*Step 1:* Check the 1968 presidential preference polls for percentages favoring each party nominee, "other party" candidates, and "undecideds." (In our illustration here, we are assuming that the nationwide presidential electorate is split exactly 50-50, with no "other party" or "undecided" preferences.)

*Step 2:* Subtract the Republican percentage from the Democratic. Divide the answer by two. This produces the National Stalemate Index. (In our illustration here, this Index is zero.)

*Step 3:* Add the quotient found in Step 2 to the number in the Predicted Stalemate Index column that most nearly produces 100.0. (In our present example, zero added to New Hampshire's 99.9 gets us closest to 100.0.) Draw a line *below* that number and state name to fix the "Electoral College cut-off point."

*Step 4:* Add up the Electoral College votes above the line for the Predicted Republican Electoral College vote and below the line for the Democratic. (In the present example, excluding the District of Columbia, this produces 207 Electoral College votes for the Republicans and 328 for the Democrats.)

What is most interesting about the Electoral College result of our hypothetical 50-50 nationwide popular vote in 1968 is the heavy lead enjoyed by the Democrats. Should the number of Democratic and Republican popular votes be the same, the

[5] See report in *San Francisco Examiner,* October 31, 1964.

Democrats would still probably receive 58 more votes in the Electoral College than they need to win; that is, with 270 Electoral College votes needed to win, the Democratic nominee would probably receive 328 as the result of a 50-50 popular vote split.

Put another way, in order to barely squeak through to victory, the Republicans would need to garner 52 per cent of the popular vote.

# 18

# Robert C. Terry
## *Secrets of Advancemanship*

### A. YOUR ROLE AS ADVANCEMAN

A visit by a presidential candidate in this jet age is a complex enterprise. Success results only from the efforts of dozens, sometimes hundreds, of people. But effort alone is not enough. As an orchestra needs a conductor, a campaign visit needs an advance man. He cannot play all the parts, but he must lead them together harmoniously.

The Advanceman, or Advance Team Captain, is the Candidate's senior representative at the scene of a coming visit. He is the diplomatic middleman between local hosts, who would program the Candidate for 24 hours a day, and the Candidate's staff, who must conserve his energies and precious time. Although the Advanceman must strive to serve the desires of local hosts, his final responsibility is to the needs of the Candidate. His challenge, both as technician and as diplomat, is to mesh the legitimate needs of many persons–local hosts, Candidate, his staff, local and travelling press, Secret Service, and Advance Headquarters–into a visit which will be successful both logistically and politically.

Good Advancemen share several qualities with good leaders:

> Learn quickly and continually. Be a good listener: people need to talk, and you need to learn.
>
> Be flexible but decisive. Try to accommodate local needs, then resolve issues firmly so that others can key their efforts to your decisions. One secret of good advancing is to start solving problems fast, even before you leave home (see Section C, below).
>
> Be tireless. Sleep after you return home.

Cultivate a passion for details—relevant details. Another secret for planning successful visits is to overplan. Prepare for every conceivable turn of events. Heed that maxim: "For want of a nail, the shoe was lost; for want of a shoe, the horse . . . the rider . . . the message . . . the battle . . . the war was lost."

Never do yourself what you can have someone else do for you. Conserve your energies, release theirs, and show that you respect their talents. Your job—the tough one—is to figure how to put others to work usefully. Delegate authority, but demand performance.

Finally, be committed but stay cool. Yes, the fuel of this campaign is enthusiasm. And more often than you expect, you'll be working with enthusiastic amateurs. But they are usually eager for professional help of the right sort. They will look upon you as a pro in your craft. So, act professionally. Put the job first. Let others blow their cool in confusion or in bickering, in the presence of the Candidate or in dangerous crowds. The Candidate dislikes being hustled around by excitable people. Your job is to think clearly, and then act smartly—against the next event, the next misunderstanding, the next day, and the next emergency.

These qualities are commonly needed by most leaders or organizers of everyday enterprises. But the organizer of political enterprises needs several qualities in addition:

Subordinate yourself to your Candidate and your cause. Build up your local hosts. (But for their work the Candidate would not even be coming.) Have them issue press releases, even if you write them, and give orders even if you decide them. You should be almost, but not quite, anonymous. There's only one Candidate, and he's not you.

Speak tactfully. Never speak ill of any political personality. Never stay in a group when such talk occurs. Why? First, only the Candidate may choose such action, and he must not be trapped by a staff man into agreeing to or denying critical comment. Second, we are campaigning not on personalities, but on issues. Third, the Candidate needs all the support he can garner, if not today then at least tomorrow. Fourth, of many ways to waste your energies, this is the worst.

Expect resentment and anger. Local hosts may be suspicious of all outsiders. Hostility may linger from the previous visit of a national staffer or from a clash by telephone with a Washington office. The press may resent being barred from an event. Try to dissipate these emotions with patience and competence, with good humor but firmness. Remember to praise in public, criticize in private.

The Advanceman is an ambassador. Even though preparations for a visit are always hectic, you must take time to be diplomatic. Even though you expect never to return to that city, the Candidate surely does. So, encourage local hosts to contribute their ideas, and work with them in resolving conflicts.

But you will sometimes encounter a local chairman who remains adamant in putting his interests before those of the Candidate. If sweet reason fails, consider the call-to-Washington ploy: Before ending at loggerheads with the locals, explain that you must clear the sticking point with headquarters. Retire to your room, brush your teeth or write your mother, and return to report that "Washington says . . ." This should preserve your authority without causing the local chairman to lose face.

In extreme cases, you may simply have to become hard-nosed. Explain to Headquarters why. Then be sure that any local animosity is directed at you, not at the Candidate.

By the time the plane lands or the motorcade arrives, the Advanceman, who must have covered every foot of ground and every detail of the schedule, must have firm control of the visit. Last-minute changes or meddling lead certainly to confusion and disappointments; these may cost votes and even negate the political aim of the visit.

During the visit, one member of the Advance Team must be available to the Candidate and his principal aides at all times. A good rule of thumb, when outside of hotels, is to stay at "eyesight distance"–keeping beyond camera range of the Candidate whenever possible, but positioned so that you can be beckoned.

## B. YOUR COLLEAGUES OF THE SECRET SERVICE

The Secret Service is wholly responsible for the Candidate's physical security, and hence for his housing and transportation. It runs an intelligence network and a system for continuous communications. (*Note:* Inform the Secret Service of *any* threatening call or letter.) It also sends out advancemen (referred to herein as Secret Service Advance Agents).

You are called by the Secret Service the "Political Advanceman" or "Staff Advanceman". You are responsible for all aspects of the visit other than the Candidate's physical security, including what the Candidate will do, when, and how. The Secret Service works within the Candidate's decisions, expressed prior to the visit through his Scheduling Director and the Advanceman, as to what he will do. But common sense requires that you work closely with the Secret Service Advance Agent in planning a reasonable compromise between security and exposure. Hence, you must work out *all* details *with* the Secret Service on such matters as travel routes, movements through hotels, crowd control, greeting committees, and press arrangements. But ultimately you, the Candidate's representative on the scene, bear final authority–and responsibility–for political aspects of the visit.

## C. BEFORE DEPARTING

You should, under the best of conditions, arrive on station four to seven days before the Candidate. But conditions are seldom ideal. In either case, as soon as you receive an assignment start advancing—in your head and by telephone.

1. The Advance Desk will give you an Advanceman's kit including:
   a. A tentative schedule for the visit, including the hotel where the Candidate will stop;
   b. Names with telephone numbers of the local host contact, other members of the Advance Team, the Secret Service Advance Agent, and the local telephone company contact;
   c. A list of other local persons important to the visit, including news media men (from the press office), personal friends of the Candidate, civic and governmental leaders, and general political information;
   d. Press kits, if needed;
   e. Two sets of work sheets, one for your use and one for you to parcel out as needed to guide your local assistants;
   f. A letter of authorization (if needed), an advance to cover expenses, and air travel tickets with return open (or pre-paid reservations from your point of departure). Be sure to learn what understanding, if any, exists between Headquarters and local hosts about paying all costs for the visit.
2. Upon completing your travel plans, inform the Advance Desk of your flight numbers, times of departure and arrival, telephone contacts, and other details. Try to coordinate your arrival time with that of the Secret Service Advance Agent; at least, upon your arrival, make him your first or second point of contact.
3. Buy yourself a pocket telephone book, solely for this assignment. Start listing all the numbers (*both* home *and* office, always) of persons with whom you'll be working, at the site and in Washington.
4. Telephone your local host contact and start working:
   a. Tell him when and where you plan to arrive; ask him to meet you, so that you can at once meet the airport manager and survey where the Candidate will arrive.
   b. If you're likely to need a car, have him borrow one for your exclusive full-time use or reserve one from Avis (with which this campaign has a national contract giving us a 20% discount).
   c. Learn all he can tell you about the *proposed* events (you make them final later), his local organization, and the problems you will face. Write notes continually and completely; this jotting will fix details in your memory faster. Always get accurate spellings, correct titles, and phone numbers at the first; you will need them often later.
   d. Ask him to be thinking of reliable local assistants whom you can make responsible for the jobs listed below in Section D. Ask him to set up a meeting, soon after you arrive, with his working committee for the visit, so that you can size them up and put them to work rapidly.

e. Check whether your local host has enough campaign materials, such as posters, buttons, pamphlets, and glossy photos for the press. If not, order them from national headquarters for immediate shipment, or check that supplies already ordered have been sent.

5. Use your flight time to advantage: Review the schedule in light of your host's briefing, and arrive with a list of questions, plans, and jobs. For example, realize that Sundays slow down advance work.

## D. ON ARRIVAL

1. *At the airport:* Familiarize yourself, together with the airport manager and your local host contact and the Secret Service Advance Agent, with proposed plans for the Candidate's arrival. Sketch the layout. Study the options. Link names with faces. List home and office phone numbers (telephone books rarely list the *important* airport numbers).
2. *At the hotel:* Register where the Candidate will stay, and on the same floor. Your room becomes the Advance Office. It's most efficient for you to work there and have others come to you; when you leave, you lose touch.
3. Call the Advance Desk *at once* to confirm your arrival, report your room and phone numbers, and get late information. Call via the incoming WATS line or, if that's too busy, *collect* on the direct lines to the Advance Desk.
4. Check in with the Secret Service Advance Agent, and work as a team on every detail of the mechanical arrangements.
5. You *must* be accessible to your Secret Service colleague and to Washington Advance Headquarters *at all times.* When you leave your local Advance Office, leave word with your Girl Friday (or with the hotel switchboard) where you can be telephoned.
6. Meet as soon as possible with your local host contact to review the schedule in detail. If he has no local staff or committee to organize the visit, put one together fast. REMEMBER: YOU CANNOT DO THIS WHOLE JOB ALONE. YOU NEED ONE PERSON TO BE RESPONSIBLE FOR EACH OF THE FOLLOWING:

   a. Airport arrangements and baggage
   b. Motorcades ("Motorcade Assistant," preferably a former police officer or Secret Service Agent)
   c. Hotel arrangements (if needed)
   d. Physical arrangements for each rally or meeting ("Program Chairman")
   e. Publicity and press facilities ("Local Press Guide")
   f. Crowds (telephone campaigns, leafletting, sound trucks, etc.)
   g. Decorations and signs
   h. Bands and music
   i. Stenographic help, including rapid mimeographing facilities and supplies during the 6 hours just prior to the Candidate's arrival.
   j. Women's chairman

Instruct each of these assistants verbally, but also give them work sheets as check lists; insist that they report to you their progress daily, and keep your own set of work sheets up to date. (*Caution:* Before the plane arrives, brief your assistants not to lose their heads when the Candidate appears. Too often, local youngsters turn to jelly, forget their jobs, and trail off behind the Candidate.)

7. Also, choose yourself, or ask your local host colleague to assign you, a legman to be at your beck and call 16 or more hours each day. He should be someone with wheels, young enough to be energetic, but old enough to be reliable and discreet. If no Girl Friday was sent with you, get one locally to watch phones, type, etc.
8. Review with your local host contact the understanding with Washington Headquarters about costs. In general, local committees must bear as many expenses as possible for the Candidate and his travelling staff, including your hotel room and meals. The travelling press pay their own room and board costs, but the campaign pays for facilities in the press working rooms.
9. Place all telephone calls to Advance Headquarters collect. If an expense simply cannot be paid locally, such as taxi fares, submit it afterwards to the Advance Desk for reimbursement. For claims of more than $5, you must attach a receipted bill. If you feel compelled to make an expenditure, which cannot be paid locally, of more than $15, you must first get specific permission from the Chief of Advance or his Administrative Assistant.

# 19

**John Bibby**
**Roger Davidson**

## *The Day of Senator Monroney*

On a pleasant August day in 1963, Senator Monroney got off the elevator at the sixth floor shortly after 9:00 A.M. and entered his suite of offices. Passing through a small reception room, he paused briefly at the desk of Mrs. Betty Lund, his personal secretary. As usual, Mrs. Lund had prepared a schedule of the day's formal engagements: Monroney follows the schedule if he can, but less important items often must be shunted aside as the day proceeds. Copies of the schedule are distributed daily to key staff members. In addition to keeping the schedule, Mrs. Lund handles Monroney's personal correspondence and serves as chief receptionist. Another woman in this room assists with these duties while serving as secretary to the senator's administrative assistant.

Monroney's schedule for this particular day was relatively simple. The Commerce Committee's Aviation Subcommittee, of which Monroney is chairman, was holding all-day hearings on the future of feeder air service in New England. Earlier in the summer, the Civil Aeronautics Board had refused to renew Northeast Airlines' lucrative New York-to-Miami run, a decision that imperiled the airline and alarmed New Englanders who depended upon it for air service. Shortly before 10:00 Monroney left his office for the hearing, which was to be held in the old Senate office building.

After conferring briefly with committee staff members, Monroney banged his gavel to open the session. Although the hearings had opened four days earlier, Monroney spent several minutes reviewing the purpose of the investigation for the benefit of witnesses and spectators attending for the first time:

> The Committee will hear testimony on the economic impact which possible discontinuance or interruption of air service will have on the communities, businesses, employees, and other affected parties. The Committee will also hear testimony and consider what may be done to provide continued, adequate, and, if possible, improved service to this region.

Monroney stressed that the CAB's decision was not specifically under review. While the committee could hardly fail to take note of the CAB action, he explained that the appropriate appeals were petitions for reconsideration and appellate review in the courts. "I do not believe it would be proper for this Committee to inquire into the merits of that case at this time," he concluded.

Throughout the morning the subcommittee heard a series of witnesses, mostly mayors from small New England cities. One by one, they reiterated the importance of air service to their communities. The witnesses had been recruited by the subcommitte staff in cooperation with the New England Council, a lobbying group which services the six New England states. At noon Monroney declared a recess until 2:00 P.M., when another set of witnesses would be heard.

Returning to his office shortly after noon, Monroney greeted two constituents from Ketchum, Oklahoma. They asked his help in a personal problem, and Monroney later made a phone call on the matter. He also greeted three young men from Muskogee, Oklahoma, one of whom was the son of a friend. At 12:30 he went to lunch with John Burzio, a Commerce Committee staff counsel assigned to work with Monroney on aviation issues.[1] They discussed progress and plans for the subcommittee hearings. On his way from lunch to the afternoon hearings, Monroney stopped to greet a family from McAlester. (During the day he missed four other sets of Oklahoma visitors, who were entertained by staff members in his absence.)

Monroney reconvened the Aviation Subcommittee at 2:00 to hear a long succession of witnesses. Among those testifying were executives of Eastern and

[1] In the Commerce Committee, staff counsels are appointed personally by Chairman Warren Magnuson (D. Wash.) and are not typically assigned to subcommittees; but in practice they develop a specialization and work with the relevant subcommittee chairman. Burzio, for example, works from desks both in Monroney's office and in the committee offices.

Northeast Airlines, the chairman of the New England Council's aviation committee, and the spokesman for a stewardesses' group. As the afternoon wore on, Monroney left the room at one point to seek out Majority Leader Mike Mansfield. In Mansfield's chambers in the Capitol Building, just off the Senate floor, they discussed scheduling of the airport bill, which Monroney would manage on the floor. They decided to schedule debate four days later, on a Friday. Two hours would be devoted to consideration of the bill, with one additional hour for each germane amendment. The time would be equally divided.[2] With this single exception, Monroney continued to preside until the witnesses had finished and the subcommittee was recessed at 7:00 P.M.

At no time during the day did Monroney actually go to the Senate floor. The Senate convened at noon; but since it was a Monday and many members were spending a long weekend in their home states, the session was relatively brief. The business began with the "morning hour"—a period when senators are free to introduce bills, insert material into the *Congressional Record*, and speak briefly on matters unrelated to the measures currently pending.

Following the morning hour, the Senate resumed consideration of the nuclear test-ban treaty. Senator Barry M. Goldwater (R. Ariz.) delivered a speech opposing the treaty, while Majority Whip Hubert Humphrey interjected the Administration's answers to Goldwater's arguments. Debate on the nuclear test ban followed the classic Senate pattern of "advising and consenting" to treaties. The sporadic debate began on August 5, when the treaty was signed in Moscow by representatives of the United States, Great Britain, and the Soviet Union. Finally, on September 24, the Senate was ready to vote. The treaty was ratified by a vote of eighty to nineteen (Monroney voted for ratification), fourteen more than the two-thirds required by the Constitution. During the intervening six weeks, Monroney was able to absorb the arguments and form his opinion; and as we shall see, some of his constituents were already asking where he stood. On this day, however, he chose not to listen to the debate.

Wearily, Monroney checked in at his office. When he departed at 7:15 P.M., his briefcase contained about 150 letters to be signed. The next morning Monroney returned the letters—signed and ready for folding and mailing.

Like the first day, the second workday began around 9:00 A.M. Within fifteen minutes Monroney was talking to a constituent about a large accelerated public works project for street improvements in Okmulgee, Oklahoma. As he left the office for a 9:30 committee session, he shook hands with another constituent and his college-age son.

. . . [A] n open hearing of the Defense Appropriations Subcommittee scheduled for 10:00. Deputy Secretary of Defense Roswell Gilpatric was on hand to continue his testimony on the fiscal 1964 defense budget.[3] The hearing was adjourned at noon. Subcommittee chairman Richard Russell (D. Ga.) scheduled an executive

[2] The bill, S. 1153, "to extend the Federal Airport Act and to authorize funds therefore, with amendment (S. Rept. 446)," was reported the next day. The date and length of time determined by Monroney and Mansfield were adopted by unanimous consent.

[3] The federal fiscal year 1964 had already begun more than a month and a half earlier, on July 1.

session for 2:00, at which time General Maxwell Taylor, chairman of the Joint Chiefs of Staff, was to explain certain classified items in the budget. Monroney was not able to attend that session.

At noon Monroney rushed to the Senate radio-TV studios in the Capitol basement, where he was to be a guest on a regular half-hour TV show filmed by Senators Joseph Clark and Hugh Scott for distribution in Pennsylvania. During the unrehearsed interview, Monroney was questioned at length about legislative reorganization. He explained the proposals then pending before the Senate Rules Committee and reminisced on the passage of the LaFollette-Monroney Act of 1946.[4] He also fielded questions concerning issues before the Commerce Committee. He reviewed the railroad labor dispute and predicted that the President's public accommodations bill would reach the Senate floor in some form.

From the studio Monroney rushed to the New Senate Office Building for a 1:00 P.M. briefing of the Aviation Subcommittee. Officials of the North American Aviation Company reported on progress of plans for the supersonic RS-70 aircraft. In midafternoon the meeting was adjourned so the senators could go to the floor and vote on a three-month extension of the existing temporary $309-billion ceiling on the federal debt. The proposal (H.R. 7824) was passed by a fifty-seven to thirty-one margin, with Monroney voting with the majority. After the vote, Majority Leader Mansfield asked for and received unanimous consent for consideration of Monroney's Federal Airport Act later in the week. The terms of the unanimous consent agreement were those that had been worked out the day before between Monroney and the Majority Leader.

Monroney's Senate appearance on this day was not typical. Often, his committee responsibilities left him no time to spend on the Senate floor. The legislative body, however, had convened as usual at noon. During the morning hour, Senator J. William Fulbright (D. Ark.) delivered a stinging attack on a recent *Life* article on "pork-barreling" that had slurred an Arkansas River navigation project in which Fulbright (as well as Monroney) was interested. Terming the article "a libel of the entire Congress," Fulbright observed that with current deficits in the Post Office Department, the government was furnishing the publishers of *Life* with a "pork" subsidy amounting to $14.5 million a year. Then Senator Lee Metcalf (D. Mont.) delivered a detailed expose of what he considered improper lobbying activities of private power companies in the upper midwestern states. Senators and representatives are sensitive to attacks on the integrity of Congress, and the *Record* is often filled with such rejoinders to outside criticism as these. . . .

At 5:30 Monroney returned to his office and consulted with John Burzio on the railroad labor bill and plans for floor debate of the airport bill. Then he returned

[4] Earlier in the session Monroney had presided over a five-man *ad hoc* committee appointed by the Democratic leadership to make recommendations. The committee recommended a) a "rule of germaneness" for regular Senate debate; b) automatic permission for Senate committees to meet during the "morning hour"; and c) specified recesses, including a fifteen-day late summer "vacation." The Senate Rules Committee later held its own hearings, and Monroney made a highly publicized appearance during which he counseled avoidance of such highly charged issues as cloture. Later in the summer, the committee reported out the first two proposals, along with another proposal to give former Presidents limited rights to appear on the Senate floor.

the eight telephone calls that had accumulated during the day (two to Oklahoma businessmen, two to government departments, one to NBC radio, one to United Press International, and two to senators concerning legislation). The day's mail was then signed, and the day on the Hill ended at 7:00 P.M.

## THE STAFF CARRIES ON

The schedule just described is relatively typical of the late days of the congressional session, when committee and floor work is at its peak. Task follows task and Senator Monroney is able to check in at his office only sporadically. While he was occupied with his schedule, however, his staff continued to perform a variety of functions. No description of Monroney's "senatorship," then, would be complete without attention to these tasks.

On one side of Monroney's private office are the offices of his administrative and legislative assistants. Carter Bradley, the administrative assistant, joined the staff early in 1963. A former Oklahoma newspaperman, Bradley handles political matters and important constituency case work requiring personal contact. He represents Monroney on all types of matters and deals with many constituents who assume they "have to see the senator" concerning their problems. (Bradley's predecessor was a lawyer who handled many legislative matters, including aviation bills. His replacement by a non-lawyer has shifted emphasis of the job to constituency relations and case work.) The aviation specialist, John Burzio, is a young lawyer also new to the staff; his duties are roughly comparable to those of Bradley's predecessor and center around Commerce Committee business. A third man in the office, Harold Messenger, specializes in Appropriations Committee affairs and applications for appointments to the military academies.

On the other side of Monroney's office is a series of four rooms, strung out like a railroad flat. The reception room is immediately adjacent to the senator's office. Next is an office occupied by Don McBride, a special assistant for natural resources; after that the office of Miss Mary Ellen Miller, who handles the bulk of the legislative mail. The final office is devoted to the press secretary and also holds current correspondence files.[5]

## KEEPING UP WITH THE MAIL

The incoming mail, which averages 350 to 500 pieces a day, first goes across the desk of Jack Yocum, whose small office adjoins the reception room. Yocum joined Monroney's staff in 1946, and as a "clean desk man" he has developed mail-answering into a fine art. First, in- and out-of-state mail is separated. Constituent mail is answered as soon as possible, while out-of-state letters are given lower

[5] Files from previous sessions are relegated to the attics of Senate office buildings, where Senator Monroney is assigned storage space, or to the National Archives, which accepts files in the hope that they may be added to its permanent collections.

priority. Letters are opened by an automatic machine that was purchased several years ago when an important issue brought several thousand letters a day. Glancing at the first sentence of the letter, Yocum classifies it and puts it in the appropriate pile, to be directed to the various staff members.

Much "casework" is handled by Yocum himself, though many matters requiring personal intervention are referred to the administrative assistant. "Casework" includes all manner of requests for assistance of one kind or another: servicemen asking for transfer of assignments; citizens with Social Security claims; veterans wanting to establish eligibility for Veterans Administration benefits; people seeking help in bringing friends and relatives into the nation under immigration quotas; and a thousand similar demands. Yocum attempts to answer, or at least acknowledge, such requests the same day the letter arrives. Because the constituent may have written to other legislators, Monroney's office is in a sense competing with other offices.

"Legislative mail" goes to Miss Mary Ellen Miller and her assistant. She prepares replies for everyone who writes in about pending legislation. These replies invariably express the senator's appreciation for the constituent's sentiments, then explain the bill's status, and finally assure the writer that his views will be kept in mind. Whenever possible, Monroney prefers to state his position on the issue being inquired about. . . .

In addition to Miss Miller and her assistant, a young woman is employed to handle all requests for government documents and publications. Another employee takes care of simple requests pertaining to appropriations and tax matters.

With the exception of the robotyped letters, which he has already approved in draft form, Monroney himself reviews each letter before it is sent out. Each letter is worded so that he can note its contents by scanning the first two or three lines. Sometimes he will affix comments and send the letter back to be redrafted. If the letter is satisfactory, he signs it personally in green ink—a long-time Monroney trademark. (As in most senatorial offices, one staff member has learned to copy the senator's signature, in emergencies, for robotyped materials.)

## "THE THIRD SENATOR FROM OKLAHOMA"

Don McBride, Monroney's special assistant for water resources, occupies a somewhat unique place in Oklahoma politics. Though he has never held elective office, McBride has been so successful in promoting the state's interests during more than a generation on Capitol Hill that he has been described as "the third Senator from Oklahoma." Few people are more knowledgeable on reclamation and public works programs. A former Oklahoma state engineer, he was appointed head of the state's Planning and Resources Board by Governor Robert S. Kerr. Then he became director of the National Reclamation Association. In 1949 McBride accompanied Kerr to the Senate, where he served first on Kerr's personal staff and then on the staff of the Senate Public Works Committee. After Kerr's death in early 1963, McBride and his secretary were brought into Monroney's office.

McBride serves as a kind of independent agent on reclamation issues. His responsibilities to Monroney include handling all mail and casework pertaining to natural resource development—that is, any federal program involving soil, water, natural resources, public works, area redevelopment, highways, recreation, and the like. Such programs are considered "bread-and-butter" issues by legislators from southern and western states. About twenty-five percent of McBride's time is spent consulting with Oklahomans who need advice on how to deal with federal agencies. He either accompanies them to the agency or arranges their appointment and tells them how to proceed. He has extensive knowledge of the laws and programs, not to mention friendships with Washington officials from Cabinet members on down. McBride also maintains liaison with state and local officials in Oklahoma, averaging seven trips a year (each of a week to ten days in length). While accompanying Monroney to Oklahoma in July 1963 for dedication of a new reclamation dam, for example, McBride consulted with several local development groups and spent an entire afternoon talking with the Regional Engineer of the Army Corps of Engineers.

Nor do McBride's activities stop there. He serves as an informal consultant to all members of the Oklahoma delegation and occasionally to other legislators from the seven-state region of the Arkansas-Big Red drainage system. A listing of most of McBride's phone calls during the first of our two days illustrates the dimensions of his job:

> 1. with a Soil Conservation Service official, discussing a report on recreational development of Four Mile Creek at El Reno, Oklahoma;
> 2. with a Public Health Service official, discussing natural salt pollution program in Oklahoma and Texas and plans for an interim report on the subject;
> 3. with a legislative assistant of Senator J. Howard Edmonson regarding a difference between the Coast Guard and the Grand River Dam Authority in Oklahoma. (Later in the week the two senators and the relevant congressman introduced a bill to straighten out the dispute.);
> 4. with an Oklahoma congressman's administrative assistant about a job for a constituent who wanted to come to Washington;
> 5. with a Senate Interior Committee staff member about disposition of certain hearings of the Senate Select Committee on Water Resources;
> 6. with an administrative assistant of an Oklahoma Congressman about an application from Jay, Oklahoma, for Area Redevelopment Administration assistance to increase the town's water supply;
> 7. discussed same problem with ARA's southwest division representative in Washington;
> 8. with a staff member of an Oklahoma congressman, who inquired whether or not the Corps of Engineers had under authorization any projects in the vicinity of Alva, Oklahoma, which could be used for municipal and industrial water supply. (McBride advised that they did not.);
> 9. with Alva, Oklahoma, businessmen (long distance). Since the Corps

of Engineers had no reservoir available to Alva, the businessmen wanted to know how to apply for a P.L.566 water project to supplement the town's water supply (information was given);

10. with the press secretary of another senator, who wanted the names of the ten largest hydroelectric power projects in the nation;

11. with a clerk of Senate Appropriations Subcommittee on Agriculture, to find out for Monroney why the agriculture bill had not yet been reported out. (The clerk said that the committee was awaiting a report on REA loans from the General Accounting Office.);

12. the clerk called back later in the day to say that the GAO report had been received and that the subcommittee would mark up the bill later in the week.

Since Kerr's death, McBride's scope of operations has narrowed somewhat. This stems primarily from the fact that Monroney does not have Kerr's unique institutional base of power in this policy area. Kerr was acting chairman of the Senate Public Works Committee during the long period when the actual chairman, Senator Dennis Chavez (D. N.Mex.), was gravely ill with cancer. Monroney is not a member of that committee, though he has been on the Public Works Subcommittee of Appropriations since 1961. McBride's functions, however, will not become obsolete so long as Oklahoma, like other western states, depends on federal funds for the development of its natural resources.

## RELATIONS WITH THE PRESS

As a former newspaperman himself, Monroney takes an unusual interest in his relations with the press. He is available to the press and has staffed his office to supply newspapers with competently prepared "copy." Like professional newsmen, however, he is suspicious of "public relations" and prefers not to "spoon-feed" reporters with publicity releases every time he delivers a speech. Rather than writing a press release, Monroney's press aide prefers to show the reporter the relevant documents and allow him to prepare the story on his own.

In charge of press relations is Mrs. Joseph Short, an Oklahoman who once covered Mrs. Eleanor Roosevelt for the Associated Press and who served as correspondence secretary to former President Truman.[6] Mrs. Short has been with Monroney for six years.

A mimeographed collection of short news releases is sent out every two to three weeks. Though written primarily for small daily and weekly newspapers, copies are also sent to the wire services and special correspondents. They must be sent out by Saturday to reach Oklahoma in time for Wednesday or Thursday deadlines (the days when most weeklies go to press). Only two or three newsletters for the general public are put out in a year.

News releases are frequently sent out on special subjects. The stories may pertain

[6] Joseph Short served as President Truman's press secretary. After his death in 1952, Mrs. Short was appointed to the White House staff.

to Monroney's activities, or they may announce a federal grant or project. (Federal agencies often allow legislators [especially those of the President's party] to announce such things, and a lively competition has developed among many Hill offices to get first crack at these announcements.) On this particular Monday, Monroney's administrative assistant received word that the Farmers Home Administration had approved the first rural water system loan for Oklahoma, a $380,000 loan to the Sapulpa Rural Water Supply Corporation. Monroney was advised of the loan, and a joint release was sent by wire to Sapulpa newspapers and officers of the local corporation. (Under the practice of "joint releases" instigated some years ago by Monroney, each federal project is announced under the names of the two senators and the congressman from the relevant district. This applies no matter which office actually sends out the information, and the courtesy extended to the state's lone Republican congressman, Page Belcher of Tulsa.) As a result of inquirics to the FHA, the office obtained more details on the project, and later in the day a comprehensive press release was sent air mail to all newspapers in the county involved (Creek County). Although sent from Monroney's office, the releases were in the form of a joint announcement by the two senators and Congressman Tom Steed. The preparation of a formal written release was fairly unusual, for announcements of federal grants or projects are usually relayed by the office directly to the papers (and the recipients) by phone or wire.

In addition to the newspapers back home, several Capitol correspondents include Monroney's office on their "beat." The two Tulsa papers, the *Tribune* and the *World*, have Washington reporters, and a third reporter represents the two Oklahoma City dailies, which are under joint management. In addition, the two major wire services have regional correspondents on the Hill who handle stories pertaining to Oklahoma and surrounding states. Mrs. Short maintains close contact with these five reporters, sometimes even covering floor debate when they are unable to attend. When Monroney is involved in floor debate or committee work of a generally newsworthy nature, the regular wire service staffs takes over.

Press releases are rarely employed during Monroney's tours of Oklahoma, except during campaigns. Reporters in the smaller cities invariably cover his appearances, and the senator's news sense often enables him to assist local reporters in extracting newsworthy "leads" from his speeches. The big city papers, which rely more heavily on press releases, give Monroney's tours somewhat less coverage.

## THE OKLAHOMA DELEGATION

The eight members of the Oklahoma delegation have developed an unusually close working relationship. In addition to the cooperative arrangement on news releases, the delegation has meetings from time to time. There is a rotating chairman and secretary to coordinate activities (Monroney was chairman in 1963). Visiting dignitaries are sometimes invited to meet with the entire delegation. Each spring the legislators and their staff assistants attend a dinner staged by the 150 or so Oklahomans attending the U.S. Chamber of Commerce convention.

If a large delegation of constituents is known to be coming, Monroney's staff sometimes reserves the Senate Post Office Committee room across the hall and orders an urn of coffee from the Senate cafeteria. Monroney then drops in briefly to speak to the group.

## CONCLUSIONS

Our accounts of the day-to-day environment of legislators are designed to illustrate the variety of tasks performed by senators and representatives. In general, these are hyperactive men whose daily schedules are cut up unmercifully into discontinuous five- and ten-minute segments. In the case of Senator Monroney, we have deliberately focused as much on the staff as on the senator himself to reflect the critical importance of staff personnel on the Senate side of Capitol Hill.

The activities of Monroney's staff encompass practically the full range of the senator's responsibilities. Most senators are inclined to stress their roles in policy-making, and their staffs can assist them by gathering information, doing a limited amount of research, and even writing speeches pertaining to policy issues. Because Monroney is a senior member of several committees, he enjoys committee staff support on such matters as aviation or post office and civil service. In fact, it is difficult at times to separate the work of his personal and committee staffs.

The most time-consuming activities of the senator's personal staff are a function of constituency interests and demands. Constituency work, as we have seen, ranges from answering legislative mail to the varieties of "casework" chores. Because senators have a state-wide constituency, the volume and variety of their tasks are quite large in comparison to those of their House colleagues. Considering Oklahoma's median size and distance from the nation's capital, Monroney's constituent work is probably about average in volume; but like most senior members, he has seen a sizeable increase in constituent communications during his legislative career. His staff expects this volume to increase further as government becomes more involved with the personal lives of citizens, and as the citizens' level of education rises.

Some senators and representatives complain that "errand-boy" functions for constituents detract from legislative deliberation. But most members nonetheless work diligently to answer constituent requests. A congressman is often in a position to give real assistance to a bewildered or troubled constituent; and a job well done can produce a grateful and loyal supporter (not to mention the constituent's family and friends).

A further function performed in part by staffs is support for the senator's communications with the public. Dissemination of news to the media is an increasingly distinct task of Capitol Hill staffs. Every legislator is newsworthy in his home state or district; but senators are more often able to command national publicity. And a senator's greater staff resources make possible the cultivation of this national exposure on a more regular basis.

The operations of NSOB 6205 are in a real sense, therefore, the expression of Monroney's "senatorship." Monroney's office staff shares this characteristic with the staffs of his ninety-nine colleagues; and, as we have intimated, his staff is probably about average in size, work load, and degree of specialization. Though many routine functions are performed without the senator's personal intervention, the office itself is heavily dependent upon his personality, organizational skills, legislative interests, and even his political style. As for NSOB 6205, Monroney's own informality and genial manner do much to preserve the loyalty, not to mention the sanity, of his staff. As in every senator's office, the work load is highly uneven and produces periods of frantic frustration. But when all is said on the matter, most staff members would not choose to work anywhere else.

# 20

## Richard E. Neustadt
## *Three Cases of Command*

In the early summer of 1952, before the heat of the campaign, President Truman used to contemplate the problems of the General-become-President should Eisenhower win the forthcoming election. "He'll sit here," Truman would remark (tapping his desk for emphasis), "and he'll say, 'Do this! Do that!' *And nothing will happen.* Poor Ike—it won't be a bit like the Army. He'll find it very frustrating."

Eisenhower evidently found it so. "In the face of the continuing dissidence and disunity, the President sometimes simply exploded with exasperation," wrote Robert Donovan in comment on the early months of Eisenhower's first term. "What was the use, he demanded to know, of his trying to lead the Republican Party . . . ." And this reaction was not limited to early months alone, or to his party only. "The President still feels," an Eisenhower aide remarked to me in 1958, "that when he's decided something, that *ought* to be the end of it . . . and when it bounces back undone or done wrong, he tends to react with shocked surprise."

Truman knew whereof he spoke. With "resignation" in the place of "shocked surprise" the aide's description would have fitted Truman. The former senator may have been less shocked than the former general, but he was no less subjected to that painful and repetitive experience: "Do this, do that, and nothing will happen." Long before he came to talk of Eisenhower he had put his own experience in other words:

> I sit here all day trying to persuade people to do the things they ought to have sense enough to do without my persuading them. . . . That's all the powers of the President amount to.

In these words of a President, spoken on the job, one finds the essence of the problem now before us: "powers" are no guarantee of power; clerkship is no guarantee of leadership. The President of the United States has an extraordinary range of formal powers, of authority in statute law and in the Constitution. Here is testimony that despite his "powers" he does not obtain results by giving orders—or not, at any rate, merely by giving orders. He also has extraordinary status, *ex officio,* according to the customs of our government and politics. Here is testimony that despite his status he does not get action without argument. Presidential *power* is the power to persuade.

This testimony seems, at first glance, to be contradicted flatly by events in the public record of Truman's own administration and of Eisenhower's. Three cases, out of many, illustrate the seeming contradiction. In 1951 Douglas MacArthur was ordered to relinquish his commands; he did as he was told. In 1952 Truman seized the nation's steel mills; they remained in government possession for some seven weeks until he ordered them released when the Supreme Court held that he exceeded his authority. And in 1957 Eisenhower ordered Federal troops to Little Rock; the mob was dispersed, and the Negro children went to school. Evidently some commands are effective; some results can be gained simply by giving orders; some actions do get taken without argument. Truman's comments seem to be belied by his own acts and those of his successor in these instances, among others.

The contradiction is superficial. It exists if Truman's words are stretched to mean that formal powers have no bearing upon influence. It disappears the moment one takes Truman to imply that mere assertion of a formal power rarely is enough. Taken in that second sense his words are actually *substantiated* by these cases of command. For the recall of MacArthur, the seizure of the steel mills, and the Federal troops at Little Rock go far to show how special are the circumstances favoring command. They also show how narrow may be its effective reach, how costly its employment. An analysis of presidential power must begin by marking out the limits upon presidential "powers." These examples tell us much about the limits.

## II

Before I turn to what these cases show, let me review the facts in each of them. Chronologically, the MacArthur case comes first, the steel seizure second, and the Little Rock case third. For purposes of factual review it is convenient to discuss them in that order. Once the facts are stated, chronology can be ignored.

When the Korean War broke out in late June 1950 with a drive on South Korea from the North, MacArthur was in Tokyo, 600 miles away, as supreme commander for the allied occupation of Japan and as commander of American forces in the Far East, posts he had assumed five years before when he accepted Japanese surrender. To him and to his forces, necessarily, Truman first entrusted military aid for South Korea. No other forces were at hand. When the United Nations made the war its own and gave command to the United States, Truman added to MacArthur's other titles a designation as the UN field commander.

By August the General had demonstrated both that he could keep a foothold in Korea and that he, personally, might have more in mind than throwing back the

North Korean Communists. In the first days of the war Washington had "neutralized" Formosa, ordering the Seventh Fleet to interpose itself between the Communist regime in mainland China and the Nationalist regime which held the island. MacArthur soon met Chiang Kai-shek, and public statements by the two of them implied some sort of underwriting for Chiang's cause and some sort of involvement by the Nationalists in Korea. These statements were at variance with policy in Washington, to say nothing of its UN associates, and Truman, ultimately, had to tell MacArthur to withdraw a further statement he had sent the Veterans of Foreign Wars.

Within three weeks of this episode Washington was ready to forgive it and forget it in delight at the successes on the battlefield. On September 15 MacArthur's forces landed at Inchon; thereafter, virtual victory came in a rush. A month later Truman met the General at Wake Island. They then agreed that they had no dispute about the Chinese Nationalists, and they looked forward confidently to an early end of fighting with the occupation of all North Korea.

Their confidence was not to last. In the first week of November it was shaken as the UN troops encountered Chinese Communists. In the last week of November it was shattered by a Chinese Communist attack that caught MacArthur unprepared and woefully deployed. To extricate his forces he was compelled to retreat two thirds of the way down the peninsula. Not until mid-January 1951 did Washington begin to feel assured that new lines could form, hold, and support real recovery. Meanwhile, MacArthur had announced the coming of a "new war." He had despaired of holding any part of the peninsula, and he had publicly blamed his defeat on Washington's insistence that the fighting should be confined to Korea. Immediately after Chinese intervention he began campaigning for war measures against the Chinese Communists on their home grounds.

Truman, and his advisers, and most allied governments had quite the opposite reaction to Peking's attack. Their eyes were fixed on Europe as the cold war's greatest stake. They hoped to minimize the risk of long involvement elsewhere, and especially the risk of World War III. If the original objective of the fighting, South Korea, could be salvaged without deepening those risks, they would be well content. By February General Ridgway, who commanded the ground forces in Korea, was assuring them it could be done. By March his troops were doing it. Before that month was out substantially the whole of South Korea was again in UN hands, and Ridgway's troops were reaching north toward natural defense lines past the border.

It now seemed likely that hostilities might end with restoration, roughly, of the situation as it had been at the start. To Washington and to its European allies this seemed the best of a bad bargain; to MacArthur, and to many fellow citizens at home, it seemed the worst. Rather than accept it he began a new barrage of public statements aimed, apparently, at pushing Washington to "win" the war. On March 7 in a statement to the press, he called for action to "provide on the highest international levels the answer to the obscurities [of] Red China's undeclared war . . . ." On March 25 he published a demand for enemy surrender, undermining a planned presidential statement that would have expressed interest in negotiated settlement. On April 5 Joseph Martin, the Minority Leader of the House of

Representatives, read into the record a letter from the General which deplored the policies of his superiors, and ended with the words "There is no substitute for victory."

By April 5 Truman's decision already had been taken; five days later MacArthur was relieved. An extraordinary burst of popular emotion heralded his homecoming. Emotion faded, and so did he, during the course of Senate Hearings which poked into every corner of official policy. Meanwhile the war remained limited. In July truce talks began; two years later these produced an armistice along a line the troops had reached by June of 1951.

So much for the facts of the MacArthur case. Next is the steel seizure case. On December 31, 1951, five months after the start of truce talks in Korea, contracts between the United Steelworkers and major steel concerns expired with a stalemate in collective bargaining. At Truman's personal request the men continued work without a contract, while he referred their dispute to the Wage Stabilization Board, a body composed equally of labor, industry, and public members, which had charge of wage control and allied functions during the Korean War. Because this Wage Board still was hearing the case, the union twice postponed a strike, again at Truman's instance. Then, with the strike set for April 9, 1952, labor and public members of the Board agreed, March 20, on terms of settlement to recommend to the disputing parties. Industry members dissented. At first sight of these majority proposals the union embraced them, the companies denounced them, and in echelons above the Board officials thought them "high."

The Wage Stabilization Board was part of a complex administrative hierarchy established in the first six months of the Korean War. At the top was the Office of Defense Mobilization (ODM), headed by Charles E. (General Electric) Wilson whom Truman had entrusted with "direction," "supervision," and "control" of the entire home-front economic effort. ODM had been superimposed on everything else in the immediate aftermath of Chinese intervention. Next in line was an Economic Stabilization Agency (ESA), which had been created before Wilson's appointment. On paper, this Agency administered discretionary powers over prices and wages conferred upon the President by the Defense Production Act. In fact, those powers were administered by two subordinate units: the Office of Price Stabilization, headed by Ellis Arnall, former governor of Georgia, and the Wage Board, itself. The Office was organized like a regular line agency. The Board was run like a regulatory commission with one of its public members in the chair. The Board had statutory authority by delegation through the ESA, to *set* maximum limits on wages. It also had a direct authorization from the White House to *recommend* solutions for nonwage issues in labor disputes. Both functions were involved in the steel case. Wage rulings by the Board were legally enforceable; its nonwage proposals were not. Theoretically, its wage ceilings were subject to revision by the Economic Stabilizer, or the Defense Mobilizer, or the President. But practically speaking, case by case, the Board's tripartite composition and quasijudicial procedures made majority decisions irreversible on wages and not even reviewable on other issues. In comparison, the Office of Price Stabilization was an administrative unit with no more independence of its nominal superiors than it could win by bureaucratic in-fighting, and with no nonprice duties to distract it from concern for price control. One thing, however, wage and price controllers had in common: they mistrusted those above them and were cool to one another.

The Wage Board proposals of March 20 precipitated a crisis in the steel case. The industry pronounced them unacceptable. The union termed them the least it would accept. The Administration could not disavow them without wrecking the machinery for wage stabilization. A strike was just three weeks away. According to the Pentagon the possibility of enemy offensives in Korea precluded any loss of steel production. In these circumstances Wilson, as Director of Defense Mobilization, took personal charge. His answer for the crisis was a *price* concession to the companies sufficient to induce a settlement of wage and other issues before the strike deadline. After hurried consultation with the President, who was ending a vacation at Key West, Wilson sounded out the industry on price relief. Unfortunately, in an impromptu press conference he had exposed a private distaste for the Wage Board's terms of settlement. This ended union confidence in him and cast doubt on his claims to act for the Administration. Immediately after, Wilson was rebuffed by industry officials who wanted higher prices than he had in mind and made no promises to settle with the union. Immediately after that, Wilson's nominal subordinate Ellis Arnall, the Price Director, won support from Truman for a firmer stand on price controls. Concessions were to be allowed for cost increases in the normal course, but only *after* costs had been incurred. A labor-management agreement must come first. So Arnall argued. Truman sympathized. Wilson resigned on March 29.

In the remaining days before the strike the White House, now involved directly, tried to press the companies and union to a settlement without a price concession in advance. Collective bargaining was resumed and mediation was attempted. Much jockeying and many misadventures then ensued but not a settlement. Finally, to escape a shutdown of production Truman seized the industry two hours before the strike deadline. He ordered the Secretary of Commerce to administer the mills and called upon the men to work as government employees.

The union honored Truman's call; the companies accepted government control—and went to court. In ordering his seizure the President had acted without statutory sanction. Indeed, he had ignored a statute on the books, the Taft-Hartley Act, which gave him the alternative of seeking an injunction against union strike-calls for another eighty days. In these circumstances the steel companies asserted that his seizure was illegal. So they argued in the press and in a Federal District Court on April 9 and after. Government attorneys answered with appeals to the necessities of national defense. They also laid claims to unlimited, "inherent" presidential powers. The President, himself, repudiated these claims. The Court, however, was infuriated by them. The fury was shared by Congressmen and editors.

On April 29 the District Judge denied Truman's authority to seize the industry. A strike began at once. Three days later the order of that Judge was stayed by an Appeals Court decision which allowed the government to put its case before the Supreme Court. The men then straggled back to work. At Truman's request, company and union leaders went into the White House to bargain with each other then and there. On May 3 while bargaining was under way, the Supreme Court took jurisdiction of the case and pending its decision ordered that there be no change in wages. White House bargaining broke down at once; all parties turned, instead, to the Court.

On June 2 a Supreme Court majority upheld the District Judge with a set of opinions so diverse as to establish nothing but the outcome. The President at once returned the mills to private hands. Again there was a strike. This time the mills remained shut down for seven weeks until collective bargaining and White House promises of price relief produced a settlement on July 24. The men gained terms a shade less favorable than the Wage Board members had proposed; the companies gained considerably more price relief than Wilson once had offered.

Such was the outcome of steel seizure. Between it and the third case there are five years and Eisenhower's two elections. The Little Rock affair began in the first months of his second term. In April 1957 a Federal Court of Appeals approved the integration plan prepared by school authorities in Little Rock, following the Supreme Court decision of 1954 that school segregation was unconstitutional. The Little Rock School Board announced that integrated schooling would begin at Central High School in September. It intensified its efforts to accustom the community to that prospect. So matters stood in August 1957, when a local citizen brought suit, successfully, in local court to halt the integration. The local court's injunction was declared void by a Federal Judge, and legally the way was cleared for integrated classes when the school reopened on September 3.

But on September 2, Orval Faubus, Governor of Arkansas, sent National Guardsmen to surround the school. These troops, at his instruction, kept all Negroes out in order to preclude the violent citizen reaction he announced might follow from their entry. Unable to carry out its integration plan, the School Board sought instruction from the Federal Judge. He ordered the Board to proceed as planned. Faubus's troops, however, barred compliance with his order. A petition to enjoin the Governor was put before the Judge September 10 with the United States Attorney General, among others, a petitioner. The next day Faubus asked Eisenhower for a conference; the President assented. He was then on vacation in Newport, Rhode Island, and a meeting was arranged there for September 14. But the meeting produced no action on either side.

On September 20, the Federal Judge enjoined the Governor from further interference with the School Board's plan. The Governor withdrew the National Guard and on the next school day, September 23, a noisy crowd broke through police lines and molested various bystanders. The Negro children who had come to school were taken home. That afternoon the President issued a proclamation to the citizens of Little Rock ordering "all persons" to cease the obstruction of justice. That night the White House and the Mayor of Little Rock held consultations. The next morning Eisenhower called the Arkansas National Guard into Federal service, thus removing it from Faubus's hands, and ordered regular Army troops to Little Rock. Order was restored and the Negro children returned to school. They remained in school, and federal troops remained on hand, through the school year until June 1958.

Thereafter, Little Rock's attempted integration entered a new phase. By school reopening in 1958, Faubus had proposed, received, and then invoked State legislation authorizing him to close the school if it were integrated. In 1959 the

Federal courts struck down that legislation, and arrangements were made to open the school on roughly the same terms as in 1957. At the time of writing, the Governor had indicated an intention to set those terms aside if he could find a way to do it. This summary concludes without an ending.

### III

The dismissal of MacArthur, the seizure of the steel mills, the dispatch of troops to Little Rock share a common characteristic: in terms of immediate intent the President's own order brought results as though his words were tantamount to action. He said, "Do this, do that," and *it was done.* From a presidential standpoint these three orders were self-executing. To give them was to have them carried out. Literally, no orders carry themselves out; self-executed actually means executed-by-others. But self-executing does describe the practical effect as it appeared to those who gave the orders. In the order-giver's eyes command amounted to compliance.

What lay behind "self-execution" of these orders? When troops were sent to Little Rock, Eisenhower's action took the form of an executive order which "authorized and directed" the Secretary of Defense to enforce the orders of the District Court in Arkansas, utilizing "such of the armed forces of the United States . . . as necessary." To implement this order there were successive delegations of authority from the Secretary of Defense through the Secretary of the Army down to units of the 101st Airborne Division and the Arkansas National Guard, the physical executors of Eisenhower's order. In form each delegation was discretionary. In fact, according to a White House participant, "The President decided which troops to use and how fast they should get there and what they should do when they arrived. That was worked out right here and all those fellows at the Pentagon had to do was turn the crank. They knew exactly what they were to do the minute the order was signed." They knew, also, that the President intended to address the nation justifying action *taken.* Under such circumstances, command and compliance are easy to equate.

In the MacArthur case the equation is even easier, for the circumstances were the simplest possible: Truman, as Commander-in-Chief, signed the order that relieved the General and the latter, himself, was its executor, transferring his commands to his designated successor. Misunderstanding was impossible; argument was precluded by publication of the order and by a presidential radio address explaining it.

As for seizure of the steel industry, Truman announced his action in a nationally televised address and at the same time, by executive order, he directed the Secretary of Commerce, Charles S. Sawyer, to take possession of the mills as government administrator. To carry out this order all that was initially required of Sawyer was a telegraphed notification to the managements and a delegation of authority to company executives, with a request that they stay on the job and fly the flag over the mills. Following the nationwide announcement the Secretary scarcely could do less and the government, thereby, was in possession without his having to do more.

This brief recital is enough to show what lay behind the ready execution of these orders. At least five common factors were at work. On each occasion the President's involvement was unambiguous. So were his words. His order was widely publicized. The men who received it had control of everything needed to carry it out. And they had no apparent doubt of his authority to issue it to them. It is no accident that these five factors can be found in all three instances. These are the factors that produce self-executing orders. Lacking any one of them the chances are that mere command will not produce compliance.

To see what happens in the absence of these favorable factors let me turn to incidents in the same factual setting as the three orders just described. These three were promptly executed. Preceding them, or following them, however, were many other orders that did not get carried out. Those others serve to illustrate what happens when a favorable factor is missing.

The first factor favoring compliance with a presidential order is assurance that the President has spoken. The three self-executing orders were given by the man himself, and not only in form but very much in fact. They were *his* orders in the double sense that they both came from him and expressed a definite decision by him personally. Recipients were left no room for doubt on either score; wording, timing, and publicity took care of that. To see what can occur when this factor is absent, one need but contrast the incident precipitating the dismissal of MacArthur: his publicized demand for enemy surrender on March 24, 1951.

The General's call for enemy surrender came at a moment when the President, in consultation with allied governments, was planning a statement that would virtually invite negotiated compromise to end the war. MacArthur got on record first with threats to spread the war. The White House statement then was set aside. To Truman, this action on MacArthur's part signified two things: deliberate sabotage of presidential policy and a deliberate violation of explicit orders. On the record there is no doubt that the President was right in both respects. For the General had been told through channels, in advance, of the impending White House initiative. And he had been under orders since the previous December to make no public statements on foreign or military policy without prior clearance from the Departments of State and Defense. "By this act," Truman writes, "MacArthur left me no choice—I could no longer tolerate his insubordination."

Truman's comment implies what the record makes plain: he virtually invited this result by tolerating a long string of prior acts nearly as insubordinate. Since the Korean outbreak, as for years past, MacArthur had regularly used press statements to counter or to influence the views of his superiors. He had not previously used this means to stop their *acts*. But no penalties of consequence had been invoked for anything he had done short of that. To Truman this extension of the General's tactic was the final straw. MacArthur may have had no notion that the White House would react so strongly.

It is true that MacArthur violated an explicit order. But on its face the order seemed another form for form's sake. Dated December 6, 1950, it was addressed to all government departments and reached Tokyo routinely from the Pentagon. The order was expressed in terms more easily construed as the concoction of press attachés to hush Assistant Secretaries than as Truman's word to his Supreme

Commander. In fact MacArthur *was* the target of this order; his press statements immediately after Chinese intervention were the cause of it. His conduct was of great concern to Truman personally. But how was the General to know? The order's widespread application and routine appearance were meant to spare him personal embarrassment (a fact which speaks volumes in itself). Their effect was to minimize its impact and to blur its source. Even had he recognized himself as addressee and Truman personally as sender, MacArthur may have noted that his press offensive at the start of the "new war" had drawn from Washington no more by way of a rebuke than this pale order. When stakes of policy and pride are high, convictions sharp (and political allies powerful), why should not a Supreme Commander try in March a somewhat bolder move than he had got away with in December?

A second factor making for compliance with a President's request is clarity about his meaning. If it helps to have respondents know that *he* wants what he asks, it also helps to have them know precisely what he wants. To shift the illustration, when the Governor of Arkansas met Eisenhower at Newport, a week before the troops were sent to Little Rock, there is no doubt that Faubus knew it was the President who wanted something done. But whether he was clear on what that something was remains uncertain; they met alone and the terms of their conversation left room for misunderstanding, apparent or real. According to an Eisenhower aide, "Faubus knew perfectly well what the President wanted: the order of the court complied with and the kids in school, peaceably . . . and he promised to produce. We were double-crossed, that's all." But Ashmore of the *Arkansas Gazette* records the impression that the Governor, believing he could "put off the dread day" until after his next gubernatorial campaign, "carried this illusion with him to Newport . . . and brought it home intact . . . ."

A somewhat comparable piece of business marked the steel crisis of 1952 and led to resignation of the Mobilization Director, Wilson. At the outset of the crisis Wilson had conferred with Truman in Key West, talking at length and alone. But scarcely a week later, in exchanging letters upon Wilson's resignation, they recorded widely different notions of their Key West conversation. Wilson charged Truman with a change of tune; Truman charged Wilson with misconstruing orders. And both may have been right. For Wilson had returned from Key West with a mandate, as he saw it, to settle the dispute by price concessions if and as he could. This was a task demanding wide discretion for effective execution, and hence some open-endedness in its assignment. When a degree of ambiguity is inescapable, as in this case, it may take but a pinch of verbal imprecision or a dash of vacation atmosphere to produce misunderstanding. Both were in the recipe at Key West—and at Newport, five years later.

A third factor favoring compliance with a President's directive is publicity. Even when there is no need for ambiguity, no possibility of imprecision, no real discretionary leeway and nothing to misunderstand, compliance may depend not only on the respondent's awareness of what he is to do, but also on the awareness of others that he has been told to do it. In sending troops to Little Rock, in seizing the steel industry, in firing MacArthur, the whole country was taken into camp, informed of the President's commitment, invited to watch the response. But the circle of observers is rarely so broad. Often it may be entirely too narrow for presidential comfort. A case in point is Secretary Sawyer's interesting behavior in his first weeks as administrator of the seized steel industry.

Having seized the mills in desperation to avert production losses, the White House wanted to be rid of them as fast as possible—which meant as fast as it could gain assurance that production would continue once they were returned to private hands. This called for some settlement of the labor dispute whose lack of settlement had led to seizure in the first place. The circle could be broken only if continued government control were made so unattractive in the eyes of both disputants that they would prefer agreement with each other. To that end a tactic was devised: the Secretary of Commerce, as administrator of the mills, was to put into effect a *portion* of the union's wage demands to which the men were automatically entitled under the existing rules of wage control (a so-called cost-of-living adjustment). At the same time, he was to ask the price controllers for the amount of price relief to which the companies were automatically entitled under "pass through" provisions of existing legislation (the so-called Capehart Amendment). Secretary Sawyer then was to announce that he would do no more. Management and labor would be faced by a *fait accompli* that satisfied neither the union's wage demands nor the company's price demands but put some things beyond dispute and foreclosed better terms for the duration. With this prospect before them both sides might conclude that more was to be gained from settlement than from continued government direction. So, at least, the White House hoped.

Within a week of seizure Truman had decided to proceed along these lines. He asked that Sawyer act at once and planned to call for bargaining by companies and union with his Secretary's action in the background. The President's intent was clear. There were no ambiguities. But Sawyer did not act. The Secretary of Commerce spoke for business in the Cabinet. Officially and personally Sawyer had no liking for the seizure. He had not wanted to administer the mills, and he had taken the assignment with distaste. He was evidently unhappy at the prospect of his signature on wage orders and price requests committing the steel industry. Although he did not refuse to act, he managed to immerse himself in preparations. Presently the District Court relieved him of embarrassment (and the government of opportunity) by denying his authority to run the mills. When the Appeals Court restored his powers, Sawyer reached the point of action only after he had won agreement from the President that in the public record his department should be seen to act on the advice of others. It was nearly four weeks after seizure when Truman brought the union and the companies together to bargain in his office. The Secretary's action was set for two days hence. By then it was too late. On the opening day of the bargaining session the Supreme Court barred changes in wages.

Had the President initially publicized his plan, Sawyer would have had to execute it promptly or resign. That was his choice upon the night of seizure. But Truman did not publicize this scheme of wage adjustments. Toward the end of the four weeks his pressure on the Secretary came to be an open secret. At the start, however, it was little known and Sawyer did not face so sharp a choice. When officials are reluctant to do as they are told, publicity spurs execution. But publicity performs this service at the risk of turning private reluctance into public defiance. Sometimes that may not matter very much, or may even promise some advantage, or the President may have no option. Here it mattered greatly. Truman had just lost his Director of Defense Mobilization (and he had just fired his Attorney General for reasons unrelated to steel). He could ill afford to lose his Secretary of Commerce, particularly on an issue involving the administration of the mills which he had just placed in the Secretary's hands. Truman had an option and he took it. He gave instructions privately and tolerated slow response.

A fourth factor favoring compliance with a President's request is actual ability to carry it out. It helps to have the order-taker in possession of the necessary means. In one respect Sawyer's situation after seizure paralleled his situation on the night of seizure: he had authority enough and resources enough to carry out the President's immediate intention. All that Sawyer needed was a staff to prepare papers, a pen with which to sign them, and access to the telegraph. Those resources were at his disposal. In this respect, on both occasions, Sawyer was in very much the same position as MacArthur when his last orders arrived, or the Secretary of the Army when the word came through on Little Rock. Each had the necessary means at *his* disposal. Without the wherewithal in his own hands a presidential agent may be unable to do as he is told no matter how good his understanding or honest his intention.

An example of a man without the means is Wilson, the Mobilization Director, in the preseizure phase of the steel crisis. Whatever Truman may or may not have said to him at Key West, it is reasonably clear that the President wanted the labor dispute settled without a strike, even at some cost to price control. But the moment Wilson tried to satisfy this want, two things became clear. The companies were in a mood to demand guarantees of price relief, but not to promise settlement. And the Price Director, Ellis Arnall, was in a mood to refuse *any* price increase save what the law would automatically require *after* settlement. In effect, Arnall's stand became "play my way or fire me," and though Wilson ranked him bureaucratically, Arnall was a *presidential* appointee. Wilson actually controlled neither the companies nor the Price Director. He could not even bring much influence to bear upon them since his claims to speak for Truman had been clouded by a clumsy press remark about the Wage Board. Wilson had no recourse but to return to the President empty-handed. When Truman leaned toward Arnall, Wilson resigned. But even had the President renewed Wilson's mandate, it is not clear what he could have done.

Another illustration of the same point can be drawn from the act of seizure itself. I have described Truman's order in this instance as "self-executing" in effect, with Sawyer the executor in fact. But Sawyer had a silent partner, the United Steelworkers. The purpose of the seizure was production. Truman's order was effective upon issuance because the men honored their union's pledge that they would work if their employer were the government. Yet until just two hours before seizure was announced, the President had planned, simultaneously, to invoke the fact-finding procedure of the Taft-Hartley Act. This plan was dropped upon the urgent plea that wild-cat strikes in protest, and thus losses of production, might result. In order to assure that Sawyer's silent partner could achieve the purpose of the presidential order, Truman had to modify it in advance.

A fifth factor making for compliance with a President's request is the sense that what he wants is his by right. The steelworkers assumed, as Truman did, that he had ample constitutional authority to seize and operate the mills. An interjection of the term "Taft-Hartley" might have altered their response, but in its absence they conformed to the convention that they would not strike against their government, accepting as *legitimate* the President's claim upon them. The sense of legitimate obligation, legitimately imposed, was present in MacArthur's transfer of his own commands and in the Army's response to its Little Rock directive, no less than in the union's action after seizure. Without a sense of that sort on the part of order-takers, those orders would not have been carried out so promptly. But judging by the illustrations offered up to now the obverse does not follow. There is no assurance that orders will be executed just because they seem legitimate to their recipients. In none of the instances cited—not even in the case of Faubus at Newport—was a President's request considered *illegitimate* by those who *failed* to carry it out.

Perhaps legitimacy exerts a stronger influence the more distinct is its relationship to some specific grant of constitutional authority. Truman's final order to MacArthur, for example, had a clearer constitutional foundation than Eisenhower's *tête-à-tête* with Faubus, where authority was shared and therefore blurred. But Truman's earlier order to MacArthur on the clearance of public statements had precisely the same constitutional foundation as dismissal did. That earlier order had no more effect upon the General than Eisenhower had upon the Governor. Whatever its source or its relative strength, a sense of legitimacy taken alone does not assure compliance with a President's request.

When MacArthur was dismissed, when the steel mills were seized, when troops were sent to Little Rock, five factors made command appear the equal of compliance. In each of these three instances an unambiguous directive from a determined and committed President was carried out by persons who were capable of prompt response and who accepted his authority. The appearance of self-execution was produced by all these things combined. And when in other instances there was no such combination, there was also no effect of automatic execution.

How often is that combination likely to occur? How much, then, can a President rely on sheer command to get him what he wants? It takes but a glance at the examples in this chapter to suggest the answers: not very often and not very much. "Do this, do that, and nothing will happen" was the rule in incidents surrounding the dismissal of the General, and the seizure of the steel mills, and the use of Federal troops at Central High School. Viewed in their surroundings these become exceptions to the rule. So it is with presidential business generally. Under midcentury conditions self-executing orders are anything but everyday affairs. Indeed, in the whole sweep of Truman's record and of Eisenhower's, those three stand out precisely for that reason: what they represent is relatively rare.

## IV

The recall of MacArthur, the steel seizure, and the dispatch of troops to Little Rock share still another notable characteristic: in each case, the decisive order was a painful last resort, a forced response to the exhaustion of all other remedies, suggestive less of mastery than failure—the failure of attempts to gain an end by softer means.

Truman records in his memoirs that in April 1951, after reading the Pentagon file, General Marshall "concluded that MacArthur should have been fired two years ago." Not everything that Marshall read is on the public record, but quite enough is there to lend substance to the view that MacArthur's dismissal was remarkably long delayed. Even if one sets aside all pre-Korean matters, ignores all questions of *professional* performance after Inchon, and scans the record only for the insubordination that provoked the firing, one finds at least two earlier cases somewhat comparable in all respects *except* the President's response. These two are MacArthur's outcry after Chinese intervention (leading to the clearance order of December 1950), and, months earlier, his public dissent from Formosa policy. The White House announcement of his recall in April 1951, could have been issued in August or December 1950, without changing a word. Yet Truman stayed his hand on those earlier occasions (though apparently dismissal crossed his mind) and tried to patch the damage, bridge the differences, without offense to anybody's dignity except his own. The record indicates that he definitely did not want to let MacArthur go. At every challenge, save the final one, before and during the Korean War, the President sought means to keep the General both contained and on the job. Whatever his reasons Truman's pursuit of this objective—at considerable risk to policy, real sacrifice of pride—seems as persistent as anything in his career. In that sense the dismissal, when it finally came, marked failure.

And so it was with Eisenhower in the Little Rock affair. There were few things he wanted *less* than federal troops enforcing the desegregation of a Southern school. Indeed he may have helped to set the stage for Faubus by observing in July of 1957:

> I can't imagine any set of circumstances that would ever induce me to send Federal troops . . . into any area to enforce the orders of a Federal Court, because I believe that common sense of America will never require it.
>
> Now there may be that kind of authority resting somewhere, but certainly I am not seeking any additional authority of that kind, and I would never believe that it would be a wise thing to do in this country.

And when, as schools reopened in September, the Governor had National Guardsmen interfere with execution of court orders, the President made a determined effort to avoid the use of force, an effort culminating in the inconclusive Newport conversation. Eisenhower agreed to meet Faubus at Newport without exacting advance guarantees. This is testimony to the President's desire for a way out other than the one he finally chose. So is the sense of "double-cross" that long persisted in the White House *after* Newport, a natural result of wanting to believe there was another way.

As for the steel seizure, the element of failure is self-evident. Truman had sought to settle the labor dispute in order to insure against a shutdown of production. When the union contract expired in December 1951, he tried to obtain settlement without a shutdown by referring the dispute to the Wage Stabilization Board. When the Board's report brought on a crisis instead, Wilson and the President took up the search for settlement. Their disagreement had to do with tactics, not the goal. After Wilson's resignation, the search continued under White House auspices right up to the day before the seizure. That drastic act was not even considered as a serious alternative until the week before, nor chosen with finality until the very day. The White House was so anxious for a settlement that Truman cancelled plans to state his case on television some days in advance of the strike deadline, lest there be an adverse effect on last-minute collective bargaining. In consequence, when seizure came, he had to combine a grave announcement with a contentious argument—hardly the choice of a President bent on seizure in the first place. But he had no such bent. Truman did not try to prepare the country for that course, because, until the last, he was intent on an alternative.

In this instance, as in the others, command became a last resort; but save in very short-run terms, it was not "last" at all. Truman did not want the steel mills; he wanted steel production and reasonably strong price controls. Those aims could only be achieved by terms of settlement between the union and the companies not inconsistent with existing control policies. The President had no power—and seizure gave him none—to gain his ends by fiat. Seizure merely staved off their abandonment and changed the *context* of his efforts to *induce* a satisfactory settlement. Initially, the new context put new inducements at the President's disposal. But seizure produced complications also, and these ultimately cost him both of his objectives. Two months' production vanished with the strike that followed judicial invalidation of his seizure. And price controls were breached beyond repair in White House efforts to conclude the strike. Yet it does not require hindsight to perceive that seizure's nature, from the start, was that of an emergency expedient, powerfully affecting possible solutions but solving nothing of itself. This would have been the case had the outcome been happier from Truman's point of view. At best, not seizure *per se*, but the added leverage it gave to his persuasion might have brought the settlement he wanted.

The same point can be made regarding Little Rock, where Eisenhower's use of troops bought time and changed the context of his appeals to the "hearts and minds" of Southerners but solved no desegregation problems, not even the local one at Central High School. As for the MacArthur case, his removal certainly resolved command relationships in the Korean War, but these were scarcely the sole concern. What was at stake was nothing less than our strategic purpose in the conduct of the war. And Truman's order did not end MacArthur's challenge to Administration policy, however much it may have changed the context of their quarrel. The General's threat to policy was ended by the Senate inquiry that followed his removal—and by the start of truce talks in Korea. Truman dug a grave, but that alone did not suffice to push MacArthur in. Without the push administered by Senate hearings it is not entirely clear whose grave it might have been.

Not only are these "last" resorts less than conclusive, but they are also costly. Even though the order is assured of execution, drastic action rarely comes at bargain rates. It can be costly to the aims in whose defense it is employed. It can be costly, also, to objectives far afield.

When he dismissed MacArthur, for example, Truman had to pay at least one price in the coin of Korean policy. The price was public exposition, at the Senate hearings, of his regime's innermost thoughts about the further conduct of hostilities. Whatever its effect on subsequent events, Peking and Moscow thus were put on notice of American intentions through the rest of Truman's term, and at home the reading public was informed that Washington saw little point in a renewed attempt to conquer North Korea. Against this background there began the long ordeal of truce negotiations. The Chinese may not have been influenced by those disclosures; Americans certainly were. Henry Kissinger, among many others, has argued with considerable justice that ". . . by stopping [offensive] military operations . . . at the very beginning of armistice negotiations . . . we removed the only Chinese incentive for a settlement; we produced the frustration of two years of inconclusive negotiations." But no one has suggested how we were to stay on the offensive after Washington officialdom had formulated for itself and then expressed in public an intense desire to have done as soon as Peking tired of hostilities. Belabored in the hearings to define a "way out" other than MacArthur's, the Administration crystallized its own responsiveness toward offers to negotiate before they were ever made. When offers came they were seized on as "vindication." Even without the whole MacArthur uproar, it would not have been easy to press the offensive as truce talks began. After Senate hearings it seems psychologically if not politically impossible.

Besides such costs as this, directly chargeable against the purpose he was trying to protect, Truman's dismissal of MacArthur involved other costs as well, charged against other policy objectives. These "indirect" costs are hard to isolate because causation is no single-track affair, but certainly they were not inconsiderable. Among others, it is possible that Truman's inability to make his case with Congress, Court, and public in the steel crisis of 1952 resulted from exhaustion of his credit, so to speak, in the MacArthur battle a year earlier. That there is something in this will be clear from later chapters.

Drastic action may be costly, but it can be less expensive than continuing inaction. Truman could no longer have retained MacArthur without yielding to him the conduct of the war. Eisenhower could no longer stay his hand in Little Rock without yielding to every Southern Governor the right—even the duty—to do what Faubus did. These consequences threatened for the obvious reason that the instant challenge openly discounted the position of the Presidency and bluntly posed the question, "Who is President?" In either case, a soft response would have been tantamount to abdication, so public was the challenge in these terms. When Truman seized the steel mills, the Pentagon was warning that a new Chinese offensive, even Soviet intervention, might be coming in Korea "as soon as the mud dries." The seizure proved a very costly venture. But on the information then available, an April shutdown of the mills could have been far more costly. By hindsight it appears that a strike instead of seizure was the cheapest course available. The Chinese did not move as forcefully as had been feared. If they had done so, seizure might have proved a notable success. Truman acted without benefit of hindsight.

Self-executing orders have their uses, however inconclusive or expensive they may be. In each of these three cases, even steel, the presidential order brought assurance that a policy objective would remain in reach just as its loss seemed irretrievable. This is a real accomplishment. But necessarily it is a *transitory* accomplishment. Even the last resorts turn out to share the character of all the softer measures they replace. They turn out to be incidents in a persuasive process whereby someone lacking absolute control seeks to get something done through others who have power to resist.

Truman is quite right when he declares that presidential power is the power to persuade. Command is but a method of persuasion, not a substitute and not a method suitable for everyday employment.

# 21

## Robert B. Semple, Jr.

## *George Romney Decides to Withdraw*

The brief saga of Gov. George Romney's decision to withdraw from the Presidential race began Monday when his campaign managers concluded—on the basis of highly sophisticated polls—that he would absorb a defeat in New Hampshire from which he could not recover in future primaries.

It ended at 7:30 Wednesday morning over scrambled eggs and toast in the Governor's suite in the Ramada Inn in Boston. Mr. Romney made a few editing changes in the withdrawal statement, told his aides they had made the right move, and then began chatting and smiling as if he had suddenly been relieved of an enormous burden.

In between, there were numerous telephone calls and an occasional secret meeting, all the paraphernalia usually associated with a momentous decision. But all in all it was a move taken with a minimum of fuss and a maximum of dispatch and conviction.

On the basis of the evidence available now, moreover, the decision does not appear to have been orchestrated with a parallel effort to begin a boom for Governor Rockefeller of New York. On the contrary, it seems clear that Mr. Rockefeller played little if any role in the decision.

### PRINCIPAL CATALYSTS

The principal catalysts were close aides who had decided that the cause was lost, that Mr. Romney must so inform his fellow Republican Governors to whom he had earlier promised a full briefing on the progress of his campaign, and that he should use the occasion to persuade the moderate wing of the party to mobilize behind another candidate.

On the basis of talks with nearly a half-dozen Romney aides, the following is a rough chronology of the key events in the final days leading up to Mr. Romney's statement of withdrawal yesterday afternoon at the Washington Hilton Hotel.

The first and perhaps most important event in the sequence took place here Monday in the office of Leonard W. Hall, the Governor's campaign chairman. The night before, Mr. Hall had called William R. Johnson, leader of Mr. Romney's New Hampshire effort, and urged him to come to Washington for a strategy session.

Both men were fully committed to the Romney effort, but both had been badly shaken by the raw data of the most recent poll taken by Mr. Romney's own polling organization, Market Opinion Research of Detroit. The poll showed Richard M. Nixon winning more than 70 per cent of the vote, Mr. Romney about 10 per cent.

### EQUALLY UNFAVORABLE

The other "inputs"—as one campaign aide described them—were equally unfavorable. From Wisconsin, Nebraska, Oregon and other areas of the nation had come reports that the Romney effort had failed to catch fire. The Governor himself, then on the way to Boston for a series of television and radio appearances, was aware of the "inputs." But he had not yet seen the latest poll.

With the evidence spread before them, the two men began a long and discursive examination of the alternatives centered on two unavoidable truths. One was the poll. The other was the fact that in less than 48 hours Mr. Romney's fellow Republican Governors would gather at the Washington Hilton.

At a meeting in White Sulphur Springs, W. Va., in December, 1966, Mr. Romney had promised the Governors a full report on the progress of his campaign. The forthcoming meeting appeared to present an excellent opportunity to honor this commitment. Mr. Johnson and Mr. Hall then set forth these possible options:

Mr. Romney could simply refuse to report to the Governors. This was ruled out because it would violate his original commitment.

He could issue a bland report implying that he still had a chance to spring an upset. This was ruled out because it would violate the truth.

He could tell the truth and, having told it, withdraw. Although the final decision would of course be left to Mr. Romney, both Mr. Hall and Mr. Johnson agreed that this was the wisest course.

A fourth alternative was that the Governor could perhaps give a full report on the current bleak state of his campaign but pledge to go on fighting. Yet both strategists believed that this would simply prolong the agony, and—more important—cut down on the time available to the Governors to rally behind another candidate.

Finally, they agreed that the time had come to present the liberal and moderate Governors with what amounted, in effect, to an ultimatum to coalesce behind a moderate candidate. A pledge by Mr. Romney to continue in the race would relieve the Governors of such an obligation; a statement of withdrawal would force the issue.

Mr. Johnson returned to Hanover, N.H., Monday night. Mr. Hall, meanwhile, called Mr. Romney's secretary and set up a meeting for Tuesday night. By this time Mr. Romney had received the raw data of the poll.

After a dinner of steak and kidney pie at the Ramada Inn, Mr. Hall gathered Mr. Romney's advisers shortly before 9 P.M. in the room occupied by one of Mr. Romney's longtime strategists, Richard Van Dusen. There were four others present: Travis Cross, the Governor's press secretary, Jonathan Moore, his foreign policy adviser, Mr. Johnson, who had flown down from New Hampshire, and Mr. Romney himself, whose suite was only a few paces down the hall.

Mr. Johnson assumed the main burden of setting forth the facts and figures—the "total input"—as well as the alternatives open to Mr. Romney. The Governor listened intently for about an hour, occasionally offering a comment or two.

"He's a great listener," one of his aides said today. "He absorbs everything. That's the tragedy of this thing. His mind is good—very good. And that night it was working well."

Everybody in the room contributed to the discussion—"some with wisdom, others with volume," one participant recalls—but, according to all participants there was little "strong opposition" to the option of immediate withdrawal.

For most of the staff, this was the first time they had openly faced that prospect—but most if not all seemed to sense that this was the only way to escape the humiliation of defeat and—of greater importance—force the party's liberals and moderates into a fresh effort.

Around 10 P.M., Governor Romney, announcing that he would "sleep on it," rose and went to his suite. He authorized the staff to prepare a draft statement of withdrawal. The statement was written by Mr. Van Dusen from a rough draft prepared by Mr. Johnson. The meeting broke up at 12:30 A.M.

There was little discussion that night of the impact of Mr. Romney's withdrawal on other candidates—Richard M. Nixon, for example, or Governor Rockefeller. It was clear to many of the aides, and to Mr. Romney, that withdrawal might blunt the impact of a Nixon victory in New Hampshire and place pressure on Mr. Rockefeller to enter the race.

But the conversation did not focus on these matters. It focused on Mr. Romney's own standing in the polls and the country and on his obligations to the Governors and the future of the party.

The same group gathered in Mr. Romney's suite for eggs and toast at 7:30 the next morning. Mr. Romney announced that he had decided to withdraw. He made a few changes in the statement. And then he relaxed.

> "Rational human beings who do the right thing are usually happy about it," one aide recalls. "Mr. Romney felt he had done the right thing and he was happy. He sensed that he had done something creative in the midst of political chaos."

LIST TO BE TOLD

The group then made a long list of Romney supporters who would be informed of the decision—Max Fisher, for example, the Detroit businessman who had been the chief fund-raiser for the campaign. Mr. Fisher, unaware of what was happening, had gone to Acapulco, Mexico, for a brief rest.

Governor Romney's list included his wife, Lenore, then campaigning in Wisconsin, and Mr. Rockefeller. There have been several reports that Mr. Rockefeller was told of the decision before Wednesday morning but these reports have not been corroborated by any member of the Romney staff.

The lighthearted atmosphere of the final breakfast in the Ramada Inn continued as the rest of the script unfolded. Mr. Romney took care of another scheduled appearance in Boston yesterday morning, flew to Washington and delivered his statement to reporters at 5 P.M. The statement formally removed him from the race. But Mr. Romney seemed almost cheerful as he read it.

Late this afternoon he went to the airport to meet his wife. As he stood in the rain, a woman thrust her way through the crowd and grasped his hand.

"I think you made a wonderful choice," she said. "I think you'll be the next President."

Mr. Romney thrust back his head and roared, "Well, we've had a candidate and a non-candidate and now we have a non-candidate-candidate," he said.

When the jet arrived, all the passengers got off except Mrs. Romney. The Governor bounded up the steps to greet her inside. As he led her into the airport he protected her head with a copy of The Chicago Tribune that an aide had given him. The headline read:

"Romney Quits G.O.P. Race."

# 22

## Jean Heller
## *An Inside View of LBJ's Decision Not To Run*

For five months, Lyndon Baines Johnson waited for the right time, the right setting, the right mood. But today was never the day.

Until March 31.

At 8:58 p.m., the President sat behind his huge mahogany desk in the White House. Bright, hot television lights etched the lines of exhaustion in his face.

His wife, two daughters and a son-in-law sat nearby, tense, waiting. They thought they knew what was coming. But even they could not be sure.

Thirty-six minutes later, Johnson raised his right hand to his head. It was a prearranged signal to his wife.

"There is a division in the American house . . ." the President said.

Across the room, Mrs. Johnson smiled knowingly.

"What we won when all our people were united must not now be lost in suspicion, distrust and selfishness or politics among any of our people," the President said. "Believing this as I do, I have concluded that I should not permit the Presidency to become involved in any partisan divisions that are developing in this political year . . ."

In Mexico City, in the library of the U. S. Ambassador's residence, Vice President Humphrey, for a fleeting moment, looked startled.

Just outside the library, Sen. Wayne Morse stared unbelievingly at a crackling short-wave radio as the voice continued: "Accordingly, I shall not seek and I will not accept the nomination of my party for another term as your President . . ."

The language was simple, the delivery matter-of-fact.

There was no hint of the months of agonizing appraisal that had gone before.

It all began, says [Press Secretary George] Christian, at the LBJ ranch last August when Johnson told his old friend, Gov. John Connally of Texas, that he might not run again.

It was no more definite than that, but over the next three months Johnson discussed the possibility with Mrs. Johnson and mentioned it to then Defense Secretary McNamara.

Still it wasn't until last November, five months ago, that the real agony of decision began.

Early that month, in San Antonio, Christian said Johnson told him that he might retire, and instructed him to go to Austin and discuss phrasing of a withdrawal statement with Connally.

"He didn't have any doubts that he could get the nomination," Christian said. "It was the feeling that the country was becoming more and more divided, that perhaps a new man could take on some of these problems more successfully than he could."

Christian, who remembers little of the session except scribbling notes on a yellow legal tablet, saw Connally on a sunny Saturday afternoon. Connally felt, said the press secretary, that if Johnson were going to withdraw, he should do it soon, on a non-partisan occasion, in a speech directly to the people.

The decision then hinged on finding the situation to meet the criteria.

Connally and Christian agreed the best time might be two months later at the State of the Union message. Johnson seemed to agree, Christian said, but nagging doubts remained: Could a decision not to run again deepen the crisis in Vietnam? How would the troops take such news? How would North Vietnam respond?

Johnson asked his commander in Vietnam, Gen. William Westmoreland. Westmoreland replied that he did not believe the war effort would suffer irreparable damage.

### ANOTHER LEAK

Work on the withdrawal statement began in earnest. Time and again, Johnson, Christian and the President's old friend, Horace Busby, talked about phrasing, time and effect as Johnson edited and discarded proposed drafts.

On Jan. 15, two days before the State of the Union Message, Busby sent Johnson a new draft. Johnson gave it to Christian to combine with earlier statements. He did so in the presence of Christian's assistant, Tom Johnson, thus letting another aide in on the secret.

Together, Christian and Tom Johnson drew up the final version. There were just two copies. One went to the President, the other to Mrs. Johnson.

The morning of the State of the Union message, the President summoned Christian to his bedroom and said he had decided that, if he was to withdraw, he should do so that night. He wanted a few words changed and Christian went to work on it.

When the Johnsons left the White House for the Capitol, the President had a copy of the withdrawal speech in his pocket. But during the one-mile limousine ride, Christian said, the President decided that withdrawing then might hurt chances for passage of legislation he was sending to Capitol Hill. He gave the statement to Mrs. Johnson.

### HAD TO KEEP UP

The next day the statement went back to Christian with orders to update it on a week-by-week basis. For 2½ months, Christian kept it ready for delivery on a moment's notice.

As the days passed, machinery geared to the reelection of the President started up. Convention votes were being lined up. Citizens for Johnson-Humphrey was raising and spending money in Wisconsin and California.

During those 2½ months, Johnson told a few more people that he was considering retirement. Among them were Humphrey, Secretary of State Rusk, and the new Secretary of Defense, Clark Clifford. But none were told definitely when, or if.

By late March the campaign for his reelection was in full swing. He knew if he was going to stop it, said Christian, he had to stop it soon.

The announcement of the de-escalation of the bombing of North Vietnam seemed as close to the perfect time as he would ever get, Christian said, and possibly the last good chance.

### LATE HUDDLE

On Saturday night, Johnson met at the White House with Christian and two special assistants, James Johnes and Marvin Watson. They discussed the decision and left, still unsure if it had finally been made.

They still were not sure at 8:58 Sunday night, when Johnson, from behind his desk, said: "The decision's made. We're going."

He did not say which way.

But Christian recalled, "We were 99 per cent sure that he was going to step out."

In Mexico City, Humphrey and his wife; Ambassador and Mrs. Fulton Freeman, and President and Mrs. Díaz Ordaz retired to the privacy of the library to hear the broadcast.

Outside the Freeman's library, 75 other dinner guests, including Sen. Morse, one of the most vocal critics of Johnson's Vietnam policy, gathered tightly around a second radio.

At 9:34 p.m., Washington time, television viewers saw the President raise his right hand to his temple, and then the bombshell fell.

Almost as one, hands in Mexico City, Chicago, Austin, New Zealand, Washington and New York reached for telephones.

Later in the evening, the President would talk to all of those callers: Humphrey, Chicago Mayor Richard Daley, Connally, Rusk, Senate Majority Leader Mansfield and UN Ambassador Goldberg.

Later in the evening he would get back to the job of being President of the United States for nine months more.

But when he had finished his speech, looking vastly relieved, Lyndon Baines Johnson wordlessly embraced his wife and his daughters and shook hands with son-in-law Patrick Nugent.

Then he and his family walked out of the White House and into the seclusion of the Rose Garden at night.

7

# The Long Arm of the Law

The "long arm of the law" is a phrase usually used to mean that a culprit may expect inevitably to be caught. Unfortunately, most culprits escape the arm of the law. We prefer to use this phrase to mean that the problems of law and law enforcement affect the whole society. The policeman on the beat is the only contact most people have with the law. He is the symbol of law enforcement. Today, the American policeman is caught in a web of difficult circumstances. The courts are proposing an ever tougher set of requirements for observing due process of law in all phases of criminal investigation, arrest, and trial. The violent code of vigilantism that permeates American ideology is stirred up by new forms of social unrest and hostility. The rapid changes in society have tended to break down belief systems and personal relationships and to encourage a large increase in lawlessness of all types. Not only is the policeman's job becoming more difficult, but he is also faced with a great many temptations. He is, after all, on top of all the tangible property in the country, and his desires for "the good life" increase along with everyone else's.

Most policemen come from families of poor or modest circumstances and were brought up under an old world or rural psychology. The limitations imposed by this kind of background on policemen in modern America are obvious. The difficulty is compounded because most local police forces are given little or no training in how to deal with persons other than motorists or hardened criminals. Arthur Niederhoffer discusses the effects on police efficiency of recent Supreme Court decisions upholding the rights of suspects and defendants. He received his law degree in 1939 and then worked as a policeman in New York City for twenty-one years. He is now a Doctor of Sociology and a professor at the John Jay College of Police Science in New York.

The Supreme Court under former Chief Justice Earl Warren was noted for increasing the judicial protection of individual liberties and minority groups. Two such cases are reprinted in this chapter. *Marchetti* vs. *United States* demonstrates this increased emphasis on individual rights. It shows how the Supreme Court may take one view, which seems to be a reasonable one, and then, in a rare step, reverse itself to take an equally reasonable, but pro individual, position. A small federal tax on gambling was designed to smoke out gamblers operating in violation of state and local laws, so that state and local police agencies could get at them on various charges. A man is trapped: he must confess to violating one law in order to obey another or be in violation of both. The Supreme Court, after watching the traps spring in some cases, decided that they should be disassembled for violating the defendant's privilege against self-incrimination. Chief Justice Warren's dissenting opinion is also included below. Which opinion do you agree with? Where do you think the line should be drawn between the rights of society to enforce its laws and the rights of the individual?

The second case, *In Re Gault*, extended to juveniles many of the rights that adult defendants had long enjoyed. When the juvenile courts were established, they were to act in the interests of the child as a good parent would if the child's parents were not acting as "good parents" as defined by the law. Gerald Gault, with the juvenile court playing the role of inquisitor father, was imprisoned in 1964 for three years for an offense carrying a maximum of two months imprisonment if committed by an adult.

In 1967 the Supreme Court ruled in *In Re Gault* that,

> We now hold that, absent a valid confession, a determination of delinquency and an order of commitment . . . cannot be sustained in the absence of sworn testimony subjected to the opportunity for cross-examination in accordance with our law and constitutional requirements.

Thirty years ago Dean Roscoe Pound wrote that the powers of the Star Chamber were a trifle in comparison with those of our juvenile courts. Juvenile judges have long played the role of "philosopher king." The Gault case concluded that children have the same legal protections under the Constitution as do adults and that no judge in the American democratic system is wise enough to play the role of "philosopher king" without the procedural safeguards afforded by the Constitution. Do you agree? Or do you think juveniles could be better handled by a friendly father figure in the person of a juvenile judge?

The first three selections deal with individual rights in courts of law. Today these rights are being demanded in other areas of society as well. Not only minorities and the young are becoming subject to due process of law requirements. Soldiers, who were once beyond the pale of law, and employees of large corporations, who were for a long time considered to work and to be disciplined only at the will of the boss, are now demanding the same rights. William M. Evan, professor of sociology at the University of Pennsylvania, discusses the provisions for due process in military and industrial organizations. All kinds of ideas about participatory democracy, self-government, and reform are also being introduced in churches and schools, especially the colleges. What do you think will be the effects of this trend?

The last two selections in this chapter discuss the lawmaking process. Congress makes laws within the limits established by the Constitution. The Supreme Court, which interprets the Constitution and can declare laws unconstitutional, delineates the limits for Congress. For many years acts of Congress which attempted to regulate the economy or promote the general welfare were declared unconstitutional on the grounds that they violated superior individual or corporate property rights. During the Depression of the 1930's, this trend was reversed, and the Court began to declare such laws constitutional. The commerce clause of the Constitution furnished the basis for many of these actions. Over the years, the meaning of this clause has been extended to cover all kinds of industrial and commercial operations that at one time were thought to be the province only of the state governments. Now, in the fifth selection below, we hear the argument of Professor Newton Morton that the commerce clause has no effect today in limiting the power of the national government. Lawmakers, practically speaking, need not concern themselves with the distinction. Any statute, no matter how remote, has some effect somewhere upon interstate commerce, and therefore Congress has sufficient constitutional authority to regulate any activity whatsoever. Consequently, there is no state sovereignty over any part of commerce and no federalism so far as the law is concerned in this area. There is only what Congress may decide to leave to the states. This article, which describes how a constitutional clause has been stretched over 150 years until it has no bounds, shows how the courts make law. When the Constitution is stretched, it usually means that government is stretched accordingly. The question arises whether the Constitution has been stretched beyond recognition, and if so, so what?

The power of the Supreme Court to define the Constitution has meant that Presidents and senators have attempted to see that men who favor their political ideology are appointed to the Court. To this end, they have attempted on various occasions to set up requirements for men to be eligible to serve on the Court. The nation was treated recently to heated arguments over the qualifications of nominees to the Supreme Court when President Nixon failed twice in a row to have "strict constructionists" who lacked a "good civil rights record" approved by the Senate. S. Sidney Ulmer, a professor of political science at the University of Kentucky, is proposing studies to determine the relationship between formal requirements that are being sought and the subsequent behavior of judges. The information obtained would be useful to Congress and the President in setting standards for judicial appointment. What standards would you propose for appointees to the Supreme Court?

# 23

## Arthur Niederhoffer
## *The Police and the Supreme Court*

In their official policy statements police administrators oppose third-degree methods. Unofficially, a time-honored occupational ideology, with which probably half the force agrees, excuses the use of force to make suspects "talk." According to this social myth the legal system affords too much protection to evildoers and hamstrings the forces of law and order. Therefore, the police must overcome this handicap with the only measures available to them.

The police want to win both ways. Offensively, they proclaim that with legal cooperation, they could handle the burgeoning crime wave. Defensively, they try to avoid responsibility by pointing out that crime is, after all, a social problem whose complexities are beyond their control. Yale Kamisar, professor of law at the University of Michigan, explains why the police hold these contradictory views.

> The police fear—and not without cause—that the public will blame them for the increase in crime. . . .
>
> But no police force can "put a stop to it." The men on the "firing line" do not greatly affect the crime rate—nor do the courts.

Kamisar also notes that David Acheson, prosecutor of Washington, D.C., does not think that the police could reduce crime if the Supreme Court gave them more leeway. Acheson has said that

> Changes in court decisions and prosecution procedures would have

> about the same effect on the crime rate as an aspirin would have on a tumor of the brain.

Even sociologists, generally liberal reformers, cannot agree to condemn the police use of force. One sociologist overstates the police handicap by concluding that the "police have no legal ways in which they can question suspects, so naturally they use illegal ones." Prominent criminologists such as the late Edwin H. Sutherland and Donald R. Cressey adopt a similar point of view.

> The American policeman is in a difficult position, for in order to do his work efficiently he must adopt more power than the law and the formal organization of his department permit. He is responsible for the enforcement of the criminal law and for the maintenance of order, yet he cannot meet these responsibilities under the power and authority granted him.
>
> Among students of the subject there is almost unanimous agreement that the criminal law and criminal procedure are inadequate for the purpose of controlling crime and administering justice.

The above argument fallaciously assumes that the police use of illegal methods necessarily results from legal restrictions on their power. Westley has demonstrated that police brutality depends on a value system that, for extra-legal reasons, and not the difficulty of obtaining evidence, condones the rough treatment of cop-fighters and sexual criminals.

There is no evidence that cop-fighters or sexual criminals, and not other offenders, require excessive force at any time during which they are in custody and the police are preparing the prosecution. It is true that for many sexual crimes some corroboration is necessary to convict the defendant. But this evidence may be of any nature, not necessarily a confession by the prisoner.

Until 1964 there were available to the police many legitimate methods of interrogating suspects before and after arrest, and many scientific instruments such as lie detectors, drunkometers, computers, and special equipment for chemical and physical tests, to supplement the questioner's efforts. What often stymied the policeman was the suspect's right to remain silent. The rich suspect with a lawyer usually did so; it was the poor man without counsel who talked or was made to talk. In 1964 this traditional privilege of the well-to-do was extended to the indigent. The Escobedo case established the right to counsel when a man became a suspect in a police investigation. In 1966 the Supreme Court in *Miranda v. Arizona* clarified a moot point, holding that the police were obligated to inform all persons in custody of their right to remain silent, and their right to the presence and assistance of counsel, which would be provided without charge to indigent prisoners.

Sutherland and Cressey state above that students of the subject almost unanimously find criminal law and procedure inadequate to control crime. I would contend, on the contrary, that there is vast disagreement on the efficacy of the law, judging by reports from newspapers, courts, law schools, and law-enforcement agencies. Naturally, thousands of prisoners believe the law to be fearfully adequate.

Many major prisons have had to establish at least a rudimentary law library to satisfy the demands of inmates who want to find some flaw in criminal law and procedure that will win them a new trial. Victims of police prejudice and brutality, as well as the civil rights experts who seek justice for them, form another group dissatisfied with the criminal law because it gives the police too much, not too little, power. Judges, lawyers, and political scientists constitute another set of students who do not unanimously agree that law enforcement is severely hampered by the law.

Although this dispute has been seething for decades, a series of Supreme Court decisions in favor of convicted defendants and against the police and the prosecutors have brought the question to a head. A brief synopsis of some significant cases will clarify the points at issue.

### MALLORY V. UNITED STATES, 354 U.S. 449 (1957)

In Washington, D. C., Mallory, a nineteen-year-old youth of limited intelligence, was arrested on a charge of rape, detained at police headquarters but not arraigned although several magistrates in session could have heard the case. After hours of fruitless interrogation the police asked the defendant to submit to a lie detector test. They did not tell him of his rights to remain silent, to have the assistance of counsel, and to appear before a magistrate, but examined him with the lie detector for an hour and a half before obtaining a confession. Only then did they arraign him. The Supreme Court reversed his conviction by the lower court principally because of the delay in arraigning the prisoner. The court strictly limited the time for interrogating prisoners, reasoning as follows:

> We cannot sanction this extended delay, resulting in confession, without subordinating the general rule of prompt arraignment to the discretion of arresting officers in finding exceptional circumstances for its disregard. In every case where the police resort to interrogation of an arrested person and secure a confession, they may well claim, and quite sincerely, that they were merely trying to check on the information given by him.
>
> Presumably, whenever the police arrest they must arrest on "probable cause." It is not the function of the police to arrest, as it were, at large and to use an interrogating process at police headquarters in order to determine whom they should charge before a committing magistrate on "probable cause."

The Mallory case was combined with an earlier decision from *McNabb v. United States*, 318 U.S. 332 (1943), to establish the well-known McNabb-Mallory rule that requires the police to arraign a prisoner in federal courts without unnecessary delay. Although this decision was not binding on state courts, it did cause consternation among local police jurisdictions because it threatened to eliminate a traditional police *modus operandi* for solving cases—extended interrogation of suspects prior to arraignment.

### SPANO V. NEW YORK,
### 360 U.S. 315 (1959)

Spano was indicted for shooting and killing a man who had previously assaulted him in a barroom brawl. He surrendered to the district attorney and, upon the advice of his attorney, who left him in the custody of several law-enforcement officers, refused to answer any questions. Six officers questioned him from 7:15 P.M. until after midnight when he was transferred to a police station house where the interrogation continued.

A probationary patrolman, Bruno, who knew Spano, entreated him to talk, pretending that this was the only way to save Bruno's job. Finally, the prisoner confessed and was convicted and sentenced to death in the state courts.

The Supreme Court reversed the conviction, holding that although no physical force was employed, the confession was, nevertheless involuntary. This decision affirms the principle that police may not use psychological pressure and fatigue to gain a confession from a prisoner.

### MAPP V. OHIO,
### 367 U.S. 643 (1961)

The police heard that Dollree Mapp was concealing in her home a large amount of gambling paraphernalia and a person wanted in connection with a bombing. Miss Mapp refused to admit the police officers without a search warrant. About three hours later the police returned and forcibly broke into the house. When she demanded to see the warrant, one of the officers waved a paper in her face which Miss Mapp grabbed and placed in her bosom. A struggle ensued during which the officer recovered the paper and handcuffed the appellant presumably because she had been belligerent. After forcing her upstairs to the bedroom, the officers searched the house thoroughly. In the basement they found some obsene material, for possession of which the appellant was convicted in the Ohio courts.

The Supreme Court reversed the conviction and established for state as well as federal courts the doctrine that illegally seized materials could not be admitted as evidence. Up to this point state courts had not excluded evidence illegally seized by state or city policemen. On the question of whether or not this decision would impair the quality and efficiency of law enforcement, the Supreme Court cited approvingly this excerpt from *Miller v. United States,* 357 U.S. 301 (1957).

> However much in a particular case insistence upon such rules may appear as a technicality that inures to the benefit of a guilty person, the history of the criminal law proves that tolerance of shortcut methods in law enforcement impairs its enduring effectiveness.

The court also pointed to the FBI that from its inception has operated on this principle.

> Yet it has not been suggested either that the Federal Bureau of Investigation has thereby been rendered ineffective, or that the administration of criminal justice in the federal courts has thereby been disrupted.

### ESCOBEDO V. ILLINOIS, 378 U.S. 478 (1964)

Escobedo is an extension of the famous case of *Gideon v. Wainwright,* 372 U.S. 335 (1963), in which the court held that every defendant in a felony case has the right to be represented by counsel in court even though he cannot pay the fees. Escobedo was being questioned at the station house in connection with a murder. The police did not inform him of his right to remain silent, and they would not allow him to speak with his attorney, who was at the station house. A policeman friend of the prisoner urged him to talk, promising that he could go home afterward. On the basis of his revelations Escobedo was indicted for the killing and convicted.

The Supreme Court reversed the conviction and extended the Gideon doctrine from the court to the station house, holding that even during the preliminary investigation

> when the process shifts from investigatory to accusatory—when its focus is on the accused and its purpose is to elicit a confession—our adversary system begins to operate, and, under the circumstances here, the accused must be permitted to consult with his lawyer.

These last two cases, Mapp and Escobedo, have become *causes célèbres.* The Mapp case produced a frantic torrent of complaints from outraged police who felt they were being deprived of their legal right to search for and obtain evidence, but the Escobedo ruling was nearly as unpopular. Professor Fred Inbau of Northwestern University Law School described it as the "hardest body blow the court has struck yet against enforcement of law in the nation." The Escobedo case has generated a nationwide debate over confessions. Among supporters of the police and critics of the Supreme Court are former Attorney General Nicholas deB. Katzenbach, Professor Inbau, and New York District Attorney Frank Hogan; on the side of the Supreme Court, Judge David L. Bazelon of the United States Court of Appeals for the District of Columbia and Professor Kamisar. Professor Kamisar's defense of the Mapp decision applies equally well to the Escobedo case:

> What law-enforcement officers were really bristling about was tighter enforcement of long standing restrictions. Not Mapp, but state and federal constitutional provisions that had been on the books for decades, banned arbitrary arrests and unreasonable searches. The police never had

> the authority to proceed without "probable cause," only the incentive. And the principal contribution of Mapp was to reduce that incentive.

In much the same spirit Donald C. Dowling, a National Defender Fellow at the University of Chicago Law School for 1964-1965, spoke for the Escobedo ruling

> In deciding Escobedo, contrary to some popular belief, the Supreme Court did not hold a wake for policemen; it did not bury the confession; nor did it alter basic principles of law enforcement. The decision did take up some of the slack which some police have heretofore enjoyed in the interrogation of criminal subjects.

The Sixth Amendment states that "In all criminal prosecutions, the accused shall enjoy the right . . . to have the Assistance of Counsel for his defense." The logic of the Supreme Court is to confer this protection upon defendants in state trials as well as federal trials, and to make it meaningful, instead of a sham. To accomplish this the majority of the court deemed it necessary to protect the accused at every stage of the proceeding. In Gideon the right to counsel during the actual trial was affirmed. In Spano a strong concurring opinion by Justice Douglas, joined by Justices Black and Brennan and supported by Justice Stewart, held that the real violation of constitutional rights was the refusal of the police to allow the accused, after indictment and awaiting trial, to confer with his lawyer. The Escobedo case in 1964 extended the right to counsel all the way back to the point when the police investigative effort shifts from investigatory to accusatory; in other words, a person in custody has the right to consult with counsel when he stops being merely a witness and becomes a suspect. On June 13, 1966 the Supreme Court carried the doctrine to its logical end in the case of *Miranda v. Arizona,* 384 U.S. 436 (1966). They held, in effect, that as soon as the police take a person into custody they must warn him of his right to remain silent and to have a lawyer, for whom the state will pay the fee if the person in custody cannot afford it. Oddly enough, the ground of this decision was not the Sixth Amendment, which guarantees the right to counsel, but the Fifth Amendment which protects against self-incrimination.

If Escobedo caused consternation among law-enforcement agencies, imagine their reaction to *Miranda v. Arizona.* It will cause no surprise to the reader to learn that proponents, both for and against the Supreme Court decisions, can cite "facts" to support their positions. For example, in analyzing one thousand consecutive indictments in Brooklyn from February through April 1965, New York Supreme Court Justice Nathan R. Sobel found that fewer than ten per cent involved official confessions made to the police. From this data, his twenty years of experience on the bench, and discussions with other judges, Judge Sobel drew the following conclusion:

> Confessions do not affect the crime rate by more than one one-hundredth of 1 per cent, and they do not affect the clearance (solving) of crime by more than one per cent.

In another study of the court system in New York City, Abraham S. Blumberg reports that in the period from 1962 through 1964, of a random sample of 724 male defendants who pleaded guilty to felony charges, fewer than six per cent had made confessions to the police. The 724 defendants were asked who influenced them most in the final decision to plead guilty. Only four placed the responsibility upon the police, whereas 411 indicated that they were following the advice of their own defense counsel. It is Blumberg's view (and one with which I agree) that the national debate over Escobedo reflects a false ideological perception of criminal proceedings. The focus of interest ought to be the bureaucratic structure of the court where more than ninety per cent of the convictions are negotiated by defense lawyers within an institutionalized setting of bargain justice.

According to police officials and prosecutors, however, official confessions are not the only type necessary to police work. They maintain that seventy-five to eighty per cent of the convictions for major crimes rest on preliminary questioning that produces clues for further investigation.

If Mapp, Escobedo, and other decisions have had the effect about which police complain so bitterly, statistics of arrests, prosecutions, and convictions, prepared and submitted by the police themselves, ought to reveal some impairment of efficiency. Table I shows that in 1950, before any of these cases became law, police efficiency as measured by these traditional yardsticks was lower than it was after 1959 when Spano and other Supreme Court decisions began to restrict the police. Assuming the validity of these figures, one can conclude from the absence of gross

**TABLE I** A MEASURE OF POLICE PERFORMANCE

| | 1950 | 1959 | 1960 | 1961 | 1962 | 1963 | 1964 | 1965 |
|---|---|---|---|---|---|---|---|---|
| Per cent of the known major offenses cleared by arrest *by Police in the United States* | 15.3 | 27.1 | 26.1 | 26.7 | 25.7 | 25.1 | 24.5 | 24.6 |
| Per cent of the known major offenses held for prosecution in court *by Police in the United States* | 12.0 | 20.5 | 19.8 | 20.8 | 21.7 | 20.9 | 19.6 | 19.3 |
| Per cent of defendants convicted in court as reported *by Police in the United States* | 53.8 | 75.4 | 76.3 | 68.7 | 76.1 | 72.0 | 71.1 | 70.2 |
| Per cent of the known felonies cleared by arrest *by the New York City Police Department* | * | 35.2 | 34.5 | 35.3 | 35.5 | 34.9 | 33.9 | 34.5 |

SOURCE: *FBI Uniform Crime Reports*—1950, p. 14, Chart 8. 1959, pp. 81, 84. 1960, pp. 83, 86. 1961, pp. 83, 86. 1962, pp. 84, 87. 1963, pp. 93, 97. 1964, pp. 95, 101. 1965, pp. 97, 103. *New York City Police Department Annual Reports, 1959–1965.*

* The New York City Police Department's figure for the year 1950 is not entered because in that year there was a change in the method of reporting, and the police department's crime statistics were so unreliable that the FBI refused to accept them for inclusion in the *Uniform Crime Reports*. See Paul W. Tappan, *Crime, Justice and Correction* (New York: McGraw-Hill Book Co., Inc., 1960), p. 36, footnote 3.

variations in any year after 1959, that the Supreme Court scarcely disturbed the even tenor of police work.

The Miranda doctrine will undoubtedly put more lawyers into the police stations to protect the rights of their clients from the very inception of police custody, and some confessions will be blocked, although it will be a very small number when compared to the total volume of cases. In a fair proportion of these cases the lawyer himself will see to it that his client pleads guilty in court. In all cases the police will be forced to improve their technique in order to gather proof of the charges without recourse to a confession. One great benefit will be to reduce the temptation to resort to illegal third degree tactics and thus to purge the police of a cardinal sin. Police practice under the Miranda rule will be routinized; the impact on arrest and conviction rates will be negligible. Any department worthy of being called professional will meet this challenge successfully and emerge the stronger for it. Within two months of the decision, evidence is accumulating to bear out this forecast, as "the police authorities of fourteen major cities conceded that it would not affect their procedures."[1]

To revert once more to our central theme, the real threat is not the shackling of law enforcement, but the probable reinforcement of cynicism among policemen. Each new reversal of hallowed legal principles upon which the code of police work rests, strips some of the majesty from the body of the law until at last the law becomes an emperor without clothes.

[1] Editorial in the New York *Times*, August 15, 1966, p. 26. Further corroboration for this point of view appeared in surveys conducted in Los Angeles and Detroit. As in the studies conducted by Judge Sobel and Blumberg, confessions to police were necessary for conviction in less than ten per cent of the cases, and "moreover, suspects are confessing despite advice by the police that they may remain silent and have free legal counsel if they are indigent." See New York *Times*, August 19, 1966, p. 20.

Ironically, despite their public protestations, in New York City detectives and commanding officers are secretly very pleased with the new state of affairs. Before these decisions higher authority always demanded better arrest and conviction rates, and no excuses could satisfy them. Now there is a perfect explanation for lower arrest and conviction rates—the necessity of observing all the safeguards and rights surrounding the suspect. This takes a great deal of pressure off them.

# 24

# A Tax on Illegality May Be Illegal: *Marchetti* vs *United States*

Mr. Justice Harlan delivered the opinion of the Court.

Petitioner was convicted in the United States District Court for the District of Connecticut under two indictments which charged violations of the federal wagering tax statutes. The first indictment averred that petitioner and others conspired to evade payment of the annual occupational tax imposed by 26 U. S. C. § 4411. The second indictment included two counts: the first alleged a willful failure to pay the occupational tax, and the second a willful failure to register, as required by 26 U. S. C. § 4412, before engaging in the business of accepting wagers.

After verdict, petitioner unsuccessfully sought to arrest judgment, in part on the basis that the statutory obligations to register and to pay the occupational tax violated his Fifth Amendment privilege against self-incrimination. The Court of Appeals for the Second Circuit affirmed on the authority of *United States v. Kahriger,* and *Lewis v. United States.*

We granted certiorari to re-examine the constitutionality under the Fifth Amendment of the pertinent provisions of the wagering tax statutes, and more particularly to consider whether *Kahriger* and *Lewis* still have vitality. For reasons which follow, we have concluded that these provisions may not be employed to punish criminally those persons who have defended a failure to comply with their requirements with a proper assertion of the privilege against self-incrimination. The judgment below is accordingly reversed.

## I.

The provisions in issue here are part of an interrelated statutory system for taxing wagers. The system is broadly as follows. Section 4401 of Title 26 imposes upon those engaged in the business of accepting wagers an excise tax of 10% on the gross amount of all wagers they accept, including the value of chances purchased in lotteries conducted for profit. Parimutuel wagering enterprises, coin-operated devices, and state-conducted sweepstakes are expressly excluded from taxation. Section 4411 imposes in addition an occupational tax of $50 annually, both upon those subject to taxation under § 4401 and upon those who receive wagers on their behalf.

The taxes are supplemented by ancillary provisions calculated to assure their collection. In particular, § 4412 requires those liable for the occupational tax to register each year with the director of their local internal revenue district. The registrants must submit Internal Revenue Service Form 11–C, and upon it must provide their residence and business addresses, must indicate whether they are engaged in the business of accepting wagers, and must list the names and addresses of their agents and employees. The statutory obligations to register and to pay the occupational tax are essentially inseparable elements of a single registration procedure; Form 11–C thus constitutes both the application for registration and the return for the occupational tax.

In addition, registrants are obliged to post the revenue stamps which denote payment of the occupational tax "conspicuously" in their principal places of business, or, if they lack such places, to keep the stamps on their persons, and to exhibit them upon demand to any Treasury officer. They are required to preserve daily records indicating the gross amount of the wagers as to which they are liable for taxation, and to permit inspection of their books of account. Moreover, each principal internal revenue office is instructed to maintain for public inspection a listing of all who have paid the occupational tax, and to provide certified copies of the listing upon request to any state or local prosecuting officer. Finally, payment of the wagering taxes is declared not to "exempt any person from any penalty provided by a law of the United States or of any State for engaging" in any taxable activity.

II.

The issue before us is *not* whether the United States may tax activities which a State or Congress has declared unlawful. The Court has repeatedly indicated that the unlawfulness of an activity does not prevent its taxation, and nothing that follows is intended to limit or diminish the vitality of those cases. See, *e.g., License Tax Cases.* The issue is instead whether the methods employed by Congress in the federal wagering tax statutes are, in this situation, consistent with the limitations created by the privilege against self-incrimination guaranteed by the Fifth Amendment. We must for this purpose first examine the implications of these statutory provisions.

Wagering and its ancillary activities are very widely prohibited under federal and state law. Federal statutes impose criminal penalties upon the interstate transmission of wagering information, upon interstate and foreign travel or transportation in aid of racketeering enterprises, defined to include gambling; upon lotteries conducted through use of the mails or broadcasting; and upon the interstate transportation of wagering paraphernalia.

State and local enactments are more comprehensive. The laws of every State, except Nevada, include broad prohibitions against gambling, wagering, and associated activities. Every State forbids, with essentially minor and carefully circumscribed exceptions, lotteries. Even Nevada, which permits many forms of gambling, retains criminal penalties upon lotteries and certain other wagering activities taxable under these statutes.

Connecticut, in which petitioner allegedly conducted his activities, has adopted a variety of measures for the punishment of gambling and wagering. It punishes "[a]ny person, whether as principal, agent or servant, who owns, possesses, keeps, manages, maintains or occupies" premises employed for purposes of wagering or pool selling. It imposes criminal penalties upon any person who possesses, keeps, or maintains premises in which policy playing occurs, or lotteries are conducted, and upon any person who becomes the custodian of books, property, appliances, or apparatus employed for wagering. It provides additional penalties for those who conspire to organize or conduct unlawful wagering activities. Every aspect of petitioner's wagering activities thus subjected him to possible state or federal prosecution. By any standard, in Connecticut and throughout the United States, wagering is "an area permeated with criminal statutes," and those engaged in wagering are a group "inherently suspect of criminal activities."

Information obtained as a consequence of the federal wagering tax laws is readily available to assist the efforts of state and federal authorities to enforce these penalties. Section 6107 of Title 26 requires the principal internal revenue offices to provide to prosecuting officers a listing of those who have paid the occupational tax. Section 6806(c) obliges taxpayers either to post the revenue stamp "conspicuously" in their principal places of business, or to keep it on their persons, and to produce it on the demand of Treasury officers. Evidence of the possession of a federal wagering tax stamp, or of payment of the wagering taxes, has often been admitted at trial in state and federal prosecutions for gambling offenses; such evidence has doubtless proved useful even more frequently to lead prosecuting authorities to other evidence upon which convictions have subsequently been obtained. Finally, we are obliged to notice that a former Commissioner of Internal Revenue has acknowledged that the Service "makes available" to law enforcement agencies the names and addresses of those who have paid the wagering taxes, and that it is in "full cooperation" with the efforts of the Attorney General of the United States to suppress organized gambling.

In these circumstances, it can scarcely be denied that the obligations to register and to pay the occupational tax created for petitioner "real and appreciable," and not merely "imaginary and unsubstantial," hazards of self-incrimination. Petitioner was confronted by a comprehensive system of federal and state prohibitions against wagering activities; he was required, on pain of criminal prosecution, to provide information which he might reasonably suppose would be available to prosecuting authorities, and which would surely prove a significant "link in a chain" of evidence tending to establish his guilt. Unlike the income tax return in question in *United States v. Sullivan,* every portion of these requirements had the direct and unmistakable consequence of incriminating petitioner; the application of the constitutional privilege to the entire registration procedure was in this instance neither "extreme" nor "extravagant." It would appear to follow that petitioner's assertion of the privilege as a defense to this prosecution was entirely proper, and accordingly should have sufficed to prevent his conviction.

Nonetheless, this Court has twice concluded that the privilege against self-incrimination may not appropriately be asserted by those in petitioner's circumstances. *United States v. Kahriger, supra; Lewis v. United States, supra.* We must therefore consider whether those cases have continuing force in light of our more recent decisions. Moreover, we must also consider the relevance of certain collateral lines of authority; in particular, we must determine whether either the "required records" doctrine, *Shapiro v. United States,* or restrictions placed upon the use by prosecuting authorities of information obtained as a consequence of the wagering taxes, cf. *Murphy v. Waterfront Commission,* should be utilized to preclude assertion of the constitutional privilege in this situation. To these questions we turn.

III.

The Court's opinion in *Kahriger* suggested that a defendant under indictment for willful failure to register under § 4412 cannot properly challenge the constitutionality under the Fifth Amendment of the registration requirement. For this point, the Court relied entirely upon Mr. Justice Holmes' opinion for the Court in *United States v. Sullivan, supra.* The taxpayer in Sullivan was convicted of willful failure to file an income tax return, despite his contention that the return would have obliged him to admit violations of the National Prohibition Act. The Court affirmed the conviction, and rejected the taxpayer's claim of the privilege. It concluded that most of the return's questions would not have compelled the taxpayer to make incriminating disclosures, and that it would have been "an extreme if not an extravagant application" of the privilege to permit him to draw within it the entire return.

The Court in *Sullivan* was evidently concerned, first, that the claim before it was an unwarranted extension of the scope of the privilege, and, second, that to accept a claim of privilege not asserted at the time the return was due would "make the taxpayer rather than a tribunal the final arbiter of the merits of the claim." *Albertson v. SACB.* Neither reason suffices to prevent this petitioner's assertion of the privilege. The first is, as we have indicated, inapplicable, and we find the second unpersuasive in this situation. Every element of these requirements would have served to incriminate petitioner; to have required him to present his claim to Treasury officers would have obliged him "to prove guilt to avoid admitting it." *United States v. Kahriger, supra.* In these circumstances, we cannot conclude that his failure to assert the privilege to Treasury officials at the moment the tax payments were due irretrievably abandoned his constitutional protection. Petitioner is under sentence for violation of statutory requirements which he consistently asserted at and after trial to be unconstitutional; no more can here be required.

The Court held in *Lewis* that the registration and occupational tax requirements do not infringe the constitutional privilege because they do not compel self-incrimination, but merely impose on the gambler the initial choice of whether he wishes, at the cost of his constitutional privilege, to commence wagering activities. The Court reasoned that even if the required disclosures might prove incriminating, the gambler need not register or pay the occupational tax if only he elects to cease, or never to begin, gambling. There is, the Court said, "no constitutional right to gamble."

We find this reasoning no longer persuasive. The question is not whether petitioner holds a "right" to violate state law, but whether, having done so, he may be compelled to give evidence against himself. The constitutional privilege was intended to shield the guilty and imprudent as well as the innocent and foresighted; if such an inference of antecedent choice were alone enough to abrogate the privilege's protection, it would be excluded from the situations in which it has historically been guaranteed, and withheld from those who most require it. Such inferences, bottomed on what must ordinarily be a fiction, have precisely the infirmities which the Court has found in other circumstances in which implied or uninformed waivers of the privilege have been said to have occurred. To give credence to such "waivers" without the most deliberate examination of the circumstances surrounding them would ultimately license widespread erosion of the privilege through "ingeniously drawn legislation." Morgan, The Privilege against Self-Incrimination, 34 Minn. L. Rev. 1, 37. We cannot agree that the constitutional privilege is meaningfully waived merely because those "inherently suspect of criminal activities" have been commanded either to cease wagering or to provide information incriminating to themselves, and have ultimately elected to do neither.

The Court held in both *Kahriger* and *Lewis* that the registration and occupational tax requirements are entirely prospective in their application, and that the constitutional privilege, since it offers protection only as to past and present acts, is accordingly unavailable. This reasoning appears to us twice deficient: first, it overlooks the hazards here of incrimination as to past or present acts; and second, it is hinged upon an excessively narrow view of the scope of the constitutional privilege.

Substantial hazards of incrimination as to past or present acts plainly may stem from the requirements to register and to pay the occupational tax. See generally McKee, The Fifth Amendment and the Federal Gambling Tax. In the first place, satisfaction of those requirements increases the likelihood that any past or present gambling offenses will be discovered and successfully prosecuted. It both centers attention upon the registrant as a gambler, and compels "injurious disclosure[s]" which may provide or assist in the collection of evidence admissible in a prosecution for past or present offenses. These offenses need not include actual gambling; they might involve only the custody or transportation of gambling paraphernalia, or other preparations for future gambling. Further, the acquisition of a federal gambling tax stamp, requiring as it does the declaration of a present intent to commence gambling activities, obliges even a prospective gambler to accuse himself of conspiracy to violate either state gambling prohibitions, or federal laws forbidding the use of interstate facilities for gambling purposes.

There is a second, and more fundamental, deficiency in the reasoning of *Kahriger* and *Lewis*. Its linchpin is plainly the premise that the privilege is entirely inapplicable to prospective acts; . . . . We see no warrant for so rigorous a constraint upon the constitutional privilege. History, to be sure, offers no ready illustrations of the privilege's application to prospective acts, but the occasions on which such claims might appropriately have been made must necessarily have been very infrequent. We are, in any event, bid to view the constitutional commands as "organic living institutions," whose significance is "vital not formal."

The central standard for the privilege's application has been whether the claimant is confronted by substantial and "real," and not merely trifling or imaginary, hazards of incrimination. We see no reason to suppose that the force of the constitutional prohibition is diminished merely because confession of a guilty purpose precedes the act which it is subsequently employed to evidence. Yet, if the factual situations in which the privilege may be claimed were inflexibly defined by a chronological formula, the policies which the constitutional privilege is intended to serve could easily be evaded. Moreover, although prospective acts will doubtless ordinarily involve only speculative and insubstantial risks of incrimination, this will scarcely always prove true. As we shall show, it is not true here. We conclude that it is not mere time to which the law must look, but the substantiality of the risks of incrimination.

The hazards of incrimination created by § § 4411 and 4412 as to future acts are not trifling or imaginary. Prospective registrants can reasonably expect that registration and payment of the occupational tax will significantly enhance the likelihood of their prosecution for future acts, and that it will readily provide evidence which will facilitate their convictions. Indeed, they can reasonably fear that registration, and acquisition of a wagering tax stamp, may serve as decisive evidence that they have in fact subsequently violated state gambling prohibitions. . . .

We conclude that nothing in the Court's opinions in *Kahriger* and *Lewis* now suffices to preclude petitioner's assertion of the constitutional privilege as a defense to the indictments under which he was convicted. To this extent *Kahriger* and *Lewis* are overruled. . . .

V.

Finally, we have been urged by the United States to permit continued enforcement of the registration and occupational tax provisions, despite the demands of the constitutional privilege, by shielding the privilege's claimants through the imposition of restrictions upon the use by federal and state authorities of information obtained as a consequence of compliance with the wagering tax requirements. It is suggested that these restrictions might be similar to those imposed by the Court in *Murphy v. Waterfront Commission.*

The Constitution of course obliges this Court to give full recognition to the taxing powers and to measures reasonably incidental to their exercise. But we are equally obliged to give full effect to the constitutional restrictions which attend the exercise of those powers. We do not, as we have said, doubt Congress' power to tax activities which are, wholly or in part, unlawful. Nor can it be doubted that the privilege against self-incrimination may not properly be asserted if other protection is granted which "is so broad as to have the same extent in scope and effect" as the privilege itself. *Counselman v. Hitchcock.* The Government's suggestion is thus in principle an attractive and apparently practical resolution of the difficult problem before us. . . . Nonetheless, we think that it would be entirely inappropriate in the circumstances here for the Court to impose such restrictions.

The terms of the wagering tax system make quite plain that Congress intended information obtained as a consequence of registration and payment of the occupational tax to be provided to interested prosecuting authorities. See 26 U. S. C. §6107. This has evidently been the consistent practice of the Revenue Service. We must therefore assume that the imposition of use-restrictions would directly preclude effectuation of a significant element of Congress' purposes in adopting the wagering taxes. Moreover, the imposition of such restrictions would necessarily oblige state prosecuting authorities to establish in each case that their evidence was untainted by any connection with information obtained as a consequence of the wagering taxes; the federal requirements would thus be protected only at the cost of hampering, perhaps seriously, enforcement of state prohibitions against gambling. We cannot know how Congress would assess the competing demands of the federal treasury and of state gambling prohibitions; we are, however, entirely certain that the Constitution has entrusted to Congress, and not to this Court, the task of striking an appropriate balance among such values. We therefore must decide that it would be improper for the Court to impose restrictions of the kind urged by the United States.

VI.

We are fully cognizant of the importance for the United States' various fiscal and regulatory functions of timely and accurate information. . . . Accordingly, nothing we do today will prevent either the taxation or the regulation by Congress of activities otherwise made unlawful by state or federal statutes.

Nonetheless, we can only conclude, under the wagering tax system as presently written, that petitioner properly asserted the privilege against self-incrimination, and that his assertion should have provided a complete defense to this prosecution. . . . If, in different circumstances, a taxpayer is not confronted by substantial hazards of self-incrimination, or if he is otherwise outside the privilege's protection, nothing we decide today would shield him from the various penalties prescribed by the wagering tax statutes.

The judgment of the Court of Appeals is

*Reversed.*

Mr. Chief Justice Warren, dissenting.

The Court today strikes down as unconstitutional a statutory scheme enacted by Congress to make effective and enforceable taxes imposed on wagers and the occupation of gambling. In so doing, it of necessity overrules *United States v. Kahriger* (1953), and *Lewis v. United States* (1955). I cannot agree with the Court's conclusion on the constitutional questions presented, and I would affirm the convictions in these two cases on the authority of *Kahriger* and *Lewis.*

In addition to being in disagreement with the Court on the result it reaches in these cases, I am puzzled by the reasoning process which leads it to that result. The Court professes to recognize and accept the power of Congress legitimately to impose taxes on activities which have been declared unlawful by federal or state statutes. Yet, by its sweeping declaration that the congressional scheme for enforcing and collecting the taxes imposed on wagers and gamblers is unconstitutional, the Court has stripped from Congress the power to make its taxing scheme effective. A reading of the registration requirement of 26 U. S. C. § 4412, as implemented by Internal Revenue Service Form 11-C, reveals that the information demanded of gamblers is no more than is necessary to assure that the tax-collection process will be effective. Registration of those liable for special taxes is a common and integral feature of the tax laws. So also is the requirement of public disclosure. And the reach of the registration and disclosure requirements extends to both lawful and unlawful activities. Because registration and disclosure are so pervasive in the Internal Revenue Code, it is clear that such requirements have been imposed by Congress to aid in the collection of taxes legitimately levied. Because most forms of gambling have been declared illegal in this country, gamblers necessarily operate furtively in the dark shadows of the underworld. Only by requiring that such individuals come forward under pain of criminal sanctions and reveal the nature and scope of their activities can Congress confidently expect that revenue derived from that outlawed occupation will be subject to the legitimate reach of the tax laws. Indeed, it seems to me that the very secrecy which surrounds the business of gambling demands disclosure. Those legislative committees and executive commissions which have studied the problems of illicit gambling activities have found it impossible to determine with any precision the gross revenues derived from that business. For example, the President's Commission on Law Enforcement and Administration of Justice reported:

> There is no accurate way of ascertaining organized crime's gross revenue from gambling in the United States. Estimates of the annual intake have varied from $7 to $50 billion. . . . While the Commission cannot judge the accuracy of these figures, even the most conservative estimates place substantial capital in the hands of organized crime leaders. President's Commission on Law Enforcement and Administration of Justice, Task Force Report: Organized Crime 3 (1967).

The Commission's observation is doubly revealing. It shows that the business of gambling is a lucrative revenue source. And it demonstrates the need for an enforceable disclosure device, such as the registration requirement of § 4412, if the revenue potential is to be realized. No one denies that the disclosures demanded by § 4412 can also be useful to law enforcement officials and that the very process of disclosure may have a regulatory effect on gamblers and their operations. But this Court has repeatedly recognized that "a tax is not any the less a tax because it has a regulatory effect."

In view of these considerations, I cannot understand why the Court today finds it necessary to strike down the registration requirement of § 4412 directed at those who derive their income from gambling. What seems to trouble the Court is not that registration is required but that the information obtained through the registration requirement is turned over by federal officials, under the statutory compulsion of 26 U. S. C. § 6107, to state prosecutors to aid them in the enforcement of state gambling laws. If that is the source of the Court's Fifth Amendment concern, then constitutional adjudication demands that the provisions of § 6107 be the focus of the Court's decision. It does not seem reasonable to me to rule that, because information derived from the registration provisions of § 4412 must be made available to state prosecutors under § 6107, the registration requirements suffer from a fatal constitutional infirmity, even though § 4412 is a necessary and proper means of assuring that the occupational tax on gamblers will be enforceable. Certainly no Fifth Amendment issue arises from the fact of registration until an effort is made to use the registration procedure in aid of criminal prosecution. To the extent that the disclosure requirements of § 6107 would raise a Fifth Amendment problem because some of the names on the public list have admitted unlawful activities, that statutory provision is severable for purposes of constitutional adjudication. In fact, in the Internal Revenue Code itself, Congress has specifically enacted a severability clause. Section 7852 (a) of Title 26 provides:

> If any provision of this title, or the application thereof to any person or circumstances, is held invalid, the remainder of the title, and the application of such provision to other persons or circumstances, shall not be affected thereby.

That clause represents a clear statutory command to this Court to wield its constitutional knife surgically, concentrating on the suspect provisions of § 6107 rather than bludgeoning the entire taxing scheme. The Court cannot evade this constitutional and statutory duty, as it seems to do, by labeling every provision of the wagering tax statutes as "interrelated" or "integral."

There is no such narrow focus to the Court's approach to these two cases. In fact, the Court impliedly rejects such an approach in dealing with the Government's suggestion that the taxing scheme at issue be saved from constitutional interment by imposing a use restriction on the information derived from registration under § 4412. Cf. *Murphy v. Waterfront Commission* (1964). The Court finds such a limitation unacceptable because the legislative history of the wagering tax system reveals a congressional purpose to make available to state and local law enforcement officials the disclosures made through registration. The Court reasons that to impose the use restriction would be to defeat the congressional purpose, and it finds the suggested saving device unacceptable. But realistically the Court's sweeping constitutional ruling has the effect of frustrating two congressional purposes—the disclosure purpose and the revenue purpose. Such a result can hardly be justified on the ground of according a congressional purpose the deference due it by this Court. Conceding that the statutory scheme is intended to assist law enforcement, the fact that taxes in the sum of $115,000,000 have flowed from the wagering tax scheme to the Treasury in the past several years is convincing evidence of a legitimate tax purpose. The congressional intent to assist law enforcement should not be the excuse for frustrating the revenue purpose of the statutes before the Court. Regardless of legislative intent, this Court has in the past refused "to formulate a rule of constitutional law broader than is required." *Garner v. Louisiana* (1961); cf. *Kennedy v. Mendoza-Martinez* (1963). This principle should prevail in this case where the Act has the wholesome objective of devising workable procedures to assure that gamblers will pay the same taxes on their profits as other citizens are compelled to pay.

I apprehend that the Court, by unnecessarily sweeping within its constitutional holding the registration requirements of § 4412, is opening the door to a new wave of attacks on a number of federal registration statutes whenever the registration requirement touches upon allegedly illegal activities. As I noted above, registration is a common feature attached to a number of special taxes imposed by Title 26. For example, the following provisions impose special registration requirements: § 4101 (those subject to the tax on petroleum products); § 4222 (registration regarding certain tax-free sales by manufacturers); § 4722 (those engaged in dealing in narcotic drugs); § 4753 (those who deal in marihuana); § 4804 (d) (manufacturers of white phosphorous matches); §§ 5171-5172 (registration of distilleries); § 5179 (registration of stills); § 5502 (manufacturers of vinegar); § 5802 (importers, manufacturers, and dealers in firearms). And § 7011 imposes a general registration requirement on all those liable for other special taxes. Heretofore this Court has consistently upheld the validity of such registration requirements, without regard to the legality of the activity being taxed. *United States v. Sanchez,* 340 U. S. 42 (1950) (26 U. S. C. § 4753); *Sonzinsky v. United States,* 300 U. S. 506 (1937) (26 U. S. C. § 5841); *Nigro v. United States,* 276 U. S. 332 (1928) (26 U. S. C. § 4722). The implications of the Court's decisions today also extend beyond the tax statutes. For example, the statute requiring narcotics addicts and violators to register whenever they enter or leave the country, 18 U. S. C. § 1407, can now be expected to come under attack. My concern that such registration requirements will now come under attack is not imaginary. This very day the Court, adhering to its decisions in *Marchetti* and *Grosso,* declares unconstitutional in *Haynes v. United States, post,* p. 85, 26 U. S. C. § 5851, which makes unlawful the possession of a firearm not registered under § 5841. The impact of that decision on the efforts of Congress to enact much-needed federal gun control laws is not consistent with national safety. In my view, the Court has failed to take account of these relevant implications in the very broad holdings of today's decisions.

# 25

## *In Re Gault*

Appellants' 15-year-old son, Gerald Gault, was taken into custody as the result of a complaint that he had made lewd telephone calls. After hearings before a juvenile court judge, Gerald was ordered committed to the State Industrial School as a juvenile delinquent until he should reach majority. Appellants brought a habeas corpus action in the state courts to challenge the constitutionality of the Arizona Juvenile Code and the procedure actually used in Gerald's case, on the ground of denial of various procedural due process rights. The State Supreme Court affirmed dismissal of the writ. Agreeing that the constitutional guarantee of due process applies to proceedings in which juveniles are charged as delinquents, the court held that the Arizona Juvenile Code impliedly includes the requirements of due process in delinquency proceedings, and that such due process requirements were not offended by the procedure leading to Gerald's commitment. . . . The petition sought the release of Gerald Francis Gault, appellants' 15-year-old son, who had been committed as a juvenile delinquent to the State Industrial School by the Juvenile Court of Gila County, Arizona. The Supreme Court of Arizona affirmed dismissal of the writ against various arguments which included an attack upon the constitutionality of the Arizona Juvenile Code because of its alleged denial of procedural due process rights to juveniles charged with being "delinquents." The court agreed that the constitutional guarantee of due process of law is applicable in such proceedings. It held that Arizona's Juvenile Code is to be read as "impliedly" implementing the "due process concept." It then proceeded to identify and describe "the particular elements which constitute due process in a juvenile hearing." It concluded that the proceedings ending in commitment of Gerald Gault did not offend those requirements. We do not agree, and we reverse. We begin with a statement of the facts.

### I.

On Monday, June 8, 1964, at about 10 a. m., Gerald Francis Gault and a friend, Ronald Lewis, were taken into custody by the Sheriff of Gila County. Gerald was then still subject to a six months' probation order which had been entered on February 25, 1964, as a result of his having been in the company of another boy who had stolen a wallet from a lady's purse. The police action on June 8 was taken as the result of a verbal complaint by a neighbor of the boys, Mrs. Cook, about a telephone call made to her in which the caller or callers made lewd or indecent remarks. It will suffice for purposes of this opinion to say that the remarks or questions put to her were of the irritatingly offensive, adolescent, sex variety.

At the time Gerald was picked up, his mother and father were both at work. No notice that Gerald was being taken into custody was left at the home. No other steps were taken to advise them that their son had, in effect, been arrested. Gerald was taken to the Children's Detention Home. When his mother arrived home at about 6 o'clock, Gerald was not there. Gerald's older brother was sent to look for him at the trailer home of the Lewis family. He apparently learned then that Gerald was in custody. He so informed his mother. The two of them went to the Detention Home. The deputy probation officer, Flagg, who was also superintendent of the Detention Home, told Mrs. Gault "why Jerry was there" and said that a hearing would be held in Juvenile Court at 3 o'clock the following day, June 9.

Officer Flagg filed a petition with the court on the hearing day, June 9, 1964. It was not served on the Gaults. Indeed, none of them saw this petition until the habeas corpus hearing on August 17, 1964. The petition was entirely formal. It made no reference to any factual basis for the judicial action which it initiated. It recited only that "said minor is under the age of eighteen years, and is in need of the protection of this Honorable Court; [and that] said minor is a delinquent minor." It prayed for a hearing and an order regarding "the care and custody of said minor." Officer Flagg executed a formal affidavit in support of the petition.

On June 9, Gerald, his mother, his older brother, and Probation Officers Flagg and Henderson appeared before the Juvenile Judge in chambers. Gerald's father was not there. He was at work out of the city. Mrs. Cook, the complainant, was not there. No one was sworn at this hearing. No transcript or recording was made. No memorandum or record of the substance of the proceedings was prepared. Our information about the proceedings and the subsequent hearing on June 15, derives entirely from the testimony of the Juvenile Court Judge, Mr. and Mrs. Gault and Officer Flagg at the habeas corpus proceeding conducted two months later. From this, it appears that at the June 9 hearing Gerald was questioned by the judge about the telephone call. There was conflict as to what he said. His mother recalled that Gerald said he only dialed Mrs. Cook's number and handed the telephone to his friend, Ronald. Officer Flagg recalled that Gerald had admitted making the lewd remarks. Judge McGhee testified that Gerald "admitted making one of these [lewd] statements." At the conclusion of the hearing, the judge said he would "think about it." Gerald was taken back to the Detention Home. He was not sent to his own home with his parents. On June 11 or 12, after having been detained since June 8, Gerald was released and driven home. There is no explanation in the record as to why he was kept in the Detention Home or why he was released. At 5 p. m. on the day of Gerald's release, Mrs. Gault received a note signed by Officer Flagg. It was on plain paper, not letterhead. Its entire text was as follows:

> Mrs. Gault:
>
> Judge McGhee has set Monday June 15, 1964 at 11:00 A. M. as the date and time for further Hearings on Gerald's delinquency

At the appointed time on Monday, June 15, Gerald, his father and mother, Ronald Lewis and his father, and Officers Flagg and Henderson were present before Judge McGhee. Witnesses at the habeas corpus proceeding differed in their recollections of Gerald's testimony at the June 15 hearing. Mr. and Mrs. Gault recalled that Gerald again testified that he had only dialed the number and that the other boy had made the remarks. Officer Flagg agreed that at this hearing Gerald did not admit making the lewd remarks. But Judge McGhee recalled that "there was some admission again of some of the lewd statements. He–he didn't admit any of the more serious lewd statements." Again, the complainant, Mrs. Cook, was not present. Mrs. Gault asked that Mrs. Cook be present "so she could see which boy that done the talking, the dirty talking over the phone." The Juvenile Judge said "she didn't have to be present at that hearing." The judge did not speak to Mrs. Cook or communicate with her at any time. Probation Officer Flagg had talked to her once–over the telephone on June 9.

At this June 15 hearing a "referral report" made by the probation officers was filed with the court, although not disclosed to Gerald or his parents. This listed the charge as "Lewd Phone Calls." At the conclusion of the hearing, the judge committed Gerald as a juvenile delinquent to the State Industrial School "for the period of his minority [that is, until 21], unless sooner discharged by due process of law." An order to that effect was entered. It recites that "after a full hearing and due deliberation the Court finds that said minor is a delinquent child, and that said minor is of the age of 15 years."

No appeal is permitted by Arizona law in juvenile cases. On August 3, 1964, a petition for a writ of habeas corpus was filed with the Supreme Court of Arizona and referred by it to the Superior Court for hearing.

At the habeas corpus hearing on August 17, Judge McGhee was vigorously cross-examined as to the basis for his actions. He testified that he had taken into account the fact that Gerald was on probation. He was asked "under what section of . . . the code you found the boy delinquent?"

His answer is set forth in the margin.[1] In substance, he concluded that Gerald came within ARS § 8–201–6(a), which specifies that a "delinquent child" includes one "who has violated a law of the state or an ordinance or regulation of a political subdivision thereof." The law which Gerald was found to have violated is ARS § 13–377. This section of the Arizona Criminal Code provides that a person who "in the presence or hearing of any woman or child . . . uses vulgar, abusive or obscene language, is guilty of a misdemeanor. . . ." The penalty specified in the Criminal Code, which would apply to an adult, is $5 to $50, or imprisonment for not more than two months. The judge also testified that he acted under ARS § 8–201–6 (d) which includes in the definition of a "delinquent child" one who, as the judge phrased it, is "habitually involved in immoral matters."

Asked about the basis for his conclusion that Gerald was "habitually involved in immoral matters," the judge testified, somewhat vaguely, that two years earlier, on July 2, 1962, a "referral" was made concerning Gerald, "where the boy had stolen a baseball glove from another boy and lied to the Police Department about it." The

[1] "Q. All right. Now, Judge, would you tell me under what section of the law or tell me under what section of–of the code you found the boy delinquent?

"A. Well, there is a–I think it amounts to disturbing the peace. I can't give you the section, but I can tell you the law, that when one person uses lewd language in the presence of another person, that it can amount to–and I consider that when a person makes it over the phone, that it is considered in the presence, I might be wrong, that is one section. The other section upon which I consider the boy delinquent is Section 8-201, Subsection (d), habitually involved in immoral matters."

judge said there was "no hearing," and "no accusation" relating to this incident, "because of lack of material foundation." But it seems to have remained in his mind as a relevant factor. The judge also testified that Gerald had admitted making other nuisance phone calls in the past which, as the judge recalled the boy's testimony, were "silly calls, or funny calls, or something like that."

The Superior Court dismissed the writ, and appellants sought review in the Arizona Supreme Court. That court stated that it considered appellants' assignments of error as urging (1) that the Juvenile Code, ARS § 8–201 to § 8–239, is unconstitutional because it does not require that parents and children be apprised of the specific charges, does not require proper notice of a hearing, and does not provide for an appeal; and (2) that the proceedings and order relating to Gerald constituted a denial of due process of law because of the absence of adequate notice of the charge and the hearing; failure to notify appellants of certain constitutional rights including the rights to counsel and to confrontation, and the privilege against self-incrimination; the use of unsworn hearsay testimony; and the failure to make a record of the proceedings. Appellants further asserted that it was error for the Juvenile Court to remove Gerald from the custody of his parents without a showing and finding of their unsuitability, and alleged a miscellany of other errors under state law.

The Supreme Court handed down an elaborate and wide-ranging opinion affirming dismissal of the writ and stating the court's conclusions as to the issues raised by appellants and other aspects of the juvenile process. In their jurisdictional statement and brief in this Court, appellants do not urge upon us all of the points passed upon by the Supreme Court of Arizona. They urge that we hold the Juvenile Code of Arizona invalid on its face or as applied in this case because, contrary to the Due Process Clause of the Fourteenth Amendment, the juvenile is taken from the custody of his parents and committed to a state institution pursuant to proceedings in which the Juvenile Court has virtually unlimited discretion, and in which the following basic rights are denied:

1. Notice of the charges;
2. Right to counsel;
3. Right to confrontation and cross-examination;
4. Privilege against self-incrimination;
5. Right to a transcript of the proceedings; and
6. Right to appellate review.

We shall not consider other issues which were passed upon by the Supreme Court of Arizona. We emphasize that we indicate no opinion as to whether the decision of that court with respect to such other issues does or does not conflict with requirements of the Federal Constitution.

## II.

The Supreme Court of Arizona held that due process of law is requisite to the constitutional validity of proceedings in which a court reaches the conclusion that a juvenile has been at fault, has engaged in conduct prohibited by law, or has otherwise misbehaved with the consequence that he is committed to an institution in which his freedom is curtailed. This conclusion is in accord with the decisions of a number of courts under both federal and state constitutions.

This Court has not heretofore decided the precise question. In *Kent v. United States,* 338 U. S. 541 (1966), we considered the requirements for a valid waiver of the "exclusive" jurisdiction of the Juvenile Court of the District of Columbia so that a juvenile could be tried in the adult criminal court of the District. Although our decision turned upon the language of the statute, we emphasized the necessity that "the basic requirements of due process and fairness" be satisfied in such proceedings. *Haley v. Ohio,* 332 U. S. 596 (1948), involved the admissibility, in a state criminal court of general jurisdiction, of a confession by a 15-year-old boy. The Court held that the Fourteenth Amendment applied to prohibit the use of the coerced confession. Mr. Justice Douglas said, "Neither man nor child can be allowed to stand condemned by methods which flout constitutional requirements of due process of law." . . .

We do not in this opinion consider the impact of these constitutional provisions upon the totality of the relationship of the juvenile and the state. We do not even consider the entire process relating to juvenile "delinquents." For example, we are not here concerned with the procedures or constitutional rights applicable to the pre-judicial stages of the juvenile process, nor do we direct our attention to the post-adjudicative or dispositional process. . . . We consider only the problems presented to us by this case. These relate to the proceedings by which a determination is made as to whether a juvenile is a "delinquent" as a result of alleged misconduct on his part, with the consequence that he may be committed to a state institution. As to these proceedings, there appears to be little current dissent from the proposition that the Due Process Clause has a role to play. The problem is to ascertain the precise impact of the due process requirement upon such proceedings.

From the inception of the juvenile court system, wide differences have been tolerated—indeed insisted upon—between the procedural rights accorded to adults and those of juveniles. In practically all jurisdictions, there are rights granted to adults which are withheld from juveniles. In addition to the specific problems involved in the present case, for example, it has been held that the juvenile is not entitled to bail, to indictment by grand jury, to a public trial or to trial by jury. It is frequent practice that rules governing the arrest and interrogation of adults by the police are not observed in the case of juveniles.

The history and theory underlying this development are well-known, but a recapitulation is necessary for purposes of this opinion. The Juvenile Court movement began in this country at the end of the last century. From the juvenile court statute adopted in Illinois in 1899, the system has spread to every State in the Union, the District of Columbia, and Puerto Rico. The constitutionality of Juvenile Court laws has been sustained in over 40 jurisdictions against a variety of attacks.

The early reformers were appalled by adult procedures and penalties, and by the fact that children could be given long prison sentences and mixed in jails with hardened criminals. They were profoundly convinced that society's duty to the child could not be confined by the concept of justice alone. They believed that society's role was not to ascertain whether the child was "guilty" or "innocent," but "What is he, how has he become what he is, and what had best be done in his interest and in the interest of the state to save him from a downward career." The child—essentially good, as they saw it—was to be made "to feel that he is the object of [the state's] care and solicitude," not that he was under arrest or on trial. The rules of criminal procedure were therefore altogether inapplicable. The apparent rigidities, technicalities, and harshness which they observed in both substantive and procedural criminal law were therefore to be discarded. The idea of crime and punishment was to be abandoned. The child was to be "treated" and "rehabilitated" and the procedures, from apprehension through institutionalization, were to be "clinical" rather than punitive.

These results were to be achieved, without coming to conceptual and constitutional grief, by insisting that the proceedings were not adversary, but that the state was proceeding as *parens patriae.* The Latin phrase proved to be a great help to those who sought to rationalize the exclusion of juveniles from the constitutional scheme; but its meaning is murky and its historic credentials are of dubious relevance. The phrase was taken from chancery practice, where, however, it was used to describe the power of the state to act *in loco parentis* for the purpose of protecting the property interests and the person of the child. But there is no trace of the doctrine in the history of criminal jurisprudence. At common law, children under seven were considered incapable of possessing criminal intent. Beyond that age, they were subjected to arrest, trial, and in theory to punishment like adult offenders. In these old days, the state was not deemed to have authority to accord them fewer procedural rights than adults.

The right of the state, as *parens patriae,* to deny to the child procedural rights available to his elders was elaborated by the assertion that a child, unlike an adult, has a right "not to liberty but to custody." He can be made to attorn to his parents, to go to school, etc. If his parents default in effectively performing their custodial functions—that is, if the child is "delinquent"—the state may intervene. In doing so, it does not deprive the child of any rights, because he has none. It merely provides the "custody" to which the child is entitled. On this basis, proceedings involving juveniles were described as "civil" not "criminal" and therefore not subject to the requirements which restrict the state when it seeks to deprive a person of his liberty.[2]

Accordingly, the highest motives and most enlightened impulses led to a peculiar system for juveniles, unknown to our law in any comparable context. The constitutional and theoretical basis for this peculiar system is—to say the

[2] The Appendix to the opinion of Judge Prettyman in *Pee v. United States,* 107 U. S. App. D. C. 47, 274 F. 2d 556 (1959), lists authority in 51 jurisdictions to this effect. Even rules required by due process in civil proceedings, however, have not generally been deemed compulsory as to proceedings affecting juveniles. For example, constitutional requirements as to notice of issues, which would commonly apply in civil cases, are commonly disregarded in juvenile proceedings, as this case illustrates.

least–debatable. And in practice, as we remarked in the *Kent* case, *supra*, the results have not been entirely satisfactory.[3] Juvenile Court history has again demonstrated that unbridled discretion, however benevolently motivated, is frequently a poor substitute for principle and procedure. In 1937, Dean Pound wrote: "The powers of the Star Chamber were a trifle in comparison with those of our juvenile courts . . . ." The absence of substantive standards has not necessarily meant that children receive careful, compassionate, individualized treatment. The absence of procedural rules based upon constitutional principle has not always produced fair, efficient, and effective procedures. Departures from established principles of due process have frequently resulted not in enlightened procedure, but in arbitrariness. . . .

It is claimed that juveniles obtain benefits from the special procedures applicable to them which more than offset the disadvantages of denial of the substance of normal due process. As we shall discuss, the observance of due process standards, intelligently and not ruthlessly administered, will not compel the States to abandon or displace any of the substantive benefits of the juvenile process. But it is important, we think, that the claimed benefits of the juvenile process should be candidly appraised. Neither sentiment nor folklore should cause us to shut our eyes, for example, to such startling findings as that reported in an exceptionally reliable study of repeaters or recidivism conducted by the Stanford Research Institute for the President's Commission on Crime in the District of Columbia. This Commission's Report states:

> In fiscal 1966 approximately 66 percent of the 16- and 17-year-old juveniles referred to the court by the Youth Aid Division had been before the court previously. In 1965, 56 percent of those in the Receiving Home were repeaters. The SRI study revealed that 61 percent of the sample Juvenile Court referrals in 1965 had been previously referred at least once and that 42 percent had been referred at least twice before. *Id.*, at 773.

Certainly, these figures and the high crime rates among juveniles to which we have referred could not lead us to conclude that the absence of constitutional protections reduces crime, or that the juvenile system, functioning free of constitutional inhibitions as it has largely done, is effective to reduce crime or rehabilitate offenders. We do not mean by this to denigrate the juvenile court process or to suggest that there are not aspects of the juvenile system relating to offenders which are valuable. But the features of the juvenile system which its proponents have asserted are of unique benefit will not be impaired by constitutional domestication. For example, the commendable principles relating to the processing and treatment of juveniles separately from adults are in no way involved or affected by the procedural issues under discussion. Further, we are told that one of the important benefits of the special juvenile court procedures is that they avoid classifying the juvenile as a "criminal." The juvenile offender is now

[3] "There is evidence . . . that there may be grounds for concern that the child receives the worst of both worlds: that he gets neither the protections accorded to adults nor the solicitous care and regenerative treatment postulated for children."

classed as a "delinquent." There is, of course, no reason why this should not continue. It is disconcerting, however, that this term has come to involve only slightly less stigma than the term "criminal" applied to adults. It is also emphasized that in practically all jurisdictions, statutes provide that an adjudication of the child as a delinquent shall not operate as a civil disability or disqualify him for civil service appointment. There is no reason why the application of due process requirements should interfere with such provisions. . . .

Further, it is urged that the juvenile benefits from informal proceedings in the court. The early conception of the Juvenile Court proceeding was one in which a fatherly judge touched the heart and conscience of the erring youth by talking over his problems, by paternal advice and admonition, and in which, in extreme situations, benevolent and wise institutions of the State provided guidance and help "to save him from a downward career." Then, as now, goodwill and compassion were admirably prevalent. But recent studies have, with surprising unanimity, entered sharp dissent as to the validity of this gentle conception. They suggest that the appearance as well as the actuality of fairness, impartiality and orderliness—in short, the essentials of due process—may be a more impressive and more therapeutic attitude so far as the juvenile is concerned. . . .

Ultimately, however, we confront the reality of that portion of the Juvenile Court process with which we deal in this case. A boy is charged with misconduct. The boy is committed to an institution where he may be restrained of liberty for years. It is of no constitutional consequence—and of limited practical meaning—that the institution to which he is committed is called an Industrial School. The fact of the matter is that, however euphemistic the title, a "receiving home" or an "industrial school" for juveniles is an institution of confinement in which the child is incarcerated for a greater or lesser time. His world becomes "a building with whitewashed walls, regimented routine and institutional hours. . . ." Instead of mother and father and sisters and brothers and friends and classmates, his world is peopled by guards, custodians, state employees, and "delinquents" confined with him for anything from waywardness to rape and homicide.

In view of this, it would be extraordinary if our Constitution did not require the procedural regularity and the exercise of care implied in the phrase "due process." Under our Constitution, the condition of being a boy does not justify a kangaroo court. The traditional ideas of Juvenile Court procedure, indeed, contemplated that time would be available and care would be used to establish precisely what the juvenile did and why he did it—was it a prank of adolescence or a brutal act threatening serious consequences to himself or society unless corrected? Under traditional notions, one would assume that in a case like that of Gerald Gault, where the juvenile appears to have a home, a working mother and father, and an older brother, the Juvenile Judge would have made a careful inquiry and judgment as to the possibility that the boy could be disciplined and dealt with at home, despite his previous transgressions. Indeed, so far as appears in the record before us, except for some conversation with Gerald about his school work and his "wanting to go to . . . Grand Canyon with his father," the points to which the judge directed his attention were little different from those that would be involved in determining any charge of violation of a penal statute. The essential difference between Gerald's case and a normal criminal case is that safeguards available to adults were discarded in Gerald's case. The summary procedure as well as the long commitment was possible because Gerald was 15 years of age instead of over 18.

If Gerald had been over 18, he would not have been subject to Juvenile Court proceedings. For the particular offense immediately involved, the maximum punishment would have been a fine of $5 to $50, or imprisonment in jail for not more than two months. Instead, he was committed to custody for a maximum of six years. If he had been over 18 and had committed an offense to which such a sentence might apply, he would have been entitled to substantial rights under the Constitution of the United States as well as under Arizona's laws and constitution. The United States Constitution would guarantee him rights and protections with respect to arrest, search and seizure, and pretrial interrogation. It would assure him of specific notice of the charges and adequate time to decide his course of action and to prepare his defense. He would be entitled to clear advice that he could be represented by counsel, and, at least if a felony were involved, the State would be required to provide counsel if his parents were unable to afford it. If the court acted on the basis of his confession, careful procedures would be required to assure its voluntariness. If the case went to trial, confrontation and opportunity for cross-examination would be guaranteed. So wide a gulf between the State's treatment of the adult and of the child requires a bridge sturdier than mere verbiage, and reasons more persuasive than cliché can provide. . . .

We now turn to the specific issues which are presented to us in the present case.

## III. NOTICE OF CHARGES.

Appellants allege that the Arizona Juvenile Code is unconstitutional or alternatively that the proceedings before the Juvenile Court were constitutionally defective because of failure to provide adequate notice of the hearings. No notice was given to Gerald's parents when he was taken into custody on Monday, June 8. On that night, when Mrs. Gault went to the Detention Home, she was orally informed that there would be a hearing the next afternoon and was told the reason why Gerald was in custody. The only written notice Gerald's parents received at any time was a note on plain paper from Officer Flagg delivered on Thursday or Friday, June 11 or 12, to the effect that the judge had set Monday, June 15, "for further Hearings on Gerald's delinquency."

A "petition" was filed with the court on June 9 by Officer Flagg, reciting only that he was informed and believed that "said minor is a delinquent minor and that it is necessary that some order be made by the Honorable Court for said minor's welfare." The applicable Arizona statute provides for a petition to be filed in Juvenile Court, alleging in general terms that the child is "neglected, dependent or delinquent." The statute explicitly states that such a general allegation is sufficient, "without alleging the facts." There is no requirement that the petition be served and it was not served upon, given to, or shown to Gerald or his parents.

The Supreme Court of Arizona rejected appellants' claim that due process was denied because of inadequate notice. It stated that "Mrs. Gault knew the exact nature of the charge against Gerald from the day he was taken to the detention home." The court also pointed out that the Gaults appeared at the two hearings "without objection." The court held that because "the policy of the juvenile law is to hide youthful errors from the full gaze of the public and bury them in the graveyard of the forgotten past," advance notice of the specific charges or basis for taking the juvenile into custody and for the hearing is not necessary. It held that the appropriate rule is that "the infant and his parent or guardian will receive a petition only reciting a conclusion of delinquency. But no later than the initial hearing by the judge, they must be advised of the facts involved in the case. If the charges are denied, they must be given a reasonable period of time to prepare."

We cannot agree with the court's conclusion that adequate notice was given in this case. Notice, to comply with due process requirements, must be given sufficiently in advance of scheduled court proceedings so that reasonable opportunity to prepare will be afforded, and it must "set forth the alleged misconduct with particularity." . . . Due process of law requires notice of the sort we have described—that is, notice which would be deemed constitutionally adequate in a civil or criminal proceeding. It does not allow a hearing to be held in which a youth's freedom and his parents' right to his custody are at stake without giving them timely notice, in advance of the hearing, of the specific issues that they must meet. Nor, in the circumstances of this case, can it reasonably be said that the requirement of notice was waived.

### IV. RIGHT TO COUNSEL.

Appellants charge that the Juvenile Court proceedings were fatally defective because the court did not advise Gerald or his parents of their right to counsel, and proceeded with the hearing, the adjudication of delinquency and the order of commitment in the absence of counsel for the child and his parents or an express waiver of the right thereto. The Supreme Court of Arizona pointed out that "[t]here is disagreement [among the various jurisdictions] as to whether the court must advise the infant that he has a right to counsel." It noted its own decision in *Arizona State Dept. of Public Welfare v. Barlow,* 80 Ariz. 249, 296 P. 2d 298 (1956), to the effect "that *the parents* of an infant in a juvenile proceeding cannot be denied representation by counsel of their choosing." (Emphasis added.) It referred to a provision of the Juvenile Code which it characterized as requiring "that the probation officer shall look after the interests of neglected, delinquent and dependent children," including representing their interests in court. The court argued that "The parent and the probation officer may be relied upon to protect the infant's interests." Accordingly it rejected the proposition that "due process requires that an infant have a right to counsel." It said that juvenile courts have the discretion, but not the duty, to allow such representation; it referred specifically to the situation in which the Juvenile Court discerns conflict between the child and his parents as an instance in which this discretion might be exercised. We do not agree. Probation officers, in the Arizona scheme, are also arresting officers. They initiate proceedings and file petitions which they verify, as here, alleging the delinquency of the child; and they testify, as here, against the child. And here the probation officer was also superintendent of the Detention Home. The probation officer cannot act as counsel for the child. His role in the adjudicatory hearing, by statute and in fact, is as arresting officer and witness against the child. Nor can the judge represent the child. . . .

The President's Crime Commission has recently recommended that in order to assure "procedural justice for the child," it is necessary that "Counsel . . . be appointed as a matter of course wherever coercive action is a possibility, without requiring any affirmative choice by child or parent." As stated by the authoritative "Standards for Juvenile and Family Courts," published by the Children's Bureau of the United States Department of Health, Education, and Welfare:

> As a component part of a fair hearing required by due process guaranteed under the 14th amendment, notice of the right to counsel should be required at all hearings and counsel provided upon request when the family is financially unable to employ counsel. Standards, p. 57.

This statement was "reviewed" by the National Council of Juvenile Court Judges at its 1965 Convention and they "found no fault" with it. The New York Family Court Act contains the following statement:

> This act declares that minors have a right to the assistance of counsel of their own choosing or of law guardians in neglect proceedings under article three and in proceedings to determine juvenile delinquency and whether a person is in need of supervision under article seven. This declaration is based on a finding that counsel is often indispensable to a practical realization of due process of law and may be helpful in making reasoned determinations of fact and proper orders of disposition.

The Act provides that "At the commencement of any hearing" under the delinquency article of the statute, the juvenile and his parent shall be advised of the juvenile's "right to be represented by counsel chosen by him or his parent . . . or by a law guardian assigned by the court . . . ." The California Act (1961) also requires appointment of counsel.

We conclude that the Due Process Clause of the Fourteenth Amendment requires that in respect of proceedings to determine delinquency which may result in commitment to an institution in which the juvenile's freedom is curtailed, the child and his parents must be notified of the child's right to be represented by counsel retained by them, or if they are unable to afford counsel, that counsel will be appointed to represent the child.

At the habeas corpus proceeding, Mrs. Gault testified that she knew that she could have appeared with counsel at the juvenile hearing. This knowledge is not a waiver of the right to counsel which she and her juvenile son had, as we have defined it. They had a right expressly to be advised that they might retain counsel and to be confronted with the need for specific consideration of whether they did or did not choose to waive the right. If they were unable to afford to employ counsel, they were entitled in view of the seriousness of the charge and the potential commitment, to appointed counsel, unless they chose waiver. . . Mrs. Gault's knowledge that she could employ counsel was not an "intentional relinquishment or abandonment" of a fully known right.

## V. CONFRONTATION, SELF-INCRIMINATION, CROSS-EXAMINATION.

Appellants urge that the writ of habeas corpus should have been granted because of the denial of the rights of confrontation and cross-examination in the Juvenile Court hearings, and because the privilege against self-incrimination was not observed. The Juvenile Court Judge testified at the habeas corpus hearing that he had proceeded on the basis of Gerald's admissions at the two hearings. Appellants attack this on the ground that the admissions were obtained in disregard of the privilege against self-incrimination. If the confession is disregarded, appellants argue that the delinquency conclusion, since it was fundamentally based on a finding that Gerald had made lewd remarks during the phone call to Mrs. Cook, is fatally defective for failure to accord the rights of confrontation and cross-examination which the Due Process Clause of the Fourteenth Amendment of the Federal Constitution guarantees in state proceedings generally.

Our first question, then, is whether Gerald's admission was improperly obtained and relied on as the basis of decision, in conflict with the Federal Constitution. For this purpose, it is necessary briefly to recall the relevant facts.

Mrs. Cook, the complainant, and the recipient of the alleged telephone call, was not called as a witness. Gerald's mother asked the Juvenile Court Judge why Mrs. Cook was not present and the judge replied that "she didn't have to be present." So far as appears, Mrs. Cook was spoken to only once, by Officer Flagg, and this was by telephone. The judge did not speak with her on any occasion. Gerald had been questioned by the probation officer after having been taken into custody. The exact circumstances of this questioning do not appear but any admissions Gerald may have made at this time do not appear in the record. Gerald was also questioned by the Juvenile Court Judge at each of the two hearings. The judge testified in the habeas corpus proceeding that Gerald admitted making "some of the lewd statements . . . [but not] any of the more serious lewd statements." There was conflict and uncertainty among the witnesses at the habeas corpus proceeding–the Juvenile Court Judge, Mr. and Mrs. Gault, and the probation officer–as to what Gerald did or did not admit.

We shall assume that Gerald made admissions of the sort described by the Juvenile Court Judge, as quoted above. Neither Gerald nor his parents were advised that he did not have to testify or make a statement, or that an incriminating statement might result in his commitment as a "delinquent."

The Arizona Supreme Court rejected appellants' contention that Gerald had a right to be advised that he need not incriminate himself. It said: "We think the necessary flexibility for individualized treatment will be enhanced by a rule which does not require the judge to advise the infant of a privilege against self-incrimination."

In reviewing this conclusion of Arizona's Supreme Court, we emphasize again that we are here concerned only with a proceeding to determine whether a minor is a "delinquent" and which may result in commitment to a state institution. Specifically, the question is whether, in such a proceeding, an admission by the juvenile may be used against him in the absence of clear and unequivocal evidence that the admission was made with knowledge that he was not obliged to speak and would not be penalized for remaining silent. In light of *Miranda v. Arizona,* 384 U.S. 436 (1966), we must also consider whether, if the privilege against self-incrimination is available, it can effectively be waived unless counsel is present or the right to counsel has been waived. . . .

It would indeed be surprising if the privilege against self-incrimination were available to hardened criminals but not to children. The language of the Fifth Amendment, applicable to the States by operation of the Fourteenth Amendment, is unequivocal and without exception. And the scope of the privilege is comprehensive. . . .

It would be entirely unrealistic to carve out of the Fifth Amendment all statements by juveniles on the ground that these cannot lead to "criminal" involvement. In the first place, juvenile proceedings to determine "delinquency," which may lead to commitment to a state institution, must be regarded as "criminal" for purposes of the privilege against self-incrimination. To hold otherwise would be to disregard substance because of the feeble enticement of the "civil" label-of-convenience which has been attached to juvenile proceedings. Indeed, in over half of the States, there is not even assurance that the juvenile will be kept in separate institutions, apart from adult "criminals." In those States juveniles may be placed in or transferred to adult penal institutions after having been found "delinquent" by a juvenile court. For this purpose, at least, commitment is a deprivation of liberty. It is incarceration against one's will, whether it is called "criminal" or "civil." And our Constitution guarantees that no person shall be "compelled" to be a witness against himself when he is threatened with deprivation of his liberty—a command which this Court has broadly applied and generously implemented in accordance with the teaching of the history of the privilege and its great office in mankind's battle for freedom.

In addition, apart from the equivalence for this purpose of exposure to commitment as a juvenile delinquent and exposure to imprisonment as an adult offender, the fact of the matter is that there is little or no assurance in Arizona, as in most if not all of the States, that a juvenile apprehended and interrogated by the police or even by the Juvenile Court itself will remain outside of the reach of adult courts as a consequence of the offense for which he has been taken into custody. In Arizona, as in other States, provision is made for Juvenile Courts to relinquish or waive jurisdiction to the ordinary criminal courts. In the present case, when Gerald Gault was interrogated concerning violation of a section of the Arizona Criminal Code, it could not be certain that the Juvenile Court Judge would decide to "suspend" criminal prosecution in court for adults by proceeding to an adjudication in Juvenile Court.

It is also urged, as the Supreme Court of Arizona here asserted, that the juvenile and presumably his parents should not be advised of the juvenile's right to silence because confession is good for the child as the commencement of the assumed therapy of the juvenile court process, and he should be encouraged to assume an attitude of trust and confidence toward the officials of the juvenile process. This proposition has been subjected to widespread challenge on the basis of current reappraisals of the rhetoric and realities of the handling of juvenile offenders.

In fact, evidence is accumulating that confessions by juveniles do not aid in "individualized treatment," as the court below put it, and that compelling the child to answer questions, without warning or advice as to his right to remain silent, does not serve this or any other good purpose. In light of the observations of Wheeler and Cottrell, and others, it seems probable that where children are induced to confess by "paternal" urgings on the part of officials and the confession is then followed by disciplinary action, the child's reaction is likely to be hostile and adverse—the child may well feel that he has been led or tricked into confession and that despite his confession, he is being punished. . . .

We conclude that the constitutional privilege against self-incrimination is applicable in the case of juveniles as it is with respect to adults. We appreciate that special problems may arise with respect to waiver of the privilege by or on behalf of children, and that there may well be some differences in technique—but not in principle—depending upon the age of the child and the presence and competence of parents. The participation of counsel will, of course, assist the police, Juvenile Courts and appellate tribunals in administering the privilege. If counsel was not present for some permissible reason when an admission was obtained, the greatest care must be taken to assure that the admission was voluntary, in the sense not only that it was not coerced or suggested, but also that it was not the product of ignorance of rights or of adolescent fantasy, fright or despair.

The "confession" of Gerald Gault was first obtained by Officer Flagg, out of the presence of Gerald's parents, without counsel and without advising him of his right to silence, as far as appears. The judgment of the Juvenile Court was stated by the judge to be based on Gerald's admissions in court. Neither "admission" was reduced to writing, and, to say the least, the process by which the "admissions" were obtained and received must be characterized as lacking the certainty and order which are required of proceedings of such formidable consequences. Apart from the "admissions," there was nothing upon which a judgment or finding might be based. There was no sworn testimony. Mrs. Cook, the complainant, was not present. The Arizona Supreme Court held that "sworn testimony must be required of all witnesses including police officers, probation officers and others who are part of or officially related to the juvenile court structure." We hold that this is not enough. No reason is suggested or appears for a different rule in respect of sworn testimony in juvenile courts than in adult tribunals. Absent a valid confession adequate to support the determination of the Juvenile Court, confrontation and sworn testimony by witnesses available for cross-examination were essential for a finding of "delinquency" and an order committing Gerald to a state institution for a maximum of six years.

The recommendations in the Children's Bureau's "Standards for Juvenile and Family Courts" are in general accord with our conclusions. They state that testimony should be under oath and that only competent, material and relevant evidence under rules applicable to civil cases should be admitted in evidence. The New York Family Court Act contains a similar provision.

As we said in *Kent v. United States,* 383 U. S. 541, 554 (1966), with respect to waiver proceedings, "there is no place in our system of law for reaching a result of such tremendous consequences without ceremony . . . ." We now hold that, absent a valid confession, a determination of delinquency and an order of commitment to a state institution cannot be sustained in the absence of sworn testimony subjected to the opportunity for cross-examination in accordance with our law and constitutional requirements. . . .

For the reasons stated, the judgment of the Supreme Court of Arizona is reversed and the cause remanded for further proceedings not inconsistent with this opinion.

*It is so ordered.*

Mr. Justice Stewart, dissenting.

The Court today uses an obscure Arizona case as a vehicle to impose upon thousands of juvenile courts throughout the Nation restrictions that the Constitution made applicable to adversary criminal trials. I believe the Court's decision is wholly unsound as a matter of constitutional law, and sadly unwise as a matter of judicial policy.

Juvenile proceedings are not criminal trials. They are not civil trials. They are simply not adversary proceedings. Whether treating with a delinquent child, a neglected child, a defective child, or a dependent child, a juvenile proceeding's whole purpose and mission is the very opposite of the mission and purpose of a prosecution in a criminal court. The object of the one is correction of a condition. The object of the other is conviction and punishment for a criminal act.

In the last 70 years many dedicated men and women have devoted their professional lives to the enlightened task of bringing us out of the dark world of Charles Dickens in meeting our responsibilities to the child in our society. The result has been the creation in this century of a system of juvenile and family courts in each of the 50 States. There can be no denying that in many areas the performance of these agencies has fallen disappointingly short of the hopes and dreams of the courageous pioneers who first conceived them. For a variety of reasons, the reality has sometimes not even approached the ideal, and much remains to be accomplished in the administration of public juvenile and family agencies—in personnel, in planning, in financing, perhaps in the formulation of wholly new approaches.

I possess neither the specialized experience nor the expert knowledge to predict with any certainty where may lie the brightest hope for progress in dealing with the serious problems of juvenile delinquency. But I am certain that the answer does not lie in the Court's opinion in this case, which serves to convert a juvenile proceeding into a criminal prosecution.

The inflexible restrictions that the Constitution so wisely made applicable to adversary criminal trials have no inevitable place in the proceedings of those public social agencies known as juvenile or family courts. And to impose the Court's long catalog of requirements upon juvenile proceedings in every area of the country is to invite a long step backwards into the nineteenth century. In that era there were no juvenile proceedings, and a child was tried in a conventional criminal court with all the trappings of a conventional criminal trial. So it was that a 12-year-old boy named James Guild was tried in New Jersey for killing Catharine Beakes. A jury found him guilty of murder, and he was sentenced to death by hanging. The sentence was executed. It was all very constitutional.

A State in all its dealings must, of course, accord every person due process of law. And due process may require that some of the same restrictions which the Constitution has placed upon criminal trials must be imposed upon juvenile proceedings. For example, I suppose that all would agree that a brutally coerced confession could not constitutionally be considered in a juvenile court hearing. But it surely does not follow that the testimonial privilege against self-incrimination is applicable in all juvenile proceedings. Similarly, due process clearly requires timely notice of the purpose and scope of any proceedings affecting the relationship of parent and child. . . . But it certainly does not follow that notice of a juvenile hearing must be framed with all the technical niceties of a criminal indictment. . . .

In any event, there is no reason to deal with issues such as these in the present case. The Supreme Court of Arizona found that the parents of Gerald Gault "knew of their right to counsel, to subpoena and cross examine witnesses, of the right to confront the witnesses against Gerald and the possible consequences of a finding of delinquency." . . . It further found that "Mrs. Gault knew the exact nature of the charge against Gerald from the day he was taken to the detention home." . . . [N]o issue of compulsory self-incrimination is presented by this case.

I would dismiss the appeal.

# 26

## William M. Evan

## *Due Process of Law in Military and Industrial Organizations*

Of the various formalized rules governing human behavior, those dealing with work relations impinge directly and decisively on the style of life and the life chances of the average person. Such rules, whether legislated by the state or by a private corporation—with or without the participation of a trade union—have a pervasive effect, not only because people spend a large portion of their waking hours at work, but also because of the relative dominance of economic institutions, particularly in industrial societies. As Beardsley Ruml has stated:

> These rules determine for the individual where he shall work, when he shall work, what he shall do, who will give him orders, who will take

orders from him, his promotion and discipline, the amount he gets paid, the time and duration of his holidays and vacation.[1]

Rules such as these are the means of achieving organizational goals. Since conflict may arise with respect to both these rules and organizational goals, what formal provisions are there for resolving them? It can be argued that conflict is endemic to formal organizations because of the absence of complete consensus on organizational goals and rules. This lack of consensus arises because of the diversity of statuses and subunits in a formal organization. This diversity, in turn, generates different perspectives on goals and rules.[2]

In Weber's ideal-typical characterization of bureaucracy he alludes fleetingly to an appeals mechanism in connection with his assertion that offices are organized according to the principle of hierarchy. In his own words: "There is a right of appeal and of statement of grievances from the lower to the higher [offices]."[3] This right of appeal of a subordinate in a formal organization may be taken as characteristic of a rational-legal model of a bureaucracy. Unlike traditional or charismatic authority systems, a bureaucracy ideally delimits the authority of all office holders. The right of appeal, which in a formal organization functions as a mechanism for resolving authority conflicts, can be related to the constitutional doctrine of "procedural due process." This doctrine refers to a complex of norms for the impartial and fair handling of conflicts between the state and the citizen.

This paper explores some facets of the authority dimension of formal organization by considering the structural provisions for due process of law in the United States Army and the attitudes of military personnel toward this institution during World War II. In the interest of developing a perspective for a comparative analysis of formal organizations we shall compare the organization of the Army in respect to this particular institutional attribute with that of industrial organizations.[4]

## DUE PROCESS OF LAW IN THE ARMY

The Inspector General (IG) system of complaints, one of the less well-known institutions of the U. S. Army, is of special interest from the viewpoint of the structure of formal organizations in general and of industrial organizations in

[1] Beardsley Ruml, Corporate Management as a Locus of Power, in Edmond N. Cahn, ed., *The Power and Duties of Corporate Management (Social Meaning of Legal Concepts, No. 3)* (New York: New York University, 1950), p. 224. Cf. Melvin M. Tumin, Some Disfunctions of Institutional Imbalances, *Behavioral Science,* 1 (July 1956), 218-223.

[2] Cf. William M. Evan, Role Strains and the Norm of Reciprocity: Alternative Role-Models in Research Organizations, *American Journal of Sociology,* 47 (Nov. 1962), in press.

[3] Max Weber, *Theory of Social and Economic Organization,* trans. by A. M. Anderson and Talcott Parsons; ed. by Parsons (New York: Oxford University Press, 1947), p. 331.

[4] The absence of comparative studies of military and industrial organizations was recently noted by Janowitz. "Not a single empirical study exists comparing the military with business or other types of organization on this question, yet such studies would seem to be a first step in assessing the relevance of so-called principles of business administration for military organization" (Morris Janowitz, *Sociology and the Military Establishment* [New York: Russell Sage Foundation, 1959], p. 88).

particular. It is but one of several functions of the Office of the Inspector General—a staff organization—to receive complaints of any kind from all personnel of the Army. All Army personnel, enlisted men and officers alike (and even civilian employees), have a right to register complaints directly with an Inspector General officer instead of taking them up with their immediate superiors.[5] After inquiring about a complaint—defined in Army regulations as "an allegation of wrong or injustice suffered by the complainant, or inconvenience, grievance, or injury incurred"[6]—the IG recommends action to the relevant commanding officer. If the complainant is not satisfied, he may appeal to an IG officer at a higher echelon or to the Office of the Inspector General at the Headquarters of the Department of the Army in Washington.[7] This established right of Army personnel to communicate grievances orally or in writing with the IG may be interpreted as involving a right of "procedural due process of law."

We are not suggesting that the IG complaint procedure is the only provision for procedural due process of law in the Army. The Uniform Code of Military Justice incorporates this set of norms and values as well.[8] But whereas the Uniform Code of Military Justice applies to courts martial in which the complainant is always the Army—or rather the United States since they are criminal proceedings—in the case of the IG procedure, the complainant is invariably an enlisted man or an officer. As a type of "constitutional guarantee" against arbitrary authority, procedural due process, as it relates to the IG complaint procedure, has not received the attention that court-martial proceedings have in recent years,[9] which is another reason for focusing on the IG system.

The above sketch of the official function of the IG complaint procedure is sufficient to suggest that this institution involves an organizational anomaly in granting all Army personnel a legal right to lodge complaints directly with IG officers, for, in effect, it sanctions the circumventing of the chain of command in certain circumstances.

In an organization such as the Army few organizational principles are as fundamental as the chain of command. This involves the ordering of virtually all the statuses of the Army in a strict hierarchy and specifies that all communication, upward and downward, shall be through channels. Except for one's immediate superior and subordinate, *indirect* communication, rather than *direct* communication, is the rule in this type of organization.[10] Thus, if X wishes to

[5] Department of the Army, *Army Regulations,* 20-1, (Washington, D.C.: U.S. Government Printing Office, 16 July 1958), p. 18. par. 24b.

[6] Department of the Army, *Army Regulations,* 20-20, (Washington, D.C.: U. S. Government Printing Office, 16 May 1951), p. 1, par. 1a.

[7] Department of the Army, *Army Regulations,* 20-1 (Washington, D.C.: U. S. Government Printing Office, 16 July 1958), p. 21, par. 32a.

[8] *United States Code,* 1958 ed., Title 10 (Washington, D.C.: U.S. Government Printing Office, 1959), pp. 997-1036.

[9] See, for example, Frederick Bernays Wiener, Courts-Martial and the Bill of Rights: The Original Practice, I, II, *Harvard Law Review,* 72 (Nov. and Dec. 1958), 1-49; 266-304; Joseph W. Bishop, Jr., Civilian Judges and Military Justice: Collateral Review of Court-Martial Convictions, *Columbia Law Review,* 61 (Jan. 1961), 40-71.

[10] See, for example, Wilbert E. Moore, *Industrial Relations and the Social Order* (rev. ed.; New York, 1951), pp. 93-95.

communicate with Y who is neither his immediate subordinate nor his immediate superior, officially he may not communicate directly but rather through his superior, who in turn contacts Y's superior until finally Y is reached. In granting all personnel the right to communicate *directly* with an IG officer, the Army has developed an institution which is incompatible with the principle of the chain of command. We may characterize the conflict of organizational principles as that between a *vertical* versus a *horizontal* (or *lateral*) principle of communication.

## OBSTACLES TO DUE PROCESS

In view of this conflict of organizational principles, we would expect to find various obstacles to the implementation of the IG complaint system. The sources of these obstacles are threefold. First, the recruitment of IG personnel involves a status sequence for incumbents which in some respects is inherently dysfunctional to the IG complaint system. The personnel of the IG are not career staff specialists, but line officers recruited to the IG for a relatively brief tour of duty, after which they return to their duties as line officers.

As line officer, the Inspector General officer has been socialized into the value and norm of operating according to the principle of the chain of command. Upon transfer to the IG, he learns of the opposing principle of direct and horizontal communication. Since he is destined soon to return to his duties as a line officer, he is not likely to repudiate the value and norm of operating according to the principle of the chain of command, much less become committed to the function of the IG complaint procedure. Moreover, he probably perceives his being "detailed" to the IG office, from his previous wholly unrelated line office, as a downgrading, which in itself obstructs socialization into the values and norms of his new status. Accordingly, he may be inclined to uphold the prevailing norm and value of the line organization of "going through channels"; and may prefer that Army personnel take up complaints with their immediate superiors rather than come to him, although it is the complainant's acknowledged right to do so.

The hypothesized orientation of the IG officer, which stems from his temporary status as a staff specialist who is otherwise pursuing a line-oriented career, may generate a hypercritical attitude toward complaints submitted to him. He may have a tendency to view complaints as being largely unjustified. Thus the decision to recruit IG officers from the line organization for a brief tour of duty may well be a major structural obstacle to the implementation of the basic principle inspiring the IG complaint procedure, which we interpret as being the right of procedural due process of law.

A second obstacle to the implementation of the IG complaint system may be the attitude of line officers in general toward the IG complaint system. Committed to the principle of the chain of command, they probably resent the IG complaint system as incompatible with this principle. Resentment may be realistically based on the belief that any complaint involving an officer casts aspersion on his leadership ability and is interpreted by higher echelons as a "strike against him." Furthermore, line officers may view all complaints lodged with an IG officer, regardless of whether they themselves are the objects of the complaint, as evidence of a lack of confidence in them by their subordinates. In fact, line officers, although aware that it is everyone's right to submit a complaint to the IG, may be inclined to view such action by subordinates as virtually disloyal conduct; otherwise the complainant would have submitted the complaint to his immediate officer. It is not surprising then to find that commanding officers tend to urge their personnel to communicate their complaints to their immediate officers first before taking them up with an IG officer.

A third impediment to the implementation of the IG complaint system probably stems from the general orientation of Army personnel toward authority vested in office of superior rank. On the one hand, Army personnel, whether enlisted men or officers, may fear that if they register a complaint with the IG they will be the object of reprisals by their officers. The fact that they can also register a complaint regarding victimization—if it should occur—may not necessarily diminish the fear of reporting complaints to the IG. On the other hand, registering any complaint with a superior in the Army, even if the complaint does not directly involve the superior's judgment or ability, probably arouses feelings of anxiety or guilt on the part of the subordinate. As an organization with a rigid and formal system of controls, the Army instills a keen sense of obligation to obey one's superior. Moreover, the elaborate system of grading of enlisted men and officers with different increments of authority, prestige, and other forms of rewards generates a sense of awe, respect, and fear of superior office. The prevalence of "office charisma" together with the orientation toward authority indoctrinated by the Army may have the consequence of inhibiting personnel from registering complaints with an immediate superior or even with an IG officer, who is generally a major or higher in rank.

In short, there are at least three obstacles to the implementation of the IG complaint system: *(a)* the recruitment of line officers to perform a temporary staff function interferes with socialization into the values and norms of the IG status; *(b)* line officers probably perceive the IG complaint system as involving a principle of communication incompatible with that of the chain of command; *(c)* the indoctrination of an attitude of awe and unquestioning obedience toward authority vested in superior rank inhibits the registering of complaints with the IG for fear of being thought disloyal or of becoming the object of reprisals.

Perhaps because of the obstacles to the implementation of the IG complaint system, the office of the chaplain seems to have unofficially acquired a function in handling complaints. Personnel who lack confidence in the IG complaint system can bring their grievances to the chaplain, who provides a type of counseling not unlike that of the Hawthorne counselor.[11] Informally the chaplain may make representations on behalf of the complainant rather than process complaints in a judicial or adjudicative manner. Another staff organization which is probably unofficially performing a similar IG function is the Mental Hygiene Consultation Service established after World War II in the Surgeon General's Office.

[11]See, for example, the President's Committee on Religion and Welfare in the Armed Forces, *The Military Chaplaincy* (Washington, D.C.: U.S. Government Printing Office, 1950), p. 15; Department of the Army, *The Chaplain as a Counselor,* Pam. 16-60 (Washington, D.C.: U.S. Government Printing Office, 22 April 1958), p. 6.

## FACTORS FACILITATING DUE PROCESS

It does not follow that, because of several barriers to the implementation of the IG complaint system, it does not contribute to the resolution of interstatus conflicts. The mere existence of this conflict-resolution mechanism probably restrains officers from acting arbitrarily against one another and against enlisted men, for even if an officer or enlisted man should not be permitted to submit a complaint to the local IG officer—which occasionally happens—there is always the possibility that he will write a letter to the Office of the Inspector General in Washington, D.C.

The due process mechanism may be more useful in preventing the occurrence of serious rather than routine grievances for at least two reasons. First, notwithstanding the structurally induced reluctance on the part of subordinates to avail themselves of the IG system, substitute channels of communication of grievances, such as the Office of the Chaplain or the Mental Hygiene Consultation Service, serve to some extent to apprise higher echelons of the existence of some of the interstatus conflicts, particularly those involving flagrant violations of the rights of subordinates. The fact that some grievances do funnel up, whether via the IG system or the ancillary and informal systems, probably serves to discourage superiors from engaging in arbitrary behavior. Second, it is well known among all commissioned officers that the rate of IG grievances is one of the criteria employed by higher echelons in appraising the performance of officers. Thus, the existence of the IG system probably serves as an incentive to officers to conform to universalistic standards in their relations with subordinates and to avoid any obvious infringement of their rights.

In juxtaposing the barriers to the implementation of the IG complaint system with the factors facilitating its implementation, the difficult problem of standards of evaluation of organizational phenomena arises. With respect to any organizational goal, at least two standards of evaluation might be used. The first is a measure of goal attainment over time—whether there is an increase or a decrease in goal attainment. The second criterion of evaluation involves a comparison of the performance of an organization relative to a particular goal with the performance of another organization relative to the same goal.

In a comparison over time the incidence of IG complaints and the mode of disposition of these complaints—taking into account possible differences in the incidence of interstatus conflicts in peacetime and wartime conditions—would be one method of evaluation. Alternatively, for a given period of time, the IG system of the Army could be compared, for example, with the IG system in the Air Force, or else with data on the grievance system of industrial organizations. Because of the absence of comparable systematic data, only a rough comparison of the Army and industrial organizations is attempted in this paper.

## ATTITUDES TOWARD DUE PROCESS

The analysis of the IG complaint system set forth above was supported by the observations of four IG colonels whom we interviewed in 1960. Three of these informants were infantry officers prior to their assignment to the IG, and one was an artillery officer. All four evidenced little commitment to the function of the IG, presumably because of their continuing loyalty to their previous status as line officers. Thus two of the colonels repeatedly expressed surprise that enlisted men did not first discuss their problems with their commanding officers instead of with an IG officer. One of the colonels even ventured the opinion that "if officers were perfect, there would surely be no need for an IG." Another colonel recalled an experience which reflects his ambivalence toward his IG function:

> I was recently on an IG inspection in Fort Wayne. Two MP's who were sergeants came into my office and complained that they were assigned to guard the gate of the Fort instead of being assigned to duty in Detroit. They felt that this was unfair because privates and corporals were usually assigned to duty at the gate and sergeants in the city. Since the commanding officer was a friend of mine, I took the MP's with me to see whether we could straighten this out unofficially. I told the commanding officer the nature of the complaint of the two sergeants. He replied that it was simply a matter of shortage of personnel. He did not have any privates or corporals on hand for duty at the gate, but expected some in a week or two, at which time the two sergeant MP's would be assigned to duty in the city. I turned to the two MP's and asked whether that was satisfactory, and they said, "Yes, very satisfactory. Thank you very much, sir." At that point the commanding officer turned to the two MP's and said, "Every morning when I come to work I pass you men at the gate and say "good morning." At noon when I go to lunch, I pass you men at the gate again and say "hello." When I come back from lunch, I pass you men again and say "hello"; and when I go home in the evening I pass you once more. Now, why haven't you men thought of talking to *me* about this problem instead of bothering the IG?" The MP's were silent for a moment and then one of them replied, "I don't know, sir; I'm sorry."

The IG colonel then asked the writer, "Can *you* tell me why these men didn't raise this problem with their commanding officer instead of coming to me?" The writer suggested the possibility that the fear of authority vested in a superior's office is so strong in the Army as to inhibit communication of problems between subordinates and superordinates.

Given the obstacles to the implementation of the IG complaint system discussed above at least two classes of factors are significant in the registering of complaints with the Inspector General: *(a)* the social-historical situation in which the Army functions; and *(b)* the status attributes and orientations of personnel.

In the peacetime Army, such as that before World War II, enlisted men as well as officers served voluntarily. Accordingly, we would expect such personnel to have a different orientation toward the Army from those who serve involuntarily, as was the case during World War II and in the postwar period. In particular, "regular" Army personnel, i.e., "professional soldiers," are likely to be more identified with the organization's goals and norms than are the personnel of a drafted Army, i.e., of "amateur soldiers." Furthermore, professional soldiers are more likely to internalize norms pertaining to duties than norms pertaining to rights, whereas the reverse is probably true of amateur soldiers.

If these hypotheses are true, it follows that Army personnel in the pre-World War II period were probably less sensitive to injustices than their counterparts during the war and hence were less disposed to register complaints with the IG. These expectations were confirmed—in the absence of systematic data—by observations based on personal experiences of the four IG informants.

In addition, the status attributes and orientations of personnel probably affect the registering of complaints with the IG. We would anticipate, on the basis of findings by the authors of *The American Soldier,*[12] that personnel whose civilian status is higher than their Army status are more likely to experience relative deprivation and hence more likely to lodge complaints than those with the reverse set of status attributes. Similarly, the higher the level of education, the greater the level of information about legal rights and the greater the sensitivity to these rights. We further predict that Army personnel who are more oriented to careers in their civilian status than to careers in their Army status are more likely to take the risk of victimization in submitting complaints to the IG. Fortunately, some data bearing on status attributes and orientations of Army personnel toward the IG complaints system are available in a survey conducted in 1945 by the Research Branch of the War Department.[13] We present a "secondary analysis" of some of these data.[14]

Of the sample of 2,908 enlisted men, representing a cross section of soldiers stationed in the United States who filled out a questionnaire containing questions on the IG, 20 per cent answered "Yes" to the question: "Have you ever taken a problem or complaint to the Inspector General?" On the other hand, 40 per cent answered "Yes" to the question: "Have you ever felt like taking a problem or complaint to the IG *but then decided not to do so?*" This appreciable discrepancy between those who did in fact submit a complaint and those who felt like doing so but did not, suggests that there were indeed obstacles in 1945 to the implementation of the IG complaint procedure. The reasons given for not registering a complaint when one felt like doing so were classified by the authors of *The American Soldier* as follows: difficulty in getting to see the IG, ueslessness of seeing the IG, and fear of reprisal.[15] Unfortunately, the reasons given for not submitting complaints to the IG when one felt like doing so were not coded on the IBM cards of this survey. We shall, therefore, restrict our analysis to the first question, namely, what factors affect the decision to avail oneself of the right of due process in the Army.

Of all the sociological variables included in the survey, one which is significantly and positively associated with submitting complaints to the IG is level of education. The higher the level of education, the higher the proportion of soldiers who

[12]Samuel A. Stouffer *et al., The American Soldier* (Princeton, N. J.: Princeton University, 1949), I, 326-328.

[13]*Ibid.*, pp. 398-401.

[14]The late Samuel A. Stouffer was kind enough to make available the IBM cards of Survey 229A of the Research Branch of the War Department for "a secondary analysis" in connection with the research for this paper.

[15]Stouffer *et al., op. cit.,* I, 399.

TABLE 1. RELATIONSHIP BETWEEN LEVEL OF EDUCATION AND SUBMITTING COMPLAINTS TO THE IG.

| *Level of education* | *Total N in category* | *Per cent who complain to the IG* |
|---|---|---|
| Grade school or less | 75 | 14 |
| Some high school | 120 | 16 |
| High school graduate | 232 | 22 |
| Some college or more | 145 | 26 |

$X^2 = 26.45$; 3 d.f.; $p < .001$.

TABLE 2. RELATIONSHIP BETWEEN LEVEL OF EDUCATION AND SUBMITTING COMPLAINTS TO THE IG WHEN BELIEF IN MILITARY JUSTICE IS HELD CONSTANT.

| *Belief in military justice* | *Level of education of those complaining to IG* — *Some high school or less* | | *High school graduate* | | *Some college or more* | | |
|---|---|---|---|---|---|---|---|
| | % | *N* | % | *N* | % | *N* | |
| Low score (0) | 25 | (53) | 27 | (82) | 30 | (58) | $X^2 = 1.22$; 2 d.f.; $p < .70$ |
| Medium score (1,2) | 17 | (75) | 24 | (105) | 27 | (60) | $X^2 = 11.12$; 2 d.f.; $p < .01$ |
| High score (3,4,5,6) | 11 | (67) | 15 | (45) | 21 | (27) | $X^2 = 10.23$; 2 d.f.; $p < .01$ |

TABLE 3. RELATIONSHIP BETWEEN LEVEL OF EDUCATION AND SUBMITTING COMPLAINTS TO THE IG WHEN SATISFACTION WITH ARMY LIFE IS HELD CONSTANT

| *Satisfaction with army life* | *Level of education of those complaining to IG* — *Some high school or less* | | *High school graduate* | | *Some college or more* | | |
|---|---|---|---|---|---|---|---|
| | % | *N* | % | *N* | % | *N* | |
| Low score (0,1,2) | 27 | (87) | 29 | (101) | 31 | (70) | $X^2 = 1.26$; 2 d.f.; $p < .70$ |
| Medium score (3,4) | 13 | (60) | 21 | (79) | 31 | (55) | $X^2 = 31.54$; 2 d.f.; $p < .001$ |
| High score (5,6,7) | 10 | (48) | 17 | (52) | 14 | (20) | $X^2 = 7.49$; 2 d.f.; $p < .05$ |

registered a complaint with the IG (see Table 1). The variable of level of education may be interpreted as bearing upon the socialization process in the Army. Soldiers with a higher level of education are more likely to learn what the rules and regulations are, including their rights and duties, and have higher reward

**TABLE 4.** RELATIONSHIP BETWEEN LEVEL OF EDUCATION AND SUBMITTING COMPLAINTS TO THE IG WHEN BELIEF IN AUTHORITARIAN LEADERSHIP PRINCIPLES IS HELD CONSTANT.

| | *Level of education of those complaining to IG* | | | | | | |
|---|---|---|---|---|---|---|---|
| *Belief in authoritarian leadership principles* | *Some high school or less* | | *High school graduate* | | *Some college or more* | | |
| | % | *N* | % | *N* | % | *N* | |
| Low score (0) | 18 | (109) | 24 | (151) | 29 | (94) | $X^2 = 16.64$; 2 d.f.; $p < .001$ |
| Medium score (1) | 13 | (58) | 22 | (66) | 25 | (40) | $X^2 = 14.97$; 2 d.f.; $p < .001$ |
| High score (2,3) | 12 | (28) | 14 | (15) | 17 | (11) | $X^2 = .95$; 2 d.f.; $p < .70$ |

expectations. They are also more likely to have a critical attitude when they discover that their rights have been infringed.

We shall further explore, with the aid of some data from the survey mentioned, the nature of the relationship between education and submitting a complaint to the IG by testing whether several attitudinal variables act as intervening or as conditional variables.[16] The attitudinal variables in question are three: (1) belief in military justice, i.e., in the just administration of law in the Army;[17] (2)

[16] Cf. Patricia L. Kendall and Paul F. Lazarsfeld, "Problems of Survey Analysis" in Robert K. Merton and Paul F. Lazarsfeld, eds., *Continuities in Social Research: Studies in the Scope and Method of "The American Soldier"* (Glencoe, Ill.: Free Press, 1950), pp. 147-165.

[17] An index of belief in military justice, constructed by the author, consists of the following three questions. An X indicates a positive response which was given a weighting of 2; a negative response was given a weighting of 0; and an "undecided" response, a weighting of 1.

Do you agree or disagree with this statement?
"Courts-martial decisions are always fair." (Check one)
__X__ Strongly agree
__X__ Agree
____ Undecided
____ Disagree
____ Strongly disagree

"In courts martial, an enlisted man will receive as fair treatment as an officer." (Check one)
__X__ Strongly agree
__X__ Agree
____ Undecided
____ Disagree
____ Strongly disagree

"Soldiers who break Army rules and regulations are nearly always caught and punished." (Check one)
__X__ Strongly agree
__X__ Agree
____ Undecided
____ Disagree
____ Strongly disagree

satisfaction with Army life;[18] and (3) belief in authoritarian leadership principles.[19]

When we hold constant each of the three attitudinal variables, we find that the original relationship between education and submitting complaints to the IG is modified. With respect to the variable of belief in military justice, among those with

[18] A Guttman scale of satisfaction with Army life, constructed by the authors of *The American Soldier,* consists of the following seven questions. An X indicates a positive response on the scale.

All things considered, do you think the Army is run about as well as possible, or do you think it could be run better?
__X__ It is run about as well as possible, everything considered.
_____ It could be run somewhat better.
_____ It could be run a lot better.

In general, do you think the Army has tried its best to see that men get as square a deal as possible?
__X__ Yes, it has tried its best.
_____ It has tried some but not hard enough.
_____ It has hardly tried at all.

In general, do you feel you yourself have gotten a square deal from the Army?
__X__ Yes, in most ways I have.
__X__ In some ways, yes, in other ways, no.
_____ No, on the whole I haven't gotten a square deal.

Do you feel that the Army has tried its best to look out for the welfare of the enlisted men?
__X__ Yes, it has tried its best.
__X__ It has tried some, but not hard enough.
_____ It has hardly tried at all.

In general, how interested do you think the Army has been in your own welfare?
__X__ Very much.
__X__ Pretty much.
_____ Not so much.
_____ Not at all.

In general, how well do you think the Army is run?
__X__ It is run very well.
__X__ It is run pretty well.
_____ It is not run so well.
_____ It is run very poorly.
__X__ Undecided.

Do you think when you are discharged you will go back to civilian life with a *favorable* or *unfavorable* attitude toward the Army?
__X__ Very favorable.
__X__ Fairly favorable.
__X__ About 50-50.
_____ Very unfavorable.
_____ Fairly unfavorable.

[19] A Guttman scale of belief in authoritarian leadership principles, constructed by the authors of *The American Soldier,* consists of the following three questions. An X indicates a positive response on the scale.

Here are some statements made about officers and their jobs. You will find that you agree with some and disagree with others.

"An officer has to be very strict with his men or else they will take advantage of him."
__X__ Agree
_____ Undecided
_____ Disagree

a low score on this index, education makes virtually no difference as to whether soldiers submitted complaints to the IG. Only among those with a medium or high score on the index of belief in military justice is the relationship between education and submitting complaints to the IG maintained (see Table 2). Similarly, when we hold constant the variable of satisfaction with Army life, among those with a low satisfaction score our original relationship is significantly attenuated (see Table 3).

These two attitudinal variables, belief in military justice and satisfaction with Army life, are in fact positively correlated. Since among those with low scores on the scale of satisfaction with Army life and on the index of military justice, a significantly higher proportion, regardless of education, submitted complaints, we may conclude that these attitudinal variables are partly affected by the experiences some soldiers had in the course of submitting complaints to the IG. Thus it is possible that these two attitudinal variables are not acting as intervening variables but rather as conditional variables. Soldiers who submitted complaints to the IG and who were dissatisfied with the disposition of their complaints may have become alienated from the Army as reflected in a decrease in their belief in military justice and in their satisfaction with Army life.

As regards the variable of belief in authoritarian leadership principles, among those with a high score on this scale education has an insignificant effect on whether one submits complaints to the IG (see Table 4). Regardless of education, those who have a high score on the scale of belief in authoritarian leadership principles are probably more likely to accept the authority of their superiors as legitimate and to internalize their duties than are those with a low score, and hence are less likely to submit complaints to the IG.

In brief, the relationship between education and submitting complaints to the IG holds under at least three conditions: *(a)* if soldiers have a medium or high degree of belief in military justice; *(b)* if they have a medium or high degree of satisfaction with Army life, and *(c)* if they have a low or medium degree of belief in authoritarian leadership principles.

In view of the structural and attitudinal obstacles to the implementation of the IG complaint system, we may conclude that the IG mechanism of due process in the Army, as of 1945, was inadequately institutionalized as well as inadequately internalized. By *institutionalization* we mean the extent to which the provision of norms and statuses contributes to the accomplishment of a particular objective; by *internalization* is meant the extent to which the status occupants of a social system are committed to the objective in question. Deficiencies in the institutionalization of the IG complaint procedure have already been considered; deficiencies in the internalization of the norms of due process may be inferred from some of the

---

"An officer who is friendly with the enlisted men loses some of his authority over them."
___X___Agree
________Undecided
________Disagree

"An officer will lose the respect of his men if he pals around with them off-duty."
___X___Agree
________Undecided
________Disagree

survey findings and the informant testimony. During World War II officers as well as enlisted men had apparently not yet internalized as a positive value the right of procedural due process via the registering of complaints with the IG. The Doolittle Board's report in 1946 took cognizance of some of the weaknesses of the Office of the Inspector General.[20] Whether its recommended structural changes have since strengthened this institution, both with respect to the institutionalization and the internalization of norms of due process, we were not able to discover.

## DUE PROCESS IN INDUSTRIAL ORGANIZATIONS

A functional approximation, if not equivalent, of the Army's IG complaint procedure in industrial organizations is the grievance procedure provided by collective bargaining agreements between trade unions and employers. A basic feature of collective bargaining agreements is the established right of workers to initiate grievances in accordance with contractually stipulated procedures which insure that conflicts are impartially adjudicated. The procedures for processing grievances involve successive stages or appeals culminating in an arbitration procedure.

Several notable differences distinguish the IG complaint system and the grievance machinery of industrial organizations. The unionized worker submitting a grievance has a shop steward or some other union official who functions as his counsel, so to speak, vis-à-vis management; the enlisted man or officer in registering a complaint with the IG has no such "third party." The stages in the grievance procedure—which often number three or four—and the amount of time required for processing a grievance through each stage, are known in advance to the aggrieved party. This is not true of the process of registering a complaint with the IG. These differences suggest that the grievance machinery is probably a more effective safeguard of the rights of due process of law of unionized workers than the IG complaint system is of military personnel. We also predict that unionized workers as well as management are more committed to the right of initiating a grievance[21] than are military personnel to the right of lodging a complaint with the IG. In other words, the norms of due process are probably more internalized among industrial personnel than among personnel in the Army. On the other hand, one of the strengths of the IG complaint system, as compared with the grievance machinery in industry, is that it applies to *all* personnel in the Army; the grievance machinery, by contrast, is confined to unionized employees, who are predominantly manual workers.

[20] U.S. War Department, *The Report of the Secretary of War's Board on Officer-Enlisted Man Relationships* (Washington, D.C.: Infantry Journal Press, 1946). pp. 19-20, 29.

[21] Pertinent and systematic evidence on this point is lacking in the literature. See, however, Harold W. Davey, *Contemporary Collective Bargaining* (Englewood Cliffs, N. J.: Prentice-Hall, 1959), p. 134: "Most employers and union leaders agree that the real heart of collective bargaining is in the administration of collective agreements. This conclusion points up the crucial importance of developing smoothly functioning equitable machinery for the adjustment of grievances." See also Neil W. Chamberlain, *Collective Bargaining* (New York: McGraw Hill, 1951), p. 99: "The spread of the grievance system can almost be measured by the acceptance of arbitration as the final stage of that system."

In comparing the IG complaint system with the grievance machinery under collective bargaining, we wish to point up a difference between industrial and military organization which may be of considerable importance. In industrial organizations, nonunionized employees—who generally include clerical workers, technical personnel, and, of course, various levels of executives—do not have any formal rights of procedural due process of law such as Army personnel have in the IG complaint system or unionized employees in the grievance machinery.[22] These categories of personnel in industrial organizations are consequently entirely subject to the authority of superiors, regardless of whether the authority is legitimate or rational. The superiors of these occupational categories have, in effect, the right to make final decisions about any technical or administrative problem, and subordinates have no choice but to obey, unless they are willing to jeopardize their chances for promotion or possibly even risk losing their jobs.[23]

The absence of norms of procedural due process for clerical, technical, and managerial employees in industrial organizations is especially significant in view of the secular increase in the absolute as well as in the relative number of employees in these occupational categories. Correlatively, the absence of unionism among them and the improbability of unionization means that the lack of protection of rights of due process may be a serious source of strain for these employees. Two mechanisms tend, however, to reduce whatever strain results from this lack of institutionalization of due process. The first is the institutionalization of the right of job transfer within the industrial organization. If such a norm exists, it enables a nonmanual and nonunionized employee, who finds himself in an unsatisfactory authority relationship with a supervisor, to transfer without having to adjust to an arbitrary supervisor. The second mechanism is "job rotation." To the extent that the latter becomes an institutionalized procedure, it affords this type of employee an opportunity to manifest his abilities to more than one supervisor and in a variety of organizational situations, thus increasing the chances of a more objective appraisal of his ability.

Two organizational devices which only superficially resemble the norms of due process are the "open door"[24] policy and the "suggestion system."[25] In a large

[22] It is noteworthy that the potential usefulness of the IG complaint procedure in industrial organizations has recently been denied. Cf. Louis Cassels and Raymond L. Randall, Help Workers' Views Come Through, *Nation's Business,* 48 (Jan. 1960), 73. On the other hand, there is also some recent expression of awareness of the need for a grievance procedure for clerical, technical, managerial, and other employees not covered by collective bargaining agreement. Cf. John B. Coyle, Setting up Effective Communication and Grievance-Procedure Systems, *Office Management,* 31 (Feb. 1960), 26-31; and How to Set up a Grievance-Procedure System in a Non-union Office, *Office Management,* 31 (March 1960), 29-38.

[23] For an analysis of the problem of due process among middle managers in industrial organizations and its relation to the ideology of the "organization man," see William M. Evan, Organization Man and Due Process of Law, *American Sociological Review,* 26 (Aug. 1961), 540-547.

[24] See, for example, Stanley J. Seimer, *Suggestion Plans in American Industry* (Syracuse, N.Y.: Syracuse University Press, 1959); Charles E. Redfield, *Communication in Management* (Chicago: University of Chicago Press, 1953), pp. 140-158.

[25] See, for example, John T. Lloyd and Robert D. Gray, *Conference Readers' Guide for Supervision of Scientific and Engineering Personnel,* Bull. No. 26A (Pasadena, Calif.: Industrial Institute of Technology, 1956), pp. 27-28.

industrial organization an "open door" policy is not likely to be perceived as an effective means for redressing wrongs because of the social and hierarchical distance between the rank-and-file employee and the higher levels of executives whose doors are allegedly open for the righting of wrongs. A "suggestion system" tends to be viewed as an equally ineffective vehicle for the airing of grievances, though it may encourage innovative ideas if an adequate incentive is provided.

## CONCLUSION

Our comparison of the IG complaint procedure with the grievance procedure in industry led us to the conclusion that in some respects the norms of due process are more *institutionalized* in the Army than in industrial organizations, but that they are less *internalized* among the personnel of the Army than of industrial organizations. This conclusion suggests the problem of comparing formal organizations on the scales of institutionalization and internalization of the norms of due process. Our exploratory effort at such a comparison in this paper suggests that once a variety of formal organizations are ordered on a composite index of institutionalization and internalization of the norms of due process, we would be in a position to develop propositions as to the conditions favoring or impeding these social processes. Such propositions would contribute to a neglected facet of the theory of formal organization.

# 27

## Newton Morton

## *The Commerce Power Without Bounds*

The more one studies the ramification of the regulations possible under the aegis of the commerce power, the more one comes to the conclusion, that as it is applied at this time, it will support practically anything in the way of controls which Congress wants to apply, much as, in the Nebbia Case the high court ruled that there is no closed class or category of business "affected with the public interest."

In the Polish Alliance Case, Justice Frankfurter attempted to allay fears along this line and to assure us as to the future of the Federal System. He said:

> The interpretations of modern society have not wiped out state lines. It is not for us to make inroads upon our federal system either by

> indifference to its maintenance or excessive regard for the unifying forces of modern technology. Scholastic reasoning may prove that no activity is isolated within the boundaries of a single state, but that cannot justify absorption of legislative power by the United States over every activity.

This would certainly indicate that there is a sphere of activity which continues to rest with the states. If this were clearly so, it would appear that it would be possible for the high court to treat with some definiteness such powers which continue under state control. Certainly, delineation of such areas in which the state is supreme does not seem to be available at this time, but if it is not now available, what is to be the source of the clarification for the enlightenment of citizens, the states, and Congress? While Justice Frankfurter's reassuring pronouncement might be taken as providing substantiation for the advocates of the federal government concept, as distinct from the nationalist concept, the unmistakable lesson of recent cases, as Dr. Corwin stated, is that the preservation of our Federal System depends today mainly upon Congress. This is to say that Congress should provide the dicta which would clarify the issue for us.

It would seem that, since the United States Supreme Court has reversed itself to draw unto the central government powers which it stated at one time the central government did not have, it is not beyond the bounds of hope and reason to have them reverse themselves once more and seize some convenient case to delineate the limits of the spheres of influence of the state governments on the one hand and the central government on the other, so that we may "regroup and advance." Otherwise, there will continue to be a morass of uncertainty wherein there will be no definitive determination of the powers which continue to rest with the states.

The situation constitutes a lawyer's paradise, but a layman's nightmare.

## IMMEDIACY OF THE PROBLEM OF THE SCOPE OF THE COMMERCE CLAUSE

Interstate Commerce presently connotes operations which precede and follow commercial intercourse; no form of state activity can thwart the regulatory power granted by the commerce clause to Congress; the power is to be considered as an instrument for other purposes of general policy and interest; it covers every species of transmission of intelligence; it covers every species of commercial negotiation.

While these relatively few cases gave a good idea of the far-reaching influence of the commerce clause, it is most interesting to emphasize that this influence is not something confined to the dim or even the relatively recent past. In the Akron Beacon Journal for Friday, January 10th, 1964, there was an article by Richard Stout concerning the House Rules Committee hearings on the civil rights bill. The seemingly jolly concept of a floor show pervaded:

> Representative Howard W. Smith and Representative Emanuel Celler traded jibes and jokes . . . (the former) questioned the extent to which

> the public accommodations part of the bill is based on Congress' right to regulate interstate commerce and asked whether baked beans shipped from Boston to another state might bring 'a groceryman' under the provisions of the bill . . . (he went on) I'm wearing a suit of clothes and I cross the river to come from Virginia to Congress every day. Does that mean my suit is moving under interstate commerce?

While this was cited in an apparent effort of Representative Smith to ridicule the idea that the commerce clause could be used to justify any such extension of power actually the clause seems to be headed that way, strange as it may seem. In one case, it was ruled that employees of a window cleaning company, the greater part of whose work is done on the windows of industrial plants of producers of goods for interstate commerce were held to be within the provisions of the Fair Labor Standards Act! Does this seem any more ridiculous than to have Representative Smith's clothes pass inspection whichever of his one or two suits according to the account, he was wearing? It does not appear so.

The frequency with which questions arise involving the basic issue of where federal authority is delimited and that of the states takes over indicates that additional clarification is necessary. Sometime, and the sooner the better, and somehow there should be a definitive determination in the most fundamental sense of that term as to whether any controls and, if so, what controls, are under the primary jurisdiction of the states. Is anything desired by the central government to be considered to be substantiated by and able to be effected under the commerce clause? If this is true, doesn't it seem that there is no longer a federal government and that the evolution into a national government has, for all practical purposes, obliterated the states as separate entities, which was pretty much along the lines which the State of Virginia and others, as well as Hamilton, wanted back in the days of the Constitutional Convention?

It is realized fully that these do not constitute original questions, but it is also apparent that their previous advancement has not elicited sufficiently clear and satisfactory answers.

# 28

## S. Sidney Ulmer
## *Congressional Predictions of Judicial Behavior*

From 1789 to 1959, from Jefferson to Jenner, criticisms of the United States Supreme Court have been commonplace. Attacks upon the Court have been motivated by dissatisfaction with various facets of the judicial process; perhaps the most important area of dissatisfaction has centered on the decisional behavior of the justices. As a result, bills designed to establish qualifications for those appointed to the Court are continually being introduced in Congress. The number of such attempts reflects concern on the part of individual congressmen over the fact that, while the position of Supreme Court Justice is among the most important in the government, neither Constitution nor statute establishes requirements for those appointed to the Court. This is indeed strange when one considers that even the President must meet certain constitutional requirements; that is, he must be 35 years of age, a naturalborn citizen, and 14 years a resident within the United States. Thus, a man such as Frankfurter [who was born abroad as an Austrian subject] may serve as Supreme Court Justice but not as President of the United States.

Of course, there is little danger that the President will appoint a blundering idiot to the Court, but there is nothing to prevent him from so doing. Since Washington's second term, the "advice and consent" of the Senate to Supreme Court nominations has meant that the Senate merely gives "consent." There is no advising function. Consent itself tends to be automatic confirmation. This is reflected in the fact that only one nomination in this century has failed to receive Senate confirmation. This failure had nothing whatsoever to do with the "quality" of the individual involved but resulted from political pressure from the labor movement.

The role of confidential adviser to the President is filled by the Department of Justice. At present, it appears that the Department considers, among other factors, (1) the experience of the individual, (2) his character, and (3) political affiliation and activity. The last factor, ironically, may actually eliminate many men who are eminently qualified under the other two. Moreover, it is not known what other factors are considered, how often the factors change, who furnishes the information upon which the judgment is based, etc. At any rate, this system is not apt to maximize the qualities one normally expects to find in Supreme Court Justices. What are these qualities?

As Willard Hurst has pointed out, one difficulty in appraising the quality of the bench in the United States has been a lack of agreement on the qualities that make a good judge. Individual congressmen, however, have held strong convictions on this score and have spelled these out in the process of advocating passage of particular "qualification" bills.

Generally speaking, bills designed to restrict or limit the Supreme Court in some formal manner represent *prediction* on the part of their sponsors. Each such bill assumes a particular relationship between the formal requirement proposed and subsequent judicial behavior. For example, those who advocate the election of judges are predicting that an elected judge will behave differently from an appointed one. Hypotheses along this line are empirically testable at the State [government] level, since one may compare elective and nonelective systems in terms of the behavior predicted. While the work done in this area is sketchy, some of the relationships have been studied. The available evidence indicates that appointment of judges does not guarantee a more conservative bench than election.

The relationships between formal requirements and subsequent judicial behavior, which are assumed in bills designed to limit or restrict the United States Supreme Court, present peculiar problems for empirical investigation. There is only one Supreme Court and its uniqueness as an institution makes comparison with any other domestic court unlikely to be fruitful. (Possibly, one might make cross-cultural comparisons.) But, if we study the Court in terms of the nine individual justices, some of the difficulties are overcome. We may concentrate upon the relations predicted between formal requirements for *individual* justices and subsequent judicial behavior. These relationships may be empirically clarified if the variable specified in the formal requirement has frequently been associated with individual judges in the past.

Congressional bills incorporating such variables are often introduced. Among the most common types are those requiring prior judicial service for all persons appointed to the United States Supreme Court. This type of bill has been quite conspicuous in post-1954 periods. In 1956-1957, for example, at least 13 bills or resolutions of this nature were presented to Congress for action. A typical bill is S-3759, which was introduced by Senator Smathers of Florida. This bill would require five years previous judicial service on a federal bench or the highest State bench for all nominees to the Supreme Court. S-3811, introduced by Senator Long of Louisiana, would require six years' service on a court of record. Senate Resolution 264, presented by Senator Stennis of Mississippi in 1956 and reintroduced in 1957, would require at least one of each two successive appointees to the Court confirmed by the Senate to have at least ten years' service on a federal bench or on a State court of general jurisdiction. Such proposals are motivated, of course, by a dissatisfaction with decisional behavior of Supreme Court justices, combined with the belief that judicial behavior may be influenced in the desired direction by the variables incorporated in the form of requirements. The sponsors of these measures assume a relationship between the variables and the desired behavior; they are predicting that the introduction of their particular variable will have a specific impact upon Supreme Court decision-making.

The impact that is predicted is spelled out in comments upon the measures by their authors. Thus, Senator Long feels that the meaning of the Constitution does not change through time. The Court, he says, should follow precedent. It should not react to political pressures. His bill, in effect, predicts that prior judicial service operates to produce precedent-following judges. Stennis wants a court composed of justices "wedded to the system of precedent." He thinks his bill will maximize such inclinations. Smathers deplores policy-making judges. The function of the judge, in his mind, is "merely to interpret the Constitution and laws passed in relation thereto."

Clearly, these three Senators are predicting that prior judicial service will tend to produce a Supreme Court of strict constructionists. The great judge, in their minds, is the strict legalist, the non-policy-making judge who makes his decisions in terms of legal rules and couches his decisional explanations in legal jargon.

In contradistinction to this view, Justice Frankfurter has declared that "one is entitled to say without qualification that the correlation between prior judicial service and fitness for the functions of the Supreme Court is zero." Students of the subject will no doubt disagree as to what constitutes "fitness for the functions" of the Court. But, all will agree to the importance of validating or disproving broad, general statements about relationships or alleged correlations. We do not have to take such statements at face value. One can discover on other than intuitional bases whether the correlation asserted by Frankfurter is fact, or a figment of his imagination fertilized by a lack of judicial service prior to taking his seat on the Supreme Court bench. Predictions of the Smathers type may be studied empirically with considerable promise of success, since the particular variable involved has frequently been present in the background of Supreme Court appointees. The inquiry should pose the question: "Have appointees to the United States Supreme Court with prior judicial service evinced a greater tendency toward strict construction of the Constitution than appointees without such service?"

Such a study might involve the following: (1) a general survey of the "qualification" problem; (2) a survey of congressional attempts to establish qualifications for Supreme Court appointees; (3) a consideration of the constitutional ramifications of such attempts; (4) the abstraction and categorization of the behavioral assumptions and predictions in total congressional effort in this area; (5) the development of a set of hypotheses in terms of which the assumptions and predictions can be empirically tested; (6) the collection of necessary data; (7) analysis; (8) conclusions.

There are clear reasons for making such a study. A positive relationship between certain social background variables and judicial behavior is freely predicted in a public forum. The existence of the relationship is a vital factor in the advocacy and support of certain suggested legislation. Yet, the relationships are assumed, not proved. An investigation of the type suggested here would be of considerable assistance to the policymaker who is attempting to formulate and articulate legislation in the public interest. A study, if successful, would likewise furnish the appointing officer (the President in this case) with needed information, permitting appointments to be made in a more intelligent setting. Nominations to the Supreme Court cannot be made without consideration of the possible consequences. A nominational decision must be made in terms of the role and function of the Court as envisaged by the executive. The President must, therefore, make a judgment or prediction in each case as to the extent to which a particular nominee will contribute to the maximization of these goals. It should be noted in passing that Eisenhower appears to have accepted the Smathers, Long, Stennis theory of what makes a great judge. His last four appointees to the Court have all had extensive judicial experience prior to taking a seat on the high bench.

# The City

It could be argued that Americans are congenitally incapable of erecting decent cities. This is the land of the cowboys and Indians, the land of the Christmas card showing the old farm. Nevertheless, the city has been the crowning glory of American culture and civilization, producing almost all of the American contributions to art, science, music, and literature. Since World War II, there has been a growing appreciation of the hard fact that America either has to master the city or the city will destroy America. And Congress, insofar as it believes in state government and the rural way of life, had better reform its ideology. A radical reconstruction of state and local government is needed. Nothing but very great plans will suffice.

The first article in this chapter shows why many people believe such radical reconstruction is necessary. This article by Richard Reeves, a reporter for the *New York Times,* is an excellent journalistic account of the progress of a highly touted reform in a great American city. It describes a twenty-month delay in the start of a huge and necessary project. This project was not blocked by private or group interests but by a great, confused bureaucratic mess. Similar situations probably exist in hundreds of other cities. No wonder some people believe it is better to tear things down and start over.

Perhaps the most important difference between the madness of our times and that of a previous generation is between the poverty pictured in Victor Hugo's *Les Miserables* and the frustration of Franz Kafka's hero in trying to penetrate the bureaucratic mazes that kept him from reaching the castle to which he had been summoned. Everything is assured; the publicity operates; but nothing happens. Movement is frozen. What could be done to prevent such situations?

The next selection, by Daniel Moynihan, points out some of the new techniques that may be used in the next few years to facilitate the delivery of social services by the government. Mr. Moynihan, an urban affairs advisor to President Nixon in 1969-1971, is a good example of the "question mark" leader in the United States. He is not really a liberal, nor a conservative, fascist, communist, or socialist. Perhaps he is a pragmatist. At any rate, he is ready to dump or to buy anything, if only the problems involved are met head-on.

Mr. Moynihan discusses the possible future relationship between the federal and the local governments. Congress holds the city in its palm and cannot yet imagine a new kind of federalism. Must we wait for reform until the power of the states is all but abolished, with all of the disadvantages that would come from a centralized government?

# 29

## Richard Reeves
## *Bureaucratic Barriers and the Exhaustion of Reform*

On March 24, 1966, Mayor Lindsay called a news conference to make this announcement:

> The city has a plan to speed the construction of a new Lincoln Hospital in the Bronx. The plan will cut through the red tape and eliminate unnecessary delays that have marked construction of public facilities in the past. By speeding action at every possible point, we plan to complete the construction of Lincoln Hospital in five years.

City officials interviewed last week, more than 20 months after that announcement, said they "hoped" the hospital would be completed five years from now.

Herman Badillo, Bronx Borough President, said that the proposed hospital is only one on 128 capital budget projects that is behind schedule in his borough. "And there are only 128 projects in the Bronx," he added.

"There is money in the capital budget for everyone of them—some of the projects have been budgeted since 1964—but nothing is being done. Nothing is being built."

As a Democrat and a possible future candidate, Mr. Badillo cannot be considered a critic of the Republican incumbent.

But the problem he is discussing is classically nonpartisan. For as long as any city employee can remember there has been a frustrating lag between the time money is allocated in the capital budget for a construction project and the time a hospital, school, park or firehouse is actually completed.

Many agencies get involved in every city job. Meridian Management Company, which is studying methods to speed up construction for the Bureau of the Budget, estimates that 12 to 20 departments are involved in most projects and that from 167 to 300 operations must be handled between a capital budget allocation and the completion of a project.

The nature of most of those operations was revealed by Richard Shively, general manager of Meridian, who said the best way to speed up a city project was to have one man assigned "to hand-carry the papers from one guy to the next."

At the moment, according to the City Planning Commission, the city has still failed to spend $1.2-billion allocated for construction in past capital budgets.

The capital budget—64 pages crammed with thousands of numbers—is the city's listing of funds to be spent for public construction, building repairs and equipment purchases.

After considering requests from municipal departments and borough presidents, the planning commission prepares a document that must be approved by the Mayor, City Council and Board of Estimate.

## TWO SEPARATE BUDGETS

The 1967-68 capital budget, which covers the year beginning last July 1, lists $1,058,775,797 appropriated for more than 600 projects. The capital budget now being prepared for 1968-69 is expected to be just under $1-billion. (The capital budget is separate from the city's expense, or operating budget, which totaled $5.2-billion for 1967-68.)

The 128 projects in the Bronx range from Lincoln Hospital, which it is estimated will eventually cost $75-million, to three bus shelters costing a total of $5,000 on Pelham Parkway.

The three-sided wooden shelters, which are expected to take 30 days to build, have been in the budget since July 1, 1966.

The Parks Department, which has the primary responsibility for the construction of the shelters near Bronx Municipal Hospital, will accept bids on the job later this month.

"We hope construction can begin this winter," said a department official, who asked not to be identified. "I don't know why it took this long.

"Look, we work in a bureaucracy, there's a lot of papers, a lot of red tape, a lot of other agencies got involved in this: the Transit Authority, the Bureau of the Budget, the Department of Water Supply, Gas and Electricity, a lot."

Another indication of the problems of the bureaucracy is the fact that Meridian employees spent three months early this year studying the capital budget problem before they learned that City Administrator Timothy W. Costello's staff had been doing the same thing for a year. The offices of both Meridian and the City Administrator are at 250 Broadway.

Dr. Costello and Mr. Shively independently came to the same conclusion—that many of the hundreds of separate operations being handled one by one could be done at the same time.

For example, the architect of a hospital could submit his preliminary plans for review by the Hospitals Department and the Bureau of the Budget at the same time.

In the past, the architect delivered the plans to the Hospitals Department, which had to approve them and deliver them to the Budget Bureau.

The advent of simultaneous—or parallel—operations has speeded construction schedules by about 10 per cent this year, according to Mr. Shively. "But almost all projects run into snags," he said. "It's like poking a big elephant—we've got it standing, but it certainly isn't moving yet."

Mr. Badillo, who was Relocation Commissioner under former Mayor Robert F. Wagner, said that capital budget projects moved faster under the Democratic Mayor.

"Most of them—maybe 90 per cent—were behind schedule under Wagner, but a few were pushed, because every Commissioner knew the Mayor was behind them."

Mayor Lindsay said, however, that he believed projects were moving faster than ever because of such techniques as parallel operations and the efforts of his new Public Works Commissioner, Eugene E. Hult. But he did not minimize the magnitude of the problem.

"Sure it takes too long," the Mayor said. "It always has within memory and still does despite our intention and intensive effort to speed things up.

"This is one of the vexing frustrations of government. Everything should be done faster but there are too many political and bureaucratic hindrances, delays and obstructions. It's an unending fight and we are fighting it constantly."

### A CASE IN POINT

The parallel submission procedure developed in Dr. Costello's office was tried for the first time on the Lincoln Hospital job. But, although the nine-acre site was acquired at the same time that early planning of the building was done, the schedule announced by Mayor Lindsay fell apart, partly because of nine months of discussions over how many beds the hospital should have.

The Mayor announced the hospital would have 850 beds and the Board of Estimate budgeted for a 920-bed hospital.

In separate interviews this week, Commissioner Hult, whose department is responsible for construction of the building, said there would be 950 beds and Dr. Costello said there would be 925.

A Department of Hospitals spokesman finally said he wasn't sure how many beds there would be.

"That hospital's been in bad shape for quite a while," he said. "There's a lot of red tape involved. You'll have to talk to Public Works to find out what's going on."

For his part, Mr. Hult said: "We're almost ready to break into preliminary planning. Public works does the planning and supervises the design and construction. I don't know what held everything up. You'll have to talk to hospitals about that."

### COSTS GO UP AND UP

During the discussions, in which Federal and state health agencies also took part, the estimated cost of the hospital climbed with rising construction costs.

When Lincoln Hospital was placed in the 1965-66 capital budget, its estimated total cost was $42-million. The 1967-68 figure is $66,742,000, of which $3,690,000 is now allocated. The Department of Hospitals proposed figure for the 1968-69 budget is $74,452,000.

Because of the accelerated program, progress is visible at the new hospital's site, an area bounded by Park and Morris Avenues and 145th and 149th Streets.

"Keep Off—Department of Real Estate" signs guard vacant stores and small apartment houses as two bulldozers move the debris of already demolished buildings.

During three interviews about the Bronx projects, Mr. Badillo repeatedly said that the city needed a top-ranking official whose sole duty would be to supervise capital projects. Mr. Shively proposed middle-management level "project managers," each of whom would be responsible for the progress of from 6 to 10 projects.

### GETTING THINGS DONE

"We need a deputy mayor for construction," the Borough President said. "A Robert Moses type, someone who gets things done. A man who is closer to the mayor than the Budget Director, so that when he speaks, Commissioners know Lindsay is speaking."

"We've got to give people the feeling that things do happen in this city," he said at another point. "We can't complain about the middle class fleeing the city when we're not doing the things that a normal citizen has the right to expect—building schools and libraries."

There are 23 new Bronx schools listed in this year's capital budget. Complaints about the length of time it takes to build them have come up again and again at a series of community meetings that Mr. Badillo has sponsored.

### CITES STUDENT NEED

At a meeting last month in Christopher Columbus High School, Mrs. Mary A. Shaw talked about the need for the proposed Herbert H. Lehman High School to bursts of applause from an audience of several hundred residents of the northeast Bronx.

"This school was built for 1,800 students," she said of Columbus High.

"Now it has 3,300 on double session. We needed the new school in 1962. . . . They've spent one year and nine months on design and I hear they're arguing about where to put the music room. We couldn't care less where they put the music department. . . . Our children need a new school."

The $13-million Lehman High School—which is to be built partly on a platform above the Hutchison River Parkway at Tremont Avenue—first appeared in the capital budget on July 1.

"We have approval for preliminary plans on that school and we're ready to go into contract plans," said Arthur Paletta, superintendent of construction for the Board of Education. "There were many problems, many people had to be brought together. We hope to put bids out in November of 1968."

## LIGHTS FOR BASEBALL

A smaller item which went into the budget on July 1, 1966 was $112,500 for lights at two baseball diamonds in Franz Sigel Park at the Grand Concourse and 153rd Street.

"We started moving on baseball lights last spring," the unidentified Parks Department official said. "There's a lot of paperwork and design involved and you have to go back and forth with Budget and with Water Supply, Gas and Electricity. I hope we can get those lights up soon."

In a memo to the City Planning Commission two years ago, Arthur F. Klein, supervisor for plans and construction of the Metropolitan Museum of Art summarized the back and forth movement involved in any capital budget project. Mr. Klein outlined 39 major steps from the budget allocation to awarding of construction contracts.

Six of thc steps were: (4) Agency prepares preliminary design contract; (5) Agency submits preliminary design contract to Mayor's office; (6) Mayor's office refers preliminary design contract to Budget Director's office; (7) Budget Director's office refers preliminary design contracts to Mayor's office; (8) Mayor approves preliminary design contract by certificate; (9) Agency awards preliminary design contract.

The steps are then roughly repeated four times with the words "preliminary design contract" being replaced successively by "preliminary design drawings," "final design contract," "final design drawings" and "bids."

The papers go back to the Bureau of the Budget at least four times during the months a capital project is moving.

The procedure was established, as Mr. Klein wrote, "to assure the people of the City of New York that the capital improvements are being done under a system of scrutiny which would eliminate unfair practices, collusion and acts which would result in the improvements being higher in cost and lower in quality."

One high city finance official viewed the constant auditing of capital projects by the Budget Bureau, Comptroller's office and sponsoring agency this way:

"The whole system is designed to protect the public against Boss Tweed. It's protection against huge graft. The only trouble is that the delays and paperwork cost more than any civil servants could possibly steal."

# 30

## Daniel P. Moynihan
## *New Moves in Federal-Local Relations*

The past is never so clear as the future, save possibly with respect to the structure of American government. Over the years, this structure has retained a measure of complexity and contradiction of such variety that the features of the system most protested by one generation often become the qualities most valued by the next. A reemphasis of this sort appears to be in the offing. The great transformation now abroad in American society is the emergence of an educated middle-class electorate. These are certain to be notably active citizens, and it is no less certain that the complexities of the American governmental structure will both generate problems that call forth such energies and provide a bewildering array of outlets for them. No doubt the "inefficiencies" of federalism will continue to be deplored and efforts made to simplify the system, but it is most unlikely that such efforts will succeed. Thirty-five years is a short time in the history of American government; the near future is almost sure to be much like the distant past. Prolonged war, economic malaise, and racial stalemate will make for a more centrally directed system; peace, growth, and assimilation will make for a more related and permissive one. But the structure of the system is likely to continue to be much the same.

A number of large developments appears to be converging in a compatible, if not always harmonious manner. Each of these is likely to add stability to the federal system, and none appears to generate disequilibrium.

First, there is the nationalization of public policy that has accompanied the achievement of a genuinely national society. If there is still a goodly supply of local problems, there are fewer and fewer specifically local "subjects." It has been agreed, as it were, that the most important national issues will be resolved in national terms and at the national level. This process is not complete with respect to the issues of race or education, but here, too, the transformation seems well under way. In this sense we have centralized decision making within a federal structure and thereby greatly reduced pressures to change the latter in order to achieve the former.

The necessity for concentrating decision-making at the national level will be enhanced if current trends in racial concentration persist. Between 1960 and 1966, the number of children under age fourteen in metropolitan areas increased by 3.3 million. Nonwhite children accounted for one third of the gain.

. . . According to one estimate, by 1970 Negroes will constitute 40 per cent or more of the population in fourteen of the nation's major cities, including Washington, D. C., Richmond, Gary, Baltimore, Detroit, Newark, St. Louis, New Orleans, and Trenton. In southern communities accustomed to taking collective measures to prevent Negro accession to power, there may be movements toward metropolitan governments in order to maintain Negroes in a minority voting status; but, in general, continued and possibly heightened racial tension is likely to inhibit greatly the development of true metropolitan governments. *A fortiori* the resolution of conflict between central cities and suburbs (which will increasingly take on "urban" qualities of their own) will have to occur at the federal level, save for the few states with sufficient political and fiscal resources to handle such matters at the level of state government.

Second, there is the rise of the federal fisc as the primary source of discretionary public expenditure. State and local revenues will continue to be committed, and overcommitted, to established programs. By contrast, federal revenues now grow at a considerable rate, and the growth is already being forecast in five-year periods. The need to expend the surplus in order to avoid fiscal drag has created within the Executive Office of the President a systematic search for new federal spending programs. . . .

Third, the tradition of decentralization and the fact of federalism is greatly inducive to the grant-in-aid as the principal form of federal expenditure on domestic programs. These have been increasing in both amount and variety. Between 1954 and 1964, federal grants to state and local governments rose 235 per cent from $3 billion to $10 billion. This was twice the rate of increase (118 per cent) of federal grants to individuals. The variety of these problems has predictably become a problem in its own right. Thus in December, 1966, the Secretary of Housing and Urban Development reported to the Chairman of the Subcommittee on Executive Reorganization of the Senate Committee on Government Operations that there were then in existence 238 federal programs having an impact on urban areas. This maze of programs will produce periodic efforts to collapse activities into larger, more general categories, but the process is most likely to be one of alternating proliferation and consolidation, and the grant-in-aid will persist.

Fourth, the diffusion of the middle-class ideal of participation in public decision-making will add a considerable and, in a sense, unanticipated utility to the complexity of the American government structure, which requires such great citizen participation in order to operate. The fourteen hundred governments Robert C. Wood discovered in the New York metropolitan area may prove none too many if the demand for committee work is to be met. This is not to say that government will become more efficient as the "quality" of the electorate improves and the proportion of persons taking an active part in public affairs increases. The opposite might well be the case: The more persons involved in making a decision, the more difficult it becomes to reach one. . . .

## SIX THEMES FOR THE LAST THIRD OF THE TWENTIETH CENTURY

### *I. Wedding Cake Federalism*

Morton Grodzins' image of "marble cake federalism" describing the mixing up of functions among the theoretically separate layers of governments may become less useful as federal fiscal power shapes more and more government activities. What seems to be evolving is a multitiered system of bureaucracies and governmental units surmounted by the person of the President (and increasingly the person of the First Lady as well). At every level, federal funds will provide much of the cake and most of the icing.

Government Employment, 1964

| | |
|---|---|
| Federal* | 1,434,000 |
| State | 1,873,000 |
| Local, excluding education | 2,645,000 |
| Local, education | 3,018,000 |

(*Excludes those employed in National Defense and international relations.)

Both employment and expenditure have been increasing much faster at the state and local levels than that at the federal. Between 1952 and 1962, the expenditures of the Federal Government rose by 25 per cent; those of state and local government by 128 per cent. In 1946, state and local expenditures constituted 44 per cent of government outgo. In 1962, this proportion had increased to 63 per cent. But where in 1940 local government tax revenues were 5.51 per cent of the national income, by 1963 they had declined to 4.64 per cent. These patterns are reflected in the numbers of public employees at the different levels of government.

*II. New Varieties of Government*

Because multipurpose metropolitan government is not likely to emerge, special-purpose governments are likely to multiply. Some of these will be created directly by the Federal Government, as in the case of the elected county committees that administer the farm program, and the elected community-action boards that share in the administration of the poverty program. Significantly, much of the rationale of the poverty program elections has been that it is *good* for people to participate in government—not just a right but a remedy. Just as significantly, the lines of authority and communication within the federal system are more and more likely to assume a triangular form in which each government has direct relations with the other two clusters of public activity. . . .

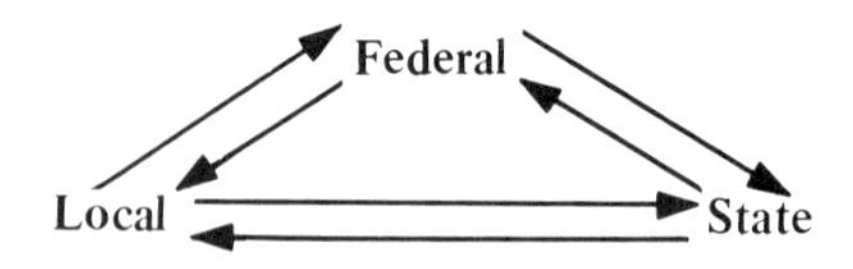


*IV. National Social Accounts*

In the middle third of the twentieth century the most powerful development in government was the emergence of a political economy capable of comprehending, predicting, and directing economic events. If this development is as yet by no means complete, its influence is already pervasive. Moreover, it provides the basis—in the form of discretionary government income—for the exploitation of what will probably be the most powerful development of the last third of the century: the emergence of a social science coupled with and based upon a system of social accounting that will give government an enlarged capacity to comprehend, predict, and direct social events. Again, it will be imperfect, but serviceable. In one political climate this may take the form of controlling society. In another it may produce a governmental system more effectively responsive to the wishes of the electorate than any society in history. . . .

### *V. The Quest for Community*

A sustained concern for the conditions under which individuals from different racial, ethnic, and class groups can establish meaningful and peaceable relationships is predictable. This concern must arise from the already begun effort to enable Negro Americans to enter the larger American society, to offset the effects of "alienation in the city, trivialization in the suburbs," and the general ecological scatteration described by Scott Greer. Programs that promote a sense of community (beautification, conservation, preservation, and so forth) are likely to be given conscious priority. This effort will further encourage the multiplication of governmental forms and activities.

### *VI. The Rediscovery of the Market*

As government tries to do more, it will find it accomplishes less. This amounts to the discovery that administrative ability is not a free good, and in the absence of it the best-intentioned programs can turn out to be calamities. This proposition has been formulated by James Q. Wilson: "There are inherent limits to what can be accomplished by large, hierarchical organizations." The limitations imposed on bureaucratic performance in the United States are notable: that it expend money efficiently, but take the utmost precautions to see that not a penny is stolen; that it be responsive to special circumstances, but rigorously consistent in its actions, and so forth. Moreover, as "easy" problems are disposed of, the more marginal, intractable ones come into prominence, and the return on government effort manifestly diminishes. All this is likely to lead to what Charles E. Lindblom has termed the "rediscovery of the market" as a means of accomplishing social objectives. The logic of events is very much on the side of Lindblom's assertion:

> That the market mechanism can be serviceable to planned and unplanned economics alike, to public and private enterprise alike, to collective and individual choice alike is a discovery the significance of which may soon dwarf what we have seen of its consequences so far.

In the future social problems are likely to be approached more often by means of an *income* strategy, than by a *services* strategy, as defined by Lee Rainwater. Thus the concept of giving the poor the money with which to purchase what they need—be it proper housing or medical care—in the market is apt to be considered far more seriously in the future than in the immediate past, which has been much influenced by ideals of professionalization in public services. In a similar vein, more and more services that have been thought to be located necessarily in the public sector will probably be contracted out to private enterprises—particularly in areas where results are more important than processes. J. Herbert Holloman foresees the development of "the public market" for just such purposes—for example, "a profit-making organization running a chain of junior colleges under contracts with the communities in which they are located."

Business organizations, which are characteristically oriented to results rather than process, are in a position to offer to contract for a wider range of such activities on a performance basis: payment to be made on delivery of the desired result, be it clean streets, fair housing, or ninth-grade achievement in mathematics on the part of ninth-grade students. In general, whatever makes for diversity in American government in the decades ahead is very likely to be given a try.

# 9

# "Happenings" in Government

Life in government can be exciting. The human companionship and dedication to ideals that are generally agreed to be in the national interest are satisfying. It can also be most frustrating. The growth of government has been reported only in several rather dull books. Otherwise, histories content themselves with a general portrayal. This treatment by the broad brushstroke leaves out the fascinating details of individual experiences with a growing agency. In the selections that follow, we are interested in problems which are both typical and peculiar.

It would probably be fair to say that the average civil servant or political appointee who spends more than three or four years in government will encounter at least one of these problems or "happenings." The clamor around the McCarthy affair—Joseph McCarthy, that is—was so great that it seemed to involve a million civil servants and political appointees. So far as political excitement was concerned, life in the civil service became rather dull afterwards until the Nixon Administration brought the postal strikes, civil rights resignations, and mass rallies of civil servants against the invasion of Cambodia. Such general storms are rare. More commonly, one agency, program, or position will experience some kind of turmoil that will shake the actors up for quite a while.

This chapter's first selection tells the story of one man's experience with the McCarthy "storm." Not one out of a thousand readers of this book will have heard of Edward Lamb, but he is a typical successful man in the American tradition. He is a legal defender of the poor and a millionaire. Yet Lamb at the height of his success was almost ruined personally and financially by political slanders. Here is his story. It is followed by the FCC ruling on the Pacifica Foundation's broadcasting licenses. In this case, a lineal descendent of the Lamb case, the Pacifica Foundation was accused by right-wing critics of being infiltrated by communists and of broadcasting subversive and obscene matter.

No society in history has ever been intelligent enough to cope with such situations. Perhaps the reader may find a way of preventing them without resorting to such old chestnuts as "the public should elect better men" or "truth will out in the end."

Next, Walter Goodman, a contributor to the *New Republic* and author of several books, tells a somewhat similar story. It concerns Peter Strobel, who resigned from a government post under charges of conflict of interest. Mr. Goodman, unlike many other journalists who have written exposes of graft and corruption in government, does us a good turn by pointing out the story of a man—very common in government—who could have grafted but did not and yet was victimized by the system.

Few government programs are killed. Here is an exception, a project so young that the action might be called infanticide. Project Camelot was sponsored by the U.S. Army to do research on counterinsurgency in underdeveloped countries. When the Chilean government found out about Project Camelot, it accused the United States of spying. Reaction against the project soon spread to other Latin-American countries and to Washington. The commotion around Camelot was enormous. Because of it, the State Department was given authority to screen all social science research projects to be conducted abroad. However, it was so inept at using its powers constructively that the situation has hardly changed, and new Camelots occur and will occur. But then, should they not? What, after all, was wrong with Camelot? But, more importantly, the State Department should have taken its new mandate seriously and asked for support for the new research that seemingly would be discouraged by the experience of the Camelot project.

Scientific research of the physical science variety has been much more successful in winning government support. Donald C. Swain, a professor of history at the University of California, describes the growth of the National Institutes of Health, which do basic research aimed at preventing disease. His account is a factual, conventional history, so much so that we do not get the smell of empire as it really happens. But we find out how a good cause gets its sturdy scientific nose into the trough and drinks every bit like the elephants of public works and armaments. In essence, there is little difference between the scientific bureaucracy and the defense, agriculture, or public works bureaucracies. The same principles of administration govern both. Growth like that of the NIH empire has occurred dozens of times with other government agencies. Judge it as you would, but judge it in relation to the total balance of government activities and in the context of the total science of administration.

There is a new animal in the zoo of government organizations that we might label the scientoid commission; it issues scientoid manifestoes and pretends to do scientific work. Usually, however, its work is conducted by a small hard-pressed staff too strapped for funds to employ much of the expertness that originally justified the existence of the commission and that could supply the factual foundation of the study.

Presidents Kennedy, Johnson, and Nixon have elevated the role of commissions in the United States to a significant level. Bold, black newspaper headlines are automatic when a commission report is leaked to the press. Crime and violence, civil disorders, pornography, and campus unrest have been subjects of concern. Readers of such newspapers must conclude that with commission reports in print, action cannot be too distant. In fact, commissions have generated high expectations but do not themselves have the authority to take action. Amitai Etzioni, professor of sociology at Columbia University, concludes that commissions today deal with the politics of issues but ignore the problems of issue-solving. Ultimately, this is bad politics. Is this conclusion warranted? Can commissions effectively help a President to pinpoint problems and propose solutions?

# 31

## Edward Lamb
### *Trial by Battle: History of a Smear*

On a quiet Saturday afternoon in 1953 an acquaintance walked over from the teletype bank in Washington's National Press Club and handed me a wire service bulletin reporting that the name Edward Lamb had been dropped by a witness testifying before Senator Joseph McCarthy.

The fateful word came from New York, where McCarthy had taken his one-man road show, ostensibly to conduct an inquiry into the affairs of the United Nations.

Without preamble, and wholly out of the context of previous testimony, McCarthy had addressed this question to a witness named John Lautner:

"Do you know Edward Lamb, the broadcaster?"

"I do not know Lamb," Lautner replied, "but I can say he was highly respected by the top Communists. I wouldn't be able to say whether Lamb himself was a card-carrying Communist."

In my turn, I had never even heard of Lautner. Nor would this total stranger, except for this brief passage, have any further connection with my affairs. Yet I soon discovered that John Lautner had great symbolic importance. His presence at Joe McCarthy's "hearing" provided a clear forewarning of the bizarre events that would occupy most of my time for the next four years.

Lautner, I found, was not an eccentric who had found his way to Joe McCarthy. On the contrary, he was a professional witness, one of a sizable pool maintained on the payroll of the Immigration and Naturalization Service of the Department of Justice. These were admitted ex-Communists retained as "consultants" with the primary duty of testifying at deportation proceedings. They also were made available to other federal agencies and Lautner, the Justice Department's hired talebearer, was on loan to Joe McCarthy for his New York opening.

The tale he bore was pretty thin stuff on its face. He had not in fact accused me of anything, and had admitted that he had no personal knowledge of me or my past. It may be that he didn't even lie under oath; for all I know, at some time in my career as a civil liberties and labor lawyer I may have been "highly respected" by some "top Communists."

But Lautner had done what Joe McCarthy knew very well he would do. The season of national hysteria marked by McCarthy's "hearings" was now well advanced, and Lautner's innocuous statement was enough to link my name to the Communist conspiracy in headlines across the land. A stock of new ammunition had been handed to powerful men in politics and business who were already gunning for Edward Lamb and his enterprises.

If the source of the accusation came to me as a surprise, the direction of the attack did not. By 1953, I had moved on from my Toledo law practice to the operation of a number of prosperous businesses. I was then owner-publisher of the *Erie Dispatch-Herald,* and had invested heavily in the development of radio and TV properties. I had become a wealthy man, and in the process had acquired the usual set of financially potent business competitors. Moreover, in the course of Adlai Stevenson's 1952 Presidential campaign, I had become prominently identified with the Democratic Party—and 1953 marked the beginning of a new Republican administration.

As far back as 1951, Republican partisans had taken note that a figure of some means and influence had arisen in Ohio and Pennsylvania and was capable of making things uncomfortable for such Old Guard demigods as Senator John Bricker. The Republican leadership of the 81st Congress decided there might be political hay to be harvested from my crusading past. A committee of the House, chaired by Representative Forest Harness but masterminded by Representative Leonard Hall, then Chairman of the Republican National Committee, paraded a long list of witnesses who attacked my character and associations. Despite my repeated requests, I was never allowed to testify in my own defense. But I had my own forum, and on November 4, 1951, I wrote in my signed column in the *Dispatch-Herald:*

> Congressman Leonard Hall, a pip-squeak congressman from Oyster Bay, recently opened up his money-hungry hands and slapped me. I have always noticed that the smaller the pip, the louder the squeak. . . .

In 1953, with Joe McCarthy's star still on the rise and my broadcasting affairs intricately involved in the decisions of a government agency, I had to recognize the Lautner testimony as something more than another skirmish in a partisan political campaign. John C. Doerfer of Wisconsin had been appointed to the Federal Communications Commission by President Eisenhower, and was known to be a protégé and close associate of Senator McCarthy. I had pending before FCC several matters that ordinarily would have been routine—applications for renewal of television licenses, for permission to extend broadcasting range or alter technical equipment, and the like. Commissioner Doerfer now sat in a place where he might determine whether I would receive favorable action on these matters—or, as it turned out, any action at all.

When I ran into the new commissioner at a Washington cocktail party he was pleasantly sociable, but seemed inordinately interested in the financial details of my television affairs. One item of unusual concern was my recent sale of Columbus TV Station WTVN to the family of the late Senator Taft for $2,000,000.

A month after this casual encounter the broadcasting trade papers reported that Commissioner Doerfer was "gunning for the liberal Democrat, Edward Lamb." At the same time the Washington rumor mill ground out the intelligence that McCarthy's Committee on Government Operations was getting ready to move against the broadcasting industry, with Edward Lamb scheduled as the first horrible example. The Lautner testimony in New York was in fact the signal that a two-pronged attack was under way.

On the FCC front my business suddenly came to a dead halt. When my attorneys pressed for action, officials at the operating level said they were now powerless since every proceeding involving Edward Lamb had been flagged to go to the desk of Commissioner Doerfer for "personal processing."

What this could mean is demonstrated by my experience in the Massillon-Canton area of Ohio, where in September 1952 I had received FCC authorization for the construction of a television station. I had bought real estate, optioned broadcasting equipment, hired personnel, and opened an office in Mansfield—in all committing myself to invest some $300,000. Engineering and technical difficulties prevented our completing construction by May 4, 1953, the date stipulated in the original authorization. Doerfer's freeze blocked our routine request for an extension, and by the time this was finally granted—on June 14, 1957, after my public "trial"—an adverse competitive situation had developed so that the great potential value of the license had literally vanished.

My broadcasting interests were then represented by the experienced and able James Lawrence Fly, a former chairman of FCC. Those wise in the ways of Washington advised me that I ought to get rid of my "New Deal lawyer." And some of these further advised me to see a certain legal middleman, or "bagman," in Washington and be ready for a pay-off. I did meet secretly with the gentleman thus designated, heard his proposition, which involved a $60,000 "legal fee," and turned him down. At no time, of course, have I ever said or implied that this lawyer, or any of the other intermediaries who approached me, actually were authorized agents of anyone in FCC or elsewhere in government. The fact that such overtures were made to me—as they often have been made, before and since, to others with difficulties before FCC and other federal agencies—is simply noted here as relevant to the atmosphere in which I had to wage a four-year campaign to clear my good name and protect my properties.

Having decided to press head-on for a showdown, I called in person on the various FCC commissioners and complained about the delay in dealing with my applications. The reaction was unanimous. Under the new regime, I was told, the key to my problems was Commissioner Doerfer.

So, on September 10, 1953, I paid a formal call on Doerfer in his Washington office—still hoping that we might talk over our problems like adult and honorable men.

Face to face, he was pleasant enough, but he promptly launched into a line of questions about my defense of trade unions in the 1930's. . . .

. . . At one point in our conversations, he intimated that he couldn't understand why a lawyer of my background would defend colored people, Communists, or labor unions. He gave me the impression that he felt anyone with all my money who was a liberal must be some kind of traitor to capitalism. I told him flatly that if helping my fellow-man made me a liberal, I intended to remain one.

Doerfer listened dubiously as I told him that I had been a Republican, like himself, until Franklin D. Roosevelt and the New Deal seemed to me to offer an appropriate, constitutional way out of many of our economic problems.

"It's too bad," he remarked as we parted, "that you aren't still a Republican."

Later, Doerfer confided to friends of mine that in our meeting I wasn't "contrite enough."

This behind-the-scenes maneuvering was already having a punitive effect on my business affairs, and the innuendo accompanying it began to be felt on the national political scene.

Adlai Stevenson had returned from the extended round-the-world tour with which he followed the 1952 campaign, and Stephen A. Mitchell, chairman of the Democratic National Committee, decided this would provide an occasion for a badly needed display of unity by the party leadership. He asked if Mrs. Lamb and I would sponsor a "welcome-home" buffet dinner in Chicago honoring Stevenson and former President and Mrs. Harry S. Truman. I agreed, and the National Committee sent out a thousand or more invitations to the top party brass.

There was, my friends intimated, a little more to the suggestion that I serve as host than the need to find someone to pay for the dinner. It was to be the occasion when plans would be announced to elect me treasurer of the Democratic National Committee.

As it turned out, my visit to Commissioner Doerfer took place just a few days before the dinner was scheduled. Immediately thereafter, word reached Steve Mitchell that the Republicans had a little surprise waiting that would permanently embarrass Stevenson and Truman. On the night of the welcoming party, Mitchell was told, Republican Chairman Leonard Hall would "expose" host Lamb's "Communist associations."

The threat came straight enough from inner Republican circles for Mitchell to accept it at face value. At an emergency session attended by Charles Murphy, one of Truman's assistants, and J. Lacey Reynolds, my Washington representative, it was decided that the most politically profitable part of valor was discretion. I accepted the judgment, even though it ran counter to my own conviction that no one, politician or not, should bow to such intimidation. Truman and Stevenson, needless to say, had nothing to do with any of this.

New invitations to the party were issued in the name of the Democratic National Committee. My name appeared only on the check for several thousand dollars that paid the bill for food and drink. No one was embarrassed, publicly at least; the Republicans made no hay; and it may be that I escaped becoming the moneybags for the Democratic National Committee—one of the few events in this history which, on second thought, I can recall with any feeling of gratitude.

This inside hatchet-job left no doubt that I was destined for the full smear treatment, and it seemed a reasonable guess that the FCC would be the chosen instrument to deliver it. I sat down with my own conscience and considered again whether I should attempt to head off the personal attack and protect my multi-million-dollar broadcasting affairs by retaining the suggested "Republican law firm." I publicly announced the result of the private deliberation in my

*Dispatch-Herald* column, under the title, "How It Feels to Be the Victim of a Frame-up":

> I have chosen to make a defense, rather than 'make arrangements' in Washington. I do this simply to preserve a good name which I hope to pass on to good children.

Committed to do battle, I retained former U.S. Attorney General J. Howard McGrath, whom I had known for many years, to take over my representation before the FCC. He asked his Providence law partner, Russell Morton Brown, to assist him in handling the details. McGrath knew everyone of any consequence in both political parties, and he had ways of finding out the background of most issues on Capitol Hill.

In March 1954 I received a so-called "McFarland letter," *after* the FCC had first released its contents to the public. ("McFarland letter" is the general term for a letter that must be sent by all federal administrative agencies to anyone whose rights are challenged, specifying the basis of action to be taken against him.) The FCC's notice stated that I was to face charges that I had misrepresented my qualifications for a television license in affidavits supporting my applications, wherein I had sworn that I had never been a Communist. It went on to say that the FCC had information in its files containing charges "that for a period of years, particularly the period 1944-1948, you were a member of the Communist Party."

Thus I was not only well-smeared, but the FCC had publicly invited my rival applicants for the valuable Toledo television license to use the Communist issue against me. The commission staff certainly knew that their false declaration could be played up in my home town, and that my business competitors and possibly a local political hatchet-man or two could be counted on to help the commission "prove" its charge that I had been a member of the Communist Party. Some of my competitors around the country did actively spread the FCC charge among the businessmen I dealt with—people who bought my products, suppliers of parts and materials to my industries—and in conservative banking circles where I would have to go for credit.

This was not true in all cases, happily. The *Toledo Blade*, although a competitor for a TV license, pointed out that it was well-informed about me, and that while "anyone would have to get up pretty early in the morning to get the best of Lamb in anything," any charge that I was a Communist was "a lot of bunk."

I answered the McFarland letter, categorically denying all such charges, and requested an early hearing. Thereafter the FCC magnanimously said that I could try to "disprove the charges."

That's quite a trick—proving a negative. But I set out to do it, if it took my last penny.

Early in May 1954, my attorneys went into the United States District Court for the District of Columbia seeking an order to compel the FCC either to renew my licenses or to issue a list of the charges it proposed to assert against me. We also asked the full membership of the commission to give me a hearing so that I could face my accusers, or at least find out what the charges were. The federal court, however, held that the FCC, as an administrative agency, at this preliminary stage of the proceedings could not be compelled to grant these ordinary rights of citizenship.

On May 6, 1954, I ran an advertisement in *The New York Times* and many other newspapers and magazines throughout the country, offering to pay $10,000 to anyone who could disprove a single one of my many non-Communist affidavits. Of course, there were no takers. The unusual advertisement caused a stir in broadcasting circles, and at least let my enemies know that I was digging in for a fight

On June 4, 1954, President Eisenhower reappointed Doerfer to a full term on the Federal Communications Commission. Senator Bricker immediately called a meeting of the Interstate and Foreign Commerce Committee of the U.S. Senate to consider the appointment. I asked for, and received, a chance to appear in opposition to Doerfer's continued presence on the federal agency regulating the broadcasting industry. There, under oath, I recited some of the experiences I had suffered at the hands of Senator McCarthy's lieutenant. Senator Estes Kefauver, also appearing at his own request, was most vehement in pointing out Doerfer's deficiencies. He emphasized that Republicans were in charge of the Senate committee, and warned that Doerfer would prove to be a real embarrassment to President Eisenhower's administration. How correct he was! The Senate approved Mr. Doerfer's appointment on June 28, 1954; six years later Doerfer resigned from the FCC, at the request of President Eisenhower, in the midst of an influence-peddling scandal.

In the meantime, we had put together a considerable staff of lawyers and special investigators, many of them drawn from my own journalistic enterprises, to work with McGrath. We now had reason to fear that the hearings might run on for years—and we had to counter a small army of government agents who were busily working in my own backyard.

The FCC sent men to Toledo, Erie, Columbus, and elsewhere to find "evidence" that I was a Communist. Drew Pearson reported that these men had caused a professional ex-Communist stool pigeon in Toledo, one William Garfield Cummings, to offer another ex-Communist, Emmett L. Wheaton, the sum of $10,000 if he would "remember" that I had attended the opening of a Toledo Communist bookstore, known as Lincoln House, in 1944.

FCC investigators went to a former secretary in my office, Evelyn Runge, who had moved to Elyria, Ohio, after leaving my employ. They asked her if she could give them any information about any possible income tax or "girl friend" problems.

"Lamb had good accountants prepare his financial returns, and his accounts were approved after especially thorough examination by the government," she told them. "And what does his sex life have to do with the charge of communism?"

She did give the FCC investigators four half-truths they tied together for later use. Fortunately, we learned about her "revelations" before she took the witness stand, and were able to explain away many of her fantasies.

These are only two of many such instances we uncovered by mounting our own diligent, widespread, and expensive counter-investigation. The FCC had asserted that it had proof that I had been a Communist—but now, after the fact, the agency was employing apparently unlimited government funds and manpower to seek any sort of "evidence" to back up the verdict already publicly rendered.

Day after day the FCC kept the headlines hot with publicity releases referring to new secret "evidence" against me. But the agency continued to reject repeated demands of my counsel for a bill of particulars—and it held to this position even after the Senate Interstate Commerce Committee formally directed the agency to provide me with details of the charges against me and the names of my accusers.

Finally, after long delays, we went into open court to face an unsubstantiated charge of what amounted to treason brought against me by an agency of my own government—and we had to go to trial on the agency's own terms.

The hearing opened on September 5, 1954, in the ornate auditorium of the Interstate Commerce Building. In those days, when someone hollered "Communist," he automatically had a circus, and the television crews and reporters were there in force.

The one encouraging sign was the presence of the Trial Examiner appointed by FCC to preside over the hearings. The assignment had fallen to Herbert Sharfman, a veteran of more than twenty years of government service. He had a reputation as a fair-minded and scholarly official, and able to make use of the independence guaranteed by his civil-service status.

Sharfman had to operate, however, within a set of procedures that ran contrary to every ordinary legal practice I had been accustomed to in my years in the courtroom. The chief prosecuter for FCC, Walter F. (Bucky) Powell, Jr., was free to introduce any charge against me he saw fit—with the burden of disproving the allegation falling upon the defendant.

To me, as a lawyer, perhaps the most shocking procedural aspect of the case was the ability of the prosecution to shift the ground of the "indictment" drastically in the course of the trial. The specific charge set forth in the McFarland letter was "that for a period of years, particularly the period 1944-1948, you were a member of the Communist Party." This we were fully prepared to refute. By the time we got to court the FCC lawyers knew as well as I did that the charge was wholly false and would never stand. But under FCC procedures they were now allowed to take out a new hunting license, and this one virtually without limits. The charge we now faced was that a dozen or more years ago I had "associated" with Communists.

Our inability to force any advance disclosure of Prosecuter Powell's list of witnesses gave him an opportunity to time their appearance for maximum publicity effect. To assist in this effort, the press agents of the FCC issued daily releases—these dealing in a highly prejudicial way with a trial the agency itself was conducting! Day after day a colorful and highly damaging piece of testimony coincided with the deadline for afternoon papers; day after day our cross-examination exploded the allegation and discredited the witness—but almost always the truth lagged the lie by a full day in the publication cycle.

And what a parade of witnesses Powell produced—perjurers, bigamists, homosexuals, and even a convicted murderer were brought on to testify against me, and most of them were paid to do so with my own government's money.

The first of the FCC witnesses was William Garfield Cummings, a Toledo informer who set the style and the tone of the entire prosecution.

Cummings asserted that he had been a member of the Communist Party during the 1940's and that he had seen me at the opening of the Lincoln House, a bookstore in Toledo, standing among a group of Communists. He testified for three days about my "contributions" to the Communist Party.

I was certain that I had never seen him before, and I knew that his specific statements were false. But, since we had discovered that he was likely to testify, we had found out plenty about Cummings. Our cross-examination began to bring out the character of this key government witness.

One of his claims to distinction was that he had recruited several people among his own family and "best friends" for the Communist Party and then reported them to the Federal Bureau of Investigation! It also came out that, in taking out a second marriage license at Bowling Green, Ohio, he had denied under oath that he had been married before. Cummings, who had five children by his second and possibly bigamous marriage, was arrested for perjury during my trial.

Our cross-examination also brought out the reason that a man of Cummings' dubious background was willing to expose himself in court. He testified that his sole current income was the $25 a day he received from FCC to testify against me. He was one of the Immigration Service's professionals. . . .

The most spectacular witness in the whole charade, and the one whose rise and fall marked the turning point in our defense, was a quiet-spoken, squat woman with thick glasses and short-cropped gray hair. She gave her name as Marie Natvig and her address as Miami, Florida. Astonishingly enough, she was cast as a *femme fatale*.

Elaborately, she spelled out her background: member of a socially prominent Cleveland family of substantial wealth, she had been educated at Eastern schools and had taught in the public schools in Cleveland.

She had first met me, she said, at a Communist meeting of agricultural workers in Chicago in 1936. She said that she had been a member of the Communist Party from 1925 to 1937, lured into the movement by the Depression, which cost her the penthouse, Rolls-Royce, and three servants she had enjoyed in the booming 1920's.

This imaginative woman claimed that she had again seen me at a Communist Party conference in Columbus early in 1936. She recalled that while I was addressing the meeting, I had pulled out of my pocket a "sketch" of my plans for setting up the National Lawyers Guild "as the legal arm of the Communist Party." She told how "Comrade Lamb" had led discussions of intricate problems of dialectical materialism, and said I had outlined practical ways to lure non-Communist lawyers into the National Lawyers Guild. She recalled that I had described the course of events to come in Asia, including the cold and hot wars raging through the 1930's.

"Didn't those terms come into existence years later?" Examiner Sharfman asked.

"No, Comrade Lamb invented them," she replied.

Mrs. Natvig built up steam when she said that I had been in favor of a modern American revolution–that I had proposed first to seize communications, then transportation, and finally prepare for insurrection in the armed forces, because "only through revolution could the intolerable living conditions of the oppressed masses be alleviated."

The mild little lady had already produced a first-class newspaper sensation, but on the second day of her testimony she found a way to make the headline type grow even larger. Testifying about the meetings I had supposedly attended in Columbus, she shyly confided that "Mr. Lamb and I had a 'liaison' in the Chittenden Hotel." Then, with bowed head, she added movingly that this was "my first infidelity and led to my divorce."

It would have seemed that a revolutionary conspiracy plus a sex scandal would have been enough to satisfy the most avid member of the FCC's staff, but Mrs. Natvig was encouraged to bring her exotic adventures up to date. Now she testified that right there in Washington, only the night before, a romantic encounter in a night club had produced the offer of a bribe of $50,000 if she would agree not to testify further against me. This sum, which she had indignantly spurned, had been proffered by a railroad-yard worker named Millings Underwood. Now the prosecution had a spy melodrama, soap opera, and detective story all wrapped up in one package.

Incredible as it now seems, this maundering tale was allowed to run into many thousands of words of testimony; with our cross-examination and her subsequent return appearances Mrs. Natvig's time on the witness stand actually ran into weeks. This at least gave us time to launch our own investigation. And here we had to start from scratch, for, as I listened in awe to these intimate details of my biography, I knew I had never seen Mrs. Natvig before, at any time, at any place, under any circumstances.

Our detectives found the first clue in the criminal records. We found that the sheltered flower had been arrested for soliciting in Madison, Wisconsin, as early as 1928, and had faced embezzlement charges in Florida. Members of her family revealed that her "socialite father" had in fact been an honest, hardworking second-hand furniture dealer in Cleveland, who had long since severed all connection with his wayward daughter. We were told that she had been married at least three times, and each of her husbands had gone bankrupt. We found a sad explanation for her violent reaction to questions regarding her children; she had been denied their custody years before and they had grown up to lead decent, respectable lives. But this delicacy did not apply to the Lamb children, who heard Mrs. Natvig accuse their father of a wide variety of immorality, scarlet and otherwise. "Let Comrade Lamb start paying for his sins!" she declaimed happily to the reporters—and we had no option but to parade her own varied history for the record in such overwhelming detail that she was later convicted of perjury.

Her testimony against me was so outlandish that we tended at first to dismiss the tale of Millings Underwood and his bribe as another cut from the whole cloth. But in the course of a routine check one of our detectives discovered that there was indeed such a person, and he delivered a highly embarrassed Virginia railroadman to the hearing room.

The hapless Underwood, with his wife sitting in the packed courtroom said that he had been "out on the town" on the night of September 24, and had picked up a lone woman sitting at one end of a hotel bar. They went down the street and had a "few beers" together at the Lotus Restaurant. They were getting a little high, when the lady excused herself to make a telephone call.

It developed that Mrs. Natvig had called Walter Leahy of the FCC staff, who was "assigned to sleuthing Lamb," and told him a man had offered her a $50,000 bribe not to testify against me. After the telephone call she insisted that Underwood take her back to her own hotel. The unsuspecting and unrequited Underwood left her at the front door—in full view of two waiting FCC witnesses.

The morning after Mrs. Natvig's story of the proffered bribe, the bewildered Underwood saw his name in newspaper stories tacked on the railroad-roundhouse bulletin board. He was kidded by his fellow-workers. But the stories didn't seem a bit funny to Mrs. Underwood.

When our attorneys called at his Arlington home about eleven o'clock the night after Mrs. Natvig's testimony, he broke down and frankly told the story from the beginning. He was quite forthright about how he had intended to entertain the lady that night. But, he said, all he did was eat chow mein and have "a few" more drinks. He was emphatic that my name wasn't even mentioned at the Lotus Restaurant.

"The only Lamb I've ever heard about is the Art Lamb I look at on television at home with my wife," he said.

The Natvig debacle put the FCC clearly on the defensive. In checking on her past we found the FBI willing to assist in such matters as establishing that she had signed non-Communist oaths in applying for federal jobs—and probably had not in fact ever been a party member. It was clear that the FBI was no longer supporting the FCC prosecutors. And it was difficult to see how anyone could. As the more than 800 printed pages of Mrs. Natvig's transcript went over to the United States attorney as the basis for perjury action, Howard McGrath pointed out that there was at least one patent and glaring contradiction on every page. The Trial Examiner finally abandoned the effort to extract any sense from her, and excused her with the stipulation that she remain under subpoena for possible recall.

This was the point where the sympathy of much of the nation's press began to swing to my side—and outspoken commentators like Drew Pearson, Robert S. Allen, Doris Fleeson, Peter Edson, and Joseph C. Harsch began to ask what the devil the government lawyers were up to in the Lamb case. In time the radio and television industry also began to lend me some support—but by and large the record of the timid broadcasters was one of extreme prudence, even though I was surely fighting their battle for freedom of the air against an overbearing bureaucracy.

The changing atmosphere had a practical effect on our conduct of the trial. Now honest men and women in government began to feed us advance information about the prosecution's "surprise" witnesses, and we were able to launch our counterattack quickly. Soon we were in position to do our own "leaking" to the reporters. On one memorable occasion we actually obtained recordings of the FCC lawyers' coaching session with a witness, and when he began to recite his well-rehearsed lines members of the audience chanted his answers before he could gulp them out.

Even though the prosecutors continued on their collision course they had lost important support in high places—even among the FCC commissioners themselves.

It was widely believed in Washington, and with reason, that for many purposes Joe McCarthy could control the commission. In addition to Doerfer, he had persuaded President Eisenhower to give a seat to Robert E. Lee, who had been a clerk for McCarthy's "un-American Committee," had been employed in the extreme right-wing propaganda enterprises of Texas oil millionaire H. L. Hunt, and was best man in McCarthy's wedding. Yet, as we were to discover later, even Joe McCarthy was getting a bellyful of the blundering ineptness of the FCC legal staff.

In 1955, in his office in the Senate Office Building, McCarthy told J. Howard McGrath, "I won't have anything more to do with investigating Ted Lamb. Let those bastards in FCC wash their own linen!" And as a manifest of his good faith he turned over to McGrath all the information he had about me in his files, including possibly confidential material obtained from government sources. This was, of course, an invaluable aid in permitting us to diagnose the opposition's strategy.

Still, the FCC attorneys showed no disposition to back away from the case. And, on our side, I was equally determined to have our full day in court. It was now clear that we had the means of laying bare the whole, despicable machinery so widely used in Washington for hiring, intimidating, and suborning witnesses in the era of the Red witch-hunt. . . .

Now the long hearing passed over to 1955. Walter Powell, the FCC prosecutor, suffered a heart attack and nervous exhaustion, and suddenly resigned. In February we went back to court to face his replacement, Joseph Kittner, an abler lawyer but one apparently no less determined to give credence to anyone who offered hope that he might sustain the indictment he had inherited.

But this was to be the season of recantation. And the first of those to hit the sawdust trail was none other than Marie Natvig. She sent word to our counsel that she wanted to set the record straight—and now it was the turn of the FCC lawyers to listen with open mouths as she primly offered her revelations from the witness stand.

"Just tell the truth," Howard McGrath instructed her, and stood aside while the lady began with the statement that all the charges she had made against me were completely false. Comrade Lamb had been replaced by Prosecutor Powell as the villain in the piece.

She testified that she had been coerced by the FCC lawyers, that she had lied about having sexual relations with me, that she had never been a member of the Communist Party. She emphasized again and again that she had been induced by Powell to relate the story of having seen me with "maps" of the "forthcoming revolution in Asia and Europe." All of her original testimony had been a fabrication bought and paid for by the prosecution.

Powell, she testified, at one point had told her: "Okay, kid, let's murder this bum, Lamb."

"The FCC lawyers told me it was my duty to testify, because Lamb's radio station could beam in enemy broadcasts," Mrs. Natvig said. "They told me to repeat over and over that Lamb had close connections with the Communist Party."

Powell, she claimed, had also dreamed up the romance between us. "Make it gory," she quoted him as telling her. "It's good for big headlines." . . .

At the end the Trial Examiner observed, perhaps with irony, that Mrs. Natvig appeared to be exercising moral courage in recanting her previous testimony. McGrath, without irony but with obvious relief, said repeatedly in open court that he would not at any time attempt to vouch for the lady's credibility, but only hoped that we had finally arrived somewhere in the vicinity of the truth. . . .

We had finally broken through the diversionary effect of sensational testimony and made the point that I was clearly being victimized by perjurers hired for the purpose—and that the government's lawyers were parties to a conspiracy to manufacture evidence against me. The *Christian Science Monitor,* the *St. Louis Post-Dispatch*, the *Washington Post*, and dozens of other influential newspapers began to cite the Lamb case as an example of justice perverted. The phrase "professional witness" came into the public vocabulary.

There were stirrings on Capitol Hill, too. Estes Kefauver, Mike Monroney of Oklahoma, Henry Jackson of Washington, John Pastore of Rhode Island, and Albert Gore of Tennessee began to speak up on the Democratic side of the Senate, and were joined across the aisle by Republicans James Duff of Pennsylvania and Margaret Chase Smith of Maine. Thomas Ludlow Ashley, Congressman from my own district in Toledo, who was in a position to know my record, ripped into the FCC for staging what he called a witch-hunt and a political frame-up.

This came directly home to the FCC when Senator Warren G. Magnuson of Washington, chairman of the Senate Interstate and Foreign Commerce Committee, invited me to appear at a public hearing and said: "I propose to make it my business to see to it that Edward Lamb at long last gets fair and equitable treatment in view of all the abuse to which he has been subjected. We will want a careful look at what happened in this case before the Federal Communications Commission. Our committee has supervision over FCC and we will want a lot of explanation about the goings-on in the Lamb case."

Magnuson went on to say that the committee would take a close look at the whole of FCC's operations to see "what it takes to get or keep a TV license." That was the moment when an unhappy new Eisenhower appointee, Ohio Republican George C. McConnaughey, came before the committee to be confirmed as new chairman of FCC.

McConnaughey backed and filled and pleaded innocent to any knowledge of the Lamb case, but the questioning was so pointed that his old friend and supporter, Senator Bricker, frequently had to ride to his rescue. Then Senator Kefauver took over with a series of incisive questions that culminated in this:

"When a matter like this, a matter of outright coercion of witnesses, comes up, Mr. McConnaughey, the entire Committee and the public has a feeling of revulsion. As chief administrator of the FCC, haven't you looked into this just a little bit?"

"I planned to," McConnaughey said. "As a result of the Lamb case, I want to look into the general principles of license renewals."

Against this background we might have been able to bring the long inquisition to a halt. My attorney, Howard McGrath, announced that we would file proceedings to have the whole case tossed out by the FCC. Prosecutor Kittner demurred—and we promptly switched our motion for dismissal to a demand for a complete hearing, which would give me a chance to take the stand and have at my adversaries under oath.

McGrath's associate, Russell Brown, argued that we should press for dismissal, and he was certain the now acutely embarrassed FCC would grant it. I said no, that I had paid dearly for my day in court and I intended to enjoy it—and maybe serve the public interest in the process.

I finally took my place in the witness chair on April 1, 1955. More than twenty-five reporters and a half-dozen photographers were on hand as the Trial Examiner called the courtroom to order for my presentation. Noticeably absent from the hearing room were the commissioners of the FCC, although their administrative assistants kept slipping in and out, carefully recording in their notebooks the details of the proceedings. One reporter observed that "history would record Lamb had the guts to face his accusers, but no one could ever claim that the FCC members had the guts to face their own hired professional witnesses."

All the members of my family were in that Washington hearing room. I was especially anxious to have them hear my testimony, given under oath.

In my opening statement to the FCC I told of my early days as a workingman's lawyer—days of depression and social upheaval, bitter strikes, hungry men, and economic disorder. I described the lunatic fringe groups that crowded into our struggles, the phony philosophers and political quacks who came not to advance the welfare of the workers or to settle strikes, but merely to obtain for themselves personal publicity and personal advancement.

A union, I pointed out, seldom chooses its own members. Thus, while I represented many unions, it was not up to me to inquire into the political, social, religious, or economic attachments of those who belonged to unions. I merely had defended strikers who were seeking their legal rights. Of course, I sought improved working conditions for them, and that meant the better life.

"I defended dozens of labor cases at the request of the American Civil Liberties Union and others," I said. "I may even have taken cases for members of the International Labor Defense, a perfectly legal organization at that time." And in connection with the American Civil Liberties Union, I testified that I had been a member since its earliest days, and "I am proud to be a member now; and I shall continue to be a member.

"Most of all, I don't want anyone to get the notion that I appear here on this public stand to withdraw from my past associations or activities on behalf of the underprivileged," I added. "I have always fought for the things that I considered to be the highest tradition of American democratic liberties."

Then, pointing at the FCC staff, I said, "My government, not I alone, is on trial here.

"I am waiving my obvious objections to the propriety of this inquiry into my opinions, so that you people, who have put on your professional witnesses, may ask me any question you want about my past activities. But don't for one second get the idea that I am here to apologize for my life, any part of my life, or any of my social, political, or economic activities." . . .

"I assure you that I am not unhappy that it has fallen to me to defend the

American freedoms which are at stake in this hearing," I said. "I have defended many minority groups, many trade unions, and many unpopular causes. I suppose any person is a 'controversial' figure who defends the rights of the unorthodox. But by defending this case, I am fighting the hysteria of this sad era while, at the same time, I am defending my own good name.

"As a result of this proceeding, I feel certain that such a violation of American liberties will not be attempted again. I have only one hope. This is that I may go down in history as a man of sufficient courage to have thwarted such encroachments on our freedoms as are represented in this attempted frame-up. I am shocked that my own government should have been used in such a dastardly fashion."

I had waited a long time for this moment, and I gave them both barrels. I said that I was prepared to stay on the witness stand as long as any person in the world had any conceivable question to ask of me, and that I was perfectly conscious of their attempt to entrap me into statements that might appear inconsistent with the millions of words of prior testimony as grounds for a possible perjury trial.

"For it is clear to everyone," I said, "that certain people high in the government, including at least one member of the Federal Communications Commission, are seeking by any means whatsoever to bring the strength of the government itself down upon my head."

Kittner and his associates met that challenge with what must be one of the most protracted cross-examinations in history. For almost three weeks we traversed the old ground as if, anticipating my clearance by the Trial Examiner, the prosecutor was trying to perfect a record for appeal to the FCC. All the infamous tricks of the McCarthy era were brought into play; at one point Kittner produced dozens of obscure left-wing publications and, even though he could not connect me with them in any way, argued that they represented the opinions of men I had somehow "been associated with."

The assault on my 1934 book, *The Planned Economy of Soviet Russia,* gave me an opportunity to place into the record a summary of the view I have held since I first began to study economics at Dartmouth, the view I have preached to the industrial leaders of the country and put into practice in dozens of my own successful business ventures:

> I have been a student of the economy of the United States. I did not believe then, and I do not believe now, that any organization or society can run without planning. In those early depression days, Americans saw the 'paradox of plenty,' when warehouses bulged with stored food even as men starved. While we have not resolved matters of equitable distribution of our resources or the paradox of farm surpluses, our country at least inaugurated during those early days many intelligent and far-reaching supports for our economy. As it is with large corporations and even with nations, so it is with smaller units such as states and communities. All of them require sensible surveying and planning.

As the hearing dragged toward a close in May 1955, I experienced one of the few moments of pleasure I had known since the FCC declared war on me in 1953. Old friends, on their own motion and without subpoena, began to come forward to testify as witnesses to my loyalty and character.

Estes Kefauver led the parade; then came Lowell Baldwin, a prominent Republican businessman of Maumee, Ohio, who is my oldest law client; Sam Sponseller of Cleveland, a regional director of the CIO who had known me in the 1930's when I took my first labor cases; David L. Lawrence, then mayor of Pittsburgh and later governor of Pennsylvania, who had known me as a labor lawyer since 1935 and testified that he was so confident of my integrity that he had once, on behalf of Philip Murray, tried to persuade me to move to Pittsburgh and become general counsel of the CIO.

And finally there was August Scholle of Detroit, as staunch an anti-Communist as any in the trade union movement. Gus Scholle told of our close association for more than two decades, and recounted the battles we had fought—some of them to head off Communist efforts to infiltrate the union movement.

The Trial Examiner asked Scholle if he had ever heard me express any anti-Communist sentiments.

"Of course I did—on a thousand occasions," replied Scholle.

"Did you ever ask Lamb if he ever belonged to any Communist-front organizations?"

"I never went to Ted Lamb and said, 'Ted, are you sympathetic to Communists?' It would be like asking the people in this room, 'Are you a bunch of traitors?' It would be stupid."

The day in court was over, but the legal in-fighting wasn't. There were delays, motions, counter-motions—and in my judgment at least one more double-cross by the prosecution, in violation of an agreement between counsel to expedite the submission of final arguments to the Trial Examiner. At one point Kittner suddenly tossed in a new document of 350 pages consisting of lengthy, violent attacks on me—and of course released this privileged matter to the press. But there were repercussions from above, and Kittner and Curtis Plummer, another member of the prosecution staff, were suddenly relieved and transferred to other posts within FCC. They had joined what finally would be a considerable list of fall guys.

In September, Trial Examiner Sharfman fell victim to the terrible strain of this fantastic hearing, and went into Georgetown Hospital with a severe heart attack. He recovered, however, and finally, on December 1, 1955, he completed his 25,000-word decision and sent it to the printers.

Every one of the issues submitted to the Examiner for finding of fact was decided in our favor. The opinion held that "Mr. Lamb possesses the qualifications necessary for a broadcast station licensee," and that the requested TV grant "would be in the public's interest, convenience, and necessity."

*TV Digest*, the leading trade publication, commented:

> Sharfman's 140-page decision, noteworthy for its literary embellishments, its curious analyses of grammar, its capsule book reviews and its sparkling of witticisms and sarcasms, concluded that: "There is no proof that Lamb personally engaged in any subversive activity." The picture of Lamb is that of a shrewd, successful and aggressive lawyer. The

> "initial decision" of the Trial Examiner gives the FCC good opportunity to get off the hook if it so chooses in a case that has been marked from beginning to end by incredible bumbling, fumbling and blundering. It is clear now that the Lamb case was conceived by an inept and fumbling Commission which bowed to pressures of the times when Communist hysteria was at its peak.
>
> The whole case with its recanting witnesses, charges of bribery, etc., was born of tortured logic within the Commission.

In one passage of the opinion Examiner Sharfman summarized the millions of words devoted to calculated assassination of my character:

> Lamb's possible naivete in allying himself with these groups cannot, on this record, be transformed into something more sinister; his professed sympathy with the underdog, his espousal of "liberal" causes, and his prominence in the community, undoubtedly made him attractive to certain organizations; and the first two factors must also have made him personally susceptible.
>
> But to say that he was starry-eyed is not to conclude that his eyes must also have been shot with malevolent gleams.
>
> That Lamb was personally sympathetic to the Soviet regime for Russia, felt that planning was indispensable to an orderly and equitable society in that country, and that we could learn from and profit from Russian experiences, is manifested from his writings; but there is nothing to indicate that he called for the importation of Communism in the United States and destruction of American institutions.

There was still room for dilatory tactics, however, and the FCC lawyers used them to the full in an effort to delay consideration of Sharfman's favorable opinion by the commission. On February 6, 1956, Howard McGrath forced the issue with a brief which stated our position in these blunt words:

> It has now been three years since Lamb's licenses expired. This proceeding has been, in our opinion, unnecessarily protracted. The chief stockholder and applicant, Edward Lamb, holds interests in other broadcasting licenses whose license renewals also have been held in abeyance awaiting the outcoming of this proceeding. These licensees, as well as Mr. Lamb's family, have suffered, and continue to suffer, economic harm beyond calculation. A favorable decision by the Commission, if rendered immediately, can do partial justice only. The economic and social damage which has been done to Mr. Lamb personally can never be repaired, and it is extremely doubtful if the expenditures of hundreds of thousands of dollars by the Government can ever be justified.
>
> The only hope of this applicant is that this entire matter will be concluded at an early date. To this end, and with the belief that oral argument is unnecessary, applicant Lamb foregoes any request therefor

> and urges that the Broadcasting Bureau exceptions be denied and that the Examiner's decision be affirmed.

And so the Lamb case came finally before the presiding members of the Federal Communications Commission. It would remain there for more than another year before, on June 14, 1957, the FCC finally and grudgingly gave me clearance and renewed my radio and television licenses.

How could such a thing happen in these United States? It is easy enough to write off the "Lamb Case" as a product of the hysteria of the McCarthy era—one not different in kind from thousands of others that were less spectacular, and had less happy endings, because the victims did not, or could not, fight back. . . .

But to blame it all on Joe McCarthy is like blaming the temperature on the thermometer. No one man could have ripped apart the fabric of our democratic processes, and so stained our national honor, without the acquiescence of those who sat in positions of power and trust.

In the beginning I did not believe that McCarthy and his kind would be allowed to run amuck with virtually no opposition from the responsible leaders of his own political party. At the outset Sherman Adams and Charles Willits, two of President Eisenhower's key White House assistants, assured me personally that they would help get the McCarthyites on the FCC to give me a fair hearing on the "unusual" charges brought against me. At one point Mr. Eisenhower himself remarked in response to a press conference question that he disliked what the government was doing with professional witnesses in the Lamb case. But there was no effective intervention against the disgraceful tactics that marked my trial until we had by our own efforts in the hearing room exposed the scandal so thoroughly that it could not be ignored—and until my own personal and political friends in the Senate and House had acted to make the Lamb case a *cause célèbre*. . . .

I must have seemed an ideal victim for those who saw an opportunity to cut me down for political purposes or financial gain. I was an outspoken liberal, a maverick businessman, and I was in a position where not only my reputation but my bank balance could be severely damaged. By simply examining my public record, which I have no disposition to hide since I am in fact rather proud of it, they could link me with causes many a conservative citizen would characterize as radical. In the Frantic Fifties it took no skill at all to bill me in newspaper headlines as a flaming Red by nudging the facts with a little innuendo, and the sly suggestion that there must be fire behind all that smoke.

Proving the charge against me turned out to be another matter, but I am sure that in the beginning those who touched off the attack were convinced that they would never have to face that necessity. There were many, as innocent as I, who did not stand and fight, but capitulated in the face of the first volley and "made arrangements" of the kind I have mentioned earlier. There were others who simply abandoned the field and let their adversaries gain the political or financial advantage they sought.

I am a fighter for causes by temperament, and always have been, which is possibly one of the reasons I am a controversial figure. But in the situation I faced the will to fight was not enough; one also had to have the means. And I was one of the few victims of that sordid era who could afford to mount a full-fledged counterattack against the massed resources of a federal agency, and stand by the guns for four grueling years. It cost me, first to last, around $900,000 to clear my name and protect my properties—a sum far beyond the reach of the hundreds of minor officials, hapless intellectuals, college professors, and innocent bystanders who were run down by the McCarthy juggernaut during the great witch-hunt.

Account must be taken, too, of the physical and emotional strain such a battle entails. I remember, without pride, the time when my self-restraint broke under the bullying of Prosecutor Powell and I yelled at him in the hearing room, "You're a lousy, lying legal prostitute." There was a riotous moment when Marie Natvig assaulted a lawyer with a water pitcher. These were symptoms of the pressures that affected all the parties during the hundreds of days of the interminable trial, the tensions that sent Examiner Sharfman to the hospital, and brought on the heart condition that removed Powell from the case.

This, then, is how this appalling thing happened to me. There remains the question of why it happened.

Venality, ambition, greed, personal malice—all these were involved, and in various combinations the deadly sins affected many of the principals. The political motivation to discredit a prominent Democrat was obvious—and it was undoubtedly compounded by the fact that I personally had crossed Joe McCarthy on occasions when I demanded that he meet the usual requirement of submitting advance scripts of his political speeches before they were broadcast over my stations. One did not easily get away with a refusal to bend the knee to the omnipotent McCarthy, and his hatchet-man, Roy Cohn.

Then, there was a great deal of money riding on the outcome of the Lamb case. This was the time when new television broadcasting frequencies were being made available by FCC, and the grant of one of those licenses in a major market area like Toledo was worth millions of dollars to the recipient. Under the circumstances there were usually several applicants for each of these plums, and the FCC had broad discretion in choosing among them. All, obviously, would be qualified so far as financial capacity, credit rating, and the like were concerned. The question would come down to an appraisal of the character of the licensee—the FCC's presumed judgment as to which of the contenders would best serve the "public interest, convenience, and necessity." Nothing could destroy character, and remove an applicant from contention, as quickly as a Red smear.

I do not suggest that all of my competitors behaved dishonorably in these circumstances; I have already cited the case of the *Toledo Blade's* editorial dismissing the original FCC charge of communism as "bunk." But there were some who were more than willing to take advantage of the situation and encourage the downfall of a man who stood between them and a multi-million-dollar property.

For these reasons, the FCC in any season operates in what amounts to the eye of a hurricane of political and financial influence, and the record is replete with cases in which commissioners—including Doerfer—and lesser functionaries have succumbed to temptation. I cannot prove, and do not charge, that any of the

$60,000 that the influence-peddler sought from me to "fix" my case would have found its way to any person connected with the FCC had I paid it. It may be that the influence he offered for sale, if he actually had any, was personal, or political, and that he was simply an opportunist lining his own pocket.

The truculence of many of the lesser figures in the trial may have been no more than the product of ambition to make a good showing in a sensational case—and, after the travesty in which they were engaged had been exposed, a stubborn pride that prevented them from admitting they had been wrong. There came a point in the hearing, certainly, when the tide turned against the prosecution in such a dramatic fashion that many of those who had rigged evidence and influenced witnesses to lie under oath had reason to fear dismissal, and perhaps even prosecution and disbarment, unless they could somehow vindicate themselves by winning their case. There were shivers in the FCC staff when one of the appellate judges hearing argument on Marie Natvig's appeal from her perjury conviction repeatedly asked if "suborning perjury is not in itself a penitentiary offense."

In the end there was no real punishment of the guilty FCC lawyers, although some undoubtedly were shunted into oblivion and lost their place on the ladder of advancement. But there was some reform of FCC procedures, and—perhaps the most important victory I can claim—as a direct result of the revelations in the Lamb case the Immigration Service's pool of professional "consultants" was disbanded and the disgraceful practice of traducing American citizens with the testimony of hired witnesses was largely ended in the federal service.

A legal system is more than laws and procedures and institutions. It must rest on a tradition of simple decency, and it must be supported by the personal commitment to justice of those who operate within its shelter. It was here that we saw the tragic and alarming failure in my own case, and it was this that raised it far above an issue between a non-conformist lawyer-businessman and a collection of bureaucrats.

I have often stood before the bar as advocate for the underdog, demanding that the case against him be tried on its merits and not in terms of prejudice against his unpopular cause. Once I had so stood in defense of the Communist Louis Budenz. Now I once again shared a courtroom with Budenz, but I no longer enjoyed the detachment of an officer of the court whose own life would go on unaffected whatever the outcome of the case at issue. Now I sat in the seat of the accused, and heard Budenz blandly lie in the service of men who sought my destruction, and believed they would attain it.

It was then, for the first time, that I fully understood the words I have tried to live by—the testament and the prophecy uttered at the beginning of this Republic by Edward Livingston in opposition to the Alien and Sedition Acts of 1798:

> If we are able to violate the Constitution, will the people submit to our unauthorized acts? Sir, they ought not to submit; they would deserve the chains that these measures are forging for them. The country will swarm with informers, spies, delators and all the odious reptile tribe that breed in the sunshine of a despotic power. The hours of the most unsuspected

confidence, the intimacies of friendship, or the recesses of domestic retirement afford no security.

The companion whom you must trust, the friend in whom you must confide, the domestic who waits in your chamber, all are tempted to betray your imprudent or unguarded fellow; to misrepresent your words, to convey them, distorted by calumny, to the secret tribunal where jealousy presides; where fear officiates as accuser and suspicion is the only evidence that is heard. We are absurd enough to call ourselves "free and enlightened" while we advocate principles that would have disgraced the age of Gothic barbarity and establish a code compared to which the ordeal is wise and the trial by battle is merciful and just.

## APPENDIX

1. The Commission has before it for consideration the above pending applications of the listed broadcast stations licensed to Pacifica Foundation. There are three aspects to our consideration: (a) certain programming issues raised by complaints; (b) issues of possible Communist Party affiliation of principals of Pacifica; and (c) a question of possible unauthorized transfer of control. We shall consider each in turn.

2. *Programming Issues.* The principal complaints are concerned with five programs: (i) a December 12, 1959 broadcast over KPFA, at 10 p.m., of certain poems by Lawrence Ferlinghetti (read by the poet himself) (ii) *The Zoo Story*, a recording of the Edward Albee play broadcast over KPFK at 11 p.m., January 13, 1963 (iii) *Live and Let Live*, a program broadcast over KPFK at 10:15 p.m. on January 15, 1963, in which eight homosexuals discussed their attitudes and problems (iv) a program broadcast over KPFA at 7:15 p.m. on January 28, 1963, in which the poem, *Ballad of the Despairing Husband*, was read by the author Robert Creeley and (v) *The Kid*, a program broadcast at 11 p.m. on January 8, 1963 over KPFA, which consisted of readings by Edward Pomerantz from his unfinished novel of the same name. The complaints charge that these programs were offensive or "filthy" in nature, thus raising the type of issue we recently considered in *Palmetto Bctg. Co.*, 33 F.C.C. 483 34 F.C.C. 101. We shall consider the above five matters in determining whether, on an overall basis, the licensee's programming met the public interest standard laid down in the Communications Act.[1] *Report and Statement of Policy Re: Commission En Banc Programming Inquiry*, 20 Pike & Fischer, R.R. 1901.

3. When the Commission receives complaints of the general nature here involved, its usual practice is to refer them to the licensee so as to afford the latter an opportunity to comment. When the Commission reviews, on an overall basis, the

[1] The Commission may also enforce the standard of Section 1464 of Title 18 (dealing with "obscene, indecent, or profane language"). See Section 312(a), (b); Section 503(b) (1) (E). In our view, enforcement proceedings under Section 1464 are not warranted, and therefore, no further consideration need be given this section.

station's operation at the time of renewal, it thus has before it a complete file, containing all the sides of any matter which may have arisen during the license period. Specifically, with respect to the programming issue in this case, the Commission, barring the exceptions noted in the *Programming Statement* (*supra*, at p. 1909), is not concerned with individual programs–nor is it at any time concerned with matters essentially of licensee taste or judgment. Cf. *Palmetto Bctg. Co., supra*, par. 22. As shown by the cited case, its very limited concern in this type of case is whether, upon the overall examination, some substantial pattern of operation inconsistent with the public interest standard clearly and patently emerges. Unlike *Palmetto* where there was such a substantial pattern (*id.* at par. 23; see par. 7, *infra*) here we are dealing with a few isolated programs, presented over a four-year period. It would thus appear that there is no substantial problem, on an overall basis, warranting further inquiry.[2] While this would normally conclude the matter, we have determined to treat the issues raised by Pacifica's response to the complaints, because we think it would serve a useful purpose, both to the industry and the public. We shall therefore turn to a more detailed consideration of the issues raised by the complaints as to these five programs. Because of Pacifica's different response to the complaints as to (i) and (iv), par. 2 above, we shall treat these two broadcasts separately (see pars. 6-7, *infra).*

4. There is, we think, no question but that the broadcasts of the programs, *The Zoo Story, Live and Let Live,* and *The Kid*, lay well within the licensee's judgment under the public interest standard. The situation here stands on an entirely different footing than *Palmetto, supra*, where the licensee had devoted a substantial period of his broadcast day to material which we found to be patently offensive–however much we weighted that standard in the licensee's favor–and as to which programming the licensee himself never asserted that it was not offensive or vulgar *or that it served the needs of his area or had any redeeming features.* In this case, Pacifica has stated its judgment that the three above-cited programs served the public interests and, specifically, the needs and interests of its listening public. Thus, it has pointed out that in its judgment *The Zoo Story* is a "serious work of drama" by an eminent and "provocative playwright"–that it is an "honest and courageous play" which Americans "who do not live near Broadway ought to have the opportunity to hear and experience. . . ." Similarly, as to *The Kid*, Pacifica states, with supporting authority, that Mr. Pomerantz is an author who has obtained notable recognition for his writings and whose readings from his unfinished novel were fully in the public interest as a serious work meriting the attention of its listeners; Pacifica further states that prior to broadcast the tape was auditioned by one of its employees who edited out two phrases because they did not meet Pacifica's broadcast standards of good taste; and that while "certain minor swear words are used, . . . these fit well within the context of the material being read and conform to the standards of acceptability of reasonably intelligent

[2] While, for reasons developed in this opinion, it is unnecessary to detail the showings here, we have examined the licensee's overall showings as to its stations' operations and find that those operations did serve the needs and interests of the licensee's areas. *Programming statement, supra,* at pp. 1913-16. In this connection, we have also taken into account the showing made in the letter of April 16, 1963.

listeners." Finally, as to the program, *Live and Let Live*, Pacifica states that "so long as the program is handled in good taste, there is no reason why subjects like homosexuality should not be discussed on the air"; and that it "conscientiously believes that the American people will be better off as a result of hearing a constructive discussion of the problem rather than leaving the subject to ignorance and silence."

5. We recognize that as shown by the complaints here such provocative programming as here involved may offend some listeners. But this does not mean that those offended have the right, through the Commission's licensing power, to rule such programming off the airwaves. Were this the case, only the wholly inoffensive, the bland, could gain access to the radio microphone or TV camera. No such drastic curtailment can be countenanced under the Constitution, the Communications Act, or the Commission's policy, which has consistently sought to insure the "maintenance of radio and television as a medium of freedom of speech and freedom of expression for the people of the Nation as a whole" (*Editorializing Report*, 13 F.C.C. 1246, 1248). In saying this, we do not mean to indicate that those who have complained about the foregoing programs are in the wrong as to the worth of these programs and should listen to them. This is a matter solely for determination by the individual listeners. Our function, we stress, is not to pass on the merits of the program—to commend or to frown. Rather, as we stated (par. 3) it is the very limited one of assaying at the time of renewal whether the licensee's programming, on an overall basis, has been in the public interest and, in the context of this issue, whether he has made programming judgments reasonably related to the public interest. This does not pose a close question in the case: Pacifica's judgments as to the above programs clearly fall within the very great discretion which the Act wisely vests in the licensee. In this connection, we also note that Pacifica took into account the nature of the broadcast medium when it scheduled such programming for the late evening hours (after 10 p.m., when the number of children in the listening audience is at a minimum).[3]

6. As to the Ferlinghetti and Creeley programs, the licensee asserts that in both instances some passages did not measure up to "Pacifica's own standards of good taste." Thus, it states that it did not carefully screen the Ferlinghetti tape to see if it met its standards "because it relied upon Mr. Ferlinghetti's national reputation and also upon the fact that the tape came to it from a reputable FM station." It acknowledges that this was a mistake in its procedures and states that "in the future Pacifica will make its own review of all broadcasts. . . ." With respect to the Creeley passage (i.e., the poem, *Ballad of the Despairing Husband*)[4], Pacifica again states that in its judgment it should not have been broadcast. It "does not excuse the broadcast of the poem in question" but it does explain how the poem "slipped by" KPFA's Drama and Literature Editor who auditioned the tape. It points out that

[3]Pacifica states that it "is sensitive to its responsibilities to its listening audience and carefully schedules for late night broadcasts those programs which may be misunderstood by children although thoroughly acceptable to an adult audience."

[4]The program containing this passage was a taped recording of Mr. Creeley's readings of selections from his poetry to students at the University of California. KPFA broadcasts many such poetry readings at the University, which are recorded by a University employee for the school's archives (and made available to the station).

prior to the offending poem Mr. Creeley, who "has a rather flat, monotonous voice," read 18 other perfectly acceptable poems–and that the station's editor was so lulled thereby that he did not catch the few offensive words in the 19th poem. It also points out that each of the nine poems which followed was again perfectly acceptable, and that before re-broadcasting the poem on its Los Angeles station, it deleted the objectionable verse.

7. In view of the foregoing, we find no impediment to renewal on this score. We are dealing with two isolated errors in the licensee's application of its own standards–one in 1959 and the other in 1963. The explanations given for these two errors are credible. Therefore, even assuming, *arguendo*, that the broadcasts were inconsistent with the public interest standard, it is clear that no unfavorable action upon the renewal applications is called for. The standard of public interest is not so rigid that an honest mistake or error on the part of a licensee results in drastic action against him where his overall record demonstrates a reasonable effort to serve the needs and interests of his community (see note 2, *supra*). Here again, this case contrasts sharply with *Palmetto* where instead of two isolated instances, years apart, we found that the patently offensive material was broadcast for a substantial period of the station's broadcast day for many years. See par. 3, *supra*.

8. We find, therefore, that the programming matters raised with respect to the Pacifica renewals pose no bar to a grant of renewal.[5] Our holding, as is true of all such holdings in this sensitive area, is necessarily based on, and limited to, the facts of the particular case. But we have tried to stress here, as in *Palmetto*, an underlying policy–that the licensee's judgment in this freedom of speech area is entitled to very great weight and that the Commission, under the public interest standard, will take action against the licensee at the time of renewal only where the facts of the particular case, established in a hearing record, flagrantly call for such action. We have done so because we are charged under the Act with "promoting the larger and more effective use of radio in the public interest" (Section 303 (g)), and obviously, in the discharge of that responsibility, must take every precaution to avoid inhibiting broadcast licensees' efforts at experimenting or diversifying their programming. Such diversity of programming has been the goal of many Commission policies (e.g., multiple ownership, development of UHF, the fairness doctrine). Clearly, the Commission must remain faithful to that goal in discharging its functions in the actual area of programming itself.

9. *Communist Party Affiliation Issue.* Under the public interest standard, it is relevant and important for the Commission to determine in certain cases whether its applicants, or the principals of its applicants, for broadcast licenses or radio operator licenses, are members of the Communist Party or of organizations which advocate or teach the overthrow of the Government by force or violence. Sections

[5] One other programming aspect deserves emphasis. Complaint has also been made concerning Pacifica's presentation of "far-left" programming. Pacifica has stated that it follows a policy of presenting programs covering the widest range of the political or controversial issue spectrum–from the members of the Communist Party on the left to members of the John Birch Society on the right. Again, we point out that such a policy (which must, of course, be carried out consistently with the requirements of the fairness doctrine) is within the licensee's area of programming judgment.

307(a), 307(d), 308(b), 309, 47 U.S.C. 307(a), 307(d), 308(b), 309; *Borrow v. F.C.C.*, 285 F. 2d 666, 669, *cert. den.*, 366 U.S. 904; *Cronan v. F.C.C.*, 385 F. 2d 288 (C.A.D.C.), *cert. den.*, 366 U.S. 904; *Blumenthal v. F.C.C.*, 318 F 2d 276 (C.A.D.C.), *cert. den.*, Case No. 1026, June 3, 1963; cf. *Beilan v. Board of Education*, 357 U.S. 399, 405; *Adler v. Board of Education*, 342 U.S. 485, 493; *Garner v. Los Angeles Board*, 341 U.S. 716, 720; *Speiser v. Randall*, 357 U.S. 513, 527. The Commission therefore has followed a policy of inquiring as to Communist Party membership in those radio licensing situations where it has information making such inquiry appropriate. Because of information coming to the Commission's attention from several sources, the Commission requested information from Pacifica Foundation on this score. On the basis of information obtained from Government sources, the Foundation, and our own inquiry, we do not find any evidence warranting further inquiry into the qualifications in this respect of Pacifica Foundation.

10. *Unauthorized Transfer of Control.* Until September 30, 1961, control of Pacifica was vested in Executive Members, who elected a Committee of Directors, who in turn elected officers and controlled the Foundation's activities. On September 30, 1961, the Executive Membership and the Committee of Directors were abolished. In their place, Pacifica is controlled–pursuant to its by-laws–by a Board of Directors, which elects officers and controls the Foundation's activities. The new by-laws which accomplished this result were appropriately reported to the Commission at the time they were adopted. However, no application for consent to a transfer of control was then filed.

11. This matter was brought to Pacifica's attention by a letter of February 7, 1963. The licensee's response of April 26, 1963, takes the position that no transfer of actual control had in fact taken place. However, in the event that the Commission deemed an application for consent to transfer of control to be necessary, Pacifica simultaneously filed such an application (BTC-4284). Pacifica argues that, in actual practice, control had been in the so-called Committee of Directors, and that this practice had been formalized in an amendment to the by-laws of October 20, 1960, which read, in relevant part:

> Except as hereinafter provided, the powers of this corporation shall be exercised, its property controlled, and its affairs conducted by a Committee of Directors which shall consist of twenty-one Executive Members of this Corporation.

The new Board of Directors, elected on September 30, 1961, was identical with the then existing Committee of Directors, and the officers of the Foundation likewise remained the same.

12. Although the September 30, 1961 revision in the by-laws does appear to have been only the formal recognition of a development in the actual control of Pacifica which had occurred over a period of years, and although there may well be merit in Pacifica's contention that changes in the composition of its Executive Membership (or, for that matter, of its present Board of Directors) should not be regarded as transfers of control, the September 30, 1961 revision in the by-laws did transfer legal control. Prior to that date, the Executive Membership elected directors, who

elected officers. After that date, the directors themselves have elected new directors, as well as officers. The fact that the legal control vested in the Executive Members did not, in practice, amount to actual control, does not mean that its existence can be ignored—any more than the legal control of a 51% stockholder in a commercial corporation can be ignored because he fails to exercise it. See *ABC-Paramount Merger case*, 8 Pike & Fischer, R.R. 541, 619; *Press-Union Publishing Co., Inc.*, 7 Pike & Fischer, R.R. 83, 96; *Universal Carloading Co. v. Railroad Retirement Board,* 71 F. Supp. 369.

13. On the other hand, it is clear that Pacifica did not seek to conceal or misrepresent any facts concerning those who control its affairs, and that the failure to file involved was an excusable one. We therefore grant the pending application for transfer of control.

14. *Conclusion.* In view of the foregoing, it is ordered, this 22nd day of January, 1964, that the above-entitled applications of Pacifica Foundation ARE GRANTED as serving the public interest, convenience and necessity.

FEDERAL COMMUNICATIONS COMMISSION
Ben F. Waple, Secretary

Concurring Statement of Commissioner Robert E. Lee

I concur in the action of the Commission in granting the several applications of Pacifica Foundation. However, I feel constrained to comment on at least one program coming to our attention insofar as it may or may not reflect these stations' program policies.

Having listened carefully and painfully to a 1½ hour tape recording of a program involving self-professed homosexuals, I am convinced that the program was designed to be, and succeeded in being, contributory to nothing but sensationalism. The airing of a program dealing with sexual aberrations is not to my mind *per se* a violation of good taste nor contrary to the public interest. When these subjects are discussed by physicians and sociologists, it is conceivable that the public could benefit. But a panel of eight homosexuals discussing their experiences and past history does not approach the treatment of a delicate subject one could expect by a responsible broadcaster. A microphone in a bordello, during slack hours, could give us similar information on a related subject. Such programs, obviously designed to be lurid and to stir the public curiosity, have little place on the air.

I do not hold myself to be either a moralist or a judge of taste. Least of all do I have a clear understanding of what may constitute obscenity in broadcasting.

# 32

## Walter Goodman
## *The Burden of Mr. Strobel*

Peter Strobel came to this country in 1925, when he was twenty-four years old. Over the next quarter century he built up, together with an enviable reputation as a structural engineer, a consulting engineering firm that brought him in a good year an income of more than $100,000. In the spring of 1954, having been cleared by the Republican National Committee, he was appointed Public Buildings Service Commissioner in the General Services Administration at a salary of $14,800. "My adopted land has treated me well," he said, "and this is my chance to prove that I am grateful."

Mr. Strobel was not in the same economic bracket as Harold Talbott, and on taking the job, which carried with it responsibility for more than one billion dollars in real estate and 200 million dollars' worth of building projects, he made clear to his boss, GSA Administrator Edmund F. Mansure, that although he was relinquishing active management of the firm of Strobel and Salzman, he was holding onto his ninety per cent interest. "I could not see my way to accept employment with the federal government," he explained later, "without being assured that the office of Strobel and Salzman could be permitted to continue, because it is my creation, and it is about the only thing I have."

He laid down several rules for the company, the main one barring it from taking on any new clients who were seeking work from the Public Buildings Service. This arrangement was to seem ominously reminiscent of Harold Talbott's arrangement with Mulligan and Company, but the similarity was more in wording than in spirit. Mr. Strobel was serious about it. For six months, he let a GSA standards-of-conduct statement remain unsigned on his desk "because I could not sign the statement just as it is." When finally he did sign it, in December, he added a note which again spelled out his connection with Strobel and Salzman. Ten months after taking these unusual pains to set the record straight, the commissioner was called before a House Committee to defend himself against conflict-of-interest charges. There were three major ones:

1. After starting in his government job, he went personally to the Army Corps of Engineers and pressed a claim for $7500 owed to his company.
2. At his suggestion, a $16,390 contract for remodeling a government building was awarded to one of his company's clients.
3. While holding public office, he personally solicited an $18,000 construction contract for his engineering company from a Manhattan architectural firm.

To the ordinary newspaper scanner, these baldly stated facts must have seemed like clear echoes of Secretary Talbott's calls on his old friends, and by the standards demanded of Caesar's wife, Mr. Strobel's reputation was lost. Less than two weeks after the charges were leveled, he resigned from his post, conforming to the Talbott pattern. The story passed quickly from the papers, and for most of the nation it was just another familiar instance of a businessman-official gone sour. But the appearances on which the case was decided did this particular businessman slight justice. The details are not exciting, barely worth a column on an inside page, but let's bear with them.

### 1. THE CORPS OF ENGINEERS

In the spring of 1955, Mr. Strobel went over to the Pentagon on his lunch hour to inquire after a payment that the Corps of Engineers owed Strobel and Salzman for a job done in 1953. Although he did not try to trade on his official status in presenting the claim, it was nonetheless a foolish move, open to the interpretation that he was acting as an "agent" in trying to collect a debt from the government, and thereby violating the oldest of the conflict-of-interest statutes. It was the act of an impatient businessman (the bill had gone unpaid for months) and would better have been left to his partner—who actually settled it after a time for $3097. It was an error of impulse, but it carried no hint of influence or of undue gain for his company.

### 2. THE CONTRACT-AWARDING

Not long after Mr. Strobel came to Washington, the Public Buildings Service was asked by the Immigration and Naturalization Service to take on a rush job of renovating its new quarters in New York City. The PBS deputy regional director was worried about the close deadline; he had only three months to get the job done, and the selection of an architect alone normally took a full month. On being apprised of the problem, Mr. Strobel asked him whether he had in mind a specific architect for the project; he said he didn't, whereupon Mr. Strobel suggested a firm—Serge Petroff and Associates, which he knew from experience was willing and able to handle rush jobs. It was not a notably desirable commission, combining a tight deadline with a modest fee, and the deputy director gladly got in touch with Petroff, who started work that same weekend.

Mr. Strobel did not mention when the decision was being made that Petroff had previously carried out assignments for Strobel and Salzman, and it was on this point—not on any suspicion of a payoff—that three Democrats on the investigating committee faulted him. "Due regard for the proprieties," they declared, "might have dictated that Mr. Strobel advise GSA officials at the time that Petroff was a regular and active client of Strobel and Salzman."

Mr. Strobel explained: "I had only one thing in mind, and that was for the government to get this particular project on the road as fast as possible, and knowing that the project was not necessarily an attractive proposition for any architect, I don't think it entered my thought that there might be any conflict whatsoever. It was a matter of getting a job done, and that is how I made my reputation, that I can get work done." (It turned out that Petroff had received a very small favor indeed. The Immigration Service project was abandoned, and the architects drew a $9200 fee for their work. A few months later, when a considerably more lucrative government project was pending, Petroff was ruled out because it had recently been awarded the other contract. Attempting to explain how he finally chose the architect for this second job from among three equally qualified contestants—who, like all architects, abhorred competitive bidding as demeaning to their profession—the deputy said candidly: "It was just an eeny, meeny, miney, mo basis.") Mr. Strobel could have played safe by not putting forward a suggestion at all. He could have left it up to his deputy, who knew nothing about architectural firms. But one of the commissioner's special assets was that he had better criteria to go by than eeny, meeny, miney, mo.

It is not hard to accept his statement that a possible conflict of interest never occurred to him. Could he have recommended Petroff in the first place if he had not had some dealings with the firm? Must we grow suspicious on learning that six of fourteen architects on a list submitted to the Central Intelligence Agency for its new office building in 1955 were clients of Mr. Strobel's company? Or may we not take at face value his explanation that "it goes to prove the high caliber of clientele Strobel and Salzman have been able to establish—in other words, it would be impossible to give fair consideration to the qualified firms without running across some people that I had business with as a partner of Strobel and Salzman"?

Peter Strobel's difficulty in this case was that he did what he had been hired to do, and used the knowledge he had been hired to do it with. Fresh from private industry where he was accustomed to being his own man, to making quick decisions based on long experience, he acted for the government as he would have acted for himself in a similar situation. This can be hazardous—but it can also be innocuous and efficient.

## 3. THE BUSINESS-SOLICITING

At the end of 1954, the business manager of Strobel and Salzman made an appointment to see the head of the architectural firm of Ferrenz and Taylor about a possible engineering contract. Mr. Ferrenz suggested that he bring along his boss, Commissioner Strobel, and as is the way with suggestions from prospective clients, the commissioner went along. No business was signed up at this meeting, but about ten months later Strobel and Salzman did take on a job for Ferrenz, which carried a fee of $18,000; Mr. Strobel did not participate in the negotiations leading to this contract.

What troubled the Congressman here was that Ferrenz and Taylor subsequently showed an interest in getting work from the Public Buildings Service—a development which would have put the commissioner in a sticky position. But, in fact, Ferrenz never did get a government contract, and Mr. Strobel promised that if ever they were considered for one, he would disqualify himself. This might be dismissed as an inexpensive verbal sacrifice, except that his behavior in another, similar case lent weight to the pledge. On learning that an architect who had recently given an engineering assignment to Strobel and Salzman was being seriously considered for a government project, Mr. Strobel had his company withdraw from its contract—thereby giving up a fee of $30,000.

One Congressman said that "perhaps Mr. Strobel was naïve in not understanding why one of the members of Ferrenz and Taylor had expressed a desire to meet him at that particular time." The observation was sensible. A politically astute man would have been wary about such a request, but Mr. Strobel was far from that—and Strobel and Salzman's need for new business was pressing. During his year and a half in Washington, his firm acquired only two new clients, including Ferrenz and Taylor. Profits dropped from more than $106,000 in 1953 to below $53,000 in 1954, and Mr. Strobel's income sank in those two years from about $87,000 to less than $35,000. "I don't want to build up my own importance," he told the Congressmen, "but it probably wouldn't be altogether unreasonable to say that I am a very important man in that outfit—in fact, I knew that all the time, and I found out that I was a lot more important to the firm than I thought I was when I came down here."

Innocence is an ambiguous virtue in a public official, but perhaps the same innocence which allowed Peter Strobel to meet with a prospective client who may have had ulterior motives could have saved him from more serious involvements had the client become a government contractor. For Strobel and Salzman to be barred from doing business with any firm that *might* some day do business with the government (GSA maintains a list of one hundred or so top architects who fall automatically into that category) would have meant either that he had to get out of government or give up "about the only thing I have." For him, he said, his business was a personal thing, "a matter of pride—not like selling dividends"; his life's major creation as well as his major source of income was at stake.

Even putting so kind an interpretation on Mr. Strobel's actions, it may seem that consciously or not he did in fact overstep the undefined bounds of propriety that the Congressmen invoked. The White House—in the person of Sherman Adams, who in those years was still handing down rulings on other people's conduct—did not feel his case was worth even a mild embarrassment in an election year. He was treated as Harold Talbott was treated, but without the march-past. Most Democrats, delighted at any stain on the Administration escutcheon, were not about to pause and make judicious distinctions between the Strobel case and the Talbott case; they cheerfully lumped them together for purposes of display and disposal. Even the Republicans on the investigating committee concluded that although the commissioner had done nothing unethical, his outside connection nonetheless placed him "in a fundamentally inconsistent and untenable position. . . ." Mr. Strobel—who declared at the start of the investigation, "If they want to get rid of me, they'll have to fire me. I'm not the kind of man who runs"—resigned with the usual letter and left Washington, unmourned and unmedaled, but with a better understanding of political rigors and of himself ("In politics I was out of my element") and impressed perhaps with Samuel Johnson's maxim that there are few ways in which a man can be more innocently employed than in getting money.

Having sent a Talbott packing, one can write him off as an extreme example of the kind of businessman who is bound to fall into difficulties in Washington. But Peter Strobel was in no way extreme. What little he did was not noble or selfless, but it was not iniquitous either and certainly not immoral; when we send him home because he was in an "untenable position," we make nonsense of the wholesome notion of inviting men who run their own businesses to try the role of Washington bureaucrat, to participate in their government.

Here, one would have thought, was the place for the friends of the businessman (and the small businessman at that) to make their stand. But Mr. Strobel was not important enough to warrant such a fuss. It was left for Representative Sidney A. Fine, a Democrat, to divorce himself from the rest of the investigating committee, and issue the most cogent statement of the hour. Emphasizing that Peter Strobel, rather than a career civil servant, had been named commissioner "because of his high qualifications and long experience in the construction and engineering industry," and that "the evidence is clear that he performed services of outstanding value to the government at great personal sacrifice," Mr. Fine went on to ask a question that has still to be answered: "What standards of conduct should be expected from individuals brought into government service for positions of responsibility when it is recognized that they cannot meet their obligations solely on government salaries, and are brought in to assist the government for relatively short periods of time with the full expectation that they will return at some future date to their own private business interests?"

# 33

## Irving Louis Horowitz
## *The Life and Death of "Camelot"*

In June of this year—in the midst of the crisis over the Dominican Republic—the United States Ambassador to Chile sent an urgent and angry cable to the State Department. Ambassador Ralph Dungan was confronted with a growing outburst of anti-Americanism from Chilean newspapers and intellectuals. Further, left-wing members of the Chilean Senate had accused the United States of espionage.

The anti-American attacks that agitated Dungan had no direct connection with sending US troops to Santo Domingo. Their target was a mysterious and cloudy American research program called Project Camelot.

Dungan wanted to know from the State Department what Project Camelot was all about. Further, whatever Camelot was, he wanted it stopped because it was fast becoming a *cause célèbre* in Chile (as it soon would throughout capitals of Latin

America and in Washington) and Dungan had not been told anything about it—even though it was sponsored by the US Army and involved the tinderbox subjects of counter-revolution and counter-insurgency in Latin America.

Within a few weeks Project Camelot created repercussions from Capitol Hill to the White House. Senator J. William Fulbright, chairman of the Foreign Relations Committee, registered his personal concern about such projects as Camelot because of their

> "reactionary, backward-looking policy opposed to change. Implicit in Camelot, as in the concept of 'counter-insurgency,' is an assumption that revolutionary movements are dangerous to the interests of the United States and that the United States must be prepared to assist, if not actually to participate in, measures to repress them."

By mid-June the State Department and Defense Department—which had created and funded Camelot—were in open contention over the project and the jurisdiction each department should have over certain foreign policy operations.

On July 8, Project Camelot was killed by Defense Secretary Robert McNamara's office which has a veto power over the military budget. The decision had been made under the President's direction.

On that same day, the director of Camelot's parent body, the Special Operations Research Organization, told a Congressional committee that the research project on revolution and counter-insurgency had taken its name from King Arthur's mythical domain because "It connotes the right sort of things—development of a stable society with peace and justice for all." Whatever Camelot's outcome, there should be no mistaking the deep sincerity behind this appeal for an applied social science pertinent to current policy.

However, Camelot left a horizon of disarray in its wake: an open dispute between State and Defense; fuel for the anti-American fires in Latin America; a cut in US Army research appropriations. In addition, serious and perhaps ominous implications for social science research, bordering on censorship, have been raised by the heated reaction of the executive branch of government.

## GLOBAL COUNTER-INSURGENCY

What was Project Camelot? Basically, it was a project for measuring and forecasting the causes of revolutions and insurgency in underdeveloped areas of the world. It also aimed to find ways of eliminating the causes, or coping with the revolutions and insurgencies. Camelot was sponsored by the US Army on a four to six million dollar contract, spaced out over three to four years, with the Special Operations Research Organization (SORO). This agency is nominally under the aegis of American University in Washington, D.C., and does a variety of research for the Army. This includes making analytical surveys of foreign areas; keeping up-to-date information on the military, political, and social complexes of those areas; and maintaining a "rapid response" file for getting immediate information, upon Army request, on any situation deemed militarily important. . . .

In a recruiting letter sent to selected scholars all over the world at the end of 1964, Project Camelot's aims were defined as a study to "make it possible to predict and influence politically significant aspects of social change in the developing nations of the world." This would include devising procedures for "assessing the potential for internal war within national societies" and "identify(ing) with increased degrees of confidence, those actions which a government might take to relieve conditions which are assessed as giving rise to a potential for internal war." The letter further stated:

> The US Army has an important mission in the positive and constructive aspects of nation-building in less developed countries as well as a responsibility to assist friendly governments in dealing with active insurgency problems.

Such activities by the US Army were described as "insurgency prophylaxis" rather than the "sometimes misleading label of counter-insurgency."

Project Camelot was conceived in late 1963 by a group of high-ranking Army officers connected with the Army Research Office of the Department of Defense. They were concerned about new types of warfare springing up around the world. Revolutions in Cuba and Yemen and insurgency movements in Vietnam and the Congo were a far cry from the battles of World War II and also different from the envisioned—and planned for—apocalypse of nuclear war. For the first time in modern warfare, military establishments were not in a position to use the immense arsenals at their disposal—but were, instead, compelled by force of a geopolitical stalemate to increasingly engage in primitive forms of armed combat. The questions of moment for the Army were: Why can't the "hardware" be used? And what alternatives can social science "software" provide?

A well-known Latin American area specialist, Rex Hopper, was chosen as director of Project Camelot. Hopper was a professor of sociology and chairman of the department at Brooklyn College. . . .

## THE CHILEAN DEBACLE

How did this social science research project create a foreign policy furore? And, at another level, how did such high intentions result in so disastrous an outcome? . . .

It was ironic that Chile was the scene of wild newspaper tales of spying and academic outrage at scholars being recruited for "spying missions." For the working papers of Project Camelot stipulated as a criterion for study that a country "should show promise of high pay-offs in terms of the kinds of data required." Chile did not meet these requirements—it is not on the preliminary list of nations specified as prospects.

How then did Chile become involved in Project Camelot's affairs? The answer requires consideration of the position of Hugo G. Nutini, assistant professor of anthropology at Pittsburgh, citizen of the United States and former citizen of Chile. His presence in Santiago as a self-identified Camelot representative triggered the climactic chain of events. . . .

Soon after Nutini arrived in Santiago, he had a conference with Vice-Chancellor Alvaro Bunster of the University of Chile to discuss the character of Project Camelot. Their second meeting, arranged by the vice-chancellor, was also attended by Professor Eduardo Fuenzalida, a sociologist. After a half-hour of exposition by Nutini, Fuenzalida asked him pointblank to specify the ultimate aims of the project, its sponsors, and its military implications. Before Nutini could reply, Professor Fuenzalida, apparently with some drama, pulled a copy of the December 4 circular letter from his briefcase and read a prepared Spanish translation. Simultaneously, the authorities at FLACSO turned over the matter to their associates in the Chilean Senate and in the left-wing Chilean press.

In Washington, under the political pressures of State Department officials and Congressional reaction, Project Camelot was halted in midstream, or more precisely, before it ever really got under way. . . .

The State Department has recently established machinery to screen and judge all federally-financed research projects overseas. The policy and research consequences of the Presidential directive will be discussed later.

What effect will the cancellation of Camelot have on the continuing rivalry between Defense and State departments for primacy in foreign policy? How will government sponsorship of future social science research be affected? And was Project Camelot a scholarly protective cover for US Army planning—or a legitimate research operation on a valid research subject independent of sponsorship?

Let us begin with a collective self-portrait of Camelot as the social scientists who directed the project perceived it. There seems to be general consensus on seven points.

■ First, the men who went to work for Camelot felt the need for a large-scale, "big picture" project in social science. They wanted to create a sociology of contemporary relevance which would not suffer from the parochial narrowness of vision to which their own professional backgrounds had generally conditioned them. Most of the men viewed Camelot as a bona fide opportunity to do fundamental research with relatively unlimited funds at their disposal. (No social science project ever before had up to $6,000,000 available.) Under such optimal conditions, these scholars tended not to look a gift horse in the mouth. As one of them put it, there was no desire to inquire too deeply as to the source of the funds or the ultimate purpose of the project.

■ Second, most social scientists affiliated with Camelot felt that there was actually more freedom to do fundamental research under military sponsorship than at a university or college. One man noted that during the 1950's there was far more freedom to do fundamental research in the RAND corporation (an Air Force research organization) than on any campus in America. Indeed, once the protective covering of RAND was adopted, it was almost viewed as a society of Platonist elites or "knowers" permitted to search for truth on behalf of the powerful. In a neoplatonic definition of their situation, the Camelot men hoped that their ideas would be taken seriously by the wielders of power (although, conversely, they were convinced that the armed forces would not accept their preliminary recommendations).

- Third, many of the Camelot associates felt distinctly uncomfortable with military sponsorship, especially given the present United States military posture. But their reaction to this discomfort was that "the Army has to be educated." This view was sometimes cast in Freudian terms: the Army's bent toward violence ought to be sublimated. Underlying this theme was the notion of the armed forces as an agency for potential social good—the discipline and the order embodied by an army could be channeled into the process of economic and social development in the United States as well as in Latin America.
- Fourth, there was a profound conviction in the perfectibility of mankind; particularly in the possibility of the military establishment performing a major role in the general process of growth. They sought to correct the intellectual paternalism and parochialism under which Pentagon generals, State Department diplomats, and Defense Department planners seemed to operate.
- Fifth, a major long-range purpose of Camelot, at least for some of its policy-makers, was to prevent another revolutionary holocaust on a grand scale, such as occurred in Cuba. At the very least, there was a shared belief that *Pax Americana* was severely threatened and its future could be bolstered.
- Sixth, none of them viewed their role on the project as spying for the United States government, or for anyone else.
- Seventh, the men on Project Camelot felt that they made heavy sacrifices for social science. Their personal and professional risks were much higher than those taken by university academics. Government work, while well-compensated, remains professionally marginal. It can be terminated abruptly (as indeed was the case) and its project directors are subject to a public scrutiny not customary behind the walls of ivy. . . .

## THE INSIDERS REPORT

Were the men on Camelot critical of any aspects of the project?

Some had doubts from the outset about the character of the work they would be doing, and about the conditions under which it would be done. It was pointed out, for example, that the US Army tends to exercise a far more stringent intellectual control of research findings than does the US Air Force. . . .

Another line of criticism was that pressures on the "reformers" (as the men engaged in Camelot research spoke of themselves) to come up with ideas were much stronger than the pressures on the military to actually bring off any policy changes recommended. The social scientists were expected to be social reformers, while the military adjutants were expected to be conservative. . . .

Another objection was that if one had to work on policy matters—if research is to have international ramifications—it might better be conducted under conventional State Department sponsorship. "After all," one man said, "they are at least nominally committed to civilian political norms." . . .

## POLICY CONFLICTS OVER CAMELOT

. . . One of the characteristics of Project Camelot was the number of antagonistic forces it set in motion on grounds of strategy and timing rather than from what may be called considerations of scientific principles.

- The State Department grounded its opposition to Camelot on the basis of the ultimate authority it has in the area of foreign affairs. There is no published report showing serious criticism of the projected research itself.
- Congressional opposition seemed to be generated by a concern not to rock any foreign alliances, especially in Latin America. Again, there was no statement about the project's scientific or intellectual grounds.
- A third group of skeptics, academic social scientists, generally thought that Project Camelot, and studies of the processes of revolution and war in general, were better left in the control of major university centers, and in this way, kept free of direct military supervision.
- The Army, creator of the project, did nothing to contradict McNamara's order cancelling Project Camelot. Army influentials did not only feel that they had to execute the Defense Department's orders, but they are traditionally dubious of the value of "software" research to support "hardware" systems.

Let us take a closer look at each of these groups which voiced opposition to Project Camelot. A number of issues did not so much hinge upon, as swim about, Project Camelot. In particular, the "jurisdictional" dispute between Defense and State loomed largest.

### *State vs. Defense*

In substance, the debate between the Defense Department and the State Department is not unlike that between electricians and bricklayers in the construction of a new apartment house. What "union" is responsible for which processes? Less generously, the issue is: who controls what? At the policy level, Camelot was a tool tossed about in a larger power struggle which has been going on in government circles since the end of World War II, when the Defense Department emerged as a competitor for honors as the most powerful bureau of the administrative branch of government. . . .

It should be plain therefore that the State Department was not simply responding to the recommendations of Chilean left-wingers in urging the cancellation of Camelot. It merely employed the Chilean hostility to "interventionist" projects as an opportunity to redefine the balance of forces and power with the Defense Department. What is clear from this resistance to such projects is not so much a defense of the sovereignty of the nations where ambassadors are stationed, as it is a contention that conventional political channels are sufficient to yield the information desired or deemed necessary.

### *Congress*

In the main, congressional reaction seems to be that Project Camelot was bad because it rocked the diplomatic boat in a sensitive area. Underlying most congressional criticisms is the plain fact that most congressmen are more sympathetic to State Department control of foreign affairs than they are to Defense Department control. In other words, despite military sponsored world junkets, National Guard and State Guard pressures from the home State, and military training in the backgrounds of many congressmen, the sentiment for political rather than military control is greater. In addition, there is a mounting suspicion in Congress of varying kinds of behavioral science research stemming from hearings into such matters as wiretapping, uses of lie detectors, and truth-in-packaging.

### *Social Scientists*

One reason for the violent response to Project Camelot, especially among Latin American scholars, is its sponsorship by the Department of Defense. The fact is that Latin Americans have become quite accustomed to State Department involvements in the internal affairs of various nations. The Defense Department is a newcomer, a dangerous one, inside the Latin American orbit. The train of thought connected to its activities is in terms of international warfare, spying missions, military manipulations, etc. The State Department, for its part, is often a consultative party to shifts in government, and has played an enormous part in either fending off or bringing about *coups d'état.* This State Department role has by now been accepted and even taken for granted. Not so the Defense Department's role. But it is interesting to conjecture on how matter-of-factly Camelot might have been accepted if it had State Department sponsorship. . . .

Further, it is apparent that Project Camelot had much greater difficulty hiring a full-time staff of high professional competence, than in getting part-time, summertime, weekend, and sundry assistance. Few established figures in academic life were willing to surrender the advantages of their positions for the risks of the project.

One of the cloudiest aspects to Project Camelot is the role of American University. . . .

The difficulty with American University is that it seems to be remarkably unlike other universities in its permissiveness. The Special Operations Research Office received neither guidance nor support from university officials. From the outset, there seems to have been a "gentleman's agreement" not to inquire or interfere in Project Camelot, but simply to serve as some sort of camouflage. If American University were genuinely autonomous it might have been able to lend highly supportive aid to Project Camelot during the crisis months. . . .

### *Military*

Military reaction to the cancellation of Camelot varied. It should be borne in mind that expenditures on Camelot were minimal in the Army's overall budget and most military leaders are skeptical, to begin with, about the worth of social science research. So there was no open protest about the demise of Camelot. Those officers who have a positive attitude toward social science materials, or are themselves trained in the social sciences, were dismayed. Some had hoped to find "software" alternatives to the "hardware systems" approach applied by the Secretary of Defense to every military-political contingency.

. . . [T]here were differing perspectives of the importance of Camelot: an Army view which considered the contract as one of several forms of "software" investment; a social science perception of Project Camelot as the equivalent of the Manhattan Project.

## WAS PROJECT CAMELOT WORKABLE?

While most public opposition to Project Camelot focused on its strategy and timing, a considerable amount of private opposition centered on more basic, though theoretical, questions: was Camelot scientifically feasible and ethically correct? No public document or statement contested the possibility that, given the successful completion of the data gathering, Camelot could have, indeed, established basic criteria for measuring the level and potential for internal war in a given nation. Thus, by never challenging the feasibility of the work, the political critics of Project Camelot were providing back-handed compliments to the efficacy of the project. . . .

The research design of Camelot was from the outset plagued by ambiguities. It was never quite settled whether the purpose was to study counter-insurgency possibilities, or the revolutionary process. Similarly, it was difficult to determine whether it was to be a study of comparative social structures, a set of case studies of single nations "in depth," or a study of social structure with particular emphasis on the military. In addition, there was a lack of treatment of what indicators were to be used, and whether a given social system in Nation A could be as stable in Nation B.

In one Camelot document there is a general critique of social science for failing to deal with social conflict and social control. While this in itself is admirable, the tenor and context of Camelot's documents make it plain that a "stable society" is considered the norm no less than the desired outcome. The "breakdown of social order" is spoken of accusatively. Stabilizing agencies in developing areas are presumed to be absent. There is no critique of US Army policy in developing areas because the Army is presumed to be a stabilizing agency. . . .

It never seemed to occur to its personnel to inquire into the desirability for successful revolution. This is just as solid a line of inquiry as the one stressed—the conditions under which revolutionary movements will be able to overthrow a government. Furthermore, they seem not to have thought about inquiring into the role of the United States in these countries. This points up the lack of symmetry. The problem should have been phrased to include the study of "us" as well as "them." It is not possible to make a decent analysis of a situation unless one takes into account the role of all the different people and groups involved in it; and there was no room in the design for such contingency analysis. . . .

## THE ETHICS OF POLICY RESEARCH

The issue of "scientific rights" versus "social myths" is perennial. Some maintain that the scientist ought not penetrate beyond legally or morally sanctioned limits and others argue that such limits cannot exist for science. In treading on the sensitive issue of national sovereignty, Project Camelot reflects the generalized dilemma. In deference to intelligent researchers, in recognition of them as scholars, they should have been invited by Camelot to air their misgivings and qualms about government (and especially Army sponsored) research–to declare their moral conscience. Instead, they were mistakenly approached as skillful, useful potential employees of a higher body, subject to an authority higher than their scientific calling.

What is central is not the political motives of the sponsor. For social scientists were not being enlisted in an intelligence system for "spying" purposes. But given their professional standing, their great sense of intellectual honor and pride, they could not be "employed" without proper reverence for their stature. Professional authority should have prevailed from beginning to end with complete command of the right to thrash out the moral and political dilemmas as researchers saw them. The Army, however respectful and protective of free expression, was "hiring help" and not openly and honestly submitting a problem to the higher professional and scientific authority of social science.

The propriety of the Army to define and delimit all questions, which Camelot should have had a right to examine, was never placed in doubt. This is a tragic precedent; it reflects the arrogance of a consumer of intellectual merchandise. And this relationship of inequality corrupted the lines of authority, and profoundly limited the autonomy of the social scientists involved. It became clear that the social scientist savant was not so much functioning as an applied social scientist as he was supplying information to a powerful client. . . .

The story of Project Camelot was not a confrontation of good versus evil. Obviously, not all men behaved with equal fidelity or with equal civility. Some men were weaker than others, some more callous, and some more stupid. But all of this is extrinsic to the heart of the problem of Camelot: what are and are not the legitimate functions of a scientist?

In conclusion, two important points must be clearly kept in mind and clearly apart. First, Project Camelot was intellectually, and from my own perspective, ideologically unsound. However, and more significantly, Camelot was not cancelled because of its faulty intellectual approaches. Instead, its cancellation came as an act of government censorship, and an expression of the contempt for social science so prevalent among those who need it most. Thus it was political expedience, rather than its lack of scientific merit, that led to the demise of Camelot because it threatened to rock State Department relations with Latin America.

Second, giving the State Department the right to screen and approve government-funded social science research projects on other countries, as the President has ordered, is a supreme act of censorship. Among the agencies that grant funds for such research are the National Institutes of Mental Health, the National Science Foundation, the National Aeronautics and Space Agency, and the

Office of Education. Why should the State Department have veto power over the scientific pursuits of men and projects funded by these and other agencies in order to satisfy the policy needs—or policy failures—of the moment? President Johnson's directive is a gross violation of the autonomous nature of science.

We must be careful not to allow social science projects with which we may vociferously disagree on political and ideological grounds to be decimated or dismantled by government fiat. Across the ideological divide is a common social science understanding that the contemporary expression of reason in politics today is applied social science, and that the cancellation of Camelot, however pleasing it may be on political grounds to advocates of a civilian solution to Latin American affairs, represents a decisive setback for social science research.

# 34

## Donald C. Swain
## *The Rise of the National Institutes of Health Empire*

Few federal agencies have prospered as greatly in recent years as the National Institutes of Health, the research branch of the U.S. Public Health Service. Every year, with uncommon enthusiasm, Congress approves larger and larger expenditures for the study of human disease. Already NIH has become the hub of an enormous research effort, and its program will probably continue to expand. The agency has grown so rapidly since the end of World War II that the prewar and wartime stages in its development are now almost forgotten. It was during the 1930's that NIH began laying the groundwork for its current research program. Before the end of World War II federal public health officials had formulated the objectives, worked out the basic organizational pattern, and gained the legislative authority for a great postwar medical research effort. Their far-sighted policy, carefully calculated to advance the cause of federally sponsored medical research, made it possible for NIH to become the giant that it is today.

### CREATION OF NIH

By 1930 the Public Health Service had achieved a proud record in medical research. Its original research laboratory, established by Joseph J. Kinyoun in 1887, contributed significantly to the success of the fight against cholera in the late 19th century. After the turn of the century the bureau's Hygienic Laboratory, an outgrowth of Kinyoun's pioneer facility, won recognition for developing a series of improved vaccines and antitoxin serums whose systematic use helped to bring the dread infectious diseases of the early 20th century under control. Within three decades smallpox and diphtheria practically disappeared. Typhoid fever became much less of a public health problem. In a great cooperative effort medical science was gradually conquering these diseases.

As the danger posed by infectious illnesses declined, top-echelon public health officers came to realize that new medical research objectives should be formulated. Accordingly, during the late 1920's a new research policy began to crystallize in the Public Health Service. Acute infectious diseases each year caused fewer deaths, but the toll taken by the so-called chronic diseases–especially cancer and heart disease–was increasing. Creation of the National Institute of Health in 1930 was one of the early indications that the Public Health Service had begun to modify its research policy. Intended specifically to supersede the Hygienic Laboratory and to carry out the bureau's reoriented research plans, this new organization became both a means of emphasizing the chronic diseases and a vehicle for the expansion of federally sponsored medical research. Thirty years ago, however, the Public Health Service received only a small amount of money for research. In fiscal year 1931 NIH operated on an appropriation of $43,000.

Research on the problem of cancer was already a well-established part of the Public Health Service program. In 1922 PHS investigators had set up a special Cancer Investigations Laboratory at Harvard Medical School, and they had conducted experiments throughout the 1920's. Moreover, the Hygienic Laboratory in Washington had periodically undertaken cancer studies. But these investigations were small-scale. In 1930 the Surgeon General, H. S. Cumming, announced that extension of the work on cancer was needed. He also announced that the Public Health Service hoped to study heart disease, "one of the major causes of premature death." Within two years, federally financed cancer research had begun to expand and NIH had initiated a pilot study of rheumatic heart disease.

During the Hoover Administration there was another significant change in PHS research objectives. Increasingly, NIH staff members thought in terms of basic studies designed to obtain "fundamental knowledge concerning the chemical conditions which control the life, growth, and multiplication" of normal and abnormal cells. This trend toward basic research paralleled the increasing emphasis on chronic diseases. Of course, studies of infectious diseases continued. In 1931 the Public Health Service established its Rocky Mountain Spotted Fever Laboratory in Hamilton, Montana, and there initiated the research which subsequently produced an effective vaccine for this indigenous disease. Investigations of tuberculosis, venereal disease, and childhood illnesses were continued and expanded.

Nevertheless, by 1932 the National Institute of Health had definitely laid out a program of increased emphasis on the chronic diseases. Lack of funds proved a severe handicap, and L. R. Thompson, then director of NIH, made the search for additional research financing his personal concern. He was able to obtain funds through the Social Security Act of 1935.

## EXPANSION OF FEDERAL MEDICAL RESEARCH

In the second year of the New Deal, Thompson and others had arranged for the President's Science Advisory Board to undertake a special study of medical research in the Public Health Service. The NIH leaders hoped that a recommendation for expansion would result. Pushed gently by Thompson, Karl T. Compton, chairman of the Science Advisory Board, designated a subcommittee consisting of Thomas J. Parran, Jr., Milton J. Rosenau, and Simon Flexner, all friends of the Public Health Service, to make the study. Getting Parran and Rosenau appointed to the Science Advisory Board in the first place had been a major but unpublicized PHS objective which was achieved at the cost of some bitterness.

In 1934 the National Academy of Sciences was already miffed at President Roosevelt for having established the Science Advisory Board without the advice and consent of the Academy. When Roosevelt decided to expand the board and to appoint Parran and Rosenau (neither of whom held membership in the NAS), a heated controversy developed, and as a consequence the Science Advisory Board was less effective than it might otherwise have been. It expired in 1935. But for as long as the Board lasted, the presence of Parran and Rosenau was of considerable benefit to the Public Health Service.

The special subcommittee, comprised of Parran, Rosenau, and Flexner, recommended increased research in cancer, heart disease, tuberculosis, malaria, venereal disease, and dental problems. It also suggested that "funds for the scientific work of the Public Health Service. . . be increased by the sum of $2,500,000 over and above the allotment for 1934–35" and that the disbursement of funds be left "to the judgment of the Surgeon General with the approval of the National Advisory Health Council." This was a powerful endorsement of medical research in the Public Health Service, and it was carefully phrased so as to recommend maximum flexibility for NIH. If Congress approved, NIH would be free to channel new funds into research in the chronic diseases.

Thompson and his colleagues organized a letter-writing campaign to generate public and Congressional support for their cause. They pointed out that the prevention of disease tended to increase the economic security of the general population. When the Social Security Act became law, in 1935, Title VI authorized the expenditure of up to $2 million annually for the "investigation of disease and problems of sanitation."

Although officials of the National Institute of Health were gratified, they remained keenly aware that Congress still had to appropriate the money. They turned to the press, hoping to keep the pressure on Congress through publicity. The director's office immediately announced: "A program of attack on disease along some 70 lines has been planned by the U.S. Public Health Service, to be put into effect if and when funds for scientific research became available as authorized by the social security legislation." The problems slated for study had been "on the doorstep" of the Public Health Service for "some time," the statement continued. "Lack of funds has made it impossible to go ahead with them so far."

Congress consistently refused to appropriate the maximum amount authorized by the Social Security Act, but NIH did get additional funds for research. From $375,000 in fiscal 1936, annual appropriations under Title VI increased to a maximum of $1.64 million in 1940 (they decreased during World War II). Thus, a key piece of New Deal social legislation allowed significant expansion of federally sponsored medical research and indirectly produced a new concentration on the chronic diseases. Congress also approved larger direct appropriations for NIH. By 1940 medical research in the Public Health Service had been securely linked to the New Deal social welfare program, and, in addition to Title VI funds, the National Institute of Health had an operating budget of more than $707,000.

## REORGANIZING CANCER RESEARCH

The Public Health Service had traditionally thought in terms of intramural research—that is, research conducted by its own experts and carried out primarily in PHS laboratories. As late as 1934, bureau officials had become disturbed at a suggestion made by Henry Wallace that the government should limit its own research programs and award grants-in-aid to university scientists. Immediately the director of NIH took action to defend the type of research work done by NIH, which, he said, "would not be duplicated by grants-in-aid to universities." But the Public Health Service's preference for intramural programs began to weaken in 1937, with the creation of the National Cancer Institute.

There had been a steady expansion of cancer research during the first 6 years of the 1930's, but the Public Health Service continued to call for more money for cancer studies; its interest in the chronic diseases had become pronounced. In 1936, when President Roosevelt appointed Thomas Parran to the post of Surgeon General, the emphasis on chronic illnesses became intense. "The acute infectious diseases," Parran stated in 1937, "have declined rapidly under the impact of public health effort." But there had been a concomitant increase "in many of the diseases of adult life, particularly the chronic diseases." Public health services should shift emphasis, he declared, to the "prevention and treatment of the chronic diseases." Such a shift was already well under way. The National Cancer Institute Act of 1937, sponsored by Congressman Warren G. Magnuson and Senator Homer T. Bone, accelerated the change and indicated congressional approval of the new Public Health Service research policy.

Organized as a division of NIH, the National Cancer Institute became a prototype of the many national institutes to follow. It had funds for intramural research. It was authorized to award grants-in-aid and fellowships to able researchers in institutions outside the Public Health Service. It had authority to establish a trainee program to increase the ability of physicians to diagnose cancer. It was even directed to establish a National Advisory Cancer Council to aid in the selection of grantees and trainees. From the beginning the Cancer Institute was a success. Its grants program foreshadowed today's large extramural research setup. Receiving about $400,000 annually, the institute stimulated cancer research before World War II and demonstrated the organizational advantages of a system of disease-oriented research agencies.

While it stepped up the study of chronic illnesses, the Public Health Service maintained a vigorous program of research in the field of infectious and contagious diseases. Its total research program became noticeably broader. One of the most valuable developments to grow out of federal medical research in the 1930's was an improved typhus vaccine; this vaccine was largely responsible for the notable fact that not a single American fighting man died of typhus during World War II. The influence of fluorides in drinking water also came under investigation. At first the objective was to find ways to reduce excessive natural fluoridation, the cause of mottled tooth enamel, but before the end of the decade PHS scientists had concluded that dental decay could be reduced by controlled use of fluorides in public water supplies.

By the end of the 1930's congressional eagerness to support NIH had become quite apparent. In 1938 Congress again endorsed the PHS research program by authorizing construction of new and larger NIH laboratory facilities in suburban Washington. In the mid-1930's Thompson had obtained jurisdiction over a choice acreage in Bethesda, Maryland—part of a private estate donated to the federal government. A few years later, when the time came to enlarge NIH, this site was available. Public Health researchers moved into their new laboratories shortly before World War II. With plenty of land for future expansion, NIH was admirably situated to become a truly national research center in the postwar years.

## RESEARCH IN WARTIME

During the early 1940's the Public Health Service dedicated almost all of its research capacity to the war effort. It started to prepare for wartime research in 1940, and in the same year it began to experience a shortage of scientifically trained personnel. Late in 1941, when the Committee on Medical Research began to function in the Office of Scientific Research and Development, the Public Health Service really moved into the wartime research program. In the rush to solve specific problems, such as the development of blood substitutes and the synthesis of antimalarial drugs, basic medical studies suffered. Yet the National Cancer Institite continued to operate, awarding grants and conducting research throughout the war. At least one significant advance in cancer research technique was recorded during the war years.

In the course of its wartime functions the Public Health Service had an opportunity to observe a large and successful extramural research program in operation. The Committee on Medical Research operated exclusively by awarding research contracts to universities, medical schools, and independent laboratories. The fact that these institutions were scattered across the country and conducted research in their own facilities did not retard the wartime research effort. The arrangement functioned quite smoothly and produced results. The operation of the Committee on Medical Research—in fact, the operation of the entire Office of Scientific Research and Development—provided an example that the Public Health Service could not afford to ignore as planning for the postwar period got under way. The National Cancer Institute had been a beginning, but now federal health officials, especially the new director of NIH, R. E. Dyer, became enthusiastic about the possibilities of extramural research. "Governmental funds for research should be available for grants-in-aid to scientific institutions," the Public Health Service proclaimed in 1944, "to ensure continuity of research and to enlist cooperation in investigations requiring a variety of professional skills. Yet the federal public health agency lacked authority to award grants-in-aid in support of general medical research. It could make grants only for cancer research.

Before the end of the war the Public Health Service had taken steps to remedy this situation, and in the process had obtained the last legal prerequisite for postwar success. It persuaded Congress to pass Public Law 410, the Public Health Service Act of 1944. Written to consolidate and revise existing public health legislation, this act attracted relatively little attention at the time. Yet it was an extremely important piece of legislation. Among other things it empowered the Surgeon General to "make grants in aid to universities, hospitals, laboratories, and other public or private institutions, and to individuals"; NIH at last had the legislative basis for its postwar program.

## ESTABLISHING A POSTWAR PROGRAM

The Public Health Service wasted no time in attempting to initiate a general grants program. It made preliminary plans to award grants during the latter half of 1944, but the Bureau of the Budget vetoed the proposal. Although a few grants were finally awarded in mid-1945, the Bureau of the Budget stubbornly refused to open the public purse for purposes of medical research. It was only when the Committee on Medical Research ceased operations, in December 1945, that the PHS finally got sufficient funds for a general extramural research program. Forty-four wartime research contracts, transferred to Public Health jurisdiction to insure their continuance, provided the impetus for the large grants program now administered by NIH.

The Public Health Service had long sensed the potential importance of these wartime research contracts as a means of expanding its own program. In fact, it was the director of NIH who originally suggested the transfer of the contracts. In August 1944 Dyer wrote to A. N. Richards, chairman of the Committee on Medical Research, proposing that the committee's medical research contracts be continued under the aegis of the Public Health Service and that they be coordinated with the public health program. In view of the importance of these medical studies, Dyer suggested, there would be little difficulty in persuading the Budget Bureau or Congress to approve the transfer. Vannevar Bush, director of the Office of Scientific Research and Development, responded favorably to Dyer's suggestion. For some time, however, Bush had been hoping to transfer medical research as well as certain aspects of military research to a postwar national research foundation. When it became clear that establishment of such a foundation would be delayed, the CMR contracts went to the Public Health Service, where they undergirded the emerging extramural research program.

Shortly after the war, also under authority of the Public Health Service Act of 1944, NIH began granting research fellowships. The object of this new program was "to encourage the development and to further the training of competent young researchers in the medical and allied fields of investigation." Since the National Cancer Institute had been awarding cancer research fellowships for more than 5 years, precedent for such a program existed, and the need was apparent: there was an acute and well-recognized shortage of competent medical researchers. As early as 1940 one highly placed PHS official expressed the opinion that only a few of the cancer investigators in the country merited financial assistance. In the end, the Public Health Service was prepared not only to stimulate medical research but to increase the number of well-trained medical research specialists as well.

In 1946 the Surgeon General created the Research Grants Office in NIH to coordinate the rapidly growing program of extramural medical research. By December 1947 the Public Health Service had awarded 1115 grants, for a total of $11,508,841. In a carefully considered organizational move the Grants Office began establishing study sections, composed mostly of civilian consultants, to give technical advice and to review applications for grants in specialized fields. As the program grew, the Grants Office set up more study sections, which served both as checks on the Public Health Service and as a means of drawing top-flight medical researchers into the NIH program in an advisory capacity. The study sections generated both participation and approval. Within a short time the grants and fellowships program had become extremely popular, and applications flowed in by the hundreds.

As the federal government enlarged its medical research effort, leaders of the Public Health Service drew on their past organizational experience. After almost 10 years of operation the National Cancer Institute was still functioning smoothly, providing a framework for both intramural and extramural cancer research. As circumstances warranted, therefore, the Surgeon General recommended authorization of new disease-oriented institutes. The National Institute of Mental Health became a part of the NIH complex in 1946. The National Heart Institute and the National Dental Research Institute came into existence in 1948. In each case, enabling legislation established advisory councils and provided authority for establishment of a large grants and fellowship program. The National Institute of Health continued to supervise these various programs. To prevent confusion NIH pluralized its name in 1948, and since then has been known as the National Institutes of Health.

The number of disease-oriented institutes continued to increase, for Congress, always eager to earmark funds for specific purposes, liked the idea of delimited research organizations. By 1951 there were seven institutes, microbiology, arthritis and metabolic diseases, and neurological diseases and blindness having joined the list. In fiscal 1951 the various institutes awarded research grants totaling $16,374,128 and operated on a budget of more than $60 million.

The Public Health Service was hardly surprised by this rapid growth. Its goal for more than 20 years had been to expand federally sponsored medical research. "New programs should emerge from the blueprint stage," Parran had announced in 1947, "and all peacetime health services promise to gather increased momentum. As the country's health workers speed their attack on vital problems, particularly those related to chronic disease of old age, wide public support may be anticipated. Never before has there been such keen and widespread interest in health matters throughout the land."

The Public Health Service did not escape criticism. It came under special attack for inequitable distribution of research funds. Westerners charged that the East received a disproportionate share of available support. "The time has arrived," one critic wrote in 1948, "when the West should shake off the stunting dominance of the northeastern seaboard in scientific matters, insisting on autonomy and a just share of public funds for its scientific development." Competent observers pointed out other weaknesses in the burgeoning NIH operation. As a result, the Public Health Service was forced to devote more time and attention to matters such as distribution of research funds, research coordination, and project continuity. Accounting procedures proved particularly troublesome. Not having fully anticipated the large financial support its program would receive, NIH tried to get by with outmoded methods of fiscal control. Keeping track of its multifarious grants became an acute problem as federal support mushroomed.

## AN AUTONOMOUS AGENCY FOR MEDICAL RESEARCH

In the final months of World War II, Vannevar Bush, Senator Harley Kilgore, and others proposed that a National Science Foundation be created to support and coordinate American scientific research, including medical research. Although the proposal received almost universal support, the Public Health Service looked upon it with some apprehension; NIH officials in particular had reservations about the wisdom of assigning medical research to a new scientific agency. Testifying at Senate hearings in 1945, Dyer explained that the Public Health Service already had "all of the authority in reference to health and medical research that is contemplated for the proposed foundation." He also pointed out that he had as much right to be "concerned with preserving the scientific integrity and independence of [his] organization [NIH] as any university administrator or director of a private foundation." Although the Public Health Service did not oppose the concept of a National Science Foundation, it was clearly anxious to protect its own well-established research interests.

Most medical administrators and researchers outside of the government, while favoring federal support for medical research, would have preferred to set up a new and completely autonomous agency to coordinate the national program of research in medicine. The Palmer Committee, appointed to make recommendations concerning medical research as a part of the Bush Report of 1945, concluded that "the Federal agency concerned with medical research should be created *de novo* and be independent of all existing agencies." This was contrary to the view of Bush himself, who believed that medical research should be included in the proposed national science foundation. After some hard talking he got the Palmer Committee to modify its position. At a meeting in Pittsburgh in October 1945, the deans of

American medical schools were also persuaded to go along with the Bush approach, but they indicated that serious deviation from the original Magnuson bill to establish NSF (S. 1285), or a lengthy delay in passage of the bill, would mean withdrawal of their support and a campaign to secure a separate medical foundation. In the end the Palmer Committee and the medical schools had their way. An agency devoted exclusively to medical research—a revamped NIH—did evolve. By the time Congress finally authorized establishment of the National Science Foundation, in 1950, the extramural program of NIH was so well known and so successful that the new foundation did not undertake the support of disease-oriented research. Instead, it subsidized basic research in the chemical and biological sciences, thus contributing indirectly to medical research.

## CONCLUSION

During the 1930's and the 1940's the Public Health Service experimented freely and prepared the way for its accelerated postwar growth. Before President Hoover left the White House, the PHS had decided to put greater research emphasis on the chronic diseases and had exhibited increasing interest in basic medical studies. By the end of the 1930's it had worked out the organizational pattern for its later period of growth. During the war years public health officials became firmly convinced of the value of extramural research and took steps to gain the authority needed to initiate a broad grants and fellowship program. Dramatic wartime medical achievements undoubtedly advanced the cause of federal support for medical research. An all-out attempt to reduce the occurrence and consequences of dread diseases proved to have extraordinary political appeal. But the Public Health Service itself, vigorous and flexible enough to capitalize on each opportunity, was largely responsible for the growth of NIH. The expansion of federally sponsored medical research was a goal the PHS had been working toward since 1930 at least. Without a proven organizational structure, without the experience gained by NIH before and during World War II, the great postwar program of federal support for medical research might have faltered in its initial stages. Instead, it matured, by a relatively orderly process, into a popular and effective scientific program.

# 35

## Amitai Etzioni
## *Government by Commissions*

As these lines go to press, the President's National Advisory Commission on Civil Disorders is expected to hand in its report on March 1, 1968, a short six months after it was instituted and a full six months before it was initially expected to complete its work. The conclusions of the Anti-Riot Commission, as it is known in Washington, are expected to be highly controversial; already the sides are arranging themselves—to contest or support its positions. Less widely asked is the question: to what extent do the statements of this and other such Commissions deserve such attention? What are they based on? Are their description of the conditions they report upon and their diagnoses of the ills—on which their prognoses are based—accurate, at least within limits of tolerable error? Do they have the membership and staff capable of research?

The Anti-Riot Commission, for instance, is headed by a Governor of Illinois, Otto Kerner. Its members are politicians, businessmen and lawyers; there is not one social scientist among its members or any other researcher. Initially there were some social scientists among its staff members, hired to investigate the causes and dynamics of riots. But most of these social scientists have resigned by now, and the Anti-Riot Commission, racing against a deadline, "farmed out" its research work to campus-based researchers and private advisory corporations. Given only a few months to conduct their work, some of these researchers simply did not complete their work; others handed in what they themselves considered half-processed or even shoddy work.

The issue is not that one Commission excluded experts from among its members and relied on busy politicans and community leaders for its membership, but the general American usage of this particular procedure for the study of public needs and issues. The work of several such commissions came recently under critical review. Daniel Bell explored the work of the National Commission on Technology, Automation and Economic Progress, of which he was a member. (His discussion was published in *The Public Interest*.) Robert Blauner, a Berkeley sociologist, blasted the McCone report in *Trans-Action* and Edward J. Epstein, a graduate of Cornell and Harvard, studied the work of the Warren Commission in a booklength report entitled *Inquest*.

### COMMON FEATURES OF COMMISSIONS

These and other commissions tend to have the following features in common which help to explain the frequently inadequate nature of their products: (a) Most of their members are eminent citizens, chosen not because of their expert knowledge but because of their civic stature. (b) The members all have some other full-time position and numerous additional commitments. (c) Lawyers are much over-represented and other relevant disciplines are often not represented at all. (For instance, the President's Commission on Law Enforcement and Administration of Justice had no criminologist or sociologist among its members. It was made up almost entirely of political and legal leaders.) (d) Much of the actual work is done by a staff, but its members too tend to be lawyers, burdened with other commitments (not the least of which is to find employment once the *ad hoc* job is completed), and usually not adequately guided by the commission itself. (e) The procedure of a semi-judicial process (of "hearings") is frequently used but it is not suited to the purposes of studying a situation, (f) and the pressure to reach consensus is considerable.

No wonder the Warren Commission report, based on less than ten weeks' work, according to Epstein, seems full of holes; the McCone report was sharply contradicted by a later study of the Watts area, and the report of the automation commission was carefully filed away and little has been heard about it since.

## BALM AND CONSENSUS

I was commenting to a friend, long active in Washington, on this haphazard way of studying major societal problems; no self-respecting corporation would open an overseas branch on the basis of such a study. Conferences and commissions, he felt, are part of the American way of life. They are not meant to provide systematic analysis, new information or deep insight (at least that is not their main purpose), but to soothe an alarmed public ("seven wise men are studying the problem"), delay the need to take action, build consensus around (i.e., public support for) a policy, and maybe learn something on the side.

That did make a lot of sense, only it seemed to me that these political ends could be served—even more effectively—in other ways, *and* if conferences and commissions are dedicated mainly to these purposes, there ought to be some other mechanism for societal learning.

The commissions' work should be clearly divided into two separate parts, one to be served by experts and the other by consensus-makers, whatever title these two groups may be given. The experts have to be numerous enough, have sufficient funds and time, and include representation of the relevant disciplines before they may be able to do their job. The efforts of the experts need to be concerted; they require a staff director who is used to working with teams of experts; and they need facilities such as access to libraries and computers. Such expert work is, for instance, as Richard H. Rovere pointed out, quite effectively conducted by the Federal Aviation Agency in investigating airplane accidents.

## AN APPROACH TO CONSENSUS

The consensus-makers ought to represent the various segments of the public, interests, values, and viewpoints. The consensus-makers may meet at first to set, as clearly as they can, the issues, the questions which are to be answered, and their pre-conceptions. Then the experts should get to work. They should sporadically brief the consensus-makers on their findings as their work progresses so as to note the additional questions these findings raise and prepare the consensus-makers for the final expert report. Such briefings as well as the report ought to be closed to the public and press; otherwise the experts may unwittingly absorb part of the consensus-makers' function by by-passing them, going directly to the public. Once the final report is completed, the consensus-makers may discuss it, draw the policy conclusions, and publish the expert report with their own interpretations, evaluations, and recommendations. Minority reports should be encouraged rather than frowned upon.

Such an approach would cost more and take longer than the present procedure; it may even produce less consensus. But action taken on the basis of such reports would be more effective and they would be more difficult to ignore.

All reports should have a built-in evaluation and revision mechanism. That is, if Commission X and its experts argue that steps a, b, and c will prevent riots in long, hot summers, they should meet again—next winter—to check to what extent their recommendations were effective, generate some pressure if their advice has been neglected (and the situation worsened as they foretold), or revise their recommendations if those were followed but did not have the desired result. More continuity in staff work, overview, and more follow-up will not solve all our problems but they could go a long way toward making our conferences and commissions more valuable. Now they mainly handle the politics of the issues rather than help handle the issues themselves, and this ultimately is even bad politics. If nothing else, that is what we can learn from the Kerner, Warren, McCone, and Automation Commissions.

10

# The Knowable and Possible

This chapter describes how the government obtains information about the nation's citizens, about what they want from the government, about how to fulfill those wants, and about the course of future events. First, however, is an article which tries to define those problems capable of political solutions. Professor Carl Friedrich of Harvard University suggests that incredible things happen in politics. It can be dangerous to believe any event is politically impossible unless it is logically self-contradictory, like a "bloodless war." What makes some problems, if not impossible, at least difficult to solve politically?

For the government to solve problems, it must first be aware of them. One of the ways public officials find out what the citizens want is through elections, and apportionment, which determines the relative value of each man's vote, is of great importance in the election process. The fierce agitation over apportionment in recent years has involved courts, legislatures, political parties, and some interested citizens. Many people, though, never heard of the matter or don't know what reapportionment is all about. As one reporter joked, "When asked how they liked it, some people say they tried it and didn't like it and others said that they had never eaten any." This article presents the elements of apportionment according to the new prevailing doctrine of equipopulous districts, known more popularly as "one man, one vote." After this principle failed to win more than modest victories in state legislatures, the Supreme Court took over the matter in 1963 and laid down very strict rules requiring legislatures, councils, the House of Representatives, and other representative governing bodies to be elected according to an apportionment that divided the population into constituencies with equal numbers of people. What have been the effects of this rule on the political process?

The government also obtains information by collecting statistics. Statistics show the dimensions of problems and provide information for developing and administering programs to solve them. Murray N. Rothbard, a "nineteenth-century liberal" economist and consultant, who is generally critical of government intervention in economic affairs, shows that negative effects may be associated with statistics. Perhaps some students may think he is joking about abolishing government statistics; let them prove it. We think that he is deadly serious. What would happen if statistics were abolished?

Research is another method that the government uses to find answers to the nation's problems. What kinds of research the federal government should support is currently a major political issue. Despite the obvious paramountcy of human relations problems in our society, over 90 per cent of all research funds go to the natural sciences. The present results of some of these, as for instance the space probes, are meagre; yet these activities cost as much as the so-called total war against poverty. In the third selection, Hubert Humphrey, then a U.S. senator, reviews the government's record on social science research support. Humphrey began his career as an instructor of political science. This selection is reprinted to present the flavor of recent discussions of the relationship between government and research. Do you think social science research could make a significant contribution to solving important national problems?

Computers can be used both to store and to retrieve data more efficiently and to manipulate data for research purposes. The next two articles discuss the application of computers to government operations. Fisher Howe is a foreign service officer who has studied computer science for its possible uses in the conduct of foreign affairs. A summary of his writing is presented here to show what might be done to improve foreign policy operations through the employment of computers. Very shortly, it may be predicted, not a single office concerned with foreign affairs will remain unaffected by the computer revolution.

It is doubtful that Lyndon Johnson knew much about computers. But he was President, and when his advisers convinced him something was really important, he went to bat in his typical fashion, saying "I want . . ." and meaning he wanted everybody in the government to consider computer applications and automation in their operations. His executive order to that effect is reprinted here. The attitude expressed is rather naïve. It is doubtful that the twenty-six hundred computers that he was talking about have reduced government payrolls at all. Probably they have added to the cost of government operations on the whole. This is not to say that they have not in some way produced a measurable return, and indeed in the future their effect may be very great.

T. W. Milburn, a professor of psychology, and J. F. Milburn, a professor of government, demonstrate how research can be used to predict the future. This article presents the conjectures of two groups of scientists, one behavioral and one physical, as to future events that would affect American strategic concerns. A group of military men were also involved. The article gives a rather good cross-section of what the expert elite believed at that time would be the future conditions of international relations. How may such predictions be used for policy making? How may they be verified?

# 36

## Carl J. Friedrich
## *The Politically Impossible*

What is meant, or at any rate ought to be meant by "politically impossible" is what is contrary to the nature of politics. That is to say, the question leads right into the heart of the mis-argued question of the possibility of a science of politics. Are there, can there be valid generalizations about established matters of fact in the field of politics? Philosophically, three kinds of the possible can be and have been distinguished: the logical, the epistemological and the metaphysical. In the first sense, all that is thinkable is considered possible, and that means the exclusion of the self-contradictory. Thus a powerless ruler would be "impossible," because it is of the essence of rule to require power. In the second, and scientifically the most important sense, that is possible which is compatible "with the formal conditions of experience, regarded in terms of intuition (*Anschauung*) and concepts" (Kant) as well as with the recognized body of experience. Finally, the metaphysical or ontological meaning of the possible is that which has the capacity to become something, in contrast to that which already is something. The possible is—and this has been recognized since Aristotle—a kind of being, and in a way lies between being and nonbeing. The impossible, then, would be something which can never become actual reality. It is evident, or ought to be, that in the field of politics this kind of impossibility is going to be linked to views on "human nature," if it is admitted at all. We find such impossibilities alleged in writings of the conservatives, for that reason, but also for instance in Machiavelli. Such views rest upon dogmatic assumptions which defy scientific testing and analysis.

The "politically impossible" is derived from all three types of impossibility, but is especially concerned with the "epistemological." Strictly speaking, it is even narrower, for two other types of impossibility, the legal and psychological, though politically relevant, can be set aside.

Thus it might be alleged that a certain proposed policy in the field of labor policy in the United States is "impossible," because the constitution of the U. S. leaves labor largely to the States, and therefore the particular proposal would require a constitutional amendment for its realization. There are in any constitutional democracy a good many such "impossibilities," especially in those with a federal structure. These "impossibilities," though political realities, ought not, strictly speaking, to be called "political impossibilities," because the obstruction is *legal*, not political.

"Psychological impossibility" is much more difficult and perplexing to distinguish. The obstacles to the occurrence may be the result of what commonly goes under the name of national character. Or they may be related to other givens of a psychological sort, *e.g.*, the entire range of issues related to psychoanalysis and psychiatry. A great many of the political procedures evisaged in the age of rationalism, and associated with such names as Bentham and his school, are actually impossible, because they rest upon erroneous psychology. A good many economic policies, recurrently advocated by economists and others, have not succeeded, or rather have not been adopted, because they presupposed men to be much more rational than they actually are. Again, I would say these are not political impossibilities, but psychological ones. Admittedly, the line is at times difficult to draw, because the political and the psychological sphere are so very closely bound up with each other. But unless an effort is made to exclude those vast issues which are strictly psychological, the realm of political possibilities (and impossibilities) is so greatly expanded as to become quite unmanageable.

If the legal and the psychological impossibilities are excluded, what remains for the political? Politics has been variously defined, since Aristotle coined the term as the realm of "what pertains to the polis." Its central field is that of government, of the control and direction of communities, of power in all its various connotations. It is true that most of the students of political science, the scholars in this field, are less concerned with generalizations than with the clarification of specific situations. They write about how particular governments function, how particular parties are run and so forth. But along with these studies of an anatomical kind there are others which seek to generalize more or less effectively. And then take as an illustration the field of international trade policy. It is often proposed by well-intentioned persons of good economic insight that free trade should be substituted for an established system of tariffs. We need not specify the many different forms this proposal has taken in the past. All of these plans have gone awry, because they were "politically impossible" (there are also psychological impossibilities involved, but we leave these aside here). They were politically impossible, because such a free trade policy would have to be enacted into law, and hence would have to pass through the established legislative channels. These channels operate according to the well-known ways of parliamentary bodies, responding as they do to pressure groups. There is a still more general "law" involved here, which might be stated thus: in the democratic process, the interests affected by a particular piece of legislation will be active in direct ratio to the degree that they are being affected. Hence, in many situations, the so-called general interest of such inchoate conglomerates as "the consumers" will be very ineffectively defended because they are inactive, whereas very specific interests will be very effective. . . .

The argument about what is "politically impossible" has played a considerable role in the field of European unification. Many of the participants in the debate are actually talking about "psychological impossibilities." But there are true "political" impossibilities involved. Thus it was politically impossible to achieve the ratification of the European Defense Treaty in France. The reason was basically not that the French were afraid of the Germans (a largely psychological reason), but that the French military did not want to lose their identity within a European defense force. This was a political impossibility, because the French military establishment is an important element in the French government (in the broad sense of the effective control system) and its position proved decisive. The proof of the correctness of this analysis was afterwards furnished by the ready acceptance of a German army by the French parliament (and public). Had they been afraid of Germany, they would have rejected that proposition even more decisively than the other.

The "impossibilities" of a true political kind that impede the unification of Europe are mostly of this type. A united Europe would do away with deep-rooted vested interests, especially of certain sectors of the government bureaucracy and the economy. But are they true "impossibilities"? The range of creative potential in the field of politics is so large, due to the possibilities of superior leadership, that one hesitates to admit this. After all, there have been numerous occasions when what seemed impossible has been made possible by such superior effort. . . .

But just because of these cases of superior leadership, one is not justified in abandoning the category of the politically impossible. For one thing, it always takes time for such political leadership to crystallize. Thus the time factor is of decisive importance. Therefore, most statements of the "politically impossible" need to be enclosed in specified time-brackets and other conditions of the type of *rebus sic stantibus.*

To sum up, I would conclude that apart from the logically impossible which results from self-contradiction, the range of the scientifically demonstrable "political impossibility" is very limited, if the sphere of the metaphysical is excluded. If it is included, and dogmatic views concerning human nature are admitted, the range will include all those matters which happen to be incompatible with the alleged "laws of human nature." For only what is contrary to nature is existentially impossible, and this realm is politically very flexible. Hence the statement: "this is politically impossible" ought always, or nearly always, be qualified by reference to the conditions and the period of time to which it is supposed to apply.

# 37

## Alfred de Grazia
## *The Rudiments of Apportionment*

Apportionment fever struck the State of Oregon last year. The Legislative Counsel Committee of the State, seeking to reduce to manageable proportions its task of assisting persons in the drafting of proposed apportionments, issued a "Legislative Reapportionment Do-It-Yourself Kit." Wrote the Committee, "Dear Do-It-Yourselfer . . . The Legislative Counsel Committee and its staff hope that this kit will answer some of your questions and afford some assistance to you in the event you wish to try your hand at formulating new apportionments."

The apportionment of legislatures is fascinating to the informed and uninformed alike. It is a task that appears simple, concrete, and logical–more a game than a task. But no sooner does one begin to play the game than he discovers how ramified its meanings, and disputed its rules. As the final discouragement, he sooner or later encounters a number of gentlemen who do not think it is funny at all and have political muscles to emphasize their seriousness–the legislators themselves.

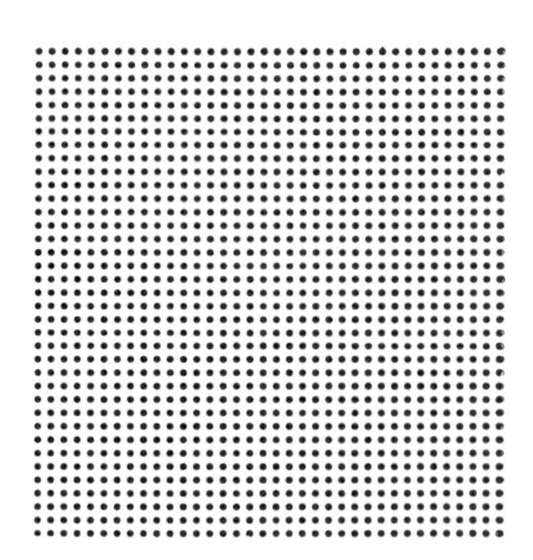

To demonstrate how apportionment begins, let us examine Figure 1. It consists of 1,565 dots more or less. Each dot stands for a person. All of them have a legislative assembly of five members. How can they be apportioned? Under the doctrine of absolute equal populations, to apportion this group, you should divide the population of 1,565 by the number of seats to be filled and then take any set of 313 people to make up each constituency, the only rule being "Don't count the same people in two constituencies." So a given constituency will be made up of 313 of the various types of persons found in the jurisdiction. The only thing they will have in common by contrast with the members of the other four constituencies is that they are charged with electing a legislator. This is superficially the most "inhuman" apportionment possible. An enormous number of different apportionments could be made under its method.

Let us change the meaning of the dots. Let each dot stand for 5,000 people. That gives 7,825,000, almost exactly the population of Michigan in 1960, by a remarkable coincidence.

Thereupon we can apportion the legislature of the State of Michigan according to the absolute principle of equal populations. If the House of Representatives consists of 100 members, then we should place 78,250 people into each district. So we take a pencil, and beginning with any dot, circle that dot and 15 other dots to give the quota for a seat in the make-believe House of Representatives.

But who are these people; why are they in groups of 5,000; where do they live; how will they vote; what will the effect be? Never mind, this is a game of numbers, not politics; people are so many potatoes in a bushel. There are, by the way, trillions of possible combinations that fulfill the requirements as here stated.

Let us structure the problem a little more than the principle of equal populations standing by itself deserves. Let us place people on a map of Michigan where they live, as in Figure 2. In it, each dot stands for 5,000 people again. Now again, the principle of equal populations says: draw any line anywhere, regardless of even the county lines you see on the map; just be sure you have only x dots. Again trillions of combinations are possible, none with any more meaning than any other, *unless additional rules are laid down.* The average intelligent person, given this task, will see the dilemma and immediately commences to set forth new rules. He says:

1. Let's make a rule that the dots have to be as close together as possible. (A rule of *community, compactness, contiguity,* and *convenience.*)

2. Let's make a rule that where other significant boundaries of going concerns exist, we should prefer to keep all the dots on one side instead of crossing back and forth. (A rule of *community* and *governmental efficiency.*)

3. Let's make a rule that we shall not count in the dots any elements that move in and out of counties and State but only those that are people who have lived there for a year. (A *residence* rule.)

4. We have to have a rule about what to do with fractions too, since, try as we may, some districts have more people than others. (A rule for *distributed fractions.*)

DISTRIBUTION OF POPULATION IN MICHIGAN BY COUNTIES: 1960

One dot represents 5,000 persons or major fraction thereof.

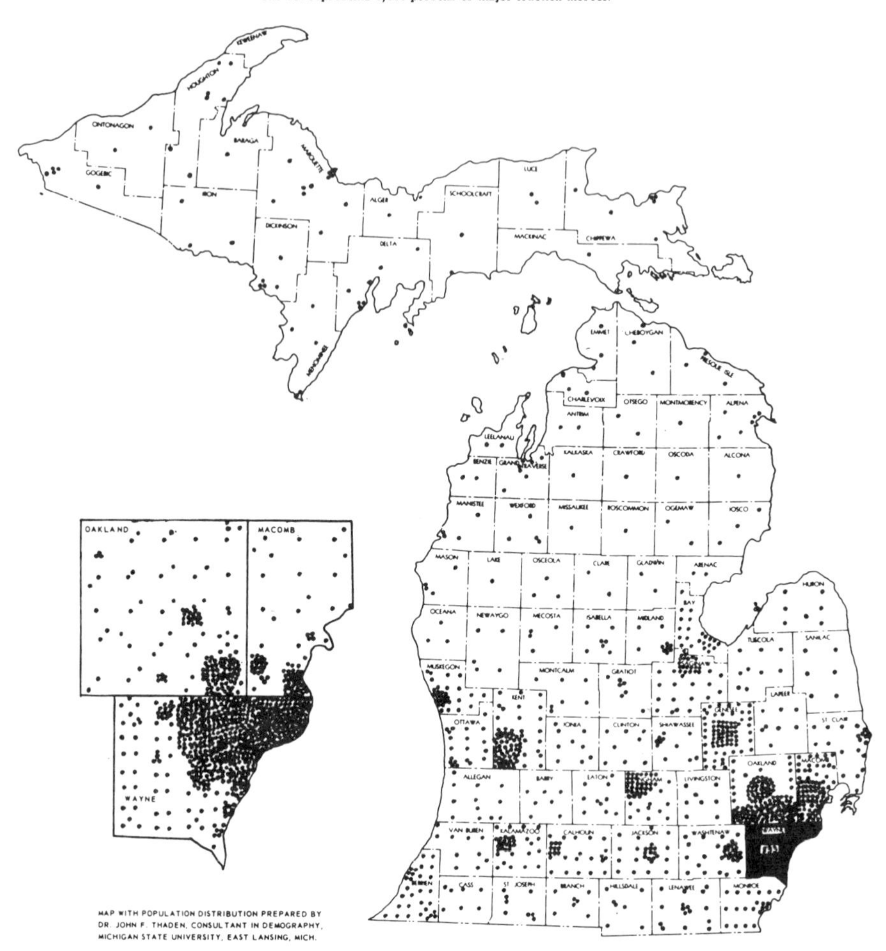


Rules 5, 6, 7, 8, etc., etc., . . . As our average intelligent person moves into the problem, he becomes of much more than average intelligence. He sees that he has to make dozens of rules, and that, starting from his very first rule, he has been making public policy, not mere calculations. As the Special Master appointed in the Wisconsin case reported: "Redistricting is not a mere exercise in mathematics or logic, nor does it involve only the finding of facts."[1] One soon discovers, if he does not surmise as much from the beginning, that public policy is heavily involved and that many other people will not agree with his policies.

Actually the whole process depicted here could be performed more flamboyantly, using electronic computers. First, we should start with a list of all people in the State and perform 99 successive lotteries. These would be random

[1] State of Wisconsin v. Zimmerman (U.S. Dist. Gt., Spec. Master Rept., Pt. II), paragraph 61.

constituencies of the State. (But note two big, debatable presumptions already. Why random? Why shouldn't steps be taken to avoid getting random groups, on grounds that we do not want each constituency to be like every other? Secondly, there would already have to be agreement on eliminating children and all others who are to be deprived of suffrage or who are non-voters.) The method would unite equal populations who would in each case mirror perfectly the population of the State. (Any random sample of 100,000 of a population of 9,000,000 would send a scientific sample survey expert into transports of joy.) Presumably, the equal-populations backers would want to add a customary rule—territorial residence. So the computer would exhibit its finer possibilities along the lines of the following simplified program.

*Drawing of State apportionment boundaries by computer:*
(Feasible for all jurisdictions, including the U.S.A.)[2]

Purpose: Place all People of State in Equal Population Districts as They Fall on the Geographical Map of the State.

A. Data (Input) to be stored in machine:

Pinpointing of location on a grid of all persons in the State eligible to vote.

B. Instructions to machine:

(1) Assign all persons with a given grid characteristic (a set of numbers) to one of x districts (x = No. of districts in the state).

(2) Subtract individual A (defined as the last individual assigned to his district) from district $X_1$, reallocate him to district $X_2$ (defined as the district into which he would have fallen had he not been picked for $X_1$).

(3) Recompute all the new district boundaries resulting from moving A from $X_1$ to $X_2$.

(4) Repeat the last two procedures until you have all possible combinations (outputs). There are many millions of them, all conforming strictly to the original purpose of creating equal population districts based on territory.

C. Query: Which of these millions should be chosen? (See 7 below)

D. Additional purpose: To create a political situation favoring one party.

(5) Assign each voter an R (Republican) or D (Democratic), designating his party (new input), with his number and instruct machine to eliminate all equal population apportionment combinations that do not concentrate the opposition party members into districts to the extent of 80 percent. Result (output): the opposition party members

[2] For those who wish not only to do their own apportionment but want to computerize the task, the following works, among others, may be recommended: Herbert D. Leeds and G. M. Weinberg, *Computer Programming Fundamentals* (New York, 1961); Robert Nathan and Elizabeth Hanes, *Computer Programming Handbook* (New York, 1962). For a detailed example of the construction of a computer model of voting behavior and its application, the interested technical reader should be sure to see pages 123-179 of W. N. McPhee and W. A. Glaser, eds., *Public Opinion and Congressional Elections* (New York, 1962).

are massed into a few districts and the party to be favored will win consistently a majority of seats.

E. Alternative purpose (instead of D above): To group people around the already existing communities.

(6) Assign a grid number to X "most important" centers of commerce and culture (new input). Instruct machine to assign people to their nearest community but not let anybody be farther than Y grid points from their center. Result (output): people are massed into districts around large centers. Districts are very uneven in population.

F. Which to be chosen?

(7) Reverting to 4, one way to choose the legal districting plan-to-be is by drawing one "winning plan" from the multitude. This could actually be done in advance by drawing one individual in the State by lot and making him or her the axis of the winning system. This would save much machine time.

Note that there would be many chances of unfavorable consequences under "B" above. Since this is applying the theory of equal territorial populations, that is all that is guaranteed. For the defenders of this belief, there is presumably no problem. For others there may be some distress owing to the possibility that the districts will not correspond to terrain differences, governmental groupings, ethnic differences, community or neighborhood groupings, economic similarities, political-historical traditions, and other characteristics that they believe should be reflected in apportionment. They may prefer plan "D" or "E" or any combination of these and other plans.

Is there then no use for the machines except to assist our theoretical thinking and to expose some logical absurdities? Yes, there may be. Following upon an initial period of research on computer possibilities in this area, it may be possible to set up some day a clear set of authoritative instructions for the machine that will electronically arrange the population into constituencies of certain traits. This "set of instructions" would be be nothing other than what we shall call in the book *the policy of the constitutional authorities* regarding "how the government should be basically organized to do what,"[3] carried over from the whole theory of representative government to the sub-sub-field of apportionment.

Until a machine can do humane work, however, it is best to limit its use strictly and so also limit the use of machine-like theories that try to organize society. American society is not a collection of faceless particles. It is composed of highly diverse and yet interconnected sets of people. A political theory suggesting that people are interchangeable like nuts and bolts is likely to be both fallacious and detrimental to the personal happiness of the citizenry.[4]

[3] Cf. Alfred de Grazia, "Law and Behavior: A Unified Approach to Their Study," III *American Behavioral Scientist PROD*, May 1960, 3.

[4] Cf. Alfred de Grazia, "Mathematical Derivation of an Election System," *Isis*, June 1953, 42.

## REPRESENTATIVE DEMOCRACY AND APPORTIONMENT THEORY

The system called democratic representative government is probably the most complicated political structure ever deliberately employed by man. An ICBM missile is simple by comparison: its arrangements of parts are tangible; cause and effects are more evident; human history does not play as large a part in its construction. It is quite necessary, therefore, to know something of the whole of representative government before attempting to examine one of its parts; apportionment cannot be understood without a larger comprehension of democratic representative government.

Politics in general is the quest for influence in government.[5] It embraces all behavior from the naked struggle for personal power to the rule-bound conduct of lawyers in a neutral court of law. We can say of politics, however, that its intent is always to discriminate; everybody involved in politics is under some necessity of seeking to preserve or change his position relative to the position of others; he must therefore act to help or to harm some interest, or else get out of politics. Good men, well-meaning men, and fanatics have often tried to destroy politics—thinking thereby to leave only the Truth, the true and one way—but they have inevitably failed or set up merely a new type of political system, screened by changes in words, where discrimination is still practiced on behalf of somebody and to the detriment of somebody else.

Representative government is an ordering of political relations. It is a system of devices and procedures (such as a legislature) intended to channel numerous opinions, interests, and abilities of a country into the making and executing of public policy. The opposite of representative government is a political order that claims all the reason, justification, and causes of its actions are beyond the scope and intelligence of all ordinary people. Nowadays the world is composed almost exclusively of representative governments; the few exceptions such as Saudi Arabia are not important enough to recall to mind the great changes of the past century. It was as late as 1822 when the leading nations of Europe declared at the Congress of Verona their resolve to crush all representative governments.

Yet, if the world of politics today is the world of representative government, it is still not a satisfactory world. Absolute governments exist that make the Congress of Verona governments appear pathetic, and they carry the forms of representative government. The Soviet Union, the People's Republic of China, Spain, and other nations are obviously of a different order of politics than the majority of Western European countries and the United States. Let us call these latter older versions of representative government *democratic* and ask what are the principal elements in their make-up.

[5] Many people are "in politics" for reasons other than influence, of course; they may merely enjoy the company of others so engaged. But the essential reason and theme of politics is influence. Lawyers may practice law to earn money but they are forced into a framework of institutions designed to test cases and make judgments.

Democratic representative government includes:

1. A pervasive doctrine of the consent of the people as the basis of government.
2. Provision for entry of various kinds of opinions and interests into the political process and legislation.
3. Limits on the extent to which dissenting groups can be coerced.
4. A rule of law, applicable to the government as well as the people.

In the American system of government, the consent of the people is implied in the widespread respect accorded to the opinions of the common man, and in the several ways provided for the population to enter individual judgments of public policies. Methods of petitioning, voting, referenda, assembly, and other devices, are designed not only to assist major popular expressions, but are also intended for every minor opinion and interest. At the same time, there are widespread attitudes against going too far in repressing minority views; furthermore, a separation of powers and checks and balances are provided in the structure of government to prevent any single group from imposing its view on the totality without enlisting extraordinary support in opinion and action from previously uncommitted leaders. Also a stability of the law is usually maintained. There is a strong effort to justify rules, regulations, and decisions upon established precedents, and to make them only according to certain procedures designed to protect the persons involved in legal contests.[6]

Four general traits then define American democratic representative government (three, if popular consent and the entry of more special opinions are conceived as shading into one another). But the machinery for working out these general design features is greatly differentiated. Hundreds of working principles (procedures) are involved. Each one of them acts to admit, foster, transform, or check some kind of opinion or behavior that is using the system.

To put it another way, practically every type of human desire has entered, been affected by, and influenced the system. And practically every kind of desire has been fabricated into a device or setting on the machinery of government to alter the inputs and outputs of opinions and behaviors.

It would be out of place here to explain the wide variety of human goals that have gone into the creation of the federal system and the division of tasks between State and local governments, of the political party system, of the system of judges and courts, of President, cabinet, and civil service, of the rights and powers of non-governmental but socially important institutions, and of the manner of conducting legislative business with its important committee system and provisions for leadership. It should be quite clear, nevertheless, that representative government of the American type rises and falls by every one of these, each consisting in turn of a great many variable procedures. All of these procedures and devices of

[6] Cf. Gaetano Mosca, *The Ruling Class* (trans. 1939) on the principles of juridical defense; A. V. Dicey, *Introduction to the Study of the Law of the Constitution* (1926); "Post-War Thinking About the Rule of Law," *Michigan Law Review*, February 1961, 485-654. Alfred de Grazia, *Elements of Political Science* (1952), Chap. 9 (rev. ed., Colliers, 2 vols., 1962, II, chap. 2).

representative government have some meaning and effect, though the difference between the most important and least important may be very large. And it must be added that there is no easy way to determine the effects of any single procedure upon the whole of representative government, even though they are all there for a purpose, that purpose being to advance somebody's idea of the good government and the good life. . . .

. . . [T]he size of the constituency varies greatly, from perhaps 20 to 180,000,000. Changes of size produce changes of many other kinds in the election process result. The only recorded intervention of George Washington in the Constitutional Convention of 1787 was a final plea for changing the Representative quota from 40,000 to 30,000, to extend the number of possible defenders of popular interests.[7] Note, too, how many ways of counting the winner there are, the majority principle being common, but many other principles such as plurality being used. As with the 26-letter alphabet that could provide us with millions of words, the basic elements of any election system can provide millions of possible effects.

All of the arrangements of representative government are operated by human beings, of course, men and women of a great many skills and different personalities and backgrounds. The structure affects them and they affect the structure. The legislators, administrators, lobbyists, judges, politicians, journalists, and citizenry work in and out of the machinery, bringing into it the tone and traits of the larger culture and taking out of it some habits and attitudes that come from the special experience of governing and politiking. Changing a formal procedure of representative government is not followed automatically by a measured response in accord with the change, but rather more often by a set of responses of a diversionary, subversive, adjusting, changing kind, so that often, the more things are changed, the more they remain the same.

To summarize thus far: politics is the process of influencing; representative government is a complex system for aiding some types of influencing and discouraging others; no single element in the system can be considered in isolation without bearing in mind all of the activity it affects or is affected by; elections are a sub-system of devices within representative government. In setting forth proposals for procedural change in a political process, the perennial risk is that important implications of the novel proposals may be disregarded, and unforeseen effects of a damaging character may be produced.

### *Apportionment Defined*

Apportionment is part of the system of elections in a representative government. It is therefore included in the list just preceding, although, as we shall show, its depth and variety are greater than indicated there. In the most abstract and general sense, apportionment is the division of a jurisdiction into groupings (constituencies) some of whose members are enabled to participate in a designation of officers of the jurisdiction.

[7] Madison in Farrand, ed., *Records of the Federal Convention of 1787* (1937), II, 644.

Each term in the definition has ramifications of significance. Expanding it, we get: "A division (*some authoritative agency must act*) of a jurisdiction (*the extent of legal control, though the population on which the apportionment is based is on occasion distinct from the jurisdiction–for example, the U. S. Constitution has an exogamous feature in that the Electors of a State are compelled to vote for either a President or a Vice President not a resident of their State*) into groupings (*of varying political or functional kind; size; degree of cohesion, from tightly organized to almost random membership; with different tasks, such as solely to vote, or to run the government–legislatures can also be constituencies; and differently qualified members–educated men, registered voters, etc.*), some of whose members (*not everyone can vote, whatever the type of grouping*) are enabled (*they are not all interested, nor are they usually compelled to be interested*) to participate (*many other things happen in an election besides the voting itself to determine the successful candidate*) in a designation (*nomination, election, preference*) of officers of the jurisdiction (*usually members of an assembly but also executives, judges, and other electors*)."

More concretely and normally in the United States, apportionment is the division of a population into constituencies whose electors will vote for members of an assembly.

# 38

## Murray N. Rothbard
## *Statistics: Achilles' Heel of Government*

Ours is truly an Age of Statistics. In a country and an era that worships statistical data as super-"scientific," as offering us the keys to all knowledge, a vast supply of data of all shapes and sizes pours forth upon us. Mostly, it pours forth from government. While private agencies and trade associations do gather and issue some statistics, they are limited to specific wants of specific industries. The vast bulk of statistics is gathered and disseminated by government. The over-all statistics of the economy, the popular "gross national product" data that permit every economist to be a soothsayer of business conditions, come from government. Furthermore, many statistics are by-products of other governmental activities: from the Internal Revenue bureau come tax data, from unemployment insurance departments come estimates of the unemployed, from customs offices come data on foreign trade, from the Federal Reserve flow statistics on banking, and so on. And as new statistical techniques are developed, new divisions of government departments are created to refine and use them.

The burgeoning of government statistics offers several obvious evils to the libertarian. In the first place, it is clear that too many resources are being channeled into statistics-gathering and statistics-production. Given a wholly free market, the amount of labor, land, and capital resources devoted to statistics would dwindle to a small fraction of the present total. It has been estimated that the federal government alone spends over $43,000,000 on statistics, and that statistical work employs the services of over 10,000 full-time civilian employees of the government.

## THE HIDDEN COSTS OF COERCED REPORTING

Secondly, the great bulk of statistics is gathered by government coercion. This not only means that they are products of unwelcome activities; it also means that the true cost of these statistics to the American public is much greater than the mere amount of tax money spent by the government agencies. Private industry, and the private consumer, must bear the burdensome costs of record-keeping, filing, and the like, that these statistics demand. Not only that; these fixed costs impose a relatively great burden on *small* business firms, which are ill-equipped to handle the mountains of red tape. Hence, these seemingly innocent statistics cripple small business enterprise and help to rigidify the American business system. A Hoover Commission task force found, for example, that:

> No one knows how much it costs American industry to compile the statistics that the Government demands. The chemical industry alone reports that each year it spends $8,850,000 to supply statistical reports demanded by three departments of the Government. The utility industry spends $32,000,000 a year in preparing reports for Government agencies . . .
>
> All industrial users of peanuts must report their consumption to the Department of Agriculture . . . Upon the intervention of the Task Force, the Department of Agriculture agreed that henceforth only those that consume more than ten thousand pounds a year need report . . .
>
> If small alterations are made in two reports, the Task Force says, one industry alone can save $800,000 a year in statistical reporting.
>
> Many employees of private industry are occupied with the collection of Government statistics. This is especially burdensome to small businesses. A small hardware store owner in Ohio estimated that 29 per cent of his time is absorbed in filling out such reports. Not infrequently people dealing with the Government have to keep several sets of books to fit the diverse and dissimilar requirements of Federal agencies.

## OTHER OBJECTIONS

But there are other important, and not so obvious, reasons for the libertarian to regard government statistics with dismay. Not only do statistics-gathering and producing go beyond the governmental function of defense of persons and property; not only are economic resources wasted and misallocated, and the taxpayers, industry, small business, and the consumer burdened. But, furthermore, statistics are, in a crucial sense, critical to *all* interventionist and socialistic activities of government. The individual consumer, in his daily rounds, has little need of statistics; through advertising, through the information of friends, and through his own experience, he finds out what is going on in the markets around him. The same is true of the business firm. The businessman must also size up his particular market, determine the prices he has to pay for what he buys and charge for what he sells, engage in cost accounting to estimate his costs, and so on. But none of this activity is really dependent upon the omnium gatherum of statistical facts about the economy ingested by the federal government. The businessman, like the consumer, knows and learns about his particular market through his daily experience.

Bureaucrats as well as statist reformers, however, are in a completely different state of affairs. They are decidedly *outside* the market. Therefore, in order to get "into" the situation that they are trying to plan and reform, they must obtain knowledge that is *not* personal, day-to-day experience; the only form that such knowledge can take is statistics. Statistics are the eyes and ears of the bureaucrat, the politician, the socialistic reformer. Only by statistics can *they* know, or at least have any idea about, what is going on in the economy. Only by statistics can they find out how many old people have rickets, or how many young people have cavities, or how many Eskimos have defective sealskins—and therefore only by statistics can these interventionists discover who "needs" what throughout the economy, and how much federal money should be channeled in what directions. And certainly, only by statistics, can the federal government make even a fitful *attempt* to plan, regulate, control, or reform various industries—or impose central planning and socialization on the entire economic system. If the government received no railroad statistics, for example, how in the world could it even start to regulate railroad rates, finances, and other affairs? How could the government impose price controls if it didn't even know *what* goods have been sold on the market, and what prices were prevailing? Statistics, to repeat, are the eyes and ears of the interventionists: of the intellectual reformer, the politician, and the government bureaucrat. Cut off those eyes and ears, destroy those crucial guidelines to knowledge, and the whole threat of government intervention is almost completely eliminated.

## WITHOUT STATISTICS BUREAUCRACY WOULD WITHER AWAY

It is true, of course, that even deprived of all statistical knowledge of the nation's affairs, the government could still *try* to intervene, to tax and subsidize, to regulate and control. It could try to subsidize the aged even without having the slightest idea of how many aged there are and where they are located; it could try to regulate an industry without even knowing how many firms there are or any other basic facts of the industry; it could try to regulate the business cycle without even knowing whether prices or business activity are going up or down. It could try, but it would not get very far. The utter chaos would be too patent and too evident even for the bureaucracy, and certainly for the citizens. And this is especially true since one of the major reasons put forth for government intervention is that it "corrects" the market, and makes the market and the economy more rational. Obviously, if the government were deprived of all knowledge whatever of economic affairs, there could not even be a *pretense* of rationality in government intervention. Surely, the absence of statistics would absolutely and immediately wreck any attempt at socialistic planning. It is difficult to see what, for example, the central planners at the Kremlin could *do* to plan the lives of Soviet citizens if the planners were deprived of all information, of all statistical data, about these citizens. The government would not even know to *whom* to give orders, much less how to try to plan an intricate economy.

Thus, in all the host of measures that have been proposed over the years to check and limit government or to repeal its interventions, the simple and unspectacular abolition of government statistics would probably be the most thorough and the most effective. Statistics, so vital to statism, its namesake, is also the State's Achilles' heel.

# 39

## Hubert H. Humphrey

## *The Need for More Behavioral Science in Government*

Virtually everyone is aware that, in recent years, science in the free world has attained the greatest freedom, the largest magnitude of support and the broadest social scope in all human history. Fewer persons seem aware or concerned about the fact that one vast segment of science continues to lag behind the others in all of these respects.

To begin with, in a certain sense, the social and behavioral disciplines are less "free" than their sister disciplines in the physical, mathematical, engineering, and biological realms. It is not that the former's academic freedom is in question;

fortunately, the right of scholars–sociologists, psychologists, anthropologists, historians, or others–to pursue the truth is less restricted than on many occasions heretofore.

Rather, the "freedom" of the social and behavioral sciences is limited in the sense that these sciences are often so little understood and esteemed that they are held back from fullest growth. The lack of understanding and of esteem are reflected in the fact that these disciplines continue to receive a disproportionately small level of financial support from public and private quarters. The support they do receive is invariably limited in scope, short-range in duration, and oriented to applied fields.

These observations do not detract in any way from the enlightened support provided by numerous foundations and by other sources, including in some instances, Federal agencies. But the social and behavioral sciences are almost in an "orphan status" in comparison to other disciplines. They are chained by circumstances and limited in their potential contribution to mankind. Many other observers have come to similar conclusions. Views such as this have been expounded on various occasions by social scientists in and outside of the Government. Report after report has been written on the need to give more Federal and other impetus to the social and behavioral sciences.[1]

## NATURE OF "MAGNA CARTA"

A "Magna Carta" is needed, a blueprint for future national support for the social and behavioral sciences. Such a pronouncement should represent the combined efforts of scientists in and outside of Government. It should express policy guidelines which will help unleash men's fullest insight and talents.

The Magna Carta should first define its terms carefully and concisely; the widest possible audience should be helped to understand both the similarities and differences between these and other sciences, as well as among the respective social and behavioral sciences themselves.

The Magna Carta should stress the value of both basic and applied research on the part of Federal "in-house" scientists and, principally, extramural sources such as University faculties. The Magna Carta should point up the facts that scholarship provides the only seed-bed for new knowledge, and that scholarship requires scholars–meaning adequate personnel, career opportunities, and facilities. Above all, the Magna Carta should stress that a climate of fullest freedom is necessary, one in which creativity is fostered.

[1]See for example, Graham, Milton D., "Federal Utilization of Social Science Research, Exploration of the Problems: A Preliminary Paper," The Brookings Institution, Washington, D.C., August 1954 and "National Support for Behavioral Science," February 1958.

## SPECIALIZED STUDIES BY SENATE SUBCOMMITTEE

Part of these personal views derive from a survey which has been conducted by the Subcommittee on Reorganization and International Organizations of the Senate Committee on Government Operations, . . .

We have touched upon these phases from the standpoint of three separate but inter-related reviews, authorized by the Senate:

(a) international medical research
(b) Federal budgeting for all types of research and
(c) science information.

## MEDICAL RESEARCH AND BEHAVIORAL SCIENCE

As far back as July 1959, we received testimony from Dr. Margaret Mead[2] on the contributions which applied anthropology and related disciplines can make in international medical programs of technical assistance and research. Dr. Mead confirmed, in my judgment, that whereas the U.S. Government had used the social and behavioral sciences to considerable advantage in the winning of World War II, it had, by and large, in the post-war years, seriously downgraded these disciplines.

A fortunate exception has been the National Institute for Mental Health which, for a decade and a half, has supported an increasingly large body of scholars engaged in basic and applied research in the behavioral sciences.[3] The Division of Social Sciences of the National Science Foundation has likewise been a valuable sponsor of basic research.

## FEDERAL BUDGETING FOR RESEARCH

In July 1961, our Subcommittee held Hearings on the $9 billion Federal budget for research, development, testing, and evaluation. Once again, a phase of the problem came to light in terms of the meager financial support provided the social and behavioral sciences.

One of the by-products of this review[4] is the chart that is reproduced herein. It shows that in the 1960 fiscal year, only around 4 per cent of total Federal *research*

[2] U. S. Senate, Committee on Government Operations, Subcommittee on Reorganization and International Organizations, Hearings on "The U. S. Government and the Future of the International Medical Research," pursuant to S. Res. 347, 85th Congress, Part 1, pages 68-81.

[3] See National Institute of Mental Health, Public Health Service, Department of Health, Education and Welfare, "Research in the Behavioral Sciences Supported by the National Institutes of Health: A Summary Description," April 21, 1961.

[4] U. S. Senate, Committee on Government Operations, Subcommittee on Reorganization and International Organizations, Hearings on "Federal Budgeting for Research and Development," pursuant to S. Res. 26, 87th Congress, Parts I and II.

support of $1.9 billion was allocated to the Social and Psychological Sciences. This estimate is about the best that could be developed under circumstances of wide differences in inter-agency definition as to what constitutes "social" and "psychological" science.

## SCIENCE INFORMATION

Meanwhile, for three and a half years, the parent Committee and the Subcommittee have intermittently, as opportunity permitted, examined the problem of science information. We have been concerned with more effective publication, abstracting, indexing, dissemination and utilization of masses of scientific data.

We have noted a number of significant efforts to secure improved management of information in the social and behavioral sciences. Regrettably, some of the most promising of these efforts have died a-borning or have been held at low plateaus. Today, in the judgment of our staff[5] information management in the social and behavioral sciences appears far less advanced than in other sciences. . . .

The fact is that much of science has only dimly perceived its new and higher responsibilities in this fantastic age.

## OPPORTUNITY AND PERIL

It is an age of supreme opportunity and supreme peril. Obviously, man can usher in a golden age of abundance–of progress, prosperity, and plenty–or he can extinguish life on this planet. If he is to avoid planetary suicide, he must do so through the mobilization of every branch of human knowledge. No branch is more significant than that which concerns man's relationship with man. The proper study of man is indeed man. The proper interest of Government is in man. The proper concern of Government should be with support of the study of man, the total organism–man, the social creature. At home and abroad, we as a nation confront awesome problems to which we must look to the social and behavioral sciences for inter-disciplinary answers.

## FOREIGN AND DOMESTIC PROBLEMS

In the field of foreign policy:

How can we best communicate to the Government of the Soviet Union, to the people of the Soviet Union, to the Government and peoples of the satellite nations in the Soviet bloc, to the Government and people of Mainland China, and of areas within Peking's domination? How can we best communicate to the Government and peoples of the developing nations? What, for example, are the very words

[5] Cahn, Julius N., Director of Scientific Research Project, Committee on Government Operations, Subcommittee on Reorganization and International Organizations, manuscript, "The Crisis in Management of Information in Science and Technology," January, 1962.

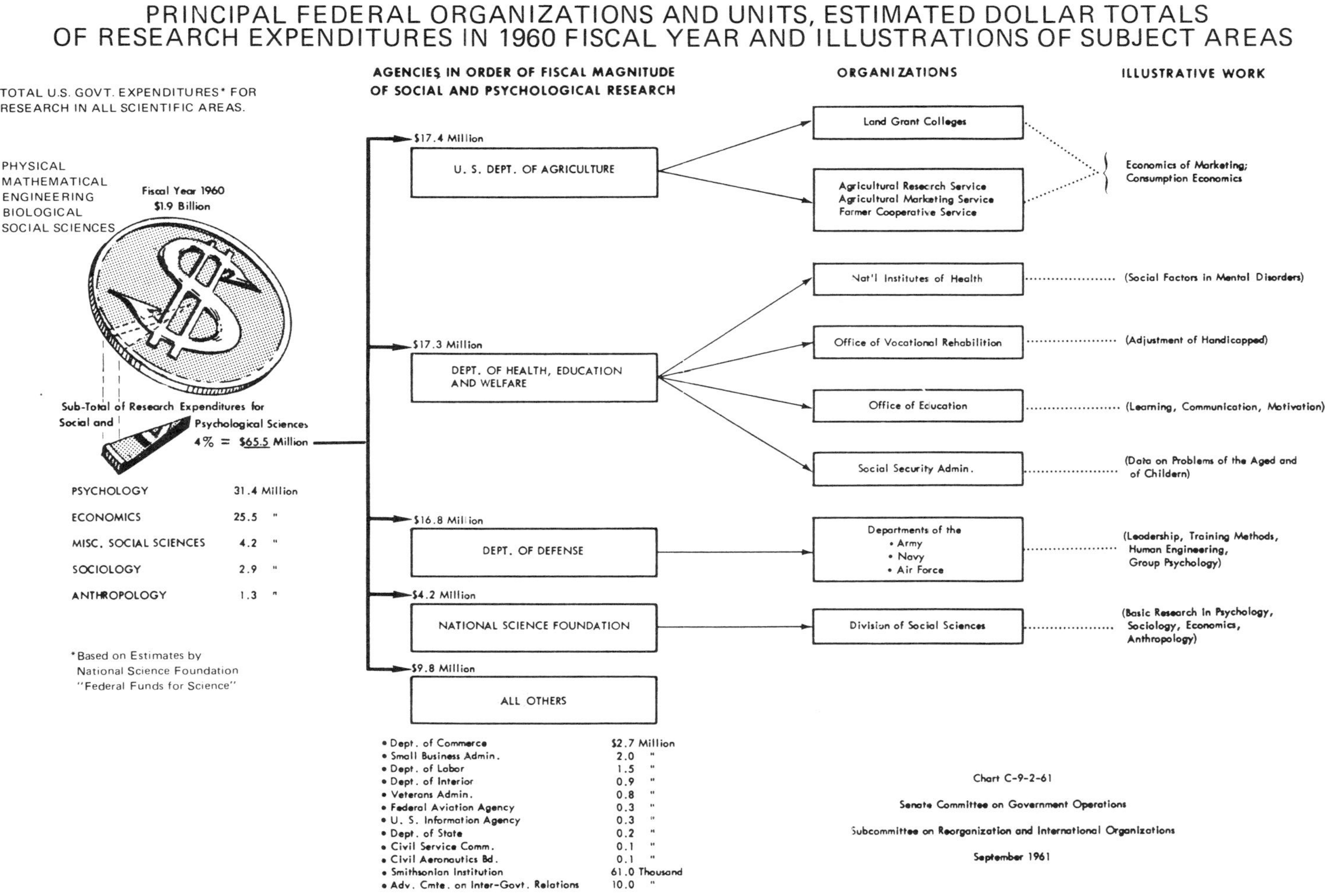
RESEARCH IN SOCIAL AND BEHAVIORAL SCIENCES IN THE UNITED STATES GOVERNMENT
PRINCIPAL FEDERAL ORGANIZATIONS AND UNITS, ESTIMATED DOLLAR TOTALS OF RESEARCH EXPENDITURES IN 1960 FISCAL YEAR AND ILLUSTRATIONS OF SUBJECT AREAS
TOTAL U.S. GOVT. EXPENDITURES* FOR RESEARCH IN ALL SCIENTIFIC AREAS.
PHYSICAL
MATHEMATICAL
ENGINEERING
BIOLOGICAL
SOCIAL SCIENCES
Fiscal Year 1960
$1.9 Billion
Sub-Total of Research Expenditures for Social and Psychological Sciences
4% = $65.5 Million
PSYCHOLOGY 31.4 Million
ECONOMICS 25.5 "
MISC. SOCIAL SCIENCES 4.2 "
SOCIOLOGY 2.9 "
ANTHROPOLOGY 1.3 "
*Based on Estimates by National Science Foundation "Federal Funds for Science"
AGENCIES IN ORDER OF FISCAL MAGNITUDE OF SOCIAL AND PSYCHOLOGICAL RESEARCH
$17.4 Million
U. S. DEPT. OF AGRICULTURE
$17.3 Million
DEPT. OF HEALTH, EDUCATION AND WELFARE
$16.8 Million
DEPT. OF DEFENSE
$4.2 Million
NATIONAL SCIENCE FOUNDATION
$9.8 Million
ALL OTHERS
• Dept. of Commerce $2.7 Million
• Small Business Admin. 2.0 "
• Dept. of Labor 1.5 "
• Dept. of Interior 0.9 "
• Veterans Admin. 0.8 "
• Federal Aviation Agency 0.3 "
• U. S. Information Agency 0.3 "
• Dept. of State 0.2 "
• Civil Service Comm. 0.1 "
• Civil Aeronautics Bd. 0.1 "
• Smithsonian Institution 61.0 Thousand
• Adv. Cmte. on Inter-Govt. Relations 10.0 "
ORGANIZATIONS
Land Grant Colleges
Agricultural Research Service
Agricultural Marketing Service
Farmer Cooperative Service
Nat'l Institutes of Health
Office of Vocational Rehabilition
Office of Education
Social Security Admin.
Departments of the
• Army
• Navy
• Air Force
Division of Social Sciences
ILLUSTRATIVE WORK
Economics of Marketing;
Consumption Economics
(Social Factors in Mental Disorders)
(Adjustment of Handicapped)
(Learning, Communication, Motivation)
(Data on Problems of the Aged and of Childern)
(Leadership, Training Methods, Human Engineering, Group Psychology)
(Basic Research in Psychology, Sociology, Economics, Anthropology)
Chart C-9-2-61
Senate Committee on Government Operations
Subcommittee on Reorganization and International Organizations
September 1961

which are most meaningful to the various societies? What are the aspirations, the felt needs of these countries?

In the field of domestic policy:

How can we come to grips with problems which are impairing the enjoyment of their birthright by vast numbers of individuals in our society—inter-group tensions, breakdown of the family unit, urban decay and suburban sprawl, adult crime and juvenile delinquency, and a wide variety of other problems? . . .

. . . Wiesner, is sensitive to the opportunities and challenges of the type which I have described, particularly as they relate to Federal decision-making.

The President's Science Advisory Committee would be an ideal forum for preparation and promulgation of the Magna Carta of which I write. The Federal Council for Science and Technology would be the logical instrumentality for follow-through, so far as Federal agency policies are concerned. The Department of Defense would be the primary agency from the standpoint of national defense and survival, as well as volume of funds, to help implement the program. Already, DOD has supported much important research in persuasion, motivation, leadership, group behavior, man-machine communication, and other areas. The National Aeronautics and Space Administration has likewise not been unaware of its responsibilities.[6] Vigorous follow-through is, however, required.

But each and every Federal Agency should make a searching self-appraisal of its responsibilities and opportunities. One such laudable self-appraisal is that which has been conducted by the Social Security Administration in the field of human welfare, under the wise leadership of Secretary of Health, Education and Welfare, Abraham Ribicoff. As his Department is aware, and as other Federal agencies should recognize, the "buck should not be passed" to the National Institute for Mental Health simply because it has had more bucks, relatively speaking, available.

Other Federal agencies, with Bureau of the Budget support, must make known their individual needs to the Congress. Our legislators, despite obvious differences of opinion which have prevailed and will no doubt continue to prevail, are far more likely to respond favorably if the Executive Branch closes ranks and if the social and behavioral sciences do likewise in communicating on the great needs of our times. . . .

In seeking the fulfillment of the Magna Carta for the social and behavioral sciences, none of us should look "to the other man alone." Nor to the agencies, whether governmental or nongovernmental. If each of us does what he can, whether in a University department, a professional society, a journal, or in the Halls of the U.S. Congress, we shall see a more dependable and broader progress of the social sciences. Ultimately, as well, we shall approach the new dawn that we seek for the family of man.

[6] Brookings Institution, "Proposed Studies on the Implications of Peaceful Space Activities for Human Affairs," prepared for the National Aeronautics and Space Administration, U. S. House of Representatives, Committee on Science and Astronautics, H. Rept. 242, 87th Congress, First Session.

# 40

## Fisher Howe
## *Using Computers in Foreign Affairs*

In the present day no activity involving information, and organization, and intellectual activity can be immune to the influence of the computer and the revolutionary changes it is bringing.

The State Department and Foreign Service is no exception. Indeed they may find more than most that the computer can assist in their critically important and infinitely complex activity. The computer can never replace professional judgment. It will never make decisions in foreign affairs. It may, however, in time give the professional a tool greatly to enhance his ability to make reliable and comprehensive judgments.

To harness the machine requires, in the first place, some familiarity with the computer functions and the manner of its operations; notably programming. More difficult by far, it requires of the user a profound, comprehensive, re-thinking analysis of his own purposes and methods; an exhausting task which, however, only the commanding substantive leaders have the knowledge and ability to perform.

Eight types of application for the computer are distinguishable. Probably each of these computer functions, with only one exception, has a place somewhere in foreign affairs activities. Conversely, seven separable processes are identifiable in foreign affairs activity and most, but not all, have a need, or at least a capacity—tomorrow if not today—to use the machine servant:

- *Administrative Support*—is already involved with, and can increasingly use, the *business data processing* capabilities of the computer. Personnel operations will come to it. In addition the widest possible use of *program evaluation* will be of concern to the administrators, both as management planners and as budget officers.
- *Information Handling*—the worldwide communications system of the State Department has need for more automation, for more system, and in particular for the *information storage and retrieval* capabilities of the computer.
- *Research*—in support of policy planning and policy direction, as other processes, has great need for computer *storage and retrieval* capability for its own files and for interagency pooling of data and information. The research activity related to foreign affairs—both within the government and outside—increasingly is exploiting the *statistical, mathematical computation* application, the *modelling and gaming,* and the *artificial intelligence* roles of the computer.

- *Programs*—such as AID, Information, Cultural Affairs, should find the optimization, the *program evaluation* activity of the computer to be a tool of enormous value. Indeed some already do.
- *Diplomatic and Consular Operations*—probably cannot use a computer in any of its varied activities although there might be a place for *program evaluation* with the representational function. Consular work can. Visa activities are already exploiting, Passport responsibilities might well utilize, the *storage and retrieval* capability.
- *Policy Planning and Direction*—has an interest in computer applications to research in the foreign affairs area and even more directly a major interest in *storage and retrieval* as part of efficient information handling which goes into, and issues from, policy formulation. In addition, both Policy Planners and Policy Action Officers will be closely involved in the *program evaluation* applications to foreign affairs: the Planner for his part in the overall policy statements which underlie the programming concepts; the Action Officer for his responsibility for the courses of action, the combined effort, in a country or functional area. Moreover, the Policy Planners, and to a lesser extent the Action Officers, in time, should be important users of the other, rapidly growing computer techniques of *modelling and gaming,* and *artificial intelligence.*
- *Education*—which in the Department and Foreign Service is focused in the Foreign Service Institute, should increasingly capitalize for training purposes on the computer tools, notably *modelling and gaming*. More importantly the Institute, through training, must lead the Foreign Service into the world of computers.

# 41

# Lyndon B. Johnson
## *"I Want . . ."*

THE WHITE HOUSE

WASHINGTON

June 28, 1966

MEMORANDUM FOR HEADS
OF DEPARTMENTS AND AGENCIES

I want the head of every Federal agency to explore and apply all possible means to

–use the electronic computer to do a better job
–manage computer activity at the lowest possible cost.

I want my administration to give priority emphasis to both of these objectives–nothing less will suffice.

The electronic computer is having a greater impact on what the Government does and how it does it than any other product of modern technology.

The computer is making it possible to

–send men and satellites into space
–make significant strides in medical research
–add several billions of dollars to our revenue through improved tax administration
–administer the huge and complex social security and medicare programs
–manage a multi-billion dollar defense logistics system
–speed the issuance of G.I. insurance dividends, at much less cost
–save lives through better search and rescue operations
–harness atomic energy for peaceful uses
–design better but less costly highways and structures.

In short, computers are enabling us to achieve progress and benefits which a decade ago were beyond our grasp.

The technology is available. Its potential for good has been amply demonstrated, but it remains to be tapped in fuller measure.

I am determined that we take advantage of this technology by using it imaginatively to accomplish worthwhile purposes.

I therefore want every agency head to give thorough study to new ways in which the electronic computer might be used to

–provide better service to the public
–improve agency performance
–reduce costs.

But, as we use computers to achieve these benefits, I want these activities managed at the lowest possible costs.

At the present time, the Federal Government

–uses 2,600 computers
–employs 71,000 people in this activity
–spends over $2 billion annually to acquire and operate this equipment, including special military type computers.

Clearly, we must devote our best efforts to managing this large investment wisely and with the least cost.

I approved a blueprint for action when I approved the Bureau of the Budget "Report on Management of ADP in the Government."

The Congress recognized this need when it enacted Public Law 89-306 (the Brooks Bill) last October. This legislation provided specific authorities to

–the General Services Administration, for the procurement, utilization and disposition of automatic data processing equipment
–the Department of Commerce, for the development of data processing standards and the provision of assistance to agencies in designing computer-based systems
–the Bureau of the Budget, for exercising policy and fiscal control over the implementation of these authorities.

These agencies are seeking actively to put into effect ways for improving and reducing the cost of this huge and complex operation.

In my Budget Message for 1967 I told the Congress of my intent to make sure that this huge investment is managed efficiently.

The Federal Government must give priority attention to

–establishing better and more effective procurement methods
–making fuller use of existing facilities through sharing and joint-use arrangements before acquiring additional equipment
–re-utilizing excess equipment whenever feasible
–achieving, with industry cooperation, greater compatibility of equipment.

I expect all agencies to cooperate fully with the Bureau of the Budget, the General Services Administration, and the Department of Commerce in accomplishing these objectives.

I want the Director of the Bureau of the Budget to report to me on December

31, 1966, and every six months thereafter, on the progress that is being made throughout the Federal Government in improving the management of this very important technology.

Lyndon B. Johnson

# 42

## T. W. Milburn and J. F. Milburn

## *Expert Predictions of Foreign Threats and Remedies*

Predicting the future is a hazardous but necessary affair. It is hazardous because we fully grasp neither the present nor the processes by which the elements of today's state of nature become tomorrow. It is hazardous because wrong guesses can be so expensive. Predicting is necessary, however, because without it we are unprepared for any future different from today. Nearly everyone agrees that predicting also can be useful, even if inaccurate, and all large organizations in the world today do some predicting. No matter how inaccurate occasional weather forecasts or sales forecasts or strategic forecasts may be, men do not and cannot stop making them. The need to predict did in fact greatly antedate the appearance of technological society. Lewinsohn[1] has traced historical changes in the mode and quality of man's various attempts at prediction, beginning with the development of astrology in Mesopotamia more than 5,000 years ago.

The rising cost of war, along with the present probabilities of war, not only increases the hazards of, but also the necessity for strategic forecasting. What dangers will face us, and how can we deal with these? The forecaster seeks to utilize as much available relevant information as he can. He often attempts to advance from intuition—the sort employed by skilled clinicians or politicians—to statements eventually susceptible to scientific validation. He would, therefore like to utilize his

[1] Richard Lewinsohn, *Science, Prophecy and Prediction,* New York: Harper & Brothers, 1961.

information as objectively as possible. One way to forecast objectively and without forcing assumptions concerning the nature of the processes (by which we get from here to there) involves extrapolation of trends. It has proved a popular way, though full of deficiencies. For example, it ignores or underplays various processes and mechanisms which produce change.[2]

Another way of forecasting involves the use of a variety of experts, each using the present as a base line. Each expert handles the processes of change by his own rules, whether implicit and intuitive or explicit and analytic. The study reported here was an exercise in strategic forecasting using this latter method. Questions and categories were the same for all judges, and instructions provided for answering in scaled form so that the results could be combined algebraically. While there is no way these authors know to avoid systematic biases which may accrue to scales resulting from combinations of data, combined judgments, *independently* arrived at, do show reductions in random errors. In this case random errors may include ones resulting from variously held premises, variously used ways of thinking (epistemologies), various kinds of categories, or even different knowledge bases. Donald Campbell has described well the virtues of the process of combining independent judgments to reduce the bias of random error.[3] In the inquiry described here, judges differed in terms of their premises, as well as their academic disciplines, their observation points, and the analytic categories they used. Such an approach should have produced a larger variety of approaches to the future so that at least some systematic biases present, *e.g.*, of a particular historical approach, may well have tended to counterbalance each other and so to have appeared as random bias, more or less correctible error. It would, of course, be extremely unlikely that all systematic bias present could be reduced or, indeed, even discerned.

Judges, of course, did not vote upon the kind of future they would like to have, although it is possible that their epistemologies and metaphysics led them in different directions. All were unusually well informed individuals, and more than a few had approached some of these problems in other contexts as systematically and knowledgeably as the systems analyst described by Albert Wohlstetter in his scholarly piece, "Analysis of Conflict of Systems."[4]

The report which follows is a summary of a questionnaire given in 1964. There is no pretense that the job is adequately done, and it seems likely that many readers of this article could think of more appropriate or useful questions to ask. The questionnaire focussed primarily on topics such as likely future threats to the United States, strategic deterrence, and weapons systems; and respondents were asked to predict in these areas to the world of the 1970's. The first of two groups consisted of thirty distinguished social scientists, preponderantly political scientists and psychologists from the academic community who were contributors or consultants to Project Michelson, a Navy-supported interdisciplinary group of over

[2] Daniel Bell, "Twelve Modes of Prediction—A Preliminary Sorting of Approaches in the Social Sciences," *Daedalus,* 93, pp. 845-880 (Summer 1964).

[3] Donald T. Campbell, "Systematic Error on the Part of Human Links in Communication Systems," *Information and Control,* 1958, 1, pp. 334-369.

[4] Albert Wohlstetter, "Analysis and Design of Conflict Systems," in Edward S. Quade (ed.) *Analysis for Military Decisions,* New York: Rand McNally & Co., 1964.

90 studies concerned with influence processes in international relations as related to strategic problems. The questionnaire was intended to exploit the talents of Project Michelson investigators in ways which would require them to stretch their knowledge beyond that of their investigations. Some of these behavioral scientists had contributed in various ways to the design of U.S. policy. A second group of twenty respondents consisted of policy-makers and scientists from the defense community, all of whom had a physical science or engineering background. The latter were participants in a Summer Study at the Naval Post Graduate School in Monterey, California in 1964. The Summer Study group was strongly interested in and informed on matters of technology and was specifically concerned with the development of weapons systems. They had less familiarity with the social sciences and with the Project Michelson studies, although many of them had read at least a few of the Michelson reports.

The questionnaire, as administered, incorporated two kinds of questions, one which required ordering statements about future events, weapons systems, deterrence, etc., along a scale according to likelihood of occurrence, importance, or extent to which the statements were considered true or less true. The second kind of question required essay-type or other open-ended answers. Only the more quantitative closed-ended responses will be included in this report. A number of scaled items on the questionnaire, dealing with beliefs about specific weapon characteristics, are also omitted as being too specialized to be of general interest.

## QUESTIONNAIRE RESULTS

Special attention was paid to examination of differences between the answers of physical scientists and the behavioral scientists in the original analysis of the results. Statistical comparisons were made between the Project Michelson group (the social and behavioral scientists) and the Summer Study group (the physical scientists) on each of the original twelve sets of mean rankings using Kendall's rank order correlation coefficient *tau*, a non-parametric statistic which varies from ±1 to zero. This analysis revealed more similarities than differences between the groups. Six of the twelve correlations were over .80, for example, and none was below .30. In addition, t-tests[5] were made between mean rankings by Summer Study participants and mean rankings by Project Michelson participants for each of the 100 individual items. These tests found that responses on 17 of the 100 items on the original questionnaire were significantly different at the .05 level, and five of the 17 items were significantly different at the .01 level. In order to establish a base line for the probability of achieving significant differences by chance, questionnaire data were subjected to a series of random t-tests using the Monte Carlo method. The probability of achieving responses on as many as 17 items significantly

[5]Student's $t$ is a more powerful parametric test often used to compare the difference between two small sample means in order to decide whether to reject the null hypothesis that they were drawn from the same population. Differences between means large enough to have occurred by chance less than 5 per cent of the time are by statistical convention considered sufficiently large to reject the null hypothesis.

different at the .05 level by chance was small (P = .012). The probability of achieving five items significantly different at the .01 level by chance was somewhat greater (P = .08). These results suggest that the two groups were quite similar in their rank orderings of items, but different in terms of intensity assigned on a number of specific items. In those cases where very little difference existed between the two groups, the data below have been combined.

The six sets of questions presented below (Figures 1 to 6) are divided into several groups. The first three sets of rankings have to do with anticipated future threats; the next two deal with beliefs about deterrence; and one set summarizes attitudes toward research priorities, a function of perceived lack of knowledge and needed knowledge. The questions have been reproduced below in the same form in which they were given to respondents, with the mean responses of each group indicated by the placement of numbers corresponding to question items on the scale below the question.

As can be seen above, there was remarkable agreement vis-à-vis the dangers to be expected in the 1970's. Respondents saw World War III or even limited strategic nuclear conflicts as extremely unlikely; both groups thereby expressed confidence

**FIGURE 1.** QUESTION I AND RESPONSES

*Anticipated future strategic (political) environment: what are the threats?*

If you were to wager, what are the chances that you would expect each of the following to occur during the era of the 1970's? That is, how likely would you find such events? (By putting these on the scale below, you will be, in part, rank ordering them. Note, however, that ties between rankings are legitimate.)

1. Small wars, *i.e.*, less than limited, largely of an intra-country sort.
2. Wars between smaller powers.
3. Various levels of economic, political and ideological competition between major powers.
4. Moderately large-scale limited strategic conflict between major powers.
5. Moderately large-scale limited strategic conflict between major powers, including the use of nuclear weapons.
6. World War III.
7. Technological breakthroughs by the Soviet Union in the areas of anti-submarine warfare and/or anti-ballistic missile defense.
8. Technological breakthroughs by the United States in the areas of anti-submarine warfare and/or anti-ballistic missile defense.

MEAN RESPONSES:

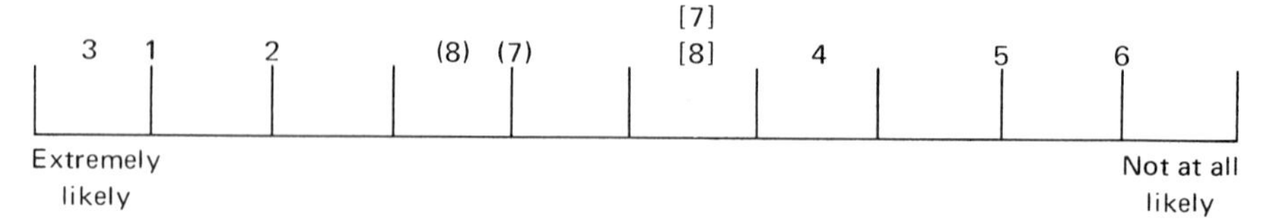


Number placements on the scale above reflect beliefs about the corresponding statements in terms of rank order and intensity. Numbers in parentheses ( ) indicate mean placement of items by Project Michelson personnel. Numbers in brackets [ ] indicate mean placement of items by Summer Study people. Numbers without brackets or parentheses are combined placements, indicating agreement.

**FIGURE 2.** QUESTION II AND RESPONSES

How likely would you expect to find each of the following events in the 1970's?

1. Warfare within the Communist world.
2. Some (at least one) presently Communist country becoming overtly non-Communist.
3. Some European country going Communist.
4. Some Latin American country (not presently Communist) going Communist.
5. Some Afro-Asian country going Communist.
6. Restoration of unity in the Communist world.
7. End of NATO, either *de jure* or de facto.
8. Functioning MLF (Multilateral Force), *i.e.*, its effective functioning in deterring or controlling aggression.
9. German neutralization.
10. Substantial disarming of strategic weapons.
11. Major technological accomplishments by the U.S. increasing the effectiveness of anti-ship or anti-aircraft defenses.
12. Major technological accomplishments by the USSR increasing the effectiveness of their anti-ship or anti-aircraft defenses.

MEAN RESPONSES:

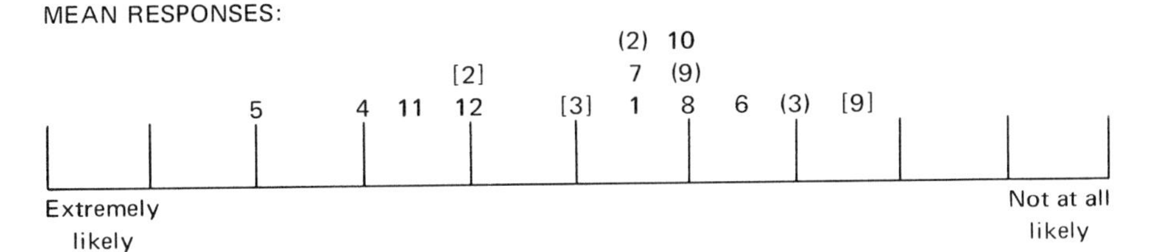


that strategic deterrence would likely work quite well into the '70's. They agreed that various levels of economic, political and ideological competition between major powers would be extremely likely. Small wars, *i.e.*, less than limited, largely of an intra-country sort, and wars between smaller powers were also seen as likely. Members of neither group felt intensely nor wished to commit themselves, nor were they in internal agreement (*i.e.*, answers of each group were most dispersed on these items) as to the likelihood of technological breakthroughs by either the Soviet Union or the United States in areas of anti-submarine warfare or anti-ballistic missile defenses, although the Summer Study people regarded them as less likely than did the Project Michelson group. (In general, there seemed to be a tendency throughout the whole set of questionnaire responses for the physical-science-oriented respondents to express themselves with more caution about physical science topics and with less caution about political topics, with the reverse being true of the behavioral scientists.)

Respondents considered it likely that some non-Communist Latin American or Afro-Asian country might turn Communist during the era of the 1970's. They disagreed, however, on the possibility of some European country becoming Communist—the physical scientists considering this much more likely than the behavioral scientists. There was disagreement also on the likelihood of German neutralization—the physical scientists seeing this as considerably less likely. There was considerable agreement that restoration of unity in the Communist world would not be likely. Respondents were not sanguine about the possibility of a

**FIGURE 3.** QUESTION III AND RESPONSES

How likely would you expect to find each of the following events?

1. A substantial UN Police Force.
2. A substantial agreement to inspection.
3. Elimination of U.S. overseas bases to a larger degree than makes them cease being major factor in U.S. defense posture.
4. Increased cohesiveness of the Western Alliance.
5. Partial disintegration of the Soviet Bloc.
6. Increased world conflict as a result of wider discrepancies in the rich-poor ratios between nations.
7. A third power bloc (U.S., USSR, and other nation or coalition).
8. "Internal wars" (not solely intra-country, but country confined) straining the international system.
9. Red China seated in the UN.

MEAN RESPONSES:

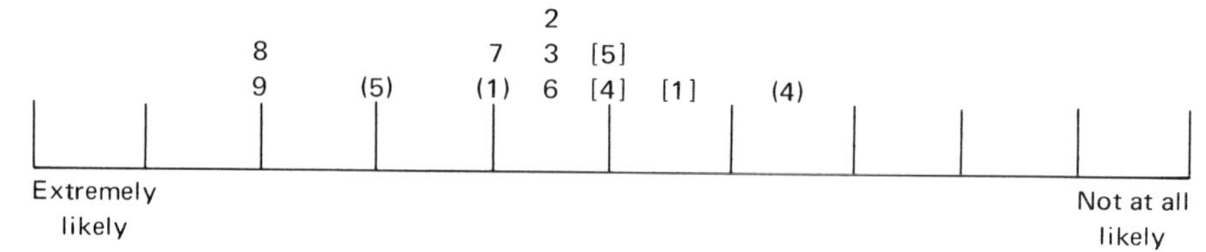


**FIGURE 4.** QUESTION IV AND RESPONSES

Which statements do you feel that you could most (or least) wholeheartedly endorse:

1. Threat of sanctions is intrinsic to effective negotiation.
2. Military threat is intrinsic to effective international negotiation.
3. Deterrence is a form of negotiation or bargaining.
4. Threat is a detriment to effective negotiation or bargaining.
5. All but the most total wars include some form or aspects of negotiation or bargaining.
6. Threats are useful or ineffectual depending upon the political and historical contexts in which they appear, *i.e.,* these latter are more important than the nature of a specific threat by itself.
7. Violence is a sign that deterrence has failed.
8. Deterrence is a form of influence process, one among many.
9. Deterrence is simply the period of waiting before violence starts.
10. Deterrence during the middle of a violent conflict is (or could be) a meaningful concept.

MEAN RESPONSES:

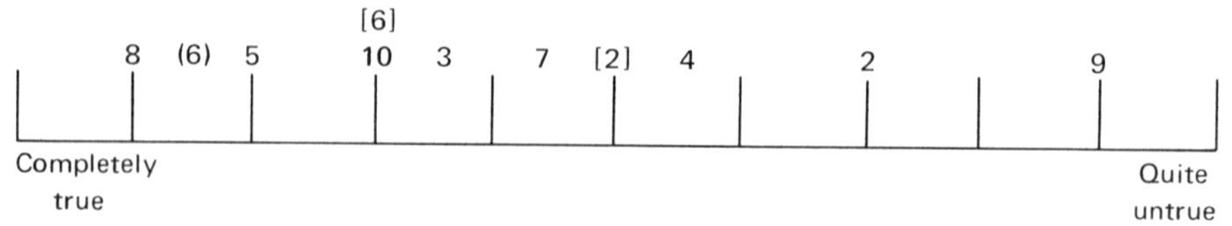


functioning Multilateral Force for use in deterring aggression, or the possibility of substantial disarming of strategic weapons during this time period.

There was agreement on the high likelihood that Red China would be seated in the UN during the 1970's and that "internal wars" (not solely intra-country, but country confined) would strain the international system. Regarded as relatively unlikely were such occurrences as increased cohesiveness of the Western Alliance (although this was considered more likely by the Summer Study group) or a substantial UN police force within the period in question (about which the Project Michelson group was more optimistic). Seen as perhaps moderately likely was the development of a third power bloc consisting of the U.S., USSR, and some other nation or coalition during the period in question. The two groups differed considerably on the likelihood of partial disintegration of the Soviet bloc, considered by the Summer Study group less likely than by the Project Michelson group.

## BELIEFS ABOUT THE NATURE OF DETERRENCE

In this series of questions concerning beliefs about the nature of deterrence, virtually all respondents agreed that deterrence is a form of influence process one among many—and that all but the most total wars include some form or aspects of negotiation. There was also agreement that threat may have some positive value in effective negotiation or bargaining. The Summer Study sample placed somewhat more importance on the role of military threat as an aid to negotiation. There was

**FIGURE 5.** QUESTION V AND RESPONSES

While there are many different approaches to the topic, some people feel that strategic deterrence is essentially a linear function of force available; others feel that such deterrence is a non-linear function (*e.g.*, depending upon context may even be discontinuous) or even a roughly curvilinear function of strategic force. Would you characterize deterrence as more nearly:

1. A linear function (roughly) of force available to the deterring party?
2. A linear function of expected surviving force of the deterred party?
3. A linear function of the values that can be destroyed by threatened (or threatening), *i.e.*, deterring party (according to the other's value scheme)?
4. A linear function of the ratio of one's superiority of strategic force available?
5. A non-linear function of force available to either side?
6. A linear function of one's potential for assuming political control?
7. A non-linear function of one's perceived intent to fight (if provoked).
8. A linear function of what the deterring party can do to the deterred beyond what the deterred can do to the deterrer.
9. A non-linear function of the mutually perceived clear superiority of one party to inflict damage.

MEAN RESPONSES:

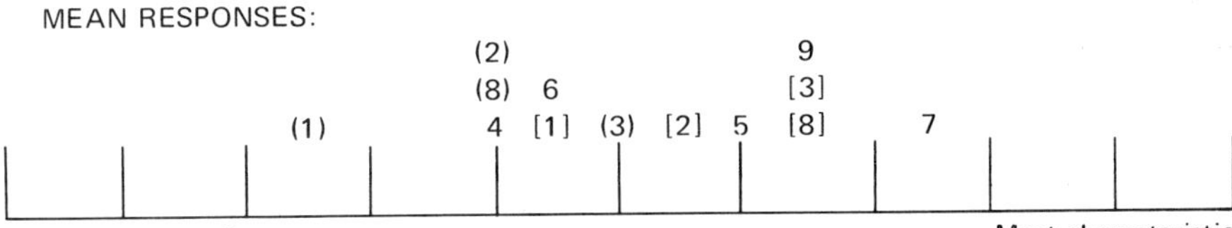

**FIGURE 6.** QUESTION VI AND RESPONSES

What research priorities should we establish for behavioral studies of use to policy-makers? Examples might include studies intended to increase the accuracy and reliability of knowledge about:

1. Perceptions by Soviets of the U.S.?
2. Responses by the Soviets to U.S. actions?
3. Perceptions by the Chinese of U.S. actions?
4. Responses by the Chinese to U.S. or other actions?
5. How we might more effectively influence our allies?
6. Limits on our ability to control or influence our allies or opponents?
7. Usefulness of weapons in arms control environments?
8. What in general influences nations?
9. Dangers which may affect the U.S. in the 1970's (*e.g.*, likely conflict areas in Latin America or the Far East) where our knowledge is now least certain?

MEAN RESPONSES:

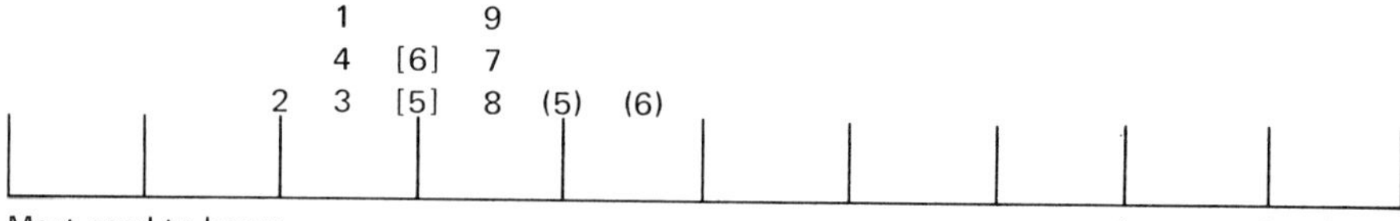


also a tendency for the physical scientists to value the importance of the political and historical context in which a threat may appear as somewhat less than the Project Michelson respondents.

It has been popular to assume that the more weapons, the more deterrence, *i.e.*, the larger our strategic force, the more effective it is as a deterrent. Such an assumption supposes that increases in international stability vis-à-vis the United States are functions of equal additive increments, direct functions, of the number of weapons or their megatonage.

One can see from Figure 5 that there is substantial agreement that deterrence might most correctly be viewed as a *non-linear* function of one's perceived intent to fight if provoked, as well as a non-linear function of the mutually perceived clear superiority of one party to inflict damage. At the same time, the Michelson group tended to view deterrence as less characteristically a linear function than did members of the Summer Study group.

## RESEARCH PRIORITIES

The concerns of these experts are probably most evident in the tight clustering of responses in Figure 6. Soviet and Chinese perceptions and responses to U.S. actions were seen by respondents as most important research areas. The only markedly different items in this group related to the importance of discerning limits on our ability to control or influence our allies or opponents (rated less important by the social scientists), and knowledge about how we might more effectively influence our allies (also rated as less important by the Project Michelson group). The general clustering of items on this scale suggests that a wider variety of concepts might have been included to produce greater differentiation.

## DISCUSSION

The few significant disagreements between the two samples appear to result from small systematic differences between the backgrounds and orientations of the groups. The physical scientist sample would appear to have less complicated views of the relation between threat and the effectiveness of deterrence. They more often see the relation as a linear one. The social scientist sample sees the effectiveness of deterrence as a function, in part, of contextual factors and tends therefore to reject the notion of simple linearity, *i.e.*, that equal and additive increments of available force produce similar increments of deterrent effectiveness. It should be emphasized that the result, while significant, was a trend and that there was still overlap between the plots of the samples.

The physical scientist group also saw the Communist world as more stable than did the sample of social scientists. It will be remembered that the 1950's was a period when U.S.-Soviet relations were relatively unstable and the two monoliths appeared to be headed for confrontation. A model of intersystem relations influenced by memories of the '50's might therefore account for some of the differences, especially if the physical scientists were somewhat more inclined to see political relations as constant. The behavioral scientists did view threat as more complex and less directly related to size or intensity of threat *per se.* They viewed the Communist world as less stable and more fragmented, less monolithic. The two great political blocs did, in fact, appear less tight as systems to that group.

The results of the questions dealing with deterrence in which differences between the groups of respondents appear in their assignment of the role of threat—particularly threat as an aid to negotiation—are of particular interest because the full set of functions of threat are neither solidly nor univocally established empirically as yet. A combination of threats and promises (the hoary "carrot and the stick") appears to change behavior and attitudes more effectively and rapidly than threat or promise used alone. Threat alone may have undesirable side effects, especially where the nature of threat and associated demands are vague. On the basis of research most carefully done on the topic thus far, World War I now appears to have been, in part, the result of unanticipated side effects of threats as employed.[6]

One could expect discontinuities in the effects of threat because the expected effect must bear some relation to *demands* made upon a deterred party. Demands which are extremely costly to meet either economically or in terms of prestige or power, as well as ones which are simply impossible to meet within the time limits

[6] Robert C. North, Ole R. Holsti, and Richard A. Brody, "Perception and Action in the Study of International Relations: The 1914 Crisis," August 1964, 62 pp., mimeo. To be published in *International Yearbook of Political Behavior Research*, J. David Singer (ed.), *Empirical Studies in International Relations.*

set by ultimata, can be expected not to be met regardless of the size of one's threat. "Impossible to meet" demands could guarantee that the world's best strategic weapons would not deter.

## SUMMARY

An exercise in prediction and related causal beliefs made use of two differently oriented and educated sets of expert respondents—behavioral scientists involved in interdisciplinary empirical investigations related to strategy for Project Michelson, and physical scientists and military colleagues concerned with making research and development recommendations about deterrent weapons. In providing rank-ordered answers to a number of sets of questions having to do with beliefs about future events, these differently trained and oriented experts tended largely to agree about the nature of threats likely to face the United States during the 1970's. They also tended to have similar beliefs about the nature of effective strategic deterrence.

World War III or limited nuclear conflicts appeared to the combined average judgment of these respondents as most unlikely, while small intra-national conflicts and ideological, economic, and political conflicts appeared extremely likely. They anticipated that some Latin American and Afro-Asian countries would turn toward Communism, but they did not expect to see Communism extended in Europe. They did not expect to see German neutralization, nor did the end of NATO seem likely to them. They anticipated neither increased cohesiveness of the Western Alliance, nor restoration of unity in the Communist world. They anticipated neither a functioning Multilateral Force, nor substantial disarmament involving strategic weapons.

The validity of this technique as an approach to looking at the future must await the passage of time. (One would expect its obsolescence as an approach to become apparent as men develop anything like a science of general forecasting or prediction.) It should prove of more than academic interest if many of the situations judged to be highly improbable come to pass, or if many of the situations deemed highly probable fail to come to pass.

# 11

# How to Torture a Public Policy

This chapter offers some insights into the problems of a bureaucracy. The articles show, alas, the now familiar picture of agencies that are established to exercise reasonable control in the public good but that eventually come into conflict with private groups and are charged with thwarting the very public interest they were established to further.

Lawrence M. Friedman discusses the failure of current public-housing policies and points out some new plans that may be effective. Mr. Friedman is not an enemy of public housing; he is pragmatic. He wants to see programs established which will solve the housing problem. His conclusion is that too little has been done, partly through sheer mismanagement and partly through failure to realize the seriousness of the problem. No one can be surprised, least of all Mr. Friedman, if there is an utter loss of faith in the ability of politics and public administration to deal with human living conditions. What must amaze anyone is the ability of the American economy to renovate the cities, and yet the absence of a will to action strong enough to bring about the radical changes that are necessary. Why is this crucial "will to action" missing? What conditions do you feel will generate it?

While Mr. Friedman's article was critical of policies, the next one criticizes agency operations—in this case, the Federal Food and Drug Administration, one of the less well-known regulatory agencies. Lloyd Cutler, a Washington lawyer with much practical experience in the recently developed field of administrative law, shows how doctors are restricted in their practice by FDA officials. He points out that the FDA scientists cannot establish absolutely that a new drug is safe or effective. He questions the mixture of formal and informal procedures that the FDA, which holds the initiative, can use alone or in whatever combination it expects to be most effective. The "terrifying armory of legal weaponry that the FDA possesses" is awesome to see, and we are told that it is practically hopeless to employ administrative hearings to reverse decisions of the agency. The drug industry is important to modern America, and the way in which the government administers and regulates it is reflected in the real income and health and happiness of every American. Do you agree that the FDA is in need of reform? Will Cutler's suggestions solve the problem?

Dr. Harold Orlans, a Brookings fellow, describes how one agency responded to public and congressional criticism of its methods. An offspring of the Manhattan Project, the Atomic Energy Commission originated as a weapons agency during World War II. It has gradually become a major civilian regulatory agency as well. Much of its work has been done by contract. Dr. Orlans reappraises the contract experience to determine whether the government should run its own laboratories or whether the experience of the AEC may be extended to other parts of the government. Do you think that the letting of contracts by the government could be a useful way of dealing with other problems?

The article by Charles Ross, a consultant for the New England Regional Commission, illustrates several problems of a bureaucracy. It shows conflict between government agencies and between an agency and the public. Because of such conflicts, activity, in the cases he describes, was slowed almost to a standstill. He also discusses the difficulties that individuals or public interest groups encounter in trying to influence agency policies. Specifically, Mr. Ross discusses the failure of the government to respond to the "new" problem of environmental pollution. He outlines a plan which he believes may help solve the pollution problem. Do you think his suggestion will be effective?

# 43

## Lawrence M. Friedman
## *Slums: Now and Hereafter*

This study has assumed that housing the poor is a matter of government concern. Some people feel that it is best to leave housing alone; the rich will build for themselves, and their houses will filter down to the poor. Some feel it is hopeless to tamper with the market. Others argue that it is senseless to single out housing. The poor need jobs and money; give them these, and they will take care of their housing themselves. These are serious points of view. This study avoids confronting them. It assumes that its readers feel a duty of government toward the poor. It also assumes that, at least for now, government will treat slum housing specially, as a problem separable from other problems of the poor; it assumes that programs specifically concerned with slum housing will be debated, evaluated, and tried. This chapter and the epilogue should be read with these assumptions in mind.

Bright promise has been followed by disenchantment several times in the history of housing. Tenement-house laws, model tenements, and public-housing programs all failed to live up to the dreams of reformers. Disillusionment with urban renewal is also running deep. The program has absorbed large amounts of money and energy; it has no serious prospect of housing the poor safely and honorably. Indeed, as we have seen, housing the poor is hardly part of its program at all. The search continues for new arms and new ideas.

Efforts are being made to intensify certain old programs, such as code enforcement. These efforts do not attack the problem at its roots. Code enforcement, for example, cannot in itself provide enough good housing for the poor. It cannot cure overcrowding in one area without creating overcrowding in another. Of course, it may be worthwhile to improve and intensify code enforcement and to reform the housing bureaucracy, even if the whole of the housing problem cannot be solved this way. There is no reason not to solve little problems merely because big ones are intractable. It is good to cure minor and sporadic injustices and to strengthen limited but useful programs. If New York City, for example, sets up a centralized, prompt, and efficient office, with a single telephone number, to handle tenants' housing complaints, one can only applaud. A phone number will never clear the slums of Harlem or integrate the poor into American society; but it might help particular people in particular ways. A war on red tape may make it possible to give tenants better service; it may keep them from freezing in winter and roasting in summer. In the long run, however, the housing problem cannot be solved by a crackdown or, for that matter, by codes or by rent strikes or receivership laws.

Existing laws, including the housing codes, are ineffective. This is due in part to defects inherent in the state of mind which led to their enactment. Programs to punish and destroy the evil slum landlord have helped to create or at least perpetuate the evil slum landlord. Intensification projects and administrative reforms run the risk of making slum housing more expensive than ever before, both financially and emotionally. A program of hatred and coercion may make some landlords give heat, make repairs, and get rid of their rats. But the crackdown approach is indirect and perhaps self-defeating. It does not provide new investment in the slums; it discourages it. Something new must be tried.

No one can complain that new tactics are not being considered. In the last few years, new programs, strategies, plans, and devices have sprouted like dandelions. Some of them are pregnant with great hope. The so-called rent subsidy or supplement is one of these. The rent subsidy is really two plans. One is a plan to pay low-income families a subsidy "equal to the difference between the amount that the applicant is able to pay and the amount of the actual rent to be charged." Public-housing rents are subsidized, but the subsidy is available only to people who live in the government's houses. Under the rent-subsidy plan proper, the subsidized poor could live in middle-income housing, if they wished. The government would pay part of their rent. Ultimately, the increased demand for decent housing at reasonable cost would stimulate private enterprise to build enough new houses, and the slums would wither away. This program has extremely avid supporters in high places. The New York Housing Authority announced in May, 1966, that it intended "to buy 2,000 to 3,000 apartments in publicly financed middle-income cooperatives and rent them as public housing at normal rates." . . .

Another kind of rent subsidy was also made part of the 1965 Housing Act. It was an attempt to goad private enterprise into building more housing for the poor. The plan thus can be compared to the model-tenement movement, but with this difference: the builder charges fair market rental, and the government picks up the difference between the rent and one fourth of the tenant's income. The program as enacted has many interesting features. For example, individuals and profit-making corporations are not authorized to build qualifying housing under the act; only nonprofit corporations, limited-dividend companies, and the like may receive the subsidy. There are important justifications for such a provision; but classic prejudices against the ordinary slum landlord are part of the reason for this provision. By now, of course, such prejudices may be warranted in many cities. One point of the act is to entice into housing a respectable class of owners and operators. Respectability, however, is equated with limited profits or no profits at all. Moreover, the act shows distinct traces of a search for the submerged and potential middle class. The Administration, in fact, had originally proposed a bill which would extend the subsidy to the lower ranks of the honorable middle class. Here Congress demurred. Under the act as passed, no one can qualify as a tenant unless his income is "below the maximum amount which can be established in the area . . . for occupancy in public housing dwellings." But Congress kept the

Administration's "categorical" approach to the selection of tenants. The rent subsidy is limited to families who have been "displaced by governmental action," to the elderly who are "sixty-two years of age or older," to the physically handicapped, and to those occupying substandard housing or housing in a "disaster area" which "has been extensively damaged or destroyed as the result of such disaster."

Success of a program like the rent subsidy cannot be measured by whether a pilot program works. Success is volume; and the most damning thing that can be said of the rent subsidy is that Congress has been desperately shy of voting any funds. . . .

. . . [I] n the short run, the rent subsidy is unlikely to provide a major solution to the housing problems of the very poor.

Another great hope has been to use some form of rehabilitation to conquer the slums. Can government, private foundations, or subsidized free enterprise provide good housing for the poor by buying and repairing existing houses? This is not the same idea as neighborhood conservation under the urban renewal laws. The idea is to fix up houses, not quarantine neighborhoods, and thus to serve the poor, not shut them out. Better housekeeping and improved community facilities will upgrade the neighborhood for those who already *live* there, not for a "better" class; people are not to be displaced merely because they are poor. It is an exciting idea in many ways: public housing without its defects of design, code enforcement without punishment and segregation, renewal without snobbery and relocation. . . .

Rehabilitation can obviously succeed in each particular instance. No "pilot programs" are necessary to demonstrate that pouring enough money and services into a building and its tenants will improve the building and the tenants. Who will provide the money? Code enforcement programs seek to make private landlords bear the cost. This is only feasible if the amounts required are such that the buildings will still be profitable after the money is spent. It may also be feasible in small sections of big cities and in big sections of very small cities. But in the heart of the slums, rehabilitation has to be nonprofit or low-profit. Private rehabilitation there is not possible without massive subsidy. Low-income householders, under the 1965 Housing and Urban Redevelopment Act, can qualify for outright grants of up to $1,500 to repair their buildings. This is a good idea and a humane one; but it probably applies more to shantytowns than to the tenement districts of big cities. The potential class of beneficiaries is probably too small for any major impact. . . .

Rehabilitation by government is another story. Philadelphia's Housing Authority has initiated a "used house" program of buying "old houses in decent communities," rehabilitating them, then furnishing them to poor families. In this way the "stigma of massive projects is . . . avoided." In 1965, the Philadelphia City Council created a nonprofit city corporation to buy and rehabilitate substandard housing for sale or rental to low-income families. Some cities are combining experiments in rehabilitation with attempts to humanize public housing, to soften the blow of urban renewal, and to increase social and racial integration, or to do all of these things. In planning the West Side Urban Renewal Area in New York City, announcement was made of provisions for "vest-pocket" public housing, for middle-income housing with slots reserved for low-income tenants who may remain in their homes even though their income rises, for extensive rehabilitation of existing houses, and for a carefully staged and phased program of construction to minimize the tortures of relocation.

. . . [T]he very fact of an outpouring of plans, proposals, demonstration projects, pilot projects, bills, laws, rules, schemes, devices, and propositions is an important *new* fact. Some proposed techniques will turn out to be better than others. None of the techniques in themselves are likely to be true solutions to the housing problem. The cumulation of them all is no solution either, but is a symptom of a *will* to succeed, which is tremendously important, and perhaps also of an inclination to devote the necessary resources, which is the *sine qua non* of success. The housing problem is not going to be solved by gimmicks, but by spending enough money on very simple things. The curse of American housing movements has been inadequate cash. Even anti-slumlord campaigns, which we have criticized here, can be analyzed as symptoms of public miserliness. It is an infinitely cheaper response to a concrete problem to pass a law and blame somebody else. If rats are a slum problem, it is cheaper to make rats a crime and landlords criminals than to take positive public action against rats. Moreover, if the rats are not eliminated, the "criminals" can be blamed and the public absolved. Public housing, in the broad sense, is the only program which might perhaps *actually* provide a significant supply of decent homes for people below the poverty level. Other programs, such as code enforcement, are not inherently incapable of making a major contribution. But they are less likely to do this because they are so strongly imbued with notions of fault and attempt to place the moral and financial burden on private shoulders.

The *scale* of housing reform is a critical factor, too, in that it indicates a shift in the alignment of political forces in regard to housing. One major point made in this study is that the problem of slum housing can be in part reduced to a problem of political leverage. The dependent poor and the Negroes have never had much social and economic power. Laws have sometimes been passed *for* them, to be sure, but usually much compromised and weakened in passage or in administration. . . .

Despite all the setbacks of the past, there are reasons for guarded optimism in the 1960's. The first of these is the militancy of the poor, particularly of the Negro poor. The militancy arose and remains strongest in the civil rights movement; but it has spilled over into other areas. The rent strikes are an example. Militancy, of course, may be and often is maddening, misguided, and ultimately self-defeating. The poor may use new-gained power only to create a whole new set of problems. The poor may turn out to foolishly misconceive their long-term self-interest and perhaps even their short-term self-interest. Yet through militant action the poor gain a chance to state forcefully their views and their wishes. And militancy may succeed by persuading the white, middle-class majority that its own self-interest requires concessions in order to avoid continued riots and confusions—a cruel but necessary calculus. In any given case, success depends upon the precise demands that are made, upon the skill of the leadership, upon the social and economic costs that the whites are asked to incur, and upon how these costs compare with the costs of resistance.

In addition, reform forces committed to the war against poverty were never stronger. Reformers have made many errors in the past; but they have played an indispensable role. Reform is difficult, and perhaps impossible, on welfare grounds alone; yet reform is unthinkable without reformers. . . .

Thus three armies–government, the reform community, and the poor themselves–are now engaged in mobilizing resources toward a solution of the problem. What these armies will accomplish remains to be seen; whether they will fight with or against each other likewise will only be revealed by the passage of time. In Syracuse, New York, in 1965, the Office of Economic Opportunity financed a Community Action Training Center, with important leadership supplied by faculty members of Syracuse University. The Center in turn mobilized tenants in public housing; and the tenants tried to wage *organized* battle against the one-sided lease, "high" rents, "pigpen" lawns, "unfair" electric bills, and other tenant grievances. The Authority, which was also a government agency, reacted with rage; government finds it hard to support attacks by its left hand on its right. In San Francisco, in 1966, angry public housing tenants turned to a legal action group–financed by OEO–for help. In October, 1965, 60 tenants "sat in" at the office of the chairman of the New York Housing Authority. In 1966, tenants and tenant groups brought numerous lawsuits against housing authorities, protesting against unfair rules and unfair governance. Some of these lawsuits have been victorious; more will be. Housing authorities and HUD are getting the messages and making some changes on their own. Political, economic, social, and administrative obstacles are enormous. But once started, protests may continue until grievances are met. We are entering a period of militancy and social action. Social forces at work will naturally be reflected in new law and in diversions of old law. But the precise directions taken remain to be seen.

# 44

## Lloyd N. Cutler
## *Drugs: The Addiction to Controls*

Of the many fascinating and highly practical aspects of federal drug legislation, I have chosen three major administrative questions for discussion. First, what are the principles that should govern official control over the development, testing, and marketing of drugs, particularly new drugs? Second, what legal and administrative procedures should be employed in exercising these controls? Third, how can the government obtain medical and scientific personnel with the qualities of mind needed to judge when a particular new drug should be made available to physicians and when a drug already on the market should be withdrawn?

### PRINCIPLES

The present drug laws give the government both the right and the duty to prevent the marketing of an unsafe or a clearly ineffective prescription drug. These laws go much further than merely requiring that the known facts as to safety and effectiveness be fully stated so that the physician can make his own decision with full knowledge of the relevant circumstances. They empower the government to decide for all physicians whether a particular drug should be available to them or not.

A good theoretical case might be made for a different type of law—a statute similar to the Securities Act of 1933, compelling full disclosure but permitting any security to be offered for sale so long as the true facts are fully stated in the prospectus. But today the point is entirely theoretical. The public, the medical profession, and the pharmaceutical industry have all accepted the proposition that the government can and should have the power to bar a drug from reaching the market. In this respect, our law is a great deal more restrictive than that of many European countries, and it raises an interesting question related to Justice Walter V. Schaefer's discussion of manufacturers' liability—whether the government itself will one day be held liable when a drug it has approved for marketing causes injury to a patient. . . .

For the most part, our drug laws are unhappily written in these absolute terms, in the confident assumption that since safety and effectiveness are matters of science, a government scientist can decide with assurance that a drug is safe or unsafe, that it is effective or ineffective, and that the risks involved in the clinical testing of an experimental new drug are or are not worth taking.

A small step away from this comfortable but inaccurate theory of absolutes was made in the Drug Amendments of 1962. Before these amendments, the government possessed the power to ban an ineffective drug only by proving that the claims of effectiveness made in labeling were false or misleading. The burden of proving falsity was on the government. Under the 1962 Act, the government is now empowered to ban the marketing of a new drug or force the withdrawal of an old drug on a finding of lack of evidence that the drug is effective in fact. The burden of proving effectiveness has thus been shifted to the manufacturer. . . .

. . . Drugs are not absolutely safe or unsafe, any more than they are absolutely effective or ineffective. Penicillin and aspirin injure or even kill a number of people every year. The "safety" of a potent drug is a relative concept, a measure of risk versus effectiveness, an expression of the judgment that on balance it is likely to do more good than harm. As with most issues of cause and effect, the evidence is rarely complete or crystal clear, and ten responsible experts may read it in ten varying ways. None of these infinite gradations is recognized by the present statute; the legal test is whether the drug has been proven "safe," and an official decision on this issue must be made one way or the other. . . .

## PROCEDURES

We have seen that the principal issues which the government's drug officials must resolve are matters of scientific judgment—whether a given drug has been proved safe and effective and, under the latest investigative regulations of the Food and Drug Administration, whether and under what conditions an experimental drug may be subjected to clinical testing.

We have seen that these issues are often very close, that responsible experts may decide them in different ways, and that there is at least a fair chance that the decision reached by any particular expert, be he government official or private citizen, may be wrong when it is first made, or proved wrong by later events. It is instructive to remember that penicillin was initially rejected as worthless by some of the leading medical authorities of the time, that Pasteur's work was rejected by the French Academy, that Galileo had to keep his experiments secret, and that Dr. Harvey Wiley firmly believed that saccharin was unsafe.

Nevertheless, our law requires that the Secretary of Health, Education, and Welfare, through his delegate, the Commissioner of Food and Drugs, make such delicate and fateful decisions, by the dozen, every week of the year. . . .

. . . Most matters are handled on an informal basis by conference or letter between FDA officials and the company involved. This is not necessarily because the FDA prefers informality but because the companies themselves are reluctant to invoke more formal procedures. The commercial consequences of an official FDA frown are so serious that most companies will acquiesce in informal suggestions of disapproval and will not resort to the types of formal hearing and review that the law provides.

My criticism is not aimed at informality as such; indeed informal conferences and correspondence are well adapted to the initial stages of new-drug proceedings. . . .

. . . But when controversies do arise, formal methods seem desirable to define the issues, to specify the grounds for the initial decision, and to provide for meaningful review.

This failure to make use of formal procedures is attributable to two principal factors. One is the terrifying armory of legal weaponry that the FDA possesses—what one of my colleagues has aptly referred to as a system of "jawbone enforcement." For any given violation of the Food, Drug, and Cosmetic Act, the FDA has a variety of enforcement weapons, ranging from a mere suit for an injunction to an outright seizure of the offending drug before trial and even to criminal prosecution. . . .

. . . The mere existence of this weaponry, coupled with the manufacturer's pathological but well-founded fear of adverse publicity, is sufficient to enable the FDA to impose its views by what has been called "the lifted eyebrow," without need to invoke formal adjudication or court proceedings.

Second, there is the utter hopelessness of invoking the formal hearing and review procedures with any degree of success. If informal discussions with FDA officials about the safety or effectiveness of a new drug prove fruitless, the sponsor has a technical right to a full administrative hearing on the record before the FDA takes final action, with a further opportunity for judicial review.

. . . [T]he chances of prevailing in the administrative hearing or in the courts are virtually nil. This is not because the FDA is always right and the companies are always wrong but because hearing examiners and judges are laymen and are loath to reverse the judgments of the FDA's medical and scientific experts where the safety and effectiveness of drugs are involved. The FDA's very competent counsel have a way of making any examiner or judge feel that reversal will harm hundreds of innocent people, and no examiner or judge is likely to take this responsibility.

Practical proof of what I am saying is the fact that in the twenty-five years since the passage of the new-drug provisions of the Act, which allow a full administrative hearing on request before any new-drug application can be denied or before the withdrawal of a previously approved drug can be ordered, not a single manufacturer has ever proceeded to a hearing on an initial new-drug application. . . .

We thus have the phenomenon of a statute which provides elaborate machinery for administrative and judicial review of regulatory action, a wide degree of disapproval within the regulated industry of the way in which it is being regulated, and a total failure of the industry to invoke the review procedures that the statute provides.

Here indeed is a practical problem of drug legislation—how to provide a meaningful form of review of FDA decisions on the safety and effectiveness of drugs, decisions that often displease the regulated industry and sometimes the medical profession, decisions that are usually made informally, without public debate, and without a formal record of detailed findings and conclusions to serve as a guide for the future. . . .

The heart of the problem, it seems to me, is that the FDA's judgments on safety and efficacy are medical-scientific judgments, and only medical and scientific experts have the capacity to review and the confidence to question the initial FDA staff decision. . . . But it is clearly practicable, and may well be desirable, to provide a mechanism for an advisory review, on the initiative of the manufacturer or the FDA, by independent medical and scientific experts somewhere between the initial FDA staff decision and the ultimate review by the head of the agency. Such a statutory procedure already exists . . . in the case of pesticides and color additives. . . .

The independent review might well confirm FDA's judgment most of the time, but at least occasionally it might not. It might be healthy for the FDA staff if the difficult and delicate medical and scientific decisions it must make were regularly subjected to independent review and scrutiny by men qualified to do so. It would be equally healthy for the industry to have the safety valve of an opportunity to seek independent review.

If such a review were available, it would be more difficult, to take two hypothetical but reasonably conceivable extremes, for an FDA staff officer to block a method of therapy which some clinicians favor but which he personally opposes, or for a disappointed company medical director to blame a justified rejection on the alleged prejudice of the FDA doctor who happened to review the application. By testing their differences before independent panels of experts, by winning some cases and losing others, both the industry and the FDA might achieve greater mutual respect and eliminate the existing and largely unfounded prejudices they now hold toward one another. . . . The availability of meaningful review is itself an important element of due process, entirely apart from the frequency with which it is invoked.

### PERSONNEL

. . . There are of course many able and dedicated people already in the FDA, and considering the conditions under which we ask them to work, we probably have more good ones than we deserve. I admire the effort, the talent, and the integrity they are putting into a tough and essential job. But the FDA's functions and responsibilities have now become so vast that a serious crisis of competence may be confronting the agency.

I have two thoughts to offer. . . . The first is to raise the question of whether the FDA is trying to do more things at one time than it or any other organization has any hope of doing competently. Is it necessary to have new-drug applications that are eight feet high? . . .

Could the agency perhaps be more effective by being more selective in the work that it does, by relying on spot checks and sampling procedures, and by relying on manufacturers and their lawyers to do more of a self-policing job themselves?

The second suggestion relates to the concept of the FDA as a separate career service, alongside the Public Health Service and its child that has now outgrown the parent, the National Institutes of Health. All three of these services have roles to perform in the advance and improvement of drug therapy. . . . It seems to me that in this separation of the policing function from the work that the Public Health Service and the National Institutes of Health are doing on the frontiers of medical knowledge, the FDA must necessarily be the loser in the constant struggle for personnel. Among the doctors and scientists who are prepared to devote a portion of their careers to government service, the PHS and NIH may present a greater challenge and a greater opportunity for service than the FDA, if only because top-flight men may prefer to work on the frontiers of discovery rather than as a cop on the beat.

I question whether this separation of functions and career services needs to continue. I think there would be a great deal to gain by creating some sort of single federal health service and by assigning doctors and scientists to successive tours of duty in each of the three agencies. This would not only give the FDA a better crack at top-flight personnel; it would also work against the inevitable tendency of any agency to think in the narrow terms of its own particular function, instead of balancing its interests against the other competing interests of the government and of society as a whole. It is possible in the name of safety to bar all drugs and all drug experiments that are not absolutely safe, and thereby frustrate the very objective of advancing the frontiers of therapy for which the NIH was established. A few men with a zeal for new-drug discovery could be a healthy infusion into the understandably cautious atmosphere of the FDA. And some of the FDA's caution and experience with the afterglow and fallout of new-drug discoveries might be a healthy influence on the exploding enthusiasm of the National Institutes of Health. A little interbreeding might improve both strains.

# 45

## Harold Orlans
## *The Atomic Energy Commission Breeds Its Power*

In 1947, the Atomic Energy Commission inherited the responsibilities of the Army's Manhattan Project and the government's wartime policy of contracting with a few of the nation's largest companies and universities to develop and produce atomic bombs. In the ensuing two decades, the Commission has spent some $40 billion on a varied program of weapons development, nuclear generation of electric power, nuclear propulsion of submarines, ships, planes, and rockets, and a broad array of fundamental and applied research in physics, chemistry, biology, medicine, and other fields. The AEC has not only contracted out R&D and procurement to industry and universities (as other agencies do) but also, to an unusual degree, it has contracted out the management of *government-owned* laboratories and production plants.

The Commission's experience has been unprecedented, not only in its scientific, technical, and military aspects, but also in its administration, politics, and economics. The AEC is the only major government operating agency headed by five full-time commissioners, rather than a single administrator or secretary. The AEC staff is the largest government bureaucracy whose main responsibility and expertise are the supervision of private contractors.

## CONTRACT POLICIES

Until recently, the two outstanding characteristics of AEC contract policy have been concentration and continuity. In the management of government-owned facilities and in R&D, more than half of the expenditures and contractor manpower were for many years in the hands of just seven contractors: Union Carbide, General Electric, Bendix, Sandia (a subsidiary of Western Electric), Du Pont, and the Universities of California and Chicago. This concentration has been due mainly to technical factors: . . .

Until 1964, changes were rarely made in the contractors managing major installations. At that time twenty large contracts (each over $10 million annually) were more than ten years old—seven of them having been signed by the AEC or its Army predecessor twenty or more years ago.

The long idyll between the Commission and its operating contractors was disturbed by congressional and industry pressures. The AEC established a new policy for selecting contractors. It had three objectives: (1) to diversify the economy of the Tri-City area around its Hanford, Washington, facilities, thereby reducing their vulnerability to cutbacks in the production of plutonium; (2) to reward companies investing in the nuclear industry; and (3) to promote competition by strengthening companies already in the nuclear industry and inducing new companies to enter the industry.

In particular, the new policy was a response to contentions by industry that firms chosen to operate AEC facilities gained a competitive advantage in the growing private nuclear industry. . . .

Implementing its new policy, the Commission announced in 1964 that the Hanford contract which General Electric had held since 1946 would be "segmented" and transferred to a number of other contractors in an effort to widen industrial participation and stimulate economic diversification in the Richland, Washington, area. Subsequently, the management contract for Hanford Laboratory was given to the Battelle Memorial Institute, and the operation of other parts of the Hanford installation was allotted to five new industrial contractors.

The Hanford case is not necessarily a clear-cut guide to future policy, since it also represented an effort by the AEC to cope with the economic crisis precipitated in January 1964 when President Johnson announced that four plutonium producing reactors, including three of nine at Hanford, would be shut down (a fourth Hanford reactor will be shut down in 1967). Nevertheless, along with changes in contractual arrangements at Argonne and Idaho Falls, it marked the end of one contract era and the beginning of a new one in which long-standing operating contracts have been questioned and an effort made to spread the work. The Commission has been well aware of the problems inherent in changing contractors and in segmentation, but has hoped that they could be reduced by vigilant contract negotiation and administration.

## THE PUBLIC AND PRIVATE SECTORS

Three related issues have been posed by the policy of contracting for the operation of commission laboratories: Should these laboratories be managed by industry or universities? Should R&D be conducted in government or private laboratories? And what effects have the government laboratories had on the development of the private nuclear industry?

It is generally agreed that the AEC's production plants and development laboratories should be operated by industry and its fundamental research laboratories by universities. But the actual situation that has developed over two decades is not this tidy. On the one hand, laboratories managed by universities have not confined themselves to basic research but, both at their own initiative and at the AEC's request, have undertaken major programs of applied research and the development of new prototypes and processes; on the other hand, industry-managed laboratories with a specific practical assignment have also undertaken fundamental scientific research. The Commission's practice has been to assign tasks on the basis of the technological qualifications of a laboratory rather than its type of management. . . .

In the field of civilian power reactors, for example, in which commercial acceptability depends on operating economy calculated to several decimal places and on the manufacturer's guarantee of performance, two firms (General Electric and Westinghouse) have been predominant, as they have been in the conventional power industry. The AEC has been reluctant to pick additional firms; rather it has given most of the work on developing advanced reactors to its own laboratories, assuming that when reactors are developed, private industry will be able to market them competitively. But the drawings and patents made available by the AEC are not the same as the "know-how" and staff acquired by AEC research and management contractors; even in the established field of water reactors, the basic drawings of which are all in the public domain, other companies have been unable to challenge GE and Westinghouse successfully because they have lacked the confidence of the electrical utilities and the experience and the people to back up the drawings.

## BIG SCIENCE AND THE UNIVERSITIES

University management of major basic research facilities, such as large particle accelerators and research reactors built and operated with public funds, has posed problems of the *location* of the facility, determination of the number of participants in the *management* group, and the assurance of equitable *access* to the machine by nonresident scientists.

*Locating Unique Facilities*

As the expense of building and operating machines for fundamental nuclear research has risen, the determination of the best site for each instrument has become more important and more hotly debated. Unfortunately, such objective considerations as the availability of land, power, water, and transportation do not narrow the range of choice sufficiently to avoid serious problems of politics, economics, and scientific morale.

Thus, in 1963, a large midwestern congressional delegation petitioned the President to endorse the construction of a 12.5-BEV accelerator at Madison, Wisconsin; and in 1965 twelve midwestern governors demanded that the proposed 200-BEV, $375 million proton accelerator be located in their region. (In December 1966, after extensive technical review, AEC picked Weston, Illinois, as the site.)

The economic issues go beyond the immediate benefits to local business and employment, to the broader cultural and economic stimulus that a major R&D center may bring to a region. Also, the AEC cannot ignore the effect of site decisions on morale at existing laboratories that contend for major new facilities so as to introduce exciting new work and talent and to counter the effect of nuclear test restrictions and production and budget cutbacks.

Regional struggles might be reduced if there were an over-all government plan for the rational geographic distribution of future R&D facilities for *all* federal agencies. . . .

*Multi-University Management*

Until recently, there was a striking contrast between the AEC practice of contracting with one university for the management of large basic research facilities and the National Science Foundation practice of contracting for this purpose exclusively with organizations representing a number of universities. The major AEC exception has been its 1947 contract with Associated Universities, Inc., to manage the Brookhaven Laboratory. As recently as 1960, the Commission designated one university, Stanford, to manage as well as construct a two-mile long, $112 million electron accelerator, with appropriate arrangements for its use by nonresident scientists.

In January 1964, following the rejection by President Johnson of midwestern university and congressional demands for a multi-university accelerator in Wisconsin, the AEC announced a new management plan for the Argonne Laboratory (near Chicago) under which a nonprofit corporation of midwest universities will formulate "policies and programs" while the University of Chicago will continue to "operate" the laboratory. . . .

The record of Berkeley and Brookhaven indicates that either one or a group of universities can successfully manage a large research installation. Logic suggests that the purer the research, the more unique the facility, and the greater the educational function, the stronger the case for multi-university management; while the more programmatic the research and the more it must be meshed with other agency functions, the stronger the case for a single responsible, and responsive, management. Experience suggests that the unique qualities of particular laboratory directors and universities are as relevant as administrative theory.

### *Allocating Machine Time.*

When, however, conditions lead the AEC to contract with a single university for the operation of a unique basic research facility, it has a responsibility to ensure that access to the facility is determined by the quality of the experiments proposed rather than by the institutional affiliation of the scientists proposing them. The managers of such machines have to face the problem of allocating time between users from their resident staff and scientists at institutions throughout the nation and the world.

Clearly, it lies within the government's power to influence the use of a facility by budgeting larger or smaller funds to the laboratory or to outside scientists. That power should be used to encourage a core group of first-class physicists in each region of the country (i.e., the minimum number required for a first-class doctoral program); but primarily to ensure that the experiments conducted at the laboratory are of the highest possible quality, variety, and originality.

## THE MULTI-PROGRAM LABORATORIES

The AEC has seven "multi-program" laboratories: Brookhaven, Argonne, Oak Ridge, Ames, Berkeley, Livermore, and Los Alamos. Together, these laboratories spend some $400 million annually on R&D. All but Oak Ridge are managed by universities or an incorporated group of universities; Oak Ridge is managed by industry. The AEC has characterized these facilities as "integrated" or "balanced," meaning, thereby, that (as a group) they have an unusually broad range of competence, conducting basic research in the physical and biological sciences as well as applied research and development in both civilian and military nuclear technology.

### *Nuclear Weapons Development.*

Although the significance of their work has given the three main weapons laboratories (Sandia, Livermore, and Los Alamos) great political, technical, and budgetary strength (in fiscal 1964 they had the largest operating budgets of all AEC laboratories), they have, nonetheless, experienced several cycles of confidence and concern. At Los Alamos, the nation's first weapons facility, both operations and morale came so close to collapse after World War II, that serious consideration was given to abandoning the site.

In the late 1950's, it seemed that a point of diminishing returns had been reached in the development of new nuclear weapons, but the advent of the missile era and the consequent need for warheads of reduced weight with reliability under the stress of missile delivery enlarged the range of fruitful R&D on nuclear weapons. In 1960 the Commission declared its intent to ensure that the three weapons laboratories will be "... maintained as strong and vigorous institutions. Should there be some decrease in weapons research and development needs, consideration will be given to expanding these laboratories' nonweapon functions. ..." How far this process of weapons improvement can fruitfully go and what expenditures should be devoted to it are questions that cannot be answered without access to classified information.

In 1962 President Kennedy noted that it is difficult to keep top-flight scientists in large laboratories on the alert for test shots which they believe will not take place, and subsequently he and President Johnson supported laboratory "readiness" for atmospheric tests as well as the current program of expensive, and extensive, underground weapons tests. Nevertheless, it cannot be said that the weapons laboratories are happy with their lot. Their drive to improve our nuclear weapons technology runs inherently counter to efforts at the highest levels of national policy to stabilize or even dismantle that technology by international agreement.

### *New Civilian Technology*

In principle, AEC laboratories are not to go beyond the line that divides the "development" of new technology from its systematic "production"; or they are to do so only temporarily, until private industry (i.e., at least two private, competitive companies) demonstrates its capacity to provide the new nuclear product or service. Where to draw the line is a problem, as was observed earlier in connection with nuclear power reactors. The Commission's R&D–and, of late, operating–contracts have been sought and, to some extent, openly used to nurse along a competitive nuclear industry until it could be sustained by a higher and more regular volume of production orders. But it presently appears that the AEC should draw the line in its own laboratories further back from the developmental end of the scale, and correspondingly increase the volume of applied research and development contracts with private industry.

### *Non-Nuclear Work*

The multi-program laboratories have made periodic efforts to diversify their activities, even by conducting non-nuclear work. The problems of atomic energy are broad but finite, so there is a question of what to do with a facility when its specific nuclear mission is accomplished. Two main answers can be given: close down the laboratory, in whole or in part, and sell it to the highest bidder or preferably to that bidder who proposes to use it for some significant public purpose; or broaden the laboratory mission to include important non-nuclear work. These are not mutually exclusive, for it may be desirable to close down or cut back some laboratories and to broaden the mission of others.

Cutbacks, let alone closings, of multi-program laboratories are not likely to be accepted meekly. There is substantial support within the Commission and the Joint Committee for their maintenance and even expansion, so as to have them "on line" and ready for any national need in either the military or civilian nuclear area. During the past six years, total AEC expenditures have been relatively stable, but, due to major cutbacks in weapons programs, the proportion devoted to military purposes declined from 75 percent in 1961 to about 50 percent in 1965.

. . . Is the time approaching when the Congress should define more clearly the proper role of all government agencies, and of their laboratories, in the realm of civilian technology? If this task is presently too large, a useful start can be made by clarifying the proper function of the AEC and its network of contractor-operated laboratories in non-nuclear science and technology.

## THE FUTURE OF THE AEC

Judged by its accomplishments, the Atomic Energy Commission's policy of contracting out all of its R&D, production, and laboratory management has worked well. AEC's contractors have turned out a steady stream of sophisticated nuclear weapons, military and civilian reactors and other nuclear hardware, and fundamental research in the physical and biological sciences. There is no reason to believe that government-operated laboratories staffed by civil servants would have done a better job, but some basic questions of public policy remain unresolved.

As some of its major tasks are completed, routinized, or turned over to industry, what should be the future of the AEC and its laboratories? Officially, the Commission appears content with its present mission but many close observers believe that a reappraisal of the mission is now called for to redefine, and perhaps enlarge, the AEC's role amidst the many governmental programs to advance the nation's science and technology.

# 46

## Charles R. Ross
## *Environmental Degradation by Government*

Beyond any doubt our environment has seriously deteriorated. Accepting this fact, we must determine how and why this happened and then, hopefully, suggest what we can do about it.

Those of us who have had the privilege of serving in the federal government must bear a good portion of the responsibility for the current sorry state of environmental affairs. In a popular phrase of the day, most of us had "tunnel vision."

How could such a thing possibly happen? It certainly was not because your government official or employee deliberately set out to ruin the nation. A review of the Department of Interior's Conservation Yearbook Number 4 for fiscal year 1967 shows that there were people in government who could talk the proper language. The Department expresses great concern for "Man . . . an Endangered Species" in the yearbook which, for the most part quotes the right persons, such as Kenneth E. Boulding, René Dubos, Robert Oppenheimer, and others. Former Interior Secretary Steward L. Udall himself says: "We need a man-centered science which will seek to determine the interrelationships of life, interrelationships whose understanding will enhance the condition of man."

President Johnson, in Executive Order 11278 establishing the President's Council on Recreation and Natural Beauty on May 4, 1966, declared. "To be isolated from that natural America is to be impoverished–no matter how different one may be. To destroy it, to treat it carelessly, is to disregard one of the profound needs of the human spirit."

Glenn T. Seaborg, Chairman of the Atomic Energy Commission, said on January 6 in the 1969 *New York Times National Economic Review:* "Many thoughtful people believe and fear that the technical civilization we have created is out of hand, that as a macro-system guided by large economic and social needs and forces, man as such is no longer in control." He suggested that our instinct for survival would carry us through, that we should not despair but must search in the deepest recesses of the human heart and conscience for the key to the future.

In the same issue of the *New York Times,* however, political scientist Zbigniew Brzezinski wondered whether our society would be able to survive the challenge posed by the technitronic society. He asserted:

> On the contrary, the instantaneous electronic intermeshing of mankind will make for an intense confrontation straining social and international peace. *In the past differences were livable because of time and distance*

> *that separated them. Today, these differences are actually widening, while technitronics are eliminating the two insulants of time and distance.*

As a former government official who has participated, I can assure you that men like Udall and Seaborg, Presidents Johnson and Kennedy, were and are sympathetic and understanding. However, as socioeconomist Robert Theobald has said, it no longer suffices for a person to have "meant well" if his intervention worsened rather than improved a situation. The right to interfere comes only through possession of information, knowledge, and wisdom.

What went wrong? Why is it we have such a faculty to ignore the wonderful speeches and reports that call our attention to the really pressing problems of the times? Way back in 1916, the National Academy of Sciences in its "Summary Report on Natural Resources" said:

> Perhaps the most critical and most often ignored resource is man's total environment .... The effects on man himself of the changes he has wrought in the balance of great natural forces and in the new microenvironment which he has created are but simply perceived and not at all well understood.

It would appear that these remarks must have had some impact in government, judging from the quotations by Udall, Seaborg, and Johnson. Yet, the Ford Foundation is willing to spend a goodly sum of money, along with Yale, to talk some more. Let us hope that there will be action as a result of these series of lectures.

Any action, of necessity, must be directed at the very institutions that sought and have been charged with the responsibility of enhancing and preserving the quality of our environment. Government, industry, and the university have let us down, and have left it up to tax-exempt foundations to carry the ball. It is really tragic that this great nation of ours has to rely upon foundations to provide the funds to those who are concerned and, in a few cases, to those who want to do something more than research or study the problem. Unfortunately, most paths lead to just a few foundations.

The relationships of industry and the university with government, in effect, have actually determined the inadvertency of the environmental degradation. In order to put together the complicated, long-range plans for tomorrow, an almost incestuous relationship between these unholy partners has developed, and such "minor" problems as the environment have been lost in the shuffle. Surely, few can be really surprised by my statement that our institutions have let us down. John Gardner, [former] Secretary of Health, Education, and Welfare, has worried about it; economist J. Kenneth Galbraith has talked about it at length. Yale Law Professor Charles A. Reich has focused on the helplessness of the individual citizen in confrontation with government and business. Andrei D. Sakharov, the Russian nuclear physicist, has written eloquently about it. In an essay which appeared in the *New York Times* on July 22, 1968, he wrote:

> The division of mankind threatens it with destruction. Civilization is

> imperiled by: a universal thermonuclear war, catastrophic hunger for most of mankind, stupefaction from the narcotic of mass culture and bureaucratic dogmatism, a spreading of mass myths that put entire peoples and continents under the power of cruel and treacherous demagogues, and destruction or degeneration from the unforeseeable consequences of swift changes in the conditions of life on our planet.

This is what I am really saying: the environmental degradation suffered by our nation has been inadvertent in the sense that our institutions have become one critical mass. The checks and balances which each institution provides for the others are no longer as effective. "I am earth's nature: no rearranging it," said Robert Browning. The unholy three, in their eagerness to rearrange nature, have failed to appreciate the dangers to the environment. However, if it is entirely inadvertent, there is hope because we may be able to do something about it.

I have spent ten years of my life in regulation of industry. During that time, I have had the pleasure of participating in the great American game of awarding certificates to the lucky holder of the right combination of experience, money, and political pressure or pull. I regret to say that regulation—one of government's technological arms, the so-called fourth branch—is as guilty as the legislative or executive branches of government in failing to understand the consequences of its decisions. These awards, which Professor Reich has discussed, are not made entirely on merit. They reflect the human characteristic of a decision-maker who understands power and mistrusts new ideas and concepts, as well as the biases of the particular agency and the deterioration of governmental process.

Let me try to substantiate the viewpoint that government agencies can be very unresponsive to new ideas, but respond much more easily to biases of the "in group," the establishment for a particular agency.

Early in my career in Washington, I had several memorable experiences with the Department of Interior. The first involved an Arizona Power Authority application to build a large hydroelectric facility in the lower Colorado River, a project known then as Marble Canyon. The case is particularly interesting because it, together with the High Mountain Sheep and the Storm King cases, illustrates the schizophrenic position in which the Department usually finds itself—a department dedicated to promoting pollution control, oil, gas and coal power, fish and national parks. It also portrays the righteous and indignant regulator who has a lot to learn.

The Marble Canyon project was expected to be the "cash register" for development of the Southwest by the Interior Department. It would provide the Department's dam builders with a beautiful project, large and massive. It would satisfy those who felt that Arizona and New Mexico deserved a better fate than Mother Nature had decreed. It would also show the Park Service who was boss.

However, the waters were muddied by the application of the Arizona Power Authority. The Arizona Power Authority was, according to some, a pseudo-public power organization fronting for the private power interests who were not about to let Marble Canyon be developed by the government. Poor California was present, gasping for its mammoth project and determined not to let its mortal enemies in Arizona win the sweepstakes. Poor Secretary Udall did not know what to do at first. Clearly, the conservationists were concerned, but the Interior Department would not support them. Finally, after the Examiner had issued a decision, the Department sought to intervene for the purpose of seeking federal development.

To make a long story short, we had oral argument; purely by chance, the conservationists were the beneficiaries rather than the victims. California and Arizona were so interested in dueling that finally Congress took hold and ordered the Federal Power Commission to slow down. Since there was a precedent in the case of the Grand Canyon from President Herbert Hoover's days, Congress was not as reluctant to step in as it often is.

Actually, the public versus private power issue became embroiled; Southern California Edison, seeking to prevent either Bridge Canyon or Marble Canyon, proposed another solution obviating the necessity of a dam on the lower Colorado. The proposal involved the construction of very large coal-generating stations in the desert. This is now underway. Knowing of the concern expressed by the Sierra Club and others, Udall has tried to make sure there would be as little impact on the environment, and especially on the Indians, as possible.

The Marble Canyon case illustrates the fairly typical bureaucratic response of someone who is challenged by an interested group seeking to present a viewpoint for which there are no supporting standard cost-benefit ratios or economic standards. The mammoth bureaucracy creaked into action. The Secretary of the Treasury issued an order to challenge the right of the impertinent conservation group, the Sierra Club (a latecomer), to dare to go to Congress to try to prevent a power development. Much to the Sierra Club's ultimate benefit, it has tentatively lost its right to claim a charitable exemption. Now the nation has a group interested in the environment which does not have to play pat-a-cake with fund sponsors. There are already too many worthwhile organizations controlling purse strings which must apologetically decline to finance action groups seeking to advance similar causes—often the reason for their very existence. Boldness is not typical of many conservation organizations and officials. Plenty of learned talk, yes; action, no. Recognizing the hand that feeds you is just as typical of man as of any other animal.

I am reminded of a day in the closing moments of the Marble Canyon controversy, when the time was running out on the congressional moratorium for the Federal Power Commission. A sincere and dedicated woman from a well-known conservation group—not the Sierra Club—was sent down by some administrative assistant on Capitol Hill to see me. She was amazed to find out that the Federal Power Commission could possibly undo all that had been accomplished. Her organization had not really focused on the FPC as one of those terrible government bodies which are the curse of society. Today, I am pleased to say, the FPC is getting its fair share of attention, although it is not very easy to follow the activities of such an agency from afar, as I personally have discovered.

While the results flowing from the Marble Canyon controversy are not as unfortunate as they might have been, most individuals would agree that it turned out as well as it did through no fault of the government. In this case, inadvertency worked to the public's benefit.

The High Mountain Sheep case is another classic conservation case. A group of private utilities proposed a power dam to be located on the Snake River, somewhat above the confluence of the Snake and the Salmon rivers, on the Idaho-Oregon border. A competing group of public power agencies proposed a much larger alternative project which would dam up both rivers. Here, the initial issue was essentially public versus private power, with federal power standing in the wings.

The principal antagonists decided early in the game that conservation, "fish," would be a factor. The private power advocates were well aware of the muscle that the fish people could exert. In fact, it has been alleged frequently that the private groups have used the fish people to kill public power projects. The public agencies decided to go whole hog and urged the largest possible projects with an attitude of "Damn the fish; full speed ahead." The Commission, with me writing the decision, elected to support the small project because it felt strongly that it was very important not to dam up the Salmon River. By this time the public power group had gotten the message that we might do this; as an alternative, it suggested that it could be talked into building the smaller project. The Feds (Interior Department) were sent into action during the closing moments of the game to pull the fat from the fire for the public bloc. They succeeded. I can still remember Justice Thurgood Marshall—then Solicitor General—arguing forcefully to Chairman Lee C. White and me that the government should take the necessary legal steps which might lead to a really large public power development, irrespective of fish.

Once again, those interested in safeguarding our environment are the inadvertent beneficiaries of governmental indecision. It now turns out that the Interior Department can prove from a fish standpoint that the High Mountain Sheep site would be prejudicial to the fish runs up the Salmon, even though it was not physically blocked. So they now want to build at another site farther upstream. The time that was bought inadvertently by the government and power interests enabled Congress to look again at the value of the Salmon River for purposes other than power, and it gave Justice William O. Douglas a chance to sound another clarion call to his nature-loving brethren. Frankly, I would not bet on any dam on the Snake. The environment-minded ladies in tennis shoes, meanwhile, are learning what it takes to survive in the cruel world of politics, where man eats man and not even gracefully at that.

These two cases, as well as the Storm King case, are really the exceptions that prove the rule. It scares me to think that the results were achieved almost by chance. I told a group of economists at the Institute of Public Utilities at Michigan State University: "You must do your job well as the guardians of our economic system. This means you may have to get your feet wet; you in turn may be accused in indignant tones of being a politician or you might even lose some good consulting jobs or the prestige of government contracts or employment. It could even involve your university in the messy but necessary life on the outside and serve as a constraint in attracting capital for the next year's building program. This is your choice. I know I got sick and tired of regulating by the seat of my pants, and it wasn't because I didn't try. Give my successors something better. But don't expect a performance under regulation better than what the so-called 'real world' can do."

The academic community concerned with the environment has a duty to see to it that the decision-maker, politician though he may be, is educated and that these decisions are not left to chance. Maybe it will not get all the glory, but its children will reap the benefits.

Now look at the other side of the coin, when society was not so fortunate. In 1912 the International Joint Commission (IJC), of which I am presently a member, was asked to explore the problems of water pollution from Lake of the Woods to the St. John River in New Brunswick, Canada. Some people may think the Department of the Interior just recently discovered that Lake Erie was a mess. It may surprise them to learn that back in 1918 the Commission officially warned the government that the situation in parts of the Great Lakes was "generally chaotic, everywhere perilous, and in some cases disgraceful." Some 51 years later, the two nations are told once again that the situation is serious. In fact, Lake Erie is said to be dead. Maybe, just maybe, this time, when the IJC comes out with its latest report on the conditions of the Great Lakes, the two governments will respond and not allow another 50 years to pass without significant corrective action.

I must mention the role of the Army Corps of Engineers. The Great Lakes provide the Corps with wonderful opportunities. Many states are bounded by the Lakes. This means many politicians. Many politicians mean many possible projects, which are proof of the individual politician's ability not only to survive in that Washington jungle, but to bring home the bacon. Just think of the harbors to be built and dredged, for example, and all the spoil that one has to get rid of. The Great Lakes "just by being there" are a challenge to any good civil engineer and politician.

For example, the IJC has a proposal before it to determine whether it is feasible to control the level of the Great Lakes. It also is supervising the dewatering of Niagara Falls; after all, we cannot let honeymooners spend the rest of their lives bemoaning the fact that the crest of the American falls is no longer the same and that those terrible boulders at the bottom destroy the spectacular effect. Furthermore, we cannot afford to let the Canadian falls be more spectacular than the American.

By the time of the origin of the Niagara Falls dewatering plan, the Commission was "on to" ecology, so we requested the Corps of Engineers to retain an ecologist to make studies of the falls before the project's start. He has assured the Commission that there is no reason to worry about an irremediable harm done by this temporary dewatering. The Commission takes pride, too, in the fact that it has managed to attach two outstanding landscape architects to its advisory boards. Hopefully, it is not too late to go back and crank into the Levels Study an ecological appraisal of such an effort. The thing that brothers me is that the happenstance leading to retention of an ecologist should not be dependent upon coincidences: a certain commissioner with an interest in the environment, or the rekindling of such interest by former Yale Law School student Frances Enseki, who belonged to what I used to call the Washington Conservation Underground—a group of young, knowledgeable, somewhat anti-establishment, diverse individuals, the real doers.

These young students and graduates, professionals if you will, actually more than anything else, give me confidence that the system can be licked. They have infiltrated all the government agencies, and tried out most of the nonprofit ones as well.

I had great pleasure recently in warning the FPC's Electric Advisory Council (one of those formidable combinations of government and business in which the consumer, the conservationist, or the man in the street is on the outside looking in). The FPC and its stepchild, the Advisory Council, were carefully discussing the future of the United States: where all the capital should be spent, and the argument of nuclear fuel versus fossil fuel. It was scarcely a simple exercise, since the power industry is the largest in the nation in terms of capital investment. Moreover, the subject dealt with energy. The Advisory Council was the same group which declined to look into air pollution a year or so earlier, jointly with the FPC. Such a subject, according to the Council, while important, was not really as necessary as discussion of how many nuclear plants could be built. Of course, the FPC could proceed on its own in such a study.

In any event, everyone understood everyone else's problem. Possibly, just to liven things up a bit and since everyone knew I was leaving the FPC, I thought I would try to leave them something to think about. There had been a lot of crying about the nasty people who did not understand the real values of life, such as cheap electricity. There were even people who insisted that power lines should be buried and some who questioned the Atomic Energy Commission about the dangers of radioactive waste, both in its discharge and disposal! Even more frustrating were those who were beginning to make a case about thermal "enrichment." Some more people were even trying to force the AEC with legislation to consider environmental factors!

The opportunity was too good to pass up. Briefly, I suggested to my fellow commissioners and the industry that the confrontation was not between them and a group of ladies in tennis shoes. Such struggles had been, and would continue to be, pretty unequal—even though individuals like Professor Frank J. Tysen of the University of Southern California, at the Thorne Ecological Institute in 1967 in Aspen, were urging these nice ladies to act like guerrillas. The new struggle would be between the establishment, in this case the FPC and the power industry (not such an unusual partnership as it seems at first glance), and the youth of today.

The young people would be armed with facts and spurred on by knowledge, not just emotion. They would be motivated by the thought that everything could end pretty quickly if too many mistakes are made. Unlike the older generations typified by those sitting in that meeting room who only have a relatively few years to live out, these youths have ahead of them most of a lifetime. Unlike us, they cannot afford the luxury of a mistake. Time has escalated, and the future becomes the present to them. "After us, the deluge" may be the motto of the industry but it is not theirs.

So I warned the industry that a revised power survey must deal with the environment, not just with natural beauty. I told them to learn something from the Bureau of Public Roads, that it would be their turn to be "on stage" during the 1970s and they should attempt to understand the ecological approach even if they did not agree with it. If they did not, I said, the youth of today would exact a stiff price, possibly going beyond dollars and cents. Their beloved institution, a semipublic business, might be forced, hopefully, to account for its mistakes.

Why such a warning should be necessary is not too hard to understand. In describing my FPC experience to the Western States Water and Power Conference recently, I said:

> It is too easy to become wrapped up in our own little world. We are too much aware only of industry and its officials. We know the latest political gossip in Washington. We are concerned about the impact of our decisions on those we happen to know. We try to be concerned about the impact of the decisions on the people we don't know, but it is difficult.

It is terribly difficult to be tough when it is necessary, if you are dealing with someone you know and like. The occasional visit to your office to say hello is a great antidote for a case of strict regulatory enforcement. As would any doctor, you pay more attention to those who complain than to those who do not complain but place their trust in you. It is good salesmanship to convince your regulator that only the two of you are capable of handling such technical and difficult problems.

To add to the soft sell, if it becomes necessary industry can turn to its true friends, those representatives or senators who understand the role of government and business. For the hard sell, discreet phone calls from distinguished senators from the "oil patch" or the current impoverished area as to the status of a particular case usually are informative enough for a good political regulator or administrator to get the message. Or possibly someone in the government needs more money which can be obtained from bonuses for offshore oil and gas concessions. There is even the possibility that upon leaving government you can secure a good consulting contract for your new firm with either industry or the local, state, or federal agencies—if you are a good boy. It is tempting. The loner who can resist the temptation finds life more satisfying but far more difficult.

Is it any wonder that to some officials and businessmen the environment or the quality of life for the average citizen is a relatively inconsequential matter when compared to the economic health of the industry?

As an example, the paper industry has successfully fought off attempts to clean up lakes and streams. In November 1963 I told the Inland Empire Waterways Association—a potent lobby for the Corps of Engineers: "To those who have been crying aloud, 'Let's clean up our streams,' I add, 'Amen.' To those who are polluting our streams, I say, 'Watch out.' "

This warning stemmed from my experience on the IJC, since for years the Commission had tried to secure some semblance of cooperation in cleaning up the Rainy and the St. Croix rivers, a fact that does not speak well for either industry or government. Here again, it is understandable; the government (in this case, local and state) was seeking to preserve jobs, and industry was trying to meet southern competition. Almost without exception, the members of industry argued that they would be forced to move to other communities which understood their problems better if pollution controls were enforced. The situation finally convinced even the most die-hard friend of the industry that the boom must be lowered on the states, even though federal-state relationships might suffer in the process. This meant taking the drastic step of removing the problem of water pollution from the Department of Health, Education, and Welfare and giving it to the Interior Department.

The solution, long in coming, was a political one which should not be forgotten. Too often the delicate ecological balance between the creature, the federal government, and its kindred creature, state government, is protected at the expense of the public.

Competition in providing citizens with the best government possible is not necessarily unfair. It should even be encouraged. In fact, we might get a government which recognizes that a place must be reserved within the decisional process for the expression of independent viewpoints by private organizations or individuals, although the average administrator or regulator does not like to be bothered by them. As a result of my experience in the Storm King case, I said in a speech to the Federal Bar Association in October 1967 that "No really satisfactory method has yet been found within the bureaucratic structure to give such expression to 'the full faith and credit' needed to expose each course of action to the fullest consideration necessary to reach the best decision."

In conclusion I said:

> The commissioners for their part will have to recognize that a greater number of appliances which provide increased leisure will be useless if there is such disharmony between man and his environment that man is unable to understand himself and his relationship to the universe.

The real action should be in local or state government, and it ought to be able to improve upon the performance of federal agencies.

I guess it is obvious that I am somewhat critical of government and its innate ability to frustrate the average man in the street, although I still think public service is the most challenging activity available to man. The real gap is the credibility gap between the youth of today and their government, although the universities—the father but not the master of the technological man—are also wanting. I said in a letter to the *New York Times* in which I was proposing an environmental institute that "An environmental institute would also re-focus the energies of the universities from the defense establishment into avenues more consistent with the concerns of their students and faculties. There would be an opportunity for students, professors, and scholars in general to apply their knowledge to real problems—something they often need to feel the relevance of their scholarship—and to help shape the environment for the years ahead.

"An environmental institute, funded by grants from Congress, private industry, foundations, and other private and public organizations, may not solve all our environmental problems but it might be a big step in that direction. Isn't it worth finding out?"

In discussing new institutions to serve the individual, William R. Ewald, Jr., observes in *Environment and Policy: The Next Fifty Years:*

> University people, as individuals, may create a stir from time to time about the future, but few communicate this and their institutions have

> somehow avoided learning how to do research on the future of the human species and environment, much less to teach it. The ring of truth is much louder and easier to follow in the hard sciences, where it is also more easily coupled with technology to find its way into the marketplace or weaponry and is more easily financed.[1]

This brings me to the methods and means which I feel can make our government more effective.

First of all, as case studies for future students, such an institute would be wise to follow a course similar to that which former Secretary of the Interior Udall suggested for Vietnam: make a behind-the-scenes study of the pressures, the influences and factors which determined some of the important environmental issues of the day.

For example, what are the whole stories on Storm King, High Mountain Sheep, Marble Canyon, the Hudson River Highway, desalinization plants, the alleged deal between the Interior Department and Corps of Engineers on the estuary study or the language concerning offshore oil and gas development in the "Marine Resources Report," the Santa Barbara incident, the slowness of the nation to focus on strip mining, the inability or delay by both industry and the scientific community to grasp the significance of thermal pollution, the failure to consider esthetics until forced to do so, and the story of the alleged threatened Udall resignation under President Johnson?

We should examine the role of federal advisory committees and should research in depth the role of the foundations in the environmental field. I recognize and pay my respects to Laurance S. Rockefeller for his service to the nation in the field of environmental study, but I wonder why it should be necessary for everyone interested in conservation to go, hat in hand, to the Fords or Rockefellers for seed money. The federal government is found wanting, possibly because it is disinclined to finance some group which would cause it trouble by raising questions about the impact of federal actions on the environment. Of course, if one has sufficient independent resources, it is a different story.

I wonder, too, whether serious thought has been given to the makeup of advisory committees. Is the public completely represented, or did we have chiefly people from Texas in the mid '60s, people from California or the West in the late '60s? Or are these committees composed of respectable, rich public members who know and understand each other?

We must analyze the role of the conservation organization, from the elite Audubon Society to the rip-roaring, gun-toting hunting clubs. Somewhere there should be an institution which the citizen can trust for sound scientific and social judgments on environmental issues. We have enough guerrillas. We need a Peace Corps type of Institute for the Environment, not a think tank for waging bigger and better wars. I could suggest men for 50 institutes tomorrow if they could be established, and the war in Vietnam would not even miss them. The world, however, might profit from their efforts.

[1]William R. Ewald, Jr., ed., *Environment and Policy: The Next Fifty Years,* (Bloomington, Indiana University Press, 1968).

It is hard to establish the need for a new institution because, of necessity, you are forced to expose the weaknesses of the old. This leaves you subject to the charge of being either an anarchist, a revolutionary, or just a frustrated old man. It helps when others have similar thoughts and your brilliant concept is not unique, although it may have been original with you. It is encouraging, too, to discover that others are also determined to prevent a multiplicity of organizations from cashing in on the ecological rage.

Through the generosity of Thomas Watson, Jr., who made one of his employees, William Ross (no relation), available, and with the cooperation and assistance of former Vermont Governor Philip H. Hoff, a Vermont Institute for the Environment is under consideration. Some might accuse us of merely seeking to emulate the university. I do not think so—at least not the type of university we know today. We would intentionally structure our institute to promote and even possibly force interdisciplinary consideration of environmental problems. We would attempt to remove the threat of domination by any single vested interest or any one individual. Like the Peace Corps, we would program a continuing renewal of personnel and the replacement of any individual after a proper period of time.

In general, we want to restore the faith and confidence of the people in the environmental decision and give them a role in shaping it. This means the youth of today, who will have to live with the mistakes of today—if the mistakes permit survival. This credibility will stem from youth's confidence in the independence of the participants, a confidence that the university sought to achieve in asking for tenure.

Last and most important, the institute would be *action oriented.* It would even include politicians! It might just get the job done if it could get off the ground. More work is required on our part, of course, but it is hard to shake the world and still earn a living, just from a time standpoint alone.

Originally, I had hopes for a national institute. A recent colloquium at Washington soon convinced me that the conservation establishment and Congress were not ready, so I lowered my sights to Vermont. Now, New Hampshire (Dartmouth University) is interested, as well as Massachusetts (Williams College). This is familiar territory—at least Vermont—and offers promise. What pleases me even more is that there seems to be a provincial northeast underground. I am exchanging ideas, including possible new legislation, with New Hampshire through a fascinating group of people who have similar opinions. I am also serving as an adviser (unpaid at my request, in order to preserve my objectivity and freedom from conflict-of-interest charges) to the Lake Champlain Committee, and through them I keep in touch with others, particularly in New York State.

We are making progress. The adversary process, the Victor Yannacones[2] and the courts are, of course, helpful. "Knowledge power," in the words of Ewald, is even more effective. Lawyers, and I confess to be one, are not known for their innovative contributions. They are essentially conservative and serve as a brake for most of society, at least for those who respect the past and are intimidated by a lawyer's ability to express himself.

[2] Victor Yannacone, a New York attorney, organized the Environmental Defense Fund in 1967 to create a new body of law by litigation on behalf of all U.S. citizens.

Loyalty to institutions, religious or otherwise, for loyalty's sake is a luxury this universe can no longer afford. We must challenge our institutions and our dogmas. Maybe, if we even challenge industry's or government's right to do as it sees fit, unless proved by others to be damaging, we would be better off.

We should require those who propose new technological advances to assume the burden of investigating and reporting the potential impact of such developments on society. Possibly, if this were to be done, the federal government would not be the inadvertent advocate of environmental degradation.

I can see progress.

12

# Budgets and the Good Life

Nothing in the world seems quite so detailed as the federal budget. We wish that perfection had resulted. As a story goes, when one of his students complained about having to master so many tiny techniques, Michelangelo retorted, "Details, my boy, add up to perfection, and perfection is no detail."

The present budget system, which has been under attack for a number of years, appears to be giving way before a much more rational system for assigning and calculating the costs of government. This new budget system, that presently carries the initials PPBS (Planning, Programming, Budget System), will soon be found throughout the government. It will probably extend to state and local governments and to industry as well.

Proper budgeting is only one aspect of the general planning of government activities. Ideally, all activities should be set up on some kind of priority basis with respect to national needs. Given a certain budget, the government could then perform the activities that are highest on the priority list. Granted, this is the great political problem of all times. Still, a great deal more can be done with it than has occurred in the past, where all too often the mode of budgeting and planning has been a composite of the successes and defeats of interested individuals, agencies, and interest groups.

Bulletin #66-3 from the Executive Office of the President, reprinted in this chapter, urges all departments to get on with the job of converting their budgeting systems to the PPBS plan. As we read through the memorandum, we notice how interested the government is in seeing that agencies give some attention to the cost-effectiveness of their spending programs. How do they know that their expenditures bring results? Truly it is difficult in many cases to show results in facts and figures. Many activities of the government are intangible, and some are secret. Nevertheless, as better methods of measuring activities are developed by the social sciences, we can expect to have some form of quantitative measurement for 90 per cent of government operations.

The effects of large government spending programs are discussed by Roland McKean, who has been one of the pioneers in new methods of public and social accounting. He is interested in measuring the impact of big government on individual freedom. Mr. McKean describes the factors found in many government activities that impede the exercise of individual desires and rights. Many of these impediments are perfectly legal and constitutional; in fact, very few of them could be protested through court action. One of the greatest failures of popular government has been the utter disregard of an accounting system for restraints on liberty. This problem has never been approached on a sufficiently specific level. We know how much is spent, and we have gross measures of what is achieved by spending, but we have few measures of the ways in which our lives are facilitated or hampered by such spending. Do you think that the situation Mr. McKean discusses is likely to develop in the future? How could it be avoided?

In the final item for reading and discussion in *Old Government/New People,* Andrew Kopkind discusses the new science of futuristics, which a great many business firms, universities, and individuals are helping to construct. It is a fascinating game, and if it evolves into a valid and reliable means of predicting and controlling the future, it will be a most useful social asset. Future planners are of all types and political persuasions. Like computers, they too must be properly "programmed" to be effectively used by society. However, the planner, unlike the computer, can potentially engage in the competition for power in the society. Could the planners eventually be a threat to the freedom of the individual? How could this be prevented?

# 47

## PPBS Or Else?

1. *Purpose.* The President has directed the introduction of an integrated Planning-Programming-Budgeting system in the executive branch. This Bulletin contains instructions for the establishment of such a system. It will be followed by additional instructions, including more explicit policy and procedural guidelines for use of the system in the annual Budget Preview.

2. *Application of instructions.* This Bulletin applies in all respects to the agencies listed in Section A of Exhibit 1. The agencies listed in Section B of that Exhibit are encouraged to apply the principles and procedures for the development and review of programs to the extent practical. (In this Bulletin, the word "agency" is used to designate departments and establishments; the word "bureau" is used to designate principal subordinate units.)

3. *Background and need.* A budget is a financial expression of a program plan. Both formal instructions (such as those contained in Bureau of the Budget Circular No. A-11) and training materials on budgeting have stressed that setting goals, defining objectives, and developing planned programs for achieving those objectives are important integral parts of preparing and justifying a budget submission.

Under present practices, however, program review for decision making has frequently been concentrated within too short a period; objectives of agency programs and activities have too often not been specified with enough clarity and concreteness; accomplishments have not always been specified concretely; alternatives have been insufficiently presented for consideration by top management; in a number of cases the future year costs of present decisions have not been laid out systematically enough; and formalized planning and systems analysis have had too little effect on budget decisions.

To help remedy these shortcomings the planning and budget system in each agency should be made to provide more effective information and analyses to assist line managers, the agency head, and the President in judging needs and in deciding on the use of resources and their allocation among competing claims. The establishment of a Planning, Programming, and Budgeting System in accordance with this Bulletin will make needed improvement possible.

While the improved system is intended for year-round use within each agency, its results will be especially brought into focus in connection with the spring Preview. It should lead to more informed and coordinated budget recommendations.

4. *Basic concepts and design.*

a. The new Planning-Programming-Budgeting system is based on three concepts:

(1) The existence in each agency of an *Analytic* capability which carries out continuing in-depth analyses by permanent specialized staffs of the agency's objectives and its various programs to meet these objectives.

(2) The existence of a multi-year *Planning and Programming* process which incorporates and uses an information system to present data in meaningful categories essential to the making of major decisions by agency heads and by the President.

(3) The existence of a *Budgeting* process which can take broad program decisions, translate them into more refined decisions in a budget context, and present the appropriate program and financial data for Presidential and Congressional action.

b. Essential to the system are:

(1) An output-oriented (this term is used interchangeably with mission-oriented or objectives-oriented) program structure (sometimes also called a program format) which presents data on all of the operations and activities of the agency in categories which reflect the agency's end purposes or objectives. This is discussed in more detail in paragraph 5, below.

(2) Analyses of possible alternative objectives of the agency and of alternative programs for meeting these objectives. Many different techniques of analysis will be appropriate, but central should be the carrying out of broad systems analyses in which alternative programs will be compared with respect to both their costs and their benefits.

(3) Adherence to a time cycle within which well-considered information and recommendations will be produced at the times needed for decision-making and for the development of the President's budget and legislative program. An illustrative cycle which does this is described in paragraph 9.

(4) Acceptance by line officials (from operating levels up to the agency head), with appropriate staff support, of responsibility for the establishment and effective use of the system.

c. The products of the system will include:

(1) A comprehensive multi-year *Program and Financial Plan* systematically updated.

(2) *Analyses,* including Program Memoranda, prepared annually and used in the budget Preview, Special Studies in depth from time to time, and other information which will contribute to the annual budget process.

d. The overall system is designed to enable each agency to:

(1) Make available to top management more concrete and specific data relevant to broad decisions;

(2) Spell out more concretely the objectives of Government programs;

(3) Analyze systematically and present for agency head and Presidential review and decision possible alternative objectives and alternative programs to meet those objectives;

(4) Evaluate thoroughly and compare the benefits and costs of programs;

(5) Produce total rather than partial cost estimates of programs;

(6) Present on a multi-year basis the prospective costs and accomplishments of programs;

(7) Review objectives and conduct program analyses on a continuing, year-round basis, instead of on a crowded schedule to meet budget deadlines.

e. The entire system must operate within the framework of overall policy guidance—from the President to the agency head, and from the agency head to his central planning, programming, and budgeting staffs and to his line managers. Fiscal policy considerations and other aspects of Presidential policy will be provided by the Bureau of the Budget in accordance with the President's program. Modifications will also have to be made from time to time to reflect changing external conditions, Congressional action, and other factors.

5. *The program structure.*

a. An early and essential step for each agency is the determination of a series of output-oriented categories which, together, cover the total work of the agency. These will serve as a basic framework for the planning, programming, and budgeting processes (including work on systems analysis, reporting, evaluation of accomplishments, and other aspects of management) and for relating these processes to each other. The following principles should guide the development of such output categories.

(1) *Program categories* are groupings of agency programs (or activities or operations) which serve the same broad objective (or mission) or which have generally similar objectives. Succinct captions or headings describing the objective should be applied to each such grouping. Obviously, each program category will contain programs which are complementary or are close substitutes in relation to the objectives to be attained. For example, a broad program objective is improvement of higher education. This could be a *program category,* and as such would contain Federal programs aiding undergraduate, graduate and vocational education, including construction of facilities, as well as such auxiliary Federal activities as library support and relevant research programs. For purposes of illustration and to aid understanding, Exhibit 2 shows some program structures as they might be applied to two organizational units within different agencies; the same approach, of course, applies to the agency as a whole.

(2) *Program subcategories* are subdivisions which should be established within each program category, combining agency programs (or activities or operations) on the basis of narrower objectives contributing directly to the broad objectives for the program category as a whole. Thus, in the example given above, improvement of engineering and science and of language training could be two program subcategories within the program category of improvement of higher education.

(3) *Program elements* are usually subdivisions of program subcategories and comprise the specific products (i.e., the goods and services) that contribute to the agency's objectives. Each program element is an integrated activity which combines personnel, other services, equipment and facilities. An example of a program element expressed in terms of the objectives served would be the number of teachers to be trained in using new mathematics.

b. The program structure will not necessarily reflect organization structure. It will be appropriate and desirable in many cases to have the basic program categories cut across bureau lines to facilitate comparisons and suggest possible trade-offs among elements which are close substitutes. It is also desirable to develop program formats which facilitate comparisons across agency lines (e.g., in urban transportation and in recreation).

c. Basic research activities may not be and frequently are not mission or output oriented. Whenever this is the case, such activities should be identified as a separate program category or subcategory as appropriate. However, applied research and development is usually associated with a specific program objective and should be included in the same program category as the other activities related to that objective.

d. To facilitate top level review, the number of program categories should be limited. For example, a Cabinet Department should have as many as 15 program categories in only a rare and exceptional case.

e. Program categories and subcategories should not be restricted by the present appropriation pattern or budget activity structure. (Eventually, however, it may be necessary and desirable for the "Program by Activity" portion of the schedules in the Budget Appendix to be brought into line with the program structure developed according to this Bulletin.)

6. *The Multi-Year Program and Financial Plan.*

a. The entire process is designed to provide information essential to the making of major decisions in a compact and logical form. A principal product of the process will be a document, the Multi-Year Program and Financial Plan of the agency.

b. Thus, the process is concerned with developing for agency head review, and, after his official approval or modification, for Bureau of the Budget and Presidential review (as summarized in Program Memoranda, per paragraph 7c) a translation of concretely specified agency objectives into combinations of agency activities and operations designed to reach such objectives in each of the stated time periods.

c. The Program and Financial Plan will:

(1) Be set forth on the basis of the program structure described in paragraph 5, above.

(2) Cover a period of years, usually five, although the number will vary with the considerations pertinent to particular agencies; for example, a longer time span would be appropriate for timber production and for large multiple-purpose water resource projects. The multi-year feature is not to be compromised by the expiration of legislation at an earlier date, since extension or renewal, with possible modification, of the legislation should be reflected in the Plan.

(3) Include activities under contemplated or possible new legislation as well as those presently authorized.

(4) Show the program levels which the agency head thinks will be appropriate over the entire period covered by the multi-year plan.

(5) Express objectives and planned accomplishments, wherever possible, in *quantitative* non-financial terms. For example, physical description of program elements might include the additional capacity (in terms of numbers to be accommodated) of recreational facilities to be built in national forests, the number of youths to be trained in Job Corps camps along with measures of the kinds and intensity of training, the number of hours of Spanish language broadcasts of the Voice of America, the number of children to receive pre-school training, and the

number of patients in Federally-supported mental hospitals. In some programs, it may not be possible to obtain or develop adequate measures in quantitative physical terms such as these but it is important to do so wherever feasible. In any case, objectives and performance should be described in as specific and concrete terms as possible.

(6) Where relevant, relate the physical description of Federal programs to the entire universe to be served. For example, a poverty program plan directed at aged poor should describe not only the numbers receiving specific Federal benefits but might well show what proportion of the entire aged poor population is being benefited.

(7) Associate financial data with the physical data to show the cost of carrying out the activity described. Cost data should be expressed in systems terms. That is, *all* costs–such as capital outlay, research and development, grants and subsidies, and current costs of operations (including maintenance)–which are associated with a program element should be assigned to that element. These component costs generally can be derived from existing appropriation and accounting categories. Where there are receipts, such as the collection of user charges or proceeds from sales of commodities or other assets, an estimate of receipts should also be included.

(8) Translate the costs and receipts used for analytic purposes, as described in the preceding subparagraph, into the financial terms used in Federal budget preparation, presentation, and reporting.

d. The Program and Financial Plan as approved by the agency head will be submitted to the Bureau of the Budget. The Bureau of the Budget will also be kept abreast of significant revisions and updatings (see subparagraphs *e* and *f*, immediately below).

e. The Program and Financial Plan, as approved or modified by the agency head in conformity with guidance received from the Bureau of the Budget and the President (usually following the annual spring Preview), will form the basis for the agency's budget requests. Therefore, it should not be changed except in accordance with a procedure approved by the agency head. Appropriate arrangements should be made for participation of the Budget Bureau in significant changes.

f. Provision will be made for a thorough reappraisal and updating of the Program and Financial Plan annually. In this process, one year is added on to the Plan. Other changes to the Plan are to be expected from time to time and a procedure may be useful for making minor changes to the Plan without requiring agency head approval.

7. *Analysis.* An analytic effort will be undertaken to examine deeply program objectives and criteria of accomplishments. Whenever applicable this effort will

utilize systems analysis, operations research, and other pertinent techniques. The analysis should raise important questions, compare the benefits and costs of alternative programs and explore future needs in relationship to planned programs. The sources of data used will be many, including most importantly, the Program and Financial Plan, special studies done throughout the agency, and budget, accounting and operating data. It is important to have continuity in the work of staffs doing this work and to build expertise in them over a period of years. As expertise is developed, more and more of the agency's activities can be subjected to these analytical techniques.

a. *Special Studies* on specific topics should be carried out in response to requests by the agency top management, the Budget Bureau, or at the initiative of the analytic staff itself. Suggestions should also be made by line operating managers. The special studies may involve intensive examination of a narrow subject or broad review of a wide field. The broad program studies envisioned here will often be hampered by a dearth of information and gaps in our knowledge which can be filled only by project studies and other micro-economic studies. Nevertheless, these broad studies should be assigned top priority in the agency's analytic effort.

b. *Questions* should be posed by the analytic staffs to other elements of the agency on program objectives, measures of performance, costs and the like.

c. A broad *Program Memorandum* should be prepared annually on each of the program categories of the agency. The Program Memorandum will summarize the Program and Financial Plan approved by the agency head for that category and present a succinct evaluation and justification. It should appraise the national needs to be met for several years in the future (covering at least as many years as the Program and Financial Plan), assess the adequacy, effectiveness, and efficiency of the previously approved Plan to meet those needs, and propose any necessary modifications in the previously approved Plan, including new legislative proposals. Thus, the Program Memorandum should:

(1) Spell out the specific programs recommended by the agency head for the multi-year time period being considered, show how these programs meet the needs of the American people in this area, show the total costs of recommended programs, and show the specific ways in which they differ from current programs and those of the past several years.

(2) Describe program objectives and expected concrete accomplishments and costs for several years into the future.

(3) Describe program objectives, insofar as possible in quantitative physical terms.

(4) Compare the effectiveness and the cost of alternative objectives, of alternative *types* of programs designed to meet the same or comparable objectives,

and of different *levels* within any given program category. This comparison should identify past experience, the alternatives which are believed worthy of consideration, earlier differing recommendations, earlier cost and performance estimates, and the reasons for change in these estimates.

(5) Make explicit the assumptions and criteria which support recommended programs.

(6) Identify and analyze the main uncertainties in the assumptions and in estimated program effectiveness or costs, and show the sensitivity of recommendations to these uncertainties.

d. In sum, the analytic effort will:

(1) Help define major agency objectives and subobjectives.

(2) Analyze and review criteria by which program performance is measured and judged, and help to develop new, improved criteria.

(3) Compare alternative programs, both in terms of their effectiveness and their costs, old as well as new.

(4) Develop reliable estimates of total systems costs of alternatives over the relevant span of years.

(5) Analyze the validity of cost data.

(6) Identify and analyze program uncertainties; test the sensitivity of conclusions and recommendations against uncertain variables.

(7) Carry out systems analyses to aid in making program choices.

8. *Relation of the system to the budget process.*

a. Two products of the system will be utilized in the spring Budget Preview: the Program Memoranda (which incorporate in summarized form the relevant portions of the Program and Financial Plan) and Special Studies.

b. All annual budget requests in the fall will be based on and related to the first year of the current multi-year Program and Financial Plan, subject to such modifications as may be required by changing circumstances since the Plan was last reviewed and approved by the agency head. Within this framework the detailed formulation and review of the budget will take place.

c. The introduction of the Planning, Programming, and Budgeting system will not, by itself, require any changes in the form in which budget appropriation requests are sent to Congress. Further, this Bulletin is not to be interpreted to set forth changes in the format of annual budget submissions to the Budget Bureau. Circular No. A-11 will be revised as needed to provide guidance on such budget submissions.

d. Over the next few years agency operating budgets used to allocate resources and control the day to day operations are to be brought into consistency with the Program and Financial Plan. Performance reports that show physical and financial accomplishments in relation to operating budgets should also be related to the basic plan.

e. The Planning, Programming and Budgeting functions are closely related and there must be close coordination in the work of the various staffs.

9. *An illustrative annual cycle.* Program review is a year-round process of reevaluating and updating program objectives, performance, and costs. The annual cycle described below is presented for purposes of illustration and will be refined and changed over time. It is intended to identify check-points to assure that essential steps are taken and that current reviews, revisions and recommendations are given consideration at appropriate times in the budget cycle. Insofar as this schedule affects internal agency operations and does not affect Bureau of the Budget scheduling, it may be modified by each agency head to suit his needs. The illustrative annual cycle shows in outline form how the system would work after it is established and operating for an agency participating in the Preview.

*January.* Changes are made by the agency to the prior multi-year program plan to conform to Presidential decisions as reflected in the budget sent to the Congress.

*March.* By March bureaus or similar major organizational units within the agency will submit to the agency head their current appraisals of approved program objectives and multi-year plans and their proposals for (a) needed modifications, including measures to meet new needs and to take account of changing and expiring needs, and (b) extension of plans to cover an added year (e.g., 1972). The Director of the Bureau of the Budget will advise the agency head of any change in the overall policies and objectives upon which the currently approved plan is based.

*April.* On the basis of instructions from the agency head following his review of bureau submissions, bureaus develop *specific* program plans.

*May.* Analytic staffs complete Program Memoranda. Agency head reviews program plans and approves Program Memoranda for submission to the Bureau of the Budget. He may want to assign additional studies on the basis of this review.

*May-June.* The budget preview is conducted by the Bureau of the Budget. The basic documents for this preview are the Program Memoranda prepared by agencies which are to be submitted to the Bureau of the Budget by May 1, and Special

Studies to be submitted over a period of several months preceding this date. Presidential guidance will be obtained, where necessary, on major policy issues and on the fiscal outlook.

*July-August.* Appropriate changes to program plans are made on the basis of the guidance received and of congressional legislation and appropriations. Budget estimates, including those for new legislative proposals, are developed on the basis of the first year of the currently approved program plans (e.g., 1968).

*September.* Budget estimates and agency legislative programs are submitted to the Bureau of the Budget.

*October-December.* Budget Bureau reviews budget estimates, consults with agencies, and makes its recommendations to the President. Presidential decisions are transmitted to agencies, the budget is prepared for submission to Congress, and the legislative program is prepared.

*January.* Changes are again made by the agency to the multi-year program plan to conform to Presidential decisions as reflected in the budget sent to the Congress.

10. *Responsibility and staffing.*

a. Personal responsibility for the Planning, Programming, and Budgeting system rests with the head of each agency. Since planning, programming, and budgeting are all essential elements of management, line managers at appropriate levels in the agency must also take responsibility for, and participate in, the system. Responsibility should be so fixed that the agency head receives the recommendations of his principal managers (e.g., bureau chiefs) on program plans as well as on the findings and recommendations of centrally prepared analytical studies. Similarly, arrangements should be made for obtaining original suggestions, recommendations, and views from other echelons in a manner consistent with the assignment of responsibility and authority.

b. Specialized staff assistance is also essential in all but the smallest agencies. Such assistance will be especially useful in the preparation and review of Program and Financial Plans and in the preparation of the appropriate analytical studies. Each agency will, therefore, establish an adequate central staff or staffs for analysis, planning and programming. Some bureaus and other subordinate organizations should also have their own analytical planning and programming staffs.

c. No single form of organization is prescribed since agency circumstances differ. Planning-Programming-Budgeting activities are functionally linked but it is not essential that they be located in the same office so long as they are well coordinated. However, it is important that the head of the central analytic staff be directly responsible to the head of the agency or his deputy.

11. *Initial action under this Bulletin.* The head of each agency listed in Exhibit 1 should see that the following steps are taken by the dates indicated. It is recognized that this is a tight schedule. Nonetheless, the President's interest in the prompt establishment of the new Programming, Planning, and Budgeting system requires that each agency exert every possible effort to adhere to this schedule.

a. *Within 10 days* after issuance of this Bulletin—the agency head should designate an official to be responsible for the development of the Planning-Programming-Budgeting system for the entire agency and inform the Bureau of the Budget of his choice.

b. *By November 1, 1965*—each agency head should have tentatively decided, in cooperation with the Bureau of the Budget, the broad program categories to be used initially in the system. Bureau of the Budget staff are prepared to make suggestions on these categories.

c. *By December 31, 1965*—agency instructions, procedures, or regulations for the Planning-Programming-Budgeting system should be issued, and a copy forwarded to the Bureau of the Budget. If it is not possible to have these in polished form by this date, they should be issued at least in such form as will allow the agency to proceed without delay on the steps necessary to produce the material required by May 1, 1966, with the more complete and polished instructions or regulations issued as soon as feasible but not later than March 31, 1966.

d. *By February 1, 1966*—each agency head should have approved the basic program structure (including program categories, program subcategories, program elements, and the nonfinancial units for measuring program objectives and accomplishments in quantitative terms) to be used in the program plan.

e. *By April 1, 1966*—a comprehensive, multi-year Program and Financial Plan should be completed for consideration and review by the agency head. The Program and Financial Plan, as approved by the agency head, will be forwarded to the Bureau of the Budget.

f. *By May 1, 1966*—for the spring Preview, Program Memoranda described above will be forwarded to the Bureau of the Budget. By this date or earlier, Special Studies will also be forwarded. More specific guidance and instructions will be provided by the Bureau of the Budget.

# 48

## Roland N. McKean
## *The Impact of Public Spending upon Freedoms*

As noted before, public spending is capable of producing numerous important effects—some that most persons would regard as desirable, others that they would regard as undesirable. So far, there has been little mention of one of the most significant effects of government spending—namely, its impact on the freedom and rights of individuals. It is so difficult to speak with any assurance on this topic that it is tempting to put the issue aside and "let George write about it." But it is such an important matter, compared to, say, efficiency in producing conventional goods and services, that even a tiny improvement in our understanding here may be worth considerable trouble. I have therefore decided to explore the possible impacts of public spending on freedom even though what is said does not carry one very far.

I shall assume here that wider range of choice is better than a narrower one, though it is impossible to show just how generally this is true. . . . This discussion will pertain mainly to the ranges of choice involved in such basic individual rights as freedom of speech, press, worship, assembly, and voting. Some expenditures, such as those to provide an acceptable, though inevitably imperfect, system of law and order and contract enforcement, work toward protecting these rights. Without those government programs, might would tend to be right, and most minority groups and individuals would fare poorly. Thus some government activities are unquestionably powerful forces to promote the freedom of ordinary individuals. It is often contended, however, that the growth of other government activities is a threat to their liberty. This is a most serious issue, for the flavor of life depends crucially on the options that individuals have in speaking, worshiping, writing, moving about, choosing jobs, and so on, especially in relation to the options they feel are technically possible.

What do government expenditures really have to do with freedom? Plenty of assertions have been made in answer to this question. Hayck and many others say that large government programs lead to serfdom. Sometimes assertions are buttressed by metaphors:

> As I have mentioned before, this is the Achilles heel which is an ideal entrance for the massive Federal octopus because the current civil rights and poverty climate tailors itself perfectly for Federal invasion of the public education field at the local level in these areas. Of course it will be said that "we only want to help in these specific areas" but soon the full blown tiger is in your tank.[1]

[1] From *The Congressional Record,* quoted in *The New Yorker,* Oct. 31, 1964, p. 202.

Others say, "Well, how has big government impaired your freedom lately? Do many persons in the United States or Great Britain feel less free today than they did several decades ago?" Actually, appallingly little is known about the connection between public spending and liberty.[2] There are inherently great uncertainties about this connection. Furthermore, people have seemingly been content with assertions about the matter and have seldom employed an analytical framework to try to sharpen their intuitive judgments about it. Here, after a fairly lengthy background discussion, I shall try to use economic theory to improve at least slightly our understanding of the connection between public expenditures and freedom.

Most people would agree that there are, inevitably, abridgments of individuals' freedoms—that inevitably there are instances of compulsion in which certain individuals or groups are given less freedom along certain lines so that they may have more of other things, or are restricted in their freedoms so that others may have a greater range of choice. Any activity supported by taxes compels some groups to give up resources for purposes they might not voluntarily support. Frequently, however, an effort has been made to render certain basic freedoms or rights—such as worship, assembly, press, or speech—widely available. In this connection, it might be noted that free speech or assembly does not mean "free resources," for if one person uses an acre of ground, an hour of television time, or a speaking platform for his purpose, he prevents someone else from devoting that resource to another purpose, unless the resource is so abundant as to be a free good. For this reason, the basic freedoms have never meant—and should never mean—that people have the right to use just any properties, whether privately or publicly owned, for assembly or worship or public speaking. These basic freedoms mean that each person has the right to buy or rent a site via voluntary exchange and speak or worship there freely without fear of criminal prosecution. Even then, of course, the activity has to be conducted without disturbing the peace or violating the rights of others, and borderline cases can easily arise. Additional abridgments of freedom by government (as well as those imposed by nature) are likely to become more numerous as population densities, urbanization, and interdependencies increase. In effect, most persons will regard it as economical to trade some freedom for additional amounts of other outputs. . . .

## IMPACTS ON CONSUMERS' SOVEREIGNTY

In most societies, past or present, government spending has involved large reductions of freedom in the sense of providing services that many individual taxpayers would not voluntarily buy. Taxes are compulsory, and we have no way of knowing just how each individual would choose to use the resources if they were left in his hands; but we know that pacifists would not buy defense, childless

[2] This view is expressed, for example, by both Francis M. Bator, *The Question of Government Spending,* Harper and Row, Publishers, Incorporated, New York, 1960, chap. 8; and George J. Stigler, "Reflections on Liberty" (unpublished manuscript).

couples would hardly spend as much as they now do on the education of other people's children, and people near Seattle would not contribute as heavily as at present toward the purchase of irrigation in Arizona.

Many government services have public-good characteristics, and it is uneconomical to charge admission and find out what consumers would voluntarily choose. As mentioned earlier, defense and flood control are examples. If these goods are to be provided at all, it is probably sensible to use compulsory assessments or taxes. In other cases, even though the government services could be sold and consumers' freedom of choice could be maintained, government uses compulsory taxes anyway and impairs this freedom. Thus for one reason or another government spending does not cater to individuals' choices in old-age insurance, education, defense, foreign aid, research and development, and so on. . . .

In addition to imposing taxes, which are directly linked with public outlays, governments restrict consumers' choices in ways that are not closely related to the volume of spending. Consumers cannot buy certain medicines without prescriptions, purchase the services of unlicensed barbers, or buy tickets to New York via San Francisco from an intra-California carrier. They cannot buy or own an eagle (according to Federal law). A few decades ago the consumer was not supposed to buy liquor. Today he may be forbidden to buy an automobile that is not equipped with a prescribed smog-control device, even if he lives in the High Sierras. If one combed our national, state and local statutes and ordinances, one could compile a tremendous list of forbidden items. And in many other countries such lists are much longer.

The reduction of choice, and any other ill effects, must be weighed against the desirable effects of these activities when each of us decides whether to support or oppose public expenditures. One thing that should be kept in mind is that, strictly speaking, consumers' sovereignty is bound to be violated to some extent in any event because of externalities and because of the interdependence among utility functions. Voluntary exchange and individual consumers' choices, as ordinarily defined, would not completely avoid coercion of other consumers either, because if Brown sells my neighbor Jones a Rolls-Royce (a voluntary exchange that makes both of *them* better off), it may thrust upon me a loss of satisfaction because of my envy of Jones.[3] This may not be as long-lived or as significant a deprivation of my freedom of choice as that represented by my annual tax bill, but such things are hard to compare.

Perhaps it should also be emphasized that innovation and economic growth have, over the last few decades, greatly increased the range of individual choice for most people. As a consequence, it may be that now the marginal loss of free choice caused by public taxation and spending is not very great. Moreover, some government programs, such as those for education, research and development, the extension of opportunity, the increase of mobility, and the prevention of deflation, may stimulate innovation and production and thereby expand the range of choice among goods for all of us. . . . As will be noted later, however, the restriction of consumers' and employees' options may have significant *indirect* effects on these

[3] Bator, *op. cit.,* pp. 86–87.

other freedoms, because these kinds of freedoms or options are to some extent substitutes, and if the cost of one kind goes up, or if it becomes relatively scarce, the price of the other tends to go up also.

## OTHER CONSTRAINTS ON INDIVIDUALS

Government places many other kinds of constraints on individuals. It may prohibit farmers from planting certain crops on certain acreages. It may prohibit growers from marketing grapefruit of less than a designated size or prohibit employers from hiring laborers for less than a designated wage. The choices of a home-builder or contractor are limited by building codes. Instead of making a flat prohibition or requirement, government often simply penalizes undesired behavior. If the farmer departs from his quota, he sacrifices the opportunity to sell at the support price. If the owner of a building fails to meet prescribed standards, he is fined. In most instances like these the government acts because of pressure from some producer organization or other group; but then *all* government action is the result of pressure from one influential group or another, for example, the majority of voters. . . .

In some governments these various restrictions have become so numerous and pervasive that they have constituted an obvious and serious impairment of freedom. In the United States they may not have seriously reduced freedom of choice; there are still numerous options. Here I shall look upon them much as I viewed the impairments of consumers' sovereignty (to which they are closely related)–I shall view them as having effects on economic efficiency but as being minor *direct* limitations on freedom.

## FACTORS THAT MAKE IT EXPENSIVE TO EXERCISE OR GUARD ONE'S BASIC RIGHTS

Let us turn to the fundamental freedoms that are enumerated in the Bill of Rights and ask what utility maximization can tell us, if anything, about the conditions under which they are likely to be eroded. As we noted in earlier chapters, our analytical tool, the basic tool of economic theory, is a simple one. It is merely the theorem that demand curves for all things are negatively inclined: If something becomes relatively expensive, individuals will take less of it, and if something becomes relatively inexpensive, they will take more of it. This basic proposition has been rather thoroughly tested and appears to be correct. . . .

### *To maintain one's rights is costly*

At best it is disturbingly expensive to guard or "purchase" one's freedoms or to stand up for the rights of individuals in general. There is the now-familiar point that, from the standpoint of each individual, voting and especially acquiring information about candidates and issues ordinarily involve costs like time and energy yet offer infinitesimal probabilities of affecting elections and therefore small expected rewards. Similar considerations apply to protesting any impairment of one's rights or of other individuals' rights. First, consider an infringement of someone else's rights. If some stranger is denied his right to vote, most persons decide that even the relatively modest effort of sending letters to their senators takes time and offers virtually no reward. If the FCC threatens a left-wing or right-wing radio station, or refuses to renew the license of one, those with relatively high stakes and those whose rights are directly threatened will complain, but few "outsiders" are likely to spend money or time protesting. The reason: one individual's action would ordinarily have little impact on (1) that particular incident or (2) the probability that those outsiders will suffer subsequent infringements of their rights.

To be sure, one can cite instances in which outsiders do enter the lists. Some do incur the high cost of forming or supporting organizations to protect individual liberties. Many persons other than those whose rights have been denied have taken up the cause of civil rights, particularly the protection of the Negro's right to vote. Sometimes this involvement is the result of a combination of events that arouses strong emotions, which then makes action have a payoff to the actor. When emotions run high, unfortunately, another high cost enters the picture. The persons concerned often lose sight of the goal of protecting all individuals' rights and become perfectly willing to sacrifice the rights of some persons to further particular objectives. If this goes far enough, it may make it still more difficult to protect the basic freedoms. At other times the action of bystanders may be prompted by a considered concern for individual rights, either for idealistic reasons or for fear that infringements may spread and affect the bystanders themselves. Nonetheless, except in rather special circumstances, individual bystanders do not find it sufficiently rewarding to intervene when someone else's rights are threatened.[4] Such behavior is not surprising or necessarily reprehensible. As the individual scans his T-account, it appears to be costly and comparatively unrewarding to act. Most of the rewards are external: decreases in the probability that *other* people's rights will be eroded. To individuals in the aggregate the reward from action, the chance of effecting a favorable outcome times the aggregate value of a favorable outcome, is large, but in such situations it is also very costly to individuals to organize group action.[5] (For these same reasons, one seldom finds consumers voicing strenuous objections to a tariff.) As a consequence, the maintenance of individual rights is at best a difficult matter, and the price of freedom is indeed high. . . .

[4] Indeed, as has been stressed in the newspapers, bystanders frequently fail to intervene to protect someone else's life.

[5] Mancur Olson, Jr., *The Logic of Collective Action,* Harvard University Press, Cambridge, Mass., 1965, especially pp. 53–97.

### *A reduction in the range of options makes it more costly to protect one's rights*

If a person has relatively few attractive options, such as alternative employers, it becomes still more expensive to him to protect his rights or those of others.[6] If, on the one hand, I can turn to alternative jobs without great sacrifice, it does not cost me much to stand up to my present employer or supervisor or colleague or client—to refuse to allow anyone to tell me what to write or say, or to tolerate discrimination against me because of my race or religion. If, on the other hand, there are only a few options of value open, it is more important for me to hold on to my present employment and not to foreclose any of my comparatively few opportunities. In other words it is more important for me to get along with employers, colleagues, and so on; I am more dependent on their opinions of me. To write or speak or worship in ways that displease them is more expensive to me than it would be if I had a better range of options. I am likely to take less of these items because their prices are higher; that is, I am more likely to speak cautiously and perhaps endure direct impairments of my freedom than I would be if I had a wide range of options. Options other than employment are pertinent too. If there are few alternatives regarding my children's schools, an apartment or house, ration coupons, recreation facilities, or permission to start a business or borrow funds, my dependence upon some persons' favors increases. I may accept more limitations on my liberty because the price of exercising my freedom has gone up. One of the most important means of keeping that price down is having the ability to vote with my feet, that is, having a diversity of stores or schools or banks or communities to which I can turn. In this indirect way consumers' choices in general are important to the basic freedoms, because they are to some extent substitutes. . . .

### *Effects of government spending on these factors*

What connection does government spending have with these factors? Public spending and government activities can, up to a point and in certain ways, increase the range of options open to most individuals. For example, certain types of spending for court systems, law enforcement, education, health, job training, employment exchanges, dissemination of information, and mobility allowances may expand the range of choices for most persons thus reducing the cost to them of exercising their independence. Some government activities expand the range of options open to particular groups, thus decreasing the cost of those persons maintaining their freedoms. Programs to offer better training to Negroes, and to reduce the barriers facing them, make it less difficult for them to acquire or protect

[6] Many of the points made in this chapter have often been made, employing somewhat different terminology, with respect to the broad extremes—socialism versus capitalism. One of the clearest presentations is Milton Friedman, *Capitalism and Freedom,* The University of Chicago Press, Chicago, 1962, pp. 1–21. To a considerable extent I have simply tried to convert such thoughts about the costs or difficulties of maintaining freedom into a continuous rather than a "two-case" cost function.

their basic freedoms. (On the other hand, constraints like the minimum-wage law reduce the options open to the "disadvantaged," who must then engage in a desperate search for ways to employ themselves at less than the legal minimum.) It seems highly appropriate to assist such groups, even though it implies reducing the range of choice facing others, in order to make the costs of protecting individual rights more nearly equal. Appropriate monetary-fiscal policy, although not necessarily correlated with the volume of public spending, is another activity that, by preventing deflation, can increase the number of job options confronting individuals. On balance, I would certainly argue that many public activities help widen the range of choices open to most people and equalize the cost of guarding their basic rights.

Beyond some point, however, government spending can begin to reduce options. At the extreme, if government were the only employer and were comparatively monolithic, I would have few job choices and would express myself rather cautiously. Even with the high levels of public spending that exist today, of course, most persons in the United States have numerous job options—multiple Federal employers, state agencies, municipal governments, semi-independent agencies, and, far more numerous, private firms. By incurring costs, one can usually send his child to the public school in his district, to a different public school, or to a private school; or, though it may entail a high cost, one can move to a different community (though clearly for some groups the options are severely limited). For services one can turn to alternative stores, banks, or apartment owners. With many options open, a person is not likely to feel unusual pressure to neglect or surrender his freedoms. Nonetheless, large additions to government spending could enlarge the role of government as an employer and a provider of services and thereby gradually raise the cost of being concerned about one's freedoms. . . .

For almost any *given* set of rules, however, greatly increased public outlays are likely to bring at least slightly higher risks—somewhat higher costs to many individuals of maintaining their basic rights. Government activities always involve hiring and firing individuals, not generalized humanity; tax and disbursement provisions differ for different groups and individuals. In real life, neither benefits nor taxes are completely general, information is not costless, and rules cannot be clear-cut. When the Sierra Club opposed the government's proposed dams in the Grand Canyon, officials *did* have a way of making this opposition expensive—namely, through the Internal Revenue Service's threat to withdraw the tax shelter previously enjoyed by the organization. Eventually various recipients of benefits might think twice about criticizing whatever coalition was in power, because the defeat of that coalition at the polls might divert benefits to other groups. It is said that in certain Communist nations patronage rather than overt coercion is now the major instrument of control—that, if one speaks too freely, he risks having his police card stamped "politically undesirable," which makes it difficult to get a car license, a good job or apartment, a passport, and so on. A large purse *can* mean power; and compared with governments, even giant corporations have small purses and little authority. A $500 billion U.S. budget might make it quite expensive to maintain checks and balances in government and the basic rights of citizens.

There is another way in which increased government spending may bring about fewer attractive options and make concern about liberties more expensive to individuals. If the government becomes a relatively large property owner or absorbs property rights by imposing heavy taxes or numerous constraints on property owners, the result may be a reduction in the range of job choices and other options open to people. The dispersal of property rights among individuals produces a multiplicity of options, giving more choices to households (with private as well as public schools to choose among), more options of setting up independent enterprises of one's own (a special sort of job option), more options of working for others who set up independent enterprises, and more ways of trading wealth for job and other options. The heavier the tax on income from properties, the less rewarding it is to set up enterprises; and if there are sufficient constraints on the use of properties, it may be costly to offer or to seek options. The fewer ways there are to trade wealth for options, the more costly it is to be a "non-preferred person"[7] (e.g., an old, colored, handicapped, inexperienced, left-wing, right-wing, or ugly person). If carried far enough, this could be a serious matter. . . .

## FACTORS THAT MAKE IT INEXPENSIVE TO INTERFERE WITH INDIVIDUALS' RIGHTS

The factors discussed so far have been those that make it more or less difficult for a person to exercise his so-called basic rights. Let us now turn to the other side of the coin—to the factors that make it more or less difficult for one person to interfere with others' basic rights. In what circumstances can someone begin to throw his weight around without sacrificing much? In part, I have already answered this question: If one can influence the direction of government expenditures, award jobs or favors to persons who have few options, or offer particularly attractive rewards or options or threats, one will find it somewhat easier than it would otherwise be to interfere with someone's basic rights. There is little point, however, in reviewing these factors merely from a different vantage point. It may be more useful to examine the roles of two particular factors—property rights and voting rights.

### *Dilution of individual property rights.*

One circumstance that may give some persons the ability to throw their weight around is the extensive attenuation of *individual* property rights. A strong tradition of maintaining such rights makes it relatively costly for persons with a reason or taste for oppression to indulge. This is because property rights give persons a base, so to speak, from which to strike back at would-be oppressors. This is true even for people who do not own property, as long as a diversity of other individuals does.

[7] Harold Demsetz, "Minorities in the Marketplace," *North Carolina Law Review*, February, 1965, pp. 271–297.

Individual property rights imply that people cannot do as they please with or on someone else's property. Thus, government or corporation officials can properly regulate my speech or other activities on *their* properties—but they cannot regulate my speech or worship on properties that *I* rent or buy (as long as I do not disturb the peace or break other laws). If they try to regulate my activities on my own property, there are fairly clear-cut steps by means of which I can sue and impose costs on them. These steps are not prohibitively expensive, and individual or small-group action has a good chance of being effective. Moreover, other persons, seeing their rights threatened, can also take similar steps to impose costs on the potential oppressor. Thus, individual property rights, if they are at least somewhat dispersed, can make extreme selfishness expensive. That is, it can make it expensive to disregard the damages one inflicts on others or to interfere with their right to speak, publish, worship, or assemble. (If only a few persons hold all the property, of course, or if the distribution of wealth is so unequal that minorities cannot possibly rent properties for their purposes, or if the wealthy can employ government to restrict entry and exchange, these cost functions will be somewhat different.)

Without individual property rights, with all properties owned by government, officials would have to decide what activities were legitimate. (It is nonsense to think that publicly owned properties would somehow become free goods.) Officials might reach decisions that infringed on people's freedoms. Through the courts people could still try to impose costs on officials who impaired their basic rights. But the rules, and the criteria of infringement, would be less clear-cut, and the cost of the information needed for a court decision would be greater. And the courts might have *even greater* difficulty in maintaining objectivity. Organizing political pressures rather than using court procedures, on the other hand, would be relatively costly to an individual or minority group and have less chance of success. If all this is correct, officials might in this milieu find it less costly to them to engage in oppressive acts. . . .

Suppose, as illustrations, that officials decided to eliminate the Pacifica Foundation, to forbid meetings of the Birch Society, to raze the house of a Negro in a white neighborhood to provide room for a small park, to ban speeches opposing U.S. defense efforts in Southeast Asia, or to forbid the advocacy of military efforts in Southeast Asia. Without a tradition of individual property rights, how could people object? Not by the *relatively* inexpensive means of lawsuits referring to their rights to use *their* properties for their own purposes. They would have to turn to comparatively difficult routes—to lawsuits contending that they had rights to use specific public properties for these purposes or to expensive attempts to sway public opinion and organize political pressures. There is nothing sacrosanct or God-given about individual property rights—but a considerable reliance on them may be an economical arrangement for making oppression of individuals or minorities expensive to oppressors. And the fact that individual property rights do not always ensure the preservation of other rights does not mean that government property rights would automatically be better.

Another important factor that makes control relatively costly to the oppressor is vigorous competition among independent enterprises. In a highly competitive industry, it is expensive for management to devote resources to purchasing nonpecuniary benefits—to emphasizing beauty more than competence when hiring secretaries, printing pamphlets supporting antivivisection, indulging in a preference for racial discrimination, indulging in a taste for right- or left-wing views, or pressuring employees to vote in a particular way. If competition is keen, the penalty for pursuing such nonpecuniary goals is bankruptcy. If competition is less vigorous, there is more room for the purchase of nonpecuniary emoluments, but even moderate competition—even rivalry among independent not-for-profit institutions or governmental units—makes it more expensive than it would otherwise be for officials to trade performance for concern about an employee's race, creed, color, manner of voting, personal life, political views, and so on. Thus, in the terminology used in the preceding section, competition makes it comparatively expensive for officials to create special options that may induce one to abandon the exercise of his rights. . . .

What does all this discussion have to do with public spending? *Beyond some level,* public spending with its accompanying taxation and constraints (1) dilutes individual property rights, and (2) reduces the degree of competition among independent enterprises. If the preceding argument is correct, these impacts can make it less expensive to men of influence to interfere with other persons' basic freedoms. Up to a fairly heavy volume of government spending and in favorable circumstances, the effects may be trivial. With further expansion of public activities, however, these effects may become cumulatively more significant. Bigger government and increased centralization may be like growing older; at any particular moment it seems a bit foolish to be alarmed about it, yet ultimately it can be fatal.

### *Lack of effective voting rights*

It presumably needs little emphasis, but a tremendously important factor in preserving other individual freedoms is the maintenance of individual voting rights. If one has a vote that is genuinely valuable to politicians and thence to officials, they will pay a price for it, and the price can include a considerable respect for basic rights. If officialdom violates the rights of individuals having such votes, the individuals can make the violations costly to officials. If an individual or set of individuals has no effective vote, however, it becomes less expensive for officials or others to interfere with those individuals' freedoms.

The effects are fairly obvious in the case of Negroes in parts of the United States where they have often had no vote at all. Since elected officials have not depended on the Negroes' votes, they have provided them with relatively poor street repairs, schools, sanitation, and public services. Perhaps more importantly, officials can dispense harsher punishments, permit inferior jury trials, and prevent Negroes from speaking freely—without paying much of a penalty. At least some difference in these respects is said to exist in cities where Negroes have begun voting. The effects are also plain to see in authoritarian societies, where citizens get to vote, but only for one set of candidates. Again, no one depends upon anyone's vote, no one is willing to trade anything for it and officials can disregard individual rights without much cost to themselves. Settling matters by majority vote may not be highly satisfactory, but democratic government has much to commend it in comparison with the alternatives. In particular, possession of votes that politicians value is essential to the preservation of individual rights.

Voting rights are, of course, an "intermediate" safeguard that depend themselves upon something else—upon some sort of consensus or agreement to live according to a set of rules. Or, perhaps voting rights are a necessary but not a sufficient condition for the maintenance of individual liberty. Another necessary condition may be an agreement to disperse power *in an operational fashion* by maintaining fairly extensive *individual* property rights. Given their other attributes and arrangements for voluntary exchange, some such property system is probably the lowest-cost way to preserve (with some designated probability) other individual rights. In the long run, a system of this sort may be especially valuable to conspicuous minorities. Such systems do not insure everyone's freedom or eliminate injustice and evil—but the relevant question is not "Is anything wrong with a particular arrangement?" but rather "What changes seem likely to offer improvements?"

## DOES THE UNSEEN HAND LEAD TO EVER-LARGER PUBLIC OUTLAYS?

Does utility maximization by voters, political parties, politicians, and officials imply ever-larger government and, if the above arguments are correct, ultimately a lower likelihood of maintaining individual rights? There is no clear-cut answer, for there are forces working in both directions. In general it may seem that spending proposals are more likely to succeed than proposals to cut spending. On the one hand, officials, politicians, and citizens who benefit from government expenditures frequently benefit considerably—enough to make active support worth its cost to those individuals. On the other hand, the ill effects are often spread over a larger group (voters who pay taxes but receive no benefits, politicians whose constituents pay taxes but receive no benefits, officials who compete for their slices of the budget), and the damages felt per individual may be slight—not enough to make active opposition worth the cost.[8] For proposals to cut spending, the lineup of forces tends to be just the opposite.

Another force that may lead to larger government spending, one that was noted earlier, is the fact that power acquisition may be a decreasing-cost output. Larger government spending may make successively larger increments of power easier to obtain. Thus for several reasons one might conclude that there are built-in tendencies for public spending to increase.

But there are clearly pressures to restrain government spending also. People recognize considerations over and above the direct effects of each proposal. The fact that public outlays do not expand so as to include the entire national

[8] See James M. Buchanan and Gordon Tullock, *The Calculus of Consent*, University of Michigan Press, Ann Arbor, Mich., 1962, pp. 164–169.

income indicates that restraining forces exist. Private consumption demands mean that beyond some point a majority would object violently to even small increases in taxes per capita. Majorities of voters in a jurisdictional unit are often unwilling, when distribution of the costs and gains are fairly clear, to provide services for minorities, unless they value the minorities' support greatly on other matters. (Older sections of a city do not like to finance facilities for annexed suburbs.) Decisions about the scale of public outlays depend upon the combination of issues that confront politicians and voters and upon the resulting bargaining network–but it is plain to see that there are constraining forces and that in the right circumstances they could even lead to cuts in public activities. Vague fears of governmental authority, which once constituted an effective restraint, may still linger. In any event there are many crosscurrents, and there is nothing predetermined about where the unseen hand will lead us regarding the volume of public spending and regarding the extent of individual liberty. We can choose–we can make use of the unseen hand rather than let it make use of us.

# 49

## Andrew Kopkind
## *The Future-Planners*

An editor of *Fortune* calls it "the greatest advance in the art of government [in] nearly a hundred years." Michael Harrington says it is "one of the most radical suggestions put forth by a responsible body in our recent history." An antipoverty official in Virginia fears it is the road to "a full-fledged socialist state"; a socialist teacher in Chicago fears it is not. Tom Hayden, the organizer in Newark, calls it "a new barbarism."

What "it" is that so excites some and horrifies others turns out to be not one thing–or at least nothing for which there are words or concepts in common usage. Rather it is a collection of vaguely related political and intellectual happenings that have to do with new ways to analyze, anticipate, and control the social environment. Involved are elements of old-fashioned central planning and new-fangled futurism; but the participants are more than planners and less than utopians. They are a new genus of social actors, something between politicians and technicians. For the most part, they do not want to push the buttons of the computerized society themselves; they are not technocrats. Instead, they would like to tell whoever is in charge which buttons to push. They dream of using social science instead of pressure politics to solve the nation's problems. Professor Bertram Gross of Syracuse, one of the few men in the business who tries to relate all the happenings into a coherent social movement, calls the new breed "technopols." But a simpler definition describes what they do: plan for the future.

Future-planning is in many ways the most fascinating, and certainly the most fashionable thing to be doing this year in both Government and the social sciences. . . .

"It's an idea whose time is coming," former Assistant Secretary of Labor Daniel P. Moynihan said recently. Politicians of the more conventional stripe are beginning to see a wave in the future. Democratic Senators Harris of Oklahoma and Nelson of Wisconsin have bills in Congress seeking Federal support, in one way or another, for future-planning. But the biggest political boost came last February when Senator Walter Mondale of Minnesota introduced legislation to set up a Council of Social Advisers in the White House, authorize an annual "Social Report" to the President, and establish a Joint Social Committee of Congress to oversee the whole thing.

The Administration is intrigued by all the activity, but cautious lest public opposition develop before a lobby for future-planning can harden its lines. "Planning" still evokes fears of creeping socialism or rampant New Dealism (although most future-planners are ideologically distinct from both doctrines), and both the regular politicians and the technopols keep their eyes trained on the right for signs of attack. But the idea remains attractive. "If the war on poverty turned out to be money without progress," a sociologist said the other day, "this could be progress without money." . . .

## SOME STICKY PROBLEMS

An impressive body of economic indicators, goals, and models has been constructed to show the state of the nation's economy and make policy objectives possible. The future-planners like to remind skeptics that it was not until economists measured unemployment that a distinct "unemployment problem" was recognized, and goals set for its alleviation. Now, Federal economists aim for certain levels of employment and use their indicators to rate success toward that end. The Council of Economic Advisers watches over a sophisticated set of national accounts, which give a fair picture of where the country stands in terms of prices, income, steel and car production, movement of goods, investment, construction, and the like. The economists use the data (weighted with their own ideas of what's good) to set economic goals. If things begin to go awry—if there are indications of inflation or an unemployment rise—the CEA will advise the President to take whatever steps he can to make the accounts come out even again. . . .

Nevertheless, to a race of underprivileged behavioral scientists, the status, influence, and political power of the macroeconomists are objects of consuming fascination and some envy. Economic data are *hard;* economic manipulation *works.* Would that the same could be said for psychology, sociology, political science, and the rest. As tokens of their esteem, the behavioral scientists choose the terminology of economics and the "harder" physical sciences and mathematics. They throw around phrases like input/output, feedback, entropy, synergism, symbosis: as if by adopting the symbols of science they could achieve it.

But they know too that the emphasis on economic accounting in Governmental planning has excluded crucial social considerations. There is altogether too much talk about Gross National Product and too little about happiness, culture, integration, participation. Bertram Gross calls the obsession with economic forces "the new philistinism."

Gross' hobby-horse is a national system of social accounting, in which aspects of the "quality of life" would be tallied along with the facts of the economy. Ways will be found to work with data on health, social relations, crime, aspirations, art and culture, conflict, mobility. In a long and difficult chapter in the anthology, *Social Indicators*, Gross outlines his ideas on the possibilities for social accounting. He concludes that it is an inevitable development.

Laymen may find social indicator prose rough going and the tables and diagrams unfathomable, but a popular statement of social accounting was made by Michael Harrington 2 months ago in *Harper's*. His formulation of social accounting is rather simple: Translate social values into economic terms (or devise a common unit for social and economic values), list the benefits on one side of a ledger, and balance them off against the social and economic debits on the other side. . . .

A Washington economist recently explained what social indicators were all about by reducing the notion to an absurdity. He fantasized a scene in the Council of Social Advisors one day in the mid-1980s:

> Dan Bell is idly watching the Dow-Jones societal wire (formerly the business wire): "Consumer Indignation Index down .04 percent. . . . Black Power Ratio steady (two percent drop in hair-straightner sales offset by two percent rise in empty seats at Miriam Makeba concerts). . . . Three youths from eastern Kentucky accepted at CCNY. . . . Participatory Democracy Determinant drops slightly (collapse of an antifluoridation organization in West Texas). . . . Gross Social Product extrapolated to 789 by December 31."
>
> Suddenly Bell calls excitedly, "Mike, Bert, come here quick. The Native Restlessness Index has hit an all-time high!" The Advisers go into special session with their staff, then report their conclusions and recommendations to the President, who the next day asks Congress for emergency legislation to install a nationwide network of plastic swimming pools. He activates the National Guard, and calls a White House Conference."

## BACK DOOR TO SOCIALISM

Much of the appeal of social indicators comes from the obvious parallel with economic accounting. . . .

The historical springs of future-planning are similarly diffuse. It has much in common with Fabianism and Keynesian economics, although there is no model for the social structure to compare with Keynes' construct of the economy. There is certainly some relevance to the concept of technocracy and managerialism. . . .

But the most direct antecedent is the systems-analysis experience which began in the '50s and was brought to the government by Defense Secretary McNamara in the '60s. A Pentagon planner fixed the origins of the "corporate society" in the Korean War:

> Major funds began to pour into research and development, stimulating the aircraft, missile and electronic industries. The rapid changes in R and D found government bureaucracy incapable of managing the complex weapons which technology declared possible, and the weapons system concept was born. The philosophy has spread throughout the economy.

PPBS—planning-program-budgeting-systems flowed out from the Defense Department. Systems men set up the guts of the poverty program. HEW took it over and put one of McNamara's whiz kids, William Gorham, in charge. But the systems approach is restricted to more or less fixed programs—a Head Start, a weapons program, a health project. And it is concerned mainly with the efficiency of the program in economic terms—according to its preset objectives and values. Cost-effectiveness analysis will not indicate which Head Start organization in Mississippi gives Negroes a better sense of their community, which helps them share in politics, or which instills more dignity in the children. It will only tell which program has more enrollees, disburses more money, and creates jobs.

Social indicators are of a different order. They are meant to quantify the intangibles of quality, and feed them into the accounting. They deal with longer-term societal trends, and lead more directly to policy goals. A social indicator system for Mississippi might find ways to quantify pride, power, and communitarianism, and so formulate objectives and measure performance. . . .

Postindustrial society (as Daniel Bell calls the current managerial, white-collared, technological state of affairs) creates the logic underlying future-planning. A case in point is the development of the supersonic transport. The fantastic size, the money, the time span, and the complex Government and corporate interests involved in the project forced planners to think about the future—what things would be like 10 or a dozen years hence when people would (or should) be hurtling around the world aboard an SST. . . .

The analysts build their futures-models, the companies fit their hardware to the models, the military men plan their strategies according to the available hardware, and the Administration chooses its foreign policy from the possible strategies. Along the way there may be some flexibility of choice: President Johnson can decide to go ahead with an antiballistic-missile program, or not. But by the time such choices are presented, many of the crucial alternatives have been eliminated. . . .

### THE "CONTRACT STATE"

As the biggest purchasing agent in the US, the Government has a special interest in seeing that its requirements are fulfilled. The Defense Department has dealings with some 17,000 subcontractors for its 12 weapons systems. Cost-accounting was obviously the only way to check on contract performance. But the "contract state" now encompasses more than military work. Increasingly, Government agencies contract out to provide social services–education, job training, health care. Performance in such areas cannot be measured in purely economic terms (although they currently are). Social indicators are needed to judge performance standards. The contract state can hardly exist without them. Defense corporations are already at work analyzing the society's domestic needs, and trying to fit their production to them. James Ridgeway has pointed out in these pages how large companies are thinking about such projects as "new towns," which they would build and (perhaps) operate, for fun and profit. In California, a traditionally nervous aerospace industry has hedged against defense appropriations cuts by working up analyses of crime, pollution, transportation, and Heaven knows what else, and selling both their models of the future and their plans for production to the state government. . . .

But model-building of future societies (almost all the planners like to "anticipate" a plurality of possible futures, rather than "predict" one specific future state) is only part of the work. It is the most fun, but also the least responsible. The serious, "scientific" future-planners are more concerned with the methods of developing social indicators, and the ways in which they will be used.

Here the most troublesome problems arise. First of all, there is precious little data available on the operation of the society in a noneconomic way. . . .

## "HUMAN VALUES"

There is no general agreement on "human values." But the people who frame the questions about the society and plan the future can easily, and unconsciously, inject their own values into the answers they receive. The Moynihan report was a good example. The assumption was that fatherless, mother-dominated families were a "bad thing." Information was collected about unemployment rates, the number of heads of households who were Negro females, education, delinquency, and other symptoms of pathology. The questions the surveyors asked were designed to find out how bad a thing it was. Such studies might be titled, "The Negroes–and what to do about them." The goals which could emerge from the collection of indicators would have to do with changing Negroes to make them conform to the model of a "healthy" family member. There might be other ways to pose questions about the condition of Negroes–for example, what is so terribly wrong with a social structure that produces racism, alienation, and gross inequality? But the policy implications of the answers to that kind of question might be too unsettling to consider. Moynihan's questions were certainly legitimate, and his data weren't at all inaccurate. The problem was that he and his fellow-surveyors were able to frame national thinking about race and poverty problems by their choice of questions. The danger is that Government and corporate elites will monopolize the business of question-asking, and so manipulate the attitudes of society they are pretending to serve as disinterested technicians.

Elitism seems to be built into the theory of social accounting. "It is an establishment position," Bauer says. "It involves amelioration of the present system, but it assumes that the system can be made to work." Future-planning serves the ideological needs of the "corporate state" to maintain itself by the manipulation of reform: not so much as to change basic economic and political relationships, but enough to take care of immediate needs. The technopols are supposed to keep the balance.

In the '50s, Daniel Bell (among others, many of whom are confirmed future-planners) proclaimed "the end of ideology" in America, and predicted its demise in the West. The theory was that ideology arises from conflict, and serious conflict (class warfare and system-wide defects) is forever resolved in the US. Furthermore, the ideological model of Marxism is discredited, and radicalism is a dead letter. What problems remain to be solved are nonideological, and could best be dealt with by intelligent, humanistic technicians. The systems analysts, the technopols, the future-planners filled the bill perfectly.

Max Ways, of *Fortune*, no modest propagandist for "liberal corporatism," sees the future-planners' role as shifting "the politics of issues to the politics of problems." Under their tutelage, business and Government will prosper, and the level of national morality will climb. As proof, he shows how the Secretary of Defense has allowed the US to avoid the twin immoralities of escalation and withdrawal in Vietnam. "McNamara, his systems analysts, and their computers are not only contributing to the practical effectiveness of US action," Ways wrote, "but raising the moral level of policy by a more conscious and selective attention to the definition of its aims."

Ways, Bell, Moynihan, Harrington and others suggest, perhaps without realizing it, that there is a definite ideology of technical problem solving. It would indeed be "known-nothing" to batter down all attempts at data collection and social accounting just to get at those ideological elements. Some of the formulators–Gross, Bauer, and Biderman–have no sharp axes to grind, and are open to arguments that their theories may be misused in practice. The "corporate state," "postindustrialism," "the contract state," or whatever US society is coming to, already tends toward elitism and a kind of totalitarianism. "The worst kind of dictatorship," Bauer said not long ago, after an evening's discussion of social indicators, "is the kind that gives people what they want, the kind in which you can't tell you're being controlled." If that is one of the possible futures, it is too important to be left only to the planners.